A Henry Wadsworth Longfellow Companion

A HENRY WADSWORTH LONGFELLOW COMPANION

Robert L. Gale

GREENWOOD PRESS
Westport, Connecticut · London

Library of Congress Cataloging-in-Publication Data

Gale, Robert L., 1919–
    A Henry Wadsworth Longfellow companion / Robert L. Gale.
      p. cm.
    Includes bibliographical references and index.
    ISBN 0-313-32350-X (alk. paper)
    1. Longfellow, Henry Wadsworth, 1807–1882—Criticism and interpretation—
Handbooks, manuals, etc.   I. Title.
    PS2288.G35 2003
    811′.3—dc22   2003057850

British Library Cataloguing in Publication Data is available.

Library of Congress Catalog Card Number: 2003057850
ISBN: 0-313-32350-X

First published in 2003

Greenwood Press, 88 Post Road West, Westport, CT 06881
An imprint of Greenwood Publishing Group, Inc.
www.greenwood.com

Printed in the United States of America

∞™

The paper used in this book complies with the
Permanent Paper Standard issued by the National
Information Standards Organization (Z39.48–1984).

10 9 8 7 6 5 4 3 2 1

Copyright Acknowledgment

Selections from *The Letters of Henry Wadsworth Longfellow,* edited by Andrew Hilen are
used by permission of the publisher from *The Letters of Henry Wadsworth Longfellow,
1814–1882, Volumes I–VI,* edited by Andrew Hilen, Cambridge, Mass.: The Belknap Press
of Harvard University Press, Copyright © 1967, 1972, 1982 by the President and Fellows
of Harvard College.

To Andrew Hilen (1913–1982) and
Edward Wagenknecht (b. 1900)

Contents

Preface

This reference "companion" has two main purposes. First, it is intended to aid in discussions, analyses, and publishable criticism of the remarkably varied writings of Henry Wadsworth Longfellow, the most popular poet in American literary history. Second, it is to make more informed, and therefore pleasurable, the reading of Longfellow's works by anyone caring to turn, or to return, to them. This reference is unique in Longfellow studies despite his having been the subject of literally countless scholars. It begins with a chronology detailing salient features in Longfellow's varied and productive life. The main part follows and presents in alphabetical order entries concerning his works, members of his family, relatives, professional associates, and a few other topics, for example, his income and his travels.

Longfellow was a companionable American poet and deserves to be honored as one at this time, almost two hundred years after his birth. In his heyday, readers hung breathless in anticipation of his latest work. After he became incredibly famous, his birthday was nationally celebrated. Persons whom Longfellow amiably dubbed "entire strangers" wrote to him for professional and personal advice, for his autograph, and even for copies of his books and for money. Other admirers reversed matters and showered him with gifts ranging from books and poems (sometimes mediocre ones they had written) to homemade jelly. He often had fifty letters at a time to be answered, and he tried to answer every one of them; when ill, he dictated his replies. He outsold in England publications by Robert Browning and Alfred, Lord Tennyson. Longfellow had a private audience with Queen Victoria, who obviously was the one to initiate the meeting (and who then, unlike his British friends, attempted to demean him). He received many honorary degrees in America and abroad. Late in his life, illustrious visitors beat a path to his door to call upon him personally. His "Excelsior" and "A Psalm of Life" sent readers into ecstasies and rank as two of the most popular poems ever written in any language. "Thanatopsis" by Longfellow's friend William Cullen Bryant and "The Raven" by Longfellow's would-be nemesis Edgar Allan Poe trail considerably. Dozens of Longfellow's poems were set to music. Only Emily Dickinson's brief, intriguing, and often short lyrics have proved more popular with composers.

Longfellow's response to the ever-increasing groundswell of his popularity is a bracing model for lesser mortals. He was appreciative, generous, and usually modest, even humble—and this in spite of his having rubbed elbows with presidents, other significant national leaders, high-ranking foreign dignitaries, and fellow writers in America and abroad (for example, John Greenleaf Whittier and Charles Dickens) almost as revered as he. Yet, august though he was in his day, Longfellow had more than a touch of Yankee shrewdness. When offered $3,000 for first-publication rights to a short poem ("The Hanging of the Crane"), he asserted to friends that he had not sought the sum but sure enough would accept it on the spot. Although he traveled broadly—and often dangerously, given the circumstances—he was happiest at home, but saddest there too. His first wife, Mary Potter Longfellow, died abroad when she was hardly more than a child; his second wife, Fanny Appleton Longfellow, a bright, beautiful, and devoted mother, suffered fatal burns before his very eyes. Longfellow responded stoically but was rarely altogether happy thereafter, although he wrote on and on, and splendidly to the very end; he also relished a few harmless May-December flirtations, details of which will never be fully documented. His children gave him love, joy, but also sometimes no little trouble; other relatives delighted him, while still others bothered him dreadfully; yet he remained with them, as with his friends and even strangers in need, loyal and generous to a fault. This companion provides biographical details concerning 97 of his close friends and an astonishing 60 of his family members, relatives, and in-laws. Longfellow was an enviably nice in-law and a model to emulate.

Longfellow the author was at his most endearing when he penned short poems and long letters. This companion discusses his 402 poems, long and short. Any devotee of Longfellow can name a dozen favorites, including several ones so lovingly handled that they are now sometimes irrationally demeaned. Many are too good to be forgotten, and yet too well remembered to be fresh. His *Evangeline* and *The Song of Hiawatha,* more popular for decades after they first appeared than they are now, seem prolix to readers with short attention spans; but they still have electricity enough to thrill many a present-date reader. The story of Evangeline is profoundly poignant—and contains a political warning of validity today. And *Hiawatha* is recognized as a pioneering treatment of Native Americans, if too bookish by half. Conscientious devotees of Longfellow should regard as ample my handling of long works by Longfellow less studied these days; they include *Christus, The Courtship of Miles Standish, Hyperion, Judas Maccabaeus, Kavanagh, Michael Angelo,* and *Outre-Mer.* And especially *Tales of a Wayside Inn,* Longfellow's entry as the best-ever American competitor to Geoffrey Chaucer's *Canterbury Tales.*

Many of Longfellow's poems have been the object of parodies, partly because of the sing-song meters of some of them but often because of their very popularity. All the same, innumerable Longfellow poems, long and short, have been translated and widely revered; without a doubt, some are being read somewhere in this troubled world this very minute, by those in need of pleasure, relaxation, or inspiration. Longfellow did more than his share of translating also. It is well known that he was a conscientious professor of foreign languages at Bowdoin College and then at Harvard; less well known, perhaps, is the fact that he skillfully translated poems originally published in at least 11 of the 15 or so foreign languages he knew. This companion treats 133 of these translations (as part of the 402-poem total). As for the 14,000 or so letters it is estimated that he wrote, 5,055 have been recovered, edited, and annotated by the late Professor Andrew Hilen of the University of Washington, and have been beautifully published by the Belknap Press of Harvard University Press (in six volumes, 1966–82).

Unfortunately, identical unreserved praise cannot also be accorded various bibliographies devoted to Longfellow over the years. There simply is no complete primary bibliography of his works. Jacob Blanck's 173-page bibliography is valuably informative but deals with Longfellow's books and identifies only in passing too few of his periodical publications; and Jacob Chester Chamberlain's bibliography concerns only first editions of Longfellow's books. This companion is therefore of incidental value for providing, in context, virtually complete bibliographical data on the pre-book appearances of Longfellow's short works.

Also absent from the scholarly world is a complete edition, embarrassingly long overdue, of Longfellow's journals and ledgers. In writing his inestimable biography of Longfellow, his devoted brother Samuel Longfellow made good use of the poet's journals, as well as many of his letters; but the Reverend Samuel was finickily nineteenth century rather than boldly twentieth or twenty-first century in his scholarly behavior, which included a bit of rewriting and more than a bit of sanitizing of the original wordings.

A massive new biography of Longfellow would be welcome, but only after his journals and ledgers are edited, annotated, and published in full, after which his letters would naturally be taken into exquisite consideration by a biographer. For now, the biographical studies by Lawrance Thompson, Edward Wagenknecht, and Andrew Hilen must sufficiently suffice. Thompson exhaustively covers Longfellow's early years. Wagenknecht's full-length biography is substantial and accurate, while his biography of Longfellow's wife Fanny is an accompanying delight. Most useful of all, however, may well be Hilen's detailed introductions to pertinent sections of his edition of the letters, as well as the letters themselves and Hilen's accompanying footnotes.

Of critics discussing Longfellow's works in general, the best are Wagenknecht, again, and Arvin Newton. George Monteiro warrants more than casual mention for his short but superb introduction to the popular 1975 republication of the long-revered "Cambridge Edition" of Longfellow's poetry. I cite, with implicit gratitude, the legions of critics concentrating on specific productions by Longfellow in end-of-entry notes and the general bibliography.

It has been a joy for me to read and reread Longfellow during the course of compiling this reference. It must be emphasized that there is no real substitute for turning and returning to Longfellow's words themselves. His skill as a prosodist is almost unmatched among American writers; his sonnets, in fact, have no American rivals. His achievement as a prose writer may not match that of his poetry; however, his shrewdness as a travel writer is perhaps still insufficiently recognized. His few efforts at fiction are also noteworthy for being almost inchoate precursors of the local-color movement he did not live to see. His best prose, in my view, is to be found in his letters. They have been informative and joyful for me to read, and something akin to an inspiration as well. Like Willa Cather's well-known Archbishop, Longfellow rhetorically positioned himself eye to eye toward everyone. His letters abundantly prove that he was, among great American writers, uniquely kind, sympathetic, patient, long-suffering, generous, surprisingly jocose and unbuttoned at times, and rarely judgmental. Taken together, they reveal to the discerning that he responded, decade after decade, to every challenge he encountered—and there were many—with dignity, forbearance, and nothing less than a spiritual radiance. Would that more of us could be like him today.

A reviewer recently sought to put down a critic who dared to praise Longfellow and his friend James Russell Lowell, and in the bargain, sought to downgrade that poetic duo as well, by defining them as "genteel versifiers upholding a moribund tradition" (David Mura, Song for Uncle Tom, Tonto, and Mr. Moto [Ann Arbor: University of Michigan Press, 2003]; his title implies his slant). Longfellow and many of his friends who were "genteel" (i.e., decent, intelligent, gracious, and, alas, conservative) sent out their bracing messages to untold millions, and people today could do worse than give their writings a fair shake. To those who might say today that Longfellow was too popular and hence inevitably a soft "versifier," my harsh reply is that they simply don't understand him. To those who say he scribbled with too much facility, I am willing to cast him as Robert Browning's Andrea del Sarto, who is made to say this about his creative efforts: "Some good son / Paint my two hundred pictures—let him try!" As for my pleasant but labor-intensive concentration on Longfellow and his works, and on his family, his friends, his letters, his rivals, and his critics as well, let me quote these apt lines from Longfellow-admirer Robert Frost's "After Apple-Picking": "I am overtired / Of the great harvest I myself desired."

Before sleep sets in, let me conclude by expressing the hope that consulting this reference will send lovers of—let's say it—old-fashioned literature to, or back to, Longfellow's texts with renewed pleasure, perhaps added understanding, and maybe surprise. Young readers, high school and college students, university graduate students, and scholars specializing in nineteenth-century American literature and social history may all gain something from my harvest here. Readers, please note that I include too many dates, hoping that they may be useful to some; I minimize them by putting most in parentheses and by abbreviating names of months, knowing that most readers will skim over them when they wish. I hope my short lists of abbreviations and use of short titles won't be troublesome. Please note the use of asterisks—thus, George Washington Greene* and Charles Sumner*—to signal cross-referencing, which should prove useful to scholars. Note that I do not cross-reference Longfellow's family members when the relationship is obvious.

I wish to express my deep thanks to the editors at Harvard University Press for their gracious generosity in permitting me to quote numerous snippets from their edition of *The Letters of Henry Wadsworth Longfellow*. Also, friendly thanks to Richard H. F. Lindeman, Director of the Hawthorne-Longfellow Library at Bowdoin College, and his hearty associates, for welcoming me and letting me consult items in their Longfellow collection. Thanks also to Anita Israel of the Longfellow House, Cambridge, Massachusetts, for answering my questions concerning Longfellow scholarship, and to George Monteiro, of Brown University, for his generous assistance. Also thanks to my colleagues at the University of Pittsburgh and its library system, especially H. David Brumble, Patricia Duff, Lois Kepes, Annette M. Krupper, Lawrence Tomikel, and Thomas M. Twiss. Thanks also to the team at Impressions Book and Journal Services, Inc. Last and always best, my love to my wife Maureen and to our family—John, Jim, Christine, Bill, and Lisette.

Chronology

1776   Longfellow's father Stephen Longfellow* (1776-1849) born.

1778   Longfellow's mother Zilpah Wadsworth Longfellow* (1778-1851) born.

1804   Longfellow's parents marry, 1 January; children: Stephen Longfellow (1805-50),* Henry Wadsworth Longfellow (1807-82), Elizabeth Longfellow* (1808-29), Anne Longfellow Pierce* (1810-1901), Alexander Wadsworth Longfellow* (1814-1901), Mary Longfellow Greenleaf* (1816-1902), Ellen Longfellow* (1818-34), Samuel Longfellow* (1819-92).

1807   Henry Wadsworth Longfellow born 27 February in Portland, Maine (then part of Massachusetts).

1813   Attends Portland Academy (to 1821).

1820   Publishes first poem, in *Portland Gazette,* 17 November.

1821   Enrolls at Bowdoin College, Brunswick, Maine, but remains home first year.

1822–25   Resides and attends classes at Bowdoin.

1824   First visits Boston, publishes poem in *United States Literary Gazette.*

1825   Briefly reads law in his father's Portland law office.

1826–29   Studies in France, Spain (meets Washington Irving,* Madrid, 1837), Italy; travels in Austria, Czechoslovakia; studies in Germany.

1829–34   Lectures on various literatures and teaches French, Italian, and Spanish at Bowdoin, is librarian there (first year).

1830   Publishes *Elements of French Grammar* (translated from French text), *Manuel de Proverbes Dramatiques, Novelas Españolas.*

1831   *Le Ministre de Wakefield, Elements of French Grammar* (2nd ed.); marries Mary Storer Potter (1812-35; *see* Longfellow, Mary).

1831–40   Contributes essays on French, Spanish, Italian, and Anglo-Saxon languages and literature, and other items to *North American Review.*

1832   *Syllabus de la Grammaire Italienne; Cours de Langue Française* (including *Le Ministre de Wakefield, Proverbes Dramatiques*); *Saggi dé Novellieri d'Ogne Secolo;* delivers poem at Bowdoin's Phi Beta Kappa Society chapter.

1833   Publishes first book, *Coplas de Manrique* (translation of *Coplas por la muerte de su padre* by Jorge Manrique).

1834   Active as member of Brunswick's Unitarian Society.

1835   Travels widely in Europe with wife and friends (meets Thomas Carlyle, London; William Cullen Bryant,* Heidelberg); studies Swedish, Finnish, Danish, Old Icelandic, Dutch; wife dies in Rotterdam; *Outre-Mer.*

1836   Continues to travel and study; meets Nathan Appleton* and his family, including Frances ("Fanny") Elizabeth Appleton (1817–61; *see* Longfellow, Fanny).

1837   Establishes residence in Craigie House.*

1837–54   Lectures at Harvard, as Smith Professor of Modern Languages and Belles Lettres, on various literatures and teaches French, German, Italian, and Spanish.

1837   Forms "The Five of Clubs" with Henry Russell Cleveland,* Cornelius Felton,* George Hillard,* and Charles Sumner.*

1839   *Hyperion.*

1840   Lectures on Dante and Jean Paul Richter at the New York Mercantile Library Association (late Jan).

1841   *Voices of the Night, Ballads and Other Poems;* records plan to write *Christus: A Mystery;* begins to contribute to *Graham's Magazine.* Edgar Allan Poe* begins to accuse him of plagiarism.

1842   Longfellow travels in Europe on leave of absence (meets Ferdinand Freiligrath,* in St. Goar, Germany; Charles Dickens,* John Forster,* and Walter Savage Landor, London and Bath); *Poems on Slavery.*

1843   Marries Fanny Appleton (*see* Longfellow, Fanny); Nathan Appleton,* Fanny's father, transfers title to Craigie House* to Fanny. Fanny's and Longfellow's children: Charles Appleton Longfellow* (1844-93), Ernest Wadsworth Longfellow* (1845–1921), Fanny Longfellow (1847-1848), Alice Longfellow* (1850-1928), Edith Longfellow Dana* (1853-1915), Anne Allegra Longfellow* (1855-1934); *The Spanish Student.*

1844   Is asked to accept nomination for Congress, declines; edits *The Waif.*

1845   Accused again by Poe of plagiarism; *Poems, The Belfry of Bruges and Other Poems;* edits *Poets and Poetry of Europe* (rev. ed., with Supplement, 1871).

1846   Edits *The Estray.*

1847   *Evangeline: A Tale of Acadie.*

1849   *Kavanagh: A Tale, The Seaside and the Fireside.*

1850   Travels to New York City, Philadelphia, and Washington, D.C. (dines with President Zachary Taylor, meets Henry Clay and Daniel Webster*); summers with family at Nahant, Massachusetts (and often later). Receives deed to Oxbow Farm, near Stockbridge, Massachusetts, from Nathan Appleton.

1851   *The Golden Legend.*

1851–53   Grows increasingly listless and restless, frustrated at lack of time and energy to write creatively.

1854   Delivers last lecture at Harvard (19 April) and resigns Smith professorship 11 Sept.

1855   *The Song of Hiawatha.*

1857   Joins The Saturday Club.*

1858   *The Courtship of Miles Standish and Other Poems.*

1859   Receives LL.D. from Harvard University.

1860   *The New England Tragedies.*

1861   Fanny Longfellow burns to death.

1863   Charles Appleton Longfellow,* Union cavalry soldier, wounded near New Hope, Virginia. *Tales of a Wayside Inn: Part First.*

1865   Longfellow founds Dante Club with James Russell Lowell* and Charles Eliot Norton.*

1866   Respectfully declines, as Protestant, Diploma and Cross of Order of SS. Maurizio and Lazzaro, Italy; *Flower-de-Luce.*

1867   Sells Oxbow Farm for $12,500.

1867–70   *The Divine Comedy of Dante Alighieri* (Longfellow's translation).

1868   *The New England Tragedies.*

1868–69   Travels with family and friends to England and the Continent; receives honorary doctorate degrees from Oxford University and Cambridge University, 1868; meets William Gladstone and Edward George Bulwer-Lytton, London, 1868; meets Alfred, Lord Tennyson,* Isle of Wight, 1868; has audience with Queen Victoria,* Windsor, 1868.

1871   Dines with President Ulysses S. Grant. *The Divine Tragedy;* re-edits *Poets and Poetry of Europe* (with Supplement).

1872   Incurs considerable investment losses because of Boston's downtown fire (9–10 Nov). *Three Books of Song, Tales of a Wayside Inn: Part Second, Christus: A Mystery.*

1873   *Aftermath,* including *Tales of a Wayside Inn: Part Third.*

1874   Receives LL.D. from Bowdoin, nominated for Lord Rector of Edinburgh University (declines); is paid $3,000 for "The Hanging of the Crane."

1875   Attends fiftieth anniversary of Class of 1825, Bowdoin; delivers "Morituri Salutamus" there. *The Masque of Pandora and Other Poems.*

1876   Publishes *Poems of Places* (8 vols.; 10 more vols., 1877; 6 more vols., 1878; 7 more vols., 1879).

1878   *Kéramos and Other Poems.*

1880   *Ultima Thule.*

1882   Dies at home of peritonitis, 24 March. *In the Harbor: Ultima Thule—Part II* (published posthumously).

1883   *Michael Angelo* (posthumous).

1884   Longfellow bust in Poets' Corner of Westminster Abbey, London, unveiled.

1886   *A Complete Edition of Mr. Longfellow's Poetical and Prose Works,* 11 volumes.

Short Titles of Works by Longfellow Cited

Aftermath   *Aftermath* (Boston: Osgood, 1873).

Ballads   *Ballads and Other Poems* (Cambridge: John Owen, 1842).

Birds   *Birds of Passage* (with date, as parts of other collections of poetry).

Bruges   *The Belfry of Bruges and Other Poems* (Cambridge: John Owen, 1845).

Coplas   *Coplas de Don Jorge Manrique* (Boston: Allen & Ticknor, 1833).

Courtship   *The Courtship of Miles Standish and Other Poems* (Boston: Ticknor & Fields, 1858).

Flower   *Flower-de-Luce* (Boston: Ticknor & Fields, 1867).

Harbor   *In the Harbor, Ultima Thule—Part II* (Boston: Houghton Mifflin, 1882).

Kéramos   *Kéramos and Other Poems* (Boston: Houghton, Osgood, 1878).

Pandora   *The Masque of Pandora and Other Poems* (Boston: Osgood, 1875).

PP.   *Poems of Places*, ed. Henry W. Longfellow (31 vols., Boston: Osgood, 1876–79).

Scudder   Horatio Scudder, ed., *The Poetical Works of Henry Wadsworth Longfellow,* Cambridge Edition (Boston: Houghton Mifflin, 1893).

S/F   *The Seaside and the Fireside* (Boston: Ticknor, Reed & Fields, 1850).

Three   *Three Books of Song* (Boston: Osgood, 1872).

Thule   *Ultima Thule* (Boston: Houghton Mifflin, 1880).

Voices   *Voices of the Night* (Cambridge: John Owen, 1839).

Short Titles of Critical and Biographical Works Cited

Arms   George Arms, *The Fields Were Green* . . . (Stanford: Stanford University Press, 1953).

Arvin   Newton Arvin, *Longfellow: His Life and Work* (Boston: Little, Brown and Company, 1963).

Brenan   Gerald Brenan, *The Literature of the Spanish People: From Roman Times to the Present Day* (Cambridge: Cambridge University Press, 1951).

Cowie   Alexander Cowie, *The Rise of the American Novel* (New York: American Book Company, 1951).

Crowninshield   Arthur Hilen, ed., *The Diary of Clara Crowninshield: A European Tour with Longfellow 1835–1836* (Seattle: University of Washington Press, 1956).

Green   Martin Green, *The Problem of Boston: Some Readings in Cultural History* (New York: W.W. Norton & Company, 1966).

Higginson   Thomas Wentworth Higginson, *Henry Wadsworth Longfellow* (Boston and New York: Houghton Mifflin, 1902).

Hilen   Andrew Hilen, *Longfellow and Scandinavia: A Study of the Poet's Relationship with the Northern Languages and Literature* (1947; Hamden: Archon Books, 1970).

Hilen, ed.   Andrew Hilen, ed., *The Letters of Henry Wadsworth Longfellow,* 6 vols. (Cambridge: The Belknap Press of Harvard University Press, 1966–82).

Hirsh   Edward L. Hirsh, *Henry Wadsworth Longfellow* (Minneapolis: University of Minnesota Press, 1964).

Little   George Thomas Little, *Longfellow's Boyhood Poems* . . . , ed. Ray W. Pettengill (Saratoga Springs: R.W. Pettengill, 1925).

S. Longfellow   Samuel Longfellow, *Life of Henry Wadsworth Longfellow,* 3 vols. (Boston and New York: Houghton, Mifflin, 1891).

More   Paul Elmer More, "The Centenary of Longfellow," in *Shelburne Essays*, 5th ser., 132-57 (Boston and New York: Houghton Mifflin, 1908).

Morison   Samuel Eliot Morison, *Three Centuries of Harvard, 1636-1936* (Cambridge: Harvard University Press, 1936).

Moyne   Ernest J. Moyne, *Hiawatha and Kalevala: A Study of the Relationship between Longfellow's "Indian Edda" and the Finnish Epic* (Helsinki: Academia Scientiarum Fennica, 1963).

Mrs. Longfellow   Edward Wagenknecht, ed., *Mrs. Longfellow: Selected Letters and Journals of Fanny Appleton Longfellow (1817-1861)* (New York: Longmans, Green, 1956).

Poe Log   Dwight Thomas and David K. Jackson, *The Poe Log: A Documentary Life of Edgar Allan Poe, 1809-1849* (Boston: G.K. Hall & Co., 1987).

Robertson   Eric S. Robertson, *Life of Henry Wadsworth Longfellow* (London: W. Scott, 1887).

Tharp   Louise Hall Tharp, *Three Saints and a Sinner: Julia Ward Howe, Louise, Annie and Sam Ward* (Boston: Little, Brown and Company, 1956).

Thompson   Lawrance Thompson, *Young Longfellow (1807-1843)* (New York: Macmillan Company, 1938).

"Tribute"   "Tribute to Henry W. Longfellow," *Proceedings of the Massachusetts Historical Society* 19 (April 1882): 266-78.

Tryon   W. S. Tryon, *Parnassus Corner: A Life of James T. Fields, Publisher to the Victorians* (Boston: Houghton Mifflin, 1964).

Wagenknecht, 1955   Edward Wagenknecht, *Henry Wadsworth Longfellow: A Full-Length Portrait* (New York: Longmans, Green & Co., 1955).

Wagenknecht, 1986   Edward Wagenknecht, *Henry Wadsworth Longfellow: His Poetry and Prose* (New York: Ungar, 1986).

Williams   Cecil B. Williams, *Henry Wadsworth Longfellow* (New York: Twayne, 1964).

Abbreviations of Periodicals Cited in Which Longfellow Published

AM   *Atlantic Monthly*

AS   *Atlantic Souvenir*

GM   *Graham's Magazine*

KM   *Knickerbocker Magazine*

NAR   *North American Review*

NEM   *New-England Magazine*

PM   *Putnam's Monthly Magazine*

SLM   *Southern Literary Messenger*

Token   *The Token and Atlantic Souvenir*

USLG   *United States Literary Gazette*

A

"THE ABBOT JOACHIM." *See Christus: A Mystery*.

"AFTERMATH" (1873). Poem, in *Aftermath*. After the main harvest comes the silent, gloomy "harvesting of ours," not "sweet" and flowery, but instead a second crop containing weeds and tangles. Longfellow placed this poetic gem last in the volume titled *Aftermath*. By the superb aftermath metaphor in it Longfellow suggests that these poems are not products of his youth or middle years, but those of the autumn of his life. Longfellow avoids adding a didactic stanza or two, and instead lets the reader harvest the moral for himself.

Bibliography: Arms; Arvin; Williams.

AFTERMATH (1873). Book of poems. I. *Tales of a Wayside Inn* [Part Third]: "Prelude," "The Spanish Jew's Tale, Azrael," "Interlude," "The Poet's Tale, Charlemagne," "Interlude," "The Student's Tale, Emma and Eginhard," "Interlude," "The Sicilian's Tale, The Monk of Casal-Maggiore," "The Spanish Jew's Second Tale, Scanderbeg," Interlude," "The Musician's Tale, The Mother's Ghost," "The Landlord's Tale, The Rhyme of Sir Christopher," "Finale." II. *Birds of Passage* [Flight the Third]: "Fata Morgana," "The Haunted Chamber," "The Meeting," "Vox Populi," "The Castle-Builder," "Changed," "The Challenge," "The Brook and the Wave," "From the Spanish Concioneros" ("Eyes So Tristful," "Some Day, Some Day," "Come, O Death," "Glove of Black"), "Aftermath." Ac-

cording to Longfellow's letter to James Ripley Osgood* (11 Jul 1873), the offer of £200 from George Routledge (1812–88) to publish an edition of *Aftermath* in England was acceptable.

Bibliography: Hilen, ed.

"AFTERNOON IN FEBRUARY" (1846). Poem, in *GM,* Sept 1845; *Bruges.* On a cold, sluggish day, the poet sees a funeral train, hears its bell, and his heart wails and tolls likewise. This intricately rhyming little poem has been likened to works by the later imagists.

Bibliography: Clark, Harry Hayden, ed. *Major American Poets.* New York: American Book Company, 1836.

AGASSIZ, LOUIS (1807–73). Scientist and educator. Jean Louis Rololphe Agassiz was born in Motier, Switzerland, was educated in Zurich, Heidelberg, and Munich (1824–30), published a monograph on Brazilian fish (1829), and began studying in Paris (1831). He was sponsored by Georges Cuvier and Alexander von Humboldt. He began to teach natural history at Neuchâtel (1832); published on fish, including extinct species (1833–34); soon concentrated on British, European, and Russian marine creatures, developing zoological nomenclature (1839–46); and studied and published on glaciers (1840–47). Financed by Friedrich Wilhelm IV of Prussia, Agassiz visited the United States (1846), lectured in the Boston area, and decided to teach at Harvard and remain in America (1848). He traveled and explored widely, in the Great Lakes region and off Florida and the Bahamas (1848-1851), publishing *Lake Superior* (1850) as one result. He wrote four volumes on the natural history of the United States, including *Essay on Classification* (1857), which was weakened by his espousal of the special-creation theory as opposed to the theories of Charles Darwin. With the help of public and private financing ($600,000 by 1859), Agassiz built the museum of Comparative Zoology at Harvard. Today it is popularly known as the Agassiz Museum. Expeditions took Agassiz to Brazil, the Rocky Mountains, Cuba, and around the Horn to California (1865-71). An apoplectic stroke (1869) slowed his professional activity.

Agassiz married Cécile Braun in Neuchâtel (1833) and had two daughters and a son with her. Incompatibility led to her return to the home of her parents with the children. She died in Carlsruhe (1848). In 1850 Agassiz sent for his children and also married Elizabeth Cabot Cary (1822-1907). Agassiz and his second wife conducted a school for young ladies in their home in Cambridge (1855-63). One of their students, in 1858 or so, was Anne Denison Wadsworth, the daughter of Alexander Scammell Wadsworth,* Longfellow's uncle. Agassiz's son, Alexander, much encouraged by his stepmother as well as Agassiz himself, became a scientist, a copper-mine manager, and the curator of the Agassiz Museum. Agassiz's practical laboratory, classroom, and pedagogical methods helped modernize American teaching of natural history.

Longfellow's journal entries record his friendship with Agassiz. They first met at the home of Cornelius Conway Felton;* at which time Longfellow describes Agassiz as "A pleasant, voluble man, with a bright, beaming face" (9 Jan 1847). The two entertained one another at dinners and were fellow guests at the homes of others. When Nathan Appleton,* Longfellow's father-in-law, entertained them at dinner, Agassiz took the occasion to praise the description of the Rhone glacier in Longfellow's *Hyperion* (3, 4 Feb 1847). Longfellow attended lectures by Agassiz. In 1851 he introduced Longfel-

low to Jean Jacques Antoine Ampère (1800-64), literary historian and Dante scholar. Longfellow sent Agassiz his poem in French titled "Noël," to accompany a 1854 Christmas basket of wines. In February 1857 Agassiz persuaded Longfellow to join the Saturday Club,* founded the year before. Longfellow wrote "The Fiftieth Birthday of Agassiz: May 28, 1857" to celebrate the event. Longfellow wrote Charles Sumner,* their mutual friend, that Agassiz was delighted with the $200,000 already raised to start building his museum (27 Apr 1859). Longfellow and Agassiz attended a Boston party hosted by Oliver Wendell Holmes* to honor Paul Charles Morphy (1838-84), the phenomenal American chess champion (1 Jun 1859). Agassiz and Longfellow met the London publisher, Alexander Macmillan (1815-96), at the home of the publisher James T. Fields.*

Beginning in 1870, Longfellow was saddened by Agassiz's illness and inability to work at his former pace. Still, the two met "Mr. Bret Harte, from California" at a Saturday Club dinner (25 Feb 1871). Longfellow drove Agassiz to a dinner to meet Ulysses S. Grant, presumably in Boston (15 Sep 1871). Longfellow, Agassiz, and John Tyndall (1820-93), the British physicist and student of glaciers and light, were guests at the home of James Russell Lowell* (26 Oct 1872). After Agassiz's death, Longfellow composed "Three Friends of Mine," a sonnet praising Agassiz, Felton, and Sumner.

Bibliography: Green; S. Longfellow; Lurie, Edward. *Louis Agassiz: A Life in Science.* Chicago: University of Chicago Press, 1960; Morison.

"THE ALARM BELL OF ATRI." *See* "The Sicilian's Tale," in *Tales of a Wayside Inn*, Part Second.

"ALLAH" (1878). Poem, translated from the German poet Siegfried August Mahlmann (1771-1826), in *Kéramos*. Allah gives light, rest, succor. The poet will gladly fly to "Allah's dwelling," where there will be no darkness and he will see again.

"ALL' ILLUSTRISSIMO SIGNOR PROFESSORE LOWELLO" (1887). Poem, in Italian.

When James Russell Lowell,* because of a sore throat, could not attend either a meeting of the Dante Club (10 Jan 1866) and or a later dinner with Longfellow (12 Jan 1866), Longfellow sent him his prescription for a quick cure: Gargle with claret or any other wine. Lowell replied in a poem concluding that he was too sick to dine out even if Horace asked him to do so.

Bibliography: Hilen, ed.; S. Longfellow.

"AMALFI" (1875). Poem, in *AM,* May 1875; *Pandora, Birds* (1875). The poet, in his snowy "north-land," remembers "Amalfi [sitting] in the heat," envisages an "indolent" monk looking down upon the town's fountains, mills, girls assigned by "inexorable fate" to a "life of toil," and remembering crusaders and pilgrims, and seeming to "swoon / In the happy afternoon."

"ANCIENT SPANISH BALLADS" (1835). Poems, translated from various sources, in *Outre-Mer;* Scudder. I. The waters of Rio Verde are mixed with much Moorish and Christian blood. II. When King Alfonso VIII of Castile (1158-1214) sought to replenish his war-depleted treasury by taxing his Castilian hidalgos, three thousand of them tied gold coins to spears, charged his highness, and all died, save three. (A longer version of this translation, when first published, in *NEM,* Apr 1932, was titled "The Ballad of the Five Farthings.") III. Charlemagne was harassing northern Spain (Roncevalles, 778); so Bernardo rallied young peasants and old—"gallant Leonese," all—to his "standard," to fight against "the false king."

Bibliography: Brenan.

"THE ANGEL AND THE CHILD" (1870). Poem, translated from French poet Jean Reboul (1796-1864), in *AM,* Sep 1870; *Three.* An angel bends over a child's cradle, notes a resemblance to himself, says the earth, unworthy of the child, has pains with joy, and shadows with nice days. No one should mourn when this "pure" child wings with the angel to "eternal realms of light!" Mother, the poet says, your son has died.

"THE ANGLER'S SONG" (1825). Poem, in *USLG,* 15 Mar 1825. The lark and the woodsman are on their way. The poet notes the glorious morning, the shadow-casting oak, and the "sultry" high-up sun, as he plies rod and "Tangling" line. Only at eventide, when "the wind sighs," does he depart.

"ANGLO SAXON LITERATURE" (1838). Article, in *NAR,* Jul 1838. This essay also is the Introduction to *Dictionary of the Anglo-Saxon Language* (1838) by Joseph L. Bosworth.*

Bibliography: Hilen, ed.; Thompson.

"ANNIE OF THARAW" (1846). Poem, translated from the German poet Simon Dach (1605-59), in *Hyperion; Bruges.* The persona addresses Anke von Tharau, his "true love," and says they will stand by each other in all weather and despite sadness. If she wanders, he will follow, even through armies. Can anything in "the turmoil of life" bother them? Only "dissension" could convert their household, where he is king, and she is queen, from a heaven to a hell.

"ANNIVERSARY POEM" (1824). Unpublished poem, which Longfellow delivered before the Peucinian Society (22 Nov 1824).

Bibliography: Little.

APPLETON, FANNY. *See* Longfellow, Fanny.

APPLETON, HARRIET COFFIN SUMNER (1802–67). The second wife of Longfellow's father-in-law Nathan Appleton* and the mother of three of his children.

APPLETON, MARIA THERESA GOLD (1786–1833). The mother of Fanny Longfellow,* Longfellow's second wife. Maria Appleton's parents were Thomas Gold, a lawyer in Pittsfield, Massachusetts, and Martha Marsh Gold. Maria was the first wife of Nathan Appleton,* and had four children with him, in addition to Fanny.

APPLETON, MARY (1813–89). *See* Mackintosh, Mary Appleton.

APPLETON, NATHAN (1779–1861). The father of Longfellow's second wife, Fanny Longfellow.* He had two older brothers, Isaac Appleton (1762–1853) and Samuel Appleton* (1766–1853), and one younger brother, Eben Appleton (1784–1833). In 1806 Nathan Appleton married Maria Theresa Gold (1786–1833; *see* Appleton, Maria Theresa Gold). They had five children: Thomas Gold Appleton* (1812–84), Mary Appleton (1813–89; *see* Mackintosh, Mary Appleton), Charles Sedgwick Appleton (1815–35), Fanny, and George William Appleton (1826–29). When his wife Maria died, Nathan Appleton married Harriet Coffin Sumner (1802–67; *see* Appleton, Harriet Coffin Sumner). Their three children were William Sumner Appleton* (1840–1903), Harriot Appleton (1841–1923; Mrs. Greeley Stevenson Curtis), and Nathan Appleton (1843–1906).

The elder Nathan Appleton was an enormously successful banker, textile industrialist, and politician, whose fortune ultimately amounted to $1,800,000. In his factories, he used water power sensibly and employed women laborers. He served in Congress (beginning in 1830), advocated better treatment of slaves, and favored a protective tariff. Gilbert Stuart (1755–1828) painted portraits of Nathan and Maria Appleton. Nathan Appleton took his children Thomas, Mary, and Fanny, and also his invalid cousin William Sullivan Appleton,* for a long European vacation (from November 1835 through the summer of 1837). When they were in Thun, Switzerland, on their way to Interlaken, Longfellow chanced to meet them (20 Jul 1836); they met again at Interlaken (31 Jul 1836). He admired the entire family, but especially Fanny, who, however, was initially less attracted to him. Longfellow's ripening friendship with the Appletons was put on hold when in August he had to escort back to America Clara Crowninshield,* who was a family friend, and also the wife of William Cullen Bryant,* and their daughter Fanny.

Nathan Appleton demonstrated his approval of Longfellow as a son-in-law when, following the wedding vacation Longfellow and Fanny enjoyed (Jul 1843), Nathan bought and gave to Fanny Craigie House,* their happy home until Fanny's death (10 Jul 1861). Already desperately ill, Nathan Appleton died (14 Jul), one day after her funeral. Fanny's and Longfellow's surviving five children inherited a considerable part of Appleton's fortune.

Bibliography: Gregory, Frances W. *Nathan Appleton: Merchant and Entrepreneur. 1779–1861.* Charlottesville: University Press of Virginia, 1976; S. Longfellow; *Mrs. Longfellow;* Wagenknecht, 1955.

APPLETON, NATHAN (1843–1906). The half-brother of Fanny Longfellow.*

APPLETON, SAMUEL (1766–1853). The brother of Nathan Appleton, Longfellow's father-in-law. In his journal (20 Apr 1850), Longfellow describes Samuel Appleton as a "gentle, glowing, benignant, happy old man, in his crimson velvet dressing gown, like a sun setting in crimson clouds, shining over all with genial, cheerful light." Longfellow admired Appleton's fiery denunciations not only of Daniel Webster* but also of the Fugitive Slave Act of 1850.

Bibliography: S. Longfellow.

APPLETON, THOMAS GOLD (1812–84). The brother of Fanny Longfellow and therefore Longfellow's brother-in-law. Tom Appleton, poet, essayist, wit, notable conversationalist, and philanthropist, was born in Boston. He attended the Boston Latin School, the Round Hill in Northampton, Massachusetts; studied law to please his father; graduated from Harvard (1831); and thereafter lived the easy life of a cultured, well-traveled bachelor. He painted, collected art, and was a benefactor of the Boston Museum of Fine Arts. Oliver Wendell Holmes* called Appleton the wittiest man of his time and place. Most of his bons mots are lost, but he is memorably alleged to have said, "All good Americans, when they die, go to Paris." His rather stilted verse is found in *Faded Leaves* (1872) and *More Leaves* (1874). His prose, often reviewed as "pleasant," is sufficiently represented in *A Nile Journal* (1876) and *Syrian Sunshine* (1877).

Longfellow met Appleton in Thun, Switzerland (20 Jul 1836), during the Appleton family's long European vacation. Tom and Fanny were devoted to each other, and Longfellow greatly relished the company of this witty bon vivant. When in the states, Tom occasionally dined at Longfellow's home and met, and held his own with, such luminaries as Louis Agassiz,* George William Curtis,* Cornelius Conway Felton,* Ralph Waldo Emerson,* Oliver Wendell Holmes, James Russell Lowell,* Dom Pedro II of Brazil, and William Hickling Prescott.* When in Europe, Appleton's path was often smoothed by commendatory letters of introduction Longfellow sent to cultivated friends of his there. In 1860 Tom and Longfellow purchased together a vacation house at Nahant, Massachusetts. Tom accompanied Longfellow and other family members on the poet's final trip to Europe (1868-69). Tom, who traveled widely, sent many letters to Longfellow from London, Paris, Italy, Egypt, Greece, Jerusalem, and elsewhere, and often included in them information about writers and scenes dear to Longfellow. In some letters, Tom commented on Longfellow's poetry; in one (1 Dec 1851) he praised the figures of speech in *The Golden Legend.* As for Longfellow on Appleton's work, among numerous chit-chat letters may be found one (3 Mar 1872) to the effect that *Faded Leaves* "is full of beautiful thoughts" but reveals "an occasional haziness of expression."

Bibliography: Hale, Susan. *Life and Letters of Thomas Gold Appleton.* New York: D. Appleton and Company, 1885; Hilen, ed.; S. Longfellow; *Mrs. Longfellow;* Wagenknecht, 1955.

APPLETON, WILLIAM SULLIVAN (1815–36). The son of Joseph Appleton (1751-95), who was the uncle of Nathan Appleton (1779-1861).* Hence, William was the cousin, once removed, of Fanny Longfellow.* Longfellow met William, who was grievously ill, during the Appleton family European tour, and was kind to him until William died in Schaffhausen, Switzerland.

Bibliography: Mrs. Longfellow.

APPLETON, WILLIAM SUMNER (1840–1903). The half-brother of Fanny Longfellow.*

"AN APRIL DAY" (1825). Poem, in *USLG,* 15 Apr 1825; *Voices.* When winter and storms end, life renews, "teeming with bright forms," birds are "quick in the bright sun," sunsets glow on the hills, the moon rises over the rock-bordered lake, and stars twinkle. Thoughts, "wedded" to April, will mature by autumn.

"THE ARROW AND THE SONG" (1846). Poem, in *Bruges.* The poet "shot an arrow into the air," could not see its flight; similarly, he "breathed a song into the air," lacked sight to discern its flight. The poet finds the fine arrow in an oak, the song in a friend's heart. This old chestnut was once unbelievably popular.

Bibliography: Kip, H. Z. "The Origin of 'The Arrow and the Song.'" *Philological Quarterly* 9 (Jan 1930): 76-78.

"THE ARSENAL AT SPRINGFIELD" (1844). Poem, in *GM,* Apr 1844; *Bruges.* The enormous arsenal has "burnished arms" piled to the ceiling; it resembles a pipe organ, silent until "the death-angel" fingers its keys and creates laments, groans, and other war-time sounds. The past—including Saxons, Norsemen, Florentines, Aztecs, and recent pillaging soldiers—was full of such "universal clamor." But

> Were half the power that fills the world
>   with terror,
>   Were half the wealth bestowed on
>   camps and courts,
> Given to redeem the human mind from er-
>   ror,
>   There were no need of arsenals and
>   forts.

Longfellow was inspired to write this effective and often-anthologized poem when he and Fanny, on their wedding journey (summer 1843), visited the arsenal at Springfield, Massachusetts, in the company of Charles Sumner.* While Sumner was asserting that money spent on weaponry might better be used to fund a comparably expensive library, Fanny observed that the shining gun barrels resembled an organ which would evoke mournful music and urged Longfellow to write a poem about peace.

Bibliography: Arvin; Wagenknecht, 1986.

"ART AND NATURE" (1832). Sonnet, translated, unsigned, from the Italian poet Francisco de Medrano (1570–1607?), in *NEM,* Nov 1832, as "Nature and Art"; *Coplas,* as "Nature and Art"; Scudder. Fountains, gardens, and like products of "human artifice" are tiresome compared to rivers, meadows, hills, and other "free and wild" natural creations, designed by the "Eternal Architect."

Bibliography: Thompson.

"THE ARTIST" (1878). Sonnet, translated from Michelangelo, in *Kéramos.* Just as the inside of a "marble block" contains everything a sculptor can imagine and make out of it, so, "fair lady," within you "hidden lie" thoughts about "death and love." It is my fault if my "humble brain . . . draw[s] but death from thee."

"THE ASSUMPTION OF THE VIRGIN" (1832). Poem, translated from Luis Ponce de León (1460?–1521), *NAR,* Apr 1832; Scudder. The "peerless Queen of air" ascends to "The opening heavens," wearing moonlike sandals, crowned with stars by angels, looking down on our "thorny valley," and drawing as by "magnet power" our "imprisoned soul[s]."

ASTOR, JOHN JACOB (1822–90). Grandson of the merchant millionaire John Jacob Astor (1763–1848) and the brother-in-law of Samuel Ward.* Ward asked Longfellow in 1839 if he would like to apply for the position of traveling companion and tutor for the young man during a six-month tour of Europe. Longfellow applied for the job, but the Astor family decided that John Astor didn't need such a companion. In 1841, when young John Astor was attending Harvard Law School, he and Longfellow had dinner together.

Bibliography: Hilen, ed.

"AT LA CHAUDEAU" (1877). Poem, translated from the French poet Xavier Marmier (1809–92), in *PP, Harbor.* The poet was happy at La Chaudeau when his "years [were] twice ten." But then he wandered. Now gray and old, he returns, where "A sweet remembrance keeps off age." He hopes that friends whom God intended not to leave La Chaudeau will realize he wants only to be back by its castle.

"AUF WIEDERSEHEN: IN MEMORY OF J.T.F." (1881). Poem, in *AM,* Jun 1881; *Harbor.* It is painful to wait until we can again see our departed loved ones. It would be terrible if they feel sorrow like ours or if they remember us no longer. Let us believe that death is a beginning and allow faith to overcome reason's "confines." This poem was written a few days after the death of James T. Fields.*

Bibliography: Wagenknecht, 1986.

"AUTUMNAL NIGHTFALL" (1824). Poem, unsigned, in *USLG,* 1 Dec 1824; Scudder. Autumn "is the year's eventide," mournful, sad, lifeless. Dead leaves remind us "of our mortality, / And of our fading years." Spring, which "shall renew with cheerful days," won't bring back the poet's "joys." The distinguished jurist, Theophilus Parsons (1797–1882), briefly editor of the *United States Literary Gazette* (in 1824), in which "Autumnal Nightfall" was published, delighted Longfellow by telling him that the poem had been attributed to William Cullen Bryant.*

Bibliography: Higginson.

"AUTUMN: 'THOU COMEST . . .'" (1846). Sonnet, in *Bruges.* Autumn arrives, "heralded by . . . rain" and standing like Charlemagne on his golden bridge. He blesses the land, receives the farmers' prayers, and is followed by the wind, his "almoner, . . . scatter[ing] . . . golden leaves." The final line is an unusual alexandrine, that is, it is in iambic hexameter not pentameter.

"AUTUMN WITHIN" (1882). Poem, in *Harbor.* "Youth and spring" are outside, and birds sing and build; but cold autumn, silence, and dead leaves reside in the poet, and the mill within him murmurs not.

"AUTUMN: 'WITH WHAT A GLORY . . . '" (1825). Poem, in *USLG,* 1 Oct 1825; *Voices.* Spring with its buds is followed by the "pomp and pageant" of autumn, which is mellow, vivid, passionate. Autumn also resembles "a faint old man," who listens to robins, bluebirds, and winter birds, and who willingly responds when death beckons with its "solemn hymn." The conclusion of this poem closely resembles the tone of "Thanatopsis" (1817) by William Cullen Bryant,* which coincidence Longfellow later acknowledged.

Bibliography: Arvin; Little; S. Longfellow; Wagenknecht, 1986.

"AZRAEL." *See* "The Spanish Jew's Tale," in *Tales of a Wayside Inn,* Part Third.

B

BACHI, PIETRO (1787–1853). Author of *Gl' Inni Giovenili della Signora Anna Letizia Barbauld, tradotti in Italiano* (Boston, 1832), an Italian reading book. Longfellow reviewed it favorably (*American Monthly Review,* Jul 1832), in the process becoming an advocate for teaching foreign languages to children. Bachi taught both Italian and Spanish at Harvard (1826–46). When Longfellow became Smith Professor of languages at Harvard (1836), he also became Bachi's admiring supervisor. Bachi went bankrupt (1844) and was later asked to resign from Harvard (1846).

"THE BALD EAGLE" (1833). Prose tale, unsigned, in *Token,* 1833.

Bibliography: Hilen, ed.; Thompson.

"THE BALLAD OF CARMILHAN." *See* "The Musician's Tale," in *Tales of a Wayside Inn,* Part Second.

"THE BALLAD OF THE FIVE FARTHINGS." *See* "Ancient Spanish Ballads."

"A BALLAD OF THE FRENCH FLEET" **(1877).** Poem, in Boston *Transcript,* 17 Mar 1877; Scudder. Standing "in the Old South" in October 1746, Prince prays that, if it be God's will, let the inimical French fleet, commanded by boastful Admiral D'Anville, be stopped so that his target, "Boston Town," would be spared. Sure enough, lightning, hail, and an "October gale" combine to break up the fleet, scatter it "as a smoke,"

and sink it "like lead in the brine." This poem was occasioned when efforts were being made to save Boston's Old South Meeting House from demolition. Longfellow's source for this episode was *History of the Colony and Province of Massachusetts* (2 vols., 1764, 1767) by Thomas Hutchinson (1711–80), colonial administrator and historian. Longfellow's references are to Thomas Prince (1687–1758), Massachusetts pastor and historian, and to Jean Baptiste Louis Frédéric de le Rochefoucauld, duc d'Anville (1709–46).

Bibliography: Frégault, Guy. *Canada: The War of Conquest.* Trans. Margaret M. Cameron. New York: Oxford University Press, 1969; Wagenknecht, 1986.

BALLADS AND OTHER POEMS (1842). A collection of poems: *Ballads:* "The Skeleton in Armor," "The Wreck of the Hesperus," "The Luck of Edenhall," "The Elected Knight," "The Children of the Lord's Supper." *Miscellaneous:* "The Village Blacksmith," "Endymion," "The Two Locks of Hair," "It Is Not Always May," "The Rainy Day," "God's-Acre," "To the River Charles," "Blind Bartimeus," "The Goblet of Life," "Maidenhood," "Excelsior."

BANCROFT, GEORGE (1800–91). Diplomat and historian. He was born in Worcester, Massachusetts, graduated from Harvard (1817), earned his Ph.D. at Göttingen (1820), tutored Greek at Harvard (1822), and with Joseph Green Cogswell (1786–

1871) established the experimental Round School at Northampton, Massachusetts (1823–31). He published the first three volumes of what was to be his *History of the United States, from the Discovery of the American Continent* (1834, 1837, 1838). A Jacksonian Democrat, Bancroft began a political career: Secretary of the Navy (1845–46) and acting Secretary of War (1845) in the cabinet of President James K. Polk; minister to England (1846–49); and minister to Germany (1867–74). Gradually came the fourth and fifth volumes of his history (1852), and the sixth, seventh, eighth, ninth, and tenth (1856, 1858, 1860, 1866, 1875). After and amid other writing, he issued his revised history (6 vols., 1875–76) and an expanded revision (6 vols., 1883–85). Bancroft married the well-to-do Sarah H. Dwight (1827); they had three children, and then she died (1837). He married Elizabeth Davis Bliss (1803–86), a widow with two children (1838); she and Bancroft had no children together.

Longfellow was always impressed by Bancroft, who advised Longfellow to study in Göttingen (1826) and gave him letters of recommendation useful there (1829). In a letter to Clara Crowninshield* (21 May 1838), Longfellow expresses surprise that Bancroft married Elizabeth Bliss, whom he defined as "too much of an icicle to want a husband"; the poet mustn't have known about her previous marriage (or perhaps he did). Longfellow saw Bancroft at Nahant (1841) and in Cambridge (1842). From England, Bancroft sent him praise of *Evangeline* (1848). According to his journal (8 Jul 1855), Longfellow dined with Bancroft in Newport, Rhode Island. Longfellow's friend George Washington Greene,* author of a biography of his grandfather General Nathanael Greene, American Revolutionary War hero, took umbrage at Bancroft's treatment of General Greene in his history; Longfellow, in 1866, 1867, 1874, 1876, and 1877, wrote Greene to sympathize, though sometimes coolly.

Bibliography: Hilen, ed.; S. Longfellow.

"THE BANKS OF THE CHER" (1877). Poem, translated from the French poet Antoine-Marin le Miérre (1723–93), in *PP,* ed. Longfellow; Scudder. The poet beholds the beautiful, ermine-white chateau of Chenonceaux, beside the Cher River, in the storied French province between Tours and Amboise. He recalls varied historical events that occurred hereabouts, from the time of Saracen defeats by Charlemagne to those of amorous Francis I and Henry II. The chateau ennobles Cher waters.

"THE BARON OF ST. CASTINE." *See* "The Student's Second Tale," in *Tales of a Wayside Inn,* Part Second.

"BARRÉGES" (1877). Poem, translated from the French lawyer-poet Jean Jacques Lefranc Pompignan (1709–84), in *PP, Kéramos.* The persona, gladly saying goodbye to cold mountains, "misty" clouds, and terrifying torrents, thinks about his own hearth near pleasant meadows, flowers, and harvests, and bids his "lazy coursers" to speed him there.

BARTLETT, ELIZABETH (1753–1825). Longfellow's maternal grandmother, after her marriage to Peleg Wadsworth (1748–1829).* Through his Bartlett and Wadsworth ancestors, Longfellow traced four pilgrims aboard the *Mayflower,* including John Alden and Elder Brewster.

"THE BATTLE OF LOVELL'S POND" (1820). Poem, signed "Henry," in Portland *Gazette,* 17 Nov 1820; Scudder. The "cold . . . north wind" provides "a requiem" over the unmarked graves of the well-remembered patriots and of their enemies. This poem was Longfellow's first publication. Its anapestic meter imitates that of "The Destruction of Sennacherib" by Lord Byron. Longfellow's poem commemorates Lovewell's Fight (9 May 1725), near Fryeburg, Maine, less than 60 miles from Brunswick, where Bowdoin College is located. Captain John Lovewell and 46 men from what is now Nashua, New Hampshire, planned to attack an Indian village near Fryeburg but were ambushed and virtually wiped out. Family tradition has it that Longfellow, aged thirteen when this poem was published, wept into his pillow when he heard unfavorable comments on it. Longfellow was inspired to write this poem by "Lovellspond," a poem by Thomas Cogswell Upham (1799–1872), a professor at Bowdoin (1824–67) who published a book of his poems titled *American Sketches* (1821). In his "Roger Malvin's Burial" (1832), Nathaniel Hawthorne* treats the moral and psychological quandary of a survivor of the battle at the pond.

Bibliography: Little; S. Longfellow; Thompson, Lawrance. "Longfellow's Original Sin of Imitation." *The Colophon,* n.s., 1 (autumn 1935); Williams.

"BAYARD TAYLOR" (1880). Poem, in *Thule.* Like a traveler eager to leave an inn before nightfall, the poet has left his body. His books gaze down at him the way "statues in the gloom / Watch o'er Maximilian's tomb." His "latest verse / Was a garland" decorating his funeral bier. Longfellow was a friend of Bayard Taylor,* travel-book writer, fiction writer, poet, diplomat, and lecturer. A memorial service for Taylor was held in Boston (9 Jan 1879). Although invited, Longfellow was unable to attend; so he sent a copy of his poem that he had written for the occasion and that was read aloud by Oliver Wendell Holmes.*

Bibliography: Hilen, ed.

BEAN, HELEN MAR (1836–95). Concord, New Hampshire, poet. When Helen Mar Bean sent Longfellow a batch of her poems, he replied (15 May 1879) and described them as having "much merit both of conception and execution." Pressed further, he invited her (27 Nov 1879) to visit him in Cambridge. Thus encouraged, she bombarded him with gifts, more verse, and a couple dozen letters. His numerous replies personify patience itself. After Helen married John Quincy Adams Bean (1818–?), also a would-be poet, in 1864, both Beans visited Longfellow. She sat for Longfellow's son Ernest Wadsworth Longfellow* to paint her portrait (1880). In his last letter to her (5 Feb 1882), Longfellow thanks her for jelly and flowers.

Bibliography: Hilen, ed.

"BECALMED" (1882). Poem, in *Harbor.* The poet, idle "upon the sea of Thought," asks for some inspiration to "fill the canvas of the mind," so that he will move forward again.

"THE BELEAGUERED CITY" (1839). Poem, in *SLM,* Nov 1839; *Voices.* The poet once read an "old, marvellous tale" about "a midnight host of spectres pale" that seemed to lay siege to Prague but vanished when cathedral bells called the faithful citizens to their morning prayers. So it is with "the human soul," which is beleaguered through hours of darkness; but when our church bells call us to prayer, "The midnight phantoms feel the spell, / The shadows sweep away," our faith shines like "a morning star," and our affrights die. Edgar Allan Poe* falsely accused Longfellow of plagiarizing from his "The Haunted Palace" in writing "The Beleaguered City." Longfellow provided clarifying details of the matter in a letter (28 Sep 1850) to Rufus Wilmot Griswold,* Poe's editorial associate and dishonest biographer.

Bibliography: Hilen, ed.; *Poe Log.*

"BELFAGOR IN BEACON STREET." Play projected by Longfellow in 1837 but never written.

Bibliography: Thompson.

"THE BELFRY OF BRUGES" (1843). Poem, in *GM,* Jan 1843; *Bruges.* The poem is divided into two parts: "Carillon" and "The Belfry of Bruges." "Carillon": The ringing of the varied bells in the Bruges carillon resembles "the poet's airy rhymes," with their images, "songs, and ditties" scattered "From the belfry of his brain." Often, literal and poetic chimes alike are ignored; at night we are sleepy, during the day, busy. Once in a while, however, some "sleepless wight," immune to the day's dins, may find pleasure in poetry, be reminded of old thoughts, and weep while dreaming. "The Belfry of Bruges": The poet recalls climbing into the belfry of Bruges early one summer morning, above the silent city, hearing swallows and "the melancholy chimes," and envisaging historic heroes of Flanders, Italian merchants, local weavers, "whiskered Spaniard[s]," and much else—until city sounds rouse him. This poem was inspired by Longfellow's visit to Europe (summer 1842). In "Longfellow's Visit to Venice" (after 1954), John Betjeman (1906-84) parodies the guidebook aspect of Longfellow's "The Belfry of Bruges" and "Nuremberg."

Bibliography: Arvin.

THE BELFRY OF BRUGES AND OTHER POEMS (1846). Collection of poems: "Carillon." "The Belfry of Bruges." *Miscellaneous:* "A Gleam of Sunshine," "The Arsenal at Springfield," "Nuremburg," "The Norman Baron," "Rain in Summer," "To a Child," "The Occultation of Orion," "The Bridge," "To the Driving Cloud." *Songs:* "Seaweed," "The Day Is Done," "Afternoon in February," "To an Old Danish Song-Book," "Walter von der Vogelweide," "Drinking Song," "The Old Clock in the Stairs," "The Arrow and the Song." *Sonnets:* "The Evening Star," "Autumn [Thou comest]," "Dante." *Translations:* "The Hemlock-Tree," "Annie of Tharaw," "The Statue over the Cathedral Door," "The Legend of the Crossbill," "The Sea Hath Its Pearls," "Poetic Aphorisms."

"BELISARIUS" (1875). Poem, in *Pandora, Birds* (1875). Belisarius, old, poor, and now blind, summarizes his military service under Justinian in Persia, Africa, Rome, Parthenope, Byzantium, and elsewhere. He is well aware that it is vain to expect gratitude or praise from the people, but is sustained by his "unconquerable will." Belisarius (505?-565), a general of the Eastern Roman Empire, served brilliantly under Emperor Justinian I (483-565) but fell out of favor (after 540). Longfellow's "Belisarius" is one of several poems lamenting the fact that fame is transitory.

Bibliography: Wagenknecht, 1986.

"THE BELL OF ATRI." *See* "The Sicilian's Tale," in *Tales of a Wayside Inn*, Part Second.

"THE BELLS OF LYNN" (1866). Poem, in *Flower.* "O Bells of Lynn!" shouts the poet repeatedly. Everyone hears this sunset curfew—fishermen, herdsmen, and even coastal waves, beneath "the spectral moon." The subtitle of this monotonous poem is "Heard at Nahant," Nahant, Massachusetts, being the location of the Longfellows' summer home.

"THE BELLS OF SAN BLAS" (1882). Poem, in *Harper's New Monthly Magazine,* Mar 1882; *Harbor.* To sailors proceeding south from Mazatlan down Mexico's west coast, the bells of San Blas are meaningless. But to the poet,

> a dreamer of dreams,
> To whom what is said and what seems
> Are often one and the same[,]

the bells are touching, searching church voices, are voices from the fading past, and though now moldy and rusted, speak querulously to him. Is the ancient faith dead? Are the old saints dead or merely forgetful? Would that we could be brought back to a world filled anew with faith. If so, our voices would resemble the return of exiled kings and lordly priests. Although these bells peal vainly,

> Out of the shadows of night
> The world rolls into light;
> It is daybreak everywhere.

Inspired by "Typical Journeys and Country Life in Mexico," by William Henry Bishop, *Harper's New Monthly Magazine* (Mar 1882), Longfellow wrote "The Bells of San Blas" only nine days before his death. It has been contrasted with "Dover Beach" (1867) by Matthew Arnold (1822-88); both "Dover Beach" and "The Bells of San Blas" deplore the diminution of religious faith in the late nineteenth century, but Longfellow finds change acceptable because of his unshaken personal faith.

Bibliography: Goss, E. H. "The Poet of the Bells." *Bay State Monthly* 1 (Feb 1884): 105-6; Williams.

BENJAMIN, PARK (1809–64). Editor, poet, and lecturer. Born in British Guiana, Benjamin was educated in New England and studied law at Harvard, under Joseph Story,* and at Yale, where he met Nathaniel Parker Willis.* Benjamin and Oliver Wendell Holmes* published some of their poetry in *The Harbinger: A May Gift* (1833). Benjamin coedited the *New-England Magazine* with Samuel Gridley Howe* (1834-35); in it he published early stories by Nathaniel Hawthorne.* When the magazine merged with the *American Monthly Magazine* (1835), he published works by Hawthorne, Holmes, and Edgar Allan Poe.* After the magazine folded (1838), Benjamin joined Horace Greeley, editor of the *New-Yorker,* and also began working with Rufus Wilmot Griswold.* Benjamin cofounded the *New World* (1839-45) and accepted works by William Cullen Bryant,* Holmes, Walt Whitman, Willis, and Longfellow. Continuing his editorial work, Benjamin was Longfellow's literary agent, married Mary Brower Western (1848; they had eight children), lectured intermittently and often oddly in verse (1849-58), and edited the *Constellation* (beginning 1858). During the Civil War, he obtained permission from President Abraham Lincoln to write Lincoln's second campaign biography (William Dean Howells* had written the first), but died before he could write it. His sister, Mary Elizabeth Benjamin, married the historian John Lothrop Motley (1814-77), whom Longfellow knew slightly.

Benjamin published Longfellow's "The Wreck of the Hesperus" in the *New World.* In the letter enclosing $25 in payment (7 Jan 1840), he asked Longfellow to write something laudatory about Richard Henry Dana Sr.,* who was soon to be lecturing in New York. He also told Longfellow he was dickering through George Stillman Hillard* for someone to write a review for him of Longfellow's *Voices of the Night.* According to a journal entry, Longfellow walked and dined with Benjamin (2 Nov 1846) and enjoyed his "capital imitations of [William Charles] Macready," the popular British actor (1793-1873) who performed in the United States (1826, 1843-44, 1849). A later journal entry (6 Apr 1850) tells of Longfellow's going to the Boston office of William Davis Ticknor and observing Benjamin's "discoursing oracular speech" in front of Cornelius Conway Felton,* James T. Fields,* and others; Longfellow adds, "He [Benjamin] is going to make lecturing his profession."

Bibliography: Hoover, Merle M. *Park Benjamin, Poet & Editor.* New York: Columbia University Press, 1948; S. Longfellow.

"BEOWULF'S EXPEDITION TO HEORT" (1838).

Poem, translated from the Anglo-Saxon *Beowulf* (tenth-century transcription), in *NAR,* Jul 1838; Scudder. When "Higelac's Thane" (Beowulf) hears about "Grendel's deeds" (the monster has raided Heort, Hrothgar's great hall), he sails "a sea-ship" with "fifteen men" and their "War-gear, Goth-like," "Over the swan's road" to "shore-cliffs shining, / Mountains steep." "The warden of the Scyldings" sees them and is amazed, for

> Ne'er saw I mightier
> Earl upon earth
> Than is your own,
> Hero in harness.

He requests a quick explanation.

"BEWARE!" (1839).

Poem, translated from the German, author unknown, in *Hyperion; Voices.* You are advised to beware of this "maiden fair," with her demure eyes, golden hair, and white bosom. "She is fooling thee!" The garland she offers is a fool's cap.

"THE BIRD AND THE SHIP" (1839).

Poem, translated from the German poet Wilhelm Müller (1794-1827), in *Hyperion; Voices.* When a "bonny boat" invites a tiny bird to perch on its mast and be merry, the bird declines, saying that it can fly "over the sails" and must "sing my weary song" beyond the knowledge of poets or printers.

"THE BIRDS OF KILLINGWORTH." *See* "The Poet's Tale," in *Tales of a Wayside Inn*, Part First.

"BIRDS OF PASSAGE" (1847).

Poem, in *The Opal: A Pure Gift for the Holidays* (New York, 1847) edited by auctioneer-wit John Keese (1805-56); *S/F.* Shadows fall, but the night is star-lit. The poet hears the "toiling, beating pinions" of invisible birds leaving lands of snow for "southern lea[s]." Their sound may be likened to that of the "wingèd words" of the poet, which like soulful cries fly through light into "our world of night."

Bibliography: Hilen, ed.

***BIRDS OF PASSAGE* (1858, 1863, 1873, 1875, 1878).** Five so-called poetic "flights," appearing thus: (l) in *The Courtship of Miles Standish and Other Poems* (1858); (2) in the first part of *Tales of a Wayside Inn* (1863); (3) in the third part of *Tales of a Wayside Inn* (1873); (4) in *The Masque of Pandora and Other Poems* (1875); (5) in *Kéramos and Other Poems* (1878).

"THE BLACK KNIGHT" (1839). Poem, translated from the German poet Johann Ludwig Uhland (1787–1862), in *Hyperion; Voices.* At glad Pentecost, the King orders Spring to break. But into the midst of playful jousts "a sable Knight" rides, opposes a youth, asks a maiden to dance, and tells a man's children to have some yellow wine. The youth falls, the girl's flowers fade, and the children drop dead. When the "fear-struck father" asks to be taken also, "the grim Guest" merely says, "Roses in the spring I gather!"

"THE BLANK BOOK OF A COUNTRY SCHOOLMASTER" (1834–35). Essays, in *KM,* 1 May 1834, Sept 1834, Jan 1835. They relate to "The Schoolmaster," some parts of which were used in *Outre-Mer.* "The Happy Man and the Lucky Dog," part of "The Blank Book of a Country Schoolmaster," went into *Hyperion.*

"BLESSED ARE THE DEAD" (1845). Poem, translated from the German poet Simon Dach (1605-59), in *Poets and Poetry of Europe,* ed. Longfellow; Scudder. In the prison of life, we are sad, worried, weeping, and in anguish. By comparison, "blest are ye whose toils are ended," who have ascended to God, whose tears Christ has dried, and who have found "joy and rest."

"BLIND BARTIMEUS" (1841). Poem, in *Arcturus,* 7 Dec 1841; *Ballads.* Bartimeus is blind at Jericho's gates. When he learns that Christ is approaching, he asks for pity. The crowd reluctantly relays his message. Christ tells Bartimeus that his faith has saved him. The poem is based on Mark: 10. The poet includes a reminder that there is spiritual as well as physical blindness. Longfellow quotes three statements—from Bartimeus, the crowd, and Christ—in Greek, and even rhymes key English and Greek words. Weaving some twenty-four Greek words into the poem may be effective enough, but only for those who know the language. In a letter to Samuel Ward* (3 Nov 1841), Longfellow encloses a copy of "Blind Bartimeus," says that while he was reading Mark in Greek the whole scene suddenly flashed before him, and adds that Nathaniel Hawthorne* has been staying overnight with him.

Bibliography: Arvin; Hilen, ed.; Wagenknecht, 1986.

"THE BLIND GIRL OF CASTÈL CUILLÈ" (1850). Poem, translated from the French dialect poet Jacques Jasmin (Jacques Boé, 1796–1864), in *S/F.* Below lofty Castèl-Cuillè (Castelculier), the road is full of merrymakers singing about a wedding. But Baptiste is sad. He loved "tender" Margaret; but she was blinded by the pestilence, and his father issued a certain order. "Wearied at home," Baptiste went away and returned much later. He then was enticed to wed Angela, but still thought about Margaret. Crippled Jane, an unerring soothsayer, enters and warns Angela that marrying "this false bridegroom" is tantamount to digging her tomb. Meanwhile, angelic Margaret thinks of Baptiste—"of my night he is the star!"—and calls out for him. If he does not come, she wants to die. He promised her. Is he weary? Ill? A man enters. But he is young Paul, her brother, announcing that Angela is to wed Baptiste tomorrow morning. Margaret, stunned, resembles "A wax Madonna," recovers, and asks Paul to dress in homespun and linen, and attend the ceremony. He leaves. Jane, the crone, enters and suggests that Margaret pray to love the lad less. Dissembling, Margaret assumes "a sweet, contented air" and talks about the weather. Jane leaves. At daybreak, behold two maidens: One decks herself with a bouquet, flaunts, flutters; the other takes something from a drawer, hides it beneath her bodice, is conducted by Paul up to the castle chapel past their father's grave. Wedding bells sound. Margaret and Paul enter the chapel; "the bridal train" and the villagers soon follow. Baptiste stands sad and mute. Onlookers delight Angela by whispering about her beauty. When the ceremony is pronounced, Margaret emerges from the confessional, raises a knife, says her blood will be Baptiste's "holy water," but falls lifeless "ere the fatal stroke descended." That night, the roads don't blossom for the bride leaving her former home; instead, a "fair . . . corpse . . . leave[s] its home" headed for the cemetery. Cornelius Conway Felton* wrote Longfellow from Strasbourg (8 Jul 1853) that he had just met the poet Jasmin and regretted not being able to give him Longfellow's translation of "The Blind Girl."

Bibliography: Arvin; S. Longfellow.

BOARDMAN, CORNELIA LUCRETIA (1845–?). Medical student. She moved from Great Barrington, Massachusetts to Boston, studied medicine in Philadelphia, and met Longfellow (1870s). Denied access to American medical schools, she studied medicine in Vienna (to 1880) and practiced in St. Louis. Late in his life, Longfellow happily followed her career.

BONNER, SHERWOOD (1849–83). Fiction writer. Katharine ("Kate") Sherwood Bonner was born in Holly Springs, Mississippi. Her father was an Irish-born physician; her mother, a Southern planter's daughter. Katharine was well educated in Holly Springs and at a boarding school in Montgomery, Alabama. Kate, as she was called, read voraciously, began writing as a teenager, and pseudonymously published a Gothic story set in Italy in the *Massachusetts Ploughman* (1869). Its editor was Nahum Capen (1804–86), a Boston publisher and phrenologist, who had encouraged her by correspondence. Kate married Edward MacDowell (1871), with whom she had a daughter, Lilian Kirk MacDowell (1871–1922). MacDowell was a dilettantish weakling who often deserted her. In 1873 Kate left Lilian with Aunt Margaret, her mother's reliable sister, and traveled to Boston. The Capen family welcomed her, and she became a controversial

temperance lecturer's secretary. She boldly wrote Longfellow (8 Dec 1873) to explain her predicament plaintively and to ask to meet him. He answered promptly, and she visited Craigie House the following week. Kate radiated beauty, charm, and enthusiasm. Longfellow was thrilled and helped her in many ways. When her daughter Lilian was baptized, Longfellow became her godfather. Kate published essays (as Katharine MacDowell and Kate MacDowell), first in the Memphis *Avalanche,* about Boston and New England celebrities, including Ralph Waldo Emerson,* whom she also wrote and then interviewed (unsatisfactorily), Oliver Wendell Holmes,* Julia Ward Howe,* and Charles Sumner* (Longfellow may have escorted her to a memorial service for Sumner), among others. Longfellow introduced her to William Dean Howells,* but Howells never encouraged her brand of realism. Kate published "The Radical Club: A Poem, Respectfully Dedicated to 'The Infinite' by an Atom" (anon., Boston *Times* [8 May 1875]; in pamphlet form, by Sherwood Bonner [1876]). It satirized effete Bostonian socialites and pseudointellectuals, and consequently made Kate the subject of varied talk. When her sister, Ruth McDowell, moved to Boston to study voice, Longfellow called on her at the Capens's home to welcome her. Later, Ruth began an unsatisfactory marriage with Edward's younger brother, David MacDowell.

Longfellow's friendship with Kate developed into platonic intimacy. He made her the central figure in "The Masque of Pandora" (1875). He engaged her as his morning secretary when he started compiling *Poems of Places* (31 vols., 1876–79). Kate went abroad for eight months in 1876, sent travel sketches about London and Italy (as by Sherwood Bonner) to the *Avalanche* and the Boston *Times,* and wrote Longfellow playfully intimate letters. In his replies, he addressed her as "Dear Aurora." She returned to America to visit relatives in Mississippi, and unhappily, her improvident husband in Texas; to be Longfellow's irregular amanuensis again; and to continue writing. Longfellow suggested that she write an autobiographical novel—together they titled it *The*

Prodigal Daughter. She published some excellent local-color stories for magazines (1876–82). The novel, retitled, became *Like Unto Like* (1878), much altered and set in Holly Springs in 1875. Longfellow liked the manuscript and recommended it to Harper and Brothers, who accepted it. Ecstatically grateful, Kate dedicated it to Longfellow. Through him she met Helena Modjeska (1840–1909), the Polish actress, and uniquely charmed that personage. Kate gave Mme. Modjeska a reception (1878), which Longfellow and other notables attended. Howells declined.

Tragedy struck. Yellow fever hit Holly Springs and endangered her father, brother, and Lilian. In August 1878, Longfellow visited Kate the morning she left Boston to hurry home. She hustled Lilian and Aunt Martha out of town, wired Longfellow for relief money, and nursed her father and brother until they died in her arms (Sep). Breaking the town quarantine, she returned to Boston, the Capens, and Longfellow. Her husband Edward arrived in Boston (Oct). Kate introduced him to Longfellow; accompanied Edward to Kentucky, where Ruth and David MacDowell, and other family members were staying; and returned to Holly Springs in November to start sorting out family finances—and to pour out her grief in letters to Longfellow. She asked Longfellow, who had already given her $100, to "loan" her $600 to start a market garden with a Mississippi neighbor. Longfellow refused. Back in Boston (late 1879), Kate became aware that she and Longfellow, now cooler, were the subject of unsavory gossip. She felt ostracized socially, moved with Aunt Martha and Lilian to southern Illinois (1880), and continued to publish. Among several innovative stories, "A Volcanic Interlude" (*Lippincott's Magazine,* Apr 1880) may be mentioned. It is a sensational tale of miscegenation, which added to Kate's notoriety. She obtained a divorce (May 1881) and wrote Longfellow again (Aug), this time not only for money but also for sympathy. She was suffering from breast cancer. He sent $500. She wrote about her pains and medical expenses (Mar 1882). From his deathbed, Longfellow replied, promised more aid, but soon died. Kate wrote Longfellow's daughter Alice Mary Longfellow,* a letter (5 Apr 1882) including this eloquent praise of him: "To me through many years he was such a friend as I can never hope to have again, strengthening faith, reanimating courage, sustaining my faltering steps, keeping hope alive in my heart. In the wild misery that followed the cruel death of my father and my brother, when it seemed as if reason itself would desert me, dear dear Mr. Longfellow sorrowed with me and helped me to live through the dark days. Now he too has gone, and my world is desolated" . Kate also wrote Alice about her daughter Lilian's needs and reminded Alice of promised financial aid, which she promptly sent. Kate consulted physicians in Boston, where she was still ostracized, and also in Holly Springs. Until within four days of when she died there, she continued to write stories—even dictating in pain—to earn money to leave Lilian. Sherwood Bonner's stories are collected in *Dialect Tales* (1883) and (posthumously) *Suwanee River Tales* (1884).

Bonner published *The Story of Margaret Kent* (1886), a sensational, best-selling novel as by "Henry Hayes." It presents a beautiful Southern female writer, her no-account husband, her move with her little daughter to a New York apartment, where her associates include artist Sarah Longstaffe (note name), Herbert Bell, famous septuagenarian poet (note poet's age), and Mrs. Townsend, patroness turned venomous gossip. Ellen Olney Warner Kirk (1842–1928) soon identified herself as "Henry Hayes." She was a minor writer and the stepmother of Sophia Kirk, who was a close friend of Kate's and who wrote a preface for *Suwanee River Tales.* The heroine of *The Story of Margaret Kent* was soon recognized as modeled on Kate. It is now even theorized that the vigorous beginning of the novel may have been written by Kate, while the vapid remainder was Ellen Kirk's work. Sherwood Bonner is now famous in large part for "A Volcanic Interlude," for being the heroine of a bestseller, and for being the most mysterious of Longfellow's late-life lady friends. Is it significant that part of the time Longfellow's letters to her were in French? Bonner wrote Longfellow at least fifty-four letters.

Bibliography: Biglane, Jean Nosser. "An Annotated and Indexed Edition of the Letters of Sherwood Bonner (Catharine Bonner MacDowell)." Master's thesis, Mississippi State University, 1972; Faranda, Lisa Pater. "A Social Necessity: The Friendship of Sherwood Bonner and Henry Wadsworth Longfellow." In *Patrons and Protegees: Gender, Friendship, and Writing in Nineteenth-Century America,* ed. Shirley Marchalonis, 184–211. New Brunswick: Rutgers University Press, 1988; Frank, William L. *Sherwood Bonner (Catherine McDowell).* Boston: Twayne, 1976; Hilen, ed.; McAlexander, Hubert Horton. *The Prodigal Daughter: A Biography of Sherwood Bonner.* Baton Rouge: Louisiana State University Press, 1981; Moore, Rayburn S. "'Merlin and Vivien'? Some Notes on Sherwood Bonner and Longfellow." *Mississippi Quarterly* 28 (spring 1975): 181–84; Sutherland, Daniel E. "Some Thoughts Concerning the Love Life of Sherwood Bonner." *Southern Studies* 26 (summer 1987): 115–27; Wagenknecht, 1955.

A BOOK OF SONNETS (1875). *See The Masque of Pandora and Other Poems,* 1875.

A BOOK OF SONNETS (1878). *See Kéramos and Other Poems,* 1878. Longfellow wrote Thomas Stephens Collier (1842–93), a New York-born poet living in Norfolk, Virginia, a letter (29 Feb 1880) in which he suggested his preference for "the strict Italian rule of the Sonnet and not the looser and perhaps more facile English method."

Bibliography: Hilen, ed.

"A BOOK OF SUGGESTIONS." A manuscript "book" in which Longfellow jotted down ideas for future writing.

"BOOK OF VANITY." A manuscript "book" in which Longfellow described how he wrote some of his early poems.

"BOSTON" (1876). Sonnet, in *PP, Kéramos.* Boston in Lincolnshire, England, developed around a priory founded by St. Botolph, "a Saxon monk." It was "pillaged by marauding Danes," but a Boston across "leagues of sea" now commemorates its "sacred name." St. Botolph's monastery was founded in 654 and destroyed in 870.

BOSWORTH, JOSEPH L. (1789–1876). English clergyman and lexicographer. He compiled *Dictionary of the Anglo-Saxon Language* (1838; abridged, 1848). He was chaplain of the English Church in Rotterdam (1835) and, when Longfellow's wife Mary was fatally ill there, helped Longfellow find a nurse for her. The two men remained in touch by letters, both after Mary's death and when Bosworth returned to England. Longfellow published an essay titled "Anglo-Saxon Literature" (*NAR,* Jul 1838), which was also used as the Introduction to Bosworth's *Dictionary.* When Longfellow was last in London (1869), he tried unsuccessfully to visit Bosworth.

Bibliography: Hilen, ed.

"THE BOY AND THE BROOK" (1871). Poem, translated from the prose version by Leo M. Alishan (1820–1901) of an Armenian song, in *AM,* Jul 1871; *Three.* A boy, washing his hands at a brook, asks it questions. The brook replies that it comes from melted mountain snows, that it visits gardens and hears nightingales, and that when a maid who loves the boy drinks from a fountain, it kisses her chin. Although Longfellow by letter (2 Mar 1871) informed James T. Fields,* then editing the *Atlantic Monthly,* that he was "disgusted" with the poem and asked him not to publish it, it appeared anyway.

Bibliography: Armenian Popular Songs Translated into English. Venice: S. Lazarus, 1852; Hilen, ed.

"BRAZEN NOSE COLLEGE" (1825). Essays, fourteen in number, in *Portland Advertiser.* Longfellow wrote two. One is titled "My School Boy Days."

BREMER, FREDRIKA (1801–65). Woman of letters, born in Åbo, Swedish Finland. Her tyrannical father, a wealthy merchant, was of German descent. In 1804 he moved his family to an estate in Stockholm, Sweden, where Fredrika was excellently tutored, but felt stifled until she could travel and study in Europe (1820–21). After her father's death, she had the means to pursue a career as social reformer, traveler, and writer. Her domestic novels were the first in Swedish literature, were widely translated, and include *Familjen H* (1831; *The H—- Family,* 1842),

Grannarna (1837; *The Neighbors,* 1853), and the semiautobiographical *Hemmet* (1839; *The Home,* 1843). Bremer traveled in the United States and Cuba (1849-51). She was especially welcome in New England because of her denunciation of slavery. American writers whom she admired the most were Ralph Waldo Emerson,* Nathaniel Hawthorne,* Washington Irving,* James Russell Lowell,* and Longfellow. Resulting from Bremer's acute observation of politicians, social leaders, writers, and living conditions in America was her popular, insightful *Hemmen i den Nya världen* (*The Homes of the New World,* 3 vols., 1853-54), which includes astute comments on various American writers. In her last dozen years, Bremer spent much time in England, on the Continent, and in Palestine, wrote many books as a consequence, and then returned to Sweden (1861), where she died near Stockholm.

While Bremer was staying in a hotel in Boston, Longfellow called on her and noted the following in his journal (6 Dec 1849): "A kindly old lady, with gentle manners and soft voice. We talked of Swedish authors. . . . [Esaias]Tegnér[*] she spoke of with affection, much moved and with tears in her eyes." Longfellow added that Bremer was going at once to stay with the Lowells. A few days later the Lowells included the Longfellows at a dinner party. Fanny Longfellow wrote her brother Thomas Gold Appleton* (17 Dec 1849) about meeting Bremer, who, she notes, is petite and gentle, sketches delicately, and "reads English, even Emerson, with remarkable comprehension and discrimination." Fanny also indicates her own thorough knowledge of characters in Bremer's novels *The Neighbors* and *The Home.* Fanny liked Bremer so much that she had Longfellow order a cast made of Bremer's hand. When Longfellow called on Bremer again, some women were present, including an ex-slave who had escaped disguised as a man and with her husband acting as "his" slave. Bremer was delighted at the woman's gumption. While Bremer was making a pencil sketch of Longfellow, he noted in his journal that an unnamed woman asked her if a woman could ever feel "fulfilled" without having children. Bremer, who in early ma-

turity had vowed to stay single, bridled and shouted, "'Yes, indeed! Those women who have no children of their own do more than those who have many'" (12 Feb 1850). Bremer wrote Longfellow (26 Feb 1850) to thank him for a gift of some of his writings, to send him some works by Truneberg (unidentified), and to thank him and his wife for their memorable hospitality. Shortly before she left New England, Bremer asked the Longfellows to come see her so that she should finish the sketch she had started of him.

Bibliography: Forsa[o]s-Scott, Helena. *Swedish Women's Writing 1850-1995.* London: The Athlone Press, 1997; S. Longfellow; Wagenknecht, 1955.

"THE BRIDGE" (1845). Poem (originally titled "The Bridge over the Charles"), in *Poems,* 1845; *Bruges.* The poet stands on the bridge (over the Charles River, between Cambridge and Boston). He sees the moon, a "flaming furnace," and seaweed brought by the tide, and recalls wishing that when in sorrow he could be floated to the sea at ebb tide. Now, however, he thinks of the sadness of others who have walked on this bridge. May the moon somehow symbolize "love in heaven," its light now "wavering" in these waters. It has been suggested that Longfellow is here contrasting his sadness while courting Fanny Appleton and his subsequent happiness after marrying her. The bridge, once called the West Boston Bridge, is now called the Longfellow Bridge. Andrew Craigie (1743-1819), the husband of Longfellow's one-time landlady Elizabeth Nancy Shaw Craigie,* built this bridge over the Charles.

Bibliography: Hilen, ed.; Wagenknecht, 1986.

"THE BRIDGE OF CLOUD" (1864). Poem, in *AM,* Sep 1864; *Flower.* The poet sits by his vision-inducing hearth, but his fancy lacks the power to build. Although "she builds me bridges / Over many a dark ravine" and he tries to follow, he is unable to go beyond "the parapets of cloud" that envelope the misty valley. He is aware that his many friends have kind thoughts, but his mood is one of despair. The bleak misery

Longfellow expresses here was occasioned by the death of his beloved wife Fanny.

Bibliography: Arvin; Wagenknecht, 1986.

"THE BROKEN OAR" (1878). Sonnet, in *Kéramos.* A tired Icelandic poet lacks a final word for his book. At sunset a wave casts a broken oar at his feet. A carving on it says, "Oft was I weary, when I toiled at thee." He writes down these words and throws "his useless pen into the sea." Longfellow wrote the following in his journal (13 Nov 1864):

> Stay at home and ponder upon Dante. I am frequently tempted to write upon my work [that of translating *La Divina Commedia*] the inscription found upon an oar cast on the coast of Iceland,—
> *Oft war ek dasa dur ek dro thick.*
> "Oft was I weary when I tugged at thee."

Bibliography: S. Longfellow; Williams.

"THE BROOK" (1833). Irregular sonnet, translated from an anonymous Spanish poem, in *Coplas,* as "To a Brook"; *Voices.* This "soul of April" laughs at mountains and mirrors mornings. Its "pure crystal" water is brighter than sand, silver, and gold, is guileless, and prefers fountains to "the haunts of man."

"THE BROOK AND THE WAVE" (1873). Poem, in *Aftermath, Birds* (1873). The brooklet, finding its way from the mountain to the rolling, howling, "briny ocean," fills its "bitter heart" with fresh, sweet water.

BROWN, CHARLES F. *See* "The Wondrous Tale of a Little Man in Gosling Green."

BRYANT, WILLIAM CULLEN (1794–1878). Poet, travel writer, and editor. Born in Cummington, Massachusetts, Bryant attended Williams College (1810-1l), studied law (1811-14), passed the bar, and practiced law in Plainfield, Massachusetts (1815) and in Great Barrington, Massachusetts (1816-25). The popularity of his "Thanatopsis" (1817, 1821) helped persuade him to quit law and develop a career in journalism and editing instead. Bryant edited the New York *Review*

and Athenaeum Magazine (1825-27) and then, momentously, the New York *Evening Post* (1827-78). Bryant married Frances Fairchild (1821) and with her had two daughters. His wife died in 1866. Bryant became part owner and editor-in-chief of the *Post* (1829), wrote in favor of abolition (from 1836), and supported the new Republican Party (beginning in 1856), the presidential candidacy of John C. Frémont (1860) but then those of Abraham Lincoln (from 1861). Writing and traveling extensively—to America's Midwest, Europe, Cuba, the Middle East, and Mexico—Bryant published several editions of his *Poems* (the best being that of 1832), books of travel, and books of reminiscence. He issued his two-volumed, blank-verse translations of the *Iliad* (1870) and the *Odyssey* (1871, 1872); wrote critical studies of several authors, notably James Fenimore Cooper (1852) and Washington Irving* (1860); published additional translations; and coedited *The Complete Works of Shakespeare* (3 vols., 1886-88). Bryant's best poetry came early, is descriptive rather than narrative, displays technical competence but little passion or realism, and concerns love, nature, mutability and death, and the need for morality. His travel writings are informative and sometimes witty.

Longfellow when young was so influenced by Bryant's poetry that some of his juvenile poems were regarded as imitative of or even mistaken for Bryant's—for example, "Autumn." Bryant read several of Longfellow's early verses, signed by his initials only, and praised them. Longfellow's "Thanksgiving" and two sonnets by Bryant appeared in the same issue of the *United States Literary Gazette* (15 Nov 1844). Longfellow, with Clara Crowninshield* along, first met Bryant, together with his wife and their daughters, in Heidelberg (Dec 1835). They walked together and often spoke German while discussing literature—to improve their knowledge of the language. Bryant returned to New York (Jan 1836). Longfellow escorted the Bryant women to the Ems baths (Jun), to Heidelberg (Aug), Paris and Le Havre (Sep), and home to America (Nov 1836). Longfellow met Bryant in New York (Jan 1839) and again when Richard Henry Dana

Sr.* lectured there on Shakespeare (Jan 1840), after which Bryant hosted a dinner with Dana, Longfellow, the poet Fitz-Greene Halleck (1790-1867), and Parke Godwin (1816–1909), critic, editor, and Bryant's son-in-law. Bryant wrote Longfellow (31 Jan 1846) to praise his works for their "exquisite music," their "depth of feeling and spirituality," and the "creative power" by means of which they present "passages from the great drama of life." Later, the two men met socially, on purpose or by chance, and also constantly praised one another in well-phrased letters. For example, when Bryant sent Longfellow a copy of his *Thirty Poems* (1864), Longfellow replied by a letter (4 Jan 1864) in which he calls the work "very consoling both in its music and in its meaning." Bryant was a lifelong influence on Longfellow.

Bibliography: Arvin; Crowninshield; Bryant, William Cullen II and Thomas G. Voss, eds. *The Letters of William Cullen Bryant.* 6 vols. New York: Fordham University Press, 1975-92; S. Longfellow; *Mrs. Longfellow.*

"THE BUILDERS" (1850). Poem, in *S/F.* We all build within "these walls of Time." What may seem useless strengthens; what seems idle supports. So, unify everything. Old-time artists "wrought with greatest care," because "the Gods see everywhere." Make everything full and clean. Work amply today, and the future will be secure and unity will prevail. This poem has been criticized for its confused symbolism. Are we the wall-maker or the wall?

Bibliography: Wagenknecht, 1986.

"THE BUILDING OF THE SHIP" (1850). Poem, in *S/F.* The merchant asks the Master to build him a sturdy vessel. The Master creates a model, thinks of historic ships and even an "airy argosy" designed by the sun, assembles all types of wood, and tells a certain "fiery youth" working for him that "the day that gives her [the ship] to the sea / Shall give my daughter unto thee!" The maiden stands at her father's door, "Like a beauteous barge," joyful and proud. At dawn the "noble" building begins. By evening the oak beam, "straight and strong," is on the slip.

That night, the tender couple hears the Master recount fearful stories of sailors far away and of the "pitiless sea," which, like Death, both "divides and yet unites mankind!" "[A]fter many a week," the skeleton of the ship looms high. Wood is hammered, tar is boiled, copper bands and an anchor are made, and finally the ship's figurehead is cunningly carved. It resembles not "a Nymph or Goddess of old" but is modeled on the Master's daughter. Its name, "the UNION," is appropriate, since, for example, in the ship "Cedar of Maine and Georgia pine / Here together . . . combine." Masts, spars, shrouds, and other parts are fixed in place; and a flag with "stars and stripes" is "Poised . . . at the mast-head." The launching day arrives. The ocean is restlessly pacing along the sands, like a strong youth. He awaits his bride. On deck is "another bride . . . by her lover's side." The Master shakes his new son's hand and kisses his blushing daughter. The pastor weds the two and comments that we all resemble ships voyaging out, homeward bound; and though often rocking, rising, falling on life's vast ocean, if we follow a true compass we can "safely reach / The Fortunate Isles." At the Master's order the ship is freed of "shores and spurs," and "leaps into the ocean's arms." That old gray bridegroom must protect the charming, youthful creature. "Sail forth into the Sea, O ship!" with never a "doubt or fear." Likewise, may this "loving, trusting wife" voyage on "the sea of life." May the "Ship of State," the UNION, similarly sail ahead. Masterfully constructed, it should therefore fear no rock, gale, tempest, false light, or fierce wave. America's hearts, hopes, prayers, tears, and faith "Are all with thee,—are all with thee!"

It has often been noted that both in its ode form and in its civic positivism "The Building of the Ship" resembles "The Song of the Bell" by the German poet-playwright Johann Christoph Friedrich von Schiller (1759-1805). Frances Kemble,* the British actress, gave several public readings of "The Building of the Ship" during her 1850 American tour, once with Longfellow sitting in the front row, utterly delighted. In his journal (12 Feb 1850), he describes his excitement.

Abraham Lincoln was moved to tears when he read "The Building of the Ship." Although made too familiar by anthologies and recitations, it has still-fresh local-color details making it resemble a Currier and Ives print, and it has been favorably compared to the mini-epic cataloging found in Walt Whitman's songs of occupations.

Bibliography: Arvin; Blainey, Ann. *Fanny & Adelaide: The Lives of the Remarkable Kemble Sisters.* Chicago: Ivan R. Dee, 2001; Lang, Hans-Joachim and Fritz Fleischmann. "'All This Beauty, All This Grace': Longfellow's 'The Building of the Ship' and Alexander Slidell Mackenzie[*]'s 'Ship.'" *New England Quarterly* 54 (Mar 1981): 104–18; S. Longfellow; Scholl, J. W. "Longfellow and Schiller's 'Lied von der Glocke.'" *Modern Language Notes* 28 (Feb 1913): 49–50; Wagenknecht, 1986.

BULL, OLE BORNEMANN (1810–80). Norwegian violinist. As a youth, he was sent to Christiania (now Oslo) to study theology, but instead devoted his energies to music and political protest. He studied the violin in Copenhagen and Kassel, Germany, played in concerts in Norway, and studied in Paris, where in 1833 he was inspired by hearing Nicolò Paganini (1782–1840). Bull performed to enthusiastic audiences in several European cities (1830s), was the first violinist after Paganini to give a concert at the Opéra in Paris (1835), married there (1836), and toured in the United States (1843–45). Bull established the first Norwegian Theatre in Bergen (1852), installed young Henrik Ibsen as its director (to 1857), and returned to the United States. He purchased 11,114 acres in Potter County, Pennsylvania, and founded a Norwegian settlement there, to be called Oleanat. It soon failed (1853). After giving more concerts in America (to 1857), he returned to Bergen to direct the Norwegian Theatre. His wife died (1862). He returned to America (1868), married Sarah Chapman Thorp (1850–1911) in 1870, and established a pattern of wintering in the United States and summering in Norway. In failing health, he returned to Lysö near Bergen (1880), and died there. Bull was long remembered for wild renditions of his own compositions, his own arrangements of other works, and fantasias on national airs.

Longfellow knew Bull in Cambridge and used him as the model for the Musician in *Tales of a Wayside Inn.* Longfellow's journal entries indicate their friendship and the Longfellows' hospitality to Bull. After dinner one evening at the Longfellows' home, with Thomas Gold Appleton,* James T. Fields,* and William Wetmore Story* as fellow guests, "in the twilight, Ole Bull played and chanted old Norse melodies, which were very striking" (4 Dec 1855). Bull, Fields, and William Makepeace Thackeray* were the Longfellows' dinner guests—with "music on the Cremona" (7 Dec 1855). After giving "a concert in Cambridge, [Bull] comes up with Fields to supper" (19 May 1857). Longfellow wrote Fields (19 Mar 1871) that after dinner "this evening . . . he [Bull] played divinely on the violin, and told some amusing stories," then adds, "What a child of Nature, and how very agreeable he is!" A final journal entry (2 May 1877) reports that "Ole Bull, with his wife and her brother, dined with us." The industrial chemist Eben Norton Horsford (1818–93) and his wife were Longellow's neighbors. Through letters from Norway which Mrs. Horsford had received and sent Longfellow, he was able to read details of Bull's funeral and wrote Fields's widow Annie Adams Fields* about the event (29 Sep 1880): "All Bergen's flags at half-mast; telegram from the King; funeral oration by the poet [Björnstjerne] Björnson [1832–1910]. The dear old musician was carried from his island to the mainland in a steamboat, followed by a line of others. No Viking ever had such a funeral." In 1885, Longfellow's daughter Anne Allegra Longfellow* married Joseph Gilbert Thorp Jr. (1852–1931), Bull's brother-in-law.

Bibliography: Bergsagel, John. "Bull, Ole (Bornemann)." In *The New Grove Dictionary of Music and Musicians,* ed. Stanley Sadie, 445–48. 20 vols, III. London: Macmillan Publishers Limited, 1980.

"BURIAL OF THE MINNISINK" (1827). Poem, in *AS,* 1827; *Voices.* As evening casts a mellow light on hill, forest, and lake, the faithful followers of the young warrior chief of the Minnisink Indians place him in his grave, cloaked in roebuck skin, with weapons and cuirass beside him. His eye-darting war horse is brought near and slain with a swift arrow into his heart, so that the chief can "grasp his steed" and ride the plains again. "Burial of the Minnisink" is regarded as Longfellow's earliest poem concerning Native Americans. While in college, he read about the Minnisink in *Account of the History, Manners, and Customs of the Indian Nations Who Once Inhabited Pennsylvania* (1819) by John Gottlieb Ernestus Heckewelder (1743–1823). "Minnisink," however, was a place name, not a tribal name.

Bibliography: Arvin; Hilen ed.; Little.

"THE BURIAL OF THE POET" (1879). Sonnet, *AM,* Apr 1879; *Thule.* During a gentle snowfall, we placed him "in the sleep that comes to all," leaving him "to his rest and his renown." The moon shines on the flowerlike flakes. The snow resembles "the winding-sheet of Saladin / With chapters of the Koran." But the cruciform shadows cast down here by bare branches are "more . . . triumphant signs." The poet was Richard Henry Dana Sr.,* the Massachusetts author who died 2 February 1879. His grandson, Richard Henry Dana II* had married Longfellow's daughter Edith the year before. Longfellow sent the poet's son, Richard Henry Dana Jr.* a tender letter of sympathy (18 Feb 1879) and enclosed a copy of this splendid sonnet, which he originally titled simply "R.H.D."

Bibliography: Hilen, ed.

C

"CADENABBIA" (1874). Poem, in *AM,* Dec 1874; *Pandora, Birds* (1875). The poet sits idly on marble steps near Como—"the loveliest of all lakes"—with leaves overhead, gleaming sunshine, barges casting "pendent shadows" on the lapping water, fishermen's bells tinkling, and villas, hills, and woods in the distance. He asks that the vision of this "land and . . . supreme / And perfect beauty" fill his heart and brain and only then "fade into the air again." This poem, like others, resulted from Longfellow's final European tour (1868–69). In guidebook fashion, Longfellow offers place names—Belaggio, Como, Somariva, Stelvio Pass, Varena. The result might make experienced travelers nostalgic and stay-at-homes envious.

"CANZONE" (1878). Poem, translated from Michael Angelo, in *Kéramos.* The artist expresses his belief that in all "the vanished years" he cannot recall a single day when he was free of false hopes, impossible wishes, and contrary passions. Now far "from the true and good," he is "infirm and weary," and shadows mount.

CAREY & HART. Philadelphia publishers. This firm, owned and managed by Edward L. Carey (?–1845) and Abraham Hart (1810–85), published Longfellow's *Poems and Poetry of Europe* (1845) and *Poems* (1845, illustrated). His 1844-54 correspondence with the firm, and after Carey's death, with Hart more directly, reveals his occasional discontent, often concerning payments due,

and also expresses his desire to issue a cheap edition in 1846 of his collected poetry. Longfellow won out, and Harper & Brothers in 1846 published such an edition, including *Poems on Slavery;* it was priced at 50 cents. Charles Sumner* negotiated the terms. In 1849, Henry Carey Baird (1825-1912) founded Henry Carey Baird & Company, successor to Carey & Hart. In that year, Baird and Longfellow began a dispute concerning the ownership of the stereotype plates of the 1845 edition of Longfellow's *Poems.* The matter went on, unresolved, into 1865 by which time the plates were worthless.

Bibliography: Hilen, ed.

"CARILLON" (1845). Poem, in *Poems,* 1845. *See* "The Belfry of Bruges."

"CARRIER'S ADDRESS" (1822). Address, in Portland *Gazette,* 1 Jan 1822. Several addresses, in poetic form and all unsigned, were published; Longfellow may have written one of them.

Bibliography: Little; Thompson.

"THE CASTLE BUILDER" (1867). Poem, in *Our Young Folks,* Jan 1867; *Aftermath, Birds* (1873). The dreamy little boy builds sky-seeking castles out of his wooden blocks and also rides on his father's knee and hears legends about brave heroes. When he is mature, may he build other towers, ride other horses, listen to higher voices, and nonetheless retain his "simple faith in mysteries."

"THE CASTLE BY THE SEA" (1839).
Poem, translated by Longfellow and Frances
(Fanny) Appleton* (later his wife), from the
German poet Johann Ludwig Uhland (1787–
1862), in *Hyperion, Voices.* Have you seen
that castle by the sea, with clouds above
and waves beneath? Yes, and also the moon
and the mist above and around it. Did you
hear the winds, waves, and minstrel too?
Yes, and the gale caused me to weep. Did
you see the King and his bride, proud in
their crimson and gold? No, I saw only "the
ancient parents" attired in mourning garb.

"CASTLES IN SPAIN" (1877). Poem, in *AM,*
May 1877; *PP, Kéramos, Birds* (1878). The
poet finds that Spanish "form[s] and countenance[s]" are altered for him by "annals of
remotest eld." Thus, the Alhambra reminds
him of Aladdin; Burgos, of the Cid; Cordova,
of "Almanzor" (Arabic for "Victorious"; i.e.,
Ibn Abi'Āmir Mohammed [939-1002]); and
Toledo, of Valladolid, Zamora, of Wamba
(Visigoth king, 697-710). Something fearful
hovers over "the enchanted landscape," as
though Torquemada (Tomás de Torquemada
[1420?-98]) or King Philip II (1527-98)
were near. Hills, orchards, rivers seem less
real than the Past, and the poet's castles in
Spain are built not of stone but of "summer
clouds" blowing into his "mist of rhyme!"
This astonishing poem, with its modified
ballad rhythms, has a challenging *abaaab*
rhyme scheme.

Bibliography: Brenan.

"CATAWBA WINE" (1858). Poem, in
Courtship, Birds (1858). In this "Song of the
Vine," the poet praises the "rich wine of the
West / That grows by the Beautiful [Ohio]
River." It is better than Isabel, Muscatel, Mus-
tang, Scuppernong, Sillery, Verzenay, or
wines coming from Danube, Rhine, or Guadalquivir vineyards. Wines from Europe
"rack our brains / With the fever pains," and
should be dumped down "sewers and
sinks," especially that devilish poison, "Bor-
gia wine." The poet hopes "The winds and
the birds" will deliver this song of his to the
West. Nicholas Longworth (1782-1863), the
American horticulturist who retired from
practicing law in Cincinnati (1828) to de-

vote himself to cultivating grapes and making wine, sent Longfellow a present of Catawba wine. Longfellow mailed this poem to
Longworth in gratitude. Its unique chauvin-
ism, though critical and excessive, is mainly
humorous.

Bibliography: Wagenknecht, 1986.

"THE CHALLENGE" (1873). Poem, in *Aftermath, Birds* (1873). The poet recalls an
old Spanish legend or chronicle. After King
Sanchez was killed during the siege of Zamora, Don Diego de Ordoñez, one of his officers, rode toward the walls to challenge
"All the people of Zamora," and to challenge
as well their relatives and friends, "the born
and the unborn." All should be aware of
"The poverty-stricken millions" that are
starving everywhere, reaching out for mere
crumbs while the traitorous few enjoy light
and warmth, feasts and songs. Ignored and
"in the camp of famine . . . [,] Christ . . . Lies
dead upon the plain!" This poem is regarded
as a rare instance in which Longfellow protests against selfish materialism and advo-
cates social democracy. The legend or
chronicle Longfellow hints at was either the
Poema del Mio Cid (c.1140), the great Spanish epic, or else one of the historical sources
or analogues thereof. Longfellow's Sanchez
was Sancho II, King of Castile and Léon
(c.1037-72), who was fatally lanced by an
assassin during his siege of the fortress-city
of Zamora, held by his rebellious younger
brother, Alfonso VI of Léon and their sister,
Urraca.

Bibliography: Arvin; Brenan; de Chasca, Edmund. *The Poem of the Cid.* Boston: Twayne,
1976; Pidal, Ramon Menéndez. *La España del
Cid.* 7th ed. 2 vols. Madrid: Espasa-Calpe, 1964;
Wagenknecht, 1986.

**"THE CHAMBER OVER THE GATE"
(1879).** Poem, in *AM,* Mar 1879; *Thule.* The
poet asks whether his listener can see, far
away, that desolate old man who sits at the
chamber over the gate lamenting the death
of Absalom, his son. Is the sound of lamentation so distant? In truth, "There is no far
or near." The echo of ancient sounds is
heard now. People are watching everywhere
for "tidings of despair." Knowing that such

grief is common provides little relief. Surely the old father wishes he had died instead of "Absalom, my son!" Longfellow sent this wrenching, tersely understated elegy with a letter of condolence (Oct 1878) to the Bishop of Mississippi, his casual friend, when he learned that the bishop's son, the Reverend Duncan C. Green, had died serving his parishioners during a yellow fever epidemic in Greenville, Mississippi. Longfellow's title has to do with David's mourning the loss of Absalom (*see* 2 Sam. 18: 33).

Bibliography: Arvin.

"CHANGED" (1873). Poem, in *Aftermath, Birds* (1873). From a hill outside town the poet sees "the oaks . . . fresh and green," bright seawater, shining sunlight. They are the same as before, but they seem different now. Is he changed? Surely he is estranged from friends who used to be with him here. The town was Portland, Maine, which Longfellow visited in 1847 and 1858, among other times.

CHANNING, WILLIAM ELLERY (1780–1842). Clergyman and publicist. He was born in Newport, Rhode Island. His father, William Channing, was attorney general of Rhode Island and a staunch Federalist. After the father's death when he was thirteen, young Channing lived with William Ellery, his maternal grandfather, and then with his uncle, Francis Dana, chief justice of Massachusetts, while attending Harvard. He graduated in 1798. For almost two years he tutored family members of D. M. Randolph, United States marshal in Richmond, Virginia, which caused him permanently to oppose slavery. Channing studied theology for three years and was pastor of Boston's Federal Street Church (renamed the Arlington Street Church) from 1803 until 1824, during which time he was a leading spokesman for emerging American Unitarianism. An anti-Calvinist, he rejected the notion of original sin, affirmed the freedom of the will, and accepted the Bible as divine revelation. He married Ruth Gibbs, his first cousin (1814); they had four children. Her family wealth helped Channing to considerable independence. He enjoyed travel in Europe, where he was esteemed as a Christian humanist and praised for advocating social, political, and cultural liberalism. After a dispute with his church leaders when they were insufficiently committed to abolition of slavery (1840), Channing declined further stipends granted during his semiretired status. His "Remarks on a National Literature" (1830) and his *Slavery* (1835) influenced American authors, including James Russell Lowell,* Charles Sumner,* and Longfellow, among many other readers.

Channing was a Harvard classmate of Stephen Longfellow, the poet's father, who was profoundly influenced by Channing's theological beliefs. A few days before leaving on his first European tour, Longfellow wrote his mother Zilpah Wadsworth Longfellow (2 May 1826) that he heard Channing in Boston deliver "a most eloquent sermon, and preached it most eloquently." Longfellow's interest in Channing's attitude toward slavery may be indicated by the fact that George Ticknor,* while he was studying Spanish literature in Europe, wrote Longfellow from Dresden (19 Feb 1836) to the effect that Channing's *Slavery* was much the rage abroad. Longfellow's *Poems on Slavery* (1842) is dedicated to Channing and begins with the laudatory "To William E. Channing." The poems caused an irate reader to write Longfellow (20 Dec 1842) and lump poet and preacher together as objects to be criticized.

Bibliography: S. Longfellow; Mendelsohn, Jack. *Channing, the Reluctant Radical: A Biography.* Boston: Little, Brown, 1971.

"CHARLEMAGNE." *See* "The Poet's Tale," in *Tales of a Wayside Inn,* Part Third.

"CHARLES SUMNER" (1875). Poem, in *AM,* Jan 1875; *Pandora, Birds* (1875). The poet offers "this verse" to the troubled, conflicted, honorable man. Like brave Winkelried, he sustained wounds "and broke / A path for the oppressed." While he was living, the design of his life seemed "incomplete"; however, "in the dark unknown," it seems perfected. Though dead, he "Inspires a thousand lives," exactly as "a star quenched" still sheds its light upon us. Shortly after the death

(1874) of his close friend Charles Sumner,* Longfellow penned this vigorous, thirty-six-line elegy, in quatrains effectively rhyming *abab*.

"CHAUCER" (1875). Sonnet, in *Pandora, Birds* (1875). Longfellow envisages an old writer in "a lodge within a park." The walls have windows of "painted glass" and pictures of hunters, hawks, hounds, and a "hurt deer." The aging poet is listening to a lark outside, laughs, and writes. Reading *The Canterbury Tales* by this "poet of the dawn" who made "his old age / . . . beautiful with song," Longfellow hears the cock crow and the linnet sing, and inhales "odors of ploughed field or flowery mead." This is one of Longfellow's most thrilling sonnets.

Bibliography: More; Tenfelde, Nancy L. "Longfellow's 'Chaucer.'" *Explicator* 22 (Mar 1964): 55.

"THE CHILD ASLEEP" (1831). Poem, translated from the French poet called "Clotilde de Surville" (perhaps Marguerite Éléonore Clotilde de Vallon Challis, dame de Surville [c.1400-?]), in *NAR,* Apr 1831; Scudder. The mother suckles her baby, watches him sleep, fears needlessly it is the sleep of death, and is relieved when he briefly rouses. Then she "sigh[s] in vain" for the child's father to return. According to one legend, Clotilde married Bérenger de Surville in 1421, and he was killed in 1428 during the siege of Orléans. According to other authorities, Clotilde de Surville never existed.

Bibliography: Arvin; Chambers, E. K. *The History and Motives of Literary Forgeries.* . . . 1891. Reprint, New York: B. Franklin, 1970.

"CHILDHOOD" (1844). Poem, translated from the Danish poet Jens Immanuel Baggesen (1764–1826), in *GM,* Apr 1844; Scudder. The persona remembers his tender mother and his rollicking father. When he was little, "gold, and Greek, and love . . . [were] unknown." He loved the stars, the moon, the sun. His mother taught him to pray "to be wise, and good," and to reverence God. He prayed for his parents, sister, townspeople. He knew neither king or beggar. Since they are all gone, along with his

happiness and peace, he prays never to lose his cherished memories.

"CHILDREN" (1858). Poem, in *Courtship, Birds* (1858). Come, children; look at the sun rising in the east, think about birds and brooks. The poet, by contrast, thinks of autumn and snows. If the world lacked children, we would fear the desertlike past even more than the "dark" future. Children resemble the "juices" of "sweet and tender" forest leaves not yet hardened into wood. May the children whisper to the poet "What the birds and the winds are singing" to them. Our schemes and our wisdom are nothing compared to childish touches and expressions. Superior to recorded words are children, who are "living poems."

Bibliography: Wagenknecht, 1986.

"THE CHILDREN OF THE LORD'S SUPPER" (1842). Poem, translated from *Nattvardsbarnen* ("The First Communion," 1820) by the Swedish poet Esaias Tegnér,* in *Ballads.* Pentecost has arrived. The decorated church resembles a garden. The children are to renew their baptismal vows. The Bible on the preacher's oaken pulpit is wreathed. Angelic tresses hang beneath "the lustre of brass, new-polished, [which] blinked from the ceiling, / And for lights there were lilies of Pentecost set in the sockets." Bells ring. Organ music rolls. The congregation, with uplifted faces, sings the hymn by Johan Olof Wallin (1779–1839) about "David's harp in the North-land / Tuned to the choral of [Martin] Luther." The fatherly old preacher greets everyone cordially. With "Many a moving word and warning," his discourse falls like dew, like manna. He catechizes the curly-haired, rosy-cheeked boys and the trembling, blushing girls, encourages them, and soon "the doctrines eternal / Flowed, like the waters of fountains, so clear from lips unpolluted." He explains "the Christian lore of salvation" to the children, "in few words, / Thorough, yet simple and clear, for sublimity is always simple." He explains that they slept in their mothers' arms at baptism but now are awake to receive the Holy Church's "light in its radiant splendor." The preacher can detect guile; so the children must answer truthfully: "believe ye in God, the Father who this world created? / Him who redeemed it, the Son, and the Spirit where both are united?" Without compulsion, many a clear "Yes" rings out, and the children become brothers and sisters, will grow strong, should remain pure. The preacher warns that they will so quickly leave "childhood's sacred asylum," mature, and so soon drop "in[to] Age's chill valley" that they must along the way pray, remain stainless, worship, and remember, as the "Son of Eternity" did when on earth, to focus on "his Father's manifold mansions." God's wrath can be awful; His voice, however, is not fiery, stormy, "but . . . in the whispering breezes." Remember that "Love is life, but hatred is death." At the crucifixion, God's Son "Solemnized Love," for "Depths of Love are Atonement's depths." If you love God, you should also love your brethren. Forgive hate. Lead the erring back to righteousness. Remember that "Love among mortals / Is but an endless sigh!" We have Hope, which is "transfigured" into the "living assurance" called Faith. "Christian works are no more than / Animate Love and faith, as flowers are the animate Springtide." Fear not death, which with "a kiss upon lips that are fading" returns the soul, like a "ransomed child," to "its father." The preacher, unafraid of death, coolly envisions an "unpolluted" heaven. No dust. All light. He reminds God that he has instructed these pure, glad children faithfully. He tearfully blesses them and tells them that next Sunday he may be dead and answering to God. The preacher recalls Adam: "in the Thought is the Fall; in the Heart the Atonement. / Infinite is the fall,—the Atonement infinite likewise." He informs his children that the sinful at communion "eateth and drinketh / Death and doom!" Not so the forgiven. As he administers the contents of "chalice and paten" to each child, it seems to the narrator that God looks down through the church windows, the trees outside bow, the grave grasses shiver, and all is radiant. As the children rise, the old man blesses their "innocent tresses" by a laying on of his hands.

By coincidence, at about the time when Samuel Ward* was urging Longfellow to translate Tegnér's *Nattvardsbarnen,* Longfellow was writing Ward (24 Oct 1841) that

Tegnér had written Longfellow to praise his earlier translation of parts of Tegnér's *Frithiofs Saga.* Later Longfellow wrote Ward (6 Nov 1841) that as he was translating "The Children of the Lord's Supper" his eyes were often blinded with tears because of its touching beauty. However, the metrical form of the poem, which he cast in the hexameters of Tegnér's original, gave him considerable trouble. In his Introduction, he says that the meter made him think that his "English muse" resembled "a prisoner dancing to the music of his chains." Still later, both Longfellow and Tegnér expressed discontent with Longfellow's handling of hexameters. Longfellow has since been praised for succeeding as well as possible in converting easy Swedish hexameters into generally recalcitrant English ones. *See also* "Tegnér's Frithiofs Saga."

Bibliography: Arvin; Hilen; Leighly, John. "Inaccuracies in Longfellow's Translation of Tegnér's 'Nattvardsbarnen.'" *Scandinavian Studies and Notes* 21 (1949-50): 171-80; S. Longfellow; Wagenknecht, 1986; Williams.

"THE CHILDREN'S CRUSADE" (1882).

Poem, in *Harbor.* It is hard to believe the accounts in history books about children hoping to achieve what "harnessed, ironmailed / Knights of Christendom had failed" to accomplish. Children "gleaned" words from the "The Hermit," and like blossoms, birds, and summer leaves were swept forward. From Cologne, to the accompaniment of church bells and the songs of nuns and monks, "Forth the young crusaders fared." Under their cross, banners, and flags, "Youths and maidens" gently sang, "Give us, give us back the holy / Sepulchre of the Redeemer!" Though urged forward, they might have heard a nearby foaming cataract tell them to return to their home, which is truly their "Holy Land." But their "dauntless leader" reminds them, when their feet bleed and they weep, that others have also suffered. Suddenly from a faraway mountain slope comes an avalanche, filling all with fear. And so "Passed they into lands unknown, / Passed to suffer and to die." The fragmentary verses end here.

Bibliography: Wagenknecht, 1986.

"THE CHILDREN'S HOUR" (1863). Poem, in *Tales of a Wayside Inn,* 1863, *Birds* (1863). "Grave Alice, and laughing Allegra, / And Edith with golden hair" attack the poet "by surprise." They climb into the "turret" of his castlelike, lamplit study. They kiss him and hug him. But he overmatches them and imprisons them in "the dungeon / In the round-tower" of his heart, where he will keep them "Till the walls shall crumble to ruin, / And moulder in dust away." "The Children's Hour" is one of Longfellow's most beloved poems, memorializing as it does his three daughters. It may be ungracious to note that the symbolism is mixed: Longfellow is likened to a castle within his study, which is also likened to a castle. In 1865 Longfellow was happy to be shown a Portuguese translation of "The Children's Hour."

Bibliography: S. Longfellow; Wagenknecht, 1955.

"CHIMES" (1882). Sonnet, in *Harbor.* The poet, sleepless late at night, hears chimes, which seem to "Salute" the slowly moving stars providing a canopy, a "vast . . . dome," above him. At such a time "The slumbering world" itself seems like a vessel "sink[ing] under us," accompanied by the tiniest little "rush of foam." Longfellow often writes of his proximity to the uncanny transcendent—best, perhaps, when he unites stars, bell sounds, and water, as he does here.

Bibliography: Arvin.

"CHRISTMAS BELLS" (1866). Poem, in *Flower.* The poet hears Christmas bells playing carols that sing "Of peace on earth, good-will to men!" But the sound of cannon fire in the South drowns out these carols. It seems as though an earthquake were splitting all our "hearth-stones," and that there is no peace. But over the despairing poet's bowed head comes the message that God lives, "The Wrong shall fail, / The Right prevail," and peace and good will shall return. This poem was written on Christmas Day 1864, when the Civil War was raging.

"CHRISTMAS CAROL" (1832). Poem, translated from one of the Neapolitan *Pas-* *torali de' Zampognari,* in Scudder. Christ was born in Bethlehem at night, but the stars were bright, especially one that guided the Magi. Peace spread everywhere, and gentle animals were not troubled by wild ones. Appearing before the shepherds, a dazzling angel quieted them and announced that the world was now "a smiling paradise."

"A CHRISTMAS CAROL" (1850). Poem, translated from the Noei Bourguignon (Christmas songs) by Gui Barôzai (Bernard de la Monnoye, 1641–1728), in *S/F.* The poet hears street minstrels playing Christmas songs, and also listens to chimes and "gleemen sing[ing]." Shepherds sang when "the Babe was born." The poet knows that nuns sing "in frigid cells," old washerwomen sing beside their "rivers cold." So the poet and his friends "by the fire / Ever higher [should] / Sing . . . till the night expire!"

CHRISTUS: A MYSTERY (1872). Poetic drama. It is in three parts: *The Divine Tragedy* (1871), *The Golden Legend* (1851), and *The New England Tragedies* (1868).

Bibliography: Arvin; Charles, St. Mary. "Longfellow's *Christus.*" Ph.D. diss., University of Pennsylvania, 1955; Wagenknecht, 1986; Williams.

The Divine Tragedy begins with an "Introitus," in which an angel, praising Habakkuk, the prophet, for his charity and his fight for truth, flies him to Babylon to give food to Daniel. Habakkuk, rejoicing, says that the world awaits the Redeemer. Habakkuk is an appropriate introductory figure, because he represents prophetic potency and because of his modest openhandedness. (*See* Hab.; Apoc., Bel and Dragon.)

"The First Passover" follows, with ten numbered scenes.

I. "Vox Clamantis." John the Baptist urges all to repent, for the Messiah is coming. A priest asks who John is. John replies that he baptizes with water, but one mightier and higher is coming who will "baptize . . . with fire." (*See* Matt. 3: 11; Mark 1: 7–8.)

II. "Mount Quarantania." Introducing himself as one who will come invisibly and with persuasive tones, Lucifer challenges the penitentially fasting Christ to turn stones to bread, to act and gesture regally, to claim

Lucifer's widespread kingdoms. Angels strengthen Christus as he shouts, "Get thee behind me, Satan!" (*See* Matt. 4: 3–10; Mark 1: 12–13; Luke 4: 1–6.)

III. "The Marriage in Cana." To the accompaniment of musicians, the bridegroom and the bride commend each other, and guests converse. As Christus enters, one guest asks this:

> Who is that youth with the dark azure eyes,
> And hair, in color like unto the wine,
> Parted upon his forehead and behind
> Falling in flowing locks?

He is identified as "The Nazarene / Who preacheth to the poor in field and village / The coming of God's kingdom," and further as one "Oft known to weep, but never known to laugh." With him is his mother, "with eyes of olive tint, / And skin as fair as wheat, and pale brown hair." Christus arranges for pots of water to turn to wine for the marriage feast. A furtive speaker is Manahem the Essenian, who foretold that Herod would be king. Manahem, aside, envisages a thorn-crowned figure and a cross in darkness. While Manahem quietly sums up life as

> A dream within a dream, a wind at night
> Howling across the desert in despair,
> Seeking for something lost it cannot find,

the bridegroom tells his beloved that she "make[s] the very night itself / Brighter than day," and adds that the very stars are her lamps while soft winds pass over gardens and fields "laden with odors unto thee, my Queen!" The Hebrew name Manahem, whom Longfellow makes into an Essenian, derives from Manaen, its Greek form. (*See* Sg [Song]; John 2: 1-11; Acts 13: 1.)

IV. "In the Cornfields." Philip tells Nathanael that they are wondrously led by Jesus of Nazareth, whose miracle at Cana has caused his fame to spread. The Pharisees shout "Rabbi" to Christus and rebuke him for breaking the Sabbath. He rebuts them but gets called a "poor demoniac" as he leaves. (*See* Matt. 12: 1–51; John 1: 43–50.)

V. "Nazareth." Queried in the synagogue by a priest, a Pharisee, and an elder who regard him as seditious, Christus says, "For Zion's sake I will not hold my peace, / And for Jerusalem's sake I will not rest." Warned that the son of the carpenter Joseph and Mary should not regard himself as a prophet, Christus replies that no one is a prophet in his own country. He is expelled. (*See* Isa. 61: 10; Matt. 5: 4, 11: 5, 13: 54–57; Mark 6: 4; Rev. 21: 2.)

VI. "The Sea of Galilee." Peter tells Andrew that by following Christus's order he miraculously caught "multitudes" of fish, then was told he would "catch men." Philip reports that Christus, while at Nain, restored a widow's only son to life. The men lament that brutish Nazarenes have driven Christus from their city. They see Christus approach, with Judas Iscariot, whom they call "unclean [in] spirit." Philip is inspired by Christus's voice as he urges the burdened to let him take their yoke. (*See* Matt. 4: 19, 11: 28–29; Mark 1-17; Luke 7: 11.)

VII. "The Demoniac of Gadara." While a demon-possessed, naked Gadarene is ranting among the rocks and hurling stones at passersby, Christus enters and compassionately orders the "unclean spirit" to leave the fellow. When a swineherd gripes that his swine suddenly grew savage, rushed to the sea, and drowned, Peter sees the event as punishment of "The apostate Jews" for consuming "abominable" pig flesh and broth. (*See* Isa. 66: 17; Matt. 8: 28–34.)

VIII. "Talitha [Tabitha] Cumi." A woman touches Christus's robe, hoping thus to be made well again. He starts, hears, and tells her that "faith hath made thee whole." To the accompaniment of minstrels, Christus restores life to the dead daughter of lamenting Jairus and his wife. (*See* Matt. 9: 18–26; Acts 9: 40.)

IX. "The Tower of Magdala." Mary Magdalene, sitting alone and disconsolate, reminisces about her "unhallowed revels" with "princes and . . . merchants" who used, paid, and left her. She fears that in the next world she will be condemned with them to "endless joy or pain, or joy in pain." Yesterday, however, she saw someone under her tower, and suddenly

> . . . the air seemed filled and living
> With a mysterious power, that streamed
>   from him,
> And overflowed me with an atmosphere
> Of light and love.

She immediately felt purified. In the morning she saw an angelic figure on the water, bidding someone of little faith to come on the water to him. Magdalene says that she must find this leader, "follow him, and be with him forever!" She will take an alabaster box of balm, spirits, and herbs, and wash his blessed feet.

X. "The House of Simon the Pharisee." Magdalene enters Simon's house while he is talking to a disbelieving guest. They see her bathe Christus's feet with her tears, wipe them with her hair, and anoint them with "precious ointment . . . of sweet odor." Christus explains: Magdalene was kinder to him than Simon was; her many sins are forgiven because "she loved much"; her faith has saved her; she may "Go in peace!" (See Luke 7: 36-50.)

"The Second Passover" has eleven numbered sections.

I. "Before the Gates of Machaerus." Manahem welcomes the wilderness, night, solitude, and crane-filled skies. The Passover moon rises over the sandy desert. Within walled Machaerus, Herod dines with Herodias, and John the Baptist is imprisoned.

II. "Herod's Banquet Hall." Sent for, Manahem predicts that Herod will rule for thirty years at least. Herod is happy to hear this, especially because he is about to hold his birthday banquet. In an aside, Manahem says that Herodias and Salome, her daughter, are angelic looking but destructive. Herod recalls that he arrested John the Baptist for saying he should not marry his brother Philip's wife. Salome dances so enchantingly that Herod promises her any gift. She demands John the Baptist's head. Regretting his "accursed oath," Herod reluctantly gives the order. (See Matt. 14: 1-11.)

III. "Under the Walls of Machaerus." Manahem, allowed to leave, is critical of that "castle of despair," housing such sinners. He sees the decapitated body thrown from the tower, hopes it is buried soon, and hears an angel curse Herod's palace.

IV. "Nicodemus at Night." One night, Christus, when asked by Nicodemus, says that one must be born again to enter God's kingdom; one born again, of the spirit, has a mysterious origin and destination, like the wind; precisely as Moses raised the serpent, one must be lifted by the Son of Man; "whosoever shall believe in Him / Shall perish not, but have eternal life"; for too long, people preferred darkness to light. Nicodemus feels reproved for questioning Christus in the darkness. (See John 3: 1-21.)

V. "Blind Bartimeus [Bartimaeus]." Bartimeus is speaking about the past to Chilion, his son, when they hear Christus coming. Bartimeus asks, "That I receive my sight!" Christus replies, "Thy faith has made thee whole!" Bartimeus finds the newly visible world bewildering, dreamlike, and tender, and rejoices to see Chilion's "beautiful" face, with his deceased mother's very eyes. (See Luke 18: 35-43 and Longfellow's poem "Blind Bartimeus.")

VI. "Jacob's Well." One hot and dusty day, a Samarian woman sees a Galilean Jew, wonders why he is here, and is surprised when he requests water. She asks why he speaks to a despised Samarian. He replies that she might well ask him for "the living water," which when taken, quenches all thirst and lifts one "Into life everlasting." She wonders if he is "greater than our father Jacob" and would surely like some of that living water. He asks her to fetch her husband. When she denies having one, he startles her by saying she had five husbands and is now living with a man not her husband. She reckons he must be a prophet. He says he is the Messiah. The disciples return and wonder why Christus talked with a foolish Samarian woman, who is now running off and saying she saw Christ. When the disciples offer food, Christus says his food is the divine command to finish God's work here. (See John 4: 4-35.)

VII. "The Coasts of Caesarea Philippi." Christus, in the mountains of Caesarea Philippi, asks John, James, and Peter who the people say he is. The first two say John the Baptist, Elias, Jeremiah, or some old prophet. When Peter says he is Christ, the Son of God, Christus calls Peter "Simon Barjona," blesses him, and says that upon Peter he will build his church. Christus adds that he must go to Jerusalem, be crucified, and rise again on the third day. He climbs a hill and shines radiantly. The three disciples mistake his two, bearded companions, seen briefly, for Moses and Elias. God's voice identifies Christus as His Son. Descending, they see a crowd, and Christus removes "unclean spirits" from an idiotically behaving son of a man who has more faith, Christus notes, than the disciples themselves. (*See* Matt. 16: 13-28, 17: 1-21.)

VIII. "The Young Ruler." Here Christus speaks about much—the cocky Pharisee and the humble Publican (tax collector); little children deserving of the kingdom of heaven; a ruler's obligation to obey the commandments to merit heaven; the need to sell possessions and give to the poor; the difficulty of the rich to gain "Eternal life." (*See* Luke 9-29.)

IX. "At Bethany." Martha complains that when the Master comes, her sister Mary sits at his feet and lets Martha do all the housework. Christus comforts Martha by saying that Mary "hath chosen that good part / Which never shall be taken away from her!" (*See* Luke 20: 39-42.)

X. "Born Blind." A Jew believes that a certain beggar, said to be cured of blindness when Jesus put clay on his eyes and told him to wash at the Pool of Siloam, was not born blind at all. His parents say that he was. The Pharisees investigate and give only God the glory, accuse the beggar of blasphemy, and cast him out. (*See* John 9: 13-34.)

XI. "Simon Magus and Helen of Tyre." At Endor, Simon cannot persuade Helen, his mistress, that this region near Mt. Tabor is pleasant; she says she was happier back in colorful Tyre. He says he is not a magician but "the Power of God, and the Beauty of God!" When he tries to elevate her thoughts, she falls asleep. He describes his varied knowledge and plans to summon spirits to restore advantageous powers to his Samaritans. When Helen awakens, he tells her that he was with the Wise Men who followed the star but avoided continuing through fear of Herod. Helen says the Nazarene is alive. When Simon says that he has heard about him but hasn't seen him, she replies that such is the excuse of those not wanting to find him. Simon wonders whether he or the Nazarene deserves to be called the King of Israel. (*See* Acts 8: 9-25 and Longfellow's poem "Helen of Tyre.")

The Simonians were rivals of early Gentile Christianity, founded by slick Simon Magnus in Samaria just before it was evangelized.

Bibliography: Arvin; Grant, R. M. *Gnosticism and Early Christianity.* 2d ed. New York: Columbia University Press, 1966.

"The Third Passover" is in twelve numbered parts.

I. "The Entry into Jerusalem." As Christus enters Jerusalem, a girl reminds her mother that he restored Bartimeus's sight. (*See* Longfellow's poem "Blind Bartimeus.") Her mother recalls that she asked Christus when he was near Tyre and Sidon to make whole again this same daughter, who was then possessed by demons, and he did so because of the mother's faith in him. The daughter sees Christus and describes his face as careworn, sweet, and compassionate. Christus enters, riding on an ass. When some Pharisees ask him to rebuke his happily shouting "followers," he answers that if they remained silent "The very stones beneath us would cry out!" (*See* Matt. 15: 21-28; Luke 19: 40.)

II. "Solomon's Porch." Gamaliel, the scribe, soliloquizes in praise of the unwritten law over the written law and recalls that "bright-eyed schoolboy" in Nazareth who told his mother he had to be about his Father's business. Then Gamaliel hears Christus tell the people outside that the scribes and Pharisees, to whom he repeatedly says, "Woe unto you," are lazy, selfish, demanding, and hypocritical. He specifies their actions in great detail. Gamaliel, aghast, regards Christus as a vile, unclean, dangerous "brawler." (*See* Matt. 23: 1-38; Acts 5: 34.)

III. "Lord, Is It I?" Christus tells the disciples that one of them will betray him. Each asks, "Lord, is it I?" To Judas he answers, "Ay, thou hast said." Judas leaves. Peter, who professes willingness to be imprisoned or even die for Christus, is told, "Ere the cock crow, thou shalt deny me thrice!" Peter says he will not. Christus adjures the disciples to sell their cloaks and buy swords. Shown two such weapons, Christus says they are "enough." (*See* Matt. 26: 20-25; Luke 22: 33-38; John 13: 21-30, 38.)

IV. "The Garden at Gethsemane." While Peter, John, and James rest under an olive tree near Brook Kedron, Christus prays and says, "Oh let this cup pass from me! Nevertheless / Not as I will, but as thou wilt, be done!" The temple captain arrives with Judas and some soldiers. Christus tells his disciples to sheath their swords. Judas kisses Christus, who led away, defines all "this [as] the power of darkness." A youth follows, wearing a linen cloth, which is taken from him. (*See* Matt. 26: 36–56; Mark 14: 32–51; Luke 22: 40–53; John 18: l-11.)

V. "The Palace of Caiaphas." While Caiaphas, the high priest, is telling some Pharisees that Christus is dangerous and must die, Christus is led in and queried, answers, is silent before false witnesses, and is struck, blindfolded, and led away. During this time, Peter denies knowing Christus, hears a cock crows, and weeps in shame. (*See* Matt. 26: 57–75; Mark 14: 53–72; John 18: 12–27.)

VI. "Pontius Pilate." In a soliloquy, Pilate recalls wintering his legions here in Jerusalem and gripes first about the "proud and self-conceited . . . Jews," whose Moses and Pentateuch are no greater than Rome's Numa and Laws, and then about this "mild enthusiast." Pilate sent him to Herod, but if necessary, can smoothly pardon and release him. Jews have a God but no goddess, such as Romans have. Pilate will let the Jews wrangle while he withdraws to read his "Ovidius on the Art of Love."

VII. "Barabbas in Prison." Barabbas, partly in humorous lingo, says he doesn't worry about his career as a robber but is now pretty sure he'll be executed because he stabbed a Roman equerry, is in jail, and is also accused of sedition. (*See* Mark 15: 7; Luke 23: 19; John 18: 50.)

VIII. "Ecce Homo." Pilate finds no fault in this "Jesus, Son of Joseph." But the crowd wants him crucified, and a messenger reveals that Pilate's wife had an unpleasant dream about Jesus. Pilate washes his hands and tries again to mollify the crowd, which, however, wants Jesus dead and is willing to "Let his blood be on us and on our children!" Pilate finds him faultless, orders him brought out, and says, "Behold the man!" When he asks the crowd if they want their king crucified, the chief priests say that their only king is Caesar and that they want Christus's cross to read not "the King of the Jews"

but merely that he said he was "the King of the Jews!" (*See* Matt. 27: 11–25; Mark 15:1–15; Luke 23: 1–24; John 18: 29–40, 19: 21.)

IX. "Aceldama." Judas, in despair, remembers his unhappy childhood, the "unclean spirit" constantly torturing him, and Christus's prediction that he would be the betrayer. Judas wonders why God or Herod did not kill Judas earlier, and hopes for the forgiveness of Christus, whose "sweet, patient face" he remembers. Judas throws himself from a cliff. (*See* Matt. 27: 5.) Aceldama is the Field of Blood, the Valley of Slaughter. (*See* Jer. 19: 6.)

X. "The Three Crosses." Manahem observes the three crosses and sees the crucified Christus, head crowned with thorns, hands and feet pierced, but now "at rest forever." How can Caiaphas explain this bloody deed? Priests, scribes, and elders wonder why Christus, or his God, cannot save him. Christus asks God to forgive his ignorant persecutors and tells the penitent thief crucified beside him, "This day thou shalt be with me in Paradise." Simon Magus notes that this punishment is due those "Who preach new doctrines." The young ruler misinterprets this action. A soldier misunderstands Christus's "Eloi" (my God) as a call to "Elias" (Elijah). When another soldier offers wormwood to thirsty Christus, he answers, "It is finished!" (*See* Matt. 27: 45–47; Mark 15: 29–36; Luke 23: 34–43; John 19: 29–30.)

XI. "The Two Maries [sic]." Mary Magdalene and James's mother, Mary, see the stone of the sepulchre rolled away. An angel tells them not to fear, that Jesus of Nazareth "is arisen!," and reminds the women that Jesus predicted his crucifixion and resurrection. The angel tells them to go see Christus in Galilee. Christus appears to Mary Magdalene, who initially thinks he is a gardener. He calls her name, and she replies, "Rabboni!" (Teacher). (*See* Matt. 28: 1–9; Mark 16: 1–7; Luke 24: 5–7; John 19: 13–16.)

XII. The Sea of Galilee." Nathaniel, John, Peter, and Thomas, while fishing unsuccessfully, discuss the resurrection and their dull future. Christus appears before them on the shore and tells them to cast their nets farther out. Their nets soon fill. The men return to land. Christus breaks bread with them.

When spoken to by Christus, Peter says he loves Christus and is told to feed Christus's lambs and sheep. Thomas in two asides regards Christus as boastful, confident, and wondering whether they love him. John detects in Christus's words Peter's death by crucifixion. Peter promises to follow his "dear Lord and Master . . . even unto death!" (*See* John 21: 1–19.)

The Divine Tragedy ends, first, with an "Epilogue," titled "Symbolum Apostolorum," in which the twelve apostles, one after another, recite successive parts of the Apostles' Creed, and second, with "First Interlude," titled "The Abbot Joachim." In the latter, the abbot reflects in his convent room, with a storm outside, on how his pilgrimage to the Holy Land inspired him to write. In his books he has divided the age of Humanity into those of the Father (fear), the Son (wisdom), and the Holy Spirit (love)— "For Wisdom that begins in Fear / Ends in Love." The third age is now beginning. He concludes that "the sole thing I hate is Hate; / For Hate is death; and Love is life." Longfellow's abbot is Joachim of Floris (c.1145– 1202?), born in Calabria, where he founded his abbey.

As early as 1841 Longfellow first thought about writing what became *Christus,* which he completed thirty-three years later. In *The Divine Tragedy,* which is its 1871 beginning, occasional songs in several different meters and rhyme schemes break up lengthy sequences in blank verse. Often Longfellow offers close and relentless paraphrases from the Gospels. Best are the powerful soliloquies of Menahem, Mary Magdalene, and Judas. Delighted with early sales of *The Divine Tragedy,* Longfellow wrote George Washington Greene* (17 Dec 1871) that 10,000 copies were published five days earlier and that 3,000 more copies were being rushed into print.

Bibliography: Arvin; Barker, Kenneth, ed. *The NIV Study Bible.* Grand Rapids: Zondervan Bible Publishers, 1985; Hilen, ed.; Jones, Howard Mumford. "Literature and Orthodoxy in Boston after the Civil War." *American Quarterly* 1 (summer 1949): 149–65; Schmidt, Alfred G. *"Longfellow's Divine Tragedy.* Lucka S.A.: Druck von Reinhold Berger, 1905; Wagenknecht, 1955.

The Golden Legend begins with a "Prologue," titled "The Spire of Strasburg Cathedral," in which Lucifer urges his "Powers of the Air" to wreck the cathedral cross, bells, windows, and doors. But they reply that they cannot since the place is protected by angels, saints, holy water, apostles, and martyrs. While Lucifer rebukes his blight-breathing spirits for cowardice and says that time will do his destroying, the bells peal out not only encouragement but also warnings for all to be vigilant.

Six numbered scenes follow.

I. "The Castle of Vautsberg on the Rhine." Prince Henry of Hoheneck in his tower chamber recalls past happiness, laments the departure of friends, and halfcalls for "the undisturbed and deep / Tranquillity of endless sleep!" Lucifer enters, "waylaid" here by the storm, and calls himself a "Travelling physician" who can keep Henry, whose malady he has heard of, from ever dying. Henry describes himself thus: "My heart has become a dull lagoon, / Which a kind of leprosy drinks and drains." He explains that "the doctors of Salern[o]" say his only cure—which is impossible—is the blood of a maiden who would willingly give it to him at the cost of her life. Lucifer thinks maybe a brainless girl might be found, but meanwhile suggests "The Elixir of Perpetual Youth, / Called Alcohol," and whips out a flask. Its shimmering, dancing, fragrant contents tempt Henry; so he enjoys a fiery, energizing draft, despite an angel's warning. Lucifer, disappearing, gloats that Henry will fall "into the dark abyss." Sure enough, Henry quaffs more and soon becomes unconscious.

In the castle courtyard, Walter the minnesinger (Walther von der Vogelweide [c.1170–1230?]; *see* Longfellow's poem "Walter von der Vogelweid"), long absent, encounters his friend Hubert, who tells him that the local priests found Henry, bleary-eyed from constant reading, in a swoon. They "mutter[ed] their hocus-pocus" over him, called him practically dead, advised him to repent, and banished him. Henry found shelter in the Odenwald. Walter watches the sun set over beautiful fields, vineyards, valleys, hills, and hamlets, and says:

The day is done; and slowly from the scene
The stooping sun up-gathers his spent
    shafts,
And puts them back into his golden quiver!

But then friendly Henry's "absence more / Than the impending night darkens the landscape o'er!"

II. "A Farm in the Odenwald." While Henry sits reading, a monk enters and is recognized by "the oldest monk of all" as Felix, who left the convent a century ago and is identified by his name in a "tome, bound / In brass and wild boar's-hide." After all, years are like a single night. Elsie, aged fifteen, enters and offers Henry some flowers. He says that when they have faded, memory of them will "re-create them from the dust." The two hold hands, and Elsie tells him about Christ and the sultan's daughter, which he remembers as "The long-forgotten legend." That girl, in her father's garden gathering a bouquet, wondered where the beloved "Master of the Flowers" lived. That night Jesus appeared, said that he left his Father's realm to visit her, and took a ring from his finger for her. When she agreed to become his bride, his wounds bled and his hands held roses, which he said he had gathered at the cross on which he died for her. Then the girl, rejoicing, "Followed Him to his Father's garden." Henry assures Elsie that "the Celestial Bridegroom / Will come for thee" and crown her head with roses, not thorns. Henry tells her to put the flowers beside Saint Cecilia's picture in the church. (In 1838 Longfellow and Nathaniel Hawthorne* thought of collaborating on a book to be called "The Boys' Wonder-Horn," but nothing came of the idea. *See* Ludwig Achim von Arnim and Klemens Brentano, *Des Knaben von Wunderhorn;* Roland Hoermann, *Achim von Arnim* [Boston: Twayne, 1984]. Longfellow mentions *Wunderhorn* here and there in *Hyperion*.)

Ursula and Gottlieb worship and shelter their Prince Henry, who gave them their farm and fruitful lands, and is now gravely ill. They are the parents of Elsie, and little Max and Bertha too, and call Elsie to bring a light. Together they sing an evening prayer. Elsie wishes that she could relieve him of his "sorrow and pain!" Gottlieb reveals that

Henry can be well again only if some maiden exchanges her life for his. Elsie says that she would volunteer, for which she is rebuked; then all are sent up to prayers and bed. Ursula comments on how strange and fragile Elsie appears, but Gottlieb predicts a long life for her.

In her chamber, Elsie devoutly prays for her Savior to let her follow him, bleed as he did, die to give life "to one who asks to live," and thus resemble her Savior.

Going to her parents' bedside, Elsie says that she would like to die for Henry, saw her sister Gertrude die, and would humbly follow her to the saints, the martyrs, "And Mary, and our Lord." She adds this:

> Why should I live? Do I not know
> The life of woman is full of woe?
> Toiling on and on and on,
> With breaking heart, and tearful eyes,
> And silent lips, and in the soul
> The secret longings that arise,
> Which this world never satisfies!

To every parental query and lament, Elsie has an answer and says she plans to go to Salerno. Gottlieb wonders whether her inspiration is from God or "the Evil One"; Ursula, when Elsie kisses her, feels touched by a ghost.

The village priest is fatigued after hearing confessions, wonders what advice he could ever give the prince other than "to deny / The tempter," and trudges off to comfort the sick and dying. Lucifer enters, in priestly garb and reciting his "Black Pater-noster." He lambastes the dust-encrusted old church, the holy water, the poor box, the hypocrisy of dead town leaders, and the sacrament of confession. He says that his present purpose is "to make a murderer out of a prince." Enter Henry, who tells his priest (really Lucifer) that his mind is driven to Salerno as though by a wild storm. Lucifer replies that violation of the commandment not to kill is sometimes expedient. If Henry died, he could no longer act bravely and courteously, and his people would lament terribly; whereas, Elsie, a lowly peasant, by giving him her life would end a life rough, barren, sorrowful, and toilsome. After all, he adds, "evil is only good perverted"; and, when asked, he gives Henry absolution for any sin or crime attached to causing Elsie's death. While Lucifer mutters not a benediction but a malediction over Henry's head, an angel warns him not to make "selfishness . . . a virtue."

Back at the farm, Elsie's parents, having prayed sadly, give Henry their daughter. Elsie offers him her life. Henry accepts and asks God's blessing on all.

In the family garden, Elsie gets Henry to promise not to dissuade her. He says that death is awful to him but not to her and predicts that from her dust lilies will spring on whose petals will be inscribed "Ave Maria."

III. "A Street in Strasburg." The town crier requests prayers for the dead; but Henry, wandering remorsefully, says that since the dead are at peace, the uneasy living are the ones needing comfort. Walter of the Vogelweid enters, and the two recognize each other. Walter, on his way to Palestine as a crusader, invites Henry to come along; but Henry replies that he is too fatally self-centered and, anyway, must go instead to Hirschau. Circling overhead, Lucifer boasts he has more "thralls" than God does in the city, which is filled with sin and anguish, all "ripen[ing] into crime."

On Easter Sunday, Henry and Elsie are in front of the cathedral to hear Friar Cuthbert preach from his open-air pulpit. He asks, in a roaring voice, who brought the news that "Christ is risen"? No one from court or from town, but one from Rome. When Christ first rose, people wondered who should tell Mary. Not Adam, Abel, ill-clad John the Baptist, or the broken-boned thief from the cross, but the angel who rolled the stone from the sepulchre. Cuthbert says that church bells best deliver the message today. Their chimes are sermons; beams holding the bells, "the Holy Rood"; their wheel, the turning "mind of man"; their three-twined rope, "the Scriptural Trinity / Of Morals, and Symbols, and History," rising to contemplation and down again to action. May Christ bring us to his joy. (Cuthbert's sermon is based on a discourse by a Dominican friar from Naples, Italy, named Gabriele Barletta [?–1470].)

In the cathedral, Henry expects his portrait will soon hang beside paintings of the saints, while Elsie is timorous in the presence of such opulence. Henry points out a statue of Erwin von Steinbach, master builder of the edifice, to Elsie, who admires a column nearby, as well as images of evangelists, angels, and Christ. When Elsie wishes she could leave a monument to Christ, Henry says her pure and loving life is greater yet. The two attend a miracle play, now beginning.

The Nativity play is in nine parts. Mercy, out-debating Justice, persuades God to send His son to redeem fallen man. The angel Gabriel tells virginal Mary at the well that she is God's "holy choice" to "conceive / A child this very day." Raphael (symbolizing light), Onafiel (hope), Anael (charity), Zobiachel (justice), Michael (prudence), Uriel (fortitude), and Orifel (temperance)—the angels of the seven planets—bring "The natal star" to Bethlehem. The three wise men, Gaspar, Melchior, and Belshazzar, enter the inn stable, offer greetings to Jesus, hear him say he is "the Son of God" and will die "That other men may live!," and receive his swaddling clothes from the Virgin to "keep . . . precious." During their flight into Egypt, Joseph, Mary, and the child Jesus are beset by robbers, who Christ says will be crucified with him thirty years hence, whereas Titus, who pays off the robbers, will "abide / In paradise with me." King Herod drains bumpers of fiery wine during the slaughter of the infants, which he has ordered to prevent usurpation of his crown; but when his own son is "cleft in twain," he writhes and is dragged by Satan into Hell. While at play, Jesus creates clay sparrows and lets them fly off, after which Judas hits Jesus and then Joseph takes the muddy Christ home. In the village school, the Rabbi Ben Israel gets nice answers from Judas Iscariot but not from Jesus, whom he calls "the carpenter's son" and would strike but for instant paralysis of his uplifted arm. During a time when his playmates crown Jesus with flowers, a man approaches with his snake-poisoned son, whom Jesus cures by touching; he then names the man Simon the Canaanite, one of his future followers. (See "Infancy Gospels," in Montague Rhodes James, trans., *The Apocryphal New Testament* . . . [Oxford: Clarendon Press, 1969]; pp. 38–90; Matt. 10: 4; Mark 3: 18.)

In an "Epilogue," it is announced that a Passion Play will follow and afterwards a martyr's bones will be displayed.

IV. "The Road to Hirschau." On their way to Hirschau in the Black Forest, Henry complains about life, calls himself a demon, and admires angelic Elsie, who praises the landscape as they approach the village and hear its church bells.

At Hirschau's convent, Friar Claus thanks God for his post-Lent wine, whose captured spirits he is happy to free. He especially savors Bacharach, Hochheim, and Würzburg wines. Preferring wine cellar to cell, he fills, drains, and refills his flagon, rationalizing all the while.

In the Scriptorum, Friar Pacificus lovingly transcribes and illuminates the Gospel of John as darkness is approaching. He washes his pen before writing the word "Lord." He modestly praises his work, says it bears comparison to that of Saint Theela or Theodosius, and wishes he could find green ink as pretty as what he sees outside.

In the cloisters, Abbot Ernestus, sad that he is aging and yet sometimes longing for death, greets Prince Henry hospitably. They discuss the counts of Calvi, who founded and support the convent, and the beauty of its transcribers' manuscripts.

In the chapel, Henry sees Count Hugo of the Rhine. Once his enemy, he is now a penitent and peaceful blind monk, who, kneeling, asks Henry to smite and then pardon him. Instead, Henry admits his own former rashness, kneels beside him, and suggests that they pray together for purification and God's pardon.

At their refectory, the friars and monks enjoy a wild midnight gaudiolum. Friar Cuthbert tries unavailingly to lower the volume of Friar Paul's Latin song and Friar John's one in English. A chorus follows. Lucifer enters, is mistaken for a visiting friar, and answers their queries by saying he is a Frenchman from "St. Gildas de Rhuys" bound for Rome. He describes activities in his diocese, including Abelard's affair with Heloise, friars with concubines, and a good deal of hunting in the forest. He advises his auditors to "Drink, and die game!" The gang toasts Heloise. The chapel bell startles Lucifer, who goes on and says that for malicious fun they poisoned Abelard's chalice, which, however, a friar drank from and died. When they spot Siebald the Refectorarius, a spying tattletale at their window, Lucifer suggests grabbing him and pummeling him. Suddenly Abbot Ernestus bursts in, criticizes the riotous monks, shouts, "Away, you drunkards! to your cells, / And pray till you hear the matin-bells," and tells Cuthbert he reserves a special punishment for him.

Meanwhile, in the neighboring nunnery Irmingard tells Elsie that she was fresh from the convent when she fell in love with Walter of the Vogelweid. Her father heard of their passion and commanded her to wed Henry of Hoheneck or enter the convent. When Irmingard and Henry fled, her father galloped in pursuit. She fell and awakened back in her room. She entered the convent reluctantly but is peaceful now, her "passion . . . now turned to heaven." She persuades silent Elsie to go "to thy slumber," while she prays down in the chapel.

Henry and Elsie, with some attendants, walk along a covered bridge at Lucerne. Paintings on it are of the Dance of Death, figures on which he interprets morosely, saying life is "lovely," death, "hateful." On the other hand, as they emerge Elsie welcomes death, saying, "The grave itself is but a covered bridge, / Leading from light to light, through a brief darkness!"

V. "A Covered Bridge at Lucerne." Next, they cross the Devil's Bridge, which is over a raging river and which a guide tells Henry and Elsie the Devil let stand after destroying other bridges nearby. Under it Lucifer gloats that it remains for criminals to use.

At the high St. Gothard Pass, Elsie thinks of St. Catherine carried by angels and wishes she could be borne aloft in death likewise. When they see Italy ahead, she likens it to "a garden of Paradise," but he labels it Gethsemane. The guide says they must get to lodgings in Belinzona.

Henry and Elsie, riding ahead of their servants, pause at the foot of the Alps. Trudging along with some pilgrims, chanting to St. Hildebert, is Lucifer. Garbed like a Carmelite, he sneers, "The sole of my feet are as hard and tanned / As the conscience of old

Pope Hilbebrand," criticizes the stupid pilgrims, and says he would quit the journey but for his extraordinary strength. Henry and Elsie see Cuthbert, who says he is pilgrimaging "to Benevent" to see an image of Mary, whose influential "example of all womanhood" Henry gratefully acknowledges.

Looking at the sea from their inn at Genoa, Henry is tempted by Lucifer's voice to end it all and muses thus:

A single step, and all is o'er;
A lunge, a bubble, and no more;
And thou, dear Elsie, will be free
From martyrdom and agony.

From her balcony, Elsie admires the starry night and "the music of the sea." Henry contrasts her purity with his demonic gloom.

Behind their south-bound felucca they see a storm brewing. The skipper points out a fleet of brigantines from Lucca loaded with oil and wine. He advises his passengers to go below decks.

VI. "The School of Salerno." At the gate of the college in Salerno a scholar attaches his theses, designed to refute Dionysius, Michael the Stammerer, and Johannes Duns Scotus ("that . . . beast") concerning God and creation. Doctors Serafino and Cherubino enter, trailing pupils and disputing about ideas, universals, and irregular verbs. A local scholar briefs a scholar visiting from Monte Cassino. Here, medical students first study logic for three years—otherwise, "how could you hope to show / That nobody knows so much as you know?" They dissect "the bodies of swine, / As likest the human form divine." They study several named tomes. They swear to peach on dishonest druggists, visit patients regularly, and attend the poor free. Finally, "crowned with . . . laurel," they march out in lordly fashion. Lucifer mutters criticism of the school's cocky and erroneous regimen, reads the theses at the gate, chortles, and says his position is secure "So long as the boastful human mind / Consents in such mills as this to grind." Scholars ignore "golden grain" in favor of "pitiful chaff." As Henry and Elsie approach, Lucifer expresses fear that the divinely innocent girl may yet escape his clutches, and introduces himself to the pair

as Fra Angelo, to whom Henry says he has written about Elsie's desire to die so that Henry may live. Henry says her example has readied him for death. She reminds him that he promised not to dissuade her, tells her servants to prepare her, and asks Henry to go tell her parents that she confessed, was absolved, and died happy. Lucifer leads her away, alone. Henry repents, rebukes himself, and rushes after Elsie.

Back in the Odenwald, Ursula, Elsie's melancholy mother, is at her spinning, while cheerless Gottlieb is out farming. Suddenly a forester enters and reports to Ursula that Prince Henry turned noble, saved Elsie, and was healed by touching the holy bones of St. Matthew. Ursula issues a prayer of thanks from "a mother's heart" to the Virgin Mary. The forester adds that Henry, vowing to marry Elsie, now named Alicia, is even now sailing to his home on the Rhine with her. While Ursula rushes out to Gottlieb, the forester helps himself to Gottlieb's handy beer and bread.

From the terrace at his Vautsberg castle on the Rhine, Henry and Elsie watch their wedding guests leave and hear the bells of Geisenheim chime for curfew. Henry recalls that proud Charlemagne listened to these same bells in distress after his wife Fastrada died. Elsie tells Henry that the bells make her think of "Of peace and deep tranquillity, / And endless confidence in thee!" Henry promises her his unending love and calls her his Fastrada, his queen. Night falls. The moon rises. They retire.

In an "Epilogue," the Angel of Good Deeds says that rain fills the brooks that cool the plains, and faith enabled Elsie, a holy, meek, unselfish maiden, to perform this now-recorded blissful action. The Angel of Evil Deeds observes that records of events in his open book keep fading, just the way threatening clouds and lightning are frustrated by a resisting wind. God permits Lucifer, His minister, to exist; he "labors for some good / By us not understood."

A "Second Interlude" features Martin Luther (1483–1546) writing at Wartburg. He praises God's strength, Christ's eternal protection of weak mankind, the ability of Christ's name to "vex the Devil," and the soothing power of God-given music. Luther recalls idly hunting but now prefers to hunt the Pope of Rome and "all his diabolic crew" of murderous priests, and to free all nuns, caged like warm, soft, young birds. Satan sometimes whispers doubts into Luther's ear. Luther reviles his enemies, including Erasmus (1466?-1536), "the vilest miscreant," and praises Philip(p) Melanc(h)thon (1497-1560), to whom he especially writes and in whose honor he will sing "a choral chant of victory!"

Published separately, *The Golden Legend* enjoyed great sales but mixed reviews. Longfellow wrote Charles Sumner* (20 Dec 1851) that "The first edition of three thousand five hundred is gone, and a second now in press." Dudley Buck (1839-1909), a Boston musician, composed "Scenes from Longfellow's *Golden Legend*," a symphonic cantata (1880). Edmund Clarence Stedman (1833-1908), the poet, critic, and Wall Street broker with whom Longfellow corresponded, provided paraphrases in English of the Latin verses in *The Golden Legend*. The composition was performed in Cincinnati, won a prize of $1,000, and was published (1880). In its early stages, Longfellow, to whom Buck wrote, replied (2 Dec 1872) to criticize the libretto as "a great mutilation of my poem." All the same, Longfellow wrote John Sullivan Dwight (1813-93), the Boston music critic (20 Jul 1879), to seek his influence, evidently without success, to have not only Buck's *Golden Legend* performed but also Buck's musical rendition of "The Nun of Nidaros" (*see* "The Musician's Tale: The Sage of King Olaf," in *Tales of a Wayside Inn*).

Bibliography: Arvin; P. A. C. "Longfellow's *Golden Legend* and Its Analogues." *Poet-Lore* 4 (1892): 91-100; Hammer, Jr., Carl. *Longfellow's "Golden Legend" and Goethe's "Faust."* Baton Rouge: Louisiana State University Press, 1952; Hilen, ed.; Krumpelmann, John T. "Longfellow's *Golden Legend* and the *Armer Heinrich* Theme in Modern German Literature." *Journal of English and Germanic Philology* 25 (2nd quarter 1926): 173-92; Wagenknecht, 1955.

The New England Tragedies comprises two five-act, blank-verse plays: "John Endicott" and "Giles Corey of the Salem Farms."

"John Endicott." In a "Prologue," the poet invites his audience to watch an old city rise before it, complete with "scenes of triumph, and . . . scenes of pain." This despite long-dead errors,

> . . . For the lessons they teach:
> The tolerance of opinion and of speech.
> Faith, Hope, and Charity remain,—these three;
> And greatest of them is Charity.

Boston, 1665. In the meeting house on Sunday afternoon, the Reverend John Norton (1606-63) tells his congregation that even though the angel of an angry God has warned this land, "Heresy uplift[s] its horrid head." Edith Christison counters that certain shepherds are ignoring their flocks and continues her criticism. Norton expels her and her fellow Quakers, and tells Governor Endicott (1589?-1665), also present, that the blasphemous "must be suppressed / By civil power." Endicott expresses sorrow at executions and banishments already accomplished but rationalizes that jailed heretics can only blame themselves. Nicholas Upsall breaks the Sabbath by staying home and, worse, by sheltering Quakers. His neighbor, Walter Merry, warns him, complains that today's meeting was disrupted by troublemakers, and opines that more of them deserve hanging. Several Quakers, including Wharton and Edith, discuss the martyrdom by hanging of four of their virtuous friends, now in God's "pleasant pastures." Young John Endicott, the governor's son, leading a marshal and Merry, enters and apprehends the Quakers, along with Upsall. Edith calls the young man Saul of Tarsus for persecuting her.

In his home, John is agitated: Edith called him Saul; he heard a voice cry for mercy; he dislikes seeing the grim prison where Edith languishes, and hopes his father will forgive the Quakers. At a tavern called the Three Mariners, Simon Kempthorn is drinking when it comes out that the *Swallow*, the ship he captains, brought some Quakers, including Edith and her father, Wenlock Christison, up from the Barbadoes. The marshal, accompanied by John, Merry, and the hangman, enters and reads Governor Endicott's proclamation—severe punishment to Quakers, those bringing them in, and those harboring them. When the hangman burns a pile of proscribed books, John objects and thus earns Kempthorn's indiscreet praise. Merry watches Kempthorn enjoying some ale, asks his name, and arrests him on Endicott's warrant to answer questions "Touching the Quakers." Merry enters Endicott's house and tells him he heard young John "vilipend" the laws for being "unjust . . . and abominable." Merry leaves. Endicott restrains his rage, and John enters. When Endicott says his son's face resembles that of his deceased mother, John beseeches him to emulate her mild, merciful nature. Endicott warns his son that heresy is like a seemingly harmless snow that engulfs its victims, turns them drowsy, and finally kills them; furthermore, that even doubts, like falling, dazzling stars, blind us fatally. John counters by asking, "Who dares / To say that he alone has found the truth?" Since we all have doubts, perhaps we are all heretics. Endicott chides John for his inexperience, threatens him, and orders him not to return until he is dutiful and submissive. Alone, Endicott envies the childless and says that God has sent John away from him.

Captain Kempthorn is brought before Endicott, who tells him to transport the Quakers back to Barbadoes. When he replies that "the law, sir, of Barbadoes / Forbids" such, he is to be committed, but first, to be pilloried because—Merry says—he swore on his way to the court. Next, Endicott questions Wharton the Quaker. When he refuses to doff his hat, take any oath, or be banished, he too is removed. Next comes Edith Christison, whose father's conduct has displeased Endicott. She also declines to take an oath, on the grounds that "Christ is the Word" and that she is ruled by "The Inner Light, and not the Written Word." Questioned, she says this: She was commanded by the Lord to attend Boston's church and to cry out against those worshipping powerless outward forms therein. Asked if she regards herself as a prophetess, she quotes the Bible about inspired "handmaidens . . . [who] shall prophesy." The judges nod, and Endicott orders Edith "Scourged in three towns, with forty stripes save one," and then banished.

Wenlock Christison, in the crowd, shouts, "Woe to the city of blood!" Endicott summons him, reminds him that he was banished, and threatens him with death. Christison replies that he is a freeborn Englishman, comes here in peace, and warns his oppressors that the wrath of God awaits them. Endicott asks the judges to render their verdict. One boasts of voting for Christison's death. Another declines. Endicott tells the naysayers to go on record and then orders execution by hanging. The condemned man warns that God, when they "put his servitors to death," will curse them. Learning that Edith has been whipped, John tells Upsall that "The town should be in mourning," to which Upsall replies that eventually the good citizens will overturn their "barbarous laws." He also defines John's father as "both loving and severe," and "upright . . . and . . . just . . . / In all things save the treatment of the Quakers." To all this, John complains that he is now homeless because of his father's cruelty; so Upsall offers his own place as shelter. John visits Edith in prison, where she is finding comfort in reading the Bible. He voices shame, asks for her forgiveness, and offers to help her escape. She resolutely declines, saying that "invisible bars" hold her here, that she has no fear of death, that from when she first saw him she "felt a [spiritual] tenderness" toward him, and that she awaits God's yet-unspoken word. Telling John not to remain, she now calls him "Paul of Damascus," not Saul any longer.

Behold Kempthorn in the stocks, with Merry and a crowd looking on. Kempthorn jeers several men who walk by and ignore him. When Ralph Goldsmith, a friendly sea captain, asks why he is punished, Kempthorn replies that in Boston "They put sea-captains in the stocks for swearing / And Quakers for not swearing." Now released, Kempthorn tells Goldsmith that he has to pay a fine if he doesn't return the Quakers to Barbadoes and wonders how he can return any, since one Quaker is banished and another about to be hanged. Goldsmith suggests that Kempthorn "slip your hawser on some cloudy night" and sail off. On the street, John sees Edith, bleeding from having been scourged but strong in her faith, and gives her some water. Merry warns him, to which John calls Edith's wounds "roses in the garden of the Lord!" and labels the Endicott residence "the household of Iscariot." Through his prison bars, Christison, Edith's father, advises courage and calls her blessed. She says she will comfort him in death. He warns the "pitiless town" of God's approaching wrath. John advises "ye sleepers" to reform their "bloody statutes." Endicott enters, hears Christison, is told that John is fomenting sedition, and orders him arrested. Even Merry wonders about this development. Endicott cries out, "O Absalom, my son!" Endicott meets with his deputy Richard Bellingham (1592?–1672), to discuss news brought by ship from England: Oliver Cromwell's body and those of two colleagues have been exhumed and hanged, ten regicides executed, and Charles II, newly crowned (actually not until 1610), has sent a mandamus stripping Endicott of authority, stopping his punishment of Quakers, and ordering them returned to England. Dutiful but feeling disgraced and close to death, Endicott tells Bellingham to carry out the order. In the street, a crowd led by Upsall complains to Norton that old William Brand is being cruelly tortured by the jailer for reviling ordinances. Norton, bravely intolerant, defends Brand's punishment, tears down a placard in which the magistrates declare that the jailer will be summoned to the court, and calls the placard a "flag of truce with Satan and with Sin!" Upsall calls Norton an "Orthodox Evangelist" and tells him to go away. Edith, scourged, banished, and wandering in the wilderness alone, lost but trusting her Lord to guide her, intends to return to Boston and martyrdom. John follows her blood-stained track, shouts her name, but hears no reply.

John returns to Boston at dawn one morning, stops at Upsall's house, and tells him that he was fined and released, vainly sought Edith in the wilderness, and has heard no recent news. Upsall explains: Edith is safe in his house; King Charles learned that local executions "a vein of innocent blood / Opened in his dominions," said, "I will stop that vein!," and issued a general pardon by mandamus. John rejoices. Kempthorn is dis-

consolately drinking at the Three Mariners when Edward Butter, a deaf official, enters and tells him that the Quakers have been pardoned, Kempthorn's bond has been voided, and he is free to leave. In Bellingham's presence, Endicott not only gripes about "rebellious children" but also regrets being misled by his own "righteous zeal." Bellingham interrupts to tell him this: Norton suddenly turned giddy and, dying, said God's hand did it; the horse of another official reared where Quakers had been scourged, and the man fell and "his brains were dashed about the street"; the castle captain was killed by lightning. When Bellingham adds that the Quakers are free and Kempthorn has sailed his *Swallow* away, Endicott wishes that his soul were as white and spotless as the *Swallow,* says, "O, Absalom, my son!" again, and falls dead. Bellingham says of Endicott that "Only the acrid spirit of the times / Corroded this true steel," and prays that Endicott may "rest forever in peace!"

Longfellow wrote his publisher James T. Fields* (1 Jun 1872) that he was dissatisfied with the title "John Endicott" and might like it changed, not to "Wenlock Christison," but to "Scourged in Three Towns." The change was not made.

Bibliography: Hilen, ed.; Tucker, Edward L. *The Shaping of Longfellow's "John Endicott": A Textual History, Including Two Early Versions.* Charlottesville: University Press of Virginia, 1985; Wagenknecht, 1955.

"Giles Corey of the Salem Farms." In a "Prologue," astonishment is expressed that in peaceful-looking Salem there could once have been witchcraft, "wonders of the world unseen," delusions, "and necromantic arts" ruining the weak and intimidating the strong. The religious and secular leaders "ruled . . . / Less in the love than in the fear of God," and believed that "the Powers / Of Darkness" employed witches, spells, and ghosts to work their evil. Nor was New England alone guilty; in many lands, witches were executed.

In the woods outside Salem, Tituba, an Indian slave, gathers deadly herbs that give her power in hand and eye greater than that of soldiers, rich men, scholars, preachers, and magistrates. The minister Cotton Mather (1663-1728) enters, lost and fearing that by trying to avoid witches he might encounter one. Tituba introduces herself as a witch. He remembers that she renounced evil and repented; so he gets his nearby horse, won't let her ride behind him, but will follow her back to Salem. Explaining that she can fly home on a stick, she exits.

Worried by talk about witchcraft, Justice John Hathorne (1641-1717), the great-great-grandfather of Nathaniel Hawthorne,* welcomes Mather to his home and asks the learned man for advice. Hathorne says he has seen children tormented by sorcerers but as a mere magistrate he can use only "weapons from the armory of the flesh" to fight back and therefore needs Mather's "spiritual weapons" to fight what Mather calls "These wonders of the world invisible." Yet when Mather advises caution in wielding any knife, to avoid cutting the innocent or sheltering the guilty, Hathorne says he will act fast and zealously, and not be bookish and meditative, like Mather. Mather would like divine guidance so that New England will not emit a "sulphurous odor" to the outside world. Tituba puts young Mary Walcot, who fears curses, into a trance by having her look into a mirror and watch, as "an Obi man," the witch's clever father in San Salvador, their former home, kills an enemy by melting a wax image of him. Jonathan Walcot, Mary's brother, brings Hathorne and Mather to see his sister, who is all "worn by devilish incantations!" Mary, startled, suddenly says that Goodwife Bishop is pinching and beating her and that Goodwife Corey is threatening her with a spindle. When Jonathan draws his sword, Hathorne says they can't see the "spectres" that are visible to Mary, whom Tituba awakens with a touch. Seeing a spindle in Mary's lap, Tituba says Mary took it from Goodwife Corey. Tituba also finds a bit of gray cloth Jonathan's sword cut from the witch's dress. Hathorne is convinced, while Mather advises prayer.

Old Giles Corey looks about his farm, praises God for its successful crops, and nails a horseshoe on his threshold to ward off "the powers of darkness." John Gloyd, his hired man, points out that Corey's cattle have broken loose. Corey thinks they are bewitched, but his young wife, Martha (?-1692), says Gloyd turned them loose. She reports that Goodwife Proctor (Elizabeth Proctor, ?-1692), wife of John Proctor (?-1692), told her that Bridget Bishop has been "cried out upon" and is to be tried today for witchcraft. Corey, who always liked Bridget, says he believes in and is fascinated by witchcraft, and asks her to attend the trial with him. When he refers to witches in the Bible, Martha replies that that was "long ago" and that she is not interested in Bridget's case. Corey tells her Richard Gardner, a sea-captain friend of his, is coming to visit and asks her to be nice to him. Corey cannot find his saddle. Martha says she hid it. When he threatens to ride bareback to town and say a witch stole his saddle, she fetches it for him. He rides off to town, where he learns Bridget has been condemned to death. A farmer warns him that Proctor is angry with Corey, who, he says, burned down his house, quarreled with Gloyd about his wages, and murdered a man named Robert Goodell. Corey furiously denies these accusations. Gloyd comes by and reports that the cattle, obviously bewitched, have jumped into the Ipswich River and been drowned. Corey, thoroughly vexed, wonders, "Why did I leave my ploughing and my reaping / To plough and reap this Sodom and Gomorrah?" and says he feels like drowning himself. Corey returns home in great anger and, telling Martha that Satan must have entered Proctor, explains that the fellow accused him of burning his house. Martha blames "crafty," "untruthful" Gloyd for fomenting trouble. Corey adds that rumor now has it he also caused Goodell's death fourteen years ago. Furthermore, his cattle, which he loved for their patience and strength, are now dead. Corey won't have any supper, plans to remain wrathful, and even declines to say the Lord's Prayer with Martha, since he cannot "forgive those who have sinned against us." He ruefully admits that "the old Adam . . . rises up" in him and inspires him to "Hate and revenge."

At breakfast Martha persuades Corey to avoid town, tells him that she dreamed they were both imprisoned and he was forced to testify against her, and says that while he goes mowing near the river she will watch for his friend Gardner. On a Salem street, Hathorne and Mather discuss witchcraft: A witch's evil spirit may enter another body when the witch is burned; the Bible orders Jews to burn witches; in England, "lawfully convicted" witches are executed; curious was evidence concerning Bridget Bishop's spectre, evil eyes, potent hand, and pin-stuck "poppets." Hathorne will let Mather read the court documents. Two deacons visit Martha in her home to tell her some children have called her a witch. She bluntly denies all charges, calls witchcraft "a delusion," and regards those accusing her as "deceit[ful]." Given permission, she summarizes the Biblical story of Jezebel, who caused two men—"sons of Belial"—to testify falsely against Naboth, who was stoned to death, thus enabling Ahab, Jezebel's husband, to seize Naboth's garden; but divinely inspired Elijah warns Ahab that the enemies of those who encourage false witnesses "will find them out." (*See* 1 Kings 21: 1–20.) While working in the meadow with his men, Corey kids them about his strength. Gloyd challenges him to a wrestling match, loses, and whispers that the Devil gave Corey strength. When Corey hoists a heavy cask of cider, Gloyd calls such lifting "Witchcraft." A lad runs up and tells Corey that Martha is jailed as a witch. Corey rides to town. Gloyd incites some of the men with tales of witches. One man, however, praises Martha as an innocent, good woman. Gloyd tells him to be quiet so he can nap.

Gloyd leads some farmers from the village green into the court house, where he expects to testify. Hathorne summons Martha, in chains, and accuses her of using sorcery and incantations against Mary Walcot, also present. Martha asserts her innocence as "a gospel woman." Mary says Martha is pinching and biting her right now, which Martha denies. When she says Corey, her husband, told her that children complained about her, he denies telling her. Martha asks to pray, but Hathorne says she would do so to "the Prince of Darkness." Mary faints, revives, says Martha has a bad bird on her finger and says Martha is crushing her right now. Mar-

tha answer questions thus: It isn't her fault if an evil spirit takes her shape to do ill to another; the magistrates are blind if they call her a sorceress; she hid Corey's saddle to keep him from wasting time in town; she is a faithful churchgoer, has taken communion with many now here, and is innocent of charges brought by this "distraught" girl. Summoned next, Corey says this: Martha seemed to impede his praying once; he blamed the Devil for drowning his cattle; but Martha is brave, charitable, forgiving, industrious, patient, and virtuous. When Martha is led away and Corey mutters "The dream!," Hathorne cannot make him say more than that both his death's and Martha's are "foreordained." His refusal to confess, together with Gloyd's statement about Corey's superhuman strength and Mary's sudden vision here of Goodell's ghost, condemns Corey to suffer execution by having weights placed on his body.

Gardner visits the Coreys' empty house, sees Tituba, and learns from her that Corey and Martha are in prison. While at sea and in danger, Gardner often thought of Corey and his pleasant life; but now Corey is "Drifting upon this sea of sorceries." In prison, Corey bequeaths his goods to his daughters and his "immortal soul to Him who made it." He finds comfort when he hears Martha, in another cell, singing a courageous hymn. Gardner enters, is Corey's only visitor, but cannot persuade Corey to "Confess and live." Praising Martha, Corey is led away. Outside, Gloyd soon hears the bell signaling Corey's death. Hathorne, at the graveyard, remarks that those dealing in witchcraft "drag death upon themselves," to which Mather replies that "mouldering statute-books" in England cause these executions and that Giles Corey one day "will be counted as a martyr!" In his journal (15, 18 Feb 1868), Longfellow notes that the subject of "Giles Corey of the Salem Farms" has taken "hold of me powerfully," that he has written two scenes, and that the work will be completed soon, assuming "this possession lasts."

In a "Finale," Saint John says that, as time passes, evil seems ceaseless. He wonders:

. . . doth Charity fail?
Is Faith of no avail?
Is Hope blown out like a light
By a gust of wind in the night?

But no. God breathes inspiringly, and "Him evermore I behold / Walking in Galilee," and he tells us to rise and follow him.

Longfellow could write very rapidly. In a letter to Charles Sumner* (9 Mar 1868), he reports that he wrote both *John Endicott* and *Giles Corey of the Salem Farms* in February 1868. While Longfellow was vacationing in Europe, George Routledge (1812–88), his London publisher, offered him £1,400, to be paid over ten years, or £1,000 within two years, for a London edition of *The New England Tragedies*. Longfellow accepted the quick £1,000 and, to secure copyright, traveled from Switzerland to London to be there on the day of British publication (10 Oct 1868).

Bibliography: Arvin; Hansen, Chadwick. "The Metamorphosis of Tituba, or Why American Intellectuals Can't Tell an Indian Witch from a Negro." *New England Quarterly* 47 (Mar 1974): 3–12; Hebel, Udo J. *Those Images of Jealousie": Identitäten und Alterit äten im puritanischen Neuengland des 17. Jahrhunderts.* New York: Peter Lang, 1997; Hilen, ed.; Japp, A. H. "The Puritan Element in Longfellow." *Living Age* 155 (4 Nov 1882): 306–15; Upham, Charles W. *Salem Witchcraft; with an Account of Salem Village. . . .* 2 vols. Boston: Wiggin and Lunt, 1867.

"CHRYSAOR" (1850). Poem, as "The Evening Star," in *Godey's Lady's Book,* Jan 1850; *S/F.* The evening star rises over the ocean, gleaming "ever refulgent, soft, and tender." Thus rose Chrysaor from the arms of his beloved Callirrhoe, "tender, soft, and tremulous." The poet, "entranced," wonders if he looks each night on "a God, or . . . a star." In Greek mythology, the parents of Geryon, one of Hercules's opponents, were Chrysaor and Callirrhoe, the daughter of Oceanus. This pure and lovely work has been highly praised by critics.

Bibliography: Arvin; Hilen, ed.

"THE CITY AND THE SEA" (1882). Poem, in *Harbor.* When the city, hot with "the flame / Of the pitiless sun," begs the sea to breathe on it, the sea replies that its breath sometimes brings life, but sometimes death. The sea agrees, but what will its "heaving breast" bring this time?

"CLASS POEM" (1825). Unpublished poem Longfellow read at the graduation ceremonies at Bowdoin (8 Sep 1825).

Bibliography: Little.

"CLEAR HONOR OF THE LIQUID ELEMENT" (1831). Irregular sonnet, signed "L.," translated from the Spanish poet Luis de Góngora y Argote (1561–1627), in *NEM,* 1 Jul 1831. The persona asks the water of the "rivulet" to remain calm while his beloved, who has "fierce extreme[s]," looks at herself in it. If the current rushes with "headlong speed," the image of her "rare charms" will be all churned up.

Bibliography: Brenan; Hilen, ed.

CLOUGH, ARTHUR HUGH (1819–61). British poet. He was educated at Rugby and Balliol College, Oxford, after which he worked in London as the principal at University Hall and then as an Education Office examiner. He assisted Florence Nightingale (1820–1910) in her philanthropic work in London. Clough's best poems are "The Bothie of Tober-na-Vuolich: A Long-Vacation Pastoral" (1848), a pastoral novelette in hexameters (adopted partly because of the hexameters popularized in *Evangeline* [1847]), and the posthumously issued "Dipsychus" (1869), a sardonic dialogue set in Venice that dramatizes Clough's renunciation of conservative Christian ideals. Clough's early death in Florence inspired "Thyrsis" (1867), an elegy by Matthew Arnold (1822–88).

Clough corresponded with Ralph Waldo Emerson,* who knew him in England and Paris. When Clough sent Emerson a copy of his "Bothie," Emerson lent it to Longfellow, who in his journal calls the poem "witty, and natural, and poetical in a high degree,—the love passages admirably wrought out" (7 Jan 1849). Longfellow wrote Emerson (9 Jan 1849) that the poem was "fascinating and in every part admirable," and mentioned his delight that it was in hexameters. Clough visited the United States (1852-53), was hospitably treated, and hoped unavailingly to establish a boys' school in America. Emerson hosted a dinner for Clough, Nathaniel Hawthorne,* James Russell Lowell,* Charles Sumner,* and Longfellow, who soon returned the favor with a dinner including Clough and Charles Eliot Norton.* The group proceeded to Norton's house, for what Longfellow says in his journal were "some private theatricals, with a nice little epilogue written by Mr. Clough" (26 Nov 1852). Longfellow took Clough to Lowell's home, commenting in his journal on Clough's "gentleness, and his bewildered look" (30 Dec 1852). Shortly before Hawthorne's departure for Liverpool and Clough's return to London, Longfellow hosted a dinner (14 Jun 1853) including both men. In June 1854 when Clough married Blanche Smith (1828-1904), a cousin of Florence Nightingale, Longfellow sent him a sweet letter expressing fond wishes (5 Jun 1854).

Bibliography: Hilen, ed.; S. Longfellow; Lowry, Howard F. and Ralph Leslie Rusk, eds. *Emerson-Clough Letters.* 1934. Reprint, Folcroft: Folcroft Press, 1969.

"THE COBBLER OF HAGENAU." *See* "The Student's Tale" in *Tales of a Wayside Inn,* Part Second.

CODMAN, SUSAN (1802–77). A beautiful young lady from Portland. She and Longfellow corresponded during his first stay in Europe. Although gossip in Portland had it that the two might soon become engaged, she evidently rejected him by a courteous but firm letter (8 Mar 1830), in which she said she missed him when he was away but didn't love him. In 1831 she married the much older Benjamin Welles (1781-1860).

Bibliography: Hilen, ed.

COLMAN, SAMUEL (?–1865). Portland publisher and bookseller. He published Longfellow's *Elements of French Grammar, Manuel de Proverbes Dramatiques,* and *Novelas Españolas.* He moved to New York, founded *Colman's Monthly Miscellany* (1839; it lasted only three months), published Longfellow's "Fragment of a Modern

Ballad" (*see* "The Happiest Land"), and his *Hyperion.* According to a letter from Longfellow to Colman (20 May 1839), Colman was to print 1,500 copies, give him 25 copies, and pay him $375 within six months. Plans were altered in July: 2,200 copies were to be printed, and Longfellow was to receive $500 plus 50 copies. But by December 1839 Colman had gone bankrupt, a victim of results of the Panic of 1837. Creditors seized much of the material of unsold, and even unbound, copies of *Hyperion,* and Longfellow lost almost all of the money promised him. Colman agreed to pay Longfellow in full but soon broke his word. According to a letter Longfellow wrote Samuel Ward* (5 Mar 1842), Colman paid Longfellow $272 and gave him fifteen copies of *Hyperion.*

Bibliography: Hilen, ed.

"COME, O DEATH, SO SILENT FLYING." *See* "From the [Spanish] Cancioneros."

"COMMENCEMENT ORATION" (1825). *See* "The Life and Writings of Chatterton" and "Our Native Writers."

"CONCORD" (1864). *See* "Hawthorne: May 23, 1864."

"CONSOLATION" (1870). Poem, translated from the French poet François de Malherbe (1555-1628), in *AM,* Sep 1870; *Three.* The poet addresses these lines to a gentleman of Aix-en-Provence after his daughter died. Will your grief be eternal? Will her burial cost you your reason? The poet will not criticize the girl by disparaging her. But after all, the world "exposes" the "fairest things," like a rose, to "the most forlorn" fate. There is no point in complaining to death, which "has . . . rigorous laws," condemning poor people and kings alike. "To will what God doth will," without any defiance, "gives us . . . rest."

"THE CONVENT OF THE PAULAR" (1834). Story, probably by Longfellow, in *Token,* 1834, signed "L." Juan Zurdo, a soldier, walks from San Ildefonso through the gloomy Sierra de Guadarrama to the convent. He spends an uneasy night. In the morning he finds the church filled with praying monks and is impressed by the vanity of all things human and by the uncertainty of the hereafter. Juan recognizes and greets one monk as Gonzalez, an old friend. Gonzalez doesn't heed him but stares devotedly at his crucifix. Juan deciphers some verses scrawled on the wall, to the effect that only death can warm the soul, and departs. The lines of poetry are from the Spanish of "Coplas a la Muerte Del Mastre De Sant Ago Don Rodrigo Manrique, Su Padre," by Jorge Manrique (1440?–79). Longfellow published (or republished) his translation of the poetry as "Ode on the Death of His Father," in his edition of *Poets and Poetry of Europe.*

Bibliography: Thompson; Thompson, Ralph. "Additions to Longfellow Bibliography Including a New Prose Tale." *American Literature* 3 (Nov 1931): 303–8.

COPLAS DE MANRIQUE (1832). See *Coplas de Manrique. Translated from the Spanish.*

COPLAS DE MANRIQUE. TRANSLATED FROM THE SPANISH (1832, 1833). Poem, translated from the Spanish poet Jorge Manrique (1440?–79). In this elegy, comprising forty stanza in iambic tetrameter broken by half-lines, the poet, later killed in battle himself, honors Rodrigo Manrique, his brave soldier father. In the first part of *Coplas* (couplets), it is made clear that whether one is rich or poor, aristocrat or peasant, good or evil, the end is death—and a better life hereafter. The poet wonders, for example:

> Qué se fizieron las damas,
> sus tocados, sus vestidos,
>   sus olores?
> Qué se fizieron las llamas
> de los fuegos encendidos
> de amadores?

Longfellow beautifully translates these lines as follows:

> Where are the highborn dames, and where
> The gay attire, and jewelled hair,
> And odors sweet?
> Where are the gentle knights, that came
> To kneel, and breathe love's ardent flame,
> Low at their feet?

The second part of *Coplas* praises "Roderic Manrique, he whose name / Is written on the scroll of Fame." Adjectives describing him are legion: He was brave, prudent, graceful, skillful, clement, eloquent, and generous. "He stood, in his high dignity, / The proudest knight of chivalry," not least in combat against the Moors. When Death speaks to him, he doesn't falter but says, "My spirit longs to flee away, / And be at rest." Rodrigo dies at last, "Encircled by his family," his soul led by God to "glorious rest," his influence remaining "Bright, radiant, blest." Interesting is Longfellow's incidental statement that "the good monk, in cloistered cell, / Shall gain it [heavenly reward] by his book and bell" but also by "His prayers and tears."

In 1833 Longfellow published his translation of *Coplas de Don Jorge Manrique à la Muerta de su Padre,* together with the Spanish original on facing pages, translations of seven Spanish sonnets, and an introduction, in *Coplas de Don Jorge Manrique, Translated from the Spanish with an Introductory Essay* . . . The seven sonnets are "The Good Shepherd," "The Image of God," "Nature and Art," "The Native Land," "To a Brook," "To-morrow: Lord, What Am I . . . ?," and "The Two Harvests." This was Longfellow's first book, of 96 pages. It followed his partial translation of Manrique's poem, in *NEM,* Dec 1832, and shows for the first time his skill as a translator.

Bibliography: Brenan; Hilen, ed.; Thompson; Wagenknecht, 1955.

CORTÉS Y SESTI, JOSÉ (1810-?). Friend. Longfellow met Cortés y Sesti in Madrid, where he was a bodyguard for King Ferdinand. He and Longfellow corresponded. At Longfellow's urging, he migrated to America (1832), stayed briefly with Longfellow and his wife in Brunswick, and taught Spanish in Portland (1833), returned to Spain (1834), and went to Italy (1836), where Longfellow helped him meet George Washington Greene.*

Bibliography: Hilen, ed.

COURS DE LANGUES FRANÇAISE (1832). Text prepared by Longfellow for his Bowdoin students. It contains *Le Ministre de Wakefield* and *Proverbes Dramatiques.*

THE COURTSHIP OF MILES STANDISH (1858). Poem in nine titled parts.

I. "Miles Standish." Behold Captain Miles Standish, a soldier seasoned in European battles, striding in front of his armor and weapons in Plymouth during the time of the Pilgrims. *See also* John Alden, his fair-haired, blue-eyed, young "household companion," at a pine table scribbling a letter. John Alden praises Miles Standish but keeps writing when the older man boasts that his equipment is shining because he has burnished it himself, adding, "Serve yourself, would you be well served." He likens himself to Caesar, his favorite author, for knowing the names of the twelve men he commands here in New England. He is proud of his howitzer, planted on the church roof; it will preach convincingly at any Indians daring to attack. He mentions Rose, his wife, "the first to die of all who came in the May Flower!" While Standish picks up Caesar's *Commentaries,* shelved near his Bible, to peruse it, Alden writes letters to be sent to England in a day or two by the returning May Flower—letters "Full of the name and the fame of the Puritan maiden Priscilla!"

II. "Love and Friendship." Standish praises Caesar for being able both to write and to fight. He adds that Caesar, while in Flanders, grabbed a shield, commanded his troops, ordered them forward, and won the day. Surely, he avers, "if you wish a thing to be well done, / You must do it yourself, you must not leave it to others!" Later, he adds, Caesar was stabbed by Brutus, "his friend, the orator." Once Alden has finished writing his letters, many of which are filled with the name Priscilla, Standish asks a favor. Ready to oblige, Alden gives Standish his "respectful attention." Standish's burden is this: Rose died; he is "weary and dreary"; a man should not be alone; he often thinks of "the angel . . . Priscilla." Complaining that he is "a man not of words but of actions," Standish asks scholarly Alden, adept "in elegant language," to propose to Priscilla for him in the "elegant" way a lover in a literary work would

pleadingly woo. Alden, "aghast" and "bewildered," reminds Standish what he just said about doing something oneself to get it right. Standish, unshaken, replies: "Truly the maxim is good, and I do not mean to gainsay it; / But we must use it discreetly, and not waste powder for nothing." He says he is not afraid of bullets or cannon shot, but he freely confesses he fears "a thundering 'No!' point-blank from the mouth of a woman." Standish strongly shakes Alden's gentle hand and requests his comradely help; Alden, agreeing, finds that "Friendship prevailed over love."

III. "The Lover's Errand." On his way through the woods to Priscilla, Alden wonders if he followed her over the ocean "to the desolate shores of New England" only to "relinquish it all" now. These emotions of love must have proceeded from a corrupt heart and be "delusions of Satan." God must be angry at his desire, and his cross must be in retribution for such sinfulness. He gathers flowers for Priscilla, who will see them as his parting gift and soon discard them, along with his heart. Alden reaches her "new-built house," hears her singing Psalm 100 as set to music by Martin Luther, and finds her carding wool, working the treadle, and feeding the spindle. Emotions whirl around him; his dreams and hopes disappear; his gloomy future is, after all, the decree of a merciful God. Priscilla welcomes him, says she was thinking about him, and accepts his bouquet. Speechless, he remembers once coming out of a snowstorm to her welcome fireplace and wishes "he [had] but spoken then! perhaps not in vain." They talk about the birds, the oncoming spring, and the May Flower's departure "on the morrow." Priscilla confides in Alden: She is so lonely that she would like to be "back in Old England." Taking this cue, Alden says that she needs a strong shoulder to lean on and blurts out that Standish, "a good man and true," wants to marry her. Abashed, Priscilla asks why, if Plymouth's good captain is so anxious, he didn't propose personally: "If I am not worth the wooing, I surely am not worth the winning!" Alden makes matters no better by saying Standish has been pretty busy. Priscilla replies that if he lacked time to propose "before he is married, / Would be he be likely to find it [leisure?] . . . after the wedding?" Men are all alike: too abrupt with a "sudden avowal," then indignant when "a woman / Does not respond at once to a love that she never suspected." Can a woman jump to a height a man takes his time climbing to? Such behavior is neither "right nor just." You can't take "a woman'a affection" by simply asking. "When one is truly in love, one not only says it, but shows it." Even though Priscilla gripes that the burly old captain went about it all wrong, Alden sings the fellow's praises, calling him a brave, skillful, noble descendent of Lancashire gentlemen, the heir of lands wrongly taken from him, and one not to be chided "because he was little of stature." At which

> Archly the maiden smiled, and, with eyes
>   overrunning with laughter,
> Said, in a tremulous voice, "Why don't you
>   speak for yourself, John?"

IV. "John Alden." Alden rushes away, lets the "wind of the East!" cool his fever, senses that love and friendship, desire and duty, are contending within him, regards the "moaning" ocean as the voice of "an awakened conscience," and fears that he has "displeased the Lord!" by allowing Satan to tempt him. Seeing the May Flower at anchor, he thinks it would be better if he were dead and buried back in England beside his mother, with the secret of his love concealed like a jewel on his hand. Alden returns to Standish and tells the impatient fellow everything, including Priscilla's asking Alden to speak for himself. Standish, exploding like "a hand-grenade," reminds Alden of his generosity in housing and feeding his socalled friend and feels tempted to run him through with his sword. A messenger reports evidence of a possible Indian revolt; straightway Standish, "frowning fiercely," grabs his sword and hastens to the assembled council. One "Elder of Plymouth" advises peace. But when Standish sees a "stern and defiant" Indian, stripped to his waist, offer a rattlesnake full of arrows as a threat of war, the captain shakes out the arrows, fills the skin "with powder and bullets," and gives it to the "glistening" Indian, who, thus challenged, departs. In Standish's opinion,

"Truly the only tongue that is understood by a savage / Must be the tongue of fire that speaks from the mouth of the cannon!"

V. "The Sailing of the May Flower." Alden, awake all night, hears Standish return, pray, swear, and mutter in turns, and then lie down, dressed. Alden is tempted to apologize but is ashamed, and so pretends he is sleeping. Standish rises at dawn, gets his weapons together, and marches his soldiers north. Alden joins his neighbors in morning prayers and goes down to the May Flower. Her sturdy master takes written and oral messages to deliver back in England, and wonders if Alden will be coming aboard. Alden, following a "mysterious instinct . . . ," suddenly says, "Here I remain!" and feels that "There is no land so sacred, no air so pure and so wholesome, / As is the air she breathes, and the soil that is pressed by her footsteps." He plans to protect her as "an invisible presence." Since he was first to step on Plymouth Rock, so he will leave last. Those on the shore watch as the May Flower, "Borne on the send of the sea, and the swelling hearts of the Pilgrims," disappears, her sail resembling "a marble slab in a graveyard." Not one New England pilgrim shipped home.

VI. "Priscilla." While Alden is musing about Priscilla, she appears. First, she wonders why he didn't speak to her just now, then apologizes for her forwardness yesterday, saying she spoke as she did because of their friendship. He replies that he was angry with himself for managing his errand badly; this she denies, saying women are supposed "to be patient and silent," with the result that "the inner life of so many suffering women" resembles "subterranean rivers," dark and quiet, "Chafing their channels of stone." When he, instead, compares women to "the beautiful rivers that watered the garden of Eden," she really complains. She says that such "common and complimentary" talk women regard "as insipid, if not . . . insulting." She misunderstands poor Alden, mute but all the more aware of her beauty; so she is bothered by his praise of Standish, offers to shake Alden's hand, and says they "must ever be friends." As Priscilla and Alden walk along, he at her request describes Standish's "direful wrath" last night on being told of Priscilla's rejection. When Alden adds that he decided, "for her sake," not to sail on the May Flower to England, her manner changes and in "a faltering accent" thanks him and calls him good. "Thus" Alden resembles a pilgrim slowly approaching "the Holy Land of his longings."

VII. "The March of Miles Standish." As he advances on the enemy, Standish turns from anger at a woman's rejection and a friend's betrayal to awareness that a tough warrior could hardly hope to woo one like Priscilla. He vows to love danger instead. After three days his squad finds an Indian camp. Pecksuot and Wattawamat, two huge warriors in "horrid . . . war-paint," approach with a gift of furs. "Friendship was in their looks, but in their hearts there was hatred." Hobomok, Standish's loyal Indian interpreter, explains that they want muskets and powder, which "the white man . . . concealed, with the plague, in his cellars" and with which he would "destroy his brother the red man." Standish offers Bibles instead. Wattawamat boasts of his magic birth, flourishes his knife, and threatens war; and Pecksuot says his knife "shall eat" soon and calls Standish "a little man" who ought to go find employment with women. Already spotting a circle of would-be ambushers, Standish answers this insult by grabbing Pecksuot's knife and stabbing him with it. Pecksuot falls dead, with an expression of "fiendish fierceness." Arrows fly, and muskets respond. Wattawamat is shot "through his brain" and falls, clutching the earth as though "to hold back from his foe the land of his fathers." Hobomok praises Standish. Plymouth hears of this first victory against the Indians, proof of which is Wattawamat's head mounted on the fort roof. All the townspeople rejoice, except for Priscilla, who wonders if Standish might come home and "claim" her as a "reward of his valor."

VIII. "The Spinning-Wheel." Months pass, and autumn brings ships with supplies. Standish gains renown for "defeating the alien armies," all the while alternately feeling angry, contrite, and bitter. Alden builds a sturdy house, cares for Raghorn, a white bull assigned him, and visits Priscilla with "Plea-sure disguised as duty, and love in the semblance of friendship." Alone, he has her ever in his thoughts, especially when he reads in his Bible about how a husband places his trust in his wife, and "How all the days of her life she will do him good, and not evil." One day while he watches her at her wheel, he calls her "Bertha the Beautiful Spinner." Pleased, she stands gracefully before him and asks him to hold "a snowy skein of her spinning" while she winds it to be knitted. She is expert; he, awkward. When she touches his hands to straighten the yarn, he feels numerous "electrical thrills." Suddenly a messenger brings tidings that Standish has been killed by a poisoned arrow during an Indian ambush. Priscilla is horrified. But Alden reacts as though that arrow had hit his heart "and had sundered / Once and forever the bonds that held him bound as a captive." Feeling "pain and regret," to be sure, he "unconscious[ly]" embraces Priscilla and says, "Those whom the Lord hath united, let no man put them asunder!"

IX. "The Wedding-Day." Over the scene, the sun rises majestically, like a priest in "garments resplendent," and with "golden bells and pomegranates" at his robe hem. At the ceremony, "The Elder and Magistrate" combine "the sanction of earth and . . . the blessing of heaven." Alden and Priscilla say their vows, when suddenly Standish appears, like "a ghost from the grave." A survivor of the ambush, he waited until the ritual was concluded, and now advances to shake Alden's hand in friendship, and to bow before Priscilla "after the manner of old-fashioned gentry in England." Praising both and wishing them well, Standish repeats this adage: "No man can gather cherries in Kent at the season of Christmas!" Though aware that "Lay extended before them the land of toil and privation," the couple start for Alden's house. The bridegroom places his wife on "his snow-white bull" and leads the wedding procession beyond the forest ford. They scent the odor of grapes and "the balm of the pine and the fir-tree," reminiscent of "the valley of Eschol," and illustrate yet again "Love immortal and young in the endless succession of lovers."

The Courtship of Miles Standish was originally titled "Priscilla." Priscilla is the central figure and dominates the action; Miles Standish (1584?–1656) does not. Longfellow's source was old New England history. His allusions are often appropriately Biblical, sometimes thrillingly so. His treatment of Native Americans is close to deplorable, however, by modern politically correct standards. Longfellow is descended from Elizabeth Alden, the daughter of John Alden (1599–1687) and Priscilla Mullens (also spelled Molines and Moleyns). To put it briefly, Elizabeth Alden Peabody's daughter Ruth Peabody Bartlett's daughter Priscilla Bartlett Sampson's daughter Susanna Sampson Wadsworth's son Peleg Wadsworth (1748–1829) was Longfellow's maternal grandfather. At first, in 1856, *The Courtship of Miles Standish* was to be a play. Then Longfellow began to write it as what he called "'Priscilla,' . . . a kind of pastoral poem." Retitled and finished (Mar 1858), this American poetic treasure was published in October, and became a bestseller—5,000 copies by the first noon, and 25,000 by Christmas.

Bibliography: Adams, Jr., Charles Francis. *The Episodes in Massachusetts History.* Boston: Houghton Mifflin, 1892; Arvin; Buchwald, Art. *Yes, Virginia . . . There Is a Miles Standish.* Philadelphia: Bulletin Co., 1981; Elliott, Charles Wyllys. *The New England History from the Discovery of the Continent . . . to the Period When the Colonies Declared Their Independence. . . .* New York: Scribner, 1857; Ferguson, Robert A. "Longfellow's Literary Fears: Civic Authority and the Role of the Artist in *Hiawatha* and *Miles Standish.*" *American Literature* 50 (May 1978): 187–215; Hirsh; S. Longfellow; Lowell, James Russell. *The Function of the Poet and Other Essays.* Boston: Houghton Mifflin, 1920; Tucker, Edward L. "Longfellow's *The Courtship of Miles Standish:* Some Notes and Two Early Versions." *Studies in the American Renaissance.* Ed. Joel Myerson, 285–321; Wagenknecht, 1986; Williams; Young, Alexander. *Chronicles of the Pilgrim Fathers.* 1841.

THE COURTSHIP OF MILES STANDISH AND OTHER POEMS (1858).

Collection of poems: *The Courtship of Miles Standish. Birds of Passage:* "Prometheus, or the Poet's Forethought," "The Ladder of Saint Augustine," "The Phantom Ship," "The Warden of the Cinque Ports," "Haunted Houses," "In the Churchyard at Cambridge," "The Emperor's Bird's-Nest," The Two Angels," "Daylight and Moonlight," "The Jewish Cemetery at Newport," "Oliver Basselin," "Victor Galbraith," "My Lost Youth," "The Ropewalk," "The Golden Milestone," "Catawba Wine," "Santa Filomena," "The Discovery of the North Cape," "Daybreak," "The Fiftieth Birthday of Agassiz: May 28, 1857," "Children," "Sandalphon," "Epimetheus, or the Poet's Afterthought."

CRAIGIE, ELIZABETH NANCY SHAW (1772–1841).

Longfellow's landlady in Cambridge, Massachusetts (1837–1843). She was from Nantucket, was well educated, read French easily, and was an eccentric freethinker. She evidently had a lover who deserted her and moved to the South, after which she married Andrew Craigie (1743–1819). During the American Revolution, Boston-born Craigie was the apothecary of the army of Massachusetts and probably the first apothecary of the Continental Army (beginning Jul 1775). He was commissioned apothecary general (1779) and was mustered out as lieutenant colonel (1883). He made a fortune speculating in government certificates, in the wholesale apothecary trade, and in land around Cambridge, and was a director of the first United States Bank. He purchased the Vassall House (1 Jan 1793) in Cambridge (*see* Craigie House), and he and Elizabeth enjoyed an opulent life thereabouts until their estrangement. He built the bridge over the Charles River, which is the subject of Longfellow's poem "The Bridge." Craigie over-extended his holdings, once had to hide in his house to avoid arrest, and died in debt. To survive, Mrs. Craigie was obliged to rent rooms in the big mansion, mostly to Harvard College students and instructors. In 1837 she began renting to Longfellow. He enjoyed their friendship, was puzzled by her admiration of the works of Voltaire and by her pantheistic beliefs, and regretted that she quirkily refused to see physicians and died untreated of breast cancer. Years later, Osmond Tiffany Jr. (1823–95), a former Harvard student turned author, sent Longfellow a copy of his novel *Brandon; or, A Hundred Years Ago: A Tale of the American Colonies* (1858). In an accompanying letter (21 Sep 1858), he explained that the character in it named Lucy was based on Mrs. Craigie, who, he added, was a relative of his. Longfellow replied (23 Sep 1858), acknowledged receipt of *Brandon,* and said, "I have often thought the life of Mrs. Craigie furnished matter enough for a romance."

Bibliography: Hilen, ed.

CRAIGIE HOUSE. Longfellow's residence in Cambridge, Massachusetts (1837–82). The original house was built about 1759 by Major (or Colonel) John Vassal(l), a British Tory. It had a yellow facade, with four white philasters topped by Ionic capitals. General George Washington used it as his headquarters (Jul 1775–Apr 1776), while planning the defense of Boston. A wealthy Newburyport man named Tracy bought the place. Then a Boston merchant named Russell owned it. Andrew Craigie (1743–1819) purchased the mansion and 150 surrounding acres (1 Jan 1793). He may have added the western wing to the mansion, with kitchen and pertinent parts, and certainly added an ell behind the house and a piazza with white columns on each side. A hollow-log aqueduct brought water from a spring to the house. The grounds to the rear had stables, gardens, and a gardener's house. Behind a grove of trees was a small lake, near which was an icehouse. Legend has it that the Craigies entertained Boston merchant princes and foreign diplomats in their home. But Craigie died in debt, after which his widow, Elizabeth Nancy Shaw Craigie* lived in the rear and rented front rooms upstairs. Three of her early lodgers were Edward Everett,* Josiah Quincy,* and Jared Sparks,* each of whom later served as president of Harvard.

In the summer of 1837 Longfellow, recently appointed professor of languages at Harvard, visited a Harvard law student rooming at Mrs. Craigie's house, immediately desired to room there himself, and introduced himself to Mrs. Craigie. She mistook him for yet another student and declined his request; but when he explained that he was a professor at Harvard and had written *Outre-*

Mer, which she had been reading, she agreed to let him have the graduating student's room and an adjoining one, front eastern corner, beginning in August. Longfellow used one room for a bedroom, the other for a library. From the start, he loved the place. He wrote in a letter (21 Sep 1837) to his sister Anne Longfellow,* "In my new abode I dwell like an Italian Prince in his villa." Well he might. He would ring a bell shortly before 8:00 A.M., and the servant wife of Mrs. Craigie's farmer would bring a tray loaded with his private breakfast. Then off to the college. Likewise at 5:00 P.M., for dinner. So the semesters passed. In March 1840 Longfellow also rented an adjacent third room and a kitchen, and hired a servant to prepare his meals and tidy his rooms. When Mrs. Craigie died, a man named Worcester handled the house for a short while. On 13 July 1843, Longfellow married Fanny Appleton;* her father, Nathan Appleton,* bought Craigie House (14 Oct 1843) and transferred title to Fanny (8 Nov 1843). The Longfellows were beatifically happy in Castle Craigie, as they often called it. In a letter (25 Jul 1843) to Anne Pierce, Fanny called it "my Eden." She wrote her brother Thomas Gold Appleton* (30 Aug 1843), "we have decided to let father purchase this grand old mansion if he will." Why not? To her father she wrote (Sep 1843), "We have duly considered and discussed the question of remaining here, and think, all things considered, we could not do better elsewhere. . . . If you decide to purchase this would it not be important to secure the land in front, for the view would be ruined by a block of houses." The Longfellow children were born in Craigie House. The Longfellows entertained lavishly there. Fanny tragically burned to death there. Longfellow slowly recovered there, remained there, and died there.

Craigie House, now known as the Longfellow House, became a national historic landmark (1962) and a national historic site (1972). Visitors may see, wonder at, and study an array of eighteenth- and nineteenth-century American and European decorative arts; works by nineteenth-century painters, including Albert Bierstadt and Gilbert Stuart; Longfellow's library and Longfellow family papers; and some 700,000 items in manuscript and archival collections. Scholars and other visitors are graciously welcomed in ways of which Longfellow himself would have been quietly proud.

Bibliography: Dana, Henry Wadsworth Longfellow. *The Craigie House: The Coming of Longfellow (1837-1841).* [Cambridge]: Cambridge Historical Society, 1939; Green, Samuel S. "The Craigie House, Cambridge, During Its Occupancy by Andrew Craigie and His Widow." *Proceedings of the American Antiquarian Society,* n.s., 13 (1900): 312-52; Hilen, ed.; *Mrs. Longfellow;* S. Longfellow; Wagenknecht, 1955.

CRAWFORD, THOMAS (1813?–57). Sculptor, born in New York City to Irish immigrant parents. From early childhood, Crawford wanted to be a sculptor; so he apprenticed himself to experienced wood and stone carvers and in 1835 went to Rome. He worked in the studios of Bertel Thorvaldsen (1768-1844), the Danish neoclassical sculptor, sketched nudes at the French Academy, studied classical sculpture in the Vatican, copied statues for American patrons, and began modeling portrait busts (1837). George Washington Greene,* then American consul to Rome, met Crawford soon after his arrival and took Charles Sumner,* then in Rome (1839), to meet Crawford, whose *Orpheus* Sumner persuaded wealthy Bostonians to buy. Crawford made a plaster bust of Greene (1840, Longfellow House). Charles Callahan Perkins,* another wealthy American traveler, also met Crawford and commissioned his *Hebe and Ganymede* (1842) and later his bronze *Beethoven.* Meanwhile, "Sir Orfeo" (as Crawford called it) arrived in Boston (1844) and was exhibited to great effect, together with other Crawford pieces, including a bust of Sumner. During a European vacation, Samuel Gridley Howe,* his wife Julia Ward Howe,* and her sister Louisa Ward (1823-97) visited Crawford's Roman studio (winter 1843-44). Crawford married Louisa in New York (1844); they were to have four children, including Francis Marion Crawford (1854-1909), the immensely popular novelist. During his stay in the United States, Thomas Crawford collected orders in several cities for more work, including a com-

mission for a bust of Josiah Quincy* (1846), president of Harvard. Back in Rome (1845-49), Crawford resumed his whirlwind career, creating busts, biblical and mythological statues, and genre pieces. While visiting in the United States (1849), Crawford entered the competition for a monument to honor George Washington in Richmond, Virginia, won the award, and was given a lucrative commission (1850) for group figures to be executed in Rome (1854). More work followed, including *Beethoven* (1854, Boston Music Hall), the marble *Progress of Civilization* (1854-56; marble pediment, east wing, U.S. Senate Building), and the bronze *Freedom* (1856, U.S. Capitol dome). Crawford's career ended when he experienced eye trouble (1856), consulted specialists in Rome, Paris, and London, and died in London of eye and brain cancer. When Crawford was buried in Brooklyn, New York, honorary pallbearers included Sumner, Greene, and George William Curtis.*

Sumner wrote letters from Rome (1839) to William Hickling Prescott,* George Stillman Hillard,* and Longfellow describing Crawford, his talent, and his need for "patronage." To Longfellow (26 Jul 1839), he specifically asked, if he could not order a statue from the meritorious sculptor, at least to write an article about him. Longfellow did what he could. Sumner also asked British friends to commission works by Crawford. In a letter (10 Jun 1841) to Greene, whose bust by Crawford he had seen, Longfellow called the young sculptor "a true man of Genius" and the bust of Greene "exquisite." With this letter, Longfellow sent Greene copies of his *Voices of the Night,* asking that one copy be forwarded to Crawford. Longfellow called *Orpheus* "a beautiful work of art; with more life in it than any modern statue I remember." In subsequent letters to Sumner, Crawford expresses gratitude to Longfellow and Cornelius Conway Felton,* among others. While Crawford was in Boston (1849), Longfellow invited him by letter (24 Sep 1849) to dinner, so that Longfellow could "behold your face once more," and asked him to bring "Louisa." Longfellow notes in his journal (26 Sep 1849) that "Crawford dined with us. Full of spirit and independence." Sumner sent Crawford a letter of congratulation (9 Feb 1850) when he heard of Crawford's Richmond commission: "This engagement will advertise you to the whole country." Longfellow was present at the inauguration of Crawford's *Beethoven* (Boston Music Hall, 1 Mar 1856). When news of the sculptor's death reached Longfellow, he recorded this in his journal (4 Nov 1857): "Crawford is dead!," compared the sculptor's career to Excelsior's, and noted that Crawford's gift of "a little sketch in clay, of a huntress . . . was thrown down and broken . . . just when he was dying so far away, in London." Decades later, Longfellow wrote Greene (21 Feb 1881) that Samuel Ward* had the day before introduced "Frank Crawford [his nephew], a fine, stalwart youth whom I liked much," to Longfellow in Cambridge.

Bibliography: Gale, Robert L. *Thomas Crawford: American Sculptor.* Pittsburgh: University of Pittsburgh Press, 1964; Hilen, ed.; S. Longfellow; Pierce, Edward L. *Memoir and Letters of Charles Sumner.* 4 vols. Boston: Roberts Brothers, 1877-93.

"THE CROSS OF SNOW" (1886). Sonnet, in Scudder. Through sleepless nights, Longfellow sees the "gentle face" of a "benedight" woman, who long ago "was led" through fire to her death. In the ravines of a western mountain is a "cross of snow," which, "sun-defying," never melts. He says that "Such is the cross I wear upon my breast," ever since she died eighteen years ago. Thus Longfellow mourns the death of Fanny Longfellow,* who burned to death in 1861, in this superb sonnet, dated 10 July 1879, but first published in the 1886 biography of Longfellow by his brother, Samuel Longfellow.*

Bibliography: Cox, J. M. "Longfellow and His Cross of Snow." *PMLA* 75 (Mar 1980): 97-100; S. Longfellow; More; Petry, Alice Hall. "Longfellow's 'The Cross of Snow' and Milton." *Essays in Literature* 11 (fall 1984): 299-304.

CROWNINSHIELD, CLARA (1811–1907). Longfellow's friend. Clara was born Clarissa Crowninshield in Salem, Massachusetts, the natural daughter of George Crowninshield Jr. and his mistress, Elizabeth Rowell. Her father was the son of a prosperous Salem merchant, whose brother, Benjamin W. Crownshield, was a congressman and Secretary of the Navy (1814-18) during the administrations of presidents James Madison and James Monroe. Clara's father loved the sea, launched an 80-foot barkentine, and christened it *Cleopatra's Barge* (1816)—the first vessel ever built in America solely as a pleasure yacht. He died aboard it (1817). In his will, he named Clarissa as his daughter and bequeathed her $16,000 and her mother $8,000. A Salem attorney named Benjamin Ropes Nichols informally adopted Clara and later sent her to a female seminary in Hingham, Massachusetts. There she studied Latin, a little French, polite literature, and good manners, and made friends with Elizabeth Ann Potter (1810-?) and her sister Mary Storer Potter (1812-35), who later became Longfellow's first wife. In 1827 Nichols placed Clara as a boarder in the home of his sister and her husband, Benjamin Peirce, librarian at Harvard. Though welcomed by both Peirces and their three children, Clara felt inferior, took up drawing and sewing, studied German, and especially enjoyed visiting the Potter sisters in Portland. Through careful financial advisers, Clara's inheritance provided a decent living for her.

Mary Potter and Longfellow were married (1831) by the Rev. Ichabod Nichols, Clara's legal guardian's brother. Clara paid long visits to the Longfellows in Brunswick, Maine (1831, 1832). When Longfellow first pondered returning to Europe to polish his already phenomenal linguistic skills, in preparation for teaching at Harvard, Clara did much to persuade Mary Longfellow to overcome her lassitude and urge her husband forward. So did Mary Caroline Goddard, a relative of Mary Longfellow who was to go along. Mary Goddard's deceased mother had been the sister of Mary Longfellow's father Barrett Potter's wife. Eventually, Longfellow, his wife, Clara, and Mary Goddard went abroad together. Clara had ample means to pay her way. Mary Goddard's family agreed to contribute money but reneged. Clara shared the joys, disappointments, and sorrows of the eighteen-month trip (10 Apr 1835–Oct 1836), and recorded in her diary events in London, Germany, Denmark, Sweden, the Netherlands, and France. In September 1836 Mary Goddard learned of her father's death and returned home at once. Clara was at Mary Longfellow's side when she died (28 Nov 1835) in Rotterdam and was, in Longfellow's words, a sister to him during his agony. He wrote in his journal (4 Dec 1835), "Clara is with me still—and in her society I find a soothing influence." The two continued traveling. Just before reaching Nijmegen, Holland, by boat, Clara wrote this in her diary (2 Dec 1835): "I talked to him [Longfellow] about my experiences and showed him that I had had my share of sorrows as well as he." They proceeded to Heidelberg (11 Dec 1835), where they soon found William Cullen Bryant,* his wife, and their daughters, under whose kind supervision Longfellow left Clara installed in a room in a boarding house run for students by a widow, and he continued his studies in other German locales. Declining his belief expressed in January that she would return to America with the Bryants, Clara noted in her diary (19 Jan 1836), "I thought [the idea] rather unkind and unnatural." Clara enjoyed a brief trip to Frankfurt with Longfellow (Apr), chaperoned by Mrs. Bryant and others. Longfellow escorted Clara and the Bryants along the Rhine (Jun), to the baths at Ems, elsewhere, and back to Heidelberg. Longfellow felt unable (25 Jun) to take Clara unchaperoned via Munich and Milan to Switzerland, and accordingly left her alone and disappointed. She summered in Heidelberg, proceeded to Paris, and was escorted by Longfellow from Paris to La Havre, where they started (12 Oct 1836) their voyage home.

Clara returned to Salem. Longfellow soon began to teach at Harvard. While Clara was in Europe, at least three young men found her attractive, but no permanent relationships developed. The intensity of Longfellow's friendship with Clara will remain a mystery. A letter Clara wrote him in German (11 Mar 1837) sheds little light; translated it goes in part thus: "You lack constancy. . . . This indifference of yours will not cause me any *eternal* sorrow. But whenever I see you or write to you I must think of it and feel it too. Otherwise I have had no complaints. That I am right about this you will have to admit." A few activities of Longfellow and Clara in Europe, and vistas they observed, found their way into his *Hyperion.*

In the early 1840s, Clara met Louis Thies (?–1871), a pleasant German immigrant art scholar. The two married (1843), lived in Germany a while, and returned to the United States (1849) to exhibit their art collection widely; Thies also lectured at Harvard, helped develop its Gray Collection of Engravings, and became its curator. Thies, Clara, their son, and their daughter returned to Germany (1866). He made a professional trip to Cambridge (1868–69), then returned to Germany, where their son died (1870) and then Thies died (1871). Clara's daughter married a distinguished European of German-Swedish extraction (1872). Longfellow wrote a letter (5 Mar 1881) to Sarah Holland Adams (1824–1916), who was the sister-in-law of James T. Fields* and was vacationing in Germany. In the letter, Longfellow wondered if she had met "an old friend of mine, Clara Thies, living in Dresden, Sidonien-strasse 11." The two ladies became acquainted, with immense pleasure. Clara died in Dresden (1907).

Bibliography: Crowninshield; Ferguson, David L. *Cleopatra's Barge: The Crowninshield Story.* Boston: Little, Brown, 1976; Hilen, ed.; Wagenknecht, 1955.

"THE CUMBERLAND" (1862). Poem, *AM,* Dec 1862; *Tales of the Wayside Inn,* 1863; *Birds* (1863). Longfellow commemorates the bravery of the sailors manning the wooden Federal sloop the *Cumberland,* which was sunk by the Confederate ironside the *Merrimac* in Hampton Roads, off Newport News (28 Mar 1862). The poet praises alike the "brave hearts" that drowned rather than surrender and the "brave land" that produced them. America's "rent" flag "Shall be one again, / And without a seam!" Each of the eight six-line stanzas, with shortened fourth, fifth, and sixth lines, displays martial verve.

Bibliography: Arvin; Selfridge, Jr., Thomas O. *The Story of the Cumberland.* Boston: Historical Society of Massachusetts, 1902.

"CURFEW" (1845). Poem, in *Poems,* 1845; Scudder. When the curfew bell tolls, it is time to bank the fire, put out the light, and rest. All is silent. When a book is finished, it is closed and laid away; "its fancies . . . / . . . darken and die." Songs cease. The fireplace turns cold. The windows turn dark. "Sleep and oblivion / Reign over all."

CURTIS, GEORGE WILLIAM (1824–92). Essayist, editor, and lecturer. He was born in Providence, Rhode Island. When widowed, his father sent him to school in Jamaica Plains, Massachusetts, remarried (1835), reassembled his family, and moved to New York City (1839). Curtis clerked for a merchant (to 1842) and then for two years participated in the Brook Farm experiment established outside Boston by New England Transcendentalists and also worked on a farm near Concord, Massachusetts. Hired by Horace Greeley, editor of the New York *Tribune,* Curtis became a widely traveling correspondent (1846-50; Europe, the Middle East, the Holy Land). Home again, he wrote for and helped edit *Putnam's Magazine* (1853-57) and various Harper Brothers periodicals (1853-88). During some of these years, Curtis was also a traveling lecturer. When *Putnam's* went bankrupt (1857), Curtis wrote, lectured, and personally repaid all debts (by 1873). As editor of *Harper's Weekly* (beginning in 1863), Curtis encouraged many authors, new and established, including Nathaniel Hawthorne,* James Russell Lowell,* Herman Melville, and Longfellow. In addition to several popular travel books, including *Nile Notes of a Howadji* (1851) and *The Howadji in Syria* (1852), and collections of essays, including *Prue and I* (1856, dedicated to Fanny Longfellow*) and *Literary and Social Essays* (1894), Curtis published studies of Charles Sumner* (1874), William Cullen Bryant* (1878), Robert Burns (1880), and Lowell (1892). Charles Eliot Norton* edited Curtis's

Orations and Addresses (1893-94). Curtis, an admirable lecturer and publicist, was an abolitionist, a Republic Party worker, a supporter of the presidential candidacies of John C. Frémont (1856) and Abraham Lincoln (from 1860), and an advocate of woman's suffrage, organized labor, and civil-service reform. "Political Infidelity" (1865), his most popular and fiery lecture, he repeated by popular demand upwards of fifty times. In it, he espoused more freedom of speech, an extension of which, he reasoned, might have prevented the Civil War (in which a brother of his was killed in action). In 1856, Curtis married Anna Shaw (the sister of Colonel Robert Shaw [1837-63], of imperishable Civil War fame); they had three children.

According to Longfellow's journal entries (22, 27 Mar; 13 Aug 1851), Norton, just back from India, brought Curtis, recently home from Egypt, to the Longfellows' residence for dinner; in gratitude, Curtis sent his host a copy of his *Nile Notes,* the style of which Longfellow praised as poetic prose. Curtis later lent Longfellow his translation of Persian poets. Soon, Longfellow and his wife Fanny began calling Curtis "Howadji" (Arabic for traveler). Curtis contributed essays on George Bancroft,* Ralph Waldo Emerson,* Hawthorne, and Longfellow to *Homes of American Authors* (1853). Longfellow heard Curtis give his "Political Infidelity" lecture at Cambridgeport (26 Jan 1860) and defined it as "stirring" in a letter to Charles Sumner (31 Jan 1860). Longfellow declined Curtis's challenge to write a national song, commenting thus in his journal (21 May 1861): "I am afraid the 'Go to, let us make a national song' will not succeed. It will be likely to spring up in some other way." When Curtis wrote in sympathy after Fanny's death, Longfellow thanked him and said he could hardly reply: "I am too utterly wretched and overwhelmed,—to the eyes of others, outwardly, calm; but inwardly bleeding to death" (28 Sep 1861). Longfellow rarely wrote anyone about his wife's death and his consequent suffering. In later years, Curtis remained friendly with Longfellow. On Longfellow's seventieth birthday, Curtis lauded him extravagantly: "I believe there is no man living for whom there is so universal a feeling of love and gratitude, and no man who ever wore so great a fame so gently and simply." Of Curtis's book on Bryant, Longfellow wrote Curtis (15 Jan 1879) that "It is not a painting of the man, but his statue, which may be seen from all sides, and represents him as he was and will be in the minds of his countrymen." In a letter to Curtis (1 Feb 1881), Longfellow calls his essay on Burns a "beautiful discourse," adding "I always find a charm in what you write." Soon after Longfellow's death, Curtis published a tender eulogy titled "Longfellow," *Harper's New Monthly Magazine,* June 1882.

Bibliography: Hilen, ed.; S. Longfellow; *Mrs. Longfellow;* Milne, Gordon. *George William Cur-tis & The Genteel Tradition.* Bloomington: Indiana University Press, 1956.

CURTIS, GREELY STEVENSON (1830–97). The husband of Harriot Appleton Curtis, the half-sister of Fanny Longfellow.* Curtis was a lieutenant colonel with the First Massachusetts Cavalry during most of the Civil War (Oct 1861–Mar 1864). He and Harriot were married (1863). He traveled with Longfellow's son Charles Appleton Longfellow to Mexico (1875).

Bibliography: Hilen, ed.

CURTIS, HARRIOT ("HATTIE") APPLETON (1841–1923). The half-sister of Fanny Longfellow.* Longfellow was on friendly terms with both Curtises.

D

DANA, EDITH LONGFELLOW (1853–1915). Longfellow's third daughter. He calls her "Edith with golden hair" in his poem "The Children's Hour." She and her sisters accompanied their father on his final tour of Europe (1868–69). When her mother, Fanny Longfellow, died (1861), Edith inherited sufficient funds, available at age twenty-one, to be independent for life. Longfellow cared for the inheritance and at the proper time transferred the sums, $136,533.45 in all, to Edith (22 Oct 1874). In 1878, Edith married Richard Henry Dana II,* the son of Richard Henry Dana Jr.* Longfellow was aware that her marriage was a joy for Edith but inevitably represented a permanent diminution of his own domestic felicity.

Bibliography: Hilen, ed.

DANA, JR., RICHARD HENRY (1815–82). He was the Cambridge-born son of poet Richard Henry Dana Sr.* Young Dana entered Harvard (1831), discontinued studies there and shipped as an ordinary seaman around Cape Horn to California (1834), returned to Harvard (1836), graduated (1837), studied law at Harvard (1837–1840), was admitted to the Massachusetts bar (1840) and began a successful practice in Boston. Using his experiences at sea and as a laborer in California as a basis, he wrote *Two Years Before the Mast.* His father and William Cullen Bryant* negotiated irresponsibly with Harper Brothers, who paid Dana only $250 (and a gift of twenty-four copies) for exclusive rights, published the book (1840), and netted perhaps as much as $50,000 on it themselves until the first copyright ran out (1869). Longfellow wrote his father (11 Oct 1840): "Have you read Dana's 'Two Years before the Mast'? It is a very interesting book, written in a simple style, which I think will please you. It reminds one of Robinson Crusoe; and has the advantage of being a record of real adventure." Fanny Appleton* and Charles Sumner* sent copies of Dana's masterpiece to friends in England (1841); Robert James Mackintosh,* Fanny's brother-in-law, lent it to a friend who recommended it to Edward Moxon (1801-58), the British publisher and sonneteer. Moxon published *Two Years Before the Mast* in London and voluntarily paid Dana more for doing so than the Harpers had contracted to pay Dana. Long interested in sailors' legal rights, Dana wrote *The Seaman's Friend* (1841), a timely, popular, and influential manual. Through his father's professional friendship with Longfellow, he met such luminaries as Arthur Hugh Clough,* Charles Dickens,* Cornelius Conway Felton,* James T. Fields,* Charles Eliot Norton,* and William Makepeace Thackeray,* among others. He helped found the Free Soil Party (1848), defended persons involved in fugitive-slave cases (1851-52, 1854), became an original member of the Saturday Club,* visited Cuba and published *To Cuba and Back* (1859, dedicated to members of the Saturday Club), was U.S. District Attorney for the District of Massachusetts (1861-66), edited *Wheaton's Elements of International Law* (1866), and represented Cambridge in the Massachusetts Legislature (1866–68). He married Sarah Watson, in Hartford, Connecticut; they had six children, including Richard Henry Dana II.* When Dana retired from law work (1878) to write a book on international law (never completed), he made over his law practice to his son; resided with his wife and two of their daughters in Paris (1878–79); vacationed in France, Switzerland, and Italy (1880–81); and lived in Rome (1881–82), where he died and is buried. Longfellow wrote Charles Sumner (25 Apr 1859) about *To Cuba and Back* that "Out of a three weeks absence he [Dana] makes a book of two hundred and fifty pages. It is not yet published, but will appear *incessantly.*" After Dana's son became engaged to Longfellow's daughter Edith, Longfellow and the young man's father became closer. They shared a common devotion to Sumner, recently deceased, and a common loathing of President Ulysses S. Grant.

DANA, II, RICHARD HENRY (1851–1931). He attended Harvard, wed Edith Longfellow (1878), and was given as a wedding present the remnants of his father's law practice. The devoted son, somewhat dominated by his father, compiled and published his father's *Speeches in Stirring Times and Letters to a Son* (1910). In a letter (14 Jan 1877) to Xavier Marmier (1809–92), French author and librarian, Longfellow writes of Dana's engagement to Edith thus: "Mr Dana is a young man of fine abilities and excellent character." Marmier had translated *The New England Tragedies* by Longfellow, as *Dramas et Poésies* (1872). Richard Henry Dana IV was the first child of Richard and Edith Dana. Some time after Edith's death (1915), Richard Henry Dana II married Helen Sherwood (Ford) Mumford (1865–1934). He published *Hospitable England in the Seventies: The Diary of a Young American 1875–1876* (1921). In 1868 Longfellow appointed Richard Henry Dana II executor of his last will and testament.

DANA, SR., RICHARD HENRY (1787–1879) Poet, born in Cambridge, Massachusetts, was sent to school in Newport, Rhode Island, was a member of the 1808 class at Harvard College, was suspended for taking part in the students' Rotten Cabbage Rebellion of 1807, refused to return to classes, but was later granted a degree. He read for the law, passed the Massachusetts bar (1811), but practiced only briefly, mostly in Sutton, Massachusetts. He cofounded the *North American Review* (1814), contributed pieces to it, and as its associate editor accepted "Thanatopsis" (1817) by William Cullen Bryant,* who was later his close friend despite being too liberal to suit Dana. In a 1819 review of William Hazlitt's *Lectures on the English Poets,* Dana alienated many of his associates by venturing to assert that Shakespeare was a better poet than Alexander Pope; Dana's comments helped Romantic idealists then emerging. He was denied editorship of the *Review* (1819). In New York Dana conducted *The Idler,* a short-lived literary magazine (1821). He returned to Boston, continued writing, began a series of classes for women on the subject of English literature, then began enjoying a substantial income by lecturing on literary topics, mostly Shakespeare, in Boston, Providence, New York, Philadelphia, and elsewhere (1838–51). During these years, he dismally failed to espouse American authors. He remained a Trinitarian during the rise of Unitarianism, was confirmed as an Episcopalian (1843), and helped found the Church of the Advent (1844). Once he turned semi-retired and reclusive, Dana continued to read assiduously. Although he published much after *The Buccaneer and Other Poems* (1827) and *Poems and Prose Writings* (1833; rev. ed., 1850), he is now known almost exclusively for "The Buccaneer." It is a long verse narrative about a vessel reappearing as a ghost ship after its passengers were massacred; its subject of retribution occasioned by a supernatural agent partly echoes "The Rime of the Ancient Mariner" by Samuel Taylor Coleridge. Dana married Ruth Charlotte Smith (1813) and with her had four children, including Richard Henry Dana Jr.; his wife died in 1822.

Longfellow knew four generations of Danas. In his review of Richard Henry Dana Sr.'s *Poems and Prose Writings* (*AM,* 1833),

Longfellow opines that "as a poetical thinker, Mr. Dana has no superior,—hardly an equal in the country," but then adds that "as a mere versifier, we could point out several who are his superiors." Longfellow met what he called the "versifier" at a supper party given by Frances Kemble* after one of her Shakespeare readings (Jan 1860) and referred to him as "the ancient poet" in his journal (5 Jan 1860). A couple of years later, seeing him again, this time with Richard Henry Dana Jr., Longfellow noted in his journal that "the old essayist . . . has somewhat outlived his fame, and . . . the present generation does not pay [him] the honor which is due him" (12 Mar 1862). The elder Dana attended a banquet (6 Nov 1867) given by James T. Fields* to honor Longfellow on the occasion of the publication of his translation of Dante's *Divina Commedia*. When Dana was a guest at a Saturday Club* dinner (1874), Longfellow jotted in his journal (28 Feb 1874) that he sat between Wilkie Collins and "the elder Dana,—the oldest of the American poets."

Longfellow socialized pleasantly with Richard Henry Dana II,* his son-in-law. Longfellow rejoiced in the birth of Richard ("Dickey") Henry Dana (1879-1933), his first grandchild (1 Sep 1879), and noted in his journal that day that the baby was "Born in the southwest chamber of the Craigie House[*]." Longfellow wrote his sister Anne Longfellow (20 Nov 1879) that every afternoon he played the piano to "The 'little Dana boy.'" Longfellow's second grandchild was Henry Wadsworth Longfellow Dana (1881-1933); Ph.D., Harvard, comparative literature [1910], pacifist author, and unofficial curator of the Craigie House [later to 1933].

Bibliography: Adams [Jr.], Charles Francis. *Richard Henry Dana: A Biography.* 2 vols. Rev. ed. Boston and New York: Houghton Mifflin, 1895; Gale, Robert L. *Richard Henry Dana.* New York: Twayne, 1969; Hilen, ed.; Hunter, Doreen M. *Richard Henry Dana, Sr.* Boston: Twayne, 1987; S. Longfellow; Lucid, Robert F., ed. *The Journal of Richard Henry Dana, Jr.* 3 vols. Cambridge: Belknap Press of Harvard University Press, 1968; Shapiro, Samuel. *Richard Henry Dana, Jr.: 1815-1882.* East Lansing: Michigan State University Press, 1961; Wagenknecht, 1955.

"DANTE'S DIVINA COMMEDIA: FROM THE GERMAN OF SCHELLING" (1850). Essay, translated by Longfellow from an essay by Friedrich Wilhelm Joseph von Schelling (1775-1854), in *GM*, Jun 1850.

Bibliography: Hilen, ed.

"DANTE: TUSCAN . . ." (1846). Sonnet, in *Bruges.* Although Dante wandered "through the realms of gloom" and "awful" thoughts rose from him, he was sympathetic, compassionate, and tender. The poet seems to see Dante at sunset near a convent. From its cloisters a voice "whispers, 'Peace!'"

"DANTE: WHAT SHOULD BE SAID . . ." **(1878).** Sonnet, translated from Michael Angelo, in *Kéramos.* His name is too splendid for anything to be said about him. It is easier to blame those who offended him. To instruct us, he "descended to the doomed and dead," then rose to God. Heaven's gates opened for him, while those of his country did not. Those who are perfect suffer the most grief. His greatness, like his exile, has no parallel.

"THE DARK AGES." See "Poetry of the Dark Ages."

"DAYBREAK" (1858). Poem, in *Courtship, Birds* (1858). At dawn, a wind from the sea tells the mists to move over, sailors to sail, the forest to hang out its leaves, birds to sing, "chanticler" to crow, corn to bow, and church bells to ring. But when the wind blows across a cemetery, it says, "'Not yet! in quiet lie.'" This poem may be religious or possibly just gruesome. In 1865 Longfellow was given a Portuguese translation of "Daybreak."

Bibliography: S. Longfellow; Wagenknecht, 1986.

"THE DAY IS DONE" (1845). Poem, as "Proem" in *The Waif: A Collection of Poems,* 1845; *Bruges.* When evening comes,

> . . . the darkness
> Falls from the wings of Night,
> As a feather is wafted downward
> From an eagle in his flight.

The poet asks his addressee to assuage his "feeling of sadness and longing" by reading to him. Not, however, from something grand or bardic—suggestive of war, work, or effort—but something humble and heartfelt, inducing quiet and rest. If such lines are read to him,

> . . . the cares, that infest the day,
> Shall fold their tents, like the Arabs,
>   And as silently steal away.

"The Day Is Done" has a somber, Puritanical tone often struck by Longfellow.

Bibliography: More; Williams.

"DAYLIGHT AND MOONLIGHT" (1858). Poem, in *Courtship, Birds* (1858). In daytime, the moon seems "faint and white, / Like a school-boy's paper kite," even ghostly. But at night, the moon is glorious and revelatory, and poetry is musical, graceful, and mysterious. The kite image, like something in a haiku, anticipates work by the later Imagists.

Bibliography: Wagenknecht, 1986.

"A DAY OF SUNSHINE" (1863). Poem, in *Tales of a Wayside Inn, Birds* (1863). A beautiful, sunny day makes one simply be, not do. On such a day, the poet "feel[s] the electric thrill, the touch / Of life, that seems almost too much." The wind is symphonic; the sun, "a golden galleon"; clouds, aiming for the "Islands of the Blest." The poet wishes the breezes would spin cherry and peach blossoms into his room. Why can't "man . . . be / Blithe as the air is, and as free?" Longfellow is unusually excited here.

Bibliography: Wagenknecht, 1986.

"THE DEAD" (1839). Poem, translated from the German poet August Cornelius Stockmann (1751–1821), in *Hyperion; Voices.* The persona's soul is "draw[n]" to "the holy ones," resting "softly." They sleep unfeelingly, and will do so "Until the angel / Calls them."

"THE DEAD BIRD" (1826). Poem, evidently never published.

Bibliography: Hilen, ed.; Little; Thompson.

"THE DEATH OF AGRICAN THE MOOR" (1832). Poem, unsigned, translated from an anonymous Spanish poem, in *NEM,* Apr 1832. Agrican, a Moslem knight, lies dying near a fountain in a forest, shattered weaponry nearby. He resembles a red-leafed oak struck down by a storm. He prays "In Christian faith to be baptized and Christian burial share." The "Peer of France," the mighty Paladin who dealt the mortal wound, hears his foe's prayer, brings cool water in his helmet, bathes the Moor's brow, and embraces "him in his mail-clad arms," thus creating "the Moslem's bier."

"DEATH OF ARCHBISHOP TURPIN" (1845). Poem, translated by Longfellow into heroic couplets from *The Chanson de Roland,* in *Poets and Poetry of Europe;* Scudder. Roland places the mortally wounded archbishop "on the verdant sod," swoons, prays for France, thinks of his beloved Aude, fights on, and then, returning to Turpin (?–c.800), also dies.

"DECORATION DAY" (1882). Poem, in *Harbor.* Soldiers killed during the Civil War once slept on the ground and leaped to action when called by shot, cannon, or drum. Their present sleep is undisturbed by sounds, fever, or aching wounds. "Yours has the suffering been, / The memory shall be ours." Longfellow wrote this poem about seven weeks before he died.

Bibliography: S. Longfellow.

"DEDICATION" (1850). Poem, preceding the selections in *S/F.* The poet fancies that he is walking in the twilight and is being encouraged by his many friendly readers. If his poems have given pleasure, the kind, sympathetic, informative responses from readers have "repaid" him "a thousand-fold." Since he imagines but won't see what these friends look like, they will remain "forever young" to him. As he ages, their voices will resemble a river gently flowing "through a leafless landscape." He hopes to "join your seaside walk" and be warmed at their lamplit fireside. Longfellow used "Dedication" as an introductory poem for *Household Poems.*

"DEDICATION" (1883). Sonnet, preceding *Michael Angelo: A Fragment.*

"DEDICATION TO G.W.G." (1880). Poem, dedicated to George Washington Greene* and preceding the poems in *Thule.* In their youth, they sailed for the Hesperides in search of "golden apples." But the ocean swept them elsewhere. Where are they now? Perhaps at "The tempest-haunted Hebrides." Hear the gulls scream, the breakers crash. See the seaweed and wrecks of ships at the shoreline. "[F]or a while," at the harbors of the Ultimate Isle, "we rest / From the unending, endless quest."

"THE DEFENCE OF POETRY" (1832). Essay-review, in *NAR,* Jan 1832. It was occasioned by the publication of an American edition of *Defence of Poesie* by Sir Philip Sidney. Longfellow complains that Americans are materialistic, utilitarian, opportunistic, and expansionistic. Education is aimed mainly at making one prosperous and worldly. The arts are tolerated as ornamental. Scholars and authors aren't highly regarded and are thought to be soft. But look at Homer, Dante, and Milton. They advanced the spirit of their respective times. Poetry is more significant than some recognize. American authors should be influenced less by books and more by their surroundings, should write more naturally, should be more graphic, should use imagery more characteristic of their nation, and should advocate morality and truth in letters. "A national literature . . . embraces every mental effort made by the inhabitants of a country, through the medium of the press. Every book written by a citizen of a country belongs to its national literature." This essay anticipates much that Longfellow's friend Ralph Waldo Emerson* expressed five years later in "The American Scholar." Two elements were against Longfellow's making this call a ringing success at once: America had too few authors he could point to as admired pioneers, and Longfellow himself was too well read in various European writers.

Bibliography: Thompson.

"DELIA" (1878). Poem, in *Kéramos, Birds* (1878). The poet compares his "darling" to perfume from "martyred flowers" and to the memory of a song not to be sung again. This tiny elegy, of six lines in couplets, was written to commemorate the death of Delia Farley (1856–73), the little daughter of a friend of Edith Longfellow.

Bibliography: Hilen, ed.; Wagenknecht, 1986.

"THE DESCENT OF THE MUSES" (1877). Sonnet, in *AM,* Mar 1877; *Kéramos.* When the nine beauteous "sisters" left their mountain home on Pierus and began living with ordinary folk, everything changed. They taught "Science and song" in country schools, so that while housewives and their farmer husbands were busy, "Their "comely daughters" were learning "sweet songs."

"DIALECT OF DALECARLIA" (1838). A chapter by Longfellow in *Dictionary of the Anglo-Saxon Language* (1838) by Joseph L. Bosworth.*

"DIALOGUE BETWEEN A NORTH AMERICAN SAVAGE AND AN ENGLISH EMIGRANT" (1823). Dialogue between two Bowdoin students. Longfellow spoke as King Philip (?–1676), Native American chief, sachem of the Wampanoags; George Bradbury was Miles Standish. In response to the emigrant's expression of annoyance at the ingratitude of the Indians, the savage expresses outrage at the white man's advance and laments the passing of his once-mighty people. Part of the dialogue was published in an anonymous article.

Bibliography: "Longfellow's First Wife and Early Friends." *Every Other Saturday* (19 Jan 1884); Thompson.

DICKENS, CHARLES (1812–70). British author, born in Portsea, Portsmouth. He soon moved with his impoverished family to London. He attended school at the Wellington House Academy (1825–27). He became a reporter and contributed articles to periodicals. Some were republished as "Sketches by Boz" (1836–37) and "The Posthumous Papers of the Pickwick Club" (1836–37). Fast success put him on easy street. *Oliver Twist* (1837–38), *Nicholas Nickleby* (1838–39), and more serial novels followed. Dickens visited the United States and Canada (from Jan through Jun 1842), during which time he was lavishly entertained, advocated international copyright law and the abolition of slavery, and observed enough to write controversially about his host country in *American Notes* (1842) and *Martin Chuzzlewit* (1843–44). *A Christmas Carol* (1843) enjoyed everlasting popularity. Dickens traveled to Italy (1844–45). He founded and contributed to the *Daily News* (1846), *Household Words* (1850), and *All the Year Round* (1859). Several great novels followed, including *David Copperfield* (1849–50), *Bleak House* (1852–53), *Hard Times* (1854), *A Tale of Two Cities* (1859), and *Great Expectations* (1860–61). During this time, he traveled with Wilkie Collins in Italy and Switzerland (1853), resided a while in Paris (1855), began an enduring relationship with Ellen Ternan (from 1857), and permanently separated from his wife (1858). Dickens returned to the United States (from Nov 1867 to May 1868) to give readings and enjoy more public adulation. Home again, he started *Edwin Drood* (1870) but suddenly died without completing this intriguing mystery.

Longfellow first met Dickens when he visited Boston (1842). Longfellow quickly entertained him. According to a letter to his father (30 Jan 1842), Longfellow and Charles Sumner* showed Dickens the sights, which included a sermon by Edward Thompson (1793–1871), the celebrated Boston sailor-turned-preacher, whom Dickens mentions in *American Notes.* Dickens played host to Longfellow for two weeks when he visited London (Oct 1842), inviting him to stay in his home, introducing him to friends, and even going with him (and John Forster*) to Bath to meet and dine with Walter Savage Landor. During Dickens's reading tour in the United States (1867–68), Longfellow often saw him in Boston. Longfellow's journal attests as much. Longfellow, Dickens, and James T. Fields,* their American publisher, dined together (21 Nov 1867). Longfellow invited Dickens to his home for "a little supper" (22 Nov) and again on Thanksgiving Day "to a quiet family dinner" (28 Nov). Longfellow attended three public readings

by Dickens (Dec), describing the first as "not reading exactly, but acting; and quite wonderful" (2 Dec). Longfellow attended a party hosted for Dickens by Fields (29 Feb 1868) and later "Gave a dinner to Dickens" (4 Mar). Longfellow's last European tour (1868–69) included calling at Gadshill, Dickens's famous London home, for a pleasant Sunday (Jun or Jul 1868); Longfellow took along his daughters, Alice Mary Longfellow, Edith Longfellow, and Anne Allegra Longfellow, and Thomas Gold Appleton,* Longfellow's deceased wife's delightful brother. Dickens revered Washington Irving* and Longfellow above all other American writers, while Longfellow regarded Dickens as the greatest English novelist. When Forster began publishing his *Life of Charles Dickens* (3 vols., 1872–74), Longfellow quickly read the first volume but was distressed. He wrote George Washington Greene* that it "is very interesting, but it made me profoundly melancholy; perhaps I can tell you why, but I hardly care to write it" (23 Dec 1871). What bothered Longfellow was Forster's detailed treatment of Dickens's unhappy marriage and separation. Concerning the second volume of the biography, Longfellow notes in his journal (5 Dec 1872) that it reveals Dickens as "The most restless of mortals,—no repose in anything; always at full speed. It is a wonder that he lived so long." It may be said that Dickens was great because of his restlessness; Longfellow, because of his almost habitual serene modesty. During their lives and for some time thereafter, Dickens was the best-selling British writer in the United States, and Longfellow was the most popular writer in English in all of England.

Bibliography: Ackroyd, Peter. *Dickens.* [London]: Sinclair-Stevenson, 1990; Hilen, ed.; Kaplan, Fred. *Dickens: A Biography.* New York: William Morrow, 1988; S. Longfellow; Moss, S. P. "Longfellow's Uncollected 'Letter to the Editor': Defending Dickens's." *American Notes, Dickens Studies Newsletter.* 10, i (1979): 4–7; Tryon; Wagenknecht, Edward. "Dickens in Longfellow's Letters and Journals." *Dickensian* 52 (Dec 1955): 7–19.

"DIRGE OVER A NAMELESS GRAVE" (1825). Poem, signed "H.W.L.," in *USLG,* 15

Mar 1825. Beside a quiet river is a grave without a name, seen by the sun, shadowed by a beech tree. She loved one man, was involved somehow in "a wrong," but would not marry elsewhere when ordered. She wasted away and died. Her "gray old" father, who wept at her grave, has died. But another man "mourns thee yet."

"THE DISCOVERER OF THE NORTH CAPE" (1858). Poem, based on a small part of the translation by Alfred the Great (849–99) of *Adversus Paganos Historiarum* by Paulus Orosius (fl. 415), in *Courtship, Birds* (1858). Othere, a Helgoland sea captain, tells Alfred, the Saxon king, how he grew restless when his seafaring friends interrupted his farm work to tell him about "the undiscovered deep" beyond Iceland, Greenland, and the Hebrides. So he sailed ever northward himself, until he "saw the sullen blaze / Of the red midnight sun." Suddenly loomed the wedge "Of that unknown North Cape." Othere sailed east along it for four days, then south "Into a nameless sea." The six of them harpooned "threescore" walruses, narwhales, and seals. Alfred, who has been writing down this account, grows suspicious. So Othere hands Alfred a white walrus tooth "In witness of the truth."

Bibliography: Sweet, Henry, ed. *Extracts from Alfred's Orosius.* Oxford: Clarendon Press, 1885.

"THE DISEMBODIED SPIRIT" (1831). Sonnet, translated from the Spanish poet Fernando de Herrera (1534?–97), in *NEM,* Oct 1831. The poet longs for his soul to rise and find rest with a certain pure one already released and at peace.

"DIVINA COMMEDIA" (1866, 1867). Six sonnets. I. Longfellow has often seen a worker put "his burden" down, leave the noisy street, enter a cathedral, cross himself, kneel, and "repeat his paternoster." Likewise, Longfellow lays his travail aside, "enter[s] here," and is "not ashamed to pray" "While the eternal ages watch and wait." II (*AM,* Jul 1866). "This mediaeval miracle of song!" rises, with its statues, doors, minster, gargoyles, and depictions of Christ, the thieves, and Judas. The structure is composed of "agonies of heart and brain," pain, tenderness, and joy. III (*AM,* Sep 1866). Longfellow tries to keep pace with the "poet saturnine," through perfumed aisles, between the dead, beside the candles. Sounds resembling Ravenna's rooks echo. He hears confessions about "forgotten tragedies" and regrets, but then hears words of forgiveness. IV. A woman with a snowy veil and flaming robes "stands before thee [Dante]," having inspired, troubled, and rebuked him, having made him weep and confess. Light breaks, like dawn through a "dark forest"; sadness is forgotten, the dream is remembered; what follows is "That perfect pardon which is perfect peace." V. Looking upward, the poet sees martyrs now "glorified," sees Christ's triumphant rise, sees "Beatrice again at Dante's side." Accompanied by organ strains, "unseen choirs / Sing the old Latin hymns of peace and love, / And benedictions of the Holy Cross," as the Host is raised. VI. Dante is the prophet of morning, liberty, the day. Many voices, in cities, by the sea, near mountains, and in forests, repeat Dante's lines; his fame fans like a wind across many nations. Translations in "wondrous word[s]" appeal to those foreign to Rome; "many are amazed and many doubt."

When Longfellow published his translation of *The Divine Comedy of Dante Alighieri,* 1867, he placed sonnets I and II as a preface to *Inferno;* sonnets III and IV to *Purgatorio;* and V and VI, to *Paradiso.*

Bibliography: Arms; More.

THE DIVINE COMEDY OF DANTE ALIGHIERI **(1867).** Longfellow translated Dante's masterpiece over a long period of time. In *Voices of the Night* (1839), he published translations from three subjects of the *Purgatorio* ("Beatrice," "The Celestial Pilot," and "The Terrestrial Paradise"). He started translating the *Purgatorio* (1843), discontinued, resumed (1852), and completed it (1853). After his wife Fanny Longfellow* tragically burned to death (1861), Longfellow resumed translating the work, partly as therapy. He finished a draft of everything (1863). He asked two friends, James Russell Lowell* and Charles Eliot Norton,* to meet with him, share problems he encountered with the Italian text, and suggest improvements (1864). The three friends founded the Dante Club (25 Oct 1865), which Longfellow hosted on Wednesday evenings; they were soon joined by James T. Fields,* George Washington Greene* and William Dean Howells.* Longfellow welcomed suggestions from the club members, listened tactfully, but, as Howells recalled later, could on occasion remain convinced that he knew best and often demonstrated that he had a mind of his own. He wrote Greene (20 Apr 1864) that he was surprised to "find the making of Notes to Dante very pleasant work"; he cleverly images his notes as "footlights of the great Comedy." One of Longfellow's journal entries (7 May 1864) reads as follows: "In translating Dante, something must be relinquished. Shall it be the beautiful rhyme that blossoms all along the lines like a honeysuckle on a hedge? Something more precious than rhyme must be retained, namely, fidelity, truth,—the life of the hedge itself." He tried to combine fidelity to Dante's precise, graphic, terse diction with what was sometimes at odds with it but always more important, that is, fidelity to his spirit.

Longfellow's translation of the *Inferno* was published in a private edition (1865), one single early copy of which Longfellow had printed at first so as to send it to Italy to be shown at the Dante Festival commemorating the six hundredth anniversary of Dante's birth. Longfellow's entire translation was published in three volumes (1867). The entire work was swelled by Longfellow's voluminous and often exceedingly erudite notes (easily four times the length of the poetry); they include glosses, commentaries by others, and quotations from many pertinent works paralleling Dante's specific subjects. Longfellow sent a letter (30 Oct 1866) to George Routledge (1812–88), his London publisher, to say that he would accept £450 in payment for a British edition of his three-volume translation. Dante's coffin was discovered (1865). Elizabeth Lawrence (1829–1905), the widow of Timothy Bigelow Lawrence (1826–1869), the U.S. consul general in Florence, sent Longfellow a piece of the coffin (1872). According to a letter Longfel-

low wrote her (20 Jul 1872), the relic was deposited at the Boston Athenaeum. Longfellow was always on the lookout to improve later editions of his translation. When William James Gillam (c.1827–1910), an English army officer turned school teacher, sent him a list of errata, Longfellow replied (9 Jul 1876) to thank him, to ask him to tell him about other errors if he found any, and to report that several of the mistakes Gillam noted he had already caught.

Reviews of Longfellow's translation ranged from complimentary to antagonistic. Some critics disliked its dictional and syntactical literalness and also the use of blank verse instead of Dante's intricate *terza rima;* others contended that Longfellow preferred Romance words rather than Anglo-Saxon ones when converting Dante's words into English. Regardless, Longfellow's enormous reputation made his work generally respected and very popular and also encouraged Americans to turn with greater devotion to Italian literature.

Bibliography: Arvin; Duberman, Martin. *James Russell Lowell.* Boston: Houghton Mifflin, 1966; Giametti, A. Bartlett, ed. *Dante in America: The First Two Centuries.* Binghamton: Medieval & Renaissance Texts & Studies, 1963; Hilen, ed.; La Piana, Angelina. *Dante's American Pilgrimage: A Historical Survey of Dante Studies in the United States 1800–1944.* New Haven: Yale University Press, 1948; S. Longfellow; Mathews, J. Chesley. "Echoes of Dante in Longfellow's Poetry." *Italica* 26 (Dec 1949): 242-59; Mathews, J. Chesley. "Longfellow's Dante Collection." *Emerson Society Quarterly,* no. 62 (winter 1971): 10-22; Mathews, J. Chesley. "Mr. Longfellow's Dante Club." *Annual Report of the Dante Society* 86 (1958): 23-35; Wagenknecht, 1955.

THE DIVINE TRAGEDY (1871). *See Christus: A Mystery.*

"LA DONCELLA" (1831). Poem, in *The Topic,* Boston, 1831. Longfellow reprinted it in *Outre-Mer,* in the chapter titled "A Tailor's Drawer." He had made one translation of "La Doncella" and copied it in his journal (17 May 1829), made another, and also copied it in his journal (18 Jun 1831). *See* "Song: She Is a Maid of Artless Grace."

Bibliography: Thompson.

DORIA, CLARA (1844–1931). British soprano. Her real name was Clara Kathleen
Branett. After she gave a concert in Boston,
Longfellow invited her to supper (17 Jan
1877), to be accompanied by Annie Adams
Fields.* Other guests included Annie's husband James T. Fields,* James Russell Lowell*
and his wife, Luigi Monti,* and Samuel
Ward.* Clara Doria and Longfellow met again
later and also corresponded. After she and
Henry Munroe Rogers (1839–1937), a Boston attorney, were married (1878), Longfellow was hospitable to both of them.

Bibliography: Hilen, ed.

DRIFT-WOOD **(1857).** Seven prose papers.
"Ancient French Romances: From the
French of Paulin Paris." Longfellow first published his translation of this essay in *Select
Journal of Foreign Periodical Literature*
(Jan 1853). The essay, by the French scholar
Alexis Paulin Paris (1800–1881), discusses
the poetry from *Romances of the Twelve
Peers of France,* including items devoted to
Bertha (?–783), wife of Pepin the Short and
mother of Charlemagne's mother; other sacred poetry; and works by poets or *Trouvères* of the Middle Ages, whose inspirations
came from classical antiquity, Briton writings, and French writings. Longfellow included extensive footnotes.

"Frithiof's Saga" is Longfellow's translation, mostly in prose but with some passages
in poetry, of the great national epic of Sweden by Esaias Tegnér.* Longfellow titles the
poetic passages "Frithiof's Homestead," "A
Sledge-Ride on the Ice," "Frithiof's Temptation," and "Frithiof's Farewell." Longfellow
first published this item in the *NAR* (Jul
1837) and in it included a brief life of Tegnér,
running commentary on the work, and several footnotes.

"Twice-Told Tales" is Longfellow's review,
first published in the *NAR* (Jul 1837), of the
1837 collection of stories by Nathaniel Hawthorne.* Longfellow praises Hawthorne as "a
new star . . . in the heavens" and as "a man
of genius." He says that Hawthorne's prose
is poetic and that, although we live in prosaic times, Hawthorne proves that "romance
still lies around us and within us." Longfel-

low delights that "the prominent characteristics of these tales is [*sic*], that they are national in their character." Finally, he praises
Hawthorne's style for its clarity.

"The Great Metropolis" is Longfellow's review, first published in the *NAR* (Apr 1837),
of *The Great Metropolis* by James Grant
(1802–79) and is reprinted in shortened
form. Longfellow calls the book vulgar, bad-
mannered, weak, undignified, without
grace, and unrefined. But he likes the title,
partly because he has "an affection for a
great city." Big cities contain a variety of real
people. When in London, he delights in
watching the tide of humanity roaring
through its thousands of streets. He loves to
see the Thames, especially by moonlight, to
hear "the great bell of St. Paul's," and to feel
the dawn air.

"Anglo-Saxon Literature": Longfellow
published a review of books about Anglo-
Saxon literature in the *NAR* (Jul 1838). In
this version, he omits comment on those
books and adds translated material. He
praises King Alfred, "The monarch minstrel," for studying the Saxon language. He
discusses the Anglo-Saxon language, the history of Saxons, their conversion to Christianity, and the style of Anglo-Saxon verse.
He comments on *Beowulf,* Caedmon, "Judith," Anglo-Saxon odes and ballads, and minor poems. He calls the *Saxon Laws* and the
Saxon Chronicle "two great works" of
Anglo-Saxon prose, and concludes with minor items, some extensively translated.

"Paris in the Seventeenth Century": This
began as an introduction to a college lecture
Longfellow presented on Molière (evidently
1838). He revised it (1857). Longfellow here
presents a long character sketch of King
Louis XIV, his curious combination of personality traits, his court, and the city of Paris
during his long reign.

"Table-Talk" contains pithy little statements about writing, reading, critics, literature, and life. Many entries project an image
of Longfellow at variance from his standard
public persona. Here are two examples:
"The first pressure of sorrow crushes out
from our hearts the best wine; afterwards
the constant weight of it brings forth bitterness,—the taste and stain from the lees of

the vat"; and "The tragic element in poetry . . . , without it no true . . . Elixir of Life . . . can be made."

Longfellow made a journal entry (2 Dec 1852) to the effect that perhaps he "shall never write anything more," and that he planned to publish some old magazine essays and reviews and to call the collection "Driftwood." He had some pieces printed, did not publish them, but later included some along with others in the 1857 so-called Blue and Gold edition of his works.

Bibliography: S. Longfellow; Scudder.

"DRINKING SONG" (1846). Poem, subtitled "Inscription for an Antique Pitcher," in *Bruges.* The poet invites an old friend to listen to "waters laugh[ing]" in this pitcher. In olden times, "ancient ethnic revels" were celebrated with strong drink. Bacchus drank vigorously, enticed "fair Bacchantes" to make music around him, and was responsible for "Bloodless victories." But Silenus was led to excess by his drunken satyrs. So now, those "Satyrs, changed to devils, / Frighten mortals wine-o'ertaken." Claudius avoids his

Rhenish; Redi, his "vaunted" Tuscan wine; and "Youth perpetual dwells in fountains" instead of in wine cellars. Oh, well, Falerian wine didn't light up the tables of Lucius Lucinius Lucullus, the Roman epicure, any better than water.

"A DUTCH PICTURE" (1877). Poem, in *PP, Kéramos, Birds* (1878). Simon Danz and his buccaneers attacked the King of Spain and sold the Dean of Jaen into slavery in Algiers. So he returns to his house by the Maese, comfortable with his "Plunder of convent and castle." In his view, his tulips are Turks; his gardener, that captured dean; his windmills, Spanish coastal towers. But when winter sets in, and Simon and his seafaring cronies sit by his fire looking like a Rembrandt painting "Half darkness and half light," and drink their stolen Spanish wine, he grows restless and begins to pace about "like a ship that at anchor rides." A voice, whispering to him like a wind at sea, urges him to sail again, tweak the King of Spain again, and kidnap another dean.

E

"THE ELECTED KNIGHT" (1842). Poem, translated "from the Danish," in *Ballads*. Sir Oluf rides along, looking for an adversary to tilt with. He finally sees a knight on a black horse. The knight has a sharp lance, birds on his spurs, wheels on his mail, and on his helmet a wreath, given to him by three maidens. Oluf tells the knight he will yield to him if he is Christ. When the strange knight, denying that he is Christ, says that he has been decorated by three maidens, Oluf challenges him. At the fourth tilt, both fall mortally bloodied. The three maidens wait in a tower, and "The youngest sorrows till death."

"ELEGIAC" (1880). Poem, in *Thule*. Ships in the misty distance resemble towers in a coastal city. The ships sail out of sight, and with them the poet's "thoughts over the limitless deep." They are "borne on by unsatisfied longings" until they vanish, as do the towers. A few ships remain, still moored, without sails and "looming . . . in the mist." Although the poet's thoughts, longings, and dreams are gone now, "in a haven of rest my heart is riding at anchor," secured by "chains of love" and "anchors of trust!" The elegiac-distich form here, creating a wave-like rhythm through its slow, four, four-line stanzas, has been highly praised.

Bibliography: Arvin.

"ELEGIAC VERSE" (1882). Fourteen epigrammatic poems, in *Harbor*. Perhaps a Greek poet long ago reproduced in his poetry "the wave of the sea, upheaving in long undulations." The heart of an aged poet, like that of a youthful one, can "Bloom into song." Some poets are tender enough but speak roughly. We should be grateful to writers who leave some works "in the inkstand." The Trinity can be explained by reference to rain, hail, and snow, which are three yet one. The poetic art transforms life into a floating mirage. The "structure" of life is best when it combines the masculine and feminine, like the rhymes of "A French poem." A child is like a mountain stream, bubbling freely, unaware of the mill in the valley below. Once one starts to write, "sluggish" thoughts begin to flow with the ink. Heaven, like the Fountain of Youth, lies within us; don't "seek it elsewhere." Aim above the mark; thoughts and arrows are attracted by the earth. Hebrews are right to have no present tense; the word, as spoken, is "already the Past." Age is like the twilight, when everything seems "phantasmal," like the landscape. Beginning something can be artful, but ending is more so; many poems are spoiled by superfluities.

"ELEGY WRITTEN IN THE RUINS OF AN OLD CASTLE" (1839). Poem, translated from the German of Friedrich von Matthisson (1761–1831), in *KM*, Sep 1839. A cricket disturbs the silence of the twilit evening. The poet is sad to see ruins of something once so "lordly." Ivy clings to an old column. Windows are blank. The poet imagines a "hoary warrior" ordering his well-armed, knightly son off to battle. The knight waves a sturdy farewell to a certain "fair one." But, now, "what changes!" Where goblets once rang, "rank grass" grows and owls roost. The mighty crusaders are gone, "their memories sunk and shattered." Only "urns [are] devoted unto Memory, / And the songs of Immortality!" Nothing leaves a trace on the earth—not raptures or comradeship. Graves cover one "common darkness" over "titles, honor, might, and glory," and all bright feelings.

***ELEMENTS OF FRENCH GRAMMAR* (1830).** Textbook, prepared by Longfellow for his Bowdoin students and published in Portland. It was reprinted in Boston (1831), this time with his name on the title page for the first time for any book.

"ELIOT'S OAK" (1877). Sonnet, in *AM,* Mar 1877; *Kéramos.* John Eliot, "the unknown / Apostle of the Indians," translated the Bible into an Indian language while sitting, "like Abraham at eventide," under an old oak tree. The language is now known only to that tree, "the myriad leaves [of which] are loud / With sounds of unintelligible speech."

"ELIZABETH." *See* "The Theologian's Tale," in *Tales of a Wayside Inn,* Part Third.

EMERSON, RALPH WALDO (1803–82). Highly significant man of letters. He was born in Boston, attended the Boston Latin School (1813–17), graduated from Harvard (1821), taught and studied at the Harvard Divinity School (1821–28), became the Unitarian pastor of the Second Church, Boston (1829; William Ellery Channing* influenced his liberal theological position at this time), and married Ella Louisa Tucker (1829). She died aged nineteen (1831), soon after which Emerson resigned his ministerial post (1832) and took a European tour (1832–33), meeting many famous authors, most notably Thomas Carlyle. Emerson returned home, moved to Concord, Massachusetts, married Lydia Jackson (1835) and with her had four children. He participated in the Transcendental Club (1836–43) and was friendly with and exerted an influence on many New England intellectuals, including Margaret Fuller* (whom he helped edit the *Dial* magazine [1840–44]), Nathaniel Hawthorne,* James Russell Lowell,* Charles Eliot Norton,* Henry David Thoreau,* and Longfellow. During the late 1830s and the 1840s Emerson lectured widely and also published steadily, including *Nature* (1836), "The American Scholar" (1837, an appeal for intellectual independence in America), "Divinity School Address" (1838, offensive to conservative Unitarians), *Essays* (1841), *Essays, Second Series* (1844), and *Poems* (1846). He toured in Europe again (1847–48), this time with an international reputation. He was lionized in England, where he met Charles Dickens* and Alfred, Lord Tennyson,* among others. Returning home, Emerson published *Nature: Addresses and Lectures* (1849), *Representative Men* (1850), *English Traits* (1856), *The Conduct of Life* (1860), *May-Day and Other Pieces* (1867), and *Society and Solitude* (1870). He went abroad a final time, to Europe and the Middle East (1872–73), and returned to publish *Letters and Social Aims* (1876). The accidental burning of his house (1872) probably triggered the beginning of his mental failures, which culminated in aphasia and senility. Other writings by Emerson were issued posthumously, not the least being numerous editions of his journals, diaries, and letters, which are of the utmost significance.

Longfellow, younger than Emerson, gained his reputation more slowly; therefore, the two did not become friends quickly and were never especially close. But the two did socialize, dined together at the Saturday Club* and elsewhere, and read each other's works; in addition, Longfellow faithfully attended many of Emerson's public lectures. In one of his many journal entries (8 Mar 1838), Longfellow labels as "good" Emerson's lecture on the Affections, which Longfellow heard; but he does go on to define Emerson as, though with "a brilliant mind," more poet than philosopher. Later (28 Mar 1838) he called Emerson's lecture on Holiness "a great bugbear" that the audience could hardly understand, adding "and who does?" Longfellow dutifully attended more lectures by Emerson and records occasional acute responses. The Great Men lecture contained "many things to shock the sensitive ear and heart" (11 Dec 1845). The Plato lecture was full of "the reveries of the poet-philosopher," while the mixed audience included "matrons and maidens, misanthropists and lovers," and some youths with "flowing transcendental locks" (18 Dec 1845). This lecture on Plato, published in *Representative Men,* was Emerson's own favorite. The Goethe lecture was "good, but not so pre-eminent as some of his discourses," with Emerson projecting "the Chrysostom and Sir Thomas Browne of the day" (22 Jan 1846). The Napoleon lecture, delivered after Emerson had tea with the Longfellows, combined "beautiful voice, deep thought, and mild melody of language" (4 Feb 1846). The lecture concerning Analogies between Mind and Matter prompted Longfellow to note that "his [Emerson's] manner has suffered a little by his visit to England" (22 Jan 1849). The Inspiration lecture provoked Longfellow's most famous response: "Emerson is like a beautiful portico, in a lovely scene of nature. We stand expectant, waiting for the High-Priest to come forth; and lo, there comes a gentle wind from the portal, . . . and we ask, 'When will the High-Priest come forth and reveal to us the truth?' and the disciples say, 'He has already gone forth, and is yonder in the meadows.' 'And the truth he was to reveal?' 'It is Nature; nothing more'" (29 Jan 1849). The Worship lecture, albeit with "touches of tenderness," was not "definite or explicit" (16 Jan 1852). The Will lecture provoked Longfellow's odd response that Emerson "did not once quote Jonathan Edwards, whose work I have never read, but mean now to read it" (3 Apr 1871). Nor did Longfellow much like Emerson's published prose either. In a letter to his father (21 Mar 1841), he opines that Emerson's recently appearing *Essays* are "full of sublime prose-poetry, magnificent absurdities, and simple truths," but aren't worth sending on to his father. Longfellow was somewhat better pleased with Emerson's poetry. The gift copy of his *Poems* (1846) Fanny Longfellow* read to her husband one evening and half the night, giving both "the keenest pleasure," according to a journal entry (16 Dec 1846); Longfellow

adds, however, that "many of the pieces present themselves Sphinx-like."

Longfellow wrote Emerson (27 Dec 1846) that he was afraid that his wife's preference for Emerson's poetry would make her stop reading Longfellow's. In turn, Emerson commented on Longfellow and his works. He wrote Longfellow (24 May 1849) that *Kavanagh* (the title of which he misspelled as "Kavangh"), had "gifts and graces," was "persuasive," induced a "serene mood," but had a disappointing conclusion; notwithstanding, "it is good painting, & I think it the best sketch we have seen in the direction of the American Novel," because it handles "our native speech & manners . . . with sympathy, taste, & judgment." After reading *The Song of Hiawatha,* Emerson wrote Longfellow, somewhat stuffily, "I have always one foremost satisfaction in reading your books—that I am safe. I am in variously skilful [*sic*] hands, but first of all they are safe hands. However, I find this Indian poem very wholesome, sweet & wholesome as maizes very proper & pertinent to us to read" (25 Nov 1855). Then, knowing nothing about Indians, Emerson goes on to demean them. By letter to Longfellow (24 Feb 1864), Emerson praises "The Birds of Killingworth," from *Tales of a Wayside Inn,* as "serene, happy, & immortal as Chaucer & speaks to all conditions." Emerson included the poem in *Parnassus* (1874), a poetry anthology he assembled and edited. Privately, however, Emerson expressed deplorable reservations about Longfellow. In his journal (c. Aug 1853), he said "If Socrates were here, we could go & talk with him; but Longfellow we cannot go & talk with; there is a palace [Craigie House*], & servants, & a row of bottles of different coloured wines, & wine glasses, & fine coats." This comment is both mean and hypocritical: Emerson lived in considerable comfort himself, partly owing to his first wife's inheritance and many parishioners' and friends' generosity. When senile and close to death himself, Emerson attended Longfellow's funeral and remarked that "the gentleman we have just been burying was a sweet and beautiful soul; but I forget his name."

Bibliography: Allen, Gay Wilson. *Waldo Emerson.* New York: Viking, 1981; Green; Hilen, ed.; S. Longfellow; Tryon; Wagenknecht, 1955.

"EMMA AND EGINHARD." *See* "The Student's Tale," in *Tales of a Wayside Inn,* Part Third.

"THE EMPEROR'S BIRD'S NEST" (1858). Poem, in *Courtship, Birds* (1858). Charles, the Emperor of Spain, while besieging a town in Flanders, in rainy, muddy weather, notices that a swallow has built a nest of clay and horsehair atop his tent—his "canvas palace." He orders the tent to remain undisturbed and calls the swallow his guest, his "Golondrina," perhaps some deserter's wife. His soldiers drink Flemish beer and joke about the event. When the siege ends, the tent remains intact though tattered.

"THE EMPEROR'S GLOVE" (1877). Poem, in *PP, Kéramos, Birds* (1878). When Emperor Charles, commanding much of Flanders, hears Duke Alva of Spain call the people of nearby Ghent traitorous "Lutheran misbelievers," Charles replies by asking how many pieces of Spanish leather it would take to make the city. This poem makes sense only when it is explained, as Longfellow did in a headnote, that the French name for Ghent is "Gand" and the French word for glove is "gant."

"ENCELADUS" (1859). Poem, in *AM,* Aug 1859; Scudder. Enceladus the giant lies under Mount Etna. He is not dead. "Though smothered and half suppressed," he is lifting his head above "the crags that keep him down." His movement turns oppressors "white with fear." Through the pines of Italy "the storm-wind shouts" for him to rise. The emerging giant is a symbol of the spirit of Italian liberty. Longfellow contributed the $50 he was paid for "Enceladus" to a fund for Italian widows and wounded soldiers. "Enceladus" is perhaps the best of Longfellow's political poems.

Bibliography: Arvin; S. Longfellow; Wagenknecht, 1986.

"ENDYMION" (1841) Poem, in *New World,* 25 Sept 1841; *Ballads.* With the "unasked, unsought" kiss by which Diana awoke Endymion, "Love gives itself, but is not bought." It lifts one's soul from leafy shadows. Even if one is cursed and lonely, a love awaits him and will respond to him. Before it was published, Longfellow copied this poem and sent it in a letter (14 Sept 1841) to Catherine Eliot Norton, mother of Charles Eliot Norton.*

Bibliography: Hilen, ed.

"L'ENVOI" (1839). Poem, in *Voices.* In conclusion, the poet asks that these voices, which many an evening "whispered to my restless heart repose," provide balm to the doubting and the fearful, and persuade them that the "Tongues of the dead . . . [are] not lost," but like pentacostal fire "Glimmer, as funeral lamps," on "the vast plain where Death encamps!"

"L'ENVOI" (1880). *See* "The Poet and His Songs."

"EPIGRAMS" (1846). *See* "Poetic Aphorisms."

"EPIMETHEUS, OR THE POET'S AFTERTHOUGHT" (1858). Poem, in *PM,* Feb 1855; *Courtship, Birds* (1858). Longfellow laments the fact that when he is inspired to write, the "wild, bewildering fancies" that dance around him like sunny "guests" often become pale, "haggard" creatures, with "cold . . . caresses!," when transferred to the page. Aspiring nobly, he falls like Icarus, is saddened like Pandora. Still, he will continue to listen to his deceptive Muse and let her make "each mystery clearer," each "unattained [object] . . . nearer," in the hope of wandering "Where no foot has left its traces." A more idealistic companion poem for "Epimetheus" is Longfellow's "Prometheus, or the Poet's Forethought."

Bibliography: Arvin.

***THE ESTRAY* (1846)** Fugitive poems, fifty-four in number, which Longfellow liked, selected, and edited in book form. He provided a "Proem," retitled "Pegasus in Pound." In an introductory note, Longfellow explains that an estray is any beast, not wild, in the property of a lord and not owned by anyone. It must be announced in the market place. If not claimed by the owner within a year and a day, the beast becomes the property of the lord. These stray poems can therefore be freely reprinted.

"ETERNITY" (1846). Poetic lines taken from Longfellow's "Phi Beta Kappa" poem (Bowdoin, 1832), in *Christian Family Annual,* 1846.

Bibliography: Thompson.

EVANGELINE (1847). Narrative poem. *Evangeline: A Tale of Acadie* is in two parts, each in five numbered sections. Its verse form is unrhymed dactylic hexameters with consideration variation.

The short introduction begins memorably:

> This is the forest primeval. The murmuring
> pines and the hemlocks,
> Bearded with moss, and in garments green,
> indistinct in the twilight,
> Stand like Druids of eld . . .

It continues by wondering where the people are, where their village is, where "the Acadian farmers" have gone. It seems that "Naught but tradition remains of the beautiful village of Grand-Pré," near the resounding ocean.

Part the First. I. The scene is "In the Acadian land, on the shores of the Basin of Minas." To the east of the village called Grand-Pré, lying in a fertile valley, are meadows and flocks. To the west and south orchards, cornfields, and growths of flax. To the north are forests, mountains, and Atlantic mists. From Normandy have come the villagers, now living in homes well thatched, dormered, and gabled. The women "spin . . . the golden / Flax for the gossiping looms." Men labor in their fields. Father Felician walks among the polite populace. Peace reigns. Just outside the village Benedict Bellefontaine, "the wealthiest farmer of Grand-Pré," has his home surrounded by his prosperous acreage. He is as hearty as an oak, at the age of seventy; with him is his daughter Evangeline, seventeen, lovely, sweet, and radiating "a celestial brightness—a more ethereal

beauty" when she walks home after confession. Many young men admire her with a kind of devotion; some dance with her; a few whisper hasty amorous compliments. But Evangeline responds only to Gabriel Lajeunesse, the son of the village blacksmith, Basil Lajeunesse. From childhood Evangeline and Gabriel have played together, often near the fiery smithy, sometimes riding their sleds down the snowy hills. Now Gabriel is grown and manly. Evangeline is his "Sunshine of Saint Eulalie," emanating light of the sort that plumps the orchards and fills households with "ruddy . . . children."

II. The sun retreats. Birds fly south. September harvests fill the barns. The villagers see signs of the approach of a "long and inclement" winter, but sense a "reign of rest and affection and stillness" too. Evangeline brings in her snow-white heifer. The watchdog rounds up his "bleating flocks from the seaside" where they have pastured. The wains come in from the marshes with "briny hay." The patient cows "yield their udders / Unto the milkmaid's hand." In their home, Evangeline spins flax, while Benedict sits by the shadow-casting fire and sings fond old Norman and Burgundian Christmas carols. And Basil, with quiet Gabriel, comes calling. Basil says that the English ships at "the Gaspereau's mouth" are now seen pointing their cannon at Grand-Pré and that the King of England is to be "proclaimed as law in the land" at a church meeting on the morrow. Benedict voices the hope that the British may be short of food and are simply coming for supplies. Not likely, counters Basil, who says the British remember defeats at Louisburg, Beau Séjour, and Port Royal, and have already disarmed the French hereabouts. Benedict says, "Safer are we unarmed," with dikes holding back the ocean and no fort threatening anyone. He adds that their notary, René Leblanc, will bring some good news.

III. Leblanc enters, old but unbroken by four years as a prisoner of the French for his friendship with the English. He is now wise and patient, loved by all, especially the children, to whom he tells stories of werewolves, goblins, ghosts, and the powers of good-luck charms. Leblanc says that he doesn't know what the English ships portend but that they can't mean harm to the peaceful French. Basil shouts back, "Daily injustice is done, and might is the right of the strongest!" Leblanc replies, "Man is unjust, but God is just; and finally justice / Triumphs." He recounts an old French tale. An orphan girl, working as a household maid, was accused of stealing her mistress's pearl necklace and was about to be hanged. But a storm came, blew down a statue of Justice in the public square, and from Justice's balance scales out fell the necklace, built by birds into their nest there. Basil turns quiet "but not convinced." Evangeline serves strong homemade ale, Benedict tosses some silver pieces on the table, and Basil pulls out his writing materials. He records names and ages of bride and bridegroom, lists dowry items, and affixes his seal. Then the old men play checkers, while the two lovers sit by the window whispering and "the moon rise[s] / Over the pallid sea, and the silvery mists of the meadows." The visitors depart, and "Silently one by one, in the infinite meadows of heaven, / Blossomed the lovely stars, the forget-me-nots of the angels." In her white-curtained bedchamber, Evangeline is unaware that Gabriel is watching from the orchard for her lamp and shadow. She thinks of him, but partly with "a feeling of sadness." The moon emerges from clouds, and a star follows it "As out of Abraham's tent young Ishmael wandered with Hagar!"

IV. By noon, village workers and "the blithe Acadian peasants" begin to assemble at Benedict's house for "the feast of betrothal." Michael, with snowy hair and a face that "Glowed like a living coal," plays his fiddle. Old and young dance before fair Evangeline and noble Gabriel. But drumbeats suddenly call the citizenry to the church. The men go in. The women wait outside. Guards come. The English commander explains that it is his painful duty to read "his Majesty's orders." All lands, dwellings, and livestock "Forfeited be to the crown"; the populace, now regarded as prisoners, are to "Be transported to other lands." The crowd turns loud, sorrowful, and angry. Basil shouts opposition to the English tyrants, to whom they never pledged their allegiance.

A soldier smashes Basil in the mouth. Father Felician rises, asks for continued loving of one another, and says, "O Father, forgive them!" The people repeat this. After evening service and the Ave Maria song, the ill tidings spread everywhere. The sun sets. From lonely Evangeline's soul rise thoughts of "Charity, meekness, love, and hope, and forgiveness, and patience!" The Angelus sounds. Evangeline calls aloud for Gabriel, unavailingly, covers her hearth fire, thinks of Leblanc's story about "the justice of Heaven," and finally sleeps.

V. Five days later, the Acadian women drive wains to the shore, loaded with their household goods. The patient men, released from confinement, join them. All pray to their Savior for "strength, and submission, and patience!"

Evangeline, silent, calm, and strong, whispers to Gabriel that nothing can harm them since their love is true. Benedict, her father, sits stunned, declining food. The loading of the English ships is confusing. Wives are "torn from their husbands"; children, left on shore; Basil and Gabriel go in separate vessels. At twilight, sentinels prevent the remnant from escaping. Herds mill untended in their pastures. That night the homes are torched. Father Felician offers words of comfort. The stars wheel above, "unperturbed by the wrongs and sorrows of mortals." In the red moonlight, with their homes flaming, the Acadians hear roosters crow in the glare of false dawn. Wild horses gallop past, frightened by the roaring flames. Evangeline turns to her father, but he has fallen. "Slowly the priest uplifted the lifeless head, and the maiden / Knelt at her father's side, and wailed aloud in her terror." The people hastily bury Benedict "by the seaside," the roar of "the returning tide" accompanying their dirge. The ebbing tide carries a final load of Acadians, who leave "the dead on the shore, and the village in ruins."

Part the Second. I. The exile of these Acadians, "without an end, and without an example in story," scatters them from city to city, from "the cold . . . North to sultry Southern savannahs," and also "to the lands where the Father of Waters / Seizes the hills in his hands, and drags them down to the ocean." Those separated seek their loved ones but often find solace only in death. One young woman "waited and wandered," is beautiful, young, and patient. Her life is "incomplete, imperfect, unfinished," like a day in June, "all . . . music and sunshine," that, rising in the east, falls into the east again. She searches in towns, cemeteries, follows rumors. She hears that Gabriel and Basil were hunters in the prairie, once that Gabriel was a boatman in Louisiana. When it is proposed that she should dream of Gabriel no more but wed the notary's son, Baptiste, nearby, she replies that her steady heart is "like a lamp, and illumines the pathway ahead." To this a wise priest tells her that her affection, if it does not nourish another, will return to her like a fountain with water returning to its base. Strengthened, she hears the ocean tell her not to despair. She wanders on, and much time passes.

II. In May Evangeline, guided and encouraged by Father Felician, goes by boat, handled "by Acadian boatmen," past the Ohio and the Wabash rivers and down "the broad and swift Mississippi." They pass sands and forests, chutes and islands, lagoons and wading pelicans. Vegetation grows luxuriant. They see planters' houses and slave cabins and groves of fruit trees, enter the Bayou of Plaquemine, and watch as the moon lights cypresses and cedars over the gleaming waters. The voyagers feel "forebodings of evil." A boatman's bugle notes go unanswered. They go on to the Atchafalaya lakes, see magnolias and roses, and rest under the willows. Meanwhile, Gabriel, "weary with waiting, unhappy and restless," passes in a fast little boat, seeking "in the Western wilds oblivion of self and of sorrow." No angel awakens Evangeline. But later she dismisses a "credulous fancy" that her Gabriel was near—until, that is, Father Felician tells her that Gabriel must be near and that she should trust her heart. As their group proceeds toward St. Maur and St. Martin, on the Têche, a mockingbird pours out "floods of delirious music," but then "Single notes . . . in sorrowful, low lamentation."

III. Evangeline and her companions stop at a cypress-timbered house beside a flowery prairie. They see a mounted, sturdy herdsman, master of a vast herd of white-horned cattle. He is Basil, the former blacksmith and Gabriel's father. Evangeline, heartily welcomed with the others from the boat, is delighted until Basil tells her that Gabriel, "restless grown, and tried and troubled, his spirit," and unable to "endure the calm of this quiet existence," departed earlier this day to go to Adayes, a mule-trading town, and then on to the Ozarks. Friends greet friends, and many dance to the tunes of Michael the fiddler. Basil explains that this Southern soil is better than Canada's, but fever is a constant danger here. Evangeline listens to the sea, "and an irrepressible sadness / Came o'er her heart." She enters Basil's moonlit garden, and "the manifold flowers . . . / Poured out their souls in odors." Evangeline, feeling "indefinable longings" as she views "the measureless prairie" under the stars, cries, "O Gabriel! O my beloved! / Art thou so near unto me, and yet I cannot behold thee?" When can she see and embrace him? In the morning, Father Felician, Evangeline, and their boatmen follow after Gabriel, who seems "Blown by the blast of fate like a dead leaf over the desert." Days later they get to Adayes, only to learn he left yesterday for the prairies.

IV. In the far West "the Oregon flows," and the Nebraska gladdens the valley of the Sweet-water. Near these and other streams are "wondrous, beautiful prairies," with grass, buffalo herds, bears that are "anchorite monk[s] of the desert," and smoky camps of "savage marauders." Gabriel hunted here but remains ahead of his fond pursuers, who are ever guided by hope. At one camp, the Shawnee widow of a murdered Canadian "Coureur-des-Bois," tells Evangeline her story. Evangeline in turn relates hers. When the Shawnee recites the legend of a maiden who wed Mowis, "bridegroom of snow," only to see him melt in the sunshine, Evangeline has fears that she too is "pursuing a phantom." But when she visits a Jesuit mission, the black-robed priest tells her that Gabriel left only six days earlier and will return in the autumn. She waits for months, and seasons pass; "yet Gabriel came not." Evangeline wanders on, seeking him in Michigan and at a Moravian mission, in army camps, in towns and cities. Years steal from her beauty, and her hair becomes flecked with gray.

V. A ship finally takes her to Philadelphia, that city founded by "Penn the apostle" and containing friendly Quakers. Once here, she decides to "recommence no more upon earth" her "fruitless search."

> Gabriel was not forgotten. Within her heart was his image,
> Clothed in the beauty of love and youth, as last she beheld him,
> Only more beautiful made by his deathlike silence and absence.

Wishing to follow "the sacred feet of her Saviour," she becomes a "Sister of Mercy" and for years comforts the lonely and the wretched, the sick and the sorrowful, wherever she finds them. It happens that a pestilence falls on the city, and "death flooded life," spreading through the city like a "brackish" tide. "Wealth had no power to bribe, nor beauty to charm, the oppressor." The friendless and unattended must creep to the almshouse, "home of the homeless." Evangeline visits these woeful ones, who look up to her as to an angel. One Sabbath morning, she brings flowers to the ill and something says to her, "At length thy trials are ended." She sees "Death, the consoler, / Laying his hand upon many a heart." Suddenly an old man, with gray locks at his temples, hears her cry out in "terrible anguish." As he lies "in the morning light," his face seems to grow younger. She whispers tenderly to him, "Gabriel! O my beloved!" A youthful Evangeline "rose in his vision." He weeps. She kneels beside him. He tries to say her name. She kisses and embraces him. "Sweet was the light of his eyes; but it suddenly sank into darkness." All ends now— hope, fear, sadness, heartache, longing, the pain of patience. "And, as she pressed . . . the lifeless head to her bosom, / Meekly she bowed her own, and murmured, 'Father, I thank thee!'"

Later, in the primeval forest,

> Side by side, in their nameless graves, the lovers are sleeping.
> Under the humble walls of the little Catholic churchyard,

> In the heart of the city, they lie, unknown and unnoticed.

Strangers of different "customs and language" now live in the old forest. But a few wandering Acadians have returned. Many of them tell the story of Evangeline, "While from its rocky caverns the deep-voice, neighboring ocean / Speaks, and in accents disconsolate answers the wail of the forest."

Once, when Longfellow invited Nathaniel Hawthorne* to dinner (27 Oct 1846), Hawthorne brought with him a South Boston church rector named H. L. Conolly, who said that he had been trying to interest Hawthorne in an incident told him by a parishioner. It concerned an Acadian maiden separated from her lover and reunited only when he was dying. Longfellow told Hawthorne that if he did not want the plot for a story, he would like it for a poem. Once Hawthorne had consented, Longfellow started what he tentatively titled "Gabrielle" (Nov 1846), finished a draft of *Evangeline* (Feb 1947), and showed it to Cornelius Felton,* Charles Folsom,* and Charles Sumner* for their suggestions. The revision was published (Oct 1847). Evangeline's story is based on fact. In 1755 the English expelled some three thousand French settlers from Acadie, near the Bay of Minas (in present-day Nova Scotia), burned their homes, and scattered them along the eastern seaboard and down into Louisiana. Longfellow consulted several sources, including *An Historical and Statistical Account of Nova Scotia* (2 vols., 1829) by Thomas C. Haliburton (1796-1865); accounts of Philadelphia, Louisiana, Jesuit missions, Mississippi valley travel; and French and Indian legends. In *The Exploring Expedition to the Rocky Mountains, Oregon, and California* (1843) by John C. Frémont (1813-90), Longfellow found useful descriptions of western prairies and also the name Basil Lajeunesse, who was one of Frémont's soldiers. Longfellow, who never traveled west of Niagara Falls, found help in describing the Mississippi valley when by good fortune John Banvard (1815-91) came to Boston (Dec 1846) and showed his painted diorama of the Mississippi River (it covered 3 miles of canvas). Evangeline's seeking her Gabriel in army camps may constitute Longfellow's hint that she survived into the period of the American Revolution. Indeed, the real epidemic of yellow fever in Philadelphia occurred in 1793, when Evangeline would have been fifty-five. It has been suggested that there are certain parallels in the plots of *Evangeline* and *Frithiofs Saga* by Esaias Tegnér,* the Swedish poet whom Longfellow admired and several of whose works he translated.

An instant success, *Evangeline* was in its sixth edition ten weeks after its initial publication. Its first-decade sales of almost 36,000 copies were outstanding, given the fact that the U.S. population in 1857 was under 30 million. Since then, more than 270 editions and upwards of 130 translations have appeared (in more than 10 languages). An indication of the absolute veneration in which *Evangeline* was once held is the fact that Frank Siller (1835-?), a German emigrant to Milwaukee, translated it into German and sent Longfellow a copy his daughter had written out. Longfellow wrote a letter to Siller (12 Feb 1879) to express his gratitude. Siller's translation was published in Milwaukee (1879). The touching story of Evangeline and Gabriel has been retold in dramatic, film, and musical versions; its verse form has been parodied, and its plot subjected to a musical travesty. *Evangeline* enjoyed the greatest success of any poem up to its time. Present-day readers, if they respond to literature making few pretensions to verisimilitude, may still find that innumerable lines in *Evangeline* are profoundly thrilling.

Bibliography: Applemann, A. H. "Longfellow's *Evangeline* and [Esaias] Tegnér's *Frithiof's Saga.*" *Anglia* 49 (1925): 153-72; Arvin; Grady, Wayne. "Acadia, Acadia!" *Queen's Quarterly* 105 (1998): 383-91; Hawthorne, Manning and H. W. L. Dana. "The Origin and Development of Longfellow's *Evangeline.*" *Publications of the Biographical Society of America* 41 (1947): 165-203. Reprint, Maine: Thomas P. Mosher, 1947; Higginson; Hilen, ed.; Hill, M. G. "Some of Longfellow's Sources for the Second Part of *Evangeline.*" *PMLA* 31 (Nov 1916): 161-80; Hirsh; S. Longfellow; MacMechan, Archibald. "*Evangeline* and the Real Acadians." *Atlantic Monthly* 99 (Feb 1907): 202-13; More; Moyne; Seelye, John. "Attic Shape: Dusting Off *Evangeline.*" *Virginia Quarterly Review* 60 (winter 1984): 21-44; Taylor, M. Brook.

"The Poetry and Prose of History: *Evangeline* and the Historians of Nova Scotia." *Journal of Canadian Studies* 23 (spring-summer 1988): 46-67; Wagenknecht, 1986; Williams; Winslow, Erving. "Historical Inaccuracies in Longfellow's *Evangeline.*" *Dial* 60 (3 Feb 1916): 105-7.

"AN EVENING IN AUTUMN" (1833). Poem, signed "H.W.L.," from Longfellow's "Phi Beta Kappa Poem" (Bowdoin, 1832), in *Token,* 1833.

Bibliography: Thompson.

"EVENING SHADOWS." *See* "Footsteps of Angels."

"THE EVENING STAR" (1846). Sonnet, in *Bruges, S/F.* The evening star resembles "a fair lady at her casement"; she shines and then, "divest[ing herself] / Of all her radiant garments, . . . reclines." Longfellow then addresses his wife Fanny directly, as "O my beloved, my sweet Hesperus!," and calls her his "morning and . . . evening star of love." "The Evening Star" is Longfellow's only poem devoted, minimally, to be sure, to sexual love.

Bibliography: Arvin; More; Wagenknecht, 1986.

"THE EVENING STAR" (1850). *See* "Chrysaor."

EVERETT, ALEXANDER HILL (1790–1847). Statesman and editor. He was the older brother of Edward Everett.* Boston-born Alexander Everett taught briefly at Exeter, was U.S. minister to Spain (1825-29), edited the *North American Review* (1830-35), and was president of Jefferson College in Louisiana (1842-43). While in Spain (1827), Longfellow made his acquaintance. Longfellow published often in the *North American Review* while Everett was its editor. Everett stayed with the Longfellows on the occasion of his delivering Bowdoin's 1834 Phi Beta Kappa address (3 Sep), publication of which as a fifty-five-page pamphlet Longfellow helped finance.

Bibliography: Hilen, ed.

EVERETT, EDWARD (1794–1865). Statesman and orator. Everett was born in Dorchester, Massachusetts, the younger brother of Alexander Hill Everett.* When their father, a minister, died (1802), his mother moved the family to Boston. Everett excelled at Harvard (B.A., 1811; M.A., 1814), served with fabled eloquence at the Unitarian church at Brattle Street, Boston (1814-15), wrote *Defence of Christianity* (1814), and prepared to teach Greek at Harvard by travel and study abroad (1815-19), obtaining in the process the first Ph.D. the University of Göttingen granted an American (1817). George Ticknor* accompanied Everett to Europe (1815). Everett taught at Harvard (1819-24), where his best-known student was Ralph Waldo Emerson.* He also edited the *North American Review* (1820-23). In 1822 he married Charlotte Gray Brooks, a rich Boston businessman's daughter; the couple had six children. Everett was a member of the U.S. Congress (1825-35), demonstrating much oratorical but little political force. He was governor of Massachusetts (1835-39), minister to England (1841-45), and president of Harvard (1846-49). Notably, he oversaw the founding of Harvard's Lawrence scientific school and brought Louis Agassiz* to it. When Daniel Webster,* his close friend, died (1852), Everett succeeded him as secretary of state in President Millard Fillmore's cabinet (1852-53). Everett wrote a biography of Webster (1852). Everett was elected U.S. senator (1853) but soon resigned (1854), allegedly on his physician's orders but more likely because he was timid during the controversy over the Kansas-Nebraska Bill (1854), concerning the extension of slavery. Everett spoke far and wide with astounding effect (1853-59) to raise money to restore George Washington's Mount Vernon home, submitted weekly articles on Washington to the *New York Ledger,* and published them as *Mount Vernon Papers* (1859). His speeches were also published (1856-1858), as was his short biography of Washington (1860). Everett ran as vice president on presidential candidate John Bell's unsuccessful Constitutional Union Party ticket (1860), after which he supported President Abraham Lincoln. Everett is now remembered in large part for his two-hour official oration at the Gettys-

burg National Cemetery dedication ceremony (19 Nov 1863), following which Lincoln presented his brief, memorable speech. While giving a public speech in Boston, shortly before the Civil War ended, to raise funds for sufferers in Savannah, Georgia, Everett caught a cold that proved fatal.

Longfellow read a poem at the Phi Beta Kappa chapter at Bowdoin (Sep 1832) that was so pleasing that members of the Harvard chapter invited him to repeat it for them (Aug 1833). John Quincy Adams was to have been the main orator; but, when he could not be there, Everett replaced him, heard Longfellow, and in his speech praised him as "the flashing sickle" in the field of education. By letter (3 Dec 1833) Longfellow courteously thanked Everett for sending him a copy of his Phi Beta Kappa address. When Longfellow rented rooms in Craigie House* (1837), he learned that Everett had rented there earlier. Longfellow's fellow guests at a dinner hosted by Abbott Lawrence, a rich Harvard donor (13 Oct 1838), included Adams, Jared Sparks,* and Everett (at that time governor of Massachusetts). Wasting no time after hearing of Everett's appointment as Harvard's president, Longfellow penned a congratulatory letter (9 Mar 1846) and got nine fellow faculty members to sign it with him. While both men were at Harvard, Longfellow often wrote President Everett about faculty matters, literature and foreign words, social invitations, and charitable matters. Longfellow sent a copy of *The Seaside and the Fireside* (1849) to Everett, who replied by letter (27 Dec 1849) praising "The Building of the Ship" as "admirable" and hinting that other poems in the book touch the feeling of parents whose children have predeceased them (*see* "Resignation" and "Suspiria"). Longfellow and Everett, along with Agassiz and Cornelius Conway Felton,* among others, attended a dinner given William Hickling Prescott* (3 May 1856) before the historian departed for Europe. By letter to "Mr. Longfellow" (4 Jun 1857), Everett delighted the poet by reporting that while in St. Louis he saw a fine steamer named *Hiawatha* and heard of another named *Minnehaha.* Longfellow privately expressed disgust with Everett's compromising politics before the Civil War. Still, he accepted Everett's invitation (Sep 1859) to dine with him and meet, as fellow guest, Sir Henry Holland (1788–1873), the physician of Queen Victoria.* When the Massachusetts Historical Society met to eulogize Longfellow (13 Apr 1882), Everett spoke.

Bibliography: Green; Handlin, Lillian. "Harvard and Göttingen, 1815." *Massachusetts Historical Society Proceedings* 95 (1983): 67–87; Mathews, James W. "Fallen Angel: Emerson and the Apostasy of Edward Everett." In *Studies in the American Renaissance*, 23–32. 1990; Morison; Reid, Ronald F. *Edward Everett: Unionist Orator.* Westport: Greenwood Press, 1990; "Tribute."

"EXCELSIOR" (1842) Poem, in *Ballads.* A restless, ambitious youth, bearing a banner with a device reading "Excelsior!," which he repeats, is warned of physical dangers by an old man and a peasant, and is also lured by a maiden, all in attempts to dissuade him from climbing to an Alpine summit. At dawn the monks of Saint Bernard at prayer hear "Excelsior!" The youth is soon found, "Lifeless, but beautiful." From the serene sky "A voice fell, . . . / Excelsior!"

Longfellow wrote Samuel Ward* (30 Sep 1841) that one night the poem came to him; he went to bed, but "That *voice* kept ringing in my ears"; he got up, lit a lamp, and wrote out the poem. He had been inspired to write this poem when he happened to see in a New York newspaper the seal of the state of New York, with rising sun, shield, and motto "Excelsior." He immediately imagined an Alpine climber with a pennant on his alpenstock bearing the motto. When queried about his Latin, he explained that his "excelsior" is part of *"Scopus meus excelsior est*

[my goal is higher]." Friends and contemporary readers praised "Excelsior" ecstatically. For example, Ward wrote Longfellow (4 Oct 1841) that its harmony was "divine," its "effect . . . magical, electrical"; Charles Sumner* wrote Longfellow (9 Sep 1857) that he saw a French translation of "Excelsior" written in a traveler's book at the hospice of Gran St. Bernard in Switzerland. In a letter to his brother Alexander Wadsworth Longfellow* (22 Sep 1857), Longfellow thanked him for sending a Spanish translation of "Excelsior" but wished the title "excelsior" had been retained and not changed to "Gloria." Longfellow wrote Sumner (8 May 1860) that on a day when a German translation of "Excelsior" appeared in an Innsbruck newspaper, students swarmed all over the translator with kisses. Longfellow mentioned in his journal (2 Sep 1871) that he had received a Hebrew translation of "Excelsior." During the ceremony when Longfellow was given an honorary degree of Doctor of Laws at Cambridge University (16 Jun 1868), the Public Orator punned with rousing success on the title "Excelsior" by suggesting that the poetry draws readers from life's ills *"ad excelsiora."* However, few of Longfellow's poems have been so severely criticized by recent and contemporary critics as this often-parodied chestnut.

Bibliography: Friederich, Richard. "Excelsior!," *Gettysburg Review* 4 (autumn 1991): 481–92; Hilen, ed.; S. Longfellow; Wagenknecht, 1986; Williams.

"EYES SO TRISTFUL, EYES SO TRISTFUL." *See* "From the [Spanish] Cancioneros."

F

"THE FALCON OF SER FEDERIGO." *See* "The Student's Tale," in *Tales of a Wayside Inn,* Part First.

FARRER, FRANCES (1801–86). English woman. Cornelius Conway Felton* met this beautiful widow in Scotland (1853), listened joyfully as she praised Longfellow's *Hyperion,* and encouraged her to write Longfellow. After she did so, a lively correspondence ensued, lasting until 1880. By letter (Sep 1856) Longfellow sent Thomas Gold Appleton,* his brother-in-law then in London, "Fanny" Farrer's address, for him to follow up with a visit. He also asked Charles Sumner,* when he was in England (Jul 1857), to go see the charming lady; Sumner reported back that he tried but failed to meet her. Soon after Felton died, Longfellow wrote her (8 May 1862) to praise him. Longfellow continued to think enough of her to send her copies of his three-volume translation of Dante's *Divina Commedia* (1867) and a copy of the British edition of his *Aftermath* (1873).

Bibliography: Hilen, ed.

"FATA MORGANA" (1873). Poem, in *Aftermath, Birds* (1873). The poet is forever lured by the "sweet illusions of Song," like a traveler in fields, streets, deserts, and prairies, toward the shining "city of song" in a "land of dreams." But everything vanishes in a mist, and he "wander[s] and wait[s] / For the vision to reappear."

FELTON, CORNELIUS CONWAY (1807–62). Scholar and educator. He was born in West Newbury, Massachusetts. The bankruptcy of his father, a harness maker, caused Felton hardship in early life. After attending public school at Saugus, the Bradford Academy, and the Franklin Academy at Andover, he began his lifelong association with Harvard. By the time he graduated (1827), the brilliant young man had a profound knowledge of Greek and Latin, and was also proficient in French, German, Italian, Portuguese, and Spanish. He taught at a high school in Geneseo, New York (1827-29), then returned to Harvard permanently—as tutor in Latin (1829-30), tutor in Greek (1830-32), professor of Greek (1832-34), Eliot Professor of Greek Literature (1834-60), regent (1849-60) during the presidency of Jared Sparks,* and finally president (1860-62). Felton combined pragmatic teaching and liberal administrative actions with assiduous writing and a robust social life. Among his students were James Russell Lowell,* Henry David Thoreau,* and the eccentric poet Jones Very (1813-80). Felton commissioned the 1837 Phi Beta Kappa address by Ralph Waldo Emerson* titled "The American Scholar." Felton published an edition of Homer's *Iliad* (2 vols., 1833; rev. ed., 1854); a 1840 translation of a three-volume study of German literature by Wolfgang Menzel (1798-1873), and a 1849 translation of a significant French book on geography by Arnold Henry Guyot (1807-84), whom Longfellow met (1851); annotated editions of *The*

Clouds of Aristophanes (1841), *The Aga-memnon of Aeschylus* (1847), *Panegyricus of Isocrates* (1847), and *The Birds of Aristophanes* (1849); textbooks, readers, anthologies, etc.; and upwards of 75 reviews for the *Christian Examiner* and the *North American Review.* He reviewed *A Year's Life* (1841) and later *Poems* (1844), both by Lowell, and also Emerson's *Essays* (1841); Felton took Lowell to task for subjective emotionalism, and Emerson for stylistic quirks and philosophical indefiniteness. Felton's *Familiar Letters from Europe* (1866) and *Greece: Ancient and Modern* (his 1850s lectures at the Lowell Institute, Boston; 2 vols., 1867) appeared posthumously. Felton married Mary Whitney (1815–45) in 1838; they had two daughters, one becoming a Civil War nurse. Felton married Mary Louisa Cary (1821–64) in 1846; they had three children.

Shortly after Longfellow began teaching at Harvard (Dec 1836), he met Felton; the two, together with Henry Russell Cleveland (1809–43), George Stillman Hillard,* and Charles Sumner,* founded "The Five of Clubs." Thus began Longfellow's delightful friendship with Felton, whom he occasionally addressed as "Feltonius." Longfellow in a letter to his father (22 Mar 1837) called Felton his "most intimate friend . . . [and] the best fellow in the world—or one of the best." Longfellow attended Felton's 1838 wedding ceremony but evidently not the l,500-guest dinner afterwards. After hearing Felton read his translation of Menzel's book on German literature, Longfellow, who later reviewed it in the *New World,* noted in his journal (24 May 1839) that the "vigorous, live book . . . [was] most faithfully done into English." When Edgar Allan Poe* accused Longfellow of plagiarism in a lecture (28 Feb 1845), the *Evening Mirror* published a quick essay in defense of Longfellow by someone signing himself "Outis [Greek, Nobody]." Felton may have been Outis. Felton wrote an essay on the Acadian background of *Evangeline* (*NAR,* Jan 1848). Felton and Sumner argued over politics when Felton defended the infamous Fugitive Slave Act of 1850. Longfellow tried to moderate, but the two didn't speak to each other until Sumner

was attacked and badly injured on the floor of Congress (1856). Longfellow included Felton in a dinner (26 Nov 1852) he gave for Arthur Hugh Clough,* the visiting poet from England. Lowell hosted Felton and Longfellow at a dinner (1853) he gave for William Makepeace Thackeray.* Shortly before one of his many departures for Europe, William Hickling Prescott,* the historian, had occasion to dine (3 May 1856) with several notables, including Felton and Longfellow. Longfellow drove from Nahant to Boston to attend a party, presided over by Felton (29 Aug 1859), to celebrate the fiftieth birthday of Oliver Wendell Holmes.* When Felton became president of Harvard, Longfellow rejoiced, was happy to see him in his academic regalia, and participated in some early ceremonies. After attending Felton's funeral, Longfellow noted in his journal (4 Mar 1862): "So passes away the learned scholar, the genial companion, the affectionate, faithful friend!" To Frances Farrer,* who knew Felton, Longfellow wrote (8 May 1862) that Felton "had a wider range of scholarship than any of us." Longfellow missed Felton dreadfully. His sonnet titled "Three Friends of Mine" concerns Felton, Louis Agassiz,* and Sumner.

Bibliography: Campbell, Killis. "Who Was 'Outis'?" *University of Texas Studies in English* 8 (Jul 1928): 107–9; Hilen, ed.; Hillard,* George S. "Memoir of Cornelius Conway Felton." *Proceedings of the Massachusetts Historical Society* 10 (1867–69): 352–68; S. Longfellow; Longfellow, Samuel. "The Five of Clubs." *Christian Science Monitor* (22 Oct 1938): 9; Wagenknecht, 1955.

"FENNEL." *See* "The Goblet of Life."

FIELDS, ANNIE ADAMS (1834–1915). Publisher's wife, hostess, and author. She was born, as Ann West Adams, in Boston and was excellently educated at the George B. Emerson School for Young Ladies in Boston, where she studied French, Italian, and Latin, literature, and much else, including documents relating to the need for fortunate people to commit themselves to unselfish charitable activities. She married James T. Fields,* the prominent Boston publisher (1854). She soon began to preside with unique brilliance over the Fieldses' literary salon at 148 Charles Street, Boston, and did so for sixty years. Her guests, too numerous to list in full, included Longfellow and all of the other writers in Boston and its environs, and their spouses if they were married; Louisa May Alcott (1832–88, Annie Fields's cousin), the poet Celia Thaxter (1835–94), and John Greenleaf Whittier,* for example, were single. The Fieldses' home featured a massive second-floor library, decorated with busts, paintings, sketches, and statues. Two trips to Europe (1859, 1869) enabled them to combine pleasure and business talk with Charles Dickens,* Alfred, Lord Tennyson,* and other British authors whom Fields was publishing in the United States. Dickens, who usually preferred American hotels to American homes, stayed with the Fieldses during his 1867–68 American tour.

No mere hostess, Annie Fields was easily as intelligent as her husband, often was his silent coeditor whose opinions not only he but also his authors sought. For example, she was partly responsible for his accepting *The Gates Ajar* (1868), by Elizabeth Stuart Phelps,* which became a best-seller; and she persuaded Sophia Peabody Hawthorne, the widow of Nathaniel Hawthorne,* to let Fields publish what became Hawthorne's *Passages from the American Notebooks* (1868). Annie Fields was, foremost, a self-sacrificing hostess and charity worker, despite her ambition to be a woman of letters herself. Before her husband's death (1881), she published a work on the Shaker movement (1872), a novel titled *Asphodel* (1866), and *Under the Olive* (1881), a collection of her poems. Her husband willed her all his properties and stocks, totaling $150,872.27. During her long widowhood, she combined work for social reform and women's rights and additional creative writing, including another book of verse (1895), a masque (1900), and almost countless uncollected periodical items. More important are her anonymous biography of Fields (1881) and her books on Whittier (1893), Thaxter (1895, coauthored), her close friend Harriet Beecher Stowe* (1897), and Hawthorne (1899). Her *Authors and Friends* (1896) became a best-seller, remains of immense value, and contains unique information

about Longfellow's popularity and friendships. Meriting mention is her long, intimate friendship with the New England writer Sarah Orne Jewett (1849–1909), beginning in 1881, involving pleasant travel, and resulting in Annie Fields's edition of Jewett's letters (1911).

Longfellow knew James T. Fields professionally and socially before his marriage to Annie and enjoyed their friendship and hospitality for years. He once gratefully wrote Fields (11 Nov 1862) thus: "You and your wife understand the divine art of entertaining, as few people do." Longfellow sent her a copy of his *Tales of a Wayside Inn* and in a letter (18 Jan 1864) thanked her for her effusive expression of pleasure in what she regarded as its almost divinely inspired music. Longfellow commented sparsely on Annie's creative work. He commended her study of the Shakers, saying in a letter to her (3 Sep 1872) that she "treated the theme with great delicacy and sympathy,—the only way in which such a theme can be treated." In another letter to her (18 Nov 1880), Longfellow praises her *Under the Olive* as a "beautiful book."

Bibliography: Green; Howe, M.A. DeWolfe. *Memories of a Hostess: A Chronicle of Eminent Friendships Drawn Chiefly from the Diaries of Mrs. James T. Fields.* Boston: Houghton Mifflin, 1922; James, Henry. "Mr. and Mrs. James T. Fields." *Atlantic Monthly* 116 (Jul 1915): 21–31; S. Longfellow; Roman, Judith A. *Annie Adams Fields: The Spirit of Charles Street.* Bloomington: Indiana University Press, 1990; Tryon.

FIELDS, JAMES T. (1817–81). American publisher and author. James Thomas Fields was born in Portsmouth, New Hampshire. His father was a ship master who died of fever in New Orleans (1819). Young Fields read widely, went to Boston (1831), clerked in what was later called the Old Corner Bookstore, attended the church of William Ellery Channing,* and joined the Mercantile Library Association. William Davis Ticknor (1810–64), a cousin of the scholar George Ticknor,* bought the bookstore (1832), retained Fields, employed him in Ticknor's publishing company, and made him a junior partner (1843) in what became Ticknor, Reed, and Fields (1849). That same year

Fields published his *Poems.* The firm was known as Ticknor and Fields (from 1854). Fields followed James Russell Lowell* as editor of the *Atlantic Monthly* (1861–71), with William Dean Howells* as his assistant (from 1866). When William Ticknor died (1864), Fields became senior partner of his firm, published the *North American Review,* edited by Lowell and Charles Eliot Norton,* and accepted an invitation to join the Saturday Club.*

For decades, Fields was busy publishing the following American authors, among others: Ralph Waldo Emerson,* Bret Harte, Nathaniel Hawthorne,* Oliver Wendell Holmes,* Julia Ward Howe,* Lowell, Harriet Beecher Stowe,* Henry David Thoreau,* John Greenleaf Whittier,* and Longfellow. Fields's first wife, Eliza Josephine Willard, died in 1851, a year after their marriage. In 1854 he married her brilliant young cousin Ann West Adams (*see* Fields, Annie Adams), and the two made their Boston home America's first real literary salon. They knew and entertained almost all of the distinctive New England authors, including Longfellow and the following, among others, all of whom Longfellow knew well: Emerson, Hawthorne, George Stillman Hillard,* Holmes, Julia Ward Howe, Lowell, Harriet Beecher Stowe, and Whittier. Fields visited Europe four times (between 1847 and 1870), always combining business and pleasure. He forced William Ticknor's son Howard Malcolm Ticknor (1836–1905) to sell his interest in the publishing firm and reorganized it as Fields, Osgood, and Company (1868), James Ripley Osgood* having been his associate (since 1855). Fields sold his share in the company for at least $100,000—and perhaps $150,000—and retired (1870). It became James R. Osgood and Company. A farewell party (New Year's Day 1871) gathered many friends, including Longfellow and Howells. Fields began to lecture widely and to write; among less important works, he wrote a splendid book of reminiscences titled *Yesterdays with Authors* (1872), and biographies of Hawthorne (1876) and his closest British friend Charles Dickens* (1876), and published a collection of his own poems (1881). In addition to publishing Dickens in the United States, Fields issued works by

Matthew Arnold, Robert Browning, Thomas De Quincey, Leigh Hunt, Alfred, Lord Tennyson,* and William Makepeace Thackeray*—and honorably paid them royalties instead of pirating their books, as he might legally have done. Thackeray entertained Fields in London, and Fields entertained Thackeray and even managed some of his lectures in Boston.

Longfellow began his professional association with Fields when Fields persuaded Longfellow (1846) to let William Ticknor publish his *Evangeline* and to transfer some earlier books by Longfellow to Ticknor's company. Longfellow publicly praised but privately criticized Fields's *Poems* (1849). Fields published Longfellow's next ten books, including *Kavanagh, The Seaside and the Fireside, The Song of Hiawatha, The Courtship of Miles Standish, Tales of a Wayside Inn, The New England Tragedies,* and popular collections, notably *Poems by Henry Wadsworth Longfellow* (2 vols., 1857). Longfellow often negotiated with Fields for better royalty scales; Fields didn't mind, accommodated him, and also advertised him skillfully. Fields introduced Longfellow to Dickens (Nov 1867). By the late 1860s, Longfellow was Fields's closest professional friend. After Fields retired, Longfellow published with Osgood and then Houghton, Mifflin, successors to Fields's publishing firm. Longfellow, Fields, and their wives were also personal friends. The two entertained one another at home, often dined together at mutual friends' homes, wrote to friends about one another—always sincerely and amiably—and discussed in person and by correspondence Longfellow's manuscripts, details of publishing his works, their sales, and reviews of them both positive and otherwise. Their letters are informative, though often bookish through their habit of paralleling personal events and literary passages, and are at times poignant; would-be poets often sought their help, to their mutual, well-expressed annoyance. When, despite its immense popularity, *The Song of Hiawatha* was the subject of ridicule in some quarters, Fields was so loyal to Longfellow that, according to an anecdote, he thought of suing one reviewer. Fields wanted to delete from a book he was publishing certain adverse comments about Longfellow's "Excelsior," but Longfellow noted this in his journal (29 Dec 1860): "I tell him he had better let them stand." Fields boldly offered changes in some of Longfellow's writings; for example, Fields actually improved the ending of "Paul Revere's Ride." Too soon after Longfellow's wife died, Fields in all sincerity asked Longfellow for a poem to be included in the January 1862 issue of the *Atlantic Monthly;* Longfellow replied, "I can neither write nor think; and have nothing fit to send you, but my love—which you cannot put into the Magazine" (8 Nov 1861). Longfellow was saddened that his friend John Gorham Palfrey* and Fields died in one week. To commemorate Fields's death, Longfellow wrote the tender poem titled "Auf Wiedersehen," subtitled "In Memory of J.T.F."

Bibliography: Austin, James C. "J. T. Fields and the Revision of Longfellow's Poems, Unpublished Correspondence." *New England Quarterly* 24 (June 1951): 239–50; Green; Hilen, ed.; Pye, John William. *James T. Fields: Literary Publisher.* Portland: Baxter Society, 1987; Tryon; Winship, Michael. *American Literary Publishing in the Mid-Nineteenth Century: The Business of Ticknor and Fields.* Cambridge: Cambridge University Press, 1995; Wagenknecht, 1955.

"THE FIFTIETH BIRTHDAY OF [LOUIS] AGASSIZ [*]: MAY 28, 1857" (1858). Poem, in *Dwight's Musical Journal,* 6 Jun 1857; *Courtship, Birds* (1858). Nature some fifty years ago took a child from his cradle in Pays de Vaud (in Neuchâtel, Switzerland) and said that God had written "a story-book" for him. Nature made the child come with her "into regions yet untrod" and to read the secrets "In the manuscripts of God." He wanders still, encouraged by song after song from Nature. When he falters and grows homesick, she continues to hold him. His mother back home wonders why he has never returned to her, for it is now "late and dark." This little poem, with sing-song rhythm and simple rhymes, was neatly set to music by the English composer John Liptrot Hatton (1809–86).

Bibliography: Hilen, ed.

"FIRE" (1878). Sonnet, translated from Michael Angelo, in *Kéramos.* Fire is needed to mould iron, to refine gold, to enable the phoenix to rise. Aging now, the poet hopes through the inspiring, renewing fire within him "to rise again with the divine" at his death.

"THE FIRE OF DRIFT-WOOD" (1850). Poem, in *GM,* Apr 1848; *S/F.* The poet is sitting with others in an old house on Devereux Farm, near Marblehead. A damp sea breeze enters through its windows, beyond which they see the port, the lighthouse, the fort, and wooden houses. Night falls, and the friends talk about "vanished scene[s]," old thoughts and words, past events, altered plans, the dead. They touch on what they felt when first aware that "Their lives . . . have separate ends, / And never can be one again." Memories stir "in the dark." They say too little, too much. Their words leap up, die down, like "the fire / Built of the wreck of stranded ships." As the flames fail, they are put in mind of ships "dismasted" at sea, hailed, and not answering. The windows rattle, the ocean sweeps the beach, and the fire crackles. These sounds penetrate their mental "fancies"—"The long-lost ventures of the heart, / That send no answers back again." Longfellow concludes:

> O flames that glowed! O hearts that yearned!
> They were indeed too much akin,
> The drift-wood fire without that burned,
> The thoughts that burned and glowed within.

It was probably for this poem that the publisher George Rex Graham* paid Longfellow $50, which sum Longfellow mentions receiving from Graham in a letter to Charles Sumner* (16 Feb 1848).

Bibliography: Arms; Hilen, ed.; More.

FITCH, CORNELIA (1838–93). Friend. Longfellow met this beautiful young woman at Nahant, Massachusetts (Jun 1864). She was from Auburn, New York. He was attracted to her, welcomed her at his summer residence at Nahant, and was flattered by her attentions. They corresponded with some frequency. Her letters to him are unrecovered. Her fiancé was killed in the Civil War. Her marriage (Feb 1865) to Brooklyn-lawyer David Ogden Bradley (1827–95) naturally put an end to any close relationship they might have had though not to rumors about their alleged intimacy (or that of his son Charles Appleton Longfellow*) with her.

Bibliography: Bush, Jr., Sargent. "Longfellow's Letters to Cornelia Fitch." *Books at Iowa,* no. 6 (Apr 1967): 13–23; Hilen, ed.

"FLORAL ASTROLOGY." *See* "Flowers."

"A FLORENTINE SONG." Poem, in Scudder. The female persona prefers not to love but does admit that a certain person is attractive. Is it love? Let lovers tell her.

"FLOWER-DE-LUCE" (1866). Poem, in *Flower.* The beautiful flower-de-luce—"the Iris, fair among the fairest"—grows by rivers and laughs at mills, spindles, looms, and wheels. It neither "toil[s] nor spin[s], / But Makest glad and radiant" everything near it. The winds lift it; rushes are "the green yeomen of thy manor"; dragonflies are its mailed attendants, challenging the field. It is the stream-haunting Muse "Playing on pipes of reed the artless ditties / That come to us as dreams." This flower sweetens the world.

FLOWER-DE-LUCE AND OTHER POEMS **(1866).** Collection of poems: "Flower-de-Luce," "Palingenesis," "The Bridge of Cloud," "Hawthorne," "Christmas Bells," "The Wind over the Chimney," "The Bells of Lynn," "Killed at the Ford," "Giotto's Tower," "To-morrow ['Tis late]," "Divina Commedia," "Nöel. . . ."

"FLOWERS" (1837). Poem, as "Floral Astrology," signed "Prof. H.W. Longfellow," in *KM,* Dec 1837; *Voices.* (Longfellow preferred the title "Flowers.") Flowers are stars shining "in earth's firmament." There is a divine linkage between mysterious stars and lowly blossoms, which present a loving message from God. Flowers flaunt their beauty, bud only to decay, bloom at night like wishes, glow, are optimistic, weep, are

lonely, congregate together. They are found in the wilderness, on graves in cathedrals, in rude cottages and old homes. The petals of flowers are "soul-like wings." Their affectionate blossoms hint at our resurrection to "the bright and better land." The opening image, that flowers are stars in the firmament of the earth, derives from "Story without an End" by the German philosopher, Friedrich Wilhelm Carové (1789–1852). "Floral Astrology" was the first poem Longfellow wrote in his Craigie House* upstairs chamber, and he sent it (Oct 1837) with a bouquet of autumn flowers to Fanny Appleton (*see* Longfellow, Fanny). Longfellow quoted part of Carové's "Story" in *Hyperion.*

Bibliography: Arvin; S. Longfellow; Thompson.

FOLSOM, CHARLES (1794–1872). American teacher, classical scholar, and librarian. He was born in Exeter, New Hampshire, graduated from Harvard (1813), taught school, and considered studying divinity and then medicine. He served in the U.S. Navy (1816–17, 1820–21) and as consul at Tunis (1817–19). Back at Harvard, he tutored Latin (1821–23), taught Italian (1825–26), and was librarian (1823–26, 1831). He married Susannah Sarah McKean (1824); they had seven children. He was associated with William Cullen Bryant* as an editor of the *United States Review and Literary Gazette* (1826–27). While he worked for the University Press at Harvard (1826–42), Folsom edited books by significant authors such as Charles Eliot Norton,* John Gorham Palfrey,* William Hickling Prescott,* Josiah Quincy,* and George Ticknor.* Folsom conducted a school for young women (1843–45). He was the librarian of the Boston Athenaeum (1845–56), to which he denied women admission.

Shortly after Longfellow married Mary Potter, he escorted her to Cambridge (Jan 1832), where he met Folsom. The two men corresponded voluminously (until Jan 1833), mostly about publishing grammars and readers Longfellow was writing at the time. Longfellow was especially concerned about the 1832 edition of his 1830 *Manuel de Proverbes Dramatiques.*

Bibliography: Hilen, ed.

"FONTENAY" (1877). Poem, translated from the French poet Guillaume Amfrye de Chaulieu (1639–1720), in *PP,* Scudder. The solitude of Fontenay is preferable to a noisy life. Let the breezes take away memories of sorrow. Let Death claim the poet, patient in the woods here.

"FOOTSTEPS OF ANGELS" (1839). Poem, in *KM,* May 1839; *Voices.* When night falls and firelight casts dancing shadows on the wall, "the forms of the departed" visit the poet. They include one who died while "young and strong," others who meekly suffered, and a beautiful person who loved him when he was young and who "is now a saint in heaven." This "messenger divine" sits near him, takes his hand, and gazes at him with deep, starry eyes. She softly rebukes and then gently blesses him. Though lonely now, the poet is grateful to remember that such a being once lived. This poem, in shorter form, was first called "Evening Shadows," was expanded, and was retitled "Voices of the Night: A Third Psalm of Life." Among other persons, Longfellow is obviously remembering his first wife, Mary. Longfellow noted in his journal (26 Mar 1839) that when his friend Cornelius Conway Felton* read "Footsteps of Angels" to his wife, he said she cried uncontrollably.

Bibliography: Hilen, ed.; Little; S. Longfellow.

"FORSAKEN" (1878). Poem, translated from a German work, in *Kéramos.* In a monologue, a mother abandoned by her husband tells her child that she will never forsake her, and that the child must learn to cherish, endure, and overcome suffering, and never be "False as thy father was to me."

FORSTER, JOHN (1812–76). English biographer and critic. Forster was born in Newcastle-on-Tyne, and was educated there and at London University. He contributed "Lives of the Statesmen of the Commonwealth" (1836–39) for *Cabinet Cyclopedia* (1829–44), edited by Dionysius Lardner (1793–1859). As literary and dramatic critic, Forster contributed to several newspapers and edited the *Foreign Quarterly Review* (1842–43), the *Daily News* (1846), and the *Examiner* (1847–56). He gained fame by publishing his *Treatise on the Popular Progress in England* (1840) and thereafter associated with many of England's leading authors, including Thomas Carlyle, Walter Savage Landor, and Charles Dickens.* Forster's finest work is *The Life of Charles Dickens* (3 vols., 1872–74). His other works include biographies of Oliver Goldsmith (1848; rev. ed., 1854) and Landor (1869).

Dickens introduced Longfellow to Forster when Longfellow was in London (Oct 1842). The three had many congenial meetings, which also included the caricaturist George Cruikshank (1792–1878), the tragedian William Charles Macready (1793–1873), and the portrait painter Daniel Maclise (1806–70). Forster gave Longfellow a copy of *The Statesmen of the Commonwealth of England* in its 1840 book form. On returning home, Longfellow sent Forster a copy of his *Poems on Slavery,* for which, even before receiving it, Forster wrote, "Heartily I thank you for having entered that field. Go on, with all our prayers!" (3 Jan 1843). He also promised to review it favorably, which he did, in the *Examiner.* Longfellow wrote Forster (28 Feb 1843) to explain that in those poems he "attempted only to invest the subject with a poetic coloring," to add glowing words about Forster's hospitality, and to point out jocosely that the figure of speech about a church shadow moving through the churchyard in Dickens's *Martin Chuzzlewit* (1843–44) was plagiarized from an identical one in Longfellow's preface to his *Ballads and Other Poems* (1841). In "American Poetry," a generally derogatory essay in the *Foreign Quarterly Review* (1844), Forster called Longfellow "unquestionably the first of her [America's] poets." According to his journal, Longfellow appreciated reading Forster's life of Goldsmith because of its "sympathy with literary labor and literary sorrow" (30 Aug 1848). In a letter to Forster (17 Oct 1848), Longfellow calls his work on Goldsmith "one of the most delicious books of biography ever penned." Forster wrote Longfellow (4 Sep 1848) to praise *Evangeline,* called it "beautiful and masterly," but quibbled about its hexameter verse form (4 Sep 1848). Forster helped negotiate terms (1868) with George Routledge (1812–88), the British publisher, for issuing Longfellow's *The New England Tragedies.* Forster even did some of the proofreading of it. When Longfellow wrote James T. Fields* from Vevey, Switzerland (5 Sep 1868), he immodestly quoted a letter from Forster on Longfellow's *New England Tragedies*—"beauty everywhere subduing and chastening the sadness," with the story of Giles Corey possessing "a strange attractiveness." In a touching letter to Forster (12 Jun 1870), Longfellow commiserated with him on Dickens's death and also thanked him for sending him a copy of Forster's biography of Landor. When his biography of Dickens appeared, Longfellow was saddened to read too many details about Dickens's unhappy marriage but praised Forster for truthfulness (13 Jun 1873).

Bibliography: Davies, James A. *John Forster: A Literary Life.* Totowa: Barnes & Noble Books, 1983; Hilen, ed.; Wagenknecht, 1955.

"FOUR BY THE CLOCK" (1882). Poem, in *Harbor.* As the world wheels its cities and ships toward the dawn, the poet sees only a lighted bark and hears only "the heavy breathing of the sea." The poem is dated 4:00 A.M., 8 September 1880, Nahant.

Bibliography: More.

"THE FOUR LAKES OF MADISON" (1882). Poem, in *Harbor.* The four lakes resemble handmaidens holding their mirrors "To the fair city in the West." During the day their waters are sipped by the sun; at night they reflect the stars. The lakes are serene; the city, "in robes of light." All seems dreamlike. The four lakes—Kegonsa, Mendota, Monona, and Waubesa—are in, or near, Madison, Wisconsin. Longfellow wrote this poem in response to a request from Amelia Chapman Thorp (1815–1908), who was president of the Women's State Centennial Executive Committee of Wisconsin. Mrs. Thorp was also the mother-in-law of Longfellow's friend Ole Bornemann Bull.*

Bibliography: Hilen, ed.

"THE FOUR PRINCESSES AT WILNA: A PHOTOGRAPH" (1878). Sonnet, in *Kéramos.* The sweet, innocent faces of four princesses look down from "pictured casements," epitomizing "youth and beauty and the fair renown / Of a great name, that ne'er hath tarnished been!" A voice from the street seems to be singing about faith, hope, and love, and to be concluding that "the greatest of the three is Love." Wilna is undoubtedly Vilnius (then in Poland), Lithuania.

"A FRAGMENT" (1882). Poem, in *Harbor.* It is necessary to respond to angels when they knock at the door. Athletes should strive, not rest. Good land, untilled, will produce "weeds at best."

"FRAGMENT OF A MODERN BALLAD." *See* "The Happiest Land."

"FRAGMENTS." Four dated poems, in Scudder, each beginning as quoted hereinafter. "Neglected record of a mind neglected": The poet can record little here about his neglected thoughts concerning past, present, and future (22 Oct 1838). "O faithful, indefatigable tides": The tides go out, hastily or patiently, bearing things from the land, then come in again, burdened, sometimes bothered by rocks (18 Aug 1847). "Soft through the silent air descend the feathery snowflakes": The snow softly whitens hills and fields; the hue of the river among the brown hills remains leaden, like what the blind see (18 Dec 1847). "So from the bosom of darkness our days come roaring and gleaming": Each day roars into light, sinks into the dark, and leaves evidence on Time's shore, which is soon washed away (4 Aug 1856).

FREILIGRATH, FERDINAND (1810–76). Man of letters. Hermann Ferdinand Freiligrath, born in Detmold, Germany, was a precocious, prolific linguist and translator, mastering Dutch, English, French, Greek, Italian, and Latin, in addition to his native German. He was educated to become a businessman, worked in an Amsterdam bank and a commercial house in Barmen, Germany, but changed careers after publishing a book of poetry titled *Gedichte* (1838). His early exotic and romantic poems soon gave way to radical political-protest verse. He married Ida Melos (1841); they had four children. He met Karl Marx in Brussels (1844). For safety, Freiligrath exiled himself to Belgium and Zurich, Switzerland (1845), and London (1846), where out of financial necessity he resumed a commercial career but where he also published an anthology of modern English poems (*Englische Gedichte aud neuerer Zeit* [1846]). Returning to Germany by way of a general amnesty (1848), he was soon arrested for publishing more incendiary verse, was tried on a charge of lèse majesté but was acquitted, and briefly edited Marx's and Friedrich Engels's *Neue rheinische Zeitung* (1848–49). Freiligrath had to flee to London (1851), where in what time he could find after long days in merchants' offices he translated assiduously. His *Der Sang von Hiawatha* appeared in 1857. He managed the London branch of a Swiss bank (1856–65), lost faith in Marxism, and became a British subject (1858). When the branch bank closed, Freiligrath faced unemployment and financial embarrassment, until friends and sympathetic readers poured excessive sums of money at him. He returned to Germany, technically a fugitive from justice but in actuality a welcomed celebrity of international renown (1868). He settled in Stuttgart. During the Franco-Prussian War (1870), he wrote in support of Germany in the belief that it was defending itself. He moved to nearby Cannstat (1875), where he died. Among the many authors whose works he translated, in addition to Longfellow, are the following: Robert Burns, Bret Harte, Victor Hugo, Molière, Walt Whitman, and William Wordsworth.

While summering at the Marienberg baths in Germany (1842), Longfellow met Freiligrath at nearby St. Goar. They immediately became firm friends. Together they read some German translations of Finnish poetry (in *Finnische Runen*), the meters of some of which Longfellow later used in *The Song of Hiawatha.* In his journal (12 Jun 1842), Longfellow calls Freiligrath "one of the best young poets of Germany," praises his poetry as "fresh and *virtuous,*" and comments favorably on Freiligrath's "agreeable" wife. A

day later, from Marienberg, he sent Freiligrath two of his own books. In a letter (20 Jul 1842), Longfellow praises his new friend for "superb[ly]" translating his "The Skeleton in Armor." Two days later he thanks Freiligrath for his "exceedingly fine" translation of "Excelsior." Longfellow wrote Freiligrath (24 Sep 1842) from "Nürnberg" and saw him a final time in St. Goar five days later. From London, Longfellow sent Freiligrath two more of his works. After returning home, Longfellow wrote Freiligrath (6 Jan 1843) to summarize his movements after leaving his German friend, whom he never saw again. He goes on to praise a couple of Freiligrath's poems. In later years, the two poets corresponded with mutual affection and admiration. Longfellow often provided Americans traveling abroad with letters of recommendation to Freiligrath and tried, unsuccessfully, to get him out of exile in London (1847) and into an American professorship of languages. Longfellow even endeavored, with others, to raise $2,000 to help defray travel and other expenses for Freiligrath. Freiligrath calls *Evangeline* "a masterpiece" (11 Mar 1848). To Freiligrath, in exile in London again, Longfellow wrote (16 Jul 1851) to express sorrow but to add that it "is the greatest compliment to the power of your song [his antiroyalist poetry]." When Longfellow was planning to resign his professorship at Harvard, he wrote Freiligrath (3 May 1854) to say he was recommending him as his replacement, adding, however, his doubt as to a favorable outcome. He wrote Freiligrath (25 Apr 1855) to report that James Russell Lowell* got the appointment; Longfellow sent this letter via Nathaniel Hawthorne,* then consul to Liverpool. Freiligrath wrote Longfellow from London (7 Dec 1855) to comment favorably on the meter and use of parallelism in *Hiawatha,* and to point to analogues in Finnish poetry. Longfellow wrote Freiligrath (11 Jan 1856) that Freiligrath seemed unaware that parallelism is common both in Indian and in Finnish songs. When Freiligrath's translation of *Hiawatha* arrived, Longfellow wrote (29 Jan 1857) in high praise and to agree with his prefatory statement that in the last canto "The contact of Saga and History is too close" but to add that he too "felt the clash and concussion, but could not prevent nor escape it" except by lengthening the poem excessively; Longfellow also lamented an error he made in describing sturgeons in his poem. In his reply to Longfellow (2 Apr 1857), Freiligrath tells him not to worry about such a petty error, since "Little inaccuracies of this kind must never be wanting in a work of genius. They are the bones for the critical curs to gnaw at." Longfellow wrote Freiligrath (14 Mar 1861) to praise an essay he had written on Samuel Taylor Coleridge. After Freiligrath wrote to express his sympathy following the death of Fanny, Longfellow tardily replied (28 Apr 1862), sending his thanks but adding that saying more "makes my fatal wound ache and bleed too much." Longfellow wrote his old friend (24 May 1867) to reminisce, to hope to meet again, preferably on the Rhine, and to say, "I have always loved you, and never for a moment has my feeling abated or changed." On the same day (24 May 1867), Longfellow, constantly generous, wrote his London publisher George Routledge (1812–88) to ask him to make £100 available to Freiligrath. He wrote Freiligrath (12 Aug 1867) to express his joy that Freiligrath had been welcomed home again to Germany. When Freiligrath died, Longfellow wrote a tender letter to his widow Ida Freiligrath (21 Mar 1876), in which he calls his friend "gentle" and "noble," and says he "loved him as a brother." Richard Henry Dana Jr.* asked Longfellow to compose an elegy on Freiligrath; the poet declined but sent a sizable contribution to his memorial. Freiligrath was Longfellow's closest European friend.

Bibliography: Appelman, Maria. *H. W. Longfellow's Beziehungen zu Ferdinand Freiligrath.* Münster: Westfälische Bereinsdrucherie, 1915; Hatfield, James Taft. "The Longfellow-Freiligrath Correspondence." *PMLA* 49 (Dec 1933): 1223–93; Hilen, ed.; S. Longfellow; Wagenknecht, 1955.

"THE FRENCH LANGUAGE IN ENGLAND" (1840). Article, in *NAR*, Oct 1840. Longfellow wrote the piece reluctantly, and doing so, he complained, caused him headaches.

Bibliography: Thompson.

FRERE, ALICE MARY (1842–?). English friend. She visited Longfellow (1867) in Boston, accompanied by her father, a judge of the High Court of Bombay. According to his journal (1 Apr 1867), Longfellow spent an evening with Miss Frere and the judge, and partly alone with her, the night before the Freres left for New York. She amiably wrote Longfellow (3 Apr 1867) from New York, enclosing her photograph; wrote again (6 Apr), thanking him for photographs of his study; and wrote again (also 6 Apr) to report her three-year engagement to Godfrey Clerk (1835–1908), a British rifle-brigade major. Longfellow sent her a letter (3 Apr), now lost, which crossed with hers. He wrote again (5 Apr), to praise her photograph; to express a wish that he were going to England too; to quote some lines of poetry in German by Novalis (Friedrich von Hardenberg [1772–1801]), about the propriety and logic of the development of love; to send her "a proof sheet of Dante," one of ten just arrived from London (of his translation of *The Divine Comedy*); and to lament her absence from a dinner (undoubtedly in Cambridge or Boston) to which she had been invited. Learning of her engagement, he replied (8 Apr) that "I rejoice in your happiness as if it were my own"; that he was sending her a copy of the Boston edition of his translation of *The Divine Comedy;* that her photograph reminded him of certain cited lines from Dante about a bird whose pre-dawn desire is appeased by hoping; that he won't go to New York to say goodbye to her aboard her steamer; that he regards the memory of their evening alone as "sacred and precious"; that he knows she'll keep secret what he told her, which was "the cry of my soul"; and that he wouldn't have told her if he had known her secret, about which he begs her to tell him more. He wrote her a sentimental reminiscence (18 May 1867) about her being in his study and about how he was checking her addresses on a London map. She wrote Longfellow (2 Jul 1867) to praise his Dante work extravagantly. He replied (18 Jul 1867) to congratulate her on her approaching marriage (30 July; she was to have at least one son); to say that he was not going to England soon; but to hope that, if he did later, he might find her there or in Egypt.

She wrote from Suez (22 Sep 1867) and sent a photograph of her husband; he gratefully replied (22 Dec 1867) and said that if he should return to England he would like to stay at the Derbyshire inn where she honeymooned! When he did get to Europe again, he replied from Paris (4 Oct 1868) to her invitation (13 Jul 1868) to visit her in Egypt; declined; said he found her name in the Derbyshire inn guest book; and said his son Charles Appleton Longfellow,* on his way to India, might see her along the route. In reply to her letter from India (24 Feb 1874), Longfellow wrote (5 May 1874) to acknowledge the receipt earlier of a copy of *Historical Tales and Anecdotes of the Time of the Early Khalifahs* (1873), which she had translated from Arabic and annotated; he also commented on his treasured photograph of her and to assure her of his abiding affection. Aspects of Longfellow's relationship with Alice Mary Frere remain missing parts of an intriguing puzzle.

Bibliography: Hilen, ed.; Wagenknecht, 1955.

"FRIAR LUBIN" (1831) Poem, translated from the French court poet Clément Marot (1495?-1544), in *NAR,* Apr 1831. Friar Lubin may be counted on to sin vilely in town, steal, woo innocent girls without benefit of panders, and drink. Don't look for evidence of piety, generosity, or sobriety in him.

FRIENDS LONGFELLOW KNEW CASU-ALLY. In addition to the scores of close friends, Longfellow made contact of a more casual sort, sometimes mainly by correspondence, with the following, several of whom visited him at his home in his later years: Thomas Bailey Aldrich (1836-1907), popular author, Boston-based editor. Grand Duke Alexis Aleksandrovich of Russia (1850-1908). Samuel Austin Allibone (1816-89), editor, biographical-dictionary compiler. Rasmus Björn Anderson (1846-1936), Norwegian author, teacher, diplomat. Duke of Argyll, George John Douglas (1823-1900), Scottish politician. Frédéric Auguste Bartholdi (1834-1909), French sculptor, whose *Statue of Liberty* was presented to the United States after Longfellow's death. Robert Bigsby (1806-73), British antiquarian, collector of memorabilia of the illustrious. William Black (1841-98), Scottish journalist, novelist. George William Childs (1829-94), distinguished Philadelphia publisher. Lewis Gaylord Clark (1808-73), editor of the *Knickerbocker Magazine* (1834-60), publisher of items by Longfellow; Lewis's twin brother, Willis Gaylord Clark (1808-41), poet, reviewer. Wilkie Collins (1824-89), popular English novelist. Moncure Daniel Conway (1832-1907), clergyman, abolitionist, author. Anthanase Laurent Charles Coquerel (1795-1868), liberal French clergyman, pastor in Paris. George Cruikshank (1792-1878), English caricaturist, illustrator. Lord Dufferin, Frederick Temple Hamilton-Temple-Blackwood (1826-1902), British diplomat, and his distinguished wife, formerly Hariot Hamilton. Charlotte Cushman (1816-76), leading American actress; and her companion, Matilda B. Hays (1820-?), actress, editor, translator. Felix Octavius Carr Darley (1822-88), Philadelphia-born illustrator of books, including those of James Fenimore Cooper, Charles Dickens,* Washington Irving,* and Longfellow. Julia Caroline Ripley Dorr (1825-1913), poet, novelist from Rutland, Vermont. Samuel Eliot (1821-98), American historian, educator. Charles Albert Fechter (1824-79), English Shakespearean actor. James Anthony Froude (1818-94), English historian. Richard Watson Gilder (1844-1909), American editor, poet. Minnie Hauk (1852?-1929), American operatic soprano. Paul Hamilton Hayne (1830-86), American poet. Sir Joseph Dalton Hooker (1817-191l), English botanist, traveler. Joaquin Miller (1841?-1913), western American poet. Lord Houghton, Richard Monckton Milnes (1809-85), English poet, generous friend of American authors. Thomas Hughes (1822-96), English jurist, reformer, author of the famous *Tom Brown* novels. Henry James Sr. (1811-82), philosopher, author, father of William James (1842-1910), philosopher, and Henry James (1843-1916), author. Charles Kingsley (1819-75), English clergyman, novelist. Johann Georg Kohl (1808-78), German geographer, author. Sidney Lanier (1842-81), Confederate Army veteran from Georgia, poet, novelist. Sara Jane Clarke Lippincott

(1823-1904), popular writer using the pen name "Grace Greenwood." Henry Cabot Lodge (1850-1924), American statesman, author, editor. George Macdonald (1824-1905), Scottish novelist, poet, lecturer. Karl August Nicander (1799-1849), Swedish poet. Christine Nilson (1843-1921), Swedish soprano, violinist. Francis Parkman (1823-93), American historian. Edward Hayes Plumptre (1821-91), English theological and classical scholar, who translated Sophocles and Aeschylus in verse. Bonamy Price (1807-88), English economist, free-trade advocate. Ede Réményi (1830-98), Hungarian violinist, who occasionally toured the United States beginning in 1849. Bernard Rölker (1816-88), Westphalia-born teacher of German at Harvard (1838-56), also New York resident. John Ruskin (1819-1900), Victorian art critic, man of letters. Tommaso Salvini (1829-1916), Italian tragedian, who frequently toured the United States beginning in 1873. Epes Sargent (1813-80), American editor, man of letters. Carl Schurz (1829-1906), German revolutionary, migrant to the United States (1852), Union Army officer during the Civil War, later liberal politician, editor. The Sedgwick family, distantly related to Longfellow's wife Fanny and including Susan Anne Livingston Ridley Sedgwick (1788-1867), author of juvenile novels, and Catharine Maria Sedgwick (1789-1867), phenomenally popular domestic novelist. Arthur Penrhyn Stanley (1815-81), English prelate, canon of Canterbury, then dean of Westminster. Richard Henry Stoddard (1825-1903), New York poet, critic, and Mrs. Richard Henry Stoddard (Elizabeth Drew Barstow [1823-1902]), novelist, poet. Mary Potter Thacher (1844-1941 [Mrs. Thomas Wentworth Higginson]), poet. Martin Farquhar Tupper (1810-89), popular English man of letters. Henry Wilson (1812-75), U.S. senator (1855-73), U.S. vice president (1873-75) during President Ulysses S. Grant's administration. Edwin Percy Whipple (1819-86), Massachusetts-born lecturer, man of letters, contributor to the *North American Review.* William Winter (1836-1917), New York drama critic, man of letters.

Longfellow also maintained an extensive correspondence with other authors, teachers, American and foreign publishers, translators, artists, and politicians, some of whom he never met. Exigencies of space prevent the inclusion here of dozens of additional names of persons, once significant, some surely less so, but all of whom Longfellow treated with admiration and to all of whom he was gracious and generous with his time. For example, when Louise Reid Estes (?-1883), wife of the Boston publisher Dana Estes (1840-1909), asked Longfellow for his signatures to be inserted into copies of a benefit publication, he sent her fifty (8 Dec 1879).

Bibliography: Hilen, ed.; Gorman, Herbert S. *A Victorian American: Henry Wadsworth Longfellow.* New York: George H. Doran, 1926.

"FRITHIOF'S FAREWELL" (1837). Poem, translated from the Swedish poet Esaias Tegnér,* in *NAR,* July 1837; Scudder. Frithiof, outlawed, laments that the ocean will be his grave and that his bones may wash ashore one day. The king tells him not to whimper like a girl but realize that everyone who is born has to die. *See Drift-Wood.*

"FRITHIOF'S HOMESTEAD" (1837). Poem, translated from the Swedish poet Esaias Tegnér,* in *NAR,* July 1837; Scudder. The hero Frithiof's farmland is extensive, as is his livestock. His banquet hall holds more than 500 men. At the ends of its polished oak table are statues of the gods Odin and Frey carved in elm wood. Thorsten, the gray-bearded bard, speaks. Stars look down on the hearth fire and the armor on the walls. Blushing maidens go about filling the drinking horns. *See Drift-Wood.*

"FRITHIOF'S TEMPTATION" (1837). Poem, translated from the Swedish poet Esaias Tegnér,* in *NAR,* July 1837; Scudder. Spring comes. Frithiof goes hunting with the gray-haired old king. Frithiof is tempted by the beautiful queen, riding along with them. When the king rests his head on Frithiof's knee to sleep, a black bird tells him to kill the king and grab the queen, who once kissed him; a white bird tells him no hero would behave this way. Frithiof throws his sword into the woods. The king wakes up, rested, and asks where Frithiof's sword is. Frithiof replies that gray hair maddens his steel sword and that other blades are available to him. *See Drift-Wood.*

"FROM MY ARM-CHAIR" (1880). Poem, in the *Cambridge Tribune,* 14 Mar 1879, and other newspapers; *Thule.* On Longfellow's seventy-second birthday (27 Feb 1879), the children of Cambridge presented the revered poet a chair made from the wood of the chestnut tree of the village blacksmith (*see* "The Village Blacksmith"). He writes them that he feels like a king "by divine right of song." He remembers the cool shade the tree cast in the summer, the bees hiving in it, and autumn winds causing it to shed "shining chestnuts." Now some of its bare branches, converted into a chair, "whisper of the past." Unlike that Danish king (Canute [994?-1035]), Longfellow can thus roll Time's tide back. He can see the children now, hear the bees, and see and hear the fire and the smithy's hammer there. His heart remembers. He is glad that the leafless, dead wood blossoms now "in song."

"FROM THE [SPANISH] CANCIONEROS" (1873). Four poems translated from the Spanish, in *Aftermath; Scudder.*

1. "Eyes So Tristful, Eyes So Tristful" is by an obscure poet named Diego de Saldaña. The sad eyes of the person addressed have awakened the poet to renewed distress. Comfortless, he dare not say "to what ye have betrayed me."

2. "Some Day, Some Day" is by the obscure poet Cristóbal de Gastillejo. If Love gives birth to grief, "Six feet of earth" provide painless rest.

3. "Come, O Death, So Silent Flying" is by "El Commendador Escriva." The persona asks death, silently approaching, to comply with his "wish" and take him away while he is "unconscious lying," because while he is awake "Life is but a task ungrateful" and dying is "a sweet delight."

4. "Glove of Black in White Hand Bare" is by an unnamed poet. The woman with black glove, white hand, pale forehead, regal attitude, and "coquettish charms" is not in mourning but aims at "killing men that live."

Longfellow found these Spanish poems in an anthology compiled by Eugenio de Ochoa (1815-72) and titled *Tesoro de los Romanceros y Concioneros Españoles* (1838); Longfellow included his translations of them in *Aftermath.*

Bibliography: Scudder.

"THE FUGITIVE" (1872). Poem, translated from the prose version of the Polish poet Aleksander Chodzko (1804?-91), in *AM,* Sep 1870; *Three.* The Khan asks his proud, rebellious only son to return home, with his hawks and his horses, and accept his father's coat of leather and steel. The son replies that he is slave only to Allah and will be cared for by Allah in deserts and mountains. Sobra, immemorially old and having seen much, advises the Khan not to seek "the star-white man." God brought him forth one dawn and gave him grace; angels taught him; he said "There is no God but God!"; he shall be king of all; God accepted his prayer, to which Gabriel said, "Amen!"

FULLER, MARGARET (1810–50). Journalist, editor, and social reformer. Sarah Margaret Fuller was born in Cambridgeport, Massachusetts, the eldest of nine children. She studied in a private girls' school at Groton (1823-24) and became friendly with several Harvard students (1824-33). When her father died (1835), Margaret became the breadwinning head of the family. She met Ralph Waldo Emerson* (1836), treasured his friendship, and also met many other New England intellectuals. She taught, tutored in German and Italian at various locales, and translated works from German originals (1836-44). She founded and briefly edited the *Dial* (1840-42). After traveling to Chicago and visiting its environs (1843), she published *Summer on the Lakes, in 1843* (1844), which impressed Horace Greeley so much that he hired her to be literary critic for the New York *Daily-Tribune* (1844-46). She published her controversial, seminal *Woman in the Nineteenth Century* (1845), collected her newspaper essays in *Papers on Literature and Art* (1846), and went to Europe as Greeley's foreign correspondent in England, Scotland, and France (1846).

Margaret Fuller supported Giuseppe Mazzine's efforts to free and unify Italy. She met and became involved with Marquis Giovanni Angelo Ossoli in Rome, and pregnant, perhaps married him (1847). She gave birth to their son Angelo Ossoli (1848). After the Roman Republic was proclaimed, the French laid siege to Rome (Apr-Jun 1849). She performed heroic hospital work. When the Republic fell, the Ossolis went from Rome to Florence, then sailed for America (1850). All three drowned in a shipwreck off Fire Island, New York. Her book-length manuscript detailing the Italian Revolution went down with the ship. Posthumous works include *Life Without and Life Within* (1859) and *Memoirs of Margaret Fuller Ossoli,* edited by Emerson and others (2 vols., 1852).

Fuller was never able to admire Longfellow's poetry. She did not greatly deviate from her early position on the subject reflected in the following passage, taken from her review of Longfellow's *Poems* (1845) in the *New-York Daily Tribune* (10 Dec 1845): "We must confess to a coolness toward Mr. Longfellow, in consequence of the exaggerated praises that have been bestowed upon him. When we see a person of moderate powers receive honors which should be reserved for the highest, we feel somewhat like assailing him and taking from him the crown which should be reserved for grander brows. . . . Mr. Longfellow has been accused of plagiarism. We have been surprised that

any one should have been anxious to fasten special charges of this kind upon him, when we supposed it so obvious that the greater part of his mental stores were derived from the work of others. He has no style of his own growing out of his own experience and observation of nature. Nature with him, whether human or external, is always seen through the windows of literature."

Longfellow, hardly ruffled when he read the review, noted only the following in his journal (11 Dec 1845): "Miss Fuller makes a furious onslaught upon me in The New York Tribune. It is what might be called 'a bilious attack.'" He had enjoyed reading her translation of *Eckermann's Conversations with Goethe* (1839). A later journal entry (11 Oct 1849) notes this: "We hear that Margaret Fuller is married in Italy, to a revolutionary marquis." Still later, after spending "an afternoon and evening" reading her *Memoirs,* he added this in his journal (12 Feb 1852): "Extremely interesting." According to a letter he wrote to Charles Sumner* (19 Feb 1852), Longfellow found that *Memoirs of Margaret Fuller Ossoli* (2 vols., 1852) "interested us deeply."

Bibliography: Blanchard, Paula. *Margaret Fuller: From Transcendentalism to Revolution.* New York: Delacorte Press/Seymour Lawrence, 1978; Brown, Arthur W. *Margaret Fuller.* New York: Twayne Publishers, 1964; Hilen, ed.; *Mrs. Longfellow.*

G

"THE GALAXY" (1875). Sonnet, in *Pandora, Birds* (1875). To some, this "Torrent of light and river of the air" is a mountain stream bared and showing golden and silvery sand. The Spaniards see it as their celestially armored patron saint's path. The fable makes it Phaeton's hoof-scorched race track. The poet, however, sees it as star dust spun from God's "invisible chariot-wheels."

"GALGANO: A TALE OF GIOVANNI FIOR-ENTINO" (1853). Poem, in *PM,* May 1853. In Siena, old Count Salvatore's young wife has a hand so beautiful that it nearly crazes rich young Galgano. She is called Bella Mano. In May, love is in the air. Galgano wears Bella's glove on his helmet at joustings. Tucked under his vest at banquets, it seems to be pressing his heart. Sadly, she stays "loyal to her wedded lord." To escape the summer heat, Salvatore takes Bella to his Tuscan mansion. Galgano comes riding along in the woods nearby, with a hooded falcon, is invited by Salvatore to spend the night, but declines and rides on. Returning to Bella, Salvatore "discoursed with liberal tongue" about Galgano's fine qualities. She blushes. They see Galgano's falcon circle in the sky, dive at a bird, kill it, then "spurn / His lifeless quarry" and fly away. Salvatore says that it was Galgano's falcon, which, he adds, Galgano "much . . . resemble[s]." Bella turns pale. As fate would have it, she becomes hopelessly enamoured of Galgano. The very winds whisper to her about his amorousness. One night, when Salvatore is away on official business, Bella sends a messenger to Galgano's house to say she will be his. Rejoicing, he gallops toward her garden gate. She repents, but "too late"; so she figures she might as well surrender to "her destiny!" When he arrives at the dark mansion, "An unseen hand" unlocks and unchains various doors. She welcomes him in her chamber, lays her beautiful hand on his, and offers herself to him. First, Galgano asks for an explanation. When she says that old Salvatore sang young Galgano's praises, the youth resists, contritely says he won't betray Salvatore's friendship, and rushes home. Ever after, Galgano feels released, aware that right has triumphed, and holds his head nobly high. Longfellow apparently replaced this poem with "The Falcon of Ser Federigo," in *Tales of a Wayside Inn.* "Galgano" remains uncollected.

Bibliography: Allaback, Steven. "Longfellow's 'Galgano.'" *American Literature* 46 (May 1974): 210–19; Hilen, ed.

"GASPAR BECERRA" (1850). Poem, in *S/F.* The sculptor is ashamed when he is unable to fashion a statue of the Virgin out of "precious wood" imported from the "distant East," finds relief of his humiliation in sleep, and hears a voice tell him to use a "burning brand of oak" from his hearth as material. He awakens, quenches "the glowing wood," and succeeds well. The moral? "That is best which lieth nearest; / Shape from that thy work of art." This poem is based on a story Longfellow found in *Annals of the Artists of*

Spain (1848) by William Stirling-Maxwell (1818–78). Longfellow wrote "Gaspar Becerra" in 1849, but as time went on he followed its lesson less and less.

Bibliography: Arvin; Wagenknecht, 1986.

"THE GHOST'S WALK." Unpublished and perhaps never-written poem. *See* Prescott, William Hickling.

"GILES COREY OF THE SALEM FARMS." *See The New England Tragedies.*

"GIOTTO'S TOWER" (1866). Sonnet, in *Flower.* Many sweet, restrained, uncomplaining persons devoted to answering the requests of the Holy Spirit lack nothing but a halo such as artists paint above saints' foreheads. So it is with Giotto's tower, that "lily of Florence blossoming in stone" but lacking "the glory of the spire."

"A GLEAM OF SUNSHINE" (1846). Poem, in *Bruges.* The horseman pauses where the past and the present seem to converge. The highway heads toward the town. A "green lane" leads to the church, which he and his beloved once attended. Her dress resembled lilies, and her heart was as pure. She was a messenger from God. The choir sang comfortingly. Sunlight streamed in. The sermon, about Ruth, was long but seemed short. During the prayer, he thought of his beloved. Now she is gone. But remembrance of her lightens his past, the way the sun, hidden by a near cloud. "Shines on a distant field."

"THE GLEANER OF SAPRI" (1871). Poem, translated from the Italian poet-professor Luigi Mercantini (1821–72), in the Supplement to *Poets and Poetry of Europe,* ed. Longfellow; Scudder. The persona, a peasant woman, paused while "glean[ing] the grain," saw three hundred young men land on the shore, kiss the sand, and march to Certosa. She saw them take weapons from guardsmen, attack suicidally, and be destroyed by a thousand enemy soldiers. Longfellow uses this refrain: "They were three hundred, they were young and strong, / And they are dead!" The military disaster was that of Carlo Pisacane, ex-Neapolitan officer, killed with his men while attacking Sapri, in Calabria, by forces loyal to the Kingdom of Naples (summer 1857).

Bibliography: S. Longfellow; Scudder.

"GLOVE OF BLACK IN WHITE HAND BARE." *See* "From the [Spanish] Cancioneros."

"THE GOBLET OF LIFE" (1842). Poem, in *GM,* Jan 1842; *Ballads.* The poet looks through tears at life's goblet, brimming with colorful bubbles. Its waters can startle the heart's fountains, which run off wastefully. Better it is to press fennel into the goblet, for its bitter juices provide a gladiatorial, fearless strength as well as "New light" to see the "foeman's face." Therefore pray "for strength to bear" care's weight "That crushes into dumb despair / One half the human race." The poet pledges "sad humanity" this fennel-laced "cup of grief." After Life's brief fight, "sleep we side by side." This unusually astringent poem, with twelve five-line stanzas has a curious rhyme scheme: *aaaab, ccccb, dddde, fffe,* and so on. Longfellow first thought of titling this poem "Fennel."

Bibliography: Arvin.

GODEY, LOUIS ANTOINE (1804–78). Publisher. Born in New York and largely self-educated, Godey moved to Philadelphia, worked for the *Daily Chronicle,* and with Charles Alexander, its editor, established the *Lady's Book* (1830). Godey married Maria Catherine Duke (1833); they had five children. He bought the *Ladies' Magazine,* edited by Sarah Josepha Hale* (1837), merged it with the *Ladies' Magazine* (1837), retitled it *Godey's Lady's Book* (1837), and retained Ms. Hale as editor until he sold it (1877). It was the first woman's periodical in the United States. Many important writers appeared in it, including Ralph Waldo Emerson,* Oliver Wendell Holmes,* Sara Jane Clarke Lippincott (1823–1904, "Grace Greenwood"), Edgar Allan Poe,* Harriet Beecher Stowe,* and John Greenleaf Whittier,* partly because Godey paid for what he published— an unusual practice then.

Through a friend Godey asked Longfellow to contribute (1846). He courteously declined, on the grounds that at that time he was publishing poems exclusively in *Graham's Magazine,* owned by George Rex Graham.* Later, however, Longfellow sold "The Evening Star" to Godey (1849). See "Chrysaor."

Bibliography: Finley, Ruth E. *The Lady of Godey's: Sarah Josepha Hale.* Philadelphia: J. B. Lippincott, 1931; Hilen, ed.

"GOD'S-ACRE" (1841). Poem, in the *Democratic Review,* Dec 1841; *Ballads.* The "Saxon phrase" for a burial ground, "God's-Acre" (sometimes printed as "God's Acre") appropriately consecrates and blesses the dead. "[T]he sleeping dust" therein is "The seed," the dead "garnered." We will all be placed in that acre's "furrows," to rise in a splendid harvest when the final trumpet will "winnow . . . the chaff and grain." "Then . . . the good" will "bloom, / In the fair gardens of that second birth," with unique fragrance. So, Death, plough away here in God's "place where human harvests grow!" Despite these nice thoughts, Longfellow wrote Samuel Ward * (24 Oct 1841) that he would like to be cremated, not buried. Longfellow wrote but then omitted a final stanza, in which the Elysian Fields and golden harvests are said to be visible beyond the Gates of Paradise.

Bibliography: S. Longfellow.

"THE GOLDEN LEGEND." *See Christus: A Mystery.*

"THE GOLDEN MILESTONE" (1858). Poem, in *Courtship, Birds* (1858). Outside, trees are leafless, smoke comes from village chimneys, and evening "lamps . . . glimmer." Beside hearths in many homes, old men muse, youths dream, and married couples are involved in tragedy, with "God the sole spectator." Many a family awaits "a well-known footstep in the passage." "Each man's chimney is his Golden Mile-stone." From it he measures the distance to every spot his life takes him in this world. Far away, he "Hears the talking flame, the answering night-wind," exactly as he once heard those dear to him but now gone. Do hope never to be exiled from your ancestral hearth. We can build more beautiful homes, "But we cannot / Buy with gold the old associations!" The *milliarium aureum* in the Forum was the mark from which the distance from Rome to anywhere was measured. The form of "The Golden Mile-Stone" is unusually effective. It has twelve, four-line rhymeless stanzas. Lines one, two, and four of each stanza are in trochaic tetrameter; all third lines, in trochaic dimeter.

Bibliography: Arvin.

"THE GOOD GEORGE CAMPBELL" (1843). Poem, translated from the German poet Oskar Ludwig Bernhard Wolff (1799–1851), in *GM,* Feb 1843. Back from the Highlands came the horse of soldier George Campbell. His mother and pregnant bride come out to greet Campbell. But the saddle is empty. The bride grieves. When Longfellow was accused of plagiarizing his version from a Scotch ballad in *Minstrelsy: Ancient and Modern, with an Historical Introduction and Notes,* ed. William Motherwell (1827), he easily refuted the charge in a letter to George Rex Graham* (19 Feb 1845).

Bibliography: Hilen, ed.

"THE GOOD PART, THAT SHALL NOT BE TAKEN AWAY." *See Poems on Slavery.*

"THE GOOD SHEPHERD" (1833). Irregular sonnet, translated from the Spanish poet Lope de Vega (1562–1635), in *Coplas; Voices.* The contrite poet asks the shepherd, whose song entices and whose guidance he needs, to "wash away these scarlet sins," and to wait for him. But why ask? He sees the Shepherd crucified and "waiting still."

GOSS, ELBRIDGE HENRY (1830–1908). Local historian living in Melrose, Massachusetts. When Goss sent Longfellow a copy of his monograph "Early Bells of Massachusetts" (1874), he initiated a long correspondence about bells in poetry. Over the next several years Longfellow, with patient affection, wrote Goss more than a dozen times, to answer queries about passages in literature, direct him to new sources, and thank him for little gifts. Goss planned an anthology to be titled "The Bells of the World," which, however, was never published. Finally Longfellow wrote (29 Nov 1881) that illness prevented him from seeing Goss again.

Bibliography: Hilen, ed.

GRAHAM, GEORGE REX (1813–94). Editor and publisher. Born in Philadelphia, Graham was apprenticed to a cabinetmaker, read for the law, and was admitted to the bar. In 1839 he became assistant of the *Saturday Evening Post,* bought *Atkinson's Casket,* and married Elizabeth Fry. In 1840 he bought *Burton's Gentleman's Magazine* and merged it and the *Casket* into *Graham's Magazine.* Among Graham's associate editors were Edgar Allan Poe,* Bayard Taylor,* and Rufus Wilmot Griswold.* Contributors included Elizabeth Barrett Browning, William Cullen Bryant,* James Fenimore Cooper, Richard Henry Dana Sr.,* Nathaniel Hawthorne,* George Stillman Hillard,* Frances Sargent Osgood, Catherine M. Sedgwick, Lydia H. Sigourney, William Gimore Simms, and especially Longfellow, who was always Graham's favorite. Graham increased the circulation of his elegant magazine. In 1840 it went from 5,000 to 25,000; by 1841, to 50,000. Graham became extravagant, overpaid his contributors, speculated disastrously, took to drink, and went bankrupt. In 1850 he sold his magazine, bought it back, and sold it again. Ruined by swindlers (1870), Graham, whose wife died (1871), deteriorated, became blind and senile, and died an invalid in a New Jersey hospital.

Poe wrote Longfellow (3 May 1841) to beg him, in fawning terms, to contribute something in poetry or prose, of whatever length he wished, once a month to *Graham's Magazine.* Longfellow contributed that same year, and often later. Graham paid $500 to an artist for a portrait of Longfellow (1843), which Longfellow found ugly and a waste of money but which was printed anyway. Graham published *The Spanish Student* by Longfellow in his magazine (Sep–Nov 1842). When Poe sent a savage review of it, Graham paid Poe $30 for the review but wrote Longfellow (9 Feb 1844) that he

wouldn't publish it and that Poe was probably jealous of Longfellow's reputation and wealth.

Bibliography: S. Longfellow; *Poe Log;* Pratte, Alf. "George Rex Graham." In *American Magazine Journalists, 1741-1850,* ed. Sam G. Riley, 153–58. *Dictionary of Literary Biography.* Vol. 73. Detroit: Gale Research, Inc., 1988.

"THE GRAVE" (1838). Poem, translated from the Anglo-Saxon, in *NAR,* July 1838. Your grave house was built before you were born. I will show you its location. "It is unhigh and low." Death holds its key. You will be cold, in the dark, with worms. No one will visit, because you will soon be ugly.

GREENE, GEORGE WASHINGTON (1811–83). Author, diplomat, and educator. Greene was born in East Greenwich, Rhode Island, attended Brown University (1825-27), and left in his junior year for Europe to improve his health and to study the French and Italian languages and literatures. Greene met Longfellow in Marseilles (1827), saw him again in Rome and Naples (1828), and thus began their lifelong friendship. In Paris (1828), Greene married an Italian teenager from Florence named Maria Carlotta Sforzosi. She accompanied him to Rhode Island (1830). Longfellow met and liked her, and wrote her a few letters in animated Italian. She returned with Greene to France (1831) and accompanied him (1832) back to Rhode Island, where he taught briefly at the Kingston Academy. He tried but failed to open a private academy. During this time, Longfellow began to lend him money. When Greene failed to gain a teaching position at Bowdoin, he and his wife returned to Europe, mainly Italy (1835). He was U.S. consul in Rome (1837–46), during which time he began a career in journalism, publishing in the *North American Review* and the *Knickerbocker.* He also translated *Histoire de la Civilisation en Europe* (1828) by the French historian François Pierre Guillaume Guizot (1787-1874). Samuel Ward,* distantly related to Greene, told Longfellow he would try to get the translation published in New York. Longfellow wrote Ward about the matter (2 Apr 1837), and asked Ward, who was holding the manuscript, to send it to Long-fellow, if New York was not interested, so that he could try with a Boston publisher. The translation was never published. Greene's lost his consulship in Rome, pos-sibly because he may have mishandled fi-nances while holding the position. He had been criticized in 1840 for exacting $4 each from Americans for visaing their passports; this procedure was legal but not always en-forced. When James K. Polk became presi-dent, Greene was quickly dismissed (1846).

A measure of the intimacy of Longfellow's friendship with Greene may be inferred from the fact that the longest Longfellow let-ter is probably the one he wrote Greene (23 Jul 1839); it is approximately 2,500 words in length. For the most part it concerns Longfellow's unhappy and unrequited love for Fanny Appleton, some years before she agreed to marry him; he goes on and on, then concludes: "That lady says she *will not!* I say she *shall!* It is not *pride,* but the mad-ness of passion." Only to a close friend would a fellow write in that manner. Greene published a biography (1846) of Nathanael Greene, the American Revolutionary general and his grandfather; it was a short book partly subsidized by Longfellow. Greene re-turned to the United States (1847). Greene may have tried to have his marriage annulled (1849); rumor also had it that his wife died of fever (May 1849). Greene's legal divorce (1850) distressed Longfellow deeply, and their friendship iced over for a dozen years.

Greene wrote manuals on French and Ital-ian, published *History and Geography of the Middle Ages* (1851), and was an instruc-tor in modern languages at Brown (1848–52). He married again (1852), this time to Catherine Van Buren Porter (1831–?); the couple had four children. Greene sought (1855–56) but failed to get a congressional subsidy to finance a six-volume edition of Nathanael Greene's works. He published *Primary Lessons in Italian* (1865). His *His-torical View of the American Revolution* (also 1865) proved popular and enjoyed later editions (1869, 1872, 1876). Longfel-low bought a house for $2,500 in East Greenwich, Rhode Island, for the Greenes (March 1866), put it in Greene's wife's name, and stipulated that it be willed to her children when she died; by June, Longfellow sent another $1,500 to cover some remod-eling costs. When in 1866 George Bancroft* published the ninth volume, which con-cerned the American Revolution, of his *His-tory of the United States from the Discovery of the American Continent to the Present Time* (10 vols., 1834–75), Greene took of-fense at the treatment in it of his grandfather and began pamphleteering against Bancroft. Greene wrote more essays and translations; and after being inexcusably dilatory, wrote and published a massive *Life of Nathanael Greene* (3 vols., 1867–71), which he dedi-cated to Longfellow, who helped subsidize its publication with check after check. In 1867 and 1868, Longfellow worked with William Greene (1797–1883), a lawyer cousin of George and the lieutenant gover-nor of Rhode Island (1866–67), to find ways to help George out of debt. William Greene wrote George's wife, affectionately but sternly, to tell her to buy nothing on credit and to use his and Longfellow's money gifts to pay bills with cash. Greene taught Amer-ican history at the Normal School of Rhode Island (1871) and lectured ineffectively on American history at Cornell (1871–74). Longfellow, who had long if irregularly gifted Greene with money, began early in 1872 sending him $50 a month until 1882, the year of Longfellow's death. In a letter to Greene (18 Feb 1875) Longfellow said his three daughters "wish to share with yours [Anna Greene, Kate Greene, and Mary Greene] equally Sumner's legacy" and ac-cordingly enclosed an extra check for $1,000 for the Greene girls to split. Longfellow sub-sidized the publication of Greene's *A Short History of Rhode Island* (1877). When a re-viewer wondered in the Providence *Eve-ning Press* (19 July 1877) if Greene's book was "history or fiction," Greene was out-raged and whined to Longfellow, who mol-lified him in a letter (5 Aug 1877) by noting that "Seneca says that malicious people have to drink most of their own venom," and add-ing that "The way to make them drink the whole of it is to take no notice of them what-ever." By 1879 Greene was planning to write a biography of Longfellow, collected materials and information, but never wrote it. When Ward came into some funds (1880), he twice in March sent Longfellow checks to transmit, one anonymously, to Greene. In numerous end-of-the-month letters to Greene, Longfellow humorously alludes to enclosed checks as souvenirs, payment for a non-existent "monthly" periodical, a leaf from the Charles River "bank," a slip of paper, one of twelve zodiacal signs, an appended paragraph, something with which to checkmate him, a "dividend," and so on.

Longfellow dedicated his *Ultima Thule* (1880) to Greene. The small volume begins with a "Dedication to G.W.G." In Craigie House,* Longfellow placed close to each other a statuette of Dante and the 1840 bust of Greene by Thomas Crawford,* the American sculptor. The voluminous correspondence of the two friends reveals their devotion to each other. In too many of his letters to Longfellow, Greene comes off as a bright, miserable griper, and a chronic, whining hypochondriac. Many of the hundreds of letters Longfellow wrote to Greene, beginning in 1828 and continuing with a final one ten days before Longfellow died, are among his most intimate and personally revealing. Longfellow bequeathed $1,000 to each of Greene's children.

Bibliography: Arvin; Hilen, ed.; S. Longfellow; Wagenknecht, 1955; Williams.

GREENLEAF, JAMES (1814–65). The husband of Mary Longfellow Greenleaf,* Longfellow's sister. Greenleaf was a businessman, often traveling to New Orleans. His brother, Patrick Henry Greenleaf (1808–69), and Longfellow were Bowdoin classmates and lifelong friends.

GREENLEAF, MARY LONGFELLOW (1816–1902). Longfellow's sister. She married James Greenleaf (1839). They lived in Cambridge. She often went with him on lengthy business trips to New Orleans. Widowed from 1865, she went with Longfellow when he visited Europe for the last time (1868–69).

GREENOUGH, HORATIO (1805–52). Sculptor. Greenough was born in Boston into a rich and talented family. He studied at Harvard, left for Rome (1825), was advised by the Danish sculptor Bertel Thorvaldsen (1768–1844), practiced sculpture, returned home ill (1827), made model busts of eminent people, returned to Italy, and established his famous studio in Florence (1828–51). Greenough created busts of important Americans, including James Fenimore Cooper, for whose daughters he carved *Chanting Cherubs.* These two nude baby angels (now unrecovered) had to be fitted with diapers before they could be exhibited in chaste Boston (1851). Prolific but dying early of "brain fever," Greenough left many works, the most famous of which is his *George Washington,* seminude, sandaled, seated à la Phidias's lost *Zeus.* It was commissioned by Cooper and Richard Henry Dana Jr.,* among others; was placed in the Capitol rotunda, Washington, D.C. (1841), until eroded by rain and settled; and is now in the Smithsonian Institution. Greenough wrote *The Travels, Observations and Experiences of a Yankee Stonecutter* (1852), espousing his theory that form follows function, which he had discussed with Ralph Waldo Emerson.*

When he was in Washington, D.C., with his wife, Longfellow went to the Capitol, where he saw Greenough's *Washington* and noted in his journal (17 May 1850) that it "has rather a grand effect under the blue sky." In his journal (31 Oct 1851), Longfellow records dining in Cambridge with his brother-in-law Thomas Gold Appleton,* Charles Sumner,* and others including Greenough, of whom he notes: "A fine, hearty, free, cordial gentleman is Horatio Greenough. Green be his laurels." A couple of months later Greenough called on Longfellow, who notes in his journal (25 Jan 1852), "we had a long chat about politics and art." The Longfellows had Greenough, Appleton, and Emerson to dinner (27 Jan 1852), "pleasantly, with some chat about art." Longfellow and Greenough were among the guests when Emerson hosted a dinner (20 Nov 1852) for the British poet Arthur Hugh Clough.* Longfellow was shocked to hear of Greenough's sudden death and the next day noted in his journal (19 Dec 1852) that "He was a noble, gallant fellow, so full of life!" Richard Saltonstall Greenough (1819–1904), Horatio Greenough's brother, was also an expatriate sculptor. Longfellow attended the inauguration of Richard Greenough's bronze *Benjamin Franklin* during a Franklin Festival in Boston (17 Sep 1856).

Bibliography: Hilen, ed.; S. Longfellow; Wright, Nathalia. *Horatio Greenough: The First American Sculptor.* Philadelphia: University of Pennsylvania Press, 1963.

GRISWOLD, RUFUS WILMOT (1815–57). Editor and anthologist. Born in Benson, Vermont, Griswold held a variety of jobs before drifting into journalism in Philadelphia, where he assembled a popular compilation titled *The Poets and Poetry of America* (1842) and where he helped edit *Graham's Magazine* (1842) until he was fired (1843) for dishonesty by its owner, George Rex Graham.* By alternately toadying to and vilifying various authors, Griswold became a wealthy, influential editor and arbiter of American taste. Edgar Allan Poe,* whom he met in 1841, was ultimately one of his victims. Poe presented his negative opinion of Griswold's 1842 anthology in an 1843 lecture. Griswold is now chiefly remembered for having written a scandal-mongering obituary of Poe and for publishing letters from Poe to him in which he inserted forged falsehoods detrimental to Poe and complimentary to himself. Griswold's checkered career also involved strange marriages. He married Caroline Searles (1837); they had two children, and she died soon thereafter (1842). He married Charlotte Myers (1845); he terminated their evidently unconsummated union by divorcing her for desertion (1852). He married Harriet Stanley McCrillis (1852); they had one son, William McCrillis Gris-

wold (1853–99), who became a fine bibliographer and indexer. Rufus Griswold died before he could try to defend himself against a charge (1856) that his divorce from Charlotte was invalid.

Longfellow had minimal contact with Rufus Griswold. Griswold asked Longfellow for biographical information, which Longfellow sent by letter (c. Nov 1841) and which Griswold included in his 1842 anthology. Longfellow wrote Griswold (27 Nov 1842) to express sympathy after Griswold's first wife died, to discuss "The Belfry of Bruges," which *Graham's Magazine* was publishing, and to say he would send George Graham exclusive "article[s]" for $50 apiece. He wrote Griswold (10 Jan 1843) about the Longfellow portrait Graham sought and used. Longfellow wrote Griswold (13 Apr 1843) "to present to you" Charles Eliot Norton* and to ask him to show Norton something of "the Literary *machinery*" operating in New York, where Griswold then worked. When Longfellow experienced difficulties in getting *The Spanish Student* published, Griswold was helpful, wrote George Stillman Hillard* on Longfellow's behalf, and curried favor with Longfellow by writing (26 Dec 1843) to warn him that Poe had sent an unfavorable review of it. Graham paid Poe $30 for the review but never published it. After Poe's death, Longfellow explained in a letter to Griswold (28 Sep 1850) that he had assuredly not plagiarized from Poe's "The Haunted Palace" in writing "The Beleaguered City."

Bibliography: Bayless, Joy. *Rufus Wilmot Griswold, Poe's Literary Executor.* Nashville: Vanderbilt University Press, 1843; Griswold, Rufus W. *Passages from the Correspondence and Other Papers of Rufus W. Griswold.* Cambridge: W. M. Griswold, 1898; Hilen, ed.; *Poe Log.*

H

HALE, SARAH JOSEPHA (1788–1879).
Editor, writer, and feminist. She was born, as
Sarah Josepha Buell, in Newport, New
Hampshire, was home-schooled, and
founded and taught in a school for children
(1806-13). She married David Hale, a lawyer
(1813); they had five children. After his
death (1822), Mrs. Hale published some poetry (1823) and a novel (1827), moved to
Boston, and edited the *Ladies' Magazine*
(1828-37). She continued to do so until
Louis Antoine Godey,* founder-editor of the
Lady's Book (1830-37), bought it, merged
it with the *Ladies' Magazine* (1837), and retitled it *Godey's Lady's Book* (1837). Mrs.
Hale edited it until it was sold (1877). She
was also owner-editor of two annuals, *The
Opal: A Pure Gift for the Holy Days* (1845,
1848) and *The Crocus: A Fresh Flower for
the Holidays* (1849). She wrote, compiled,
and edited much else. She compiled
Woman's Record . . . (1854), about distinguished women, and edited the letters of
Madame de Sévigné (1856) and Lady Mary
Wortley Montague (1856). She is mainly remembered, however, as the author of "Mary
Had a Little Lamb," which appeared in her
Poems for Our Children (1830). As editor of
Godey's, she accepted a few of Longfellow's
poems for publication. He published "The
Twilight" in *The Opal* and knew Horatio Em-
mons Hale (1817-96), her son, who was a
distinguished explorer and ethnologist.

Bibliography: Entrikin, Isabelle Webb. *Sarah
Josepha Hale and "Godey's Lady's Book."*

Philadelphia: University of Pennsylvania, 1946;
Hilen, ed.

**"A HANDFUL OF TRANSLATIONS"
(1870).** Five translations, in the *AM,* Sep
1870; Scudder: "The Angel and the Child,"
"Consolation," "My Secret," "Remorse," and
"Wanderer's Night Songs."

"THE HANGING OF THE CRANE" (1874).
Poem, in the New York *Ledger,* 28 Mar 1874;
Scudder. The feasting, happy, jolly guests
hang a crane (i.e., an iron arm) in the fireplace of the poet's new house (a ceremony
to celebrate a wedding). They depart and
leave the poet to his musing. A new house
is like "a new star just sprung to birth." The
poet sees "shadows passing into deeper
shade" and eluding him. (This magic-lantern
sort of vision sequence continues.) He sees
two together, sharing their lives and needing
no guests. A regal-looking baby appears at
the table. The infant needn't talk to assert
his rule. Soon the guest list swells to include
a sister, curly and rosy, for the boy. "Nor care
they for the world that rolls / With all its
freight of troubled souls." More guests swell
the table: Young maidens, with "restless
hopes and fears," resemble "timid birds"
about to fly; lads eager to let seas, countries,
cities, and solitudes challenge their strength.
Time passes like a brook flowing toward
"The gloomy mills of Death." The table
shrinks, and only two are there. The jewels
of their crown now "shine in other homes
and hearts." One is in the Far East; another,
at war, news of which the mother reads

"with a secret dread." After rain one day comes the sun, then a ruby-red sunset. That evening, guests celebrate "the Golden Wedding day." Children race along the floors, go up and down the stairs, and drum spoons at the table. The aged couple smile to see their own "forms and features multiplied," which gleam like "the reflection of a light / Between two burnished mirrors" or like bridge lamps "Stretch[ing] on and on" and making a seemingly endless vista at night. "The Hanging of the Crane" is well structured, somewhat gloomy in the middle, but pleasant at its brilliant close.

After his friend Thomas Bailey Aldrich, who had married in New York (1865), soon moved with his wife to Boston, Longfellow visited the Aldriches (1867). When Longfellow was about to depart, he told Aldrich that their dining table was small, would expand to accommodate their children, but would shrink again when the children grew up and flew away to nest elsewhere; he called this sequence the simple story of life, which could be the subject of a charming fireside poem. When Aldrich didn't take Longfellow's offer of the idea for a poem, Longfellow kept it in mind and worked it up later, in spades. Robert Bonner (1824–99), the owner of the New York *Ledger,* paid Longfellow $3,000 for "The Hanging of the Crane." It quickly generated adverse commentary. Bonner was criticized in at least one rival newspaper for paying Longfellow too much while being too little charitable elsewhere. For acting as broker in the deal, Samuel Ward* received $1,000 from Bonner. Longfellow was ridiculously accused of plagiarizing a couple of lines. Other reviewers thought it commonplace. All the same, it was published again in fancy book form (1875), illustrated by Mary Hallock (later the western writer Mary Hallock Foote [1847–1938]) and also in smaller form (1875). These editions also proved to be money trees. Longfellow dickered with James Ripley Osgood,* their publisher, and received $862.50 from him (Jan 1875), together with a promise of $1,100 more a little later. Still another edition of the poem, celebrating Longfellow's centenary, appeared (1907), more lavishly illustrated, with the most ex-

pensive of its three forms commanding $20 (upwards of $500 in twenty-first-century purchasing power).

Bibliography: Arvin; Greenslet, Ferris. *The Life of Thomas Bailey Aldrich.* Boston and New York: Houghton Mifflin, 1908; Hilen, ed.; S. Longfellow; Wagenknecht, 1986.

"THE HAPPIEST LAND" (1839). Poem, translated from an anonymous German work, as "Fragment of a Modern Ballad," in *Coleman's Monthly Miscellany,* Jul 1839 (*see* Colman, Samuel); *Hyperion; Voices.* Four stalwarts are drinking at a tavern on the Rhine. A Swabian toasts his land as the best, with strong men and pretty girls. A Saxon prefers his region, where he has many girlfriends. A Bohemian says that if there is any heaven on earth it is in Bohemia, with jolly workers. But the landlord's daughter points to heaven and says "There lies the happiest land!"

"HAROUN AL RASCHID" (1878). Poem, in *Kéramos, Birds* (1878). In a book of poetry Haroun Al Raschid reads about kings and others who once possessed the world but are now gone. He reads on: You should grab your share, called fair, of the world before you die. He bows his head and weeps. This poem, deriving from the *Arabian Nights,* has been rightly called simple but precise.

Bibliography: Arvin.

"THE HARVEST MOON" (1878). Sonnet, in *Kéramos.* The "mystic splendor" of the harvest moon rests on roofs, nests of birds, windows, lanes, and fields. These things and others are symbolic of mental images. Vegetation falls. Songbirds leave. Quails remain to pipe.

"THE HAUNTED CHAMBER" (1873). Poem, in *Aftermath, Birds* (1873). Every heart has a "haunted chamber." The poet's is haunted by ghosts from the past, like shadows cast by the moon. There is a form by the window, vanishing at dawn. Beneath "a gloomy pine" outside is the grave of a tiny child that died without ever smiling or crying. These "pallid phantoms" haunt the poet when night returns. They resemble statues on the bridge over the "river of death."

"HAUNTED HOUSES" (1858). Poem, in *Courtship, Birds* (1858). Houses where people have lived and died are haunted by phantoms gliding in, by uninvited ghostly dinner guests, by strangers sitting by the fire. We don't hold titles to houses; the dead "stretch their dusty hands" and clutch old holdings "in mortmain." A world of spirits surrounds our sensible world and breathes "ethereal air" through it. We are balanced between "attractions and desires," and vacillate between enjoyment and aspiration. Just as the moon throws "a floating bridge of light" across the sea, so the spirit world provides a connection to our world, along the swaying floor of which our thoughts wander "above the dark abyss." It has been suggested that when Longfellow wrote his "Haunted Houses" he was in unacknowledged debt to "The Haunted House" by Thomas Hood (1799-1845).

Bibliography: More.

"HAWTHORNE: MAY 23, 1864" (1864). Poem, in *AM,* Aug 1864, as "Concord"; *Flower.* The day of the funeral of Nathaniel Hawthorne* was sunny, after a week of rainy weather. The mourners, whose familiar faces seemed strange and whose words had altered meanings, could see the old manse nearby. The difference was that his face was gone, his voice silenced; all that was heard was the whisper of pines, which "hearsed" the hills near his resting place and which resembled his own "troubled" "longings." His pen dropped "and left the tale half told."

> Ah! who shall lift that wand of magic
>   power,
>   And the lost clew regain?
> The unfinished window in Aladdin's tower
>   Unfinished must remain!

The scene of this magnificent threnody is the Sleepy Hollow Cemetery, in Concord, Massachusetts. Hawthorne's mourners, in addition to Longfellow, made up an impressive group and included Louis Agassiz,* Ralph Waldo Emerson,* James T. Fields,* George Washington Greene,* George Stillman Hillard,* Oliver Wendell Holmes,* Charles Eliot Norton,* and former president Franklin Pierce. At his death, Hawthorne left

many manuscripts in fragmentary form, notably "The Ancestral Footstep," *The Dolliver Romance, Dr. Grimshaw's Secret,* and *Septimius Felton.* Sophia Amelia Peabody Hawthorne (1809-71), the author's widow, wrote Longfellow (24 Jul 1864) to praise his poem for its "Eolian delicacy, sweetness and pathos."

Bibliography: Arvin; Hilen, ed.; S. Longfellow; Wagenknecht, 1986.

HAWTHORNE, NATHANIEL (1804-64). American man of letters. Hawthorne was born in Salem, Massachusetts, attended Bowdoin College, and graduated with the class of 1825, which included Longfellow. *Fanshawe* (1828), Hawthorne's immature college romance, was followed by *Twice-Told Tales* (1837; enlarged ed., 1842), and several books for children. His literary career was interrupted by employment in the Boston Custom House (1839-41), indifferent participation for a few months in the liberal Brook Farm experiment (1841), and marriage (1842) to Sophia Peabody (1809-71). They had three children, one of whom was Julian Hawthorne (1846-1934), a popular writer whose *Nathaniel Hawthorne and His Wife* (1884) and *Hawthorne and His Circle* (1903) shed sidelights on Longfellow. Nathaniel Hawthorne published *Mosses from an Old Manse* (1846), was a surveyor in the Salem Custom House (1846-49), was obliged to accept financial aid from friends, and gained fame by publishing *The Scarlet Letter* (1850). While Hawthorne and his family lived in Lenox, Massachusetts, close to Herman Melville, he wrote *The House of the Seven Gables* (1851), after which he and his growing family resided in West Newton and then Concord (1851-53). Hawthorne wrote the campaign biography (1852) of his friend Franklin Pierce, who when he became president appointed Hawthorne U.S. consul at Liverpool, England (1853-57). After traveling and living in England, France, and Italy (1857-60), Hawthorne published *The Marble Faun* (1860), and returned home. With declining creative energies and dismayed by the Civil War, Hawthorne toiled over inchoate romances concerned with the elixir or life and with an

American claimant to a British estate, published posthumously in various fragmentary forms. Much of Hawthorne's most important writing is contained in his voluminous English, French, Italian, and American notebooks.

Hawthorne, who had not associated much with Longfellow at Bowdoin, sent him a timid letter (7 Mar 1837) praising *Outre-Mer* and alerting him that a gift copy of *Twice-Told Tales* would be arriving separately. Longfellow replied with characteristic celerity (9 Mar 1837), expressing delight in Hawthorne's work and discussing several stories in detail. Hawthorne answered by a letter (4 June 1837) often quoted because in it he compares himself to a dismal owl living back home with his mother and long fearful of re-entering "the main current of life." Longfellow favorably reviewed Hawthorne's *Twice-Told Tales* (*NAR*, July 1837), noting with pleasure national characteristics in the individual works. Thus began one of Longfellow's most celebrated literary friendships. The two men met occasionally, wrote each other frequently, and commented on one another's writing discerningly.

Various passages in letters from Hawthorne to Longfellow are illuminating. The two planned what Hawthorne called "that book of fairy tales, which you spoke of at a previous interview" (21 Mar 1838); they planned to call it "The Boys' Wonder-Horn" after *Des Knabens Wunderhorn*, but Hawthorne soon told Longfellow that he should develop the idea by himself. (*See The Golden Legend* in *Christus: A Mystery.*) In a charming letter (26 Dec 1839), Hawthorne told Longfellow this: "I read your poems over and over, and over again . . . Nothing equal to some of them was ever written in this world—this western world, I mean." As for *Poems on Slavery,* "You have never poetized a practical subject hitherto" (24 Dec 1842). "I have read Evangeline with more pleasure than it would be decorous to express. It cannot fail, I think, to prove the most triumphant of your successes" (11 Nov 1847). In an unsigned review of *Evangeline* (*Salem Advertiser,* 13 Nov 1847), Hawthorne says that Longfellow "stand[s] . . . at the head of our list of native poets." (There

is evidence that Hawthorne regretted abandoning the subject of Evangeline and the Acadians to Longfellow. Soon after *Evangeline* was published, Longfellow wrote Hawthorne [29 Nov 1847] to thank him and graciously add the following: "This success I owe entirely to you, for being willing to forego the pleasure of writing a prose tale, which many people would have taken for poetry, that I might write a poem which many people take for prose.") Hawthorne wrote Longfellow that *The Estray* is "a beautiful collection" (23 Jan 1847). Discussion in the Salem Custom House of "The Wreck of the Hesperus" "was very queer, and would have amused you much" (11 Nov 1847)— perhaps because of factual inaccuracies in it? *Kavanagh* "is a most precious and rare book—as fragrant as a bunch of flowers, and as simple as one flower" (5 June 1849). "'Weariness' . . . seem[s] to me profoundly touching. I too am weary, and begin to look ahead for the Wayside Inn [death?]" (24 Oct 1863). "I have read the 'Wayside Inn' with great comfort and delight. I take vast satisfaction in your poetry, and take very little in other men's, except it be the grand old strains that have been sounding all through my life [i.e., those of William Shakespeare, John Milton, and Edmund Spenser]" (2 Jan 1864). More candidly, and perhaps with a touch of jealousy, Hawthorne wrote a letter (5 Mar 1849) to their mutual friend George Stillman Hillard* about *Kavanagh:* "I see that Longfellow has written a prose-tale. How indefatigable he is!—and how adventurous! Well he may be, for he never fails."

Shedding light on Hawthorne are comments by Longfellow in his journal and in letters to others. He wrote George Washington Greene* that Hawthorne "is a strange owl; a very peculiar individual, with a dash of originality about him very pleasant to behold" (22 Oct 1838). In his journal (10 Oct 1839), Longfellow notes that he "passed the evening with Hawthorne in his attic. He is a grand fellow, and is destined to shine as 'a bright particular star' in our literary heavens." After entertaining Hawthorne, Hillard, and Felton at dinner, Longfellow notes in his journal that "Hawthorne is a taciturn youth . . . [who] never speaks . . . much" (5 Apr

1840); later he writes "I am more and more struck with Hawthorne's manly beauty and strange, original fancies" (27 Oct 1846). Journal entries describe *The Scarlet Letter* as "a most tragic tragedy" (16 Mar 1850) and *The House of the Seven Gables* as "a weird wild book . . . with passages and pages of extreme beauty" (16 Apr 1851). Longfellow gave a dinner honoring Hawthorne (14 Jun 1853) before he left for Liverpool; other guests included the British poet Arthur Hugh Clough,* Ralph Waldo Emerson,* James Russell Lowell,* and Charles Eliot Norton.* From Liverpool, Hawthorne wrote Longfellow (11 May 1855) that "my personal knowledge of you sheds a lustre on myself. Do come over and see these people!" Longfellow comments in his journal (1 Mar 1860) that *The Marble Faun* is "wonderful . . . but with the old, dull pain in it that runs through all Hawthorne's writings." Soon after attending Hawthorne's funeral, Longfellow wrote "Hawthorne: May 23, 1864," one of his finest poems, certainly his finest elegy.

Bibliography: Gale, Robert L. *A Nathaniel Hawthorne Encyclopedia.* Westport: Greenwood Press, 1991; Green; Hawthorne, Manning. "The Friendship Between Hawthorne and Longfellow." *English Leaflet* 29 (Feb 1940): 25–30; Hawthorne, Nathaniel. *The Centenary Edition of the Works of Nathaniel Hawthorne.* 23 vols. Columbus: Ohio State University Press, 1962–94; Higginson; Hilen, ed.; S. Longfellow; Macdonald, John J. "Longfellow in Hawthorne's 'The Antique Ring.'" *New England Quarterly* 46 (Dec 1973): 622–26; Miller, Edwin Haviland. *Salem Is My Dwelling Place: A Life of Nathaniel Hawthorne.* Iowa City: University of Iowa Press, 1991; Tryon; Turner, Arlin. "Hawthorne and Longfellow: Abortive Plans for Collaboration." *Nathaniel Hawthorne Journal* 1 (1971): 3–11; Wagenknecht, 1955; Woodson, Thomas. Introduction to *The Letters, 1813–1843.* Vol. 15. *The Centenary Edition of the Works of Nathaniel Hawthorne.* Columbus: Ohio State University Press, 1984.

"HELEN OF TYRE" (1880). Poem, in *AM,* Feb 1880; *Thule.* Who is this misty, cloudy, fiery woman? Some in the streets of Tyre called her Jezebel. When Simon Magus spoke, she paused and heard him say that he would convert her from Queen Candace and Helen of Troy to "The Intelligence Divine!" Blandished by these tempting, deceiving lies, she followed him from place to place, like "a leaf . . . blown by the gust," until she, as well as Tyre itself, vanished into nothing but "A name upon men's lips." The reader is invited to "stoop down and write" her name "in the dust."

Bibliography: Arvin; Benton, Richard P. "Longfellow's 'Helen of Tyre.'" *Emerson Society Quarterly.* No. 10 (1958): 25–28; Benton, Richard P. "Helen of Tyre." *Explicator* 16 (Jun 1958): 54; Wagenknecht, 1986.

"THE HEMLOCK TREE" (1846). Poem, translated from an anonymous German poet, in *The Gift: A Christmas, New Year, and Birthday Present* (1845); *Bruges.* The branches of the faithful hemlock are green throughout the seasons. However, fair maidens love the persona only in prosperous times, the nightingale sings only in the summer, and the brook in the meadow flows only in rainy weather.

Bibliography: Hilen, ed.

"HERMES TRISMEGISTUS" (1882). Poem, in *Century Illustrated Monthly Magazine,* Feb 1882; *Harbor.* The Nile still flows, and the "imperious" pyramids and the stony-eyed Sphinx still stand. But where is Hermes Trismegistus, who held the secrets of now-absent Egyptian kings and demi-gods? His many books, "By the Thaumaturgist plundered," are lost forever. The poet sees misty ghostliness in this wonder-worker. Was he one person or several? He appears, near the Nile, to be thinking about "the mystic union . . . / Between gods and men"; also at Thebes, to be listening, while in crowded streets, to "celestial voices."

> Who shall call his dreams fallacious?
>   Who has searched or sought
> All the unexplored and spacious
>   Universe of thought?

Trismegistus should be happy that his name has come down to us as something "sublime" despite the fact that his pages have crumbled. When the poet found that name in the weedy "Grave-yard of the Past," he briefly sensed a gloomy presence, like a breeze, which was then "no more." Hermes Trismegistus is the Greek name for Thoth, the Egyptian god of wisdom. This poem was one of the last poems Longfellow wrote.

Bibliography: Arvin; Wagenknecht, 1986.

"THE HERONS OF ELMWOOD" (1878).

Poem, in *Kéramos, Birds* (1878). The warm summer night is quiet. The only sounds come from the herons and the crickets. The herons "winging their way / O'er the poet's house in the Elmwood thickets" should call him and sing about "the green morass" and reed-watering tides. They should interpret their "sound of lament." They should sing about the joy of free flight, the sight of landscapes below and the blue above. They should ask the poet if their songs are not "sweeter and wilder and better" than those of troubadours and minnesingers. They should sing about that person who meditated near his gate. He should be assured that silent messages pay him profound "homage." The poet of Elmwood was James Russell Lowell.* Although he was not dead but merely absent from Elmwood when Longfellow wrote this poem in 1876, its tone is elegiac.

Bibliography: Wagenknecht, 1986.

HILLARD, GEORGE STILLMAN (1808–79).

Lawyer, politician, and writer. He was born in Machias, Maine. After graduating from Harvard (1828), he read law in Northampton, Massachusetts, and taught in the Round Hill School established there by George Bancroft,* and then returned for an A.M. at Harvard (1831) and an LL.B. at the Dane Law School in Cambridge (1832). He coedited the Unitarian *Christian Register* (1833–34) and edited the *Jurist* (1834). He and Charles Sumner* established a long-lasting, amiable law partnership (1834–56). Hillard had somewhat contrary ambitions. He was a conscientious, honest, but not brilliant lawyer, even though he was the first dean of the Boston Law School. He had political aspirations. He and Sumner spent a great deal of time, in and out of their offices, discussing literature, often with writers, including two of Hillard's clients, Nathaniel Hawthorne* and Longfellow. Hillard held many political offices (1835–55), both at the Boston city level and as a state representa-

tive. He became a lifelong member of the Massachusetts Historical Society (from 1843). Sumner's favoring a more militant stand in the 1850s against slavery left the more temperate Hillard out of favor, although after the Civil War he served as U.S. attorney for Massachusetts (1866–71). Hillard published numerous reviews, articles, poems, and translations, a biography of Captain John Smith (1834, as part of *The Library of American Biography,* edited by Jared Sparks*), a meticulous edition of the works of Edmund Spenser (5 vols., 1839), a memorial of Daniel Webster* (1853), a campaign biography of General George B. McClellan (1864), and a eulogy of the sculptor Thomas Crawford* (1869). Hillard's only remembered work was his popular *Six Months in Italy* (1853; 21st ed., 1881). Dedicated to his friend Crawford and his wife, Louisa Ward Crawford, the book is based on letters Hillard sent back to his wife during an 1847–48 trip he took. He had married Susan Tracy Howe, a judge's daughter, in 1835; they had one child, a son who died in 1838, after which their marriage was strained. Hillard suffered a paralytic stroke (1873) and never completely recovered. He edited the papers of George Ticknor* (1876), his and Longfellow's friend, planned a biography of Ticknor, but died before completing it.

Once Longfellow arrived in Cambridge (Dec 1836) to teach at Harvard, he quickly established friendships with Hillard, Henry Russell Cleveland (1809–43), Cornelius Conway Felton,* and Sumner. Their group became known as "The Five of Clubs." Cleveland, the husband of an heiress and a lavish host, died, after which Samuel Gridley Howe* replaced him in the club. The fivesome socialized frequently. Their intimacy is indicated by the fact that Longfellow in letters calls Hillard "St. George" and "Geordie." On the eve of Longfellow's departure for Europe (1842), Hillard published a poem in the Boston *Advertiser* titled "To the Ship Ville de Lyon," admonishing the vessel to be careful with "that loved and laurelled head" aboard. In his journal (23 Oct 1846) Longfellow notes attending a lecture Hillard gave at the Cambridge Lyceum and calls it "noble and elevated in its tone, and very well written and spoken." Others criticized Hillard's manner as ineffective through being effeminate. From Rome (1848) Hillard wrote Longfellow, touchingly, to compare Longfellow's poetic imagination and Italy's natural beauty. By letter (30 Dec 1849) Hillard thanks Longfellow for sending an early copy of *The Seaside and the Fireside,* comments on poem after poem in it, subjectively praising "The Fire of Drift-Wood" and "Resignation," but venturing to criticize a few other items. Hillard, Longfellow, Ralph Waldo Emerson,* and other notables, attended a celebration of Sir Walter Scott's birthday, held in Boston at the Massachusetts Historical Society (15 Aug 1871).

Bibliography: Palfrey, Francis W. "Memoir of the Hon. George Stillman Hillard, LL.D." *Massachusetts Historical Society Proceedings* 19 (1881-82): 339-45; Wagenknecht, 1955.

"HISTORY OF THE ITALIAN LANGUAGE AND DIALECTS" (1832). Essay, in *NAR,* Oct 1832.

"HOLIDAYS" (1877). Sonnet, in Boston *Transcript,* 27 Sep 1877; *Kéramos.* The poet feels that the most holy holidays are those one celebrates alone, "in silence and apart," in remembrance of "anniversaries of the heart." At such times, he can recall "sudden joys," flaming into brightness and "swift desires," like swallows moving in the wind, like white sails, like fading clouds, like floating lilies. These are elements from an enchanting, dreamy "fairy tale."

HOLMES, OLIVER WENDELL (1809–94). Physician, medical-school professor, and man of letters. Holmes was born in Cambridge, Massachusetts, attended Phillips-Andover Academy, graduated from Harvard (1829), and then attended Harvard's Dane Law School (1829-30), Tremont Medical School in Boston (1830-33), and medical school in Paris (1833-35). Awarded an M.D. by Harvard (1836), Holmes taught anatomy at Dartmouth College (1838-40), then practiced medicine in the Boston area (1840-47). He married Amelia Lee Jackson (1840). They had four children, including Oliver Wendell Holmes Jr. (1841-1935), who after a splendid career with the Union Army during the Civil War became a distinguished lawyer, professor of law at Harvard, and associate justice of the U.S. Supreme Court. The elder Holmes was a lyceum lecturer (1841-57), published medical works (1840s), and enjoyed a long career in medicine at Harvard (1847-82) as professor and dean. He joined the Saturday Club* (1857), helped establish the *Atlantic Monthly* (1857), provided its name, and contributed more than 120 items to it.

Creative writing was this versatile man's fruitfully indulged hobby. Among his best poems are "Old Ironsides" (1830), which saved the historic frigate the *Constitution* from demolition; "The Last Leaf" (1830), which Abraham Lincoln memorized; "The Chambered Nautilus" (1858), about material and spiritual progress and evolution; "The Deacon's Masterpiece; or, the Wonderful 'One-Hoss Shay'" (1858), a subtle, comical satire on Calvinism; and "The Song of the Stethoscope" (1849). Many of Holmes's liveliest essays, together with some verse, are collected in *The Autocrat of the Breakfast-Table* (1858), *The Professor at the Breakfast-Table* (1860), *The Poet at the Breakfast-Table* (1872), and *Over the Teacups* (1890). His so-called "medicated novels" are *Elsie Venner* (1861), about the influence on a person whose mother was bitten by a snake when she was pregnant; *The Guardian Angel* (1867), concerning heredity and psychology; and *A Mortal Antipathy* (1885), about reflexes conditioned by environment. These novels anticipate Sigmund Freud in some ways. Holmes wrote biographies of the historian John Lothrop Motley (1879) and Ralph Waldo Emerson* (1885). *One Hundred Days in Europe* (1887) narrates his trip aboard with his daughter. Holmes's host of friends, in addition to Motley and Emerson, include Louis Agassiz,* Richard Henry Dana Jr.,* Cornelius Conway Felton,* James T. Fields,* Margaret Fuller,* Nathaniel Hawthorne* (whose last physician he was), George Stillman Hillard,* James Russell Lowell,* Herman Melville (whose physician he was, briefly), John Greenleaf Whittier,* and Longfellow.

Longfellow knew Holmes intimately over the years, beginning when Longfellow was teaching at Harvard. Letters from Longfellow to Holmes are graciousness itself. When Holmes sent the Longfellows a copy of his *Poems: New and Enlarged Edition* (1849), Longfellow thanked him in a charming letter (28 Nov 1848), indicating that both Longfellows had planned to dip into the book but found themselves "read[ing] all the afternoon, till we had gone over all the new, and most of the old, which is as good as new." When Holmes sent Longfellow "Astraea . . ." (1850), his Yale Phi Beta Kappa poem, he received this dazzling compliment, which must have appealed to the scientist in him: "I have read [it] . . . with that tingling along the veins which is the sure indication of poetic electricity in the atmosphere of a book. . . . It is lightning from the air, and not galvanism from earthly acids" (28 Oct 1850). Longfellow and Holmes often attended special dinners, ceremonies, and similar events for which Holmes composed and read poems to commemorate the occasion. These events included a Cambridge Lyceum meeting, hosted by Hillard (23 Oct 1846); a dinner party to celebrate Agassiz's fiftieth birthday, hosted by Longfellow (28 May 1857); a farewell dinner party for Motley (7 Aug 1857), before one of his several trips abroad; a Harvard Musical Association dinner (18 Jan 1858); a party (1 Jun 1859) to honor the American chess genius Paul Charles Morphy (1838–84); a party hosted by Felton (29 Aug 1959) for eighteen guests to celebrate Holmes's fiftieth birthday; a dinner honoring Agassiz, about to leave for Brazil (23 Mar 1865); Longfellow's sixtieth birthday party, held at the Dante Club (27 Feb 1867); and a farewell party (23 May 1868) before Longfellow left for his final trip to Europe. The May 23rd poem for Longfellow, one of Holmes's finest of its special genre, begins "Our Poet, who has taught the Western breeze / To waft his songs before us o'er the seas," and goes on to hint at their mutual aging—"After the snows [now] no freshening dews descend, / And what the frost has marred, the sunshine will not mend." The two friends, however, often met again. Longfellow quickly got hold of Holmes's biogra-

phy of Motley and wrote him (22 Dec 1878) to say, "I have read it from beginning to end with deepest interest. It is admirably well done." Holmes's occasional verses, which he composed with unusual care, graced many a birthday party, class reunion, civic event, wedding, birth, funeral, etc., and are unquestionably the best in the English language. Longfellow sometimes referred to Holmes as "the Autocrat." When the Massachusetts Historical Society met to eulogize Longfellow (13 Apr 1882), Holmes spoke tenderly and at great length.

Bibliography: Green; Hoyt, Edwin P. *The Improper Bostonian: Dr. Oliver Wendell Holmes.* New York: William Morrow, 1979; "Tribute"; Wagenknecht, 1955.

HOSMER, HARRIET (1830–1908). America's first female sculptor. Harriet ("Hattie") Goodhue Hosmer was born in Watertown, Massachusetts. Her widowed physician father encouraged her to be a tomboy; sent her to school at Lenox, where she met the actress Frances Kemble* and other female role models; encouraged her to study art in Boston and anatomy in St. Louis; and financed her first trip to Rome (1852), to join the American art colony. Hosmer soon made friends with residents there and travelers passing through, including the expatriate American sculptors Thomas Crawford* and William Wetmore Story,* George Eliot and William Makepeace Thackeray,* and later socialized with members of royalty. She worked productively in England and back the United States, eventually had her own house and studio in Rome, and created *Puck on a Toadstool* and *Zenobia, the Queen of Palmyra, in Chains,* her most popular statues. Nathaniel Hawthorne,* who met her in Rome (1858), mentions her in his preface to *The Marble Faun,* while in the novel, Miriam admires the rendition by Hosmer (though unnamed) of the clasped hands of Elizabeth Barrett Browning and Robert Browning, both of whom Hosmer knew.

Longfellow mentions in his journal (21 Oct 1854) going to an exhibit of two of Hosmer's busts, a *Daphne* and a *Medusa.* He was struck especially by the "peculiarly brilliant . . . conception and execution" of the latter, and goes on to describe its serpentine hair, its agonized face, and "its strange beauty." A decade later is this journal entry (3 Oct 1864): "In the [Cambridge-Boston] car met Miss Harriet Hosmer, the sculptor, full of spirit and energy."

Bibliography: Sherwood, Dolly. *Harriet Hosmer: American Sculptor, 1830-1908.* Columbia: University of Missouri Press, 1991.

HOUSEHOLD POEMS (1865). Republication of 58 of Longfellow's most popular poems, with "Dedication" as an introduction.

HOWE, JULIA WARD (1819–1910). Author and reformer. She was the daughter of Samuel Ward Sr., a wealthy banker, and Julia Rush Cutler Ward, a nonpublished poetess who died in 1824. Young Julia's siblings were Samuel Ward,* who became the famous lobbyist; Louisa Ward Crawford, who married Thomas Crawford,* the sculptor; and Anne Eliza Ward, who married Adolph Mailliard, grandson of Napoleon Bonaparte's son Joseph Bonaparte (1768-1844), ex-king of Naples and Spain. The three sisters, all beautiful, were later known as "The Three Graces." Julia Ward was superbly educated by governesses and in private schools. While still a child, she wrote poems and romances. In 1841, at the Perkins Institute for the Blind, she met Samuel Gridley Howe,* the dashing, versatile humanitarian, eighteen years her senior. They married (1843). His sobriquet for her was "Diva"; her two for him, "Chevalier" and "Chev." They spent a year in Europe (1843-44), then resided in Boston. They had six children, of whom four, all distinguished, survived them: Florence Marion Howe Hall (writer, lecturer), Henry Marion Howe (metallurgist), Laura Elizabeth Howe Richard (writer), and Maud Howe Elliott (writer). Samuel Gridley Howe was long a champion of underdogs and unfortunate ones, including slaves, the blind, mute, and deaf, and the mentally challenged. He and Julia founded and edited an antislavery periodical called the *Commonwealth* (1851-52) and opened their beautiful home to abolitionists, notably Charles Sumner* and the incendiary John Brown. Her husband selfishly discouraged her writing, on the grounds that she should be mainly a homemaker. She took her children to Rome (1850) for a year away from him. She thought seriously of divorce (1854, 1857). Her pre–Civil War publications include an assembly of poems titled *Passion-Flowers* (1854, written in Rome, issued anonymously), considered racy for the times; *Words of the Hour* (1857), more poetry; *The World's Own* (1857; also titled *Leonora; or, The World's Own* [1857]), a mediocre play about a lover-abandoned woman, performed very briefly in New York and Boston; *Hippolytus* (first published 1941), another play about an unfulfilled woman; *A Trip to Cuba* (1860), a travel account, critical of slavery but also, strangely, of Caribbean slaves. She penned "The Battle Hymn of the Republic" in a candle-lit tent one dark night early in the Civil War. She claimed the poem was divinely inspired. It was published in the *Atlantic Monthly* (Feb 1862) and earned her only $4 but also international acclaim.

After the war, and once her husband became agreeable again (1868), Julia Ward Howe supported a variety of liberal causes, led the American Woman Suffrage Association (beginning 1869) with Lucy Stone (1818-93), founded the weekly suffragist *Woman's Journal* (1870), and participated in prison reform and international peace movements. After her husband died (1876), Julia Ward Howe became involved in a whirlwind round of speaking tours. Her fluency in French, German, Greek, and Italian helped her greatly. Later books include *Later Lyrics* (1866); *From the Oak to the Olive* (1868), travel sketches; *Sex and Education . . .* (1874), a symposium about coeducation which she edited; biographies of her husband (1876) and of her friend Margaret Fuller* (1883); *Is Polite Society Polite? And Other Essays* (1895), lectures; *From Sunset Ridge: Poems Old and New* (1898); *Reminiscences 1819-1899* (1899); *Sketches of Representative Women of New England* (1905); and finally *At Sunset* (1910). Julia Ward Howe knew many establishment figures during her long life, and until the end she made literary salons of her homes in New York and Newport, Rhode Island.

When Samuel Ward was visiting New England (1838), he introduced Longfellow to all three of his sisters. At Newport Longfellow and Julia discussed the round tower near which the skeleton had been found that inspired his poem "The Skeleton in Armor." He saw Julia and her sisters again (Jan 1840), at Sam's fancy New York home, while Longfellow stayed there during his engagement to lecture on Dante and Jean Paul Richter. Julia nicknamed Longfellow "Longobardus" and "Longo." Members of her family also called him Longo. He briefly tried to interest Anne in himself, with no success. Later, Cornelius Conway Felton,* Longfellow's friend who had also met the sisters, urged him by letter (15 Jun 1842) to try for any one of the three but singled Julia for unique praise: "Julia is the most remarkable person I ever knew." He added that it would be glorious if Longfellow, Charles Sumner,* and Samuel Gridley Howe should severally wed "that band of graces." Howe did soon marry Julia (1843), after which the Longfellows and the Howes often socialized and in that way moved in some interesting circles. For example, when the Howes welcomed Louis Kossuth* and Ferencz Pulszky (1814–97), Polish and Hungarian exiles respectively, and their wives, the Longfellows met them; further, according to Longfellow's journal (11 May 1852), "The Pulszkys, and Mrs. Howe, dined with us." In *White, Red, and Black* (1852), Ferencz and Theresa Pulszky described their travels in England and the United States and lauded the "natural nobility" of Longfellow and his wife, "a lady of Junonian beauty and the kindest of hearts." In his journal (24 Aug 1852), Longfellow highly praises Julia by dubbing her "our Madame de Sévigné" (the original being the splendid, fashionable French writer [1626–96]). Longfellow and Julia attended a concert of German music (Dec 1853), mostly that of Richard Wagner. She probably enjoyed it more than he did. As for her *Passion Flowers*, he found the verses "full of genius, full of beauty; but what a sad tone! Another cry of discontent. Here is [pro-feminist] revolt enough, between these blue covers" (24 Dec 1853). Nathaniel Hawthorne,* also moving in the Howe circles, reflected the harsher negative criticism her writings often evoked. He wrote (24 Apr 1857) to

William Davis Ticknor, the cousin of George Ticknor,* that "delightful" though *Passion Flowers* were, "she [Mrs. Howe] ought to be soundly whipt for publishing them." He added that in *The World's Own* she reveals "no genius or talent, except for making public what she ought to keep to herself—viz. her passions, emotions, and womanly weaknesses." Longfellow noted in his journal (15 Jan 1858) that he attended a performance of *The World's Own* but made no comment on it. Years later he noted in his journal (14 Apr 1871) that Julia and Samuel Ward visited him and that he was glad to see Sam! It is not too much to say that Julia Ward Howe was an enigma to Longfellow, who by comparison was too serenely conservative.

Bibliography: Tharp; Thompson; Wagenknecht, 1955.

HOWE, SAMUEL GRIDLEY (1801–76). A distinguished humanitarian, Howe was born in Boston, graduated from Brown (1821), earned a Harvard medical degree (1824), and then fought and worked with the Greeks in their struggle for independence (1825–31). He combined chivalric adventure and practical philanthropy. He published *Historical Sketch of the Greek Revolution* (1828). He was hired to establish a school for the blind in Boston. To prepare, he studied schools for the blind in England, France, and Germany (1831–32), during which time he was briefly jailed in Berlin for giving Polish refugees supplies and money (1831). Home in Boston, and bringing along a teacher from Paris and another from Edinburgh, he opened a school in his father's home. It grew and was eventually moved. With financial support mainly from a prominent Bostonian named Thomas H. Perkins, Howe expanded it into what became the Perkins Institute for the Blind. He gained international acclaim, in part for educating Laura Dewey Bridgman (1829–89), deaf, blind, and mute, by means of his invention of a raised alphabet. He visited several states and helped establish other schools. Meanwhile, this vigorous man coedited the *New-England Magazine* (1834–35) with Park Benjamin;* married Julia Ward Howe* (1843); had six children with her; proved rancorous, if not more, when she succeeded as a writer; worked with Horace Mann (1796–1859; the brother-in-law of Nathaniel Hawthorne*) in the field of educational reform; and extended his influence into improving schools for the then-labeled "feeble-minded young," prison conditions, and mental institutions (with Dorothy Dix [1802–87]). Howe and his wife founded and briefly edited the abolitionist *Commonwealth* (1851–52). He gave material comfort to John Brown, then denied having done so, and after Brown was hanged (1859), felt it expedient to escape to Canada briefly. Howe worked for the Sanitary Commission during the Civil War, after which he lent his voice to that of his friend Charles Sumner* in demanding rights for African Americans freed in the South but suffering under deplorable Reconstruction conditions. Howe tried to help Cretans in their unsuccessful fight for freedom from Greece (1866–67). He also tried to help President Ulysses S. Grant when he sought to annex Santo Domingo (1871). Howe was aggressive, generous and brave, and moodily quixotic; a chorus of blind girls sang at his funeral.

Longfellow met Howe (Jul 1837), during a vacation in the White Mountains with George Stillman Hillard,* who delivered an oration at Dartmouth College. When Longfellow sent Howe a copy of *Evangeline,* the good doctor in an effusive letter (8 Nov 1847) thanked him for writing "a book that pleases, instructs, improves people," said that he couldn't "appreciate the *literary* merits of Evangeline," and added that "ordinary verse" (not its hexameters) might have "pleased" him "better." Longfellow was less interested in Howe's politics than in Howe's wife's writing. The following note in Longfellow's journal (22 Dec 1850) provides sufficient evidence: "Dr. Howe dashed out on horseback, and sat an hour,—a long visit for him. The conversation took a philanthropico-political turn." Longfellow adds (5 Jan 1851): "After dinner Sumner read to us . . . Dr. Howe came in the midst of it, and we talked politics as usual." Longfellow does praise Howe, in a journal entry, for hosting a children's party: "Howe has so much sympathy with children that he manages such

matters admirably well" (28 May 1852). In another entry (4 Jan 1860), Longfellow skirts the problem of Howe's involvement with John Brown: "He [Howe] said nothing about the Virginia tragedy or his being summoned as a witness." If Longfellow knew of the Howes's serious marital problems, he would have sided with Julia.

Bibliography: S. Longfellow; Schwartz, Harold. *Samuel Gridley Howe: Social Reformer, 1801–1876.* Cambridge: Harvard University Press, 1956; Tharp; Thompson.

HOWELLS, WILLIAM DEAN (1837–1920).

Man of letters of editor. Howells was born at Martin's Ferry, Ohio, was a typesetter in his printer-publisher father's printing office, wrote for the Columbus *Ohio State Journal* (1856–61), published some minor writings, and studied literature and languages on his own. In gratitude for writing Abraham Lincoln's campaign biography (1860), Howells was named American consul to Venice, Italy (1861–65). Before going to Europe, Howells took a literary pilgrimage to New England and New York and met a dozen or so established writers, including Ralph Waldo Emerson,* James T. Fields,* Nathaniel Hawthorne,* Oliver Wendell Holmes,* James Russell Lowell,* George Ticknor,* and Longfellow. In Paris (1852), Howells married Elinor Gertrude Mead (1837–1910), a cousin of Rutherford B. Hayes, later the president; the Howellses had three children. While in Italy, Howells wrote two travel books and studied Italian literature assiduously. After returning home, he became an astute editor, first of the *Nation* in New York (1865–66), then Fields's assistant at the *Atlantic Monthly* (1866–71), and finally its editor (1871–81). Howells joined the Saturday Club* (1874). During the 1880s, he associated with other magazines, wrote extensively (novels, critical essays, and reviews), and promoted both the cause of realism and morality in it. He and his family, including his gravely ill daughter Winifred, moved to New York (1888; she died in 1889). Violent labor unrest and a study of the writings of Leo Tolstoy (1828–1910), the Russian novelist and moral philosopher, and Henry George (1839–1897), the liberal

American economist, inspired Howells to become an anti-imperialistic, moderately progressive socialist. He traveled frequently, and often with his wife. The bulk of Howells's prodigious literary production, much of which was popular and influential after Longfellow's death, includes novels, travel books, and books of criticism. His books of reminiscence, all of which illuminate the age of Longfellow and his contemporaries, are *My Literary Passions* (1895), *Literary Friends and Acquaintances: A Personal Retrospective of American Authorship* (1900, 1910), *Heroines of Fiction* (1901), *Literature and Life* (1902), and *My Mark Twain* (1910). Howells's brand of realistic fiction, now considered timid, was in his day regarded as rather daring by conservative readers and critics, especially in Boston.

Howells applied (1860) for the job as assistant editor of the *Atlantic Monthly* under Fields, did not get it, and went to Italy. Otherwise, Longfellow would surely have met him earlier than he did. In his journal (1 Oct 1864), Longfellow records his admiration for Howells's article on "Modern [Recent] Italian Comedy" (*NAR,* Oct 1864). When Howells became Fields's assistant editor of the *Atlantic,* Longfellow met him. Longfellow invited Howells to a Dante Club meeting and jotted in his journal (28 Jan 1866) that he was "formerly consul at Venice, poet and prose-writer; a very clever and cultivated young man." He attended the last Dante reading (13 June 1866). During these meetings, he associated with Fields, George Washington Greene,* Oliver Wendell Holmes,* James Russell Lowell,* and Charles Eliot Norton,* among others. Howells sent Longfellow a copy of his *Venetian Life* (1866), eliciting a letter (25 Aug 1866) in which Longfellow says that the work "is full of light and color, and . . . insight into life." By letter (11 Apr 1867), Longfellow thanked Howells for his favorable review (*NAR,* Apr 1867) of the seven-volume trade edition of Longfellow's works (1867). In 1870, Longfellow obtained a translation by Howells of "St. Ambrosio" by Giuseppe Giusti (1809–50) for inclusion in the Supplement to Longfellow's edition of *Poets and Poetry of Europe* (1871). In later meetings including

Longfellow, often hosted by him, and sometimes written about in his journal, Howells associated with Thomas Gold Appleton,* Richard Henry Dana Sr.,* Bret Harte, John Gorham Palfrey,* Bayard Taylor,* John Greenleaf Whittier,* and many other writers. Longfellow wrote Greene (7 Dec 1874), "Have you seen Howells' new novel, 'A Foregone Conclusion' [1874]? The scene is Venice [he continues], and the character of the priest Don Ippolito is very powerfully drawn. In that respect this book is a stride forward." Longfellow evidently didn't comment on Howells's two earlier novels or on three later ones available to him before his death. Longfellow might have felt that American realism was evolving too perilously to suit him. Longfellow attended a performance in Boston (1878) of Howells's play *A Counterfeit Presentiment;* was prevented by chronic neuralgia from attending in Boston *Yorick's Love,* Howells's adaptation of *Un Drama Nuevo* by the Spanish playwright Manuel Tamayo y Baus (1829–98; pen name, Joaquín Estébañez); and in his letter of regret to Howells (18 Jan 1880) said that he "enjoyed so much" *A Counterfeit Presentiment* earlier. In his *Literary Friends and Acquaintances,* Howells wrote about Longfellow more skillfully and at greater length than any of their contemporaries did. Comparing Longfellow, Holmes, and Lowell, he concludes that "Longfellow was easily the greatest poet of the three"; he adds that Longfellow's "beautiful genius . . . was not to know decay while life endured." In him, Howells saw "a final dignity . . . delicate and . . . inviolable," further, a "gentle and exquisitely modest dignity." When Mark Twain, Howells's closest friend, satirized Emerson, Holmes, and Longfellow at Whittier's birthday party, Howells called the speech "the amazing mistake, the bewildering blunder, the cruel catastrophe," observed Longfellow's "regarding the humorist with an air of pensive puzzle," and recalled Longfellow's later comment that Twain "'is a *wag.*'" Howells sufficiently sums up his devotion to Longfellow thus: "All men that I have known . . . have had some foible . . . , or some meanness, or pettiness, or bitterness; but Longfellow had none, nor the suggestion of any.

No breath of evil ever touched his name; he went in and out among his fellow-men without the reproach that follows wrong . . ." Howells comments on many specific works by Longfellow, especially those written "during the eighteen years that I knew him," when he wrote "the best of his minor poems, the greatest of his sonnets, the sweetest of his lyrics." More specifically, "The Challenge" reinforced Howells's awareness that Longfellow's "heart was open to all the homelessness of the world." The six sonnets inspired by Dante's *Divina Commedia* Howells calls "noble." When Longfellow read parts of "The Theologian's Tale: Elizabeth," from *Tales of a Wayside Inn,* aloud to Howells, "he liked my liking its rhythmical form [in hexameters], which . . . he had used . . . with so much pleasure and success."

Bibliography: Green; Howells, William Dean. *Literary Friends and Acquaintances: A Personal Retrospective of American Authorship.* Eds. David F. Hiatt and Edwin H. Cady. Bloomington and London: Indiana University Press, 1968; S. Longfellow; Tryon; Wagenknecht, 1955; Wagenknecht, Edward. "Longfellow and Howells." *Emerson Society Quarterly,* no. 58, part 1 (1st quarter 1970): 52–57.

"HYMN FOR MY BROTHER'S ORDINATION" (1850). Poem, *S/F.* Long ago Christ told a man to sell his possessions, give to the poor, and follow Him. Today He says the same to another, who obeys, and acts so as to hope for approval at "fair" wedding scenes and at "midnight prayer." The man trusts Christ as "the beloved John" did. Longfellow wrote this devout poem (1848) on the occasion of the ordination of his brother Samuel Longfellow in the Unitarian Church in Portland, Maine. In his journal (8 Feb 1848) Longfellow calls this poem a "chant" and "a midnight thought." It was sung as part of the ordination service.

Bibliography: S. Longfellow; Wagenknecht, 1986; Williams.

"HYMN OF THE MORAVIAN NUNS OF BETHLEHEM" (1825). Poem, in *USLG,* 1 Jun 1825; *Voices.* At sunset, candles are lighted in the church, the censer swings, and the nuns sing before the consecrated "crimson banner." The hymn asks the warrior to take the banner, be brave, reverent, and merciful in battle, and adjures him to believe that, should he fall, "this crimson flag shall be / Martial cloak and shroud for thee." This stirring juvenile work was written (1825) on the occasion of the consecration of the banner of Casimir Pulaski (1748?– 79), the American Revolutionary War hero. The "nuns" were in reality Moravian sisters, of Bethlehem, Pennsylvania.

Bibliography: Arvin; Little.

"HYMN TO THE NIGHT" (1839). Poem, in *Voices.* The poet begins memorably: "I heard the trailing garments of the Night [with 'sable skirts'] / Sweep through her marble halls!" He sees nearby light, hears sad and happy sounds, and drinks "repose" from the cool air. From Night he uncomplainingly "learn[s] to bear / What man has borne before!" He prays for peace and the descent of "best-beloved Night!" The first title of this poem was "Night."

Bibliography: Arms, George. "Longfellow's 'Hymn to the Night.'" *Explicator* 1 (Oct 1942): 7; Arvin; Engstrom, A. G. "Baudelaire and Longfellow's 'Hymn to the Night.'" *Modern Language Notes* 74 (Dec 1959): 695–98; More; Thompson; Wagenknecht, 1986; Williams.

HYPERION (1839). Novel in four numbered Books.

Book I. Paul Flemming, our hero, is emerging from sorrow caused by his girlfriend's death. In December he is traveling along the Rhine, which he saw one May a while ago, to southern Germany. His drift through life resembles the river's flow.

At Andernach he sees the tower, thinks of the innkeeper's dead daughter, and listens to her great-grandmother's legend about Christ. The Savior walked with ladder and lantern through the town, repaired a roof, some hogsheads, a windmill, a gate, and a boat, then nailed himself back on the church's huge crucifix. Flemming proceeds by post-chaise to Capellen.

He observes the ruin of Stolzenfels. It warns him to beware of dreams, illusions, desires, and tells him not to seek unique wisdom, as a clerical alchemist here did, but to study "the book of Nature." Handsome Flemming's good heart was hurt when death took "the sweet blue flower that bloomed beside him." He now acts more from impulse than principle, but deep down he has solid common sense.

At Salzig, Flemming is rowed on the Rhine by his landlady's teen-aged daughter, who agrees to relate the tale of the Liebenstein: Lady Geraldine was loved by two brothers, whose duel was stopped when she appeared before them as a nun—and Heaven's bride.

On to Mayence. Flemming dines lavishly and with an intelligent fat man discusses at great length the unique personality of Jean Paul Richter (1763–1825), whose writings, they agree, have "ten thousand beauties of thought and expression." After visiting the cathedral, Flemming proceeds to Heidelberg. He drives through the Hauptstrasse and calls on the Baron of Hohenfels, a friend he will winter with.

Behold Heidelberg: towers, palaces and gardens, chapel with carvings, valley and the Neckar. Flemming chats with the Baron, his dilettantish, eclectically studious host, who tells him how the castle has been haunted ever since a lady of the court and a monk disguised themselves as the Virgin Mary and Satan, respectively, to frighten a nobleman, whose guard, however, killed the monk.

A snowstorm pleases Flemming. After the Baron relates the history of the University of Heidelberg, they discuss scholarship, medieval monks' preservation of manuscripts, the value to a nation of its great authors, the dangers to writers not only of seclusion but also of popular disrespect, and their need to enjoy life and develop common sense.

Flemming muses: Time's Doomsday-Book has few names "never to be effaced." Oblivion awaits most of us; so let's worry less about gaining fame than about working dutifully. The best writers, though usually unhappy, carry on. The Baron offers and praises his wine. Many fine writers have drunk a lot (Schiller adored Rhine wine, for example). The two friends, debating whether life in town or country inspires writers more, agree that both environments pose dangers. The best authors—for example, Dante, Cervantes, and Byron—defy public criticism. Literary biographies shout a single word of advice: "Wait!" Flemming studies "the ancient poetic lore of Germany" all through the winter.

Book II. Spring—"What a thrill of delight" everywhere—comes to Heidelberg.

The Baron asks Flemming his opinion of *Urania* (1801), the didactic poem by Christoph August Tiedge (1752–1841), and is pleased when Flemming calls it "poor and pious." They discuss the love affair of old Goethe and young Bettina Brentano (von Arnim, 1785–1859), whose brother, Klemens Brentano (1778–1842), published *Des Knaben von Wunderhorn,* the ballads in which Flemming adores. The Baron calls ballads "the gypsy-children of song." The two men mention a dozen or more writers, but Flemming never mentions "the sorrow with which his heart was heavy."

They observe several people at the Hauptstrasse: Frau Himmelauen, who gossips critically about Flemming and American women; Anton Friedrich Justus Thibault (1772–1840), civil-law scholar; a wild-haired professor who believes in metempsychosis; Frau von Ilmenau, her convalescent daughter Emma, and an exiled Polish count attending her; Edgar Quinet (1803–75), author of *Ahasuerus* (1833), which Flemming calls "very wild." When the Baron voices dislike of modern French authors, Flemming theorizes that they write out of ennui. He waxes so rhapsodic about an American tree transplanted in Heidelberg, and glowing like bronze in the sunset, that the Baron says he ought to write an epic poem about it.

The two enter a student beer tavern, which is noisy, smelly, and foul with tobacco smoke. The students sing a wild song about a postilion bringing a fox to a family—papa reading, mamma making tea, daughter knitting, rector kidding scholar, fox smoking and "So grows the Fox a Bursch [student]!" One student drinks three big goblets of beer, thus defeating his rival, who sinks unconscious "midway in his third glass." A contentious student kicks several glasses, is challenged, soon fights six duels, and is nicely scarred in lip and eyelid.

Emma of Ilmenau gently asks Madelaine, her old French chambermaid who is "virtuous, because she had never been tempted," to leave her alone to her sorrow. In a letter, the Polish count, though married, avows his love. While he serenades her from outside, Emma says to herself that she hates him but will pray for him.

The wild-haired professor visits Flemming and the Baron, who falls asleep, bored by the professor's harangue "in a half-intelligible strain for two hours," which Flemming thinks is mostly based on *Die Bestimmung des Menschen* (1800) by Johann Gottlieb Fichte (1762–1814) and *Die Geschichte der Seele* (1830) by Gotthilf Heinrich von Schubert (1780–1860). The professor criticizes Flemming's age for lacking faith and for paying too much attention to the "earthly" past, present, and future and too little to radiant "Eternity." Flemming counters by quoting Thomas Carlyle to the effect that much current philosophical mumbo-jumbo can be reduced to old-fashioned knowledge "so familiar as to be a truism." The professor dilates on time being "the Life of the Soul," or else, "what is Time?" To which, the Baron rousing, says, "near midnight!" The meeting breaks up.

The Baron invites Flemming to go to Ems and meet his sister. They go by the Baron's coach through beautiful scenery to an inn at Birkenau, which has a busy mill. The Baron says that understanding German poetry, such as Goethe's song about a mill, depends on loving German landscapes. He recites some poems by Wilhelm Müller (1794–1827). One has a didactic conclusion Flemming labels "dull . . . commentary." Next morning, on to Frankfort and a thrilling performance of *Don Giovanni* by Mozart. Its ballet features a "sylph-like" dancer. A prude in the audience seems so displeased by the ballet that Flemming says she probably would agree with the French priest that called dancing satanic. The prosaic quality of life after a theatrical show is made obvious when the lithe ballerina's whiskery husband says he will "run her six nights at Munich," then take her to Vienna.

In Frankfort, the two friends discuss Goethe, born there. They admire the "indifferentism" Goethe displayed in old age. Flemming dislikes Goethe's sensuality; disagreeing, the Baron cites his marble-cold Iphigenia and says Goethe's merely copied nature; Flemming says so did the filthy Pompeiians. He calls Eckermann Goethe's Boswell, making "a Saint Peter out of an old Jupiter," then quotes Heine's calling Goethe a "majestic tree." The Baron says Johann Wilhelm Ludwig Gleim (1719–1803) regarded Goethe as a devilish youth.

On to Langenschwalbach, for the waters and a walk through the tumble-down church. Next morning, to Ems, by the river Lahn. The Baron's sister left word that she is in Franconia. The friends attend "an aesthetic tea" given by Frau Kranich, who married a rich old banker hoping, unsuccessfully, that he would die and will her a fortune. Guests include "The Grand Duke of Mississippi," rich and affected; Prince Jerkin of Moldavia, whose English is so bad he asks Flemming what he thinks of Frau Kranich's "leather" (i.e., skin); an old Frenchman who likes waltzing, of which Flemming disapproves; and so on. When old Kranich totters in, half dressed and calling himself "Mahomet, the king of the Jews!," the party ends miserably. At sunset, the two friends see Emma of Ilmenau led by Madelaine and the Pole into the woods—and to love-sick Emma's ruin.

In June, the friends are back in Heidelberg, about to part, perhaps forever. The Baron wonders why Flemming, young and from the New World, revels in moldy old places, and says doing so resembles "falling in love with one's grandmother." Flemming counters that he is more at peace now than he was 10 years ago. The city clocks strike midnight. The Baron is going to his sister in Berlin, and lonely Flemming heads for Switzerland.

Book III. The narrator summarizes the glories of summer, of day, of night, mentions the Charles River near the sea, and presents a poem about a silent evening near Mont Blanc with moonlight on Lake Leman.

Flemming presses on, beyond the Saint Gothard Pass, chats with and extravagantly tips a young herdsman, plucks a lonely blue flower, sees the Rhone glacier, sleeps at

Grimsel Hospital, next day gets to a tavern in Meyringen, boats on the Brienz, and stops at Interlachen. Much will happen to him here.

Interlachen and its environs are beautiful. The bells are eloquent. Sunset bathes valley and mountains. The main hotel is full, but the frog-like landlord promises to find Flemming a room in town. Flemming encounters Mr. Berkley, a bright, eccentric British bachelor he recently met at Goldau. Tourists return. A young woman, in black, sits by a window. Her voice thrills Flemming. Berkley tells him that she is Mary Ashburton, an English girl (aged 20) traveling with her widowed mother. Flemming accepts a spare room in a cloister across the street.

In the morning, Flemming sees Mary Ashburton again. Delighting in her quiet face, serious expression, steadily luminous eyes, striking figure, and heavenly soul, he falls in love at once. He tells Berkley that one minute all is gladness, then comes sorrow. The two men have breakfast, share a carriage for a day in the icy Grindelwald mountains, and return to Interlachen, where he converses ecstatically with Mary.

Rain the next day spoils Berkley's planned drive for all four. Flemming reports to Mary anyway. While her mother is "absorbed in the follies of a fashionable novel," he praises Mary's book of sketches, offering apt quotations from poetry the while. He opines that "Art and Nature are more nearly allied than by similitudes only. Art is the revelation of man; and not merely that, but likewise the revelation of Nature, speaking through man. Art pre-exists in Nature, and Nature is reproduced in Art." Flemming "spake" so well that Mary lets him read her well-composed diary, about Roman churches, art works, and medieval illuminated manuscripts.

After an early dinner together, Flemming finds a book by Johann Ludwig Uhland (1787-1862) and offers to tutor Mary in German from it, but she prefers to let him improvise some translations and recite others. Selections concern death disguised as "a sable knight" (*see* "The Black Knight"), a royal couple mourning their daughter's death, the need for souls to commune. Flemming discusses the elegy by Friedrich von Matthies-

son (1761-1831—*see* "Elegy Written in the Ruins of an Old Castle") on Baden-Baden's ruined castle, which Mary saw last summer; recites a poem by Johann Gaudenz Salis (1762-1834) about "the Silent Land" of death; and is so moved by Mary's tears that, caught in the "silken wings" of love, he longs "to possess" her. That night he hears that poor Emma, "tempted in her weakness," has died.

Flemming drives Mary and her mother to the valley of Lauterbrunnen. Mary is surprised that he had not yet seen Mont Blanc and its glaciers and frustrates him by telling him he should go see the place at once. A guitar player capers in, gets a gold coin from Flemming, and sings a song in German to the effect that Flemming should "Take care!" because the "maiden fair"—who knows how to show just enough bosom—"is fooling thee!" (*See* "Beware!")

Flemming, hopelessly in love, goes with Mary—Beatrice to his Dantesque feelings—to the Burg Unspunnen. While sketching, she asks him to make up a story about the place. He improvises: Hieronymus, an impoverished student, loves but has been spurned by Hermione. He has a magic lamp, given him by a Spanish astrologer. When he tells its "midnight Divinity" he wants peace, she tells him to go to the Fountain of Oblivion in the Black Forest and throw a scroll with Hermione's name on it into its waters. The student finds the fountain, sees Hermione in its waters, and tells her he will treasure her memory instead of seeking peaceful oblivion. Flemming ends his story by telling Mary that he is Hieronymus and she is Hermione. He concludes, "Alas! I found . . . love."

Confusion! Mary turns pale and silent. The two return to the hotel. Flemming finds Berkley and tells him everything. Berkley says he once loved and lost and is now glad, and advises Flemming to forget Mary. No! He will always admire and love her but has no hope. They debate for a while about whether likes or contraries attract more, then head next morning toward Innsbruck. Berkley is determined to console his friend.

Book IV. The narrator, in lovely, summery Cambridge now, pauses to humor the sleepy reader by a distracting question. This story, "which is a shadow upon the earth"—will it end in a marriage? This chapter resembles a miserere in the "authorling['s]" church-like art work.

One can become stronger because of a sad disappointment. A week passes, and Flemming suffers quietly. While he and Berkley are traveling by carriage, Berkley quotes the poem by John Suckling beginning "Why so wan and pale, fond lover?" Flemming responds that he admires Mary and wishes her well. At night they pass a village church, and Flemming dreams about a funeral. They sightsee in Innsbruck briefly and proceed to Salzburg.

Flemming develops a severe fever, hallucinates about Mary, sleeps, and after two weeks begins to recover. Berkley discusses biographies of German writers, most of whom had nice grandfathers, austere or dead fathers, and sickly mothers. The biography of E. T. A. Hoffmann (1776–1822) was different. Berkley calls Hoffmann "this unfortunate genius," says that he saw him once at an aesthetic tea, and concludes that "tobacco, wine, and midnight did their work like fiends" on him. When paralyzed and dying, Hoffmann dictated fiction and asked his wife to sit beside him. Flemming, declining to judge him harshly, says we can learn much from "a man's errors."

Berkley reads a story by Hoffmann in which Johannes Kreisler Kepellmeister (one of Hoffmann's pen names) describes an aesthetic tea he attended. He played numerous variations on the piano while other guests played cards, listened to dreadful singing by the host's daughters, Marie and Nanette Rödelein, and a few guests, downed several glasses of Burgundy, and even wrote on some handy blank paper. His conclusion? Writers, composers, and painters should be allowed to work without distractions.

Flemming and Berkley change horses at Hof. The natives remind Flemming of "Indians in the frontier villages of America." On to a town called Saint Gilgen, beside Saint Wolfgang's lake. After eating at the inn, the two stroll into the cemetery. Those resting there "heed no more the blandishments of earthly friendship." Musing that "Death

brings us again to our friends," Flemming quotes Henry Vaughan's "They Are All Gone into the World of Light!," feels tranquil at last, and lets Berkley go to Ischel alone.

Days pass. Flemming admires a widow with a deformed son, whom she loves tenderly; Flemming muses on "the beauty and excellence of the female character." Berkley suddenly reappears, and he and Flemming hire boatmen to show them the lake. Berkley scoffs at two local stories: Saint Wolfgang saved a butcher from drowning; a bridal party danced on the ice, fell through, and drowned. He also shouts blasphemies in the echo chamber of the saint's hermitage. They are rowed to the village of Saint Wolfgang, where Berkley rudely talks Latin to the local priest until the confused man bolts, but only to return with a wild-looking friend. This fellow, Brother Bernardus, says he has been "chosen by Heaven" to become a missionary to the Indians near Lake Superior and "unite all nations and people in one church!"

Bernardus tells how he became a Franciscan friar; was encouraged by a vision of his deceased mother; pronounced Prince-Abbot Berthold's funeral sermon; taught biblical hermeneutics in Klagenfurt for 10 years; found prejudices in the writings of Gregory Sixteenth (1765–1846; Pope, 1831–46); saw comparative philology as an instrument for uniting Christianity "in one Church"; found reinforcements in a star, in a meteor, and in "Luther, Melancthon, Calvin, and other great men . . . [who] fought with Satan in the Church"; and like Christ avoided Satan's snares. Bernardus determines to "excommunicate the Pope" and leave for America, inspired by Frederick Baraga (1797–1868), the Austrian-born Catholic missionary to the Great Lakes area. Flemming judges Bernardus to be "another melancholy victim of solitude and overlabor of the brain." Berkley cautions Flemming "Never [to] mind trifles" and says he is leaving early tomorrow. That night Flemming learns that the widow's deformed child has died.

On Sunday, Flemming attends church, appreciates the sermon text—"I know my Redeemeth liveth"—and watches as a child, dying only hours after its birth, is buried. This prompts him to ponder on numerous artistic representations of death, from youthful angel to dancing skeleton. He enters a chapel, weeps, prays, and is inspired by a tablet with a message challenging the reader not to mourn "the Past" but "improve the Present." Flemming "almost miraculous[ly]" comes to terms with his "wounded pride and unrequited love," and resolves to return to America, and "live . . . wisely."

Past Munich, Augsburg, and Ulm to a Stuttgard hotel goes Flemming. On Sunday he attends church but leaves before the long sermon on the history of the Reformation ends. He calls on Johann Heinrich von Danneker (1758–1841), the famous sculptor, and is impressed by the old man's devout thoughts. Danneker mentions Germany's poet-physician Paul Flem(m)ing (1609–40). Inspired by Danneker's career, Flemming longs to accomplish something himself, returns to his hotel, and happens to hear the voice of a woman in the adjoining room. She is Mary Ashburton. He dreams about her that night but, having "drunk the last drop of the bitter cup," departs quietly by postilion next morning.

Longfellow titled his work *Hyperion* not to suggest a character but because it expresses man's lofty spiritual aspirations. He made abundant use of memories of his 1835–36 experiences in Germany and Switzerland. In his first letter to Samuel Ward* (3 Apr 1836), he alludes to Jean Paul. Longfellow was in Ems, Mayence, and Heidelberg (summer 1836), met a man who told him about Jean Paul, and went on to Switzerland; conversed with Danneker in Stuttgart; at Ischel and Saint Gilgen, met a "Mr. K.," who becomes Berkley. Details from Longfellow's 1838 Harvard lectures on "The Lives of Literary Men"—on Jean Paul, Hoffmann, expatriates in Rome, and medieval scholars' work—also found their way into *Hyperion.* More important, in Thun, Switzerland (Jul 1836), Longfellow met Nathan Appleton* and his family, including his daughter Fanny (*see* Longfellow, Fanny), saw them again in Interlaken, renewed his mild friendship with Fanny next year in Boston, made her the model for Mary Ashburton, and miffed Fanny in the process when she was embarrassed to see traces of herself in print when *Hyperion* was published two years later.

One of the purposes of the novel was to acquaint American readers with German literature, just as several earlier works by Washington Irving* had told them about English life and literature. Longfellow's personal aim was to create a Bildungsroman à la Goethe's *Wilhelm Meisters Lehrjahre,* but stressing only Flemming's spiritual maturing. Longfellow wrote George Washington Greene* (10 Jun 1841) that *Hyperion* shows "the passage of a morbid mind into a purer and healthier state." Briefly lacking other ideas, Longfellow (May 1849) pondered the idea of a sequel to *Hyperion.* By 1857, *Hyperion* had sold 14,550 copies. He revised it for a new edition published in London with illustrations (1864). A revised edition was also made part of Longfellow's *Complete Works* (1866). The original edition was translated into French (1840, again with *Kavanagh* [1860]), Swedish (1853), German (1856), and Dutch (1881). *Hyperion* is virtually unread nowadays; though relentlessly pedantic, and often flowery and stilted, it has fine descriptive passages and many effective similes and metaphors. Part of "The Happy Man and the Lucky Dog," an excerpt of "The Blank Book of a Country Schoolmaster" (*which see*), was made part of Book 4 of *Hyperion.*

Bibliography: Cowie; Crowninshield; Deiml, Otto. *Der Einfluss von Jean Paul auf Longfellows Prosatil.* Ph.D. diss., Erlangen, 1927; Higginson; Hilen, ed.; Hirsh; S. Longfellow; Stowe, William W. "*The Heidenmauer* and *Hyperion:* Uses of Central Europe in [James Fenimore] Cooper and Longfellow." In *Images of Central Europe in Travelogues and Fiction by North American Writers,* ed. Waldemar Zacharasiewicz, 51–59. Tübingen: Stauffenburg Verlag, 1996; Thompson; Wagenknecht, 1955.

"IDEAL BEAUTY." Sonnet, translated from the Spanish poet Fernando de Herrera (1534?-97), in Scudder. The poet, still mortal, hopes for immortal love. Her beauty, while veiled in flesh, hints at her ideal glory.

"THE IMAGE OF GOD" (1833). Poem, translated from the Spanish poet Francisco de Aldana (1537-78), in *Coplas; Voices*. The Lord sees me, fashioned in His image but obscured by the world. The sun's warmth lessens. Although my days are wintry, my faith remains green and I hope to see the image of the merciful "Celestial King" as I, created by "the gazer . . . ," look "in a glass." *(See also Outre-Mer.)*

INCOME FOR LONGFELLOW. Longfellow's starting salary as Professor of Modern Languages at Bowdoin (1829-35) was $800 a year, with $100 in addition for his service as librarian that first year. Longfellow's annual salary as professor at Bowdoin was soon raised to $1,000. In his fourteen years as Professor of Modern Languages and Belles-Lettres at Harvard (1840-54), he was paid $1,800 the first year, $1,500 for each of the next five years, and $1,800 for each of the last eight years. The total was $23,700, or an average of $1,693 per year. Magazines (1840-44) paid him almost half the money he made by writing; but during all those years, magazine payments (only 3 a year) netted him about a tenth of what book sales paid him. Income from his books and magazine publications (1840-54) totaled $19,068 (or $1,362 per year). He was paid from $15 to $20 per poem (1840-41). But George Rex Graham,* the owner and editor of *Graham's Magazine,* soon thereafter contracted to buy poems from Longfellow for $50 apiece; however, Graham objected (1845) that a sonnet Longfellow submitted cost nearly $4 per line without filling up much of a page.

At the end of the 1853-54 academic year, Longfellow resigned from Harvard to devote himself exclusively to writing. His writings earned him $1,700 (1854). For the next few years he was averaging almost as much by writing as he had averaged by teaching, and enjoyed life more. His income was $25,343 (1855-64). In one journal entry (31 Mar 1857) he lists eleven of his books and the sales figure of each, totaling $326,308. He negotiated a new contract with Houghton Mifflin, his publishers in Boston (1865). Collected editions of his works for the next decade earned him an annual average income of $3,284. Major James Redpath (1833-91), the successful lecture agent, asked Longfellow (Aug 1875) to go on a circuit involving something like fifty evening lectures (or readings) over some thirty weeks for $25,000, less Longfellow's travel expenses and a commission to Redpath's Boston Lyceum Bureau. Longfellow declined the offer, as well as an offer for 3 trial appearances, and even one such appearance, for proportionately less money. In 1875 and on until 1882, the year of his death, Longfellow's publishers paid him an annual fee of $4,000 to reissue his former books. Although his short poems are more favorably viewed by present-day readers, his two long narrative poems, *Evangeline* and *The Song of Hiawatha,* sold steadily and well for decades after their publication; the latter, for example, earned $7,000 in its first decade. By 1864, his three books of fiction and fictional autobiography, *Outre-Mer, Kavanagh,* and *Hyperion,* had sold more than 35,000 copies in various editions; and for many years, *Hyperion* alone outsold *Evangeline.* Longfellow's immense drawing power is indicated by the fact that Robert Bonner (1824–99), the editor of the *New York Ledger,* paid $3,000 to publish "The Hanging of the Crane" (1874) a 196-line poem.

Converted to their equivalent in current purchasing power, some of the dollar figures above would be roughly as follows: $4 would be $100; $20, $500; $50, $1,250; $100, $2,500; $1,000, $25,000; $4,000, $100,000; and $25,343, upwards of $600,000!

Bibliography: Green; Hilen, ed.; S. Longfellow; Bruccoli, Matthew J., ed. *The Profession of Authorship in America, 1800–1870: The Papers of William Charvat.* Columbus: Ohio State University Press, 1968; Thompson, Lawrance R. "Longfellow Sells *The Spanish Student." American Literature* 6 (May 1934): 141–50.

"THE INDIAN HUNTER" (1825). Poem, in *USLG,* 15 May 1825; Scudder. When summer ends, the Indian sees the white man's progress in farming. Autumnal winds follow. Harvesters dance "by the greenwood tree." The Indian leaves his ancestral haunts with bitter thoughts "Of the white man's faith, and love unkind." The Indian throws himself into a "misty lake." Years later a fisherman spies, "A skeleton wasted and white," washed ashore, and in its hand "a hunter's bow." Longfellow wrote James T. Fields* (12 Apr 1852) asking him to omit this poem from the 1852 London edition of *The Poetical Works of Henry Wadsworth Longfellow.*

Bibliography: Hilen, ed.; Little.

"THE INDIAN SUMMER" (1831). Prose tale, signed "L," in *Token,* Boston, 1831.

"INSCRIPTION ON THE SHANKLIN FOUNTAIN" (1882). Poem, in *Harbor.* The weary traveler is invited to have a drink of "pure and sweet" water, leave refreshed, and remember the well "in his [Christ's] name."

"IN THE CHURCHYARD AT CAMBRIDGE" (1853). Poem, *Courtship, Birds* (1858). A beautiful woman lies buried in the cemetery, and "At her feet and at her head / Lies a slave to attend the dead." Was this an act of pompous vanity or of "Christian charity"? Not by the dead "will the mystery be unmasked." At Judgment Day we will be too busy accounting for our "secret sins and terrors" to wonder whether the lady was angry or proud. Legend has it that Madame Vassal(l), wife of John Vassal(l), the original owner of Craigie House* in Cambridge, was buried thus with two slaves in the graveyard next to Christ Church. This controversial poem was first published, as "In the Churchyard at Cambridge. A Legend of Lady Lee.—H.W.L.," in *Autumn Leaves: Original Pieces in Prose and Verse* (1853), compiled by Anne W. Abbot.

Bibliography: Arms; Arvin; Elliott, G. R. *The Cycle of Modern Poetry: A Series of Essays Toward Clearing Our Present Poetic Dilemma.* Princeton: Princeton University Press, 1929; Richards, I. A. *Practical Criticism: A Study of Literary Judgment.* New York: Harcourt, Brace and World, 1929; Wagenknecht, 1986.

"IN THE CHURCHYARD AT TARRYTOWN" (1877). Sonnet, in *AM,* Mar 1877; *Kéramos;* Scudder. The "gentle humorist," who livened tired hours "with mirth" and pleased hearts with "romantic tales," came "Here in the autumn of his days" to rest by "The river that he loved and glorified." The subject is Washington Irving.*

IN THE HARBOR: ULTIMA THULE— PART II (1882). Collection of poems: *Poems:* "Becalmed," "Hermes Trismegistus," "The Poet's Calendar," "Mad River, in the White Mountains," "Auf Wiedersehen," "The Children's Crusade," "The City and the Sea," "Sundown," "President Garfield," "Decoration Day," "Chimes," "Four by the Clock," "The Four Lakes of Madison," "Moonlight,"

"To the Avon," "Elegiac Verse," "A Fragment," "The Bells of San Blas." *Translations:* "Prelude [as treasures . . .]," "From the French [will ever the dear days . . .]," "The Wine of Jurançon," "At La Chaudreau," "A Quiet Life." *Personal Poems:* "Loss and Gain," "Autumn Within," "Victor and Vanquished," "Memories," "My Books." "Possibilities."

"THE IRON PEN" (1879). Poem, in *Harper's New Monthly Magazine,* Dec 1879; *Thule.* The poet imagines that the iron pen would rise by itself and inscribe his gratitude, that its inlaid gems would shine like thoughts, and that its wood would write some verses on the sky. The pen, however, lies in its "casket" like a mitred bishop. The poet remembers "that summer day" when "Helen of Maine" stood in the garden and gave him this pen. Her "blessing" to him was like a dew drop on "an aged tree." A girl named Helen Hamlin, of Bangor, Maine, gave Longfellow a uniquely attractive pen (Jun 1879). It was made of iron from the prison of Chillon, where François de Bonnivard (1496-1570) languished (1532-36); of three gems from Siberia, Ceylon, and Maine, respectively, all set in a gold circlet; and of wood from the U.S. frigate *Constitution.*

IRVING, WASHINGTON (1783–1859). Born in New York City, Irving was the first American writer to achieve an international reputation. He began his prolific and varied career by writing satirical pieces for newspapers, collaborated with two others (all anonymously) in the uproarious *Salmagundi; or, the Whim-whams and Opinions of Launcelot Langstaff, Esq. & Others* (1807-8), and under the pseudonym Diedrich Knickerbocker wrote the popular social satire titled *A History of New York, from the Beginning of the World to the End of the Dutch Dynasty* . . . (1809). Partly financed by his indulgent brothers, Irving moved to England (1815). While there he published his greatest work, *The Sketch Book of Geoffrey Crayon, Gent.* (1819-20), which included "Rip Van Winkle" (often called the first American short story) and "The Legend of Sleepy Hollow." After continued successes in England, Irving moved to Spain

(1826), where he produced several books, including a biography of Christopher Columbus (4 vols., 1828) and essays and sketches assembled in *The Alhambra* (2 vols., 1832). Welcomed home again, Irving toured and then did research about the West; the literary consequences included *A Tour on the Prairies* (1835), *Astoria, or, Enterprise Beyond the Rocky Mountains* (3 vols., 1836), concerning the western commercial ventures of his rich old friend John Jacob Astor (1763-1848), and a two-volume book about Benjamin Louis Eulalie Bonneville (1796-1878), American army captain who explored the Northwest (1832-35). Irving, who had been on the staff of the U.S. embassy in Madrid (1826-29) and was secretary of the U.S. legation in London (1829-32), capped his diplomatic career as U.S. minister to Spain (1842-45). Irving lived at "Sunnyside," in Tarrytown, New York (from 1846), where he wrote and published *Mahomet and His Successors* (2 vols., 1850), a five-volume life of George Washington (1855-59), and minor items.

From his early years, Longfellow delighted in reading works by Irving. *The Sketch-Book* and *Salmagundi* pieces inspired some prose items Longfellow published during and just after his college years in the *United States Literary Gazette* and the Portland *Advertiser.* Before he left on his first European tour (1826), Longfellow took letters of recommendation to Irving, including one written by George Ticknor.* Soon after Longfellow first went to Paris (Jun 1826), he met Irving's nephew, Pierre Irving (1803-76). Longfellow met Irving himself in Madrid at the American consul's home. Irving was then at work on his biography of Columbus. In a letter to his father (20 Mar 1827), Longfellow described Irving in detail as unceremonious, mirthful, and handsome, and as delivering interesting conversation in a halting manner. From Cadiz, Longfellow wrote Irving a letter (24 Sep 1837) combining cocky humor and perhaps presumptuous advice in a description of his arduous, dangerous trip via Seville to Cadiz. During his first time abroad, Longfellow began to formulate what became *Outre-Mer* in conscious, partial imitation of *The Sketch-Book.*

Of everything by Longfellow that Irving read, he liked *Hyperion* best, according to a letter (3 Oct 1852) their mutual friend Charles Sumner* wrote to Longfellow. Irving was undoubtedly pleased by its American content and tone. Longfellow notes in his journal (31 Jul 1859) being amused by anecdotes in Irving's biography of George Washington concerning the general's Cambridge camp—understandably, since his headquarters there were in Craigie House.* At a meeting of the Massachusetts Historical Society (5 Dec 1859), Irving, recently deceased, was honored in a series of resolutions. Longfellow spoke and said that Irving's *Sketch-Book* was the first book he read that fired his imagination.

Bibliography: Hilen, ed.; S. Longfellow; McFarland, Philip. *Sojourners.* New York: Atheneum, 1979; *Proceedings of the Massachusetts Historical Society, 1858-1860* vol. 4 (Dec 1859, Jan 1860): 393-95, 422-23; Wagenknecht, 1955.

"ITALIAN SCENERY" (1824). Poem, in *USLG,* 15 Dec 1824; Scudder. The poet describes a lovely scene as twilight turns to darkness. Music sweeps across the water. A gondola moves past an oak so old that "those who saw its green and flourishing youth / Are gone and are forgotten." A storm, now "wearied," leaves peace behind it. The autumnal moon rises from the sea. An "eagle screams in the fathomless ether" above the Apennines. The poet's spirit looks down on tombs and muses on the significance of the "mysterious language" audible from the heights. A voice tells him that the earth is not his home. But then cheerful dawn comes. Ten place names dot this juvenile work.

Bibliography: Little.

"IT IS NOT ALWAYS MAY" (1842). Poem, in *Ballads;* Scudder. In the sunlight and fresh air, swallows and bluebirds sing. Anchored at the river, clouds await a wind from the west. Blossoms and leaves appear anew. "Maiden," take pleasure in your perfumed times. "Enjoy the Spring of Love and Youth" while you can; "For Time will teach thee soon the truth, / There are no birds in last year's nest!" This last line comes from "No hay pájaros en los nidos de antaño," the Spanish proverb that Longfellow quotes as his epigraph.

J

"JECKOYVA" (1825). Poem, in *USLG,* l Aug 1825; Scudder. His men placed Jeckoyva's body in a "warrior's grave." This mighty hunter died before any "mist of age" overtook him. Where was he when the sun scorched him, thirst distressed him, strong winds buffeted him, and darkness misled him and he fell? He was found below a barren rock. A headnote explains that Mount Jeckoyva, near the White Hills, is named after this Indian chief, who was also known as Chocorua.

Bibliography: Little.

"JEP[H]THAH'S DAUGHTER" (1824). Poem, signed "H," in Portland *Advertiser,* 22 Sep 1824. Jephthah's daughter laments the fact that in accordance with the "sacred vow" of a warrior "that from Tubia came" she must bow before his face and be killed. She asks the "Daughters of Mizpeh" to weep for beautiful ones like herself, whose "nuptial song" none will ever hear. She, "poor dove of heaven," will soon die. This jumbled juvenile poem is based on the biblical story of Jephthah, one of the judges of Israel. He vowed to the Lord that the would offer as a sacrifice the first person to come out of his house back home in the land of Tob to welcome him if he triumph in battle against the Ammonites. He returned home victorious, but the first to greet him was his only child. (*See* Judg. 11: 1–40.)

Bibliography: Little.

JEWETT, SARA (1847–99). Actress. She debuted in New York (1872). Late in his life, Longfellow met this beautiful young actress, popular in Cambridge and elsewhere for ingénue roles. He wished her well when she went briefly to London on tour (1879), suggested that she call on his sister-in-law, Mary Appleton Mackintosh,* there, and relished her later attentive visits. Sara Jewett was no relation to the Maine fiction writer Sarah Orne Jewett (1849–1909).

Bibliography: Hilen, ed.

"THE JEWISH CEMETERY AT NEWPORT" (1854). Poem, in *PM,* Jul 1854; *Courtship, Birds* (1858). It seems strange that the buried "Hebrews" are at rest and silent near noisy waves and city bustle. They are "keep[ing] / The long, mysterious Exodus of Death." The "sepulchral stones" paving their graves resemble "the tablets of the Law," thrown down / And broken by Moses." Their recorded names reflect "different climes." Their mourners thanked God for death but also for "life that nevermore shall cease." Their synagogues are closed, their hymns unsung, their survivors gone. But the dead are here, and "their graves and their remembrance [are kept] green." They came here over desertlike seas, to avoid persecution; lived in dirty, crowded streets, fed on "bitter herbs of exile"; learned endurance "in the school of patience," and were famished and thirsty. They were cursed, "mocked and jeered, and spurned by Christian feet." Wherever they wandered, they combined "Pride and humiliation," and yet remained "unshaken as the continent." They kept alive, for their future, images of their grand, traditional "patriarchs and . . . prophets." By reverting to the past, they have read "The mystic volume of the world . . . / . . . backward, like a Hebrew book"—so much so that "life became a Legend of the Dead." What used to be will not be reborn. Although the earth gives birth to races, "the dead nations never rise again." This beautiful poem was the result of Longfellow's guided visit to the cemetery, described in his journal (9 Jul 1852). Often anthologized, it is weakened only by its closing prediction, since disproved, despite the fiendish efforts of Adolf Hitler and his followers.

Bibliography: Arvin; Fitzig, Irving. "Longfellow and 'The Jewish Cemetery at Newport.'" *American Heritage* 13 (Feb 1962): 60-63; Smith, Hammett W. "A Note on Longfellow's 'The Jewish Cemetery at Newport.'" *College English* 18 (Nov 1956): 103-4; Stock, Ely. "Longfellow's 'The Jewish Cemetery at Newport.'" *Rhode Island History* 20 (1961): 81-87; Wagenknecht, 1986.

"JOHN ENDICOTT." *See The New England Tragedies.*

JUDAS MACCABAEUS (1872). Drama in five acts and in blank verse.

Act I. In his citadel at Jerusalem, Antiochus Epiphanes, Syria's Hellenistic king, boasts about Antioch, his city, won back from Ptolemy, Antiochus's sister Cleopatra's husband. Antiochus talks to Jason, who was formerly Joshua, a Greek, but is now Hellenized and is Antiochus's high priest. Antiochus plans to Hellenize all the Jews here and give them "more gods than one," plus some goddesses, as well as hippodromes, plays, and festivals, including "The Dionysia." (*See* 2 Macc. 2: 19-23.) He gets Jason to admit that the Jews, inspired by the seven crazy sons of Máhala, a strange woman, call him "Antiochus the Mad."

Ambassadors from Samaria enter, bearded and bowing. Though Jewish, they please Antiochus by asking and receiving his permission to name their temple after "Jupiter Hellenius" (*see* 2 Macc. 6: 2). They also ask him to order his procurator, Nicanor, to quit molesting them.

When Antiochus gloats that it was easy to handle these Jews, Jason warns him that those of Judah are more stubborn. In fact, old Eleazer among them chose death by torture rather than "eat the flesh of swine" (*see* 2 Macc. 6: 18-31); moreover, many from Judah have fled to Ephraim, where Judas Maccabaeus is raising an army against Antiochus. Antiochus promises to bleed the opposition, burn their city, and salt their land until it resembles Sodom.

Act II. Máhala is in her dungeon and hears six of her rebellious sons tortured to death. She identifies the voices of two of them—Adaiah and Avilan—as they express faith, courage, resignation, and threats.

Antiochus shows Máhala the six mutilated corpses and also Sirion, her youngest, still alive. She asks Antiochus how can "a man do such deeds, and yet not die / By the recoil of his own wickedness?" Antiochus says he will give treasures to and share secrets with Sirion if he will forswear "your Mosaic Law" and be Hellenized. Urged by his mother to die bravely, Sirion rebukes Antiochus, "O godless man," and says his pride will earn him punishment. The mother calls for death to visit her. (*See* 2 Macc. 7: 1-41.)

Act III. Judas Maccabaeus is at the battlefield of Beth-horon, armored and courageous. He tersely pledges to "Serve the designs of Him who giveth life."

Jewish fugitives stream in and tell Judas that their temple is destroyed, their enemies are reveling in the courts, many Jews are forced to participate in "the festivals of Dionysus," and there is much wailing and weeping. Judas says that women should do the lamenting but that men should fight and die. Hearing about Eleazer, Máhala, and her sons, Judas says that God will pursue Antiochus and urges the fugitives to buckle on whatever armor they can find and cry out "The Help of God."

Nicanor sneaks into Judas's camp, is recognized by Judas, urges him to make "peace between us," and warns him that 40 thousand foot soldiers and 7 thousand horsemen are between Judas and Jerusalem. Judas says that after such slaughter of his people there can be peace only when Antiochus is returned to dust and Judas's banner floats over

Jerusalem. Nicanor leaves under safe conduct.

Judas's captains express fear of the enemy and are reluctant (as Nicanor thought they would be) to charge the formidable foe on this Sabbath day. Judas says he dreamed that an old man, the prophet Jeremias, accompanied by Onias, the old Jewish priest, brought a golden sword from God, and adjured Judas to smite the enemy. Remembering God's help in times past, Judas exhorts his eager troops. (*See* 2 Macc. 8: 18; 15: 3.)

Act IV. Judas, victorious against Nicanor, has flown his flag over Jerusalem, executed Nicanor, and put his head over a gate, where it "Blackens in wind and sun" (he says). (*See* 1 Macc. 7: 47; 2 Macc. 15: 32.) Antiochus remains defiant; so Judas orders the Sanctuary cleaned and repaired, and Antiochus's citadel attacked.

Some Jews find Jason and bring him to Judas, who likens the deceit on his face to "heathen images" which the Greeks have written all over the damaged "volumes of the Law." Jason says that he was simply obeying Antiochus, asks for justice or at least mercy, and when queried, reports that Antiochus has retreated with many soldiers "into the far East." Judas orders Jason to be driven out to "wander / Among strange nations," where he will "perish / In a strange land" unmourned.

Jason soliloquizes to the effect that he is "neither Jew nor Greek," sees from a safe distance Jewish ceremonies that cause nostalgia to swell in him, and determines to go find "Antiochus / Upon his homeward journey, crowned with triumph." Jason misses the comfort of familiar faces and voices. (*See* 1 Macc. 7: 47; 2 Macc. 9: 1-2; 15: 32.)

Act V. In the mountains of Ecbatana, Antiochus, driven out and with his forces "melted away" by the enemy Persians, is comforted by Philip, who says that "thou has lost / But what thou hadst not" and adds that unmarred "Syria remains" for him. But Antiochus misses the pleasures of his court and feels mocked.

A messenger from Lysias in Antioch informs Antiochus that Judas has taken Jerusalem, Emmaus, Bethsura, Ephron, and Galaad, and is heading for Carnion. Antiochus summons his charioteers for a rush to Antioch and promises to wipe out Judas, "this dreadful Jew." Suddenly, however, he staggers as though stabbed and wants to pray to "Jove, or Jehovah, or whatever." Asking help from the "God of Israel," Antiochus promises to release the Holy City, decorate its temple, make its citizens the equal of Antioch's, become a Jew, and proclaim God the world's ruler. He faints and appears, Philip says, as though dead. (*See* 1 Macc. 3: 38-59; 4: 1-34; 6: 5-16; 2 Macc. 9: 3-5, 13-20, 28-29.)

A source for *Judas Maccabaeus* in addition to 1 Maccabees and 2 Maccabees was *The Jewish Antiquities* of Flavius Josephus (37-95?). It took Longfellow only 12 days to write this disappointing play, the theme of which is unprepossessing to begin with.

Bibliography: Arvin; Hirsh; Wagenknecht, 1986.

"JUGURTHA" (1879). Poem, in *International Review,* Jan-Jun 1879; *Thule.* Jugurtha, the captured "African monarch," shouts that the baths of Apollo are cold, as he steps down into the dark Roman dungeon where he later died. The unknown, friendless poet says that his baths of Apollo are also cold, as he descends into a similar darkness, lured by a failed dreamy vision. Lucius Cornelius Sulla captured Jugurtha, the king of Numidia, in 106 B.C. and put him in a dungeon in Rome. He died, miserably, in 104 B.C. In his life of Caius Marius, Plutarch quotes Jugurtha, perhaps insane, who shouted, "O Hercules! how cold your bath is!" Longfellow may have misquoted Plutarch or, more likely, made his deranged poet aptly invoke Apollo, the god of sunlight, prophecy, music, and poetry, rather than brawny Hercules. In this late poem, Longfellow is implicitly expressing a sense of gloom because of his diminished poetic power.

Bibliography: Amacher, R. E. "Longfellow's 'Jugurtha.'" *Explicator* 6 (Feb 1948): 29; Arms; Arvin; Wagenknecht, 1986.

K

"THE KALIF OF BALDACCA." *See* "The Spanish Jew's Tale: Kambulu," in *Tales of a Wayside Inn,* Part Second.

"KAMBULU." *See* "The Spanish Jew's Tale," in *Tales of a Wayside Inn,* Part Second.

KAVANAGH **(1849).** Novel, whose full title is *Kavanagh: A Tale.* Mr. Churchill, the schoolmaster of Fairmeadow, thinks he is great, while the villagers compare him to a plodding beetle. On his way home one Saturday afternoon in September, he broods about ancient Romans and also worries about his unruly pupils and their unreasonable fathers. He sees the Reverend Mr. Pendexter, a dour Calvinist, and also an "ill-looking" fellow with a boot collection festooning his person.

Churchill's sweet wife, Mary, greets him at tea time. Lucy, their servant girl, a gypsy-looking orphan of fifteen, puts the Churchills' baby boy to bed while Alfred, aged three, romps around. Lucy asks to go to town for a bonnet ribbon. Churchill comments about the man with the boots.

Churchill looks at the book-lined wall of his study and tells Mary he would like to resemble all these scholars, poets, and authors. When he says he wants to write a Romance, she encourages him, thinking he will become famous.

He kids his wife, whom he calls "my young girl with beautiful locks," by posing mathematical questions out of a Hindu text: Find the square root of a flock of geese, the depth of pond where a lily sank two cubits away, et cetera. Mary labels Churchill "my beautiful youth with a bee in your bonnet."

Having to write some letters prevents Churchill from starting his Romance just yet. Mary's "blue orbs" show signs of sleepiness. He looks briefly at the stars, thinks a moment about "the great miracle of nature, decay and reproduction, ever beginning, never ending," and follows Mary upstairs. In due time he has a dream that combines grammatical declensions and people young and old reading his completed Romance.

Meanwhile, Pendexter, whom Churchill regards as a dull, negligent preacher, is toiling on his farewell sermon while all the village lamps are extinguished. After 25 years of service, he is retiring tomorrow. The sexton, whose wife is sick, interrupts Pendexter, who says he will pray for her.

Pendexter preaches violently, reminding his stingy parishioners of their many "social, political, and ecclesiastical" failings, but then thanking the ladies who were kind to his wife during an illness.

Alice Archer, who arrived late for church service, returns home to her mother and to Sally Manchester, their chambermaid-cook. Alice is pale, thoughtful, and thin. Her mother is widowed, querulous, and weak-eyed. Sally, big and strident, is in love with Martin Cherryfield, a traveling dentist. The only sunshine in the house enters when Alice's lovable bosom-friend, Cecilia Vaughan, pops in.

One bright autumn day, Alice returns from church to discover that her mother has gone permanently blind. Sally abruptly enters with a letter from Cherryfield. He is marrying elsewhere. Alice tells Sally she's better off. Mrs. Archer is happy that Sally will remain to serve them. Sally bitterly turns against all men.

Next morning Pendexter and his wife pack their old chaise and leave town for his childhood home. He soon becomes a militia minister.

On Sundays Churchill finds his children too noisy to permit him to write his Romance. On Mondays, early, he buys meat from the cart of Wilmerdings, the butcher. This rosy man also helps mothers by weighing little babies on his scales. While walking to school Churchill reads a placard in which William Bantam offers to make profiles.

During the winter, the churchmembers choose Arthur Kavanagh from among several candidates as their new minister. One schoolgirl writes a long, gossipy letter to an absent, "dearest" girlfriend: Billy Wilmerdings is expelled from school for truancy; Mr. Churchill poses impossible arithmetical questions; he bought Pendexter's pulpit for his own study; Mr. Kavanagh, tall, pale, and handsome, preaches beautifully; the girls enjoy sleigh riding and dancing; an Irish maid asked her dying mistress if she wanted to be buried with her false teeth; Hester Green prefers a warm bed to walking in the moonlight.

Billy runs off to sea. On his pulpit's white panels, Churchill writes pithy maxims concerning morality, sensational fiction, time, pleasures, the mingling of country lyricism and town activities to compose a "perfect musical drama," the virtue of "simplicity" in character, and the meanness of critics.

Spring, lovely spring, arrives, and so does Kavanagh, whose first sermon is about the spring of the soul. Audience response is generally cheerless; however, Kavanagh is pleased by Alice's attentiveness.

Kavanagh makes do with a room in the church tower, sallies forth on Monday to buy some bits of necessary furniture, and enters Moses Merryweather's shop. That birdlike fellow sells singing birds and stuffs other birds. Kavanagh is struck by the wondrous beauty of Cecilia Vaughan, who buys a pretty pigeon, is told how she and a friend can send it back and forth to each other, and departs. Merryweather sells Kavanagh a canary and a cage, and then mumbles to himself that Miss Vaughan would never think of marrying a poor minister.

Cecilia lives with her indulgent father, a scholarly but vapid judge, in the family mansion just out of town. Long motherless, the girl has one firm and loving friend, pale, shy little Alice, and bought the carrier-pigeon to convey their messages to each other.

Cecilia, passively courted by many unsuccessful suitors, is especially bothered by Hiram A. Hawkins, who deals in English carpets and linens, changed his name to H. Adolphus Hawkins, dresses and postures like a dandy, and writes poetry much admired by his sister, Martha Amelia Hawkins. He has Martha send Cecilia anonymous letters praising him; this, when Celia finds out about it, bothers her. She brings the pigeon to Alice, kisses her forehead a few times, shows her the "sybylline leaves" from Martha, and persuades her to write Martha to quit. Kavanagh happens to stroll past. Both girls, from the upstairs window, see him. He looks up to them. Alice blushes. She is already secretly in love with him.

Kavanagh came from a Catholic family on the seacoast of Maine. Their land was part of a royal French charter. His devout mother taught him to read lives of the saints. Her illustrated book linked "the world of spirits and the world of art," while the biographies linked "faith and good works." St. Christopher inspired young Kavanagh to be charitable and to serve Christ. Kavanagh studied the principles of Catholicism, theology, and philosophy in a Jesuit college in Canada, returned home each summer, and mourned when his mother died. He became subject to "strange and dubious thoughts," read Calvin among other writers whose "Reason" he saw as "a light in darkness," sought "Truth and Freedom" and shed certain "dogmas . . . [and] superstitions," converted to Protestantism, and left Catholic "bigotry," "fanaticism," and "intolerance" behind, even while retaining its "zeal," "self-devotion," "aspirations," "sympathies," and "endless deeds of charity." Only after his father's death did Kavanagh become a clergyman.

Kavanagh likes his church-tower room. The pigeon starts delivering letters. Martha stops writing Cecilia about Hawkins. Edward Dimple advertises his decorous bath-house for ladies. Several traveling shows come to Fairmeadow, through which a new railroad is built. By August, Kavanagh has visited all the parish families, and he and Churchill have become friends. Kavanagh's liberal sermons emphasize Christian love, are "kindly," and advocate one universal Christian church. He annoys some worshippers by criticizing intemperance, militancy, and slavery, and by recommending beautiful, not gloomy, organ music. One day old Pendexter and his wife arrive by chaise at Churchill's house. Pendexter, whose horse has "a very disdainful fling to its hind legs," gripes that Kavanagh's "liberality" is "Arianism and infidelity." Kavanagh, when warned later, tells Churchill he is unafraid. The parishioners commission a great itinerant artist to draw Kavanagh's portrait, during the progress of which Martha offers suggestions.

Churchill orders Bantam to sketch everyone in his family, including himself—holding his finger in a book. Lucy, their lively maid, has decamped with the boot salesman. One evening Mr. Hathaway, an out-of-town editor, calls on Churchill, whose locally published pieces he has admired. Wanting "to raise the character of American literature," Hathaway is establishing a national magazine himself. The two discuss what American literature should be. Hathaway wants it to be more "national" and says he is working on a "national drama" featuring the Spanish in New Mexico and also a cockfight. Hathaway prefers the universal to the national and also voices less respect for critics than Churchill does. But when Hathaway asks Churchill to provide an article for every issue of his magazine—gratis, but only at first—he agrees and promises essays on "the unrecorded and life-long sufferings of women." He must therefore delay writing his Romance.

Accompanied by his wife, their son Alfred, Cecilia, and Alice, Churchill takes Kavanagh in the Churchills' one-horse chaise, on a summer morning, for a picnic beside Roaring Brook, in the neighboring town of Westwood. The stream sings along like an Icelandic saga. Cecilia, lingering, needs Kavanagh's help to step on stones to cross the brook. When does love begin? It has begun here. After sandwiches and a huge pastry, the group approaches the nearby sawmill, about which Churchill plans to write a poem. The party returns home. Only Alfred is cross.

Autumn brings changes in nature and in the people. Lucy returns, abandoned by that "Briareus of boots" and oddly wishing she were a Christian so she could kill herself. A wandering preacher announces the end of the world.

In the Archer house, the blind mother and Sally, her servant, grumble; but Cecilia and Alice hold hands and talk—but not about love, for "while Alice, unconsciously to herself, desired the love of Kavanagh, Cecilia, as unconsciously, assumed it as already her own." Alice languishes. Cecilia blooms. Their pigeon has carried letters back and forth, but not about love.

Since Hathaway's magazine dies aborning, Churchill thinks again of turning to his Romance. Again an interruption. Clarissa Cartwright, whose poems have appeared in magazines, loans him a bundle of her manuscripts, tied up in crimson velvet, and begs him for a candid critique and a preface. Mary Churchill opines that he won't ever start his Romance.

One night, while walking in the forest, Churchill and Kavanagh hear a noisy camp-meeting hymn about the end of the world. But they don't see Lucy as she calmly wades into the water, floats deliberately away, and drowns herself. Kavanagh, back in his tower, asks the future if he will get what he desires. Everything will be fine, comes the answer.

Next morning, Kavanagh is sitting in his tower when the girls' carrier-pigeon, attacked by a king-bird, flies in for safety. Atop its "billet," labeled "Cecilia," Kavanagh places a note about his love, wraps everything, and releases the pigeon. Confused, it flies to Alice, who swiftly reads Kavanagh's love message, thinks briefly it is for her, glows, but then sees it is addressed to Cecilia, faints, comes to, sends everything to

Cecilia, prays, and resigns herself to secret sorrow. Cecilia gets Kavanagh's love message and replies, "Come to me!"

First, Cecilia rushes to Alice, tells her everything, is nonplussed by Alice's impassivity only momentarily, and kisses and caresses the glum girl. Kavanagh seeks Cecilia at Alice's place, and off they go. News of their plan to wed in the spring rushes through Fairmeadow. Churchill invites the couple for a lavish, cookbook-inspired dinner, which his patient wife prepares.

Winter comes. Alice dies. Here indeed was Churchill's subject. "The Romance he was longing to find and record had really occurred in his neighborhood, among his own friends." But he researched elsewhere, rationalized that "the familiar seems trivial," delayed, and wrote nothing. He walks by the frozen river and recalls bits of Scandinavian literature.

After their wedding, Kavanagh and Cecilia travel for three years in Italy and the Holy Land. He longs to establish a universal church. Returning to Fairmeadow, they find much changed. The railroad has converted "the simple village" into "a very precocious town." Alice's mother has died; her house is empty, for Sally, her servant, has bought a place of her own. Silas, the servant of Cecilia's father, who remains his same dreamy self, proposed to Sally. Bitten by leeches while walking barefoot, he wrote to her in his blood, "using his feet as inkstands." She refused, still thinking of her long-gone dentist. Wilmerdings has become a drunkard; his wife says their son is on a whaler in the Pacific. Hawkins has died, leaving two maidens thinking they were engaged to him; his sister remains unwed. Merryweather resembles one of his parrots more than ever.

Kavanagh visits Churchill. He and his fair-cheeked wife, plumper now, have five children. Churchill, lacking will power, calls himself a trifling failure now. When queried, he tells Kavanagh his still-nameless Romance remains unbegun. Kavanagh advises him to write about his own experiences: "Give what you have. To some, it may be better than you dare to think." Churchill replies that all he could do was "labor faithfully" as a teacher, that some of his pupils may thus

be "incited . . . to do what I shall never do." He accepts his God-accorded "destiny." The Churchills promise to call on the Kavanaghs this evening. Kavanagh tells himself to make the present moment count.

Kavanagh is of little value as a novel, even though Emily Dickinson (who must have seen herself in Alice), Ralph Waldo Emerson,* Nathaniel Hawthorne,* and William Dean Howells,* among other contemporaries, admired it greatly. In many of its humorous touches, the work anticipates aspects of the local-color movement. Also, it is of worth for its subtle autobiographical revelations. Thus, Longfellow himself shared the best traits of both Churchill and Kavanagh while rightly seeing himself as the reverse of Hawkins. Longfellow had his wife Fanny in mind when he portrayed both peppy Cecilia and Churchill's sweet wife. Longfellow rendered Mrs. Archer's blindness tenderly, in part because he feared the same fate for his own weak eyes. Other characters are partly based on real-life models. Hathaway slightly resembles Cornelius Mathews (1817–89), the energetic New York editor-author whom Longfellow knew. Longfellow's frank criticism of the proposed contents of a magazine planned by an editor named Alexander H. Smith of North Adams, Massachusetts, sounds much like Churchill's opposition to some of Hathaway's ideas (*see* Longfellow's letter to Smith, 24 Jul 1844). For Kavanagh's sermons, Longfellow echoed some of those of his ministerial brother Samuel Longfellow.* Pendexter slightly resembles Nathanael Howe (1764–1837), a Congregational clergyman from Hopkinton, Massachusetts. Would-be writers, including the originals of Clarissa Cartwright, often pestered Longfellow for opinions on their effusions. *Kavanagh* and Herman Melville's *Pierre; or, The Ambiguities* (1852) have striking parallels, especially with respect to Kavanagh and Plotinus Plinlimmon.

Bibliography: Allaback, Steven. "Voices of Longfellow: *Kavanagh* as Autobiography." *Emerson Society Quarterly,* no. 58, part 1 (1970): 3–14; Arvin; Cowie; Downey, Jean, ed. *Kavanagh: A Tale* [abridged]. New Haven: College & University Press, 1965; Faderman, Lillian. "Female Same-Sex Relationships in Novels by Longfellow, Holmes, and James." *New England Quarterly* 51 (Sep 1978): 309-32; Higginson; Hilen, ed.; Miller, Perry. *The Raven and the Whale: The War of Words and Wits in the Era of Poe and Melville.* New York: Harcourt, Brace, 1956; Reynolds, David S. *Beneath the American Renaissance: The Subversive Imagination in the Age of Emerson and Melville.* New York: A. A. Knopf, 1988; Seelye, John. "*Pierre, Kavanagh,* and the Unitarian Perplex." In *Melville's Evermoving Dawn,* eds. John Bryant and Robert Milder, 375-92. Kent: Kent State University Press, 1997.

"KEATS" (1875). Sonnet, in *Pandora, Birds* (1875). The young shepherd his "tale . . . left half told," sleeps like Endymion, his "pipe shattered," a nightingale singing nearby. A gleaming marble, which reads, "Here lieth one whose name / Was writ in water," should read instead, "The smoking flax before it burst to flame / Was quenched by death, and broken the bruised reed."

KEMBLE, FRANCES (1809–93). British actress and author. Frances ("Fanny") Kemble Butler was born Frances Anne Kemble in London. Her parents and siblings were successful actors. She made her first appearance as Juliet in Shakespeare's *Romeo and Juliet* at Convent Garden (1829). She played many leading women's roles. Perhaps her most notable success was as Julia in *The Hunchback* (1832) by James Sheridan Knowles (1784-1862); he wrote the play for her. While on tour in the United States (1832-34), Frances Kemble in 1834 married Pierce Butler (1807-67). Although they had two children, their marriage was miserable. After she returned alone to England, he sued for divorce and obtained it (1849). She was in demand to give dramatic readings in England and the United States, resided in America off and on (1849-77), summered in Switzerland often, and finally settled in London. Her daughter, Sarah Butler Wister (1835-1908), was the mother of Owen Wister (1860-1938), author of the seminal western novel, *The Virginian* (1902). Frances Kemble wrote plays, travel books, poetry, translations from French and German, and autobiographical volumes. She wrote her first novel when she was eighty. She was immensely popular in London society, and her salty conversation was greatly relished. A list

of her friends would run into the dozens and certainly included Longfellow.

When Frances Kemble stopped at Boston on tour, Longfellow and his wife called on her at her hotel (25 Jan 1849) and attended her dramatic reading of Shakespeare's *The Tempest* the following evening. According to his next-day journal entry, she combined "tears and great emotion" to create a "glorious reading!" Many journal entries follow concerning her. While attending her reading from Shakespeare's *Much Ado about Nothing,* Longfellow experimented by listening while not seeing and pronounced "the effect of the voice alone . . . a complete failure" (31 Jan 1849). He noted that she "read from 'King Lear,' and wonderfully well; with great power and pathos. It was her best reading, so far" (5 Feb 1849); however, attending her repeat reading, he noted that the play is "too tragic . . . for those who have any sorrows of their own" (7 Feb 1849). He heard her read from *Hamlet* "sublimely; with the only true comprehension and expression of the melancholy Dane I have ever had the good fortune to hear." He continued, "What nights these are!—with Shakespeare and such a reader" (16 Feb 1849). Instead of hearing her read from *Othello* a few days later, Longfellow wrote a sonnet on her performances (*see* "Sonnet on Mrs. Kemble's Readings from Shakespeare"). Longfellow was especially thrilled when he watched her captivate an audience of 3,000 at the Mercantile Library Association in Boston by reading from Shakespeare's *As You Like It* and then from Longfellow's "The Building of the Ship," with "book in hand, trembling, palpitating, and weeping" (12 Feb 1850). Longfellow heard her read from *King John* (2 Mar 1850, 13 Apr 1857), heard her read from *King Henry IV* (part one) and dined as one of her guests afterwards (6 Mar 1850), heard her read from *Macbeth* (18 Feb 1857) and an evening later welcomed her as a dinner guest, heard her read from *The Merchant of Venice* for a charity event (19 Nov 1857), heard her "stupendous" reading from *Antony and Cleopatra* (16 Dec 1859), and heard her read from *Cymbeline* (16 Feb 1860). For a few of these readings, Longfellow took Frances Kemble's hand and led her to the stage.

Fanny Appleton, before her marriage to Longfellow, enjoyed the friendship of Frances Kemble in Newport, Rhode Island (1834), London (1837), and Lenox, Massachusetts (1838, 1839). She played Viola to Frances Kemble's Olivia in a Lenox tableaux (1839). After marrying Longfellow, she became even better acquainted with the actress's ability and personality. In her journal, she defines some of Frances Kemble's poems as "'rammed with life' and suffering, but too bitter and morbid for a Christian woman . . . [and] Less poetical than I expected from her geyser-like soul" (15 May 1844). She also attended many of Frances Kemble's Shakespeare readings and commented on them in beautiful detail in her journal and in letters. Both Longfellows sympathized with Frances Kemble when she lost custody of her two children, in accordance with the terms of her divorce. (After all, she deserted them.)

Bibliography: Blainey, Ann. *Fanny & Adelaide: The Lives of the Remarkable Kemble Sisters.* Chicago: Ivan R. Dee, 2001; *Mrs. Longfellow;* Ransome, Eleanor, ed. *The Terrific Kemble: A Victorian Self-Portrait from the Writings of Fanny Kemble.* London: Hamish Hamilton, 1978; Wagenknecht, 1955.

"KÉRAMOS" (1875). Poem, in *Harper's New Monthly Magazine,* Dec 1877; *Kéramos.* The potter is under a hawthorn tree in the mottled sunshine, looking like a magician and controlling his clay. He urges his soundless wheel to spin away like "the flying world," which is also made of clay. The potter's song transports the poet "to regions far remote." By the north shore of France is Delft, its homes filled with plates, flagons, tankards, tiles, and so on—all products of "the Potter's trade." The poet glides south to "blue Charente" and the suburbs of Saintes, where Bernard Palissy (c.1510–89) the wild potter, neglecting his children to feed his kiln fire with pieces of furniture, delights to make "Some new enamel, hard and bright." The potter interjects this comparison: The jar is as ignorant in the hands of his creator, and has as little business querying him, as the potter is—and has—in the hands of his world-planning God. The poet floats, as on the wings of song, above the Pyrenees and down over Majorca, sees some "blazing fur-naces" there, and proceeds to Italy. The splendid finish of pottery from Gubbio, Faenza, Florence, and Pesaro is snow-white, sky-blue, and brilliantly iridescent. At Urbino, Francesco Xanto Avelli of Rovigo (fl.1530–45) designed pottery inspired by some of Raphael's paintings. Francesco di Giorgio (1439–1502) worked there too in "madre-perl [*sic*] and golden lines / Of arabesque"; a woman named Cana is known today only because of a Giorgio portrait of her on a cup. On to Luca della Robbia's work in his "pleasant Tuscan town." Behold his "choristers with lips of stone, / Whose music is not heard, but seen," religious figures on hospital walls, a bishop's patient figure on his tomb, and so on. Next, to "fair Ausonian shores," and nearly speaking, almost moving images of chiefs, Achilles, Alcides, his bull, Aphrodite, Helen, and demigods. The potter sings to his wheel about children, youths, adults, and oldsters. The poet wings his way to the Nile—ah, Cairo, "perfume[s] of Arabian gales," jars big enough for the Forty Thieves to hide in, memories of Scheherezade's "fascinating tales," and more wondrous ones concerning the Egyptian gods Ammon, Emeth, Osiris, Ibis, the Sphinx, and more. The potter reminds his wheel that everyone is "kindred and allied by birth, / And made of the same clay." On to the "Ganges and . . . Himalay," and the "burning town" of King-te-tching, with its thousands of glowing furnaces, out of which their porcelains are "whirled / To all the markets of the world." And also willow-patterned, "coarser household wares," with figures fondly remembered from the days of our childhood. Below tiled roofs in Nankin hang melodiously chiming bells of porcelain. The potter reminds his wheel that the nearby "furnace flame" will make, alike, honorable or shameful "vessels . . . of clay." Past the villages of Imari in Japan, where "Fusiyama's cone," stars, leaves, lakes, pale dawns, flaming sunsets, birds, and much else find their "counterpart[s]" all "painted on . . . lovely jars." The poet concludes that "Art is the child of Nature," and

He is the greatest artist, then,
Whether of pencil or of pen,
Who follows Nature.

A pealing church bell causes both the poet and the potter to pause. Both realize that today will soon be yesterday, and everything will be "trodden into clay!"

Kéramos is Greek for *pottery*. For this fine poetic expression of his art credo, which doubles as a little guidebook, Longfellow remembered a potter he enjoyed watching when he was a boy in Portland. He also made use of several literary sources as well, including 2 Timothy 2: 20, Romans 9: 21, *The Rubáiyát of Omar Khayyám, The Arabian Nights,* and "Rabbi Ben Ezra" by Robert Browning. Harper and Brothers paid Longfellow $1,000 for magazine-publication rights to "Kéramos." Longfellow gloated in a letter to James T. Fields* (3 Aug 1877) that "the Harpers . . . will harp it [the poem] in one hundred and fifty thousand households, or say half a million ears." Longfellow wrote a letter (4 Aug 1877) to Henry Mills Alden (1836–1919), long-time editor of *Harper's* (1869–1919), with eight suggestions for illustrating his poem. Alden followed one suggestion. The popularity of this poem is indicated by the fact that Charles Lanman (1819–95), a writer and artist, sent Longfellow a Japanese translation of part of it; Longfellow acknowledged receipt in a letter to Lanman (28 Nov 1877).

Bibliography: Arvin; Hilen, ed.; Wagenknecht, 1986; Williams.

KÉRAMOS AND OTHER POEMS (1878).

Collection of poems. "Kéramos." I. *Birds of Passage* (Flight the Fifth): "Herons of Elmwood," "A Dutch Picture," "Castles in Spain," "Vittoria Colonna [Once More]," "Inarimé," "The Revenge of Rain-in-the-Face," "To the River Yvette," "The Emperor's Glove," "The Ballad of the French Fleet," "The Leap of Roushan Beg," "Haroun al Raschid," "King Trisanku," "A Wraith in the Mist," "The Three Kings," "Song [Stay]," "The White Czar," "Delia." II. *A Book of Sonnets:* "Nature," "In the Churchyard at Tarrytown," "Eliot's Oak," "The Descent of the Muses," "Venice," "The Poets," "Parker Cleaveland," "The Harvest Moon," "To the River Rhone," "The Three Silences of Molinos," "The Two Rivers," "Boston," "St. John's, Cambridge," "Moods," "Woodstock

Park," "The Four Princesses at Wilna," "Holidays," "Wapentake," "The Broken Oar." *Translations:* "Virgil's First Eclogue," "Ovid in Exile," "On the Terrace of the Aigalades," "To My Brooklet," "Barréges," "Forsaken," "Allah."

Seven Sonnets and a Canzone, from the Italian of Michael Angelo: "The Artist," "Fire," "Youth and Age," "Old Age," "To Vittoria Colonna [Lady]," "To Vittoria Colonna [When]," "Dante," "Canzone [Ah me!]."

"KILLED AT THE FORD" (1866). Poem, in *Flower.* A young soldier, handsome, honorable, truthful, and cheerful, rides out one night. He hums a song about two roses on his cap and another on his sword tip. A bullet whistling from the woods kills him. His comrades take him back to the camp. His cheeks have two white roses. Over his heart is a third one, bright red. The poet sees "in a vision" the same deadly bullet reaching a northern town, street, house, and hitting a heart. Neighbors wonder how it is that, "without a cry," she "passed from cross to crown."

Bibliography: Arms.

"KING CHRISTIAN: A NATIONAL SONG OF DENMARK" (1838). Poem, translated from Johannes Evald (1743–81), in *KM,* Apr 1838. When King Christian and also Nils Juel wield their swords, the enemy shouts that it must escape and seek shelter. The skies thunder, and the dark waves roll to welcome the heroic Danes.

Bibliography: Kabell, Inge and Hanne Lauridsen. "Translating 'Kong Christian'. . . ." *George Barrow Bulletin* 17 (1999): 56–79.

"KING ROBERT OF SICILY." See "The Sicilian's Tale," in *Tales of a Wayside Inn,* Part First.

"KING TRISANKU" (1878). Poem, in *Kéramos, Birds* (1878). The magician Viswamitra raises Trisanku, "king of nations," to Indra's elysian regions. Indra becomes offended and casts Trisanku down, until he is poised and balanced between the two opposing forces. Thus it is with us, raised by hopes, dashed by doubts—suspended "Midway between earth and heaven." The source of this terse, twelve-line epigrammatic gem, was a translation of the *Ramayana,* the Hindu epic.

Bibliography: Arvin.

"KING WITLAF'S DRINKING-HORN" (1850). Poem, in *GM,* Jan 1850; *S/F.* Witlaf, a Saxon king, bequeaths his drinking horn to Croyland's jovial monks. Now, when they have revels, they toast Witlaf and pray for him. They do so at Christmas, with red wine. They drink to his soul, to Christ, and to each and every apostle. They drink to saints and martyrs. Readings are solemnly intoned from the pulpit, midnight chimes are heard, and the abbot dies in front of the yule log in the fireplace clutching "the golden bowl." The monks' merriment continues unabated, because now they "must drink to one Saint more!" Longfellow's source was *The Dark Ages . . .* (1844) by Samuel R. Maitland (1792–1866). In it, mention is made of Wichtlaf, King of Mercia in the ninth century; elsewhere is a description of how some monks continue their libations after their abbot has dropped dead of too much drink.

Bibliography: Wagenknecht, 1986.

KOSSUTH, LOUIS (1802–94). Hungarian politician whose original name was Lajos Kossuth. Soon after entering the National Diet (1830), Kossuth began to argue fiercely for Hungarian autonomy, either within the Austrian Empire or independent from it. For his political actions, he was imprisoned (1837–40). He campaigned successfully for a separate Hungarian constitution, became the new government's finance minister (1848), led the July 1848 insurrection and became Hungary's virtual dictator and then its president (1849). His army was defeated by Austria, with Russian assistance (1849), and he escaped to Turkey. Kossuth was honorably interned there and nearby (1849–51). He went by an American man-of-war to Marseilles, France, then proceeded to Southampton, England, briefly, and on to the United States (with the writer-politician Ferencz Pulszky [1814–97]), where Kossuth was applauded as a fiery patriot (1851–52).

His later career was marred by protests from rival Hungarian exiles, his association with the exiled Italian patriot Giuseppe Mazzini, abortive recruiting during the Crimean War and, later, self-imposed exile in Italy, refusal of amnesty offered by the new Hungarian government, and finally a denial of citizenship. He died in Turin, Italy, but was buried in Budapest.

Longfellow, caught up in the pro-Kossuth frenzy in America, records in his journal (25 Oct 1851) that when conversation at a certain dinner turned to politics, it was "disheartening to see how little sympathy there is in the hearts of young men here for freedom and great ideas. Instead of it, quibbling and criticising style and phrase of Kossuth's address to the democracy of France." John Forster* wrote Longfellow (18 Nov 1851) to warn him that Kossuth struck him as more interested in himself than in Hungary. Longfellow notes in his journal (13 Dec 1851) that he read Kossuth's speech in New York appealing to "the United States to give up its principle of non-intervention in European politics, and to help fight the battles of liberty in Europe." Longfellow notes Kossuth's "power of oratory and the pleading of a sincere heart," but wonders "why need people go *clean daft?*" (19 Dec 1851). Longfellow observed (27 Apr 1852) a reception for Kossuth on the Boston Commons; Longfellow and George Stillman Hillard* met Kossuth and his wife, Therese von Meszlényi Kossuth, at their hotel and that evening attended Kossuth's two-hour lecture in Faneuil Hall, Boston. In his journal (30 Apr), Longfellow comments not on Kossuth's politics but only on his command of English and his manner— "not impassioned this evening, but rather calm and historic." Longfellow dined with Kossuth, his wife, Pulszky, and his wife Terézia Walder Pulszky, among others, in the home of Samuel Gridley Howe*; he notes in his journal that "Kossuth at table was rather silent, like a man fatigued" (2 May); during the evening, Kossuth's wife gave Longfellow, "in German, a long and animated description of her wanderings and escape." It seems that, to join her husband, she had fled, disguised, into Turkey, with a price on her head. Longfellow and Cornelius

Conway Felton,* escorted Kossuth, together with George Sewall Boutwell (1809–1905), then governor of Massachusetts, to Harvard chapel (4 May), where he gave a short speech and received long applause; afterwards, Kossuth and his wife called at the Longfellows' home. They could not remain for dinner, but Pulszky and his wife did.

Pulszky later fought alongside Giuseppe Garibaldi in Italy (1862), returned to Hungary (1866) to serve in its Diet, and became the national museum director in Budapest.

Bibliography: Hilen, ed.; Komlos, John H. *Louis Kossuth in America, 1851–1852*. Buffalo: East European Institute, 1973; S. Longfellow.

L

"THE LADDER OF SAINT AUGUSTINE" (1858). Poem, in *Courtship, Birds* (1858). Saint Augustine wisely said that we can make a ladder of our vices and rise by stepping on our shameful deeds, which include ignoble thoughts and desires, too much wine, and abandoning "the dreams of youth." If we cannot fly, we can at least "scale and climb." Stony pyramids and mighty mountains have stairs and paths. Strive day and night. Rise on the wrecks of the past.

"LADY WENTWORTH." *See* "The Poet's Tale," in *Tales of a Wayside Inn,* Part Second.

"LAFAYETTE" (1825). Poem, signed "Pulci," in *American Patriot,* 1 Jul 1825. Faithful hearts surround this hero. America's flag is firmly planted. Since Europe sees "Empire's fast-westering star / Shine" here, why is Europe not free? We grandly crown our "Father"—that is, General Marie Joseph Lafayette (1757-1834), who visited Portland (25 Jun 1825) during his triumphal tour in the United States. Longfellow took a letter of introduction to Lafayette with him when he went first to Europe, sent it, and met Lafayette (1826) and again later (1829).

Bibliography: Hilen, ed.

LANGUAGES AND LONGFELLOW. Longfellow studied Latin and Greek in preparatory school and at Bowdoin College. While at Bowdoin, he studied French with a tutor. He wrote his father (5 Dec 1824) of his desire to study Italian for a year "at Cambridge." Instead, before teaching modern languages at Bowdoin, he went to France, Spain, Italy, Austria, Czechoslovakia, and Germany (1826-29), where he studied French, Italian, Portuguese, Spanish, and German. He wrote his father (19 Dec 1828) that he was fluent in French, Italian, and Spanish, and could also read Portuguese easily. After teaching French, Italian, and Spanish at Bowdoin (1830-34), Longfellow revisited Europe, traveling in England, Germany, Denmark, Sweden, the Netherlands, Germany, and Switzerland (1835-36); during this time he studied Swedish, Norwegian, Finnish, Danish, Old Icelandic, Dutch, German, and Provençal. He taught modern European languages at Harvard (1836-54). In a lecture titled "History of the Modern Languages" (1 Sep 1844), he quotes this comment attributed to King Carlos V of Spain: "Autant de langues que l'homme sait parler, autant de fois est-il homme [As many languages a man can speak, that many times he is a man]." Later vacation time in various European countries only improved Longfellow's already phenomenal linguistic skills, shown best, perhaps, in his translation of Dante's *La Divina Commedia*. In all, Longfellow translated poems in full or in parts from Danish, French, German, Greek, Italian, Latin, Old English (Anglo-Saxon), Old French, Portuguese, Spanish, and Swedish. He also versified prose translations by others from Armenian and Persian. Longfellow wrote (29 Mar 1876) his friend Elihu Burritt

(1810-79), an American linguist and language teacher, editor, and internationally known pacifist, to thank him for his textbook on teaching Sanskrit, to praise it, but also to imply that he was too old to study "this majestic old language."

Bibliography: Arvin; Doyle, H. G. "Longfellow as Professor at Harvard." *Hispania* 27 (Oct 1944): 320-29; Dunn, E. C. "Longfellow the Teacher." *North American Review* 211 (Feb 1920): 259-65; Hilen, ed.; Johnson, Carl L. "Longfellow's Beginnings in Foreign Languages." *New England Quarterly* 20 (Sep 1947): 318-19; Wagenknecht, 1955.

"THE LAY MONASTERY" (1825). Five essays, in the Portland *Gazette:* "The Author" (1 Mar 1825); "Winter Months" (15 Mar 1825); "The Literary Spirit of Our County" (1 Apr 1825); "Poets and Common-sense Men" (1 June 1825); and "Valentine Writing" (1 Oct 1825). In these essays, Longfellow's argument is that although American literary talent is advancing, it cannot flourish if it is not nurtured. Persons of talent cannot support themselves by writing alone. So, fearing poverty, they become lawyers or preachers, scholarly in those fields, and take up poetry only as a hobby.

Bibliography: Hilen, ed.; Little; Thompson.

"A LAY OF COURAGE" (1849). Longfellow took a translation by William Sidney Walker (1795-1846), titled "On Fortitude," of a five-stanza poem by Ove Malling (1746-1829), historiographer to the King of Denmark, altered three stanzas of it slightly, and submitted them to *Whelan's Magazine,* which published it (Oct 1849). The poem suggests that it is better to sing while cold and hungry but free, than it is to be in the midst of luxury; furthermore, only courage and patience win battles and gain glory.

Bibliography: Flanders, B. H. "An Uncollected Translation." *American Literature* 7 (May 1935): 205-7; Hilen, Jr., Andrew R. "Longfellow's 'A Lay of Courage.'" *PMLA* 67 (Dec 1952): 949-59.

"THE LEAP OF ROUSHAN BEG" (1878). Poem, in *PP, Kéramos, Birds* (1878). Kyrat is the beautiful chestnut horse of Roushan Beg, the bold bandit leader. To escape his myriad pursuers, led by the Arab Reyhan, Roushan Beg's nimble Kyrat must leap a thirty-foot chasm, far below which "the torrent roars unseen." Kyrat, after being kissed, caressed, and wildly sung to, measures the distance, then leaps "into the air's embrace" and beyond, to safety.

> Thus the phantom horseman passed,
> And the shadow that he cast
> Leaped the cataract underneath.

Reyhan feels obliged to praise his successful enemy as Koordistan's bravest man. In this stirring ballad, with each of its 14 stanzas rhyming aabcca, Longfellow outdoes his source, which is a prose translation by Aleksander Borejko Chodzko (1804-91), a Polish man of letters, of a popular Persian poem.

Bibliography: Arvin; Christy, Arthur, ed. Introduction to *The Leap of Roushan Beg.* . . . New York: William Edwin Rudge, 1931.

"THE LEGEND BEAUTIFUL." See "The Theologian's Tale," in *Tales of a Wayside Inn,* Part Second.

"THE LEGEND OF RABBI BEN LEVI." See "The Spanish Jew's Tale," in *Tales of a Wayside Inn,* Part First.

"THE LEGEND OF THE CROSSBILL" (1843). Poem, translated from the German poet Julius Mosen (1803-67), in *GM,* Apr 1843; *Bruges.* Christ while on the cross, seemingly forsaken by all, sees "at the ruthless nail or iron / A little bird is striving there." Christ blesses the bird and says that "as token of this moment" it will be marked by "blood and holy rood." It is called the crossbill, and its singing is legendary.

"LET ME GO WARM" (1831). Poem, translated from the Spanish poet Luis de Góngora y Argote (1561-1627), signed "L.," in *NEM,* 1 Jul 1831; Scudder. The poet prefers to enjoy muffins, hot puddings, nuts, apple tarts, and ale; to watch fountains and hear birds; and to walk over bridges. Let others fill thrones, brave wintry blasts, seek wealth abroad, and dangerously swim the Hellespont. Yes, "let the world laugh, an' it will."

LIEBER, FRANCIS (1800–1872). German immigrant political philosopher and translator. Lieber was a professor of history and political economy at South Carolina College, in Columbia (1835-56), then taught history at Columbia College, in New York (1856-72). About 1840 he started writing Longfellow. Lieber, his wife Matilda Lieber, and Longfellow met on occasion. Lieber criticized Longfellow's use of hexameters and in addition sent him original poems for commentary. Longfellow encouraged him and tried without success to get his poem "Ship-Canal" published in the *Atlantic Monthly.* Longfellow's wife Fanny liked Lieber and his wife.

Bibliography: Hilen, ed.; *Mrs. Longfellow.*

"THE LIFE AND WRITINGS OF CHATTERTON" (1825). Topic originally chosen by Longfellow for his Bowdoin commencement oration. He abandoned the topic, spoke instead on "Our Native Writers," but later wrote about Thomas Chatterton (1752-70) in "Reminiscence of Genius."

Bibliography: Thompson.

"LIFE IN SWEDEN." *See* "Tegnér's Frithiofs Saga."

"LIFE IS ITSELF A MIMIC SHOW" (1982). Poem. Since life is a show, this pretty comedy "Will be a play within a play." Longfellow wrote this prologue for a private theatrical his three daughters prepared and put on. Longfellow wrote his son Ernest Wadsworth Longfellow* (10 Mar 1866) about it.

Bibliography: Hilen, ed.

"THE LIGHTHOUSE" (1850). Poem, in *S/F.* The lighthouse, by day cloudlike, at night is a massive "pillar of fire." The giant structure seems to be "wading far out among the rocks and sands, / The night-o'ertaken mariner to save." Ships leave, waving farewell to it, and return, offering "silent welcomes." The lighthouse is attacked by sand, winds, waves, and scourging rain-storms. Birds, "maddened" by its light, fly into it and die. It resembles "A new Prometheus," rock-chained, grasping Jove's fire,

and ever hailing ships' crews to sail away— "to bring man nearer unto man!" Metaphors, separately effective, are mixed poorly here, and the moral seems tacked on.

"THE LIGHT OF STARS." Poem, apparently lost, written at Bowdoin and perhaps related to his Phi Beta Kappa poem, delivered at Bowdoin (Sep 1832).

Bibliography: Thompson.

"THE LIGHT OF STARS" (1839). Poem, by "L.," as "A Second Psalm of Life: The Light of Stars," in *KM,* Jan 1839; *Voices.* Night comes. The tiny moon falls "behind the sky." Cold stars come out. Then red Mars. Does Mars symbolize love, dreams? No. Mars exemplifies strength, indifference to pain, "the unconquered will." Reader, gain resolution, realize "how sublime a thing it is / To suffer and be strong."

Bibliography: Arvin; Thompson.

LIND, JENNY (1820–87). Swedish operatic, coloratura soprano. She was born Johanna Maria Lind, in Stockholm. Jenny Lind began studying voice at the Royal Theater of Stockholm (1830), debuted in opera (1838), studied in Paris (1841), and sang in operas in Berlin (1844) and London (1847). She was praised for her versatile voice, breath control, and range. After starring throughout Europe, Lind began to criticize the immorality of the stage and toured the United States (1850-52) under the auspices of P. T. Barnum. She enthralled her audiences. In Boston (1852) she married her accompanist, Otto Moritz David Goldschmidt (1829-1907), a German pianist, composer, and conductor. Lind gave many benefit and charity performances but also amassed a fortune of $150,000 or more, much of which she donated to worthwhile Swedish causes. She and her husband lived (from 1852) in Dresden and England, where she became a citizen (1859). After a final public appearance (1883), Lind taught at London's Royal College of Music (1883-86). She saw fit to criticize American women for their poor diet and lack of exercise.

Longfellow attended Lind's first concert in Boston and noted this in his journal (27

Sep 1850): "She is very feminine and lovely. Her power . . . takes her audience captive before she opens her lips. She sings like the morning star; clear, liquid, heavenly sounds." Her late visit with Goldschmidt at Longfellow's house prompted this journal entry (26 Jun 1851): "There is something very fascinating about her; a kind of soft wildness of manner . . . and floating shadows over her face." Longfellow attended at least four more concerts given by Lind and called on her at least once in 1851.

An inveterate lover of music, especially opera, Longfellow also appreciated the singing of Marietta Alboni (1823–94), Italo Campanini (1846–96), Etelka Gerster (1855–1920), Giulia Grisi (1811–69), Giovanni Matteo Mario (1810–83), Adelina Patti (1843–1919), Carlotta Patti (1840–89), Marie-Hippolyte Rôze (1846–1926), and Henriette Sontag (1806–54).

Bibliography: Hilen, ed.; Kyle, Elisabeth. *The Swedish Nightingale: Jenny Lind.* New York: Holt, Rinehart and Winston, 1965; S. Longfellow; Wagenknecht, 1955.

LITERARY REMAINS OF THE LATE WILLIS GAYLORD CLARK (1844).
Book edited by Willis's twin brother, Lewis Gaylord Clark (1808–73), and reviewed by Longfellow (*NAR,* Jul 1844).

"THE LITERARY SPIRIT OF OUR COUNTRY." *See* "The Lay Monastery."

LONGFELLOW, ABIGAIL (1779–?). LONGFELLOW'S AUNT. *See* Stephenson, Mrs. Samuel.

LONGFELLOW, ALEXANDER WADSWORTH (1814–1901). Longfellow's brother. He attended Bowdoin (1830–32), briefly studied medicine there (1833), and served under his uncle, Commodore Alexander Scammell Wadsworth,* as his secretary in the Pacific Fleet (to 1836). He became a civil engineer (beginning in 1837), served on the Joint Boundary Commission (1843–47), then worked for the United States Coast Survey in waters off Maine, South Carolina, and Georgia. He established a residence near Portland. In 1851 he married his third

cousin, Elizabeth Clapp Porter (1822–?). They had five children: Mary King Longfellow (1852–1945), Alexander Wadsworth Longfellow (1854–1934),* Lucia Wadsworth Longfellow (1859–1940), Elizabeth (Bessie) Porter Longfellow (1856–91; in 1878 she married Edward Sherman Dodge [1852–1934]), and Richard ("Dick") King Longfellow (1864–1914). Longfellow bequeathed his brother Alexander $5,000.

Bibliography: Hilen, ed.

LONGFELLOW, ALEXANDER WADSWORTH (1854–1934). Longfellow's nephew, nicknamed Wad and Waddy. He entered Harvard (1872), pleased Longfellow by his steadiness there, and graduated (1876). The adoring uncle attended his commencement. Wad studied architecture in Paris (1879).

Bibliography: Hilen, ed.; Wagenknecht, 1955.

LONGFELLOW, ALICE MARY (1850–1928). Longfellow's second daughter. He treated her, just the way he treated all his children, with exceptional love, kindness, and generosity. In his poem "The Children's Hour," she is "Grave Alice." She and her sisters, Anne Allegra Longfellow* and Edith Longfellow Dana,* accompanied Longfellow when he toured in Europe (1868–69). The will of their mother, Fanny Longfellow,* who died in 1861, provided her daughters with total financial independence, when each arrived at age 21. For example, Longfellow, Alice's guardian while she was a minor, transferred $131,755.45 from his deceased wife's estate to her as legal inheritor (Sep 1871).

Bibliography: Hilen, ed.; Longfellow, Alice M. "My Father." *Carrell* 1 (Dec 1960): 1–4; Wagenknecht, 1955.

LONGFELLOW, ANNE (1810–1901). Longfellow's sister. *See* Pierce, Anne Longfellow.

LONGFELLOW, ANNE ALLEGRA (1855–1934). (Nicknames: Annie, Pansie, Panzie.) Longfellow's fourth daughter. In "The Children's Hour," Longfellow calls her "laughing Allegra." She and her sisters went with Longfellow when he visited Europe (1868–69). The will of their mother, Fanny Longfellow,* provided her daughters, Anne Allegra, Alice Mary Longfellow,* and Edith Longfellow Dana,* with total financial independence, the funds to become available to each at age 21. During Longfellow's last years, Anne Allegra often acted at his secretary and prepared numerous letters which he dictated and signed. In 1885, some years after the poet's death, Anne Allegra married Joseph Gilbert Thorp Jr. (1852–1931), the brother of Sarah Chapman Thorp (1850–1911), who back in 1870 had married Longfellow's good friend Ole Bornemann Bull.*

Bibliography: Hilen, ed.; Wagenknecht, 1955.

LONGFELLOW, CHARLES APPLETON (1844–93).

(Nickname: Charley, Charlie.) Longfellow's first son. He was unruly as a boy. Not long after the Civil War began, Charles was itching to join the Union Army. Longfellow wrote his brother Alexander Longfellow* (30 Aug 1862), then serving in the Coast and Geodetic Survey, to try to hire him as an assistant—"to keep him quiet"— and even offered to pay his salary. Charles unnerved Longfellow to such an extent when he ran off and joined the Union Army (Mar 1863) that Longfellow wrote him (14 Mar 1863) to come home, since he was "too young to go into the army." Longfellow followed up by writing to Charles Sumner,* James T. Fields,* and probably others as well, to try to get Charles a commission. Still, Charles served as an artillery private and (from 1 Apr) a cavalry second lieutenant. He contracted camp fever (June), and Longfellow went to Washington, D.C., to assure himself that his treatment was satisfactory, then got him to Nahant to recuperate (Jul, early Aug). Charles suffered a shoulder and back wound near New Hope Church, Virginia (Nov); again, Longfellow went to Washington to help tend to him and then escort him to Cambridge to recuperate. Charles received an honorable discharge (Feb 1864). Rumor had it that, still recovering from his wound (1864), he overly admired the beautiful Cornelia Fitch,* whom Longfellow also briefly found attractive. She married elsewhere (Feb 1865). Charles soon

traveled a good deal: to Italy and North Africa (Nov 1864–Jun 1865); to Europe again, allegedly to study, with his uncle, Samuel Longfellow,* in the role of guide-mentor; to Cuba (Mar 1866); and to Europe with Thomas Gold Appleton,* in part aboard vivacious Uncle Tom's yacht (Jul 1866–Sep 1867), and partly with Tom's half-brother, Nathan Appleton (1843–1906).*

Longfellow from time to time wrote Charles, often about the condition of the young man's finances. One tactful letter (13 Dec 1866) dealt with expenses he was incurring (Longfellow sent a London bank $4,000 for him to draw on) and to enclose a card from Bayard Taylor* for Charles to use in St. Petersburg. Charles accompanied Longfellow during part of his final tour of Europe (1868–69) but split off to visit India (1868–69). In later years, he branched out on his own, became a troublesome spend-thrift and a dandy, and indulged himself in yacht voyages and fun abroad, as far away, for example, as Japan and China (May 1871–Jun 1874). During this time Longfellow checked on Charles's bank balances and deposited substantial sums from his son's inherited investments to his credit. Charles was so self-indulgent that he regularly overdrew, finally to such an extent that Longfellow wrote him (19 Nov 1873): "How much I lament you have not limited yourself to your income, which was ample to your needs. Now your fortune is half gone, and consequently half your annual income." On that identical day Charles was writing home to report he had hurt his leg during a shooting episode in the Philippines. In due time, he answered Longfellow's complaint to express shame and to explain that he would skip Burma, Siam, and Java, among other planned stops, and return from China more directly. Longfellow did some arithmetic and sent Charles news (19 Feb 1874) of his having spent more than $20,000 in 1873. Meanwhile, Charles was shipping home 18 cases of Japanese and Chinese screens, other curios, and sundry gifts. He took a six-week pleasure trip to London and Paris (beginning 22 Jan 1876). Next, he enjoyed a trip to Mexico, Panama, and Colón. He applied (1878) to join the ill-fated Arctic expedition of

George Washington De Long (1844-81) but then withdrew his application (1879); this was fortunate, because De Long and some of his crew died when their ship was crushed by Arctic ice. Charles enjoyed a summer of yachting in England (1880), to help for which Longfellow cabled him £1,000; father mentioned to son, "Pray do not be extravagant; for this is one third of my income, and neither you nor I can afford any lavish expenses." Unrepentant, Charles drew on his father via a Boston bank for $633.55; Longfellow wrote "Dear Charlie" at his Boston club (20 Apr 1881), "I have paid it, but do not understand it, and am much troubled by it." In many ways, Charley Longfellow, though admittedly a brave wounded veteran, was a spoiled and self-indulgent brat in later years.

Bibliography: Hilen, ed.; Hilen, Jr., Andrew R. "Charley Longfellow Goes to War." *Harvard Library Bulletin* 14 (Winter, Spring 1960): 58-81, 283-303; Longfellow, Samuel. "Longfellow with His Children." *Wide Awake* 24 (Feb 1887): 161-65; Wagenknecht, 1955.

LONGFELLOW, EDITH (1853-1915). Longfellow's third daughter. *See* Dana, Edith Longfellow.

LONGFELLOW, EDWARD. Longfellow's paternal great-great-great-great-great-grand-father. He was a yeoman in Horsforth or perhaps Ilkley, Yorkshire, England. He purchased a house in Horsforth (1625) and bequeathed it with his lands (1647) to his son William Longfellow (1620-1704).*

LONGFELLOW, ELIZABETH WADSWORTH (1808-29). Longfellow's sister. Longfellow was devoted to her, wrote more letters to her than to their siblings during their tragically brief years of affection, and received welcome encouragement from her.

William Pitt Fessenden (1806-69) while studying law in Portland in 1826 began courting Elizabeth, became engaged to her (1829), and would have married her but for her death. Three years later he married Ellen Maria Deering (1809-57). Fessenden became a U.S. senator. Longfellow knew and liked Fessenden very much.

Bibliography: Hilen, ed.

LONGFELLOW, ELLEN (1818-34). Longfellow's sister. Since she was much younger than their sister Elizabeth Longfellow,* Longfellow evidently was less close to her.

Bibliography: Hilen, ed.

LONGFELLOW, ELLEN THEODORA (1838-1927). Longfellow's niece. *See* Longfellow, Stephen (1805-50), his brother.

LONGFELLOW, ERNEST WADSWORTH (1845-1921). (Nickname: Erny.) Longfellow's second son. As a young adult, he displayed moderate artistic skills. Longfellow asked Charles Sumner* to pull strings and get Ernest, then a science student in Cambridge, appointed to West Point (1863). Sumner did so, but Ernest declined to go. A hypochondriac, Ernest was pampered by his father and vacationed in western Europe with his uncle, Samuel Longfellow* (Oct 1865-Oct 1966). Shortly before Ernest returned home, Longfellow wrote him (2 Sep 1866) about $10-$12,000 in cash coming to him when "you are of age" and wondering "how far you still cherish the artistic project." Ernest married Harriet (Hattie) Maria Spelman (1848-1937) in May 1868, and the couple accompanied Longfellow during the first part of his final tour of Europe (1868-69); the rest of the time, they travelled and then returned home by themselves (Nov 1869). Ernest, his wife, and his sister Alice summered in Europe (Jun-Oct 1872); he and his wife vacationed extensively abroad again (Jul 1876-Aug 1879; in London, Paris, Athens, Constantinople, for example); he and the expatriate American artist Francis Boott (1813-1904) studied (1876) with the French painter Thomas Couture (1815-79). Ernest became an artist, exhibited in Boston, and, among other works, painted landscapes and portraits, including one of Helen Mar Bean* (1880) and another of Longfellow (1881).

Bibliography: Hilen, ed.; Longfellow, Ernest Wadsworth. *Random Memories.* Boston: Houghton Mifflin, 1922; Wagenknecht, 1955.

LONGFELLOW, FANNY (1817–61). (Full name: Frances Elizabeth Appleton Longfellow.) Longfellow's second wife. She was the daughter of Nathan Appleton (1779-1861)* and Maria Theresa Gold Appleton;* the sister of Thomas Gold Appleton,* Mary Appleton Mackintosh,* Charles Sedgwick Appleton, and George William Appleton; the step-daughter of Harriot Coffin Sumner Appleton;* the half-sister of William Sumner Appleton,* Harriott Appleton Curtis, and Nathan Appleton (1843-1906);* and the cousin, once removed, of William Sullivan Appleton.* By every account, Fanny was a bright, attractive, friendly, observant, charming, gentle, and devout daughter, sister, wife, and mother. She was born at 54 Beacon Street, Boston (6 Oct 1817), and during her youth resided at 39 Beacon Street. Her father was considerate and exceedingly rich. The deaths of Fanny's mother (1833) and of her brother Charles (1845) sadly matured her emotionally and spiritually. From her earliest years, she enjoyed traveling. Her first extensive trip was to Europe (Nov 1835–summer 1837), during which she enjoyed the usual Grand Tour attractions. She also met Longfellow in Thun, Switzerland (20 Jul 1836). In her diary she identifies him as "Mr. L" and "the Prof." She walked and talked with him, was read to by him, and listened to his comments on scenery, literature, and languages. She was attracted to him, but on occasion his manner was off-putting. When she read his *Hyperion* (1839), she recognized herself as the model for Mary Ashburton in it and was annoyed. Probably because of this, Fanny in a letter (29 Dec 1839) to her cousin Isaac Appleton Jewett (1808-53) criticized Longfellow's *Voices of the Night* as less the work of "a night-bird and . . . more of a mocking-bird than a nightingale." Fanny and her brother Thomas visited Mary Mackintosh, their sister, in England (1841). Fanny and Longfellow were guests (Apr 1853) at the home of Andrews Norton (1786-1853), a Harvard Divinity School professor and the father of Longfellow's friend Charles Eliot Norton.* Fanny's brother Thomas was also there, shortly before another of his departures for Europe. Fanny told Longfellow, long in love with her, that she would be lonely and added, "You must come and com-

fort me, Mr. Longfellow." He responded eagerly. They wrote each other and fell in love forever. They were married in her father's home (13 Jul 1843). Her father bought and soon gave her Craigie House,* the mansion in Cambridge she called "Castle Craigie," as a wedding present. During the years between the time of Longfellow's first wife's death (29 Nov 1835) and Fanny's acceptance of his proposal of marriage (10 May 1843)—which date a year later in his journal Longfellow called "this *Vita Nova* of happiness"—Longfellow was often emotionally unstable. Marriage to Fanny (13 Jul 1843) brought him emotional and spiritual tranquillity and also contributed to his material security and ease.

The Longfellow marriage was one of the most joyous in literary annals. In two letters (24 Jul 1860) Fanny calls her husband "Best Beloved." She was his constant inspiration. They had six children: Charles Appleton Longfellow (1844-93),* Ernest Wadsworth Longfellow (1845-1921),* Fanny Longfellow (1847-1848),* Alice Mary Longfellow (1850-1928),* Edith Longfellow Dana (1853–1915),* and Anne Allegra Longfellow (1855–1934).* When Fanny gave birth to her daughter Fanny under the influence of ether, she was the first woman in the Western World to do so. Little Fanny's death was an agony for both parents. Fanny and Longfellow worried when their son Charles joined the Union Army during the Civil War, were terrified when it was reported (1 Dec 1863) that he was wounded, and were enormously relieved when he recovered. Fanny was sealing a thin paper containing a lock of one of her children's hair (9 Jul 1861), when it caught on fire and began burning her light summer dress. Longfellow rushed in and threw a small rug over her. Hysterical, she dashed to the doorway, horribly burned. A physician came and administered ether. She regained consciousness during the night. She asked for coffee in the morning. She died at 10:10 A.M. (10 Jul). Longfellow, his hands and face badly burned, was treated with ether and laudanum, became dreadfully deranged, and could not attend Fanny's funeral three days later. He grew his famous white beard to conceal burn scars.

Fanny's letters, diaries, and religious journals reveal a woman of intelligence, consideration, and wit. Through her father's political and cultural connections, and later through Longfellow's, she observed, sometimes talked with, and often recorded her impressions of many important, interesting, and unusual people. Everyone who knew her spoke and wrote kindly of her. Longfellow rarely expressed his long, long agony after his loss. He did write a letter (18 Aug 1861) to Fanny's sister, Mary Appleton Mackintosh,* extolling Fanny in unique and touching language. Exactly 18 years after Fanny's death, he wrote "The Cross of Snow," a sonnet that poignantly expresses his interminable anguish.

Bibliography: Hilen, ed.; S. Longfellow; *Mrs. Longfellow;* Wagenknecht, 1955.

LONGFELLOW, FANNY (1847–48). (Nickname: Fan.) Longfellow's first daughter. Her mother, Fanny Longfellow,* gave birth to her under ether, then still considered an experimental and risky procedure. The child's early death (on 9/11—now a dreadful set of numbers) was a terrible blow to both Longfellows.

Bibliography: Wagenknecht, 1955.

LONGFELLOW, HENRY WADSWORTH, II (1839–74). (Nickname: Harry.) The son of Longfellow's brother, Stephen Longfellow (1805-1850)* and his wife, Marianne Preble Longfellow;* hence, Longfellow's nephew. After Stephen's death, Anne Longfellow Pierce,* Henry's aunt, became his legal guardian, with the financial help of the Longfellow family. Though willing to do so, she did not also become the legal guardian of young Henry's sister Ellen Theodora Longfellow (1838-1927).* By letter to Anne (31 Dec 1850), Longfellow for obvious reasons wondered whether Harry would be willing to drop his last name and become Henry Wadsworth. Evidently nothing came of this hope. Longfellow, who felt that Harry was somewhat smothered by his aunt (as well as by Lucia Wadsworth,* his great-aunt, who also lived with Annie at the time), was happy when he went off to school. Longfellow financially supported his doing so.

Harry later entered Harvard (1857), and Longfellow paid all the bills. Harry was evidently lazy, reckless, and delinquent in school; troubled Longfellow by flirting briefly with Anne Denison Wadsworth, the daughter of Commodore Alexander Scammell Wadsworth,* Longfellow's uncle; got nervous and smoked so incessantly that he jeopardized his health; withdrew from school (1859); and was placed in a sanatorium near Northampton, Massachusetts, where he smoked and took laudanum. Longfellow tried unsuccessfully to wangle him a clerkship aboard an American naval vessel (1859). Harry was briefly aboard commercial ships (1860). During the Civil War years, he continued to be dissipated and cadge money from Uncle Henry, Aunt Anne, and other relatives (1863). He married Frances Elizabeth Gammon, of Portland (1863), and was in the army for a while (1865?).

Bibliography: Hilen, ed.

LONGFELLOW, MARIANNE PREBLE (1812–88). The wife of Stephen Longfellow (1805-50),* Longfellow's brother. They had six children: Stephen Longfellow (1832-33), Stephen Longfellow (1834-1905),* William (Willie) Pitt Preble Longfellow (1836-1913), Ellen (Nell) Theodora Longfellow (1838-1927),* Henry (Harry) Wadsworth Longfellow (1839-74),* and Marian Adele Longfellow (1849-1924). Soon after her husband died (19 Sep 1850), Marianne married George F. Fuller (7 Dec 1850) and later moved to Louisville, Kentucky.

Bibliography: Hilen, ed.

LONGFELLOW, MARY (1812–35). (Full name: Mary Storer Potter Longfellow.) Longfellow's first wife. She was the second daughter of Barrett Potter,* a Portland judge. She read assiduously in the standard fare of the times, was a pupil at a girls' school in Hingham, Maine, was discouraged by her father from learning Latin and Greek, but evidently did study a little French and work on problems in mathematics and astronomy. By all accounts, Mary was a bright, lovely, and graceful young woman, but also very fragile. When Longfellow returned from Europe (1829), family tradition has it that he saw

Mary at church, admired her appearance and manner, quietly followed her to her home, and persuaded one of his sisters to call on Mary with him. The two were married (14 Sep 1831) and lived together happily while Longfellow taught at Bowdoin. She had a miscarriage (Oct 1832). They went together to Europe for her first (and only) such trip—she was reluctant to go—and for Longfellow's second. They left New York (10 Apr 1835). One of her fellow-travelers was her friend Clara Crowninshield,* whose diary indicates that Mary was utterly devoted to her husband. Aspects of their travel, especially in Sweden and Denmark, were grueling for Mary, who was pregnant and suffering from ague. The group had a rough trip from Hamburg to Amsterdam. Five days later (5 Oct 1835), she suffered a miscarriage. They proceeded (20 Oct) to Rotterdam, where Longfellow engaged two physicians and a nurse; but Mary died of infection there (28 Nov 1835). At her side were Longfellow and Clara. Longfellow wrote a tender letter (1 Dec 1835) to Barrett Potter, in which he expressed personal consolation owing to "the goodness and purity of her [Mary's] life, and the holy and peaceful death she died." Longfellow had her body embalmed and sent by vessel to Boston. In prolonged anguish, he left (2 Dec) with Clara for Heidelberg, arranged rooms in separate houses there, and buried himself in the study of German. His letters and journal entries indicate heartbreaking grief and a considerable sense of personal guilt. He burned her journals and whatever correspondence they had accumulated.

Bibliography: Crowninshield; Higginson; Hilen, ed.; S. Longfellow; Wagenknecht, 1955; Williams.

LONGFELLOW, MARY (1816–1902). Longfellow's sister. *See* Greenleaf, Mary Longfellow.

LONGFELLOW, SAMUEL (1819–92). Longfellow's brother. He was born in Portland, Maine, where he attended the First Parish Church, which was moving away from Congregationalism to Unitarianism at the time. He was a student at Portland Academy, entered Harvard (1835), and graduated (1838).

After tutoring awhile, he studied at the Harvard Divinity School (1842–43), tutored for an American diplomat's family in the Azores (1843–44), completed his divinity studies at Harvard (1844–46), living in Craigie House* part of that time (1844–45). During these years, he was at most only slightly influenced by Transcendental thinkers of the time. After graduation, he became a mild, tolerant, unsettled Unitarian minister in Falls River, Massachusetts (1848–51), Brooklyn, New York (1853–60), and Germantown, Pennsylvania (1878–82). While in Brooklyn, Samuel Longfellow instituted vespers services for the first time in Unitarian worship. He and a close friend, Samuel Johnson (1822–82), a Unitarian clergyman, produced two books of hymns (1846 and 1864, the latter published by James Ripley Osgood*). Some of the hymns were original, while others were modified from works of other churches and other writers. He and his friend Thomas Wentworth Higginson (1823–1911), clergyman and author, collaborated on *Thalatta: A Book for the Seaside* (1853), a book of poems. Samuel Longfellow enjoyed a lengthy sojourn in Europe (1860–62). As a break from later professional duties, he happily accompanied Longfellow and other members of his family on the poet's last European tour (1868–69). In the 1870s, Samuel Longfellow published two essays downplaying the importance of Jesus and suggesting that Christianity has been but one expression of many effusions of the human religious impulse. Since he never married, he was a frequent and welcome guest in his poet-brother's hospitable home. After the poet's death, Samuel Longfellow collected masses of papers and used them extensively in writing *The Life of Henry W. Longfellow* (2 vols., 1886) and *Final Memorials of Henry Wadsworth Longfellow* (1887, added in 1891 as vol. 3 of the *Life*). Although these volumes have been criticized for occasional inaccuracy, for concealing facts, and for generally sanitizing and idealizing its subject, they are still indispensable. In *Kavanagh,* the minister who preaches against the Mexican War is considered to be based on Samuel Longfellow. Longfellow bequeathed $500 a year to his brother Samuel "during his life."

Bibliography: Hilen, ed.; May, Joseph. *Samuel Longfellow: Memoir and Letters.* Boston and New York: Houghton Mifflin, 1894; Putnam, A. P. *Singers and Songs of the Liberal Faith.* Boston: Roberts Brothers, 1875; Wagenknecht, 1955.

LONGFELLOW, STEPHEN (1685–1764).

Longfellow's paternal great-great-grandfather. He was a blacksmith in Newbury, married Abigail Tompson of Newbury, and with her had five sons, including Stephen Longfellow (1723-90),* and four daughters. Longfellow commemorates him in "The Village Blacksmith."

Bibliography: S. Longfellow.

LONGFELLOW, STEPHEN (1723–70).

Longfellow's paternal great-grandfather. He earned two degrees at Harvard (1742, 1745). He taught school in York, then moved to Falmouth (now Portland), Maine, to be the town's schoolmaster. He held other town offices. He married Tabitha Bragdon of York (1749), and with her had two sons, including Stephen Longfellow (1750-1824),* and two daughters. When British forces burned Portland, including their family home (1775), they moved to Gorham, Maine.

Bibliography: S. Longfellow.

LONGFELLOW, STEPHEN (1750–1824).

Longfellow's paternal grandfather. He inherited the farm of his father, Stephen Longfellow (1723-70),* and married Patience Young of York (1773). They had two sons, including Stephen Longfellow (1776-1849),* and four daughters. For eight years the elder Stephen represented his town in the state legislature and thereafter represented his county as a state senator. He was a judge of the Court of Common Pleas (1797-1811).

Bibliography: Higginson.

LONGFELLOW, STEPHEN (1776–1849).

Longfellow's father. He was the son of Stephen Longfellow (1750-1824)* and Patience Young Longfellow (1745-1830); the brother of Abigail Longfellow Stephenson (1779-?; wife of Colonel Samuel Stephenson [1776-1858]); and the brother of Samuel Longfellow (1789-1818; Sophia Storer's husband). Abigail's daughter Elizabeth Ware Stephenson (1802-?) in 1825 married Randolph A. L. Codman (1796-1853), a lawyer in Waterville, Maine. Born in Gorham, Maine, Stephen Longfellow graduated from Harvard College (1798), where he was a classmate of William Ellery Channing* and Joseph Story.* Stephen Longfellow studied law in Portland, Maine, and was admitted to the bar of Cumberland county (1801). In 1804 he married Zilpah Wadsworth (*see* Longfellow, Zilpah Wadsworth), the daughter of General Peleg Wadsworth (1748-1829)* and Elizabeth Bartlett Wadsworth (1753-1825), of Portland. They were to have eight children: Stephen Longfellow (1805-50),* Longfellow the poet, Elizabeth Longfellow (1808-29),* Anne Longfellow Pierce* (1810-1901; wife of George Washington Pierce* [1805-35]), Alexander Wadsworth Longfellow (1814-1901),* Mary Longfellow Greenleaf* (1816-1902; the wife of James Greenleaf* [1814-1865]), Ellen Longfellow (1818-34),* and Samuel Longfellow (1819-92).* Stephen and Zilpah Longfellow lived for a short while in a brick house built in Portland by General Wadsworth. The future poet was born in a nearby house in which the family later lived and which was owned by Colonel Stephenson. In 1814 Stephen Longfellow, a Federalist, served as a delegate to the Hartford Convention (1814) and to the Massachusetts General Court (1814, 1815). He served one term (1823-25) as a Federalist representative in the U.S. Congress and spent much time in Washington, away from his family. He was awarded an L.L.D. by Bowdoin (1828), where he was an overseer (1811-17) and trustee (1817-36). He became president of the Maine Historical Society (1834). At first, he wanted Longfellow to be a lawyer and not a man of letters, but soon encouraged and supported his son's literary ambitions, and undoubtedly helped him obtain teaching positions at Bowdoin and then Harvard. Longfellow always respected and even revered his father. But at the taciturn, self-disciplined man's death, Longfellow privately expressed sorrow at his father's finally having been restricted to living as an often

unpaid Portland lawyer. Longfellow cata-
logued his father's library for sale and purchased several of the law books listed. Some
of his father's properties in and around Portland were appraised by the Cumberland
County commissioners at $6,880 but were
sold for $8,000 (1853). His surviving chil-
dren inherited the sum, exclusive of which
the children of his deceased son Stephen received separate sums. At least as late as
1854, Longfellow paid taxes on other land
his father had owned. Properties remained
undivided (to 1856 or somewhat later).

Bibliography: Higginson; Hilen, ed.; S. Longfellow; Wagenknecht, 1955.

LONGFELLOW, STEPHEN (1805–50).
Longfellow's older brother. He and Longfellow attended Bowdoin at the same time. Stephen was a troubled adolescent, misbe-
haved at Bowdoin but graduated (1825),
read law inefficiently in his father's office
(1825), and tried without success to become a soldier. He was married (1831) to
Marianne Preble (1812–88), the daughter of
Judge William Pitt Preble (1783–1857), under whom he had served as secretary when
the judge was ambassador extraordinaire to
the Hague (1829–30). Judge Preble had
been associate justice of the Supreme Court
of Maine and a Bowdoin trustee and was to
be a railroad president. His wife was Nancy
Gale Tucker Preble (1786–1849). Longfellow had occasion to express dislike of the
judge for his bad temper. Stephen Longfellow and his wife Marianne had six children:
Stephen Longfellow (1832–33), Stephen
Longfellow (1834–1905),* William (Willie)
Pitt Preble Longfellow (1836–1913), Ellen
(Nell) Theodora Longfellow (1838–1927),
Henry (Harry) Wadsworth Longfellow
(1839–74),* and Marian Adele Longfellow
(1849–1924). Longfellow and his sister
Anne Longfellow Pierce* grew increasingly
fearful that Stephen was mentally deranged.
He became a drifter, hoped vainly to recover
his fortunes in California gold mines, was divorced (12 Jan 1850), tried the water cure
at Brattleboro, Vermont (July), and died a
dreamy, shiftless alcoholic, in Portland (19
Sept).

After Stephen's death, Judge Preble asked
the Longfellow family to help support Ste-

phen's children. Soon after Stephen's
widow remarried (1850) and went to Louisville, Kentucky. Nell joined her there. Anne
Longfellow Pierce, Harry's loving, long-
tolerant aunt, became his legal guardian.
The widowed judge, when aged sixty-nine,
nonplussed the Longfellows by remarrying
(1852); his second wife, Sarah Forsaith
Preble (1815–?), 32 years his junior, gave
him a baby boy, whom they named Edward
Preble (1855–?). Longfellow advised Willie
Preble from time to time and was happy
when he graduated from Harvard (1855)
and received a degree in architecture from
the Lawrence Scientific School (1859).
Meanwhile, Longfellow was appealed to
again (1857), probably by Judge Preble, this
time to shoulder the responsibility for Nell.
Instead, she went with her mother, then in
Washington, D.C. At one point during this
controversy, Longfellow, for too long too tolerant, returned a letter from Judge Preble
unopened (before 6 Oct 1857). Judge Preble
soon died (11 Oct 1857). Longfellow bequeathed $1,000 to each of his brother Ste-
phen's children.

Bibliography: Hilen, ed.; Wagenknecht, 1955.

LONGFELLOW, STEPHEN (1834–1905).
Longfellow's nephew, the son of Longfellow's brother Stephen Longfellow (1805–
50).* After his father's death, the boy came
under the guardianship of his grandfather,
William Pitt Preble (1783–1857). Longfellow's efforts to help "Little Steve" get settled
at schools were often frustrated by the lad's
obstinacy, recklessness, and shiftlessness.
Longfellow's brother Alexander Longfellow*
lost patience with their nephew and called
him "the Vandal S" in a letter (19 Feb 1855)
to Alexander's wife. The fellow was in the
navy briefly (1859), was a private in the
Union Army during part of the Civil War
(wounded three times), was hospitalized for
surgery for an infected leg (1865), and held
a customs-collector's job in Machias, Maine
(1865–67). He was a hopeless alcoholic, was
married (by 1876) to a woman named Garcia
I. Longfellow (they had a child that died of
cholera [1879]) but had marital difficulties,
lived in St. Louis and Philadelphia, and
"drew" in St. Louis on Longfellow's name for

money, which actions Longfellow felt obliged to honor for a time. Longfellow frequently communicated with a St. Louis attorney named Robert S. Voorhis and sent money through him to Stephen (1876, 1877). Stephen freely accepted more money, and got Longfellow to send upwards of $1,200 (1877-78) to finance an invention (a mariner's compass) in Philadelphia. Longfellow wrote Stephen (19 Jun 1877), sent two money orders ($50 each), and said they contributed to what had become a total of $250. This time he added (prematurely), "You must not expect any more. / You must not draw upon me. I do not like that. / Hoping that your Compass will prove a great success." Longfellow had occasion to summarize his April-to-November 1877 gifts to Stephen in a letter to Voorhis (20 Nov 1877), totaled the sum at $600, and enclosed $50 more. The following day he sent Stephen $100 more. He telegraphed Stephen in St. Louis (28 Jan 1878) to draw on him for more, and $100 more (30 Mar 1878), and finally $50 more (5 May 1878) for Garcia's expense to proceed to Philadelphia, to join the inventive Stephen presumably there. The compass invention failed utterly. For good measure, Stephen broke and mangled a leg while drunk in Boston (28 Nov 1878) and soon had it amputated. Longfellow had written at least one unidentified correspondent (by Apr 1879) that he was no longer honoring Stephen's drawing upon him at banks. Next, though already presumably married to Garcia, Stephen married Anna J. Hennessy, a sixteen-year-old from Charlestown, Massachusetts, in Jersey City (11 Apr 1879), got the bigamous matter hushed up through Longfellow's intervention nine days later by way of the influential Philadelphia publisher George William Childs (1829-94), yielded to family pressure, and agreed to enter a home in Boston to be treated for alcoholism (Nov 1879). He finally exhausted Longfellow's saintly patience, by forging Longfellow's name on a check for $1,000 (Dec 1879 or Jan 1880). He was taken into custody, was released on bond, appeared in court, and relieved the family by sailing for Australia (9 Feb 1880) and out of historical record.

Bibliography: Hilen, ed.

LONGFELLOW, WILLIAM (1620–1704). Longfellow's paternal great-great-great-great-grandfather. He was a well-to-do clothier in Horsforth, England, where he owned a total of four houses or cottages. He had two sons, Nathan (?-1687), and William Longfellow (1650–90),* and four daughters.

Bibliography: S. Longfellow.

LONGFELLOW, WILLIAM (1650–90). Longfellow's paternal great-great-great-grandfather. He left Yorkshire, England (c.1676), settled in Newbury, Massachusetts, and engaged in mercantile pursuits. He married Anne Sewall, of Newbury (1676); she was the daughter of Henry Sewall and the sister of Samuel Sewall (1652-1730), the colonial magistrate and diarist. William and Anne Longfellow had three sons, including Stephen Longfellow (1685-1764),* and two daughters. William Longfellow was an ensign in the Newbury company of the Essex regiment, participated in the 1690 unsuccessful expedition of Sir William Phipps against Quebec, and during the return voyage was shipwrecked and drowned.

Bibliography: Higginson; S. Longfellow.

LONGFELLOW, ZILPAH WADSWORTH (1778–1851). Longfellow's mother. In 1804 she married Stephen Longfellow (1776–1849).* They had eight children. She was justifiably proud of her Plymouth Pilgrim ancestors and of her father, General Peleg Wadsworth (1748-1829),* an American Revolutionary War hero. She was knowledgeable about religion and books and encouraged young Longfellow in his literary ambitions. She was the victim of an unspecified chronic illness. Longfellow was devoted to his mother.

Bibliography: Hilen, ed.; Wagenknecht, 1955.

"LOSS AND GAIN" (1882). Poem, in *Harbor.* When the poet compares losses and gains, attainments and misfirings, he is aware that time is often "idly spent." However, "Defeat may be victory in disguise."

"THE LOVER'S COMPLAINT" (1831). Sonnet, translated from the Spanish poet Fernando de Herrera (1534?-97), in *NEM,* Dec 1831; Scudder. The poet asks whether the sun, the winds, and the moon have seen anything resembling the eyes and golden hair of the "cruel," cold object of his affections.

"LOVER'S ROCK" (1825). Poem, in Portland *Advertiser,* 10 Jun 1825; Scudder. Some love never dies, though on occasion doomed like a star that "burn[s], and set[s]." Notice "yon dark rock that swells above / Its blue lake"; it concerns such love. When the lover of a faithful "Indian maid" proved false, she climbed to the rock, observed his "bridal feast" down below, sang a dirge, and plummeted into the lake.

LOWELL, JAMES RUSSELL (1819–91). American man of letters, educator, and diplomat. Lowell was born in "Elmwood," the conservative Lowell family's home on the outskirts of Cambridge, Massachusetts. His father, Charles Lowell, was the pastor of the West Unitarian Church of Boston. Young Lowell graduated from Harvard College (1838) and then obtained a degree from Harvard Law School (1840). He became an abolitionist, published a thin book of undergraduate verse titled *A Year's Life, and Other Poems* (1841), then published his popular *Poems* (1843), briefly coedited *Pioneer: A Literary and Critical Magazine* (1843), and published a book of literary criticism titled *Conversations on Some of the Old Poets* (1844). He was married (1844) to Maria White (1821-53), a poet, abolitionist, and disciple of Margaret Fuller.* Lowell moved with his delicate wife, briefly, to Philadelphia; she encouraged him to join reform movements and write antislavery essays. Their first daughter died aged two (1847), the year a second daughter was born and survived. In 1848, Lowell published *Poems: Second Series,* his brilliant satirical poem titled *A Fable for Critics,* and the first series of his popular *Biglow Papers.* A third daughter was born in 1849 but died the following year. His only son, born in 1850, died in 1852. Lowell and his family went to Europe (1851-52).

The health of Lowell's wife Maria, long an invalid, was no better upon their return to Elmwood, where she died (1853). Lowell, who had turned conservative again, published critical works on several British poets. Appointed to succeed Longfellow as professor of languages and literature at Harvard, Lowell placed his daughter in the care of Frances Dunlap (a niece of Robert F. Dunlap, the former governor of Maine), returned to Europe to hone his considerable linguistic skills (1855-56), then returned to teach at Harvard (1856-72). When a literary dinner club later called the Saturday Club* was founded in Boston (1856), Lowell was one of the original members, along with Louis Agassiz,* Ralph Waldo Emerson,* and several other distinguished men of letters. The group founded the *Atlantic Monthly* (1857) and added Longfellow, Oliver Wendell Holmes,* and Cornelius Felton* to their membership. Lowell married Frances Dunlap in 1857 (they had no children), served as the first editor of the *Atlantic* (1857-61), then coedited the *North American Review* (1863-72), initially with Charles Eliot Norton* (until 1868). Later coeditors were Ephraim Whitman Gurney (until 1870) and Henry Adams (until 1872). Lowell assembled additional literary essays in *Fireside Travels* (1864) and issued the second series of *Biglow Papers* (1866). He delivered his "Ode Recited at the Harvard Commencement" (1865) at the close of the Civil War. Other short poems included "The Cathedral" (1869, dedicated to James T. Fields*) and "Agassiz" (1874, shortly after the death of Louis Agassiz). Meanwhile, the public enjoyed the first series of Lowell's *Among My Books* (1870; 2nd series, 1876, which includes an essay on Dante) and *My Study Windows* (1871). After revisiting Europe (1872-74), Lowell taught again at Harvard (1874-77). Next Lowell began a distinguished diplomatic career. He was the American minister to Spain (1877-80) and then to Great Britain (1880-85). His second wife, Frances, long ill and occasionally insane, died in London (1885). From his home base, he spent several summers thereafter in England, published *Democracy and Other Addresses* (1886) and *Heartsease and Rue* (1888), and supervised a 10-volume edition of his extensive writings (1890). In poor health for some time, Lowell had started to write a biography of Nathaniel Hawthorne* shortly before dying in Elmwood.

Longfellow didn't meet Lowell for some time after the two men were famous. Lowell's *A Year's Life* resulted in his being invited to write for a Boston annual to be co-edited by Longfellow. Lowell favorably reviewed Longfellow's *Poems on Slavery* in the *Pioneer*. Lowell wrote Edgar Allan Poe* (27 Jun 1844) to say that John Forster,* English man of letters and editor of the *Foreign Quarterly Review*, was "a friend of some of Longfellow's clique here" and to hint that Forster thought too highly of Longfellow's poetic talents. But the two men became friends after Longfellow visited Lowell (29 Oct 1846), and the two discussed the slavery problem. According to Longfellow's journal (15 Jun 1848), Lowell read him part of *A Fable for Critics,* which Longfellow later described in his journal as "full of wild wit and deviltry, and amazingly clever" (4 Nov 1848). In his famous *Fable,* Lowell includes many witty and uncannily apt estimates. William Cullen Bryant:* "as quiet, as cool, and as dignified, / As a smooth, silent iceberg, that never is ignified." Richard Henry Dana Sr.*: "Here comes Dana, abstractedly loitering along, / Involved in a paulo-post-future of song." Emerson: "A Greek head on right Yankee shoulders, whose range / Has Olympus for one pole, for t'other the Exchange." Rufus Wilmot Griswold*: "here comes Tityrus Griswold, and leads on / The flocks whom he first plucks alive, and then feeds on." Hawthorne: "with genius so shrinking and rare / That you hardly at first see the strength that is there." Oliver Wendell Holmes: "A Leyden-jar always full-charged, from which flit / The electrical tingles of hit after hit." Washington Irving*: "thrice welcome, warm heart and fine brain, / You bring back the happiest spirit from Spain." Poe: "with his raven, like Barnaby Rudge, / Three fifths of him genius and two fifths sheer fudge." John Greenleaf Whittier*: "whose swelling and vehement heart / Strains the strait-breasted drab of the Quaker apart." And Lowell on Lowell: "The top of the hill he will ne'er come nigh reaching / Till he learns the distinction 'twixt sing-ing and preaching." In his journal (22 Nov 1848), Longfellow tersely defined Lowell's series of *The Biglow Papers* as "very droll." Longfellow's daughter, Edith Longfellow,* was born (22 Oct 1853), five days before Lowell's first wife, Maria, died. In response, Longfellow wrote "The Two Angels," a touching poem in which the angel of life is described as visiting Longfellow while the angel of death calls at the Lowells's door. Longfellow's wife Fanny socially welcomed Lowell's second wife, Frances, but told friends she wished Lowell had instead married Jane Norton, Norton's more accomplished sister. Longfellow notes in his journal (29 Nov 1861) that Lowell, with their mutual friend Norton along, brought Anthony Trollope,* the English novelist, to meet him. When Longfellow resumed translating Dante's *Divine Comedy,* Lowell and Norton met with Longfellow at his house many a Wednesday evening (from 25 Oct 1865, given as the date their Dante Club was established), to discuss his ongoing work. Lowell, long a specialist in Dante and teacher of an advanced course at Harvard on his works, had by this time read *La Divina Commedia* more than 20 times. Longfellow completed translating the *Paradiso* (Jun 1866); so the friends, sometimes having admitted other Dante scholars, discontinued their Dante Club meetings, until Longfellow's translation of the *Purgatorio* came under scrutiny (Dec 1866). Longfellow invited Lowell and Norton to Saturday evening sessions (until early 1867) to go over Norton's translation of Dante's *Vita Nuova.* For Longfellow's sixtieth birthday, Lowell published "To H.W.L. (On his birthday, 27th February, 1867)" in the *Advertiser.* It is a charming, seven-stanza poem, of which this stanza is the most insightful:

Some suck up poison from a sorrow's core,
  As naught but nightshade grew upon
    earth's ground;
Love turned all his to heart's-ease; and the
  more
Fate tried his bastions, she but forced a
  door
    Leading to sweeter manhood and more
    sound.

Longfellow never saw Lowell again after he left to become minister to Spain (1875); he wrote "The Herons of Elmwood" to express his mild sadness because of their separation. In his essay "Dante" (1876), Lowell calls Longfellow's translation of *La Divina Commedia* the best among complete ones. When Longfellow's bust was unveiled at Westminster Abbey in London (2 Mar 1884), Lowell, in his capacity as the American minister to England at that time, gave a lengthy speech. One of his main points was to compare Longfellow and Thomas Gray for their similar "subdued splendor," "transparency of diction," ability at "assimilating the beauties of other literature without loss of originality," and "sympathy with universal sentiments and the power of expressing them so that they come home to everybody, both high and low." Lowell also said of Longfellow, "Never have I known a more beautiful character."

Bibliography: Arvin; Duberman, Martin. *James Russell Lowell.* Boston: Houghton Mifflin, 1966; Green; Higginson; Hilen, ed.; Morison; *Poe Log;* Tryon; Wagenknecht, 1955.

"THE LUCK OF EDENHALL" (1840). Poem, translated from the German poet Johann Ludwig Uhland (1787-1862), in *Boston Notion* (24 Apr 1841). At a banquet, the young Lord of Edenhall orders his frightened old seneschal to bring out the Luck of Edenhall. The Luck is a tall crystal goblet, which was given to his ancestors by a fountain sprite and inscribed with a warning that if it breaks, the luck of Edenhall will be dashed as well. Before offering it for drinks, the Lord rings it, "Kling! klang!" It breaks into pieces; the hall cracks and falls at once, dames are startled, guests fly into dust, foe-

men charge in, and the Lord is smitten dead, holding part of the crystal. Next morning, the seneschal ruminates that the earth itself, lucky and proud like glass, "In atoms shall fall" one day.

During his last trip abroad (1868-69), Longfellow landed in Liverpool, traveled north to the environs of Carlisle, and visited Corby Castle and Eden Hall, where he saw the famous goblet, unbroken despite the ballad. The legend of the Edenhall glass is touched on in one of the selections in Sir Walter Scott's *The Minstrelry of the Scottish Border,* with which Longfellow was familiar.

Bibliography: S. Longfellow; Wagenknecht, 1986.

"THE LUNATIC GIRL" (1825). Poem, in *USLG,* 1 Jan 1825; Scudder. Despite care and sympathy, a "chill frost" one autumn blighted this "beautiful, most gentle" girl. She "drooped" like a fair flower. Some die of love, they say; some kill themselves in desperation. This girl and her lover parted, they say, somewhat coldly. He went to sea and was drowned. The poet saw her afterwards. She tossed pebbles in a fountain and watched them sink. To her ear she held a seashell her lover had given her. When it told her "The tides are out!," she fancied she saw his corpse washed ashore. She mused over his other gifts—a necklace, a halcyon-feathered fan. She once imagined that wind-bent branches were signaling her lover's approach. She tried to embrace him, failed, smiled, and wept. She pointed to a cloud in the west, fancied it was her lover's "wandering bark," then turned away, despondent. After three months, ever displaying "warm love and deep sincerity," she died.

Bibliography: Little.

M

MACDOWELL, KATHARINE SHERWOOD BONNER. *See* Bonner, Sherwood.

MACKENZIE, ALEXANDER SLIDELL (1803–48). U.S. Naval officer and author. After service taking him to Spain, the Baltic, Russia, and Brazil, he was the captain of the *Somers,* a small brig, with a few junior officers, and young sailors, including cadets on their first outward-bound voyage (1842). While the *Somer* was returning home from Africa, three cadets planned to kill Mackenzie, his lieutenant, and anyone else resisting, convert the brig into a pirate ship, and raid American commercial shipping. Anticipating their action, the officers seized the three ringleaders, tried them by drumhead court, and hanged them (1 Dec 1842). One victim was Philip Spencer, aged 18, the son of John C. Spencer, the secretary of war (1841–43) in President John Tyler's cabinet. Mackenzie was court-martialed but acquitted (28 Mar 1843). Charles Sumner* wrote a long, spirited defense of Mackenzie's conduct aboard the *Somer* during the tragedy (*NAR,* Jul 1843). Others rankled, however. Partisan controversy and commentary continued for decades, even after Mackenzie died while serving under Commodore Matthew Galbraith Perry at Vera Cruz during the Mexican War. Mackenzie wrote *A Year in Spain, by a Young American* (2 vols., 1829), *Popular Essays on Naval Subjects* (1833), *An American in England* (2 vols., 1835), *Spain Revisited* (2 vols., 1836), *Two Years in Spain* (2 vols., 1939), and biographies of John Paul Jones (2 vols., 1841), Oliver Hazard Perry (2 vols., 1840), and Stephen Decatur (1846).

In Madrid (1827), Longfellow met Mackenzie when he was a lieutenant on leave in Spain and calling himself Alexander Slidell (he added Mackenzie in 1837); they took a tour to Segovia together and corresponded later. Longfellow read at least parts of Slidell's *Year in Spain* in an 1832 Swedish translation. He wrote Mackenzie (3 May 1837) asking him to collect songs in any "outlandish tongues" for him during his cruises. After Mackenzie's death, Longfellow wrote in sympathy to his widow Catherine A. R. Mackenzie (30 Oct 1848) and also to express his gratitude that Mackenzie in a deathbed letter to her had asked her to thank Longfellow for his highly valued friendship.

Bibliography: Hayford, Harrison, ed. *The Somers Mutiny Affair.* Englewood Cliffs: Prentice-Hall, 1959; Hilen, ed.

MACKINTOSH, MARY APPLETON (1813–89). The sister of Fanny Longfellow* and Thomas Gold Appleton,* and therefore Longfellow's sister-in-law. Mary married Robert James Mackintosh (1806–64),* son of the eminent philosopher Sir James Mackintosh (1765-1832), in December 1839 in the home of her father, Nathan Appleton.* The couple moved to England, where they had four children: Ronald Mackintoch (1840-70), Eva Mackintosh (1843-1935), Angus Mackintosh (1846-?), and James Mackintosh

(1846–?). Mary was a hypochondriac, disliked her husband's desire for a diplomatic career, but accompanied him to Antigua (1850), when he became governor general of the Leeward Islands. Fanny's letters to Mary reveal a steady sisterly love. When Fanny burned to death, Mary, then in London, wrote Longfellow a comforting letter, to which he replied with haunting poignancy (18 Aug 1861).

Bibliography: Hilen, ed.; *Mrs. Longfellow.*

MACKINTOSH, ROBERT JAMES (1806–64). The businessman husband of Mary Appleton Mackintosh,* who was the sister of Fanny Longfellow.* At first, Fanny didn't much like Mackintosh, whom she described as "a puzzle not Chinese but English." Later, however, she liked him well enough but was sad that his work took her sister far away from her.

Bibliography: Mrs. Longfellow.

"MAD RIVER, IN THE WHITE MOUNTAINS" (1882). Poem, in *AM,* May 1882; *Harbor.* The traveler asks the Mad River why it doesn't take it easy, since rest is best in this restless world. The river wonders why this city fellow wants to know. Because the traveler would like to learn the river's song. The river explains that at first it was a brooklet, ventured out irresolutely like a child, left the forest, and raced across fields as though pursued. Hearing the ocean calling, it must carry logs from the hills to the mills, "water[s cattle] with these arms," and earns the name "Mad" for breaking sand and clay banks and washing bridges away. It invites the traveler to write his "little rhyme" and let him go on to the mills. "Mad River" was one of the last poems Longfellow wrote.

"MAIDEN AND WEATHERCOCK" (1880). Poem, in *Youth's Companion,* 27 May 1880; *Thule.* The maiden asks the weathercock what he sees from his church-tower perch. The answer: a ship with a sailor on deck, "blowing . . . kisses toward the land." The maiden says the fellow is her lover, heading home, and chides the weathercock for veering about, unlike her steady lover. The weathercock says he was built to "change with all the winds that blow," and adds she'll be glad if he looks the other way when she and her lover meet. Hezekiah Butterworth (1839–1905), editor of *Youth's Companion,* paid Longfellow $100 for this poem and "The Windmill" together.

Bibliography: Hilen, ed.

"MAIDENHOOD" (1842). Poem, in *SLM,* Jan. 1842; *Ballads.* The poet compares the brown-eyed, golden-haired girl to a brook about to become a river, to a dove afraid of the falcon's shadow, to morning nearly noon, to May nearly June, to a tree bough with birds but soon covered with snow. He asks her to preserve her "dew of youth" and especially her "smile of truth," which, darting into "sunless heart[s]," is divine. This poem, though in charming rhymed triplets, offers an image of the feminine surely unacceptable in both his epoch and, especially, ours of political correctness.

Bibliography: Arvin; Williams.

***MANUEL DE PROVERBES DRAMATIQUES* (1830).** Reader, prepared by Longfellow. A second, expanded edition soon appeared (1832). Longfellow corresponded with Charles Folsom,* publisher and editor, concerning this work.

Bibliography: Hilen, ed.

"THE MASQUE OF PANDORA" (1875). Masque in eight scenes, in *Pandora,* 1875.

I. "The Workshop of Hephaestus." When Hephaestus finishes a beautiful clay statue, Zeus breathes mortal life into it but also a spirit "of diviner essence," with gifts of song, eloquence, beauty, and that "nameless charm" which enslaves "all men." A chorus of graces sings of the moving, breathing creature's beauty, and calls her Pandora (translation: "having all gifts").

II. "Olympus." Hermes happily obeys Zeus's command to escort Pandora to Prometheus and to tell him to marry her. This, even though Hermes is aware that "Who thinks of marrying hath already taken / One step upon the road to penitence."

III. "Tower of Prometheus on Mount Caucasus." While Prometheus is seeing evil omens in the stars, Hermes brings in timid Pandora. After some verbal fencing, Hermes tells Prometheus that Zeus ordered him to present Pandora as a gift. Prometheus, though acknowledging Pandora's beauty, says he distrusts any gift from the unfriendly gods. She says Prometheus is known for being "humane." He says, rather, he is unfortunate, being punished by "the rock and vulture" for bringing "to man the fire / And all its ministrations." He prefers his thoughts of "ideal beauty" to anything merely real. Hermes warns that the gods don't "solicit"; they offer irrevocable "Choice and occasion." Pandora says she and Hermes should leave. They do so. In a chorus of the three fates, the first calls Prometheus "defiant" and predicts confusion; the second says that through pain Prometheus "the highest shall attain"; the third suggests that Pandora, a "new toy," should be presented to Epimetheus to tempt him.

IV. "The Air." Noting that tough Prometheus's tender-hearted brother Epimetheus is now forge-hot with love, Hermes springs off the earth, which immediately "rocks [like] the bough from which a bird takes wing."

V. "The House of Epimetheus." Epimetheus praises Pandora for her melodic voice, delicate form, "tender eyes," and "whole presence," adds that Eros not Hermes must have brought her, and expresses his love. She loves him too but says he doesn't really know her. He replies that it seems he always knew her and only just now found her. She adores everything about his beautiful, hospitable house. She observes his carved, embossed oak chest, which he says an oracle has forbidden him ever to open. He suggests a stroll in his garden, where the nightingales will teach him how to woo her. She says he needs no teacher. A chorus of the Eumenides starts thus:

What the Immortals
Confide to thy keeping,
Tell unto no man.

They caution silence, pronounce the gods unforgiving, and cite the fates of Tantalus, Sisyphus, and Ixion.

VI. "In the Garden." While Epimetheus is optimistic and daring, Pandora is fearful if coy. The birds sing of love and their consequent fledglings. Echo seconds all this. A chorus of reeds sounds a warning, to which Epimetheus says Pan made a pipe of reeds and asks Pandora to stop being coy. Pandora retorts that he should not be "rude and mannerless," like Pan. As Prometheus enters, the Dryades warn Pandora to hide from him. Prometheus tells Epimetheus that she is a dangerous gift from the gods and should be refused. The two madden each other with a few taunts. Then, calling Epimetheus a descendant of Titans and hence more than a mere man, Prometheus invites him to visit his tower, enjoy working at the forges in his caverns, and study the stars and agriculture. Epimetheus laments thus:

O my brother!
I am not as thou art. Thou dost inherit
Our father's [the Titan Iapetus's] strength,
    and I our mother's [a sea-nymph's]
    weakness:
The softness of the Oceanides,
The yielding nature that cannot resist.

But Prometheus persuades him to pep up and leave. Choruses mention "wrinkled" mountains ("Solemn, eternal, and proud"), "impetuous" waters ("Hurrying onward" to fountains), "rush[ing]" winds ("Trumpets of terrible breath"), and shadowy forests ("Filled with the breath of freedom"), and then urge "endless endeavor" toward victory and renown.

VII. "The House of Epimetheus." Pandora is tempted "by powers invisible / and irresistible" to accept Epimetheus's sumptuous house as hers, and his love too. She resists lifting the chest lid, since she shouldn't and also since shadowed faces in numerous wall mirrors would be watching. Lying down to sleep, she awaits her lover, her "Helios." Zephyrus bids sentinels of the Ivory Gate to hold back its "evil dreams of fate / And falsehood and infernal hate," and bids other sentinels to open the Gate of Horn and release "dreams of truth," and "wondrous prophecies / And visions of the morn." Instead, dreams emerge from the Ivory Gate, fatally ordered out of "gloomy Tartarus" to whisper into the sleeper's ear

A Tale to fan the fire
Of her insane desire

To know a secret that the Gods would keep.

Pandora awakens, says the oracles told only Epimetheus, not her, to keep the chest shut. Anyway, mirrors can't see anything. And after all, the Gods, who know good and evil, created her and filled her "with desire / Of knowing good and evil like themselves." Willy-nilly, she opens the chest. A mist fills the room. She faints. A storm bursts outside. A chorus from the Gate of Horn says that the secret is out and is flying all around, and that what follows "on every side" is sickness, sadness, pain, sounds of misery and "maniac laughter"—in fact, "All the evils that hereafter / Shall afflict and vex mankind." Nothing but "Hope remains behind."

VIII. "In the Garden." Epimetheus observes ruinous change everywhere and fears for the future. Pandora confesses that she opened the chest, and asks to be punished, killed, not pardoned. He takes the blame, and says he shouldn't have revealed the oracle's secret admonition, shouldn't have left her alone to be tempted, and loves her all the more now, because she is weak and therefore worthy of pity in addition to love—rather than mere "worship." When she doesn't like the idea of pity, he counters that she is still his goddess and that ahead of them are

> Youth, hope, and love:
> To build a new life on a ruined life,
> To make the future fairer than the past,
> And make the past appear a troubled dream.

The two see an omen in a storm-wrecked nest and a bird working on a new nest. Epimetheus adjures the Eumenides to get lost. Pandora hopes to be punished only by suffering, since only thus will they be reconciled "To the immortal Gods and to ourselves." The Eumenides, however, sing out that "souls like these" won't escape their torches and their scourges, because

> Never by lapse of time
> The soul defaced by crime
> Into its former self returns again.

Only when Helios purifies the guilty will recovery occur, the lost be regained, and

"nobler passions and desires" begin to guide the penitent toward a "new life."

Longfellow's source for his Pandora story is *Works and Days* by Hesiod. Longfellow first thought of calling his one and only masque "The Legend of Prometheus" and then "The Masque of Epimetheus." The finished work was published in *The Masque of Pandora and Other Poems* (1875). By year's end the volume had sold 5,000 copies and a new edition was being prepared. A musical version of the masque was written by Alfred Cellier (1844–91), the English composer; it was performed, unsuccessfully (10 Jan 1881), by Blanche Roosevelt's English Opera Company, at the Boston Theater, featuring the poet's friend Blanche Roosevelt Tucker-Macchetta* as Pandora. Although Longfellow wrote a special song and chorus for Blanche's appearance, he had his friend Sherwood Bonner* in mind when the image of Pandora was developing in his imagination. He admired Blanche's singing but disliked the way Rowe had "mutilated and mal-treated" his poem, as he puts it in a letter to Blanche's actress friend Sara Jewett* (7 Mar 1881).

Bibliography: Arvin; Hilen, ed.; Lamberton, Robert. *Hesiod.* New Haven: Yale University Press, 1988; Wagenknecht, 1986.

***THE MASQUE OF PANDORA AND OTHER POEMS* (1875).** Collection of poems: *The Masque of Pandora.* "The Hanging of the Crane," "Morituri Salutamus." *Birds of Passage. Flight the Fourth:* "Charles Sumner," "Travels by the Fireside," "Cadenabia," "Monte Cassino," "Amalfi," "The Sermon of St. Francis," "Belisarius," "Songo River." *A Book of Sonnets:* "Three Friends of Mine," "Chaucer," "Shakespeare," "Milton," "Keats," "The Galaxy," "The Sound of the Sea," "The Tides," "A Shadow," "A Nameless Grave," "Sleep," "The Old Bridge at Florence," "Il Ponte Vecchio di Firenze."

MASSACHUSETTS HISTORICAL SOCIETY. Founded in 1791 by Dr. Jeremy Belknap (1744–98), author and minister of the Federal Street Church in Boston, it is the oldest historical society in the United States. Its purpose, agreed to by Belknap's friends, was to provide a central depository in Boston for historical books, pamphlets, manuscripts, and records, and to publish copies of rare items. Membership was limited to 30 residents of Massachusetts and 30 non-residents; but when incorporated in 1794 through the efforts of James Sullivan (1744–1808), then the Attorney General of Massachusetts, it increased resident membership to 60, later increased to 100 (1857). The Society moved from a bank library (1791) to the attic of Faneuil Hall (1793) to part of a building on Arch Street (1794), and next to the ample attic of a savings institution building on Tremont Street (1833). At first, materials were donated, sometimes by badgered owners. The Society immediately began publishing copies of donations in a massive way. Chronically meagre funds, from dues and small gifts, were improved by a $10,000 legacy (1854) from the estate of Samuel Appleton (1766–1853),* the older brother of Nathan Appleton,* Longfellow's father-in-law. Longfellow was elected to membership and accepted (Dec 1857). He invited the Society (17 Jun 1858) to meet at Craigie House,* his residence, which was especially attractive to members because it had been General George Washington's headquarters at one time. Longfellow spoke at a Society meeting (Dec 1859) to commemorate the death of Washington Irving.* After Longfellow's death, the Society met (13 Apr 1882) to eulogize their faithful companion; Edward Everett,* Oliver Wendell Holmes,* Charles Eliot North,* and a few others spoke with tender affection. When the new building for the Society was completed on Boylston Street (1899), its library contained about 40,000 books and about 100,000 pamphlets. Society holdings were made available to nonmember scholars and other readers (1910). It has steadily continued to grow, flourish, and foster scholarship and publishing.

Bibliography: Riley, Stephen T. *The Massachusetts Historical Society 1791–1959.* Boston: Massachusetts Historical Society, 1959; "Tribute."

"THE MEETING" (1873). Poem, in *Aftermath, Birds* (1873). When we get older and meet the few friends we have left, we think and talk more about the dead than about the living, can "hardly distinguish / Between the ghosts and the guests," and experience "a mist and shadow of sadness" when we try to joke.

"MEMORIES" (1882). Sonnet, in *Harbor.* The poet says the memories he has of friends he was once close to are "overgrown / With other thoughts and troubles of my own," a little the way grass, moss, and lichens spread over a grave. Are friends' memories of him likewise going? No, our memories are all pleasant, like withered flowers, perhaps, but with "the root perennial."

"MEZZO CAMMIN" (1886). Sonnet, Scudder. Longfellow realizes that half his life "is gone" and he has not "fulfilled" his ambition "to build / Some tower of song with lofty parapet." What held him back was not laziness, pursuit of pleasure, "restless passions," but rather "sorrow and a care that almost killed." Behind him lie roofs, bells, lights of a city. Above him "Death" thunders. Longfellow penned these lines, the last of which is an unusual alexandrine (i.e., is in iambic hexameter not pentameter), at Boppard, on the Rhine River (25 Aug 1842), soon after which he returned home. This splendid sonnet was first published in Stephen Longfellow's* 1886 biography of his brother.

Bibliography: S. Longfellow; Williams.

MICHAEL ANGELO: A FRAGMENT **(1883).** Drama in three parts, each with titled subdivisions.

"Dedication," in sonnet form. Longfellow says that nothing dies but instead is simply revived. For example, the land steams up into clouds that fall as rain. Similarly, he now "build[s] this verse" out of "old chronicles."

Part First. I. "Prologue at Ischia." The vibrant Julia Gonzaga (Duchess of Trajetto), whose old husband died in her arms, must leave the weary Vittoria Colonna, whose young husband (Marchese di Pescara) died in battle. Julia is returning to Fondi, where Fra Sebastiano will paint Julia's portrait as a gift to the accomplished young Cardinal Ippolito (de' Medici). He rescued her once from the Moors. Vittoria praises the ever-working Michael Angelo. Vittoria thinks he may covet Julia, who says not so. Sunset falls over nearby Naples, Sorrento, and Vesuvius.

(Longfellow appears to have planned to have Fra Bernardino enter this scene and tell Vittoria that he has been summoned to Rome and may preach dangerously there. *See also* "Vittoria Colonna.")

II. "Monologue." In his studio, Michael Angelo laments the fact that the Pope has ordered him to follow the Sistine ceiling paintings with a depiction of the Last Judgment. Sebastiano might have painted it. Michael Angelo can do so, if his imagination is thrillingly alerted, as it now is by thoughts of a certain angelic face. But he is now seventy, with a face like "Laocoön's, full of pain," and a forehead resembling "a ploughed harvest-field."

III. "San Silvestro." At a Roman chapel one afternoon, Vittoria Colonna sends for Michael Angelo. She and some others await him. As he approaches, he views Vittoria as "Saint or Goddess." When she says the Pope is permitting her to build a convent and needs his advice, Michael Angelo, delighted, theorizes that paintings and statues are shadowlike compared to architectural realities. He saw the Laocoön unearthed and seemed to hear the serpents' victims cry in agony; but if he could build a temple for God half as fine as what the Forum once was, he would be uniquely thrilled. Agreeing, Vittoria says,

> Art is the gift of God, and must be used
> Unto His glory. That art is highest
> Which aims at this.

(Longfellow appears to have rejected a greatly expanded version of this scene.)

IV. "Cardinal Ippolito." Jacopo Nardi comes from Florence to ask help of Cardinal Ippolito, awaits the pretentious man in his luxurious palace, and is startled when Ippolito enters dressed like a fancy Spaniard. The bright fellow says he prefers not to wear petticoats "Like an old dowager." He praises Nardi's translation of Titus Livius's histories of Rome. They agree that Ippolito's "obscene" cousin, Duke Alessandro, is destroying the morals, the liberty, and the "Tuscan tongue" of Florence. Saying Lucifer himself now reigns there, Nardi says that Alessandro

is strengthening his position by planning to marry Margaret, daughter of the Emperor of Spain. Ippolito says he will go aid the Emperor in fighting the Turks and thus gain his support against Alessandro. Nardi leaves. Sebastiano, the portrait painter, enters. Ippolito praises his portrait of Julia, gives him a beautiful Turkish scimitar, wishes Sebastiano could paint Julia's escape on horseback from the brigands, says he is tired of Rome, a "dead old city" with convent bells ringing day and night, plans to help the Emperor, but tonight invites Sebastiano to dine with him on eels, oysters, and wine. Sebastiano warns that certain eels once poisoned a pope.

V. "Borgo delle Vergine at Naples." In her Neapolitan palace, Julia asks a close friend, Giovanni Valdesso, for advice. She feels uneasy, frustrated, and disgusted with her lot. Aware of her beauty, she says she is indifferent to her numerous suitors and yet prefers lively friendship, which she calls Paradise, to living part of the time, as she does, in a convent, which she calls Purgatory. Valdesso tells her to "tune your heart-strings to a higher key / Than earthly melodies," and to be sincere in her faith, not ostentatious about it. He criticizes her for her friendship with Ippolito and for her giving him her portrait. She says she did so out of gratitude for his saving her from the Moors under Barbarossa. Suddenly word comes that Ippolito has been poisoned.

VI. "Vittoria Colonna." Julia visits Vittoria at Torre Argentina. Vittoria is sorry for Julia's loss and says Michael Angelo is going to do her portrait. He enters, is introduced again to Julia, and lavishes such praise on her beauty that Vittoria asks for praise too. To this he says she "conceal[s] / Your manifold perfections from all eyes." While he is outlining his portrait, she asks about his Sistine commission. He says,

> Old men work slowly. Brain and hand alike
> Are dull and torpid. To die young is best,
> And not to be remembered as old men
> Tottering about in their decrepitude.

The two women continue their gossip. Vittoria talks about Duke Ercole of Ferrara, who is cold and intolerant; to which Julia wonders how the French princess could ever marry him. Michael Angelo responds,

> The men that women marry
> And why they marry them, will always be
> A marvel and a mystery to the world.

When Vittoria praises Ercole's wife and her court of noble, talented women, and says Boccaccio couldn't have written accurately about them, Michael Angelo praises Boccaccio's rendition of Griselda. While praising the duke's wise male courtiers, Vittoria adds that no poets there could match dead Ariosto, who, she reminds Michael Angelo, called him "less man than angel, and divine." Michael Angelo turns modest and then a little bitter.

Part Second. I. "Monologue." At home, Michael Angelo thinks about the painting of Christ he created and sent to Vittoria, now hiding in a convent in Viterbo from Cardinal Caraffa, who hates all Colonnas. She wrote praising Michael Angelo's art and predicting that he will sit at Christ's right hand in Heaven. Michael Angelo loves Rome, moldy and old like himself. Though "Trodden by priestly feet" here, he loves the city where Virgil and Trajan lived. He misses Vittoria. Opening the *Divina Commedia,* he calls Dante

> . . . the great master of our Tuscan tongue,
> Whose words like colored garnet-shirls in
>   lava
> Betray the heat in which they were engen-
>   dered.

He deplores Dante's being criticized here and in Florence. Also mocked, Michael Angelo concludes that "There's not room enough / For age and youth upon this little planet." As he seeks to sketch Dante's Beatrice, he thinks of Vittoria, his own womanly guide.

II. "Viterbo." At her convent window, Vittoria relishes "Silence and solitude," asks her sacred dead to look at her, and says that after a few more prayers and sighs she will join her Francesco.

III. "Michael Angelo and Benvenuto Cellini." Gaily dressed and cocky, Cellini visits Michael Angelo, says he is leaving Rome for Florence, and asks Michael Angelo to come with him and work on the unfinished sac-

risty. Declining, Michael Angelo says Rome has infected him with the malarial fever of wanting to do nothing but work. He recalls art masterpieces in Florence by Brunelleschi, Ghiberti, Giotto, and Ghirlandajo, and laments that, now old, he can look back on little he has done. Cellini commends Michael Angelo's varied works and asks about his *Last Judgment.* Nearly done, says Michael Angelo; he adds that Biagio, the papal master of ceremonies, was so critical of it that Michael Angelo painted the fellow in it as Minos, guardian of Hell. Cellini says he would have killed the fellow, then boasts of his shooting the constable of Bourbon France and also of being pardoned by Pope Clement after shooting a Spaniard during the siege of St. Angelo. Michael Angelo wonders who absolved the Pope. The two agree that Sebastian, now busy stamping lead seals on papal bulls, has grown fat and lazy. Michael Angelo advises Cellini to "Have faith in nothing but in industry" and to create "greater things" than a mere goldsmith's "pretty" objects. Cellini admits that while imprisoned at St. Angelo he had a vision of a splendid crucifix of radiant sunshine and felt divinely touched. He adds that he has been summoned to France, will make a gold salt-cellar for the king, and envisions a statue of Mars for Fontainebleau. When Cellini departs, Michael Angelo wonders where Dante would place Cellini. His passions have hurt his virtues, but he is not a hypocrite hiding his sins under "leaden cloaks."

IV. "Fra Sebastiano del Piombo." Fat Sebastiano puffs his way up Michael Angelo's stairway and asks whether he ever plays in the Campagna and the Alban hills, visible from his window. No, says Michael Angelo; he never plays. Sebastiano says he likes to rest, and invites Michael Angelo to dine with him and Francesco Berni, who will read from his *Orlando Inamorato.* No. Sebastiano says that the jovial, wine-bibbing Rabelais, creator of Gargantua, will be there. Not interested in mirth or wine, says Michael Angelo, who prefers to read Dante, "greatest of all poets." Berni calls Dante dull and prefers Petrarca. Michael Angelo doesn't like "Tinkling . . . little sonnets." They discuss Aretino, a poet whom Michael Angelo says

Berni describes "as having one foot in the brothel / And the other in the hospital." He adds that Aretino even offered suggestions for his *Last Judgment.* He praises Sebastiano's portrait of Vittoria, gripes about Jan Van Eyck's introducing oil in paints, and says he prefers frescoes. Sebastiano compares the sharp outlines of Roman buildings at this sunset to Cimabue's art. Michael Angelo says nature, "always right," provides such scenes and, further, "That picture that approaches sculpture nearest / Is the best picture." When he tells Sebastiano that he should continue working, that money and children don't last, but, that, for example, Ghiberti's baptistery gates will "keep his name and memory green," Sebastiano replies that he is content to let other painters work faster than he ever could. Michael Angelo says "Sebastiano del Piombo" is called leaden for good reason and recalls his once wishing to compete with Baldassare and Raphael. Michael Angelo denies Sebastiano's retort that he is alive but Raphael is "dust and ashes," and adds that Raphael, lucky to have died young, "Caught strength from me, and I some greater sweetness / And tenderness from his more gentle nature." Saying he prefers fun to earning short-lived compliments, Sebastiano leaves Michael Angelo alone and wondering what the future commentators will think of himself. Remembering his wrinkles, "marred countenance," rude speech and manners, and "uncouth rhymes," they will be unaware of his womanlike tenderness but "will estimate / His influence" on his era.

(Longfellow wrote but rejected a scene dramatizing the supper Michael Angelo declined to attend. In it, Rabelais says that

> . . . behind my mask of folly
> I utter certain verities, which spoken
> In soberness would bring me to the faggot.

Cellini also enters, to escape some pursuers.)

V. "Michael Angelo and Titian." Titian visits Michael Angelo in Rome, and, with Giorgio Vasari mostly just listening, discusses art with him. Titian finds Roman ruins depressing and prefers to be near the sounding sea. Michael Angelo praises three superb Venetian artists—Giorgione, Tintoretto, and, of course, Titian. Titian says Tintoretto "paints with fire, / Sudden and splendid." Vasari wonders if Tintoretto is still conceited. Titian doesn't care. When Michael Angelo wonders whether any artist could well follow Titian and Tintoretto, Vasari ventures to name five lesser painters. Titian thinks the next generation "will possess the world that we think ours, / And fashion it far otherwise," then praises, somewhat jealously, a newcomer called Veronese, who has "rare promise." Michael Angelo "rejoice[s] / To see the young spring forward in the race," eager and audacious. Titian agrees that age "must make room for others." When asked, he undrapes *Danaë,* his painting, the varied colors of which Michael Angelo praises for brilliantly reflecting its artist's Venetian natural environment of sunshine, showers, and the Adriatic. Vasari asks Michael Angelo whether painting or sculpture is "the greater of the sister arts." After hedging, he answers, "I account that painting as the best / Which most resembles sculpture," and likens *Danaë* to "a statue with a screen behind it!" As he leaves with Vasari, Michael Angelo whispers that Venetian painters have more knowledge of color than of drawing.

VI. "Palazzo Cesarini." Julia visits Vittoria. Ten years have passed since they were both at Ischia. Vittoria looks at her fading beauty in a mirror. She recalls that Catullus and Ippolito have died. Other friends have been banished for holding unwelcome religious beliefs. Vittoria asks Julia to read Petrarca's "Triumph of Death" aloud. While hearing it, she drops her mirror and dies. Michael Angelo enters, praises her features, saintly in death, kisses her hand, and prays for her repose.

(Longfellow wrote but rejected a revised scene at Palazzo Cesarini in which the two women discuss "pitiless . . . Caraffa.")

Part Third. I. "Monologue." Michael Angelo addresses his model for St. Peter's Cathedral, which follows Brunelleschi's plan, and wishes it could expand and become the real structure. It will take long to build, especially since materialistic cardinals keep interfering. Michael Angelo should not have outlived merry Sebastiano, now dead. "When men are old, the incessant thought of Death / Follows them like their shadow" but is a friend.

II. "Vigna di Papa Guilio." Pope Julius praises Michael Angelo to Cardinal Salviati and Cardinal Marcello, who both contend that the artist is incapacitated by old age. Michael Angelo enters and tells Pope Julius that Baccio Bigio, an architect whom the cardinals like, sabotaged St. Mary's bridge by stealing expensive stones with which Michael Angelo strengthened its piers. He laments thus:

> Men have become
> Iconoclasts and critics. They delight not
> In what an artist does, but set themselves
> To censure what they do not comprehend.

Proof soon comes. The cardinals say he departed from plans by Bramante and San Gallo. Michael Angelo exalts Bramante but says San Gallo's additions wrecked Bramante's lighting plans, mentions his new window plans, and tells the cardinals he won't share his every design idea with them. They call him rude. Michael Angelo recites his noble pedigree, asks Pope Julius to cancel his contract and let him return to Florence, is firmly refused, agrees to stay to prevent Bigio's further damage, but complains about "the sure decline / Of art, and all the meaning of that word." Pope Julius blesses him and orders the cardinals never to mention Bigio's name to him again.

III. "Bindo Altoviti." From his doorstep in Rome, Bindo Altoviti saddens Michael Angelo by reporting that Cosimo the tyrant reigns supreme in their beloved Florence, where freedom-fighter Philippo Strozzi and others have been jailed. Michael Angelo says the miseries "Of Florence are to me a tragedy / Deeper than words, and darker than despair." But Bindo adds that Cellini, after long years away, is returning to Rome. Bindo shows Michael Angelo a superb bronze bust of himself done by Cellini. Michael Angelo says Cellini has happily thus revealed his amazing "genius," praises the "power and feeling" the bust demonstrates, but says it should be placed in better light.

IV. "In the Coliseum." Michael Angelo is in the Coliseum to express wonder at its long-standing architecture and to absorb something of the genius of Gaudentius, its builder. Tomaso De' Cavalieri is with him, praises the old master as a teacher himself, and decries the bloody uses to which the place was put. Michael Angelo says he is concerned with its beauty, and calls it "The queen of flowers, / The marble Rose of Rome!" Cavalieri says Michael Angelo's art is "nobler." Michael Angelo suddenly describes a dream he had, in which "a great hand out of heaven" put an end to the earth, the seas, forests, and fields; the graves opened; cities fell "like jewels from a broken crown"; the earth, at first like "A skeleton of stone," began to resemble a ship buffeted by huge waves, and sank into the darkness "with her dead crew." When Cavalieri says the earth doesn't move, Michael Angelo cites "A certain man, Copernicus," who says otherwise; therefore, his own dream may presage the coming truth.

V. "Benvenuto Again." After 12 years, Cellini returns to Rome, visits Michael Angelo, and tells him much: France's king welcomed and pensioned him; he received Michael Angelo's letter praising his Bindo bust, but tells him his bronze *Perseus* is better still. He describes it, says it will be placed in Florence's Ducal Square near Michael Angelo's *David* and Donatello's *Judith,* then laboriously explains how difficult *Perseus* was to cast. When he says Cosimo has invited Michael Angelo to come to Florence, not to work but merely to advise other artists if he pleases, Michael Angelo says this:

> The Grand Duke Cosimo now reigns supreme;
> All liberty is dead. Ah, woe is me!
> I hoped to see my country rise to heights
> Of happiness and freedom yet unreached
> By other nations, but the climbing wave
> Pauses, lets go its hold, and slides again
> Back to the common level, with a hoarse
> Death rattle in its throat.

He adds that Rome is friendly, whereas Baccio Valori, Guicciardine, and Strozzi—his old Florentine friends—have all been killed. Moreover, Aretino bothered him by writing him a letter criticizing his *Last Judgment* for being too graphic and taunting him for delaying Pope Julius's mausoleum. Suddenly praising himself, he calls his work a marvel of boldness, thanks Nature for giving him his talent, and likens his critics to those boys who threw stones at Dante. He asks Cellini to tell Cosimo he will remain in Rome to work on St. Peter's dome. The two friends agree that sculpture is more lifelike than painting but that architecture is the best art form, because it "is that which builds" and creates. Michael Angelo says that when St. Peter's is ready, stations will be assigned for statues; meanwhile, there are administrative hindrances, and eventually he may return to Florence for burial.

VI. "Urbino's Fortune." While Michael Angelo is chipping away at marble for a statue, Urbino, who has been his color grinder for 26 years, stands near and praises him. Michael Angelo says he can see in a block of marble every feature of the "lovely" statue he labors to free from "the stone walls that imprison" it. To guarantee Urbino's secure old age, he gives the faithful servant two thousand crowns in gold.

VII. "The Oaks of Monte Luca." Alone in a forest, Michael Angelo reveres the aged oaks and wishes he had spent more time with "Nature, gentle mother," and less in stifling cities. He interrupts the thoughts of a wrinkled old monk nearby. The fellow wishes he could see Rome and the Pope, whom Michael Angelo identifies as the former Cardinal Caraffa, now eighty, with old eyes "burning like carbuncles," cursing Spaniards and Jews, and guarded by German Lutherans. The monk would also like to see the Sistine Chapel's *Last Judgment,* which Michael Angelo says is already blackened by incense and candle smoke. He adds that Luther of Wittenberg has disturbed Rome, now full of discordant, jealous strife. So, stay here. At vespers, the two pray for peace.

VIII. "The Dead Christ." While working on a statue of the Dead Christ, Michael Angelo longs for sleep. His friends are all gone, especially Vittoria, touched by "the great sculptor Death . . . into marble." He kissed her cold hand. Why not her "dead, dumb lips?" Vasari enters. The Pope wants to see the Basilica dome plans. Michael Angelo will look for them. Meanwhile, he says what he is carving now is his own tomb. He lets his lamp fall, calls life "An empty theatre," with lights out, music ended, actors gone, and

Death pulling at his cloak. He will soon be "extinguished" like his lamp, which he drops. "Ah me! ah me! what darkness of despair! / So near to death, and yet so far from God!"

(Longfellow wrote but rejected a scene in which four friends attend Michael Angelo on his deathbed. The old artist says,

> The ninety years
> Of my long life collapse and fall together,
> Like tents of soldiers, who are breaking camp
> When the long war is over.)

For his long *Michael Angelo: A Fragment,* Longfellow diligently researched the life and times of Michelangelo. His main sources were Ascanio Condivi, *Vita di Michelangelo Buonarroti* (1823); Giorgio Vasari, *Vite dé Piú Eccelenti Pittori, Scultori, ed Architetti Italiani* (1550); Benvenuto Cellini's autobiography; Hermann Grimm, *Leben Michelangelos* (1879); Ermanno Ferrero and Joseph Müller, *Carteggio di Vittoria Colonna* (1889); Anna Brownell Murphy Jameson, *Memoirs of the Early Italian Painters, and of the Progress of Painting in Italy* (2 vols., 1845); Jacopo Nardi, *Istorie della Cittá di Firenze* (1858); James Northcote, *The Life of Titian* (1830); Lorenzo Pignatti, *Storia della Toscana* (1813–14); Leopold von Ranke, *The History of the Popes* (1847); Felice Rizzardi, *Rime e lettere di Veronica Gambara* (1759); *Some Memoirs of Renée of France, Duchess of Ferrara* (1859); Juan de Valdéz, *Alfabeto Christiano* (1861); and Benedetto Varchi, *Storia Fiorentina* (1852).

Michael Angelo is in blank verse, sometimes conversational, at times ringingly eloquent, on occasion rising to lyric fervor. Its hero's emphasis on age and death is overdone but understandable. Longfellow was sixty-five when he started the work (6 March 1872). At first it was to be a dramatic poem concentrating on Michael Angelo and Vittoria Colonna. Longfellow let his grief over his wife Fanny's death find indirect expression in Michael Angelo's lamentations after Vittoria dies in the play. Longfellow wrote but rejected material not only on Rabelais but also on Charlemagne, added and then deleted translations of some of Michael Angelo's sonnets, completed a preliminary draft (18 May 1872), added intercalary scenes thereafter, but left the entire huge manuscript in fragmentary form at his death. Longfellow also planned but rejected a scene depicting Tomaso comforting Michael Angelo as he dies.

Bibliography: Arvin; Goggio, Emilio. "The Sources of Longfellow's *Michael Angelo.*" *Romanic Review* 25 (Oct-Nov 1934): 314-24; Wagenknecht, 1986.

"MIDNIGHT." Sonnet, unrecovered. Longfellow noted in his journal (29 Feb 1876) that he had written a sonnet titled "Midnight."

Bibliography: S. Longfellow.

"MIDNIGHT MASS FOR THE DYING YEAR" (1839). Poem, as "Psalm, the Fifth: Midnight Mass for the Dying Year," in *KM,* Oct 1839; *Voices.* Death is pulling the bleary-eyed old year's beard. Leaves fall. Rooks call woefully. Winds chant "solemn masses" under friarlike, hooded clouds. The dying year resembles "despised" King Lear. Here comes a summery day—too briefly. Let the winds not vex the old year's ghost, as a howling wind sweeps away the red leaves but not the soul's sins. May Christ help when "a mightier blast" comes. Although the message of this poem is undistinguished, its verse form is original: five-line stanzas, each rhyming *abab,* followed by a two-beat, refrainlike fifth line. In the poem, Longfellow identifies "The storm-wind from Labrador" as "Euroclydon." When a reader wrote Lewis Gaylord Clark, the *Knickerbocker* editor, to object, Longfellow sent Clark an elaborate, philological defense, which Clark published (*KM,* Dec 1839) and which he said was sent in by a "Southern correspondent." Longfellow was distressed when Edgar Allan Poe* in an anonymous review of *Voices of the Night* (*GM,* Feb 1840) wrongly accused him of plagiarizing from "The Death of the Old Year" (1832) by Alfred, Lord Tennyson.*

Bibliography: Hilen, ed.; Thompson; Williams.

"MILAGROS DE NUESTRA SEÑORA" (1832). Poem, translated from the Spanish poet Gonzalo de Berceo (1180–after 1246),

in *NAR,* Apr 1832; Scudder. The poet comes upon a meadow. It has fragrant flowers, a fountain, fruit trees, and the sound of harmonious songs. Each of the six four-line stanzas of this poem rhymes *aaaa.*

MILLER, FRANCES ROWENA (1856–c.1926). (Pen name: Fran Mille.) Opera singer and author, from Wisconsin. Out of the blue, she visited Longfellow (1874). He was flattered by her attention, and they began to write each other. When she went to Milan (1875) to study voice for almost six years, they continued to correspond. In one letter (30 Dec 1876), Longfellow commented on her poem "The Poisoned King" (1876), calling it "a little bit mystical" but adding that he "had no great difficulty understanding it." An intimate part of another letter (2 Feb 1877) he wrote in Italian. He sometimes addressed her as "Cara la mia Francesa" or "Cara Signora," and once signed himself as "Vostrissimo / L." On occasion, he sent her money. During the last five months or so of his life, she occasionally asked to see him at his home or in Boston, but his increasing feebleness prevented their meeting.

Bibliography: Hilen, ed.

"MILTON" (1875). Sonnet, in *Pandora, Birds* (1875). Waves hit the beach and recede. Each ninth wave turns the sand to gold. So it is with England's "sightless bard," whose undulating poetry has many a ninth wave that "Floods all the soul with its melodious seas."

MISCELLANEOUS POEMS SELECTED FROM THE UNITED STATES LITERARY GAZETTE, 1826. Collection of 82 poems by several poets, including the following by Longfellow: "Dirge over a Nameless Grave," "Thanksgiving," "Sunrise on the Hills," "Hymn of the Moravian Nuns at the Consecration of Pulaski's Banner," "The Indian Hunter," "The Angler's Song," "An April Day," "Autumn [With what glory . . .]," "Autumnal Nightfall," "Woods in Winter," "A Song of Savoy," "Italian Scenery," "The Venetian Gondolier," and "The Sea Diver."

"THE MONK OF CASAL-MAGGIORE." See "The Sicilian's Tale," in *Tales of the Wayside Inn,* Part Third.

"MONTE CASSINO: TERRA DI LAVORO" (1875). Poem, in *AM,* Feb 1875; *Pandora, Birds* (1875). The poet first describes the scene: river, towns, hills and mountains, old walls. He touches on historical persons: Pope Boniface (VIII, 1235?-1303; reigned 1294-1303, disgraced), and Sciarra Colonna (?-1329), and his enemy; Manfred (1232?-66), betrayed and killed at Benevento, the Volscian town where Juvenal was born. Now for the convent. Longfellow recalls climbing the path to its gate, hearing vesper bells, entering as darkness fell and the river below "Sheathed itself as a sword, and was not seen." He recalls how Saint Benedict (of Nursia; 480-543), 13 centuries earlier, founded the convent and based its order on "prayer and work, and counted work as prayer." It doesn't matter that Boccaccio mocked the supposedly "lazy brotherhood." Longfellow recalls discussing "such themes . . . with one young friar" there, then resting half in dreams until daylight. Bright sunlight shone on the mountains and the valley. As he happens to see a steaming railroad, he ponders "The conflict of the Present and the Past, / The ideal and the actual in our life"; thus are "this world and the next . . . at strife." Longfellow was inspired to write "Monte Cassino" after seeing Italy a final time during his trip to Europe (1868-69). In a letter to William Dean Howells* (9 Dec 1874), then editor of the *Atlantic Monthly,* Longfellow said he wished the poem "were better and shorter."

Bibliography: Hilen, ed.; Sabatino, Iannetta. *Henry W. Longfellow and Montecassino.* . . . N.p., n.d.; Wagenknecht, 1955.

MONTI, LUIGI (1830–1914). Italian teacher and diplomat. Monti, a native of Palermo, took part in the Sicilian revolution against Naples (1848); after the Italian revolution (1848–49) failed, he migrated to Boston (1850). He soon met Longfellow. They talked about Italy and enjoyed Italian music and wine together. Monti became a naturalized American citizen. Because of Longfel-

low's recommendation, Monti taught Italian at Harvard (1854-59). He was married (1856) to Frances A. Parsons (?-1906), the sister of Thomas William Parsons (1819-92), an amateur Dante scholar whom Longfellow knew well. Monti gave readings to small audiences at Craigie House,* and elsewhere nearby, for money (Mar–May 1861). Longfellow recommended Monti for the consulship at Palermo, unsuccessfully at first (1856) but later successfully (1861), because of the influence of Charles Sumner.* Monti served in that office 12 years. When Longfellow went abroad (1868-69), Monti visited him in Naples (Mar 1869). While in Palermo, Monti started translating some novels by Francesco Domenico Guerrazzi (1804-73). Monti left his wife and daughter in Palermo, returned to Boston (1874), and taught Italian there. Longfellow entertained Monti at his home, tried to get him teaching posts (unsuccessfully at Cornell and Johns Hopkins, successfully at Wellesley), and lent him money. Monti was the model for the Sicilian in *Tales of a Wayside Inn.* He published a short story titled "Benedetto Civiletti" in *Harper's New Monthly Magazine* (June 1881).

Bibliography: Hilen, ed.

"MOODS" (1878). Sonnet, in *Kéramos.* The poet wishes a song, fresh and perhaps with a medicinal bitterness, might sing out of Nature's heart, to dispel his moody lethargy. But songs don't always breathe on us when we wish. They come, "sudden and swift and strong," like a wind out of who knows where; nor do we know their "wayward course" when they leave.

"MOONLIGHT" (1882). Poem, in *Harbor.* As the moon climbs into and out of clouds, it looks like "a phantom with a lamp" climbing stairs, behind walls, then peering out of windows. Its light touches everything magically, changing a forest into a foreign town, the ground into a street of marble. The spirit relishes such illusions, and "We see but what we have the gift / Of seeing; what we bring we find."

"MORITURI SALUTAMUS" (1875). Poem, in *Harper's New Monthly Magazine,* Aug

1875; *Pandora.* It begins with the quotation of the gladiators' greeting: "O Caesar, we who are about to die / Salute you!" Longfellow praises the present well-remembered scene—trees, river, sea nearby, halls. None answers, since "we are only as the blast, / A moment heard, and then forever past." But the teachers, one of whom is still living, are heard yet. The poet praises the dead, as Dante did. Those teachers "live[d] / In the delight that work alone can give." The poet salutes students full of "illusions, aspirations, dreams!" To them everything is possible. The oldsters, however, resemble Priam's aged friends sitting on Troy's walls chirping at the fight they can't engage in. Who among the new generation towers highest? Don't boast. Study instead. Aim high, but don't be too bold. Fewer than half of the former classmates still live. A salute to those now gone, whom there is no need to name, "For every heart best knoweth its own." The poet gives "tender thought[s]" as he walks from their graveyards "unto these scenes frequented by our feet / When we were young, and life was fresh and sweet." Faces now before him are the same, yet not so. Shall the poet depart or tarry? He will stay and greet his "companions, comrades, classmates, friends!" Time has written 50 volumes about them all—about tragedies, comedies, joys, griefs, victories, defeats, struggles, temptations, retreats, regrets, doubts, fears, and cause for tears, and

> . . . sweet, angelic faces, what divine
> And holy images of love and trust,
> Undimmed by age, unsoiled by damp or
> dust!

Rather than peruse those volumes, however, think of what is yet unwritten. The poet adverts to a story from medieval Rome. A clerk saw a statue; on the finger of an upraised hand was a ring. Where its shadow fell, the clerk dug and found a hall lit by a blazing jewel; it revealed a statue of an archer who warned of his unavoidable aim. At a banquet sat brave knights and lovely ladies—all of stone. When the clerk greedily seized a golden knife, the archer shot the jewel to pieces, all turned dark, and the clerk died. The poet explicates: The statue with the finger is "the Adversary old" and tempts the

clerk to turn greedy; the archer is Death; the flaming gem, Life; avarice hardened the knights and the ladies; the clerk, in abandoning books, betrayed "his nobler self." The scholarly life is forever at odds with the busy "market-place . . . [and] love of gain." It's never too late: Sophocles, Simonides, Theothrastus, and Goethe were creative octogenarians; Chaucer too wrote when old. They are exceptions, perhaps; however, they reveal "How far the gulf-stream of our youth may flow / Into the arctic regions of our lives." Sure enough, "Whatever poet, orator, or sage / May say of it, old age is still old age." It is waning moon, dusk, weakness, surcease, embers and ash. So? Lights are fading but not gone. Old trees can bear "some fruit." Some opportunities are left. When "twilight fades away, / The sky is filled with stars, invisible by day."

"Morituri Salutamus," for which he was paid $1,000 for its magazine publication, is by all odds Longfellow's finest long ode. Longfellow read it at Brunswick to celebrate the fiftieth anniversary of his class at Bowdoin (7 Jul 1875). It appeared the following day in *Harper's.* The older Longfellow's readers become, the more sound his bracing advice seems—often. The poem may have been inspired by Longfellow's seeing a copy of *Gladiators before Caesar,* the painting by Jean Léon Gérôme (1824-1904). The poem is a ringing success in vigorous heroic couplets, marred only by the medieval tale, which he found in the *Gesta Romanorum.* Longfellow, who regularly declined innumerable invitations to speak on special occasions or to read from his works, obviously had to make an exception at his Bowdoin class ceremony. He was pleased with his performance, and so was the reporter for the Portland *Daily Press* (8 Jul 1875) who said that Longfellow's "delivery though low was mellifluous." Longfellow wrote George Washington Greene* (10 Jul 1875) to report what the *Press* said and to add that he was "as proud as a peacock."

Bibliography: S. Longfellow; Wagenknecht, 1986.

"THE MOTHER'S GHOST." *See* "The Musician's Tale," in *Tales of a Wayside Inn,* Part Third.

"MS ACCOUNT BOOK." Book in which Longfellow recorded his income, from royalties, fees, and investments. Entries prove that from 1872 until 1882 he took in about $16,000 per annum.

Bibliography: Hilen, ed.

"MS BOOK OF DONATIONS, 1874–82." Book in which Longfellow recorded many of his charitable gifts, to relatives, friends, applicants, memorials, and various causes. During this period, he gave away more than $16,500.

Bibliography: Hilen, ed.

"MS LEDGER." Book in which Longfellow kept track of financial matters.

"MS LETTER CALENDAR." Book in which Longfellow kept a record of some of his correspondence.

MULCHINOCK, WILLIAM PEMBROKE (1820–64). Irish poet who came to the United States and while in New York City bothered Longfellow by writing him frequently (1849–52), for money and for help in getting work published. Longfellow responded with reluctance. Mulchinock's "Aileen Aroon" was published in *Graham's Magazine* (Apr 1850).

Bibliography: Hilen, ed.

"MURMURING WIND THAT EVERY-WHERE . . ." See "Song: Murmuring Wind That Everywhere . . ."

MUSICAL SETTINGS OF LONGFELLOW'S POEMS. Numerous composers have set to music upwards of 200 poems and poetic passages by Longfellow. Their favorites have been "The Arrow and the Song," "Beware," "Daybreak," "Good night! Good night, Beloved!," "The Rainy Day," "The Sea Hath Its Pearls," "Stars of the Summer Night!," and passages from *The Song of Hiawatha.* Among the finest efforts are those by Michael William Balfe (1808–70), Irish opera composer and singer; of 16 Longfellow poems Balfe set to music, the best include "The Arrow and the Song," "The Day Is Done,"

"Excelsior," "Good night! Good night, Beloved!," and "The Village Blacksmith." The only American poets to come close to inspiring composers to the degree Longfellow has done are Emily Dickinson, Langston Hughes, and Walt Whitman.

Bibliography: Hovland, Michael. *Musical Settings of American Poetry.* Westport: Greenwood Press, 1986.

"MUSINGS" (1825). Poem, in *USLG,* 15 Nov 1825; Scudder. At his "window one night," the poet sees stars, moon, sea, and "autumn wood[s]." One after another, the village lights are extinguished, except one. Then that one is also. But the poet's inner light still shines. Yes, joys must die, after which each of us "turn[s] . . . / To the lamp that burns brightly within."

Bibliography: Little.

"MY BOOKS" (1882). Sonnet, in *Harbor.* When Longfellow looks at his old books, he compares himself to an aging knight looking at weapons he can "no longer wield." His books, "My ornaments and arms of other days," aren't exactly useless, but they are "no longer used." They remind his "clouded and confused" mind of when he was more able and joyful. Longfellow dated this poem "December 27, 1881," a few months before his death. It may be a touching farewell to arms; however, Longfellow pleased and comforted others by writing, and rarely used his pen as a weapon against adversarial readers or critics.

Bibliography: More.

"MY CATHEDRAL" (1880). Sonnet, in *Thule.* The poet's place of worship has pines for towers, an arch of vines, with the wind for the organ, and no "martyr's bones" anywhere. The reader is invited to walk on a pavement of leaves, to hear a choir of birds, and to discover "worship without words."

"MY DEAR LITTLE *MARGE*" (1967). Poem. In a letter from Göttengen (Mar 1829), Longfellow sent this little ditty to Margaret Louisa Potter (1817–?), the sister of Mary Storer Potter (*see* Longfellow, Mary

Storer). Its subject is his gift of a bottle of eau de cologne.

Bibliography: Hilen, ed.

"MY LOST YOUTH" (1855). Poem, *PM,* Aug 1855; *Courtship, Birds* (1858). When Longfellow thinks of his youth, the lines of a Lapland song haunt him: "A boy's will is the wind's will, / And the thoughts of youth are long, long thoughts." He thinks of his seaside town (Portland), its trees, the gleam of water in the distance, wharves, slips, tides, bearded Spanish sailors and their mysterious ships, the old fort and its gun sounding at sunrise, and drums and bugles. He remembers seeing "the sea-fight far away," with the rival captains both brought ashore, dead. He remembers the forest nearby, with Sabbath sounds reminding him of "the friendships old and the early loves." He remembers his youthful plans, fears, and longings, his undying dreams he cannot speak of now. Now, when he visits the town of his youth, he sees strangers but still breathes the same fresh air, hears the trees whispering that same old song, and can find his "lost youth again" in the nearby woods.

"My Lost Youth," for which Longfellow received $50, is one of his most beloved poems. He learned of the Lapland song in a translation by the German poet Johann Gottfried von Herder (1744–1803) in Herder's anthology *Die Stimmen der Völker in Liedern* (1779). Herder's version of the refrain is "Knabenwille ist Windeswille, / Jünglings Gedanken lange Gedanken." In Longfellow's refrain, "will" rhymes often with "still," and once each, effectively, to "thrill" and "chill." The naval battle was between the victorious American *Enterprise,* with Captain William Burroughs in command, and the defeated British *Boxer,* with Captain Samuel Blyth in command (5 Sep 1813). Both captains were killed; and Longfellow, aged six, saw their spectacular joint funeral in Portland.

Bibliography: Arms, George. "The Revision of 'My Lost Youth.'" *Modern Language Notes* 61 (Jun 1946): 389–92; Arvin; Eberwein, Jane D. "'The Wind's Will': Another View of Frost and Longfellow." *Colby Library Quarterly* 16 (Sep 1980): 177–81; Hatfield, James Taft. "Longfellow's 'Lapland Song.'" *PMLA* 45 (Dec 1930): 1182–92; Hickey, Donald R. *The War of 1812: A Forgotten Conflict.* Urbana and Chicago: University of Illinois Press, 1989; Hilen, ed.; Wagenknecht, 1986; Williams.

"MY SCHOOL BOY DAYS" (1825). Essay, in "Brazen Nose College." It includes Longfellow's account of writing and publishing "The Battle of Lovell's Pond," his first poem.

"MY SECRET" (1859). Irregular sonnet, translated from a poem by the French poet Félix Arvers (1806–50), in *Gifts of Genius; A Miscellany of Prose and Poetry by American Authors,* 1859; *AM,* Sep 1870; Scudder. The persona, who has led a mysterious life, has a secret. He fell permanently in love in one moment. "Hopeless the evil is." The woman causing it all "nor knew it nor believed." He sometimes is near her. He asks nothing, has gained nothing. This "gentle and endearing" woman will, though "distraught," be "faithful still unto her austere duty." When she reads this poem, she will uncomprehendingly wonder, "Who can this woman be?"

N

"A NAMELESS GRAVE" (1875). Sonnet, in *Pandora, Birds* (1875). A grave at Newport News, Virginia, without name or date, simply reads "A soldier of the Union mustered out." Was this "unknown hero" a sentinel, a scout, a soldier killed while attacking or retreating? The poet senses a "secret shame," because the soldier gave him so much and the poet can "give thee nothing in return."

"THE NATIVE LAND" (1833). Sonnet, translated from the Spanish poet Francisco de Aldana (1537–78), in *Coplas; Voices.* The poet writes of the sorrow of a person "in this prison-house of clay" exiled from his native land, which he regards as a place of light, unfading glory, truth, and "holy quiet." His soul lovingly aspires to dwell in its divine equivalent. (*See* also *Outre-Mer.*)

"NATURE" (1877). Sonnet, in *AM,* Mar 1877; *Kéramos.* When day ends, a loving mother leads her tired child to bed. He is reluctant to leave his broken toys. She promises new ones, but he may not especially like them. So it is with Nature. She takes our playthings away, and we are too sleepy to distinguish between "the unknown . . . [and] the what we know." "Nature" is one of Longfellow's best sonnets, with a well-controlled, one-sentence, Homeric simile. When Elizabeth Stuart Phelps* wrote Longfellow to praise this poem, he graciously replied (22 Mar 1877), "You call it an anthem, and an anthem henceforth it shall be."

Bibliography: Aspiz, Harold. "Longfellow's 'Nature.'" *Explicator* 42 (fall 1983): 22–23; Rea, John D. "Longfellow's 'Nature.'" *Modern Philology* 18 (May 1920): 48; Wagenknecht, 1986.

"NATURE AND ART." *See* "Art and Nature."

"THE NATURE OF LOVE" (1832). Poem, translated from the Italian poet Guido Guinizelli (1240?–74), in *NAR,* Oct 1832; Scudder. Love seeks shelter in a "noble heart," which, however, doesn't exist before love. Similarly, light didn't exist before the sun was formed. Heat exists solely to warm "its allotted place." When the sun draws out "what was vile," starlight "impart[s] / Strange virtue" to love-like gems. Thus "Nature doth create" nobility of heart, which is rewarded by "love . . . from woman's eye." Imagery in this poem is unsatisfactorily jumbled.

NEAL, JOHN (1793–1876). Maine author, born in Falmouth (now Portland), Maine, into a Quaker family. Neal, after attending local schools until he turned twelve, became self-taught and developed a varied career, as clerk, itinerant teacher, dry goods merchant, and lawyer and editor in Baltimore. He published five novels (1816–23), including *Randolph* (1823), which was so critical of the behavior of a diplomat named William Pinkney (1764–1822) that his son Edward Coote Pinkney (1802–28), a poet, challenged Neal to a duel. Declining, Neal decamped to London (1823–27) where he published extensively, including dozens and dozens of articles in *Blackwood's Magazine* about American writers (including himself!). Returning to New York, he founded the short-lived *Yankee,* mainly to advocate utilitarianism. Once back in Portland (1828), he began to practice law, was invited to establish a gymnasium at Bowdoin, and married his cousin Eleanor Hall (1809–77); they had five children. Neal wrote three more novels and many short stories (1828–35). He continued to write and edit, practiced law, ran unsuccessfully as a Whig for the state senate (1838), sold real estate, and championed the rights of women and African Americans. He encouraged early efforts by Nathaniel Hawthorne,* Edgar Allan Poe,* and John Greenleaf Whittier.* His autobiography is aptly titled *Wandering Recollections of a Somewhat Busy Life* (1869). His *Portland Illustrated* (1874) was a kind of popular guidebook.

Beginning when he was a student at Bowdoin, Longfellow followed Neal's zigzag career, in later years occasionally saw him in Boston, Cambridge, and Portland, and corresponded with him. Longfellow read enough of *Randolph* to label it in a letter to his mother (4 Dec 1823) "a compound of reason and nonsense—drollery and absurdity—wit and nastiness" and yet "the work of Genius." He wrote Jared Sparks* (9 Oct 1825), then editor of the *North American Review,* offering, without success, to write an adverse review of Neal's *Brother Jonathan* (1825), a three-volume novel about colonial New England. He wrote George Stillman Hillard* (16 Aug 1838) that he had just seen Neal, that Neal wanted to run for U.S. Congress, and that he would fail. Neal wrote Longfellow (13 Jan 1840) to express admiration for some of the poems in *Voices of the Night* but dislike of others, because they "are . . . respectable," and because "they cannot be found fault with"! Longfellow wrote to thank Neal (26 Oct 1869) for sending him a copy of his *Wandering Recollections,* and said he had read it in one sitting and liked it because it was—like Neal himself—"frank and fearless, and full of vigor." Longfellow wrote George Washington Greene* (12 Nov 1874) that Neal had sent him a copy of *Portland Illustrated,* which he found "written in

his peculiar style, and interesting to me, who am fond of local history." He tried to help Neal get his American Revolutionary War novel *Seventy-Six* (1823) republished and wrote one of Neal's daughters (9 May 1876) to sympathize with her after James Ripley Osgood* declined to do so. In a letter to Greene (24 June 1876), Longfellow quotes Neal's preface to his novel *Rachel Dyer* (1828), in which he criticizes the stilted English of some English writers. Other evidence indicates that Longfellow also knew Neal's Gothic novel *Goldau; or, the Maniac Harper* (1818), his five-act tragedy *Otho* (1819), and his two-volume novel *Logan: A Family History* (1822).

Bibliography: Cowie; Hilen, ed.; Lease, Benjamin. *That Wild Fellow John Neal and the American Literary Revolution.* Chicago: University of Chicago Press, 1972; S. Longfellow; Sears, Donald A. *John Neal.* Boston: Twayne, 1978.

"A NEAPOLITAN CANZONET" (1832). Poem, evidently a translation, in *NAR,* Oct 1832; Scudder. The poet's heart dropped on the beach. Sailors say they saw it in a woman's bosom. The poet asks her to keep it and give him hers.

"NEGLECTED RECORD OF A MIND NEGLECTED." *See* "Fragments."

***THE NEW ENGLAND TRAGEDIES* (1868).** *See Christus: A Mystery.*

"NIGHT." *See* "Hymn to the Night."

"NIGHT" (1880). Sonnet, in *Thule.* When darkness comes, petty daytime actions and worries vanish. What follows is important, because at night we can blot out the trivial, which may be likened to a palimpsest text concealing "the ideal, hidden beneath."

"NIGHTFALL IN NOVEMBER" (1824). Poem, signed "H.," in Portland *Advertiser,* 1 Dec 1824. The night is calm. The sun is setting silently. A seabird flies over the bay. The mountain turns purple. More distant is the sight of snow. Ocean winds rush and fill a "lagging sail." As night falls, the lighthouse "presides / Over . . . full-flowing tides." A family circle safe at home hopes a certain person, now distant, is calm with "his own thoughts." Just as gravity draws together "worlds of this vast system," so the magnetic attraction of love draws "All . . . towards one point."

Bibliography: Little.

"NÖEL" (1865). Poem in French, in the *AM,* Oct 1865; *Flower.* Longfellow sent this poem to accompany an 1864 Christmas "panier de vins divers" to his friend Louis Agassiz.* In it, the poet sings the praises of various wines included. Each of its 11 rollicking stanzas ends with "Bons amis / Allons donc chez Agassiz!" or a variation thereof, using in place of "Allons," "J'ai dansé," "chanté," "diné," "soupé," "couché," and ending "Bons amis / Respectez mon Agassiz!"

"THE NORMAN BARON" (1845). Poem, in *Poems,* 1845; *Bruges.* A Norman baron lies dying. A storm blast shakes his castle. Death is winning this battle, despite the old baron's vassals, servants, plundered lands, and monk praying beside him. "[S]erf[s] and vassal[s]" are holding "their Christmas wassail" in the hall below. They sing that "Christ is born to set them free!" Lightning shows the trembling baron his paintings of holy figures on his casement. He feels contrite, pomp vanishes, reason strips the truth bare. He frees his vassals, his serfs, and all whom he wronged. Death no longer seems terrifying. Centuries pass, but his "good deed" remains bright in the history books. The source of "The Norman Baron," which is in four-line trochaic stanzas with complicated rhymes, is an anecdote recorded by Augustin Thierry (1795–1856) in his *Conquête de l'Angleterre par les Normands* (1825).

Bibliography: Wagenknecht, 1986.

NORTON, CHARLES ELIOT (1827–1908). Educator and man of letters, Norton was born in Cambridge, Massachusetts, the son of Andrews Norton (1786–1853), an anti-Emersonian Harvard professor of sacred history, and Catherine Eliot Norton (1793–1879), the daughter of Samuel Eliot, a wealthy Boston merchant-banker. Cather-

ine's sister, Anna Eliot Ticknor, was Charles's aunt and the wife of George Ticknor.* Charles had three sisters: Louisa Norton, Jane Norton, and Grace Norton. He attended Harvard (B.A., 1846; M.A., 1849); two of his professors were Cornelius Conway Felton* and Jared Sparks.* Norton worked in the East India trade (late 1840s), published a variety of essays, and established a night school for Irish immigrants. He traveled (1849–51) on business and for pleasure, rubbed elbows with a variety of people at most levels of society, and was especially fascinated by European culture, notably Venetian. In Boston again, Norton did accounting work, taught, wrote, edited, vacationed, and developed lifelong friendships, particularly with George William Curtis,* James Russell Lowell,* and Longfellow. When his father died (1853), Norton became the leader of the wealthy family, took his mother and two single sisters (Jane and Grace) to Europe, and became the best of all possible culture seekers—meeting innumerable intellectuals in London (notably John Ruskin), Paris, Florence, and Rome, and absorbing numerous artistic delights there before returning home (1857). He published articles and reviews in the *Atlantic Monthly,* translated Dante's *Vita Nuova* (partly, 1859; fully, 1867), and gained immense renown for his *Notes of Travel and Study in Italy* (1859) and later works. He was invited to join the Saturday Club* (1860), where he associated amiably with Ralph Waldo Emerson,* Oliver Wendell Holmes,* and others. He married (1862) Susan Ridley Sedgwick (1838–72); they moved to Ashfield, in western Massachusetts. Norton and Lowell coedited the *North American Review* (1864–68) in such a way as to give it a liberal, nonregional manner. Off to Europe again (1868), this time with his wife and their three daughters and two sons. Norton continued studying and observing, matured old and new intellectual friendships (for example, with Charles Dickens*), and made himself an expert in medieval and Renaissance art, literature, history, and non-Christian spiritual development. Soon after giving birth in Dresden to their third son (1872), Norton's wife died. In silent misery, Norton moved with his children to Paris and

London before returning home. Invited to teach at Harvard by Charles William Eliot (1834-1926), his cousin and Harvard's president (1869-1909), Norton became America's first professor of art history (1875-98). His influence was incalculable, as professor, author, public lecturer, organizer of art exhibits, adviser of art collectors, and propagandist against the vices of machine politicians and leisure-class showiness. He organized the Dante Society (1880) and published *Historical Studies of Church Building in the Middle Ages* . . . (1880) and a prose translation of the *Divina Commedia* (1891-92). In addition to other literary work, he edited the letters of Thomas Carlyle (1883-91), Curtis (1893-94), John Donne (1895), Emerson (1883, 1884), Lowell (1894), and Ruskin (1904).

Longfellow, soon after arriving in Cambridge (Dec 1836) to begin teaching at Harvard, made the acquaintance of Charles Eliot Norton when he visited the home of Charles's parents. Charles's father had retired from teaching in the Harvard Divinity School (1830) but was still an active scholar and writer. Longfellow felt closer, however, to Charles's mother Catharine Norton, talked with her about poetry, and when apart enjoyed a lively correspondence with her. Some 30 letters from Catharine to Longfellow have survived. In letters he wrote her from Marienberg, Germany (25 Jun, 26 Aug 1842), he says he is keeping his promise to Charles (then aged 14) to collect foreign coins for him. In other letters he sends his love to Charles. Longfellow followed details of Norton's first adult trip abroad (1849-51) with keen interest. He wrote Norton (5 Feb 1850), then in India, about Norton family news, politics, and sacred Indian literature. Home again, Norton dined at the Longfellows' home, together with Curtis, back from Egypt himself. Soon thereafter, Longfellow and his wife Fanny firmed up their friendship by often spending pleasant Tuesday evenings at the home of the hospitable, articulate Nortons; in addition, the Longfellows were often hosts to Norton. For one example, when Nathaniel Hawthorne* was leaving to become the American consul at Liverpool, Longfellow hosted a dinner party

that included Norton (14 Jun 1853). Longfellow read Norton's preliminary essays (in 1857) on Dante's *Vita Nuova* and his 1859 book on Italy. According to his journal (29 Nov 1861), Longfellow, Norton, and Lowell briefly associated with Anthony Trollope,* the Victorian novelist then in the United States on business. (*See* Lowell, James Russell, for details.) When Longfellow was well along with his translation of Dante's *Divina Commedia* (1863), Norton asked him to delay publication so as to coincide with the 600th anniversary of Dante's birth (1865). A note in his journal (25 Oct 1865) records Longfellow's first meeting with Norton and Lowell in what became the Dante Club, to discuss revisions in his translation. Norton valuably participated in many such meetings at the Longfellows' home, on successive Wednesdays, followed by pleasant dinners. This entry in Longfellow's journal (17 Oct 1867) indicates Norton's professional level: "Walk up to Norton's. He shows me some of [Joseph Mallord William] Turner's sketches—originals, which he has just received from Ruskin." (Longfellow may well have been puzzled by Turner's unconventional artistry. Ruskin once said that, of all the Americans he knew, he liked Norton and Longfellow best.) Longfellow and Norton continued to socialize, once at what must have been a marvelous dinner hosted by James T. Fields* (23 May 1868), with fellow guests including not only Norton and Longfellow, but also Louis Agassiz,* Richard Henry Dana Sr.,* George Washington Greene,* Lowell, and Holmes (who read a poem). Longfellow's and Norton's correspondence generally concerns favors and gifts, bits of social gossip, and opinions. To commemorate Longfellow's death, the Massachusetts Historical Society held a meeting (13 Apr 1882) at which Norton spoke eloquently and tenderly. Later, Norton wrote *Henry Wadsworth Longfellow: A Sketch of His Life* . . . (1907).

Bibliography: Green; Morison; *Mrs. Longfellow;* S. Longfellow; Turner, James. *The Liberal Education of Charles Eliot Norton.* Baltimore and London: Johns Hopkins University Press, 1999; Tryon; Vanderbilt, Kermit. *Charles Eliot Norton: Apostle of Culture in a Democracy.* Cambridge:

The Belknap Press of the Harvard University Press, 1959; "Tribute."

"N'OUBLIEZ PAS DEMAIN . . ." (1982).

Poem in French. Longfellow sent an eight-line poem in French to James Russell Lowell* (28 Feb 1870), telling him not to forget tomorrow's luncheon of oysters, lobster salad, venison, and wine; so "N'arrivez pas trop tard!"

Bibliography: Hilen, ed.

"NUREMBERG" (1846).

Poem, in *GM,* Jun 1844; *Bruges.* In the Pegnitz Valley, with the Franconian mountains for background, is old Nuremberg. It is a place of gabled houses, work, song, art, birds, and memories. Royal rulers and busy burghers combined to make the city influential. The main market has a beautiful fountain. The churches of Saint Sebald and Saint Lawrence are elaborately decorated with stone and bronze sculptures. One artist is worthy of special praise: "Here, when Art was still religion, with a simple and reverent heart, / Lived and labored Albrecht Dürer, the Evangelist of Art." He may have departed, but "Dead he is not, . . . for the artist never dies." Special too are the Mastersingers, especially Hans Sachs, "the cobbler-bard." These chanting poets of Nuremberg gathered in "Fame's great temple" the way swallows do in the spouts of buildings. Sachs's house is now a tavern, frequented by thirsty workers in the evening. Nuremberg's "ancient splendor" lives on, not because of its political rulers but because of its creative, "pedigree[d]" toilers.

In complex, mainly trochaic, fifteen-syllable lines, "Nuremberg" was inspired by Longfellow's visit to Europe in the summer of 1842. In "Longfellow's Visit to Venice" (after 1954), John Betjeman (1906–84) parodies the guidebook aspect of Longfellow's "Nuremberg" as well as his "The Belfrey of Bruges."

Bibliography: Arvin; Wagenknecht, 1986; Williams.

O

"THE OCCULTATION OF ORION" (1845).
Poem, in *GM,* Nov 1845; *Bruges.* The poet
has a "sublime," dreamlike vision. He sees
Time balancing the waning day and the advancing night. Mysterious stars rise, and he
hears their music. One after another appear
"The Samian's . . . lyre," "Dian's circle," Sir-
ius, and then Orion the hunter—with sword
and radiant lion's skin. The pale moon,
seemingly in response to God's voice, steps
on the fiery stars, unafraid because of "Her
holiness and her purity." When she reaches
Orion, he drops the lion's skin and stops
beating the bull's head. An angel pierces the
silence with a cry, echoed by "the heavenly
lyre": "Forevermore, forevermore, / The
reign of violence is o'er!"

Bibliography: Arvin; Wagenknecht, 1986; Zim-
merman, Michael. "War and Peace: Longfellow's
'The Occultation of Orion.'" *American Literature*
38 (Jan 1967): 540-46.

"ODE ON THE DEATH OF HIS FATHER"
(1834). *See* "The Convent of the Paular."

"ODE WRITTEN FOR THE COMMEMO-
RATION AT FRYEBURG, MAINE, OF
LOVEWELL'S FIGHT" (1825). Poem, in
Eastern Argus, 23 May 1825 (and elsewhere,
May 1825); Scudder. Years have passed since
"our fathers bled" here. Now "a holier faith"
has supplanted that of "the red men." The
story must be preserved of that terrible battle—full of war cry, shot, smoke, shattered
tree bark, and "death wail." Our liberty,
which we celebrate here today, must never

"decay." The well-managed rhyme scheme of
each of this ode's six stanzas is a difficult
aaabcccb. This poem was the first to be published over Longfellow's name.

Bibliography: Little; Thompson.

"O FAITHFUL, INDEFATIGABLE TIDES."
See "Fragments."

"OLD AGE" (1878). Sonnet, translated from
a sonnet by Michael Angelo, in *Kéramos.*
The poet's bark is in "The common harbor"
now. He must give an accounting of his
"long life." Art was his illusory, vain "idol
and . . . king." What are his sweet dreams of
love now, when "two deaths may be mine"?
He is now not pleased by "Painting and
sculpture." His soul turns to the embrace of
the opening arms of the crucified "Love Divine."

"THE OLD BRIDGE AT FLORENCE"
(1875). Sonnet, signed "H.," in *AM,* Jan
1875; *Pandora, Birds* (1875). Built by Tad-
deo Gaddi (1300?-66), I am five centuries
old. My foot, like St. Michael's foot on the
dragon, is on the Arno River, which "struggles" under me and shows waving scales.
Steadfast, I remember wars involving the
Medici, the Ghibellines, the Guelfs. I am bejeweled. I thrill to recall that Michaelangelo
"leaned on me."

"THE OLD CLOCK ON THE STAIRS"
(1846). Poem, in *Bruges.* On the stairs in an
old, tree-shadowed country seat is "An an-

cient timepiece," the pendulum of which says, "Forever—never! / Never—forever!" With its hands it "points and beckons," like a monk crossing himself, and says that same refrain. The clock repeats it softly by day, loudly at night; in times of fun and sorrow, birth and death, like a watchful God; like a warning skeleton at hospitable feasts; in front of children and youths, like a gold-counting miser; once, when a bride was up-stairs and a corpse below. When the poet asks about a possible reunion of all who have heard the clock, its answer is "For-ever—never!" Ah, "Never here, forever there" is the incessant message of this "hor-ologe of Eternity." There are two sources for this poem. The maternal grandfather of Fanny Longfellow* had an old-fashioned clock with a pendulum in his home in Pitts-field, Massachusetts, which Longfellow and Fanny visited during their wedding journey (1843); in addition, Longfellow read in a work by a French missionary named Jacques Bridaine (1701–67) the definition of eternity as "une pendulum dont le balancier dit et redit . . . Toujours, jamais! Jamais, toujours!"

Bibliography: S. Longfellow; Wagenknecht, 1986; Williams.

"OLD ENGLISH ROMANCES" (1833). Es-say, in *NAR,* Oct 1833.

"OLD PARISH CHURCH" (1824). Poem, in Portland *Advertiser,* 25 Sep 1824. This tem-ple is hallowed. Holy light has warmed its walls, near which its builders no longer "shall throng." Time, which has "pluck'd thy strength away," will soon "waste our own vitality." Its spire points toward "our resting place." The tower bell bids farewell "To per-ishing mortality." The poet seems to see and hear the old church's patriarchs at the altar. He hears choirs "of peace and sins forgiven." Won't the deceased church leaders reach down a hand to save this temple? Time, peace, and mercy ought to help. The poet hopes "our Fathers' Temple" will be spared. Longfellow wrote this poem when he heard that the aged church was going to be razed to make room for a new one.

Bibliography: Little; Thompson.

"OLD ST. DAVID'S AT RADNOR" (1880). Poem, in *Lippincott's Magazine,* Jun 1880; *Thule.* The church is peaceful, surrounded as it is by graves. Troubled persons can find rest here. Ice caresses the church stones the way a child would caress "the wrinkled cheeks of age." Inside are old aisles, pews, and a pulpit. The minister, a combination of "Poet and Pastor," makes the place radiant. What makes it splendid is faith's conquest of doubt, love's defeat of hate. The poet says that if he were a pilgrim or a pastor, he would prefer this place to any other. Here he would remain. No storm can tear the furled sail, no wind loosen "the anchored soul." Longfellow wrote a letter (4 Jun 1880) to William F. Halsey (1807–82), rector of St. David's, Radnor, Pennsylvania (1866–82), to explain that this poem was inspired by Long-fellow's visit to Radnor (May 1876), at which time Halsey "so courteously greeted me and my companions."

Bibliography: Wagenknecht 1986.

"OLIVER BASSELIN" (1855). Poem, in *PM,* May 1855; *Courtship, Birds* (1858). On a stone by a window of a mill in Val-de-Vire (Normandy) is carved this: "Oliver Basselin lived here." Only the donjon-keep of the chateau above it remains. The convent on a neighboring hill is gone. In that stony mill, Basselin once sang the songs that made the region splendid. Content here, he never sought to "soar . . . higher." Here his songs were merrily in tune with his "green earth," and they rang out in local taverns and hos-tels. They didn't resemble songs about Agin-court's knights or high-aiming monk chants. The names of the old barons, knights, squires, and friars have vanished. Basselin's memory, however, is a part of this place, like its landscapes and rivers; for his songs live in many hearts and are "Haunting still / That ancient mill." Olivier Basselin (c.1400-c.50), a fuller by occupation, is regarded as the au-thor of French drinking songs. Guillaume Stanislas Trebutien (1800–1870), a scholar-editor from Caen, Normandy, wrote Long-fellow (20 Jun 1861) to thank him for this poem lauding Basselin.

Bibliography: S. Longfellow.

"ON A LOCK OF HAIR" (1825). Poem, in Portland *Gazette,* 1 Oct 1825. Like a pilgrim treasuring a relic from a shrine, the persona will keep "this sweet gift" as a token of unbroken love. It is more valuable to him than robes, diadems, and thrones. This unsigned poem was published together with another poem ("Valentine") in an essay titled "Valentine Writing."

Bibliography: Little.

"ON MRS. KEMBLE'S READINGS FROM SHAKESPEARE." *See* "Sonnet on Mrs. Kemble's Readings from Shakespeare."

"ON THE TERRACE OF THE AIGALADES" (1877). Poem, translated from the French poet Joseph Méry (1798–1865), in *PP, Kéramos.* From a high portal we can see "three things,—/ The Sea, the Town, and the Highway." The Sea says it drowns brave men. The Town says it works too hard, is smoky. The Highway says it leads to dangerous northern "climates." So we stay up here, where life "glides by" nicely. We see tiled roofs, olive trees, grape vines, and mountains flowery in an eternal "springtime." We can sleep under the trees beside rainbow-tinted, sunny waterfalls. We live languidly, "Forget to-morrow in to-day," and leave to others the sea, the town, and the highway.

"THE OPEN WINDOW" (1849). Poem, in *SLM,* Nov 1849; *S/F.* The old house is quiet. No children are looking out of the nursery windows. The dog is there. Birds are singing. But the children's voices will be heard only in dreams now. The little boy walking beside the poet cannot understand why his warm hand is held so tightly.

"ORIGIN AND PROGRESS OF THE FRENCH LANGUAGE" (1831). Essay, in *NAR,* Apr 1831.

"ORIGINS AND GROWTH OF THE LANGUAGES OF SOUTHERN EUROPE AND THEIR LITERATURE" (1830, 1907). Longfellow's inaugural address, Bowdoin College (21 Sep 1830); published in Brunswick (1907).

OSGOOD, JAMES RIPLEY (1836–92). Editor. Osgood was born in Fryeburg, Maine, graduated from Bowdoin (1854), was a law clerk for a year, and then began clerking for Ticknor and Fields, owned and managed by William Ticknor, the brother of George Ticknor,* and by James T. Fields.* William Ticknor died (1864); Osgood was named Fields's junior partner the following year. The firm was reorganized (1868) as Fields, Osgood and Company. Fields retired (1870), whereupon Osgood and others bought Fields's interest for $100,000 or more. The firm became James R. Osgood and Company (1871). Osgood continued the earlier firm's work, published the *Atlantic Monthly,* the *North American Review,* other periodicals, and also works by the earlier firm's star authors, including Longfellow, William Cullen Bryant,* Ralph Waldo Emerson,* Nathaniel Hawthorne,* Oliver Wendell Holmes,* William Dean Howells,* James Russell Lowell,* Harriet Beecher Stowe,* Bayard Taylor,* John Greenleaf Whittier,* and Bret Harte, whom Osgood had "discovered" (1868). Osgood continued publishing many British authors, including Charles Dickens,* Alfred, Lord Tennyson,* and William Makepeace Thackeray.* He brought aboard younger writers, notably Elizabeth Stuart Phelps* and Sarah Orne Jewett (1849–1909), both of whom Longfellow knew. Fields had been a better manager of finances and a more congenial friend of authors than Osgood was. Osgood paid authors less handsomely, experimented with manufacturing innovations ineffectively, suffered a warehouse fire (1872), sold off many of the firm's periodicals (1873–77), and even released rights to Dickens and Thackeray to other firms (1875). Osgood merged with the publishers Hurd and Houghton to create Houghton, Osgood and Company (1878–80), after which, owing to his mammoth debts, Osgood withdrew and Houghton, Mifflin and Company was formed. Osgood established a new James R. Osgood and Company (1880), published a posthumous work by Hawthorne, new works by Howells and Mark Twain, among others, and started some biographical series. Creditors foreclosed on Osgood's firm (1885). Ticknor and Company sought to help, survived a while, went bankrupt, and was taken over by Houghton, Mifflin (1889). Osgood's final years were marked by other professional ventures, in New York and London.

Longfellow felt that Osgood was a newcomer to the firm publishing his works and preferred to deal with Fields. In his early letters to Osgood, Longfellow maintains a rather cool tone. However, it was with Osgood that he cannily arranged for the revised firm to pay him $4,000 per year for his in-print books (1875). All the same, his last letter to Osgood (6 Feb 1881) was addressed to "Dear Mr. Osgood."

Bibliography: Hilen, ed.; Tryon; Wagenknecht, 1955; Webber, Carl Jefferson. *The Rise and Fall of James Ripley Osgood: A Biography.* Waterville: Colby College Press, 1959.

"OUR NATIVE WRITERS" (1825, 1884). Oration. As part of graduation ceremonies at Bowdoin (7 Sep 1825), Longfellow spoke about his hope (and probably that of some of his professors) that emerging native writers would enjoy success and not retain "allegiance to Old England." The speech was published in *Every Other Saturday,* 12 Apr 1884.

Bibliography: Every Other Saturday 1 (12 Apr 1884): 116–17; Thompson.

OUTRE-MER **(1835).** (Full title: *Outre-Mer: A Pilgrimage Beyond the Sea.*) Travel book. This work comprises 28 titled, unnumbered sections.

"The Epistle Dedicatory": The unnamed author hopes that his unknown readers, including "the wise and great," may find amusement in the "trifles" that follow and will desire to become better acquainted with him.

"The Pilgrim of Outre-Mer": Pilgrims and troubadours used to be given hospitality and invited to tell "tales of wonder." Times have changed, but we are still curious. The author has visited "The Pay d'Outre-Mer," that is, "the Land beyond the sea." He has traversed France, smoked in Flanders, boated in Holland, studied in Germany, seen Italian sights, and heard music in Spain. He wishes to jot down his impressions before they fade.

"The Norman Diligence": First comes France. Everything "was like a dream"—the landscape, trees, birds, fields, hospitality. He sits atop the diligence for the view. Inside it are "motley groups" of travelers. The officious "*Conducteur*" displays "comic gravity" while bustling on errands. The postilion, smelling of tobacco and wine, manages his five horses well as the diligence passes peasants, shepherds, flocks, girls in wooden shoes, and mendicants, some old, others blind. Scenes flit before the author "like the shifting scenes of a magic lantern." They stop at a cabaret, then proceed to Rouen.

"The Golden Lion Inn": They spend the night at the *Lion d'Or.* The author leaves his seventh-floor room to ramble unguided through the city streets. Everything "breathed of the Middle Ages." Coming upon the stupendous cathedral, he admires its "awful sublimity" both outside and within. In the morning he goes to the Palais de Justice, sees an illuminated manuscript in the public library, strikes up a conversation at dinner with a congenial fellow-traveler, strolls with him, and enjoys his story about Martin Franc of times past.

"Martin Franc and the Monk of Saint Anthony": Martin Franc, a Rouen tradesman, is poverty-stricken, but grows proud and lazy. His wife Marguerite is a flirtatious beauty. All their friends desert them except Friar Gui, St. Anthony's disreputable, leering sacristan. When he turns amorous toward Marguerite, Martin tosses him out. Marguerite prays for good fortune at the St. Martin altar in the church. Gui listens in, says her prayers are answered, and offers her a purse of money. She says that Gui shouldn't give her money in the church but at her home, and adds that Martin is away. She and Gui whisper something. At midnight he enters her place, is assured Martin is gone, takes her hand, and tosses his purse on the table. Martin steps up and clubs him dead. The two planned only to stun, rob, and oust him. Well, Martin takes his corpse to the convent garden and seats him under a statue of the Madonna. A monk seeks Gui for midnight prayers, finds him, slaps him to wake him up, thinks he has killed him, and carries him to Marguerite's door, figuring everyone will reckon one of her lovers got jealous and killed Gui. Martin and Marguerite find him, conclude that the Devil himself has betrayed them, and Martin plans to drop Gui into the river but pauses to rest. A robber happens by, thinks the two are waiting to waylay him, drops his sacked booty, and vanishes. Out rolls the head of a hog stolen from the butcher. Martin sacks Gui in place of the hog and returns home with the hog. Earlier that robber and his two cohorts stole and sacked a hog hanged by the butcher for tomorrow's market. The robbers now locate and open their sack, see Gui, and regard him as Satan assuming a monk's shape to get them hanged. They hang Gui at the butcher's place. In the morning the butcher finds him, fears arrest for murder, carefully fastens Gui onto his horse, makes it gallop, and shouts that Gui is a horse thief. The townspeople join in pursuit of horse and rider, but they plunge together into the river and are "seen no more!" (When Longfellow was accused in an article in the *New York Atlas and Constellation* [1833] of having plagiarized this story from George Colman, "The Knight and the Friar," Longfellow replied in a letter to the editors [Bowdoin, 1833] that he explained in the story itself that the plot was taken from a manuscript of the Middle Ages and adds that Colman, whose work he had never seen, "evidently drew . . . from the same source.")

Bibliography: Hilen, ed.; S. Longfellow.

"The Village of Auteuil": Summer makes one prefer the country to the city. The author accordingly spends a summer month at a *maison de santé* at Auteuil, outside Paris and near the Bois de Boulogne. In the *maison,* managed by monkey-faced Dr. Dentdelion, are invalids, sick people, and lazy ones. The Bois reminds the author of lines from La Fontaine, Racine, and Molière. From his second-floor chamber, he sees a neighbor's pleasant garden. An English colonel in a next-door room has a fever and often raves at night. The author takes morning and evening walks and donkey rides, and at noon rests by a "little silver pool," with flies, insects, and frogs. He enjoys observing rural dances, swains and maidens riding wooden

carrousel horses, and happy throngs—from Passy, Billancourt, Sèvres, Brétigny, and Saint-Yon—at the annual midsummer fair. Under his window passes a blind fiddler, led by a clear-eyed boy. Their evident happiness would teach "the crabbed and discontented rich man" much. One day the author witnesses a colorful village wedding—joyful bridegroom in blue suit, blushing bride dressed in white and with white roses in her hair, master of ceremonies scattering sous and sugarplums. The couple will live far from "the gilded misery and the pestilential vices of the town." That evening the author also sees a melancholy funeral procession and comes to the obvious conclusion that "joys and sorrows of this world are so strikingly mingled!," and that "all is mutable, uncertain, and transitory." He also feels that in the city we study others, while in the country we will learn instead about ourselves.

"Jacqueline": Jacqueline, whose sister Amie has died before her, is ill. She has been brought from Tours by her widowed mother to the Auteuil *maison de santé* for treatment but is dying. Hearing church bells one Sunday morning, Jacqueline tells her mother that her pains are terrible and that she's happy to be going to heaven. She asks her mother to pray for her next Sunday, because she'll be gone. The priest comes, accompanied by a few devout villagers, and quickly hears the child's confessions. This "meek and lowly heart" confesses a former desire to live, whereas "the wise providence of God" specified otherwise. The priest solemnly asks her questions concerning her faith. "I believe," "I pardon," and "I do" are her answers. He administers extreme unction. As twilight deepens, no one can tell precisely when her "spirit took its flight . . . to a better world than this."

"The Sexagenarian": The author often strolls with Monsieur d'Argentville, an old fellow in the *maison.* Far from being ill, he has a famished dog's appetite. The author learns that d'Argentville came from a wealthy royalist Nantes family, studied law in Paris, prided himself on having been a "dangerous" lover, was threatened by a girlfriend's brother and changed lodgings, was wounded in a duel in the Boise de Boulogne, and courted a woman but decamped when her supposed castles were all "Chateaux en Espagne." During the Revolution he escaped the guillotine by going to Boston, where he taught fencing, French, and dancing. During the Bourbon restoration, he returned home and litigated for his lost fortune without success. He is now "A petulant, broken-down old man," aware of having misspent his life.

"Père la Chaise": This cemetery in Paris is both like and unlike Westminster Abbey. It also houses the dead but is green and open. The author enters the cemetery and walks along gravel paths under foliage, sighing breezes, and bird notes to the monument over the often-reburied ashes of Abélard and Héloïse. It seems that God treats the "weak and simple" tenderly but the markedly intelligent with "displeasure." The author proceeds to the crowded tombs of historians, musicians, philosophers, politicians, scholars, and warriors. Their influences are upon the living. Expensive monuments here wrongly intrude "into the sanctuary of genius." Lower down are graves of the poor, often "dislodged to give place to another." Affection sometimes decorates these spots. But planted rose bushes are not "fitter objects" than "sculptured marble." The graves of those who were good, great, noble, pure, virtuous, and wise are properly distinguished. Death is not a leveler after all. The buried are not equal. Beautiful urns and busts do not "create . . . distinctions, but . . . mark them." Still, fancy marble and brass only mock buried pride, falsity, and wealth. From a hill the author sees and hears restless Paris. Contrasting it and this "metropolis of the dead," the author looks back at the cemetery, now "dim and indistinct" under the summer stars. (Longfellow appropriately quotes from Sir Thomas Browne in this section.)

"The Valley of the Loire": In beautiful October the author proceeds, mostly on foot, from Orléans to Tours. During the first day he talks with an old woman gathering grapes. She is distressed when he says he left his mother to journey a thousand leagues here. He talks with a *vieille moustache,* a loyal veteran of the Napoleonic wars. He spends the night at an ugly inn by a mill near

a ravine. Next morning he sees a wine press and passes vintagers, breakfasts at Mer, and while inspecting the chateau of Chambord seems to step "back into the precincts of the feudal ages." Third day—Blois, with beautiful views and an uncompleted castle, symbol of "the power and weakness of man." Next—to Amboise and "voluptuous" Francis the First's chateau of Chenonceau, and then a view of the bedchamber of the "fascinating" Diane de Poitiers (1499–1566), amid other objects of value to antiquarians. On to a tavern called the Boule d'Or. In the morning, dismal rain, but still a view of the "delightful environs" of Tours. The author's "listless . . . pen" cannot improve on descriptions by others of the city and "the delicious plain" around it. At Vendôme he visits the ruined chateau of Jeanne d'Albret, Henry the Fourth's mother. Finally, a diligence to Paris.

Bibliography: Bardon, Françoise. *Diane de Poitiers et le Mythe de Diane.* Paris: Presses Universitaires de France, 1963.

"The Trouvères": In "this paper," Longfellow discusses the literature of medieval France, touching on Charlemagne's encouragement of learning as well as of chivalry, the ballad collection called the *Heldenbuch,* the *Chansons de Geste,* "Rowland and Olivir," obscene fabliaux, and lyrics of Southern troubadours. The minstrel Taillefer and Turpin, the chronicler, are mentioned. Strangely, "ancient historical romances" of the northern Trouvères were ignored until recently. Their sources probably include Arabian and Scandinavian narratives as well as Southern lyrics. Longfellow offers translations of a few early "simple and direct" Northern love poems. They tell how spring and birdsongs inspire the lover to express "*les douces dolors*" he feels when he thinks of his beloved. Two "ancient lyric poets of France" merit special treatment: Charles d'Orléans (1391–1465) and Clotilde de Surville. Longfellow outlines the former's life and translates two of his delicate poems about spring; he also translates the latter's poem about nursing her infant son (*see* "The Child Asleep"). Longfellow says he is not writing for scholars or critics and heretofore provides no footnotes. ("Clotilde de Surville" may be Marguerite Élénore Clotilde de Vallon Challis, dame de Surville [c.1400–?], the supposed author of the *Poésies de Clotilde,* including the original of "The Child Asleep.")

"The Baptism of Fire": Anne Du Bourg has been imprisoned for six months. He was a judge who refused to condemn persons "for conscience' sake," and has been therefore condemned as "a convicted heretic" to be burned to death. De Harley, Du Bourg's "former colleague," calls on him in prison, and tells Du Bourg, suspected of conspiring with Huguenots, can still save himself if he renounces "this abominable heresy." Eloquently refusing, Du Bourg, who has comforted himself by reading Tertullian's *Apologeticus* in praise of Christian martyrs, is led to the scaffold, suspended over "quivering flames" of smoky fagots, and dies shouting, "My God! forsake me not, that I forsake not thee!" (Anne [*sic*] Du Bourg, a magistrate, offended King Henri II of France [Jun 1559] when he opined that Huguenots who prayed directly to Christ were less sinful than adulterers, blasphemers, and murderers. Henri, an adulterer with his mistress, Diane de Poitiers, ordered Captain Gabriel de Montgommery to arrest Du Bourg. Ironically, Montgommery fatally wounded Henri in a friendly joust [Jul 1559]. François, duc de Guise, Henri's son Francis II's mentor, said that it would be an affront to Henri's memory not to go ahead and hang and burn Du Bourg, which was accordingly done [Dec 1559].)

Bibliography: Baumgartner, Frederic J. *Henry II: King of France 1547–1559.* Durham: Duke University Press, 1988; Cloulas, Ivan. *Henri II.* N.p.: Fayard, 1985.

"Coq-à-L'Âne": As rainy winter ends, the author takes a five-day, four-ride coach-and-horses journey from Paris to Bordeaux. The rocky motion induces daydreams, in which the real and the imaginary worlds mix. At night, the moonlight renders the dull landscape beautiful. Some nights, a certain "garrulous traveller" would mutter on and on, until his questions fail to arouse his sleeping companions. At relay stations, talk between "drowsy hostler" and postilion is punctuated by ribaldry. Sleepers in the coach

"cage" assume odd postures and make for "a living caricature of man." From Orléans the author "struck across" the Indre, Haute-Vienne, and Dordogne toward Périgueux. The landscape is dotted with "objects of art and antiquity"; they, plus conversation, "lighten the tedium." Most of the talk concerns "affairs of church and state." One fellow traveler blames the Jesuits for controlling "the mind of our imbecile monarch [Louis Philippe]." When the author ventures to criticize the frequency of revolutions in "mercurial" France, he gets rebuked. During breakfast at Limoges, they see the foppishly dressed son of a notary public, which triggers talk about French fashions, the excesses of Madame de Pompadour and others like her, and more politics. To change the subject, a skinny fellow in "a black, seedy coat" tells the following coq-à-l'âne [cock-and-bull story].

"The Notary of Périgueux": A certain Périgueux notary public, from a fine family but now poor, is so henpecked that he must occasionally escape to the suburban *Café Estaminet,* where he smokes his pipe, drinks, plays dominoes, and gossips. A special companion there is a bachelor wine dealer, who gets him to sample his wares so much that he winds up sick at home. When his unsympathetic wife breaks his long-stemmed pipes, he puts a short-stemmed one in his vest pocket and escapes to his office. While there, he is told by a friend that the wine dealer has a dreadful fever and wants the notary to draw up his will. He rushes to the dealer's home, where he finds the apothecary and the housekeeper in much confusion. The notary prepares the will. The dealer signs it, raves a combination of prayers and "dram-shop and . . . card-table" talk, and dies. The apothecary explains that contagious scarlet fever killed him, its main symptom being a pain in the right side. The notary pockets his little pipe, takes the apothecary's horse, and gallops "three mortal miles" home through the windy, snowy night with a burning sensation in his side. He doesn't see shadows of two heads in his house, rushes in, greets his wife, but finds his pain was caused by the hot ashes of his pipe. When asked, the tale-teller says, yes, the notary died later. What of? He answers, "he died—of a sudden!"

"The Journey into Spain": Spring comes, bringing dreamy thoughts of leaves, fresh air, blue skies, clouds, and birds. As the Bordeaux carnival ends, the author proceeds to Bayonne, past dirty hovels, wind-shaken pines, and villages. Valleys are "delicious," and "the sea flashes." With a pretty, colorfully dressed Basque girl as his guide, he rides horseback on the balanced double saddle to St. Jean de Luz, "a smoky little fishtown." In the morning by carriage, on through hills, past a rough chapel, to Vitoria. The author rambles through its nondescript streets. Next noon, they pause at a "dilapidated tenement" in Old Castile resembling an out-at-elbows old don. Beside it is a combination court and stable, littered with lumber, clothes, wineskins, etc. In the kitchen, food is hanging. A wildly garbed fellow guest is a Maragateri'a muleteer. Another guest discusses regional costumes and says those of Andalusian are the best and costliest. The author cites *Gil Blas* in response. Soon, on by mule-drawn diligence to Burgos. Next day they enter "the Heróica Villá of Madrid."

"Spain": Back home again in sunny June, the author remembers Spain, the vigor of its North, the sensuousness of its South, its musical language, its poetry and fiction, and, sadly, the present-day oppression of its "brave and generous people." Spaniards combine pride and "superstitious devotion to . . . the Church." Even its holidays are sad. He declines to describe a bullfight but quotes several lines from the translation by John Gibson Lockhart (1794–1854) of "The Bull-fight of Ganzul." (Longfellow deplored the tradition of bullfighting.)

"A Tailor's Drawer": This chapter is a sweeping together of separate little essays, just the way a tailor's drawer has jumbled contents. In Madrid, the author rents a third-floor room looking down on the Puerta del Sol, in the same house where Gil Blas lived. From its balcony, he views a parade of people selling fruit, chickens, oil, water, religious pictures, and various services. He sees a beauty from Malaga. She is coquettish but is guarded by an armed brother. In a certain

Spanish song, sailors, cavaliers, and "swains" never saw anything "half so fair as she!" (*see* "La Doncella," retitled "Song: She Is a Maid of Artless Grace"). A miller whacks his patient donkey. A gallant fop falsely fancies himself a ladies' man. The author wonders: Is a barefooted, mendicant monk, with no home on earth, "nearer God?" On a sultry day, the author sees a nobleman reading his newspaper but prefers to enjoy a *siesta* himself. When evening brings "dewy freshness," the city turns lively. Midnight comes, and the night is lovely.

"Ancient Spanish Ballads": Every nation has its popular songs. Spain's ballads are often splendid. A good thousand have been collected in *Romancero General* (4 vols., 1604). During seven centuries, the Moors dominated Spain; what warriors won, and died for, their minstrels sang about. There are three main groups of Spanish ballads—historic, romantic, and Moorish. The historic celebrate the deeds of early heroes. The finest concern Roncesvalles, for example, Bernardo del Carpio's march there. The best of the romantic ones concern Charlemagne's Twelve Peers. An especially touching poem tells about the Conde Alarcos, who jilted the king's daughter, married another woman, and was ordered by the king to prove his loyalty by killing his wife—which he did. Again, Longfellow quotes Lockhart. Moorish ballads present "a new world, more gorgeous and dazzling than that of Gothic chronicle and tradition." Moorish knights are "resolute in camps" but "effeminate in courts." Longfellow presents Lord Byron's translation of "The Siege and Conquest of Alhama," in which a lawless king summons his knights to help him, only to be told off for his previous cowardice. Longfellow concludes by agreeing with Robert Southey that many Spanish ballads are inferior; notes the excellence of such English ballads as "Sir Patrick Spence" and Michael Drayton's "Battle of Agincourt"; but insists, in opposition to Southey, that the one about Bernardo is as good as "Chevy Chase," and that the one about Alarcos "has hardly a peer in all English balladry."

"The Village of El Pardillo": When maidenly spring ripens into womanly summer, the author leaves Madrid for El Pardillo, one of the few northern villages with much charm. It even has a few trees. Rural towns have "a beautiful moral feeling" and teach much about the seasons. He stays with Lucas, an honest farmer, whose Tartar wife, Matina, is meddlesome. The author trades cigars to villagers for stories and gossip. In the gloomy church he watches the priest catechize sincere but "roguish" little kids, who sing beautifully but who must be puzzled by aspects of the Holy Trinity, if adults are. The inhabitants of El Pardillo include the priest, his talked-about housekeeper, the alcalde, the pedantic physician, the sacristan, a griping politician, and a notary public. On Sundays after Mass, the villagers enjoy rural dances, during which they can briefly lay aside their troubles. The author joins a group to visit Villafranca, a fifteenth-century Moorish castle fallen into ruins. Fellow tourists remind him of several of Chaucer's Canterbury pilgrims. A legend of the castle has it that a certain lawyer, tempted by a Jew, sold his soul to the devil and was burned by the Inquisition.

"The Devotional Poetry of Spain": Moral poetry in all Christian lands is similar. But devotional poetry is different, "shadowing forth . . . various creeds and doctrines." In Catholic countries, poetry about the Virgin Mary is different from Protestant treatments of her. In Spain there is unique poetry about Santiago, "her patron saint," and about the Crusades and "the crescent of Mahomet." The "foremost" Spanish devotional poet was Gonzalo de Berceo (1180?–after 1246), whose "upwards of thirteen thousand alexandrines" are a monument. Longfellow quotes from his translation of "Vida de San Millan" (*which see*) and mentions his *Miraclos de Nuestra Señora,* the vulgar style of which is "at variance with the elevated character of the subject." But in truth no literary treatment—or painterly or sculptured, for that matter—of an ardently imagined religious subject can do more than suggest "moral sublimity." Only the "enlightened mind," not "the dark and superstitious" one, can truly judge religious art. Sincere devotion can occasionally result in glorious poetry, for example, two sonnets by Lope de

Vega (1562–1635), which Longfellow translates (*see* "The Good Shepherd" and "Tomorrow"). Spanish poetic dramas originated from medieval miracle, morality, and mystery plays. Many mix solemnity and buffoonery. Longfellow summarizes the elaborate plot of *La Devocion de la Cruz* by Pedro Calderon de la Barca (1600–1681), a noteworthy sacred drama. Much Spanish religious poetry, when not espousing any dogma or creed, is uniquely beautiful. Longfellow offers translations from Francisco de Aldana (*see* "The Image of God" and "The Native Land"), both of which characteristically display "warmth of imagination and depth and sincerity of feeling." (This essay is an abbreviated version of one Longfellow published earlier and titled "Spanish Devotional and Moral Poetry," *NAR,* Apr 1832.)

"The Pilgrim's Breviary": After Madrid comes a long trip. First, to Aranjuez and the big, sad La Mancha plains, rendered famous by Cervantes, who has made fiction of history and history of romance. On to Córdova. After four days, Manzanares, and a "sombre-looking inn" there. In the courtyard, muleteers and maids from the inn dance a fandango to the tunes of three blind musicians. A Spanish student boldly strides up, helps himself amiably to food and wine that the author and his friends are having, and relates the story of his life: When orphaned, he was reared by an uncle, sent to the University of Alcalá, became a charity student upon his uncle's death, and then alternated between "want and extravagance." Sometimes he went to gambling tables, filched a nonplussed winner's earnings, and lost "the nice distinctions of right and wrong." Accepting the author's bread, sausage, Vich wine, and a Cuban cigar, the saucy fellow says he is no worse than a mendicant friar. After "desolate and sad" La Mancha comes "lively and picturesque" Valdepeñas, and on to Andalusia. The author calls a portrait of Christ, saved from St. Veronica's handkerchief, a "monument of superstition." Along the Guadalquivir River on a highway threading through orchards and gardens, to Córdova, once boasting Saracen magnificence. The author laments the fact that all along the road to Seville he was never robbed. The pleasant city is famous for its oranges and lovely women. At last, Cadiz, where he takes rooms overlooking the public square. The city is enchanting. As he writes in his journal, he imagines that when old he will reread it with tears in his eyes. Devotion to the Virgin Mary is "ardent and enthusiastic" here. As twilight falls, disputes cease, walking about and even conversation stop, tranquillity reigns, as Ave Maria is sounded. Longfellow writes: "though I may differ from the Catholic in regard to the object of his supplication, yet it seems to me a beautiful and appropriate solemnity, that . . . the voice of a whole people . . . should go up to heaven in praise, and supplication, and thankfulness." On the way to Granada, the author's group overtakes a handsome smuggler on horseback, gaily bedecked and singing a song of "pleasing melancholy." In Granada, "the moon, rising behind the Alhambra," baptizes the author with the "spirit of the night." He wonders how he can, like other artists of earlier times, leave his creative mark. He feels free, but "an infinite and invisible power overrules" him. We all have "hopes and fears." Others have accomplished their missions and departed. In the morning he visits the exquisite Alhambra, which defies description. What luxury, for its occupants to be wooed by music, near lush gardens, beside softly gushing fountains, cooled by gentle mountain breezes. The structure is "an earthly paradise,—a ruin, wonderful in its fallen greatness!"

"The Journey into Italy": With four companions, the author leaves Marseilles (15 Dec 1827), for 10 days by road to Genoa. He remembers every scene and every incident—private carriage from Toulon, landscapes and peasants, amphitheatre at Nice, inn at Monaco—altogether "*un spectacle admirable!*" Christmas Eve at Genoa brings him to a hotel terrace, into the dark streets, and to a midnight mass. Altar lights shine on supporting columns of red marble. When he sees communicants kneeling in prayer, he wonders how many are sinful. One girl reminds him of Goethe's Margaret. After examining Genoa's streets, piazzas, and palaces, he proceeds to Lucca and Pisa. In

Florence he stays near the Piazza Novella, is reminded of Boccaccio, and visits a museum with statues depicting the plague. He becomes acquainted with an English tourist who avoided St. Peter's in Rome and Pompeii near Naples and aimed simply "to complete the grand tour." By contrast, the author meets an American who in a single day can visit a dozen sights mentioned in his guidebook. On, after six misty, rainy days, "with a vetturino" via Siena to Rome, silent and desolate in January.

"Rome in Midsummer": The Carnival season is over, and the author remains in Rome to study, "domiciliated" with a family (*see* Persiani, Giulia) near the beautiful Piazza Navona. His routine is this: mornings, museums and libraries; midday rest; dinner at eight; conversation with travelers, artists, and writers; reading Dante and other authors "till the morning star is in the sky." Longfellow presents a typical travelogue concerning the Piazza Navona market, Saturday water pleasures, the environs of the Janiculum including adjacent villas, Torquato Tasso's tomb, humble Holy Week activities of the nobility, the Roman habit of combining "*Panem et circenses* [bread and circus sports]," the oppressive hot wind from Africa (and its cure, ale), female fortune-tellers and beggars and saints'-lives hawkers, the melancholy sound of church bells during rainstorms, gossip concerning the "bad reputation" of Catholic churchmen from cardinals on down, and shadows cast by midnight moonlight into the Coliseum and elsewhere. His conclusion? "I was a citizen of Rome!"

"The Village of La Riccia": The author spends September in slovenly La Riccia, in the beautiful Albanian hills outside Rome, near the lakes of Alban and Nemi. Near his inn little moral lessons are enacted. This gentle-eyed spaniel of a condemned murderer wanders in to be petted; could a dog love a killer? Why does that cruel man beat his overloaded donkey when it falls? Do these pilgrims heading for the shrine at Loretto march out of Bunyan's book for him to see? The author describes his various "woodland walks"—to Albano, to the lakes, to Castel Gandolfo and its Capuchin convent, to the uniquely high peak of Monte Cavo. The view of the Campagna and Rome reminds him of locations in the *Aeneid*. He converses with a Capuchin friar, here for 30 years, about Roman literature and early Christian history. The friar shows him a treasured copy of *Octavius* by Marcus Minutius Felix (i.e., Minucius Felix), a third-century Christian convert, of whom the author had never heard. The author mentions foreign artists staying here for the summer to sketch the beauty of local women and the glorious sunsets. At the convent again, the author talks with an Irish-born friar who, with a friend, has studied six years at the Jesuit College in Rome. The friend, whom the author meets, is dying of "consumption" but dreams of returning to his family back home.

"Note-Book": Now that it is autumn, Longfellow rushes his concluding paragraphs. He provides skimpy descriptions of Venice (moonlight, a singing gondolier), Trieste ("busy, commercial"), Vienna and "the lordly Danube" and Greifenstein, several German cities, and Holland.

"The Pilgrim's Salutation": Longfellow bids goodbye to his patient readers—"fair dames and courteous gentlemen"—and confesses that he had many sweet "dreams of home [while] in a foreign land" and often longed to return "to the paternal roof." He thanks his readers for hospitably welcoming "these tales of my pilgrimage" and wishes them peace.

"Colophon": Saying that his "pilgrimage is ended," Longfellow confesses that he stole "a feather . . . from the sable wing of night" and wrote "when the duties of the day were over." Why "all this toil," though? It is vain to dream of fame, for his "little book is but a bubble on the stream" of time.

Outre-Mer is based in large part on Longfellow's 1826–29 stay in Europe. He wrote his father from Göttingen (15 May 1829) that he was already preparing "a kind of Sketch-Book of scenes in France, Spain, and Italy"—obviously in admired imitation of *The Sketch Book* (1819–20) by Washington Irving.* When Joseph Tinker Buckingham, editor of the *New-England Magazine,* asked Longfellow for contributions; he sent Buckingham a total of six installments (Jul 1831–Feb 1833), with "The Schoolmaster" as their general title and narrating in the first person the man's travel in Europe. Longfellow wrote George Washington Greene* (9 Mar 1833) that he was preparing "a kind of Sketch-Book of France, Spain, Germany, and Italy," with descriptions, character sketches, and tales, and had plans to publish it in parts, if at all. The finished book appeared, first in two anonymous parts (No. 1, 1833; No. 2, 1834), then as an anonymous two-volume book (New York, 1835; London, as by "An American," 1835). It is noteworthy that Mrs. Elizabeth Shaw Craigie* (1772–1841), the initially unobliging owner of Craigie House,* rented two rooms to Longfellow only after she learned that he was the author of *Outre-Mer.*

Bibliography: Arvin; Higginson; Hilen, ed.; S. Longfellow; Pauly, Thomas H. "*Outre-Mer* and Longfellow's Quest for a Career." *NEQ* 50 (Mar 1977): 30–52; Wagenknecht, 1955; Williams.

"OVID IN EXILE" (1876). Translation of the tenth and twelfth elegies in Book III of Ovid's *Tristia*, in *PP, Kéramos.* In a letter to George Washington Greene* (24 Feb 1878), Longfellow wondered at considerable length if there were any poetic translations of Ovid's *Tristia* and also expressed thoughts about including a translation of Ovid's "lamentations from the shores of the Black Sea" in his *Kéramos and Other Poems* (1878). The result is upwards of 120 lines in irregular trochaic and dactylic hexameters—for example, "I have beheld the vast Black Sea of ice all compacted, / And a slippery crust pressing its motionless tides."

Bibliography: Hilen, ed.

OWEN, JOHN (1806–82). Publisher. He was born in Portland, Maine, graduated from Bowdoin (1827), and attended Harvard Divinity School. He settled in Cambridge and sold books for James Munroe and George Nichols there. Owen took over the firm and established it as his own (1836). He published *The Evidences of Genuineness of the Gospels* (vols. 2 and 3, 1837–44) by Andrews Norton, father of Charles Eliot Norton;* *The History of Harvard University* (1840) by Josiah Quincy;* and *Poems* (1844) and *Conversations on Some of the Old Poets* (1845) by James Russell Lowell.*

When Samuel Colman* published *Hyperion* in a manner Longfellow regarded as unsatisfactory (1839), Longfellow turned to his friend Owen, whose firm published *Voices of the Night, Ballads and Other Poems, Poems on Slavery, The Spanish Student, The Waif,* and *The Belfry of Bruges and Other Poems.* Longfellow went (after 1845) with the firm headed by William D. Ticknor, brother of his friend George Ticknor,* and then to its successors. Longfellow remained Owen's devoted and sociable friend. Owen's company failed (1848). When John Gorham Palfrey* became postmaster of Boston, Longfellow wrote him (3, 9 Apr 1861), to ask that he consider employing Owen.

Bibliography: Hilen, ed.; Thompson.

P

PALFREY, JOHN GORHAM (1796–1881).
Unitarian minister, professor, and historian.
Palfrey was born in Boston, attended Phillips
Exeter Academy and then Harvard (B.A.,
1815; M.A., 1818). He succeeded Edward
Everett* as Unitarian pastor of the Brattle
Street Church in Boston. He resigned to
teach sacred literature at Harvard and be
dean of its theological faculty (1831-39).
Both earlier, during this time, and until
1859, Palfrey contributed numerous articles
to the *North American Review.* He edited it
while his friend Jared Sparks,* the regular
editor, was abroad (1825). After purchasing
it (1835), Palfrey managed it (until 1843). He
served in the legislature of Massachusetts
(1842-43), was its secretary of state (1844-
47), was a member of the U.S. House of Representatives (1847-49), and was Boston's
postmaster (1861-67). Palfrey married Mary
Ann Hammond (1823); they had six children, and two of their sons were Union
Army generals during the Civil War. Palfrey
was a member of the Massachusetts Historical Society but resigned on two different occasions over trivial controversies. He published his sermons and treatises, and also
essays on linguistics; his main written production was his *History of New England* (4
vols., 1858-75; 5th vol., 1890).

Soon after arriving at Harvard (Dec 1836)
to begin teaching there, Longfellow met Palfrey, probably after one of Palfrey's Sunday
afternoon divinity lectures at the college
chapel. The two became friends, and Palfrey
published Longfellow's essay on and partial

translations of *Frithiofs Saga* by Esaias Tegnér* (*NAR,* Jul 1837). After Longfellow took
rooms in Craigie House* (1837), Palfrey and
others often visited him there for food,
drink, and conversation. They were also
welcome guests together elsewhere. An indication of Palfrey's political influence lies in
the fact that the Palfreys invited Longfellow
to a special dinner (Jun 1847), other guests
being John Quincy Adams and his son
Charles Francis Adams; Longfellow was unfortunately too occupied with class work to
accept. When Palfrey was expressing his abolitionist politics in Congress, their friend
Charles Sumner* defended him in discussions with Longfellow, who, however, was
pained to observe—and note in his journal
(3 Sept 1848)—that "the life political begins
to make its mark on him . . . [,] the mark of
struggle and defiance." Sumner later quarreled with Palfrey over political issues. Longfellow wrote Sumner (26 Apr 1859) that the
first volume of Palfrey's *History of New England* "is very successful" and that he was
busy writing the second volume. Longfellow
continued to delight in Palfrey's friendship,
noting in his journal (30 Dec 1859) that he
"is an excellent companion; full of learning,
mellow, and lenient in judgment." Palfrey
sent a copy of the third volume of his *History* to Longfellow, who replied graciously
(28 Dec 1864): "I shall read it, as I did the
other volumes, with a feeling of gratitude to
you, for having ground and sifted the husky
and dusty old records into wholesome
food." He was deeply saddened when both

Palfrey and James T. Fields* died in one week.

Bibliography: Gatell, Frank Otto. *John Gorham Palfrey and the New England Conscience.* Cambridge: Harvard University Press, 1963; Hilen, ed.; S. Longfellow.

"PALINGENESIS" (1864). Poem, in *AM,* Jul 1864; *Flower.* The poet lies on "the headland-height," watches the glistening waves melt into mist, and suddenly seems to see friends from "days departed," with faces lovely as in dreams. Not so. He sees the lonely shore again, and a wind strips nearby wild roses of their petals. Is the legend true that alchemists could "re-create the rose" out of its ashes, though not fragrantly blooming? "Ah me!," can "The rose of youth [be] restore[d]" out of the heart's ashes? The poet wants his youth back. But the sea answers, "Alas! thy youth is dead!" The poet accedes, won't try to disinter it, only to gain pain. He will remember, look ahead, and "weep no more." He wonders into what autumn, after what sunsets, under what "midnight skies," into what houses once occupied by friends, he might carry his cross. He knows not but will reverently read "the mystic book" of his future until he comes upon "The End." This remarkable poem contains 11 stanzas. The following exemplifies the captivating form of each:

"O, give me back," I cried, "the vanished
    splendors,
The breath of morn, and the exultant strife,
    When the swift stream of life
Bounds o'er its rocky channel, and surrenders
The pond, with all its lilies, for the leap
    Into the unknown deep!"

Bibliography: Arvin.

"PARKER CLEAVELAND; WRITTEN ON REVISITING BRUNSWICK IN THE SUMMER OF 1875" (1878). Sonnet, in *Kéramos.* Parker Cleaveland (1780–1858), the author of a respected scientific book titled *An Elementary Treatise on Mineralogy and Geology* (2 vols., 1822), was Professor of Natural Philosophy at Bowdoin College when Longfellow was a student there. Long-

fellow admired Cleaveland, benefited from his continued friendship, and kept in touch with him and members of his family. In this sonnet, Longfellow eulogizes Cleaveland as "serene and sweet," as one whose life was "rounded . . . and . . . complete." He graced his teacher's chair as a king might his throne. In his classes, he made "A pastime of the toil of tongue and pen." He sleeps here "amid the groves he loved so well" and awakens with God.

Bibliography: Cleaveland, Nehemiah and Alpheus Spring Packard. *History of Bowdoin College, with Biographical Sketches. . . .* Boston: J. R. Osgood & Company, 1882; Hilen, ed.

PARODIES. Given Longfellow's popularity, his occasional simplicity of subject matter and treatment, and his sometimes relentless metrics, it was inevitable that he should be parodied. Longfellow was not pleased with parodies. When Henry Clay Lukens (1838–?), a Philadelphia journalist, sent Longfellow his parody of *Lenore* (1870) by Gottfried August Bürger (1747–94), Longfellow replied at some length (6 Oct 1870), of which this was his central point: "A parody or travesty of a poem is apt to throw an air of ridicule about the original, though made with no such intention." Longfellow was the victim of countless parodies, with the following among the most frequent targets: *The Courtship of Miles Standish,* "The Day Is Done," *The Song of Hiawatha,* and "The Village Blacksmith."

Bibliography: Brett, Simon, ed. *The Faber Book of Parodies.* London: Faber and Faber, 1984; Lowrey, Burling, ed. *Twentieth Century Parody: American and British.* New York: Harcourt, Brace, 1960; Falk, Robert P., ed. *American Literature in Parody. . . .* New York: Twayne, 1955; Hilen, ed.; Parrott, E. O., ed. *Imitations of Immortality: A Book of Literary Parodies.* Harmondsworth, Middlesex, England: Penguin Books, 1986.

"PASSAGES FROM FRITHIOF'S SAGA BY ESAIAS TEGNÉR." *See Drift-Wood.*

"PASSAGES FROM JEAN PAUL" (1841). Translations by Longfellow from works by Jean Paul Richter (1763–1825), one of his longtime favorites. The selections, for which

Longfellow received $15, appeared in the *Boston Notion* (13 Mar 1841).

"THE PAST AND THE PRESENT." *See* "Phi Beta Kappa Poem."

"PAUL REVERE'S RIDE." *See* "The Landlord's Tale," in *Tales of a Wayside Inn,* Part First.

"PEDESTRIAN." *See* "Reminiscence of Genius."

"PEGASUS IN POUND" (1847). Poem, as "Proem," in *The Estray: A Collection of Poems; S/F.* Pegasus, "the poet's winged steed," strays into "a quiet village." Boys find him, and supposedly "wise men" put him into the pound. Plans are made to sell the "estray." A variety of "country people" hurry in "to see this wondrous / Winged steed, with mane of gold." Neither "food nor shelter" is provided. Pegasus patiently looks through the pound bars at the moon and the stars. A bell tolls midnight. A cock crows. Pegasus breaks free, "unfold[s] . . . his pinions," and soars away. Villagers find nothing but his hoofprints "upon the greensward," from which springs a fountain of invigorating waters and soothing sounds. The source is "Pegasus im Joche" (1795), a poem by Johann Christoph Friedrich von Schiller (1759–1805).

PERKINS, CHARLES CALLAHAN (1823–86). Art critic, philanthropist, and administrator. Perkins was born in Boston, the son of a wealthy merchant. After attending schools in Boston and Cambridge, Massachusetts, and Burlington, New Jersey, Perkins attended Harvard (graduating 1843). A sizable inheritance financed an extended stay in Rome (1843–46), where he studied art and commissioned (1842) a marble *Hebe and Ganymede* by the American sculptor Thomas Crawford.* Perkins studied painting and music in Paris (1846–49). Back in Boston (1849–51), he was active in musical societies, heard his own compositions performed, and commissioned Crawford (1851) to create the bronze *Beethoven* for the Boston Music Hall. Perkins studied music in

Leipzig (1851–56), returned home, and married Frances D. Bruen (1855). The couple had three children. Perkins lectured on painting at Trinity College, Hartford (1857). He took his family to Europe, where he studied art history in Florence, Italy, and published *Tuscan Sculptors* (2 vols., 1864) and *Italian Sculptors* (1868). Perkins resided in Boston (from 1869), where he focused his considerable energies on enterprises for the public good. He was an official of the Boston Art Club (1869–80), was an early planner of the Museum of Fine Arts (from 1870), lectured on Greek and Italian art and on engraving at the Lowell Institute (intermittently 1871–78), was an innovative official on the Boston School Board (1871–84), was a member of the American Academy of Arts and Sciences (from 1874), and was president of the Handel and Hayden Society (1875–86). In addition to other publications, Perkins wrote *Raphael and Michelangelo* (1878), which he dedicated to Longfellow and in which he included translations by Longfellow of Michelangelo's sonnets. He expanded his earlier works on sculpture into *Historical Handbook of Italian Sculpture* (1883). He wrote *Ghiberti et on École* in French (1886) and helped edit *Cyclopedia of Painters and Paintings* (4 vols., 1885–87). While Perkins was visiting his son's summer home in Windsor, Vermont, he was thrown from a runaway horse-drawn carriage and killed instantly.

Longfellow knew Perkins casually and admired him greatly. In a letter to Charles Eliot Norton* (5 Feb 1850), Longfellow mentions enjoying matinee musicals given by Perkins. According to his journal (13 Jan 1855), Longfellow went to Boston, called on Perkins, and "Saw his pictures." Perkins illustrated many of his lectures with pictures. In a much later journal entry (12 May 1872), Longfellow reminds himself that his poem on "Charlemagne" is based on a lecture by Perkins, in which he mentioned "a story in an old chronicle, *De Factis Caroli Magni,* quoted by Cantù, *Storia degli Italiani,* ii. 122." Longfellow attended Perkins's final lecture for the season (29 May 1872) on Italian art.

Bibliography: Eliot, Samuel. "Memoir of Charles Callahan Perkins, A.M." *Proceedings of the Massachusetts Historical Society,* 2d ser., 3 (Feb 1887): 223–46; S. Longfellow.

PERSIANI, GIULIA (1804–?). Italian woman, married when thirteen to Antonio de Cesaris and widowed not long thereafter. When Longfellow first went to Rome, he was introduced to the Persiani family by George Washington Greene,* who was living with them. Longfellow roomed with them (Feb–Dec 1828) and became friendly with the father Innocenzo, the mother Marianna, their son Fabio, and their three daughters, Giulia (the eldest), Virginia, and Luisa. Longfellow developed a serious romantic relationship with Giulia. After Greene had become U.S. consul in Rome (1837), Longfellow pestered him for information about her, and learned that she was married (by 1838) to a Frenchman named De Launoy and was in Paris with her husband (by 1839). In three letters to Greene, Longfellow referred to "my romantic passion for Madame Julia" (1 Oct 1839), to the Persiani family's "*hot* daughter" (9 Jan 1840), and to his "*antiqua flamma,*" whom "I want to see once more" (2 Aug 1842, from Marienberg, Germany). While last in Rome, Longfellow wrote Greene (7 Feb 1869) that he had sought out remnants of the Persiani family, saw Fabio, learned that Virginia was in Paris, "called" Luisa, but saw neither her nor Giulia.

Bibliography: Hilen, ed.

"THE PHANTOM SHIP" (1851). Poem, in *GM,* Feb 1851; *Courtship, Birds* (1858). In Cotton Mather's *Magnalia Christi Americana* (1702), Book I, Chapter VI, is the story of a "ship [that] sailed from New Haven," with its canvases full of frosty wind and with a cargo of "heavy . . . prayers," including those of the minister (the Rev. Mr. Davenport). Master Lamberton was afraid that his "crank and walty" vessel would sink. Winter passes. No tidings. The people ask God to explain what He did with the ship. One June day just before sunset they finally see her, "steadily steering landward" but with falling masts, sails "blown away like clouds," and rigging dropping. Suddenly "the hulk dilated and vanished, / As a sea-mist in the sun!" The pastor concludes that God responded to their prayers by sending "this . . . mould of their vessel!," "this Ship of Air," in order "to quiet their troubled spirits." Longfellow received a long letter from Samuel Ward* (12 Jan 1841) detailing Mather's account of the missing vessel and its ghostly reappearance following prayers. Ward offered to send Longfellow a copy of the pertinent passage. Longfellow finally got around to reading Mather in the Harvard library and wrote the poem the same evening (11 Oct 1850).

Bibliography: S. Longfellow.

PHELPS, ELIZABETH STUART (1844–191L). Novelist. She was born in Boston and was baptized Mary Gray Phelps. She was the daughter of Elizabeth Stuart Phelps (1815–52) and Austin Phelps, an Andover Theological Seminary professor. Her mother wrote popular religious stories and semi-autobiographical novels under the pen name "H. Trusta" ("Trusta" being an anagram of "Stuart"). One of her novels, *The Sunny Side* (1851), sold more than 100,000 copies. Her daughter, when her mother died, changed her name to that of her mother and published under that name. Her invalid father's nervousness, combined with the death during the Civil War of a young man she loved, made her a recluse for some time, after which she published *The Gates Ajar* (1868). It concerned the future life and offered comfort to other women whose loved ones died in the war. Phelps followed its success with two sequels: *Beyond the Gates* (1883) and *The Gates Between* (1887). Earlier than these were four works, each daring for the times. *Hedged In* (1870) concerns illegitimacy. *The Silent Partner* (1871) deals with capital-labor strife in polluted factories. *The Story of Avis* (1877) innovatively dramatizes domestic love rather sadly triumphing over a heroine's desire for a career. *Dr. Zay* (1882) heaps praise on the heroine, who is a physician. Phelps married Herbert Dickinson Ward (1888), and they coauthored several romances, the best being *Come Forth* (1890), about Jesus and Lazarus. She wrote a biography of James T. Fields* (1881), a couple of novels—*The Ma-*

donna of the Tubs (1877) and *Jack the Fisherman* (1887)—deriving from summers she spent in Gloucester, Massachusetts, and also *Friends: A Duet* (1881), among other novels. In her autobiography, *Chapters from a Life* (1896), Phelps discusses not only her many New England friends but also nervous disorders that both marred and vivified much of her work.

Longfellow replied in a letter (12 Mar 1876) to "Miss M.S. Phelps," when she asked about any possible historical background of the building in which the heroine of his *Evangeline* had found her Gabriel. In answering her "kind letter," he told her about a secluded old almshouse in Philadelphia that he "chose . . . for the final scene." When he read *The Story of Avis* by Phelps, he jotted his impression in his journal (30 Oct 1877): "A fresh, original style of writing, very interesting and peculiar." According to his journal (1 Feb 1878), he had lunch with the following: Helena Modjeska (1840–1909), the Polish actress then on tour in the United States; her son; Annie Adams Fields,* the wife of his publisher James T. Fields; and "Miss Phelps, author of Avis." In his journal (6 Aug 1878) he notes that he and the Fieldses "Drove to Gloucester to see Miss Phelps in her cottage, just as large as my study,—twenty feet square." A couple of weeks later he sent her a letter (21 Aug) lamenting the fact that he did not remain with her "long enough to see the fog lift and Norman's Woe rise to view. I have never seen those fatal rocks." This was the locale of the wreck in "The Wreck of the Hesperus." He goes on to mention her "paragraph on Co-education" and "In School Days" by John Greenleaf Whittier.* Rather clearly, Mary Stuart Phelps's feminist precepts and examples were too advanced for Longfellow to do much more than bow at. Nonetheless, his praise of *The Story of Avis* thrilled her, and she wrote him (27 Feb 1879) to thank him profoundly. In a letter to her (21 Aug 1881), Longfellow says that *Friends: A Duet* shows "your power of delineating female character" and praises her book on Fields as "by far the best I have seen." Many years after Longfellow's death, Phelps wrote an essay titled "Longfellow, Whittier, and [Oliver Wendell] Holmes,[*]" *McClure's Magazine* (Jul 1896).

Bibliography: Hilen, ed.; Kessler, Carol Faley. *Elizabeth Stuart Phelps.* Boston: Twayne Publishers, 1982; S. Longfellow.

"PHI BETA KAPPA POEM" (1829). Longfellow delivered this poem, called "The Past and the Present," at Bowdoin's 1829 commencement ceremonies. He repeated it at the annual fall meeting of Bowdoin's Phi Beta Kappa Society three years later. He used it again at Harvard's fall 1833 meeting of the Society. The poem praises the progress of modern, more liberated education when compared to the consequences of restrictions on medieval intellectualism. The first three six-line stanzas became "Sunset after Rain," in *A Practical Grammar of the English Language* (Portland: Shirley and Hyde, 1839), by Roscoe Goddard Greene. Longfellow took four sections from the 1833 version, called them "The Dead," "The Soul," and "Truth," and sent them to various periodicals, fruitlessly. "The Warning," a fourth part taken out later, was published in his *Poems on Slavery.*

Bibliography: Thompson.

PHOTOGRAPHS OF LONGFELLOW. *See* Portraits and Photographs of Longfellow.

PIERCE, ANNE LONGFELLOW (1810–1901). (Nickname: Annie.) Longfellow's favorite sister. She encouraged his friendship with Mary Storer Potter, who became his first wife (1831). When Anne's and Longfellow's sister, Elizabeth Longfellow,* died (1829), Anne may have suffered a nervous breakdown. In 1832 she married Longfellow's Bowdoin classmate and friend George Washington Pierce,* who died (1835) two weeks before Longfellow's wife Mary died. Never remarrying, Anne lived during her long, long widowhood in the Longfellow home on Congress Street in Portland. Until their deaths, she cared lovingly there for her parents and also for Lucia Wadsworth,* her aunt. After the death of Stephen Longfellow (1805–50),* her brother, Anne offered to become the legal guardian of two of his children, Ellen Longfellow (1838–1927)* and

Henry Wadsworth Longfellow II,* if the Longfellow family would help financially; she became only Henry's guardian. She was always a welcome visitor at Longfellow's home. She was a valuable companion when Longfellow took his three daughters, among others, with him on his last European tour (1868-69). Many of Anne's letters concern family matters, notably complaints about not only her nephew Henry but both also Henry's mother, Marianne Preble Wadsworth Longfellow,* and her father, Judge William Pitt Preble, neither of whom she liked. For decades, Longfellow supported Anne financially in considerable part. He bequeathed her $500 a year "during her life." Her old Portland home is now a beautiful, popular, and valuable museum.

Bibliography: Hilen, ed.; Thompson; Wagenknecht, 1955.

PIERCE, EDWARD LILLIE (1829–97). Attorney and biographer. Pierce was born in Stoughton, Massachusetts, was educated at the normal school in Bridgewater, Massachusetts, and graduated from Brown University (1850) and Harvard Law School (1852). During the 1850s, he worked for Salmon P. Chase in Cincinnati and then in Washington, D.C., met Charles Sumner,* and was impressed by his work for the civil rights of oppressed fugitive slaves, immigrants, and Catholics. During the Civil War, Pierce was a Union Army private briefly, worked on behalf of "contraband" slaves escaping to Union-controlled land and trying to farm there, and was appointed an internal-revenue tax collector in Boston. He also developed expertise in railway law. He was a county district attorney in Massachusetts (1865-69), the secretary of the Massachusetts State Board of Charities (1869-74), lecturer at Boston University Law School (1872-82), a member of the state legislature (1875, 1876, 1897), and the author of *Enfranchisement and Citizenship: Addresses and Papers* (1896), which reflects his liberal thought, and of a genealogical sketch of his mother Elizabeth Lillie's ancestors (1896). Pierce's finest publication was his edition of *Memoirs and Letters of Charles Sumner* (4 vols., 1877-93), the result of 20 years of

work on some 30,000 letters by Sumner, and including his speeches and news accounts concerning him. Pierce married Elizabeth H. Kingsbury of Providence, Rhode Island (1865); they had four children. Two years after his wife's death (1880), Pierce married Maria L. Woodhead, of England; they had two children. Pierce's brother was Henry Lillie Pierce (1825-96), a successful manufacturer, a mayor of Boston (1873, 1878), and a member of Congress (1873-77). Edward Pierce died in Paris.

Longfellow didn't know Edward Pierce well. However, soon after the death in 1874 of Sumner, whom Longfellow knew intimately, Sumner's vast array of papers was sent to Cambridge; Longfellow, a cotrustee of Sumner's literary estate, helped locate a place for them and was asked by the trustees to examine them and to consider writing Sumner's biography. He courteously—and sensibly—declined; but, evidently in charge of finding a biographer for Sumner, he first wrote their mutual friend John Lothrop Motley (1814-77), the eminent historian. Motley, who had visited Longfellow shortly after his wife Fanny burned to death, replied from Paris (1874) that chronic illness prevented him from undertaking the assignment; in addition, Motley's own wife was ill and died later that year. Pierce was eventually assigned the formidable task of writing Sumner's biography, to which Longfellow offered steady moral support and assistance. He checked many transcriptions, provided some translations where needed, and wrote Pierce numerous helpful letters. In the resulting massive work, Sumner's and Pierce's innumerable connections to Longfellow and his circle of friends are made evident. When the first volume appeared, Longfellow wrote Pierce (8 Nov 1877) to congratulate him and to "prophecy a brilliant success for the book."

Bibliography: Hilen, ed.; S. Longfellow; Rhodes, James F. "Memoir of Edward L. Pierce." *Proceedings, Massachusetts Historical Society,* 2d ser., 18 (Jun 1904): 363-69.

PIERCE, GEORGE WASHINGTON (1805–35). Longfellow's brother-in-law. After Longfellow graduated from Bowdoin, he briefly studied law in his father's office with Pierce, Patrick H. Greenleaf, Frederic Mellen, and his brother Stephen Longfellow. For diversion they wrote a series of essays, after the manner of *The Sketch Book* (1820) by Washington Irving,* and purportedly by students studying at the Temple Bar and enjoying membership in a social club called Brazen Nose College. The essays, 14 in number, were published in the Portland *Advertiser* under pseudonyms. Longfellow's pen name was Nathan Bonithan. Pierce married Longfellow's sister Anne (1832; *see* Pierce, Anne Longfellow). Pierce was a member of the House of Representatives in Maine (1832–33) and was closely acquainted with Franklin Pierce, Bowdoin graduate and future president of the United States. Longfellow greatly liked George Pierce, wrote numerous letters to him—often addressing him as "Geordie"—and was saddened when he died two weeks before Longfellow's wife Mary died. Longfellow always remembered George Pierce fondly. Anne Pierce asked Longfellow (1854) to write a biographical sketch of George, to be included in *History of Bowdoin College, with Biographical Sketches of Its Graduates from 1806 to 1879, Inclusive,* then being prepared by Nehemiah Cleaveland (1796-1877, Bowdoin graduate [1813]). Declining, Longfellow said that Josiah Pierce (1827-1913), George's nephew and a Portland lawyer, could do a better job. Longfellow did send Anne (24 Oct 1854) pages and pages full of his tender "reminiscences and impressions" of George, which he said Josiah could "insert in the form of a letter" if he wished. But Josiah didn't wish. *History of Bowdoin College* (1882) was completed by Alpheus Spring Packard (1798-1884), one of Longfellow's teachers at Bowdoin, and included Josiah Pierce's sketch—without evident use of Longfellow's memoir.

Bibliography: Hilen, ed.; Little.

POE, EDGAR ALLAN (1809–49). Poet, fiction writer, and critic. Poe had a productive but tragically brief life. He was born in Boston to actor parents. His father soon disappeared. When his mother died (1811), he was taken into the home of, but never formally adopted, by John Allan, a wealthy Richmond merchant, and his wife. They took Poe to England, where Allan developed overseas business concerns and where Poe was an excellent student (1815-20). The three resided again in Richmond (1820-25). Poe gave himself "Allan" as his middle name (after 1826), enrolled briefly at the University of Virginia (1826), disputed with John Allan over money, traveled to Boston and published his first poetry (1827), served well in the U.S. Army as Edgar A. Perry (1827-29), and attended West Point (1830-31), lived obscurely in Baltimore and New York (1831-34), and published his first short fiction (1832). In Richmond he edited the *Southern Literary Messenger* (1835-37); in 1836 married his cousin Virginia Clemm (1823-47; they had no children); lived in New York (1837-38) and then Philadelphia (1838-44) while coediting *Burton's Gentleman's Magazine* (1839-42) and editing *Graham's Magazine* (1841-42; owned by George Rex Graham*), and returned to New York (1844-49), part of the time editing the *Broadway Journal* (1845-46). Poe's final days are still clouded in mystery. He went from Richmond intending to proceed to New York but stopped in Baltimore, where, perhaps after drinking too much, he fell into a coma, was taken to a hospital, and died. Poe was spectacularly creative and vastly influential in poetry, fiction, and criticism. His collections of poetry include *Tamerlane and Other Poems* (1827), *Al Aaraaf, Tamerlane and Minor Poems* (1829), *Poems* (1831), and *The Raven and Other Poems* (1845). Collections of his short stories are *Tales of the Grotesque and Arabesque* (1840), *Prose Romances of Edgar A. Poe* (1843), and *Tales* (1845). His critical essays and reviews, not collected in his lifetime, are often perceptive, especially his reviews of *Twice-Told Tales* by Nathaniel Hawthorne* (1842, 1847), "The Philosophy of Composition" (1846), and "The Poetic Principle" (1850). Occasionally they were vituperative, for example, his ill-natured attacks on Longfellow.

Poe briefly and harmlessly reviewed Longfellow's *Outre-Mer* in the *SLM* (Jun 1835) but adversely reviewed *Hyperion* in *Bur-*

ton's *Gentleman's Magazine* (Oct 1839), calling it "a profusion of rich thought" but "without design, without shape, without beginning, middle, or end," and viciously reviewed *Voices of the Night* in *Burton's* (Feb 1840), accusing Longfellow of plagiarizing "Midnight Mass for the Dying Year" from "The Death of the Old Year" by Alfred, Lord Tennyson.* By letter (5 Jul 1840), Longfellow asked his friend Lewis Gaylord Clark (1810-41), poet and twin brother of Willis Gaylord Clark (1810-73), editor of the *Knickerbocker Magazine,* to try to identify the author of those anonymous reviews; Clark incorrectly named the publisher William Evans Burton (1804-60) as the culprit. Acting as Graham's editor and agent, Poe obsequiously wrote Longfellow (3 May 1841) asking him to contribute to *Graham's Magazine* on any terms. Longfellow replied (19 May 1841), respectfully declined on the grounds of being too busy, and added this: "all that I have read from your pen has inspired me with a high idea of your power; and I think you are destined to stand among the first romance-writers of the country, if such be your aim." In a letter (29 May 1841) to Rufus Wilmot Griswold,* who was briefly to succeed Poe as editor of *Graham's* (1842), Poe falsely accused Longfellow of plagiarizing from "The Haunted Palace" by Poe when Longfellow wrote "The Beleaguered City." Longfellow clarified the matter in a letter to Griswold (28 Sept 1850). To Griswold, Poe submitted an unfavorable review of *The Spanish Student* by Longfellow. Griswold wrote Longfellow (26 Dec 1843) to curry favor by telling him how "malignant" the review was and what a "poor critic" Poe was. Graham bought the review but never published it. In the New York *Evening Mirror* (13, 14 Jan 1845) Poe's unsigned review of *The Waif,* Longfellow's assembly of poems, caused additional controversy by foolishly contending that Longfellow not only beefed up the book by anonymously adding some of his own works but also made other selections that wouldn't show up Longfellow's. Poe lectured in New York (26 Feb 1845) on American poets and poetry, in the process called Longfellow a plagiarist, and for saying so was roundly criticized by various defenders, best by "Outis" in the *Mirror.* At this time, Nathaniel Parker Willis* was the editor and co-owner of the *Mirror.* "Outis" may have been Longfellow's close friend Cornelius Conway Felton.* Poe in an unsigned essay ("The American Drama," in *American Review: A Whig Journal of Politics, Literature, Art and Science* [Aug 1845]) included ridicule of *The Spanish Student,* the plot of which, however, he summarized skillfully. After reading the essay, Longfellow wrote James Russell Lowell* (18 Aug 1845), "I see he [Poe] is braying at me again." Poe downgraded Longfellow's *Hyperion* when a second edition appeared, for being a mere "book . . . and not a dream to boot" (*Broadway Journal,* 27 Dec 1845). Poe took pleasure in the adverse criticism of Longfellow's poetry published by Margaret Fuller* (1845). Three days after Poe's death, Longfellow wrote a letter (10 Oct 1849) to John Reuben Thompson (1823-73), editor of the *Southern Literary Messenger,* containing this muted tribute to Poe: "His prose is remarkably vigorous, direct, and yet affluent; and his verse has a peculiar charm of melody, an atmosphere of true poetry, about it which is very winning. The harshness of his criticisms, I have never attributed to anything but the irritation of a sensitive nature chafed by some indefinite sense of wrong." Thompson published Longfellow's entire letter (*SLM,* Nov 1849). After Poe died, Maria Poe Clemm (1790-71), Poe's aunt and the mother of his deceased wife, wrote to Longfellow some 15 letters (1850-66), usually asking for money. She also wrote to Charles Sumner* for the same purpose. Longfellow contributed a sum of $50 gathered from several people for her, sent it to her by letter (2 Jul 1860), and sent her $10 more (4 May 1863).

Bibliography: Allaback, Steven. "Mrs. Clemm and Henry Wadsworth Longfellow." *Harvard Library Bulletin* 18 (Jan 1970): 32-42; Campbell, Killis. "Who Was 'Outis'?" *University of Texas Studies in English* 8 (Jul 1928): 107-9; Hilen, ed.; S. Longfellow; *The Poe Log;* Moss, Sidney P. *Poe's Literary Battles.* Durham: Duke University Press, 1963; Ostrom, John Ward, ed. *The Letters of Edgar Allan Poe.* 2 vols. Cambridge: Harvard University Press, 1948; Pollin, Burton R. "Longfellow and Poe: An Unnoted Hexameter Exchange." *Mississippi Quarterly* 37 (Fall 1984): 475-82; Shuman, R. Baird. "Longfellow, Poe, and *The Waif.*" *PMLA* 76 (Mar 1961): 155-56; Wagenknecht, 1955.

POEMS OF PLACES (1876–79). A massive collection of poems describing many places, country by country, edited by Longfellow in 31 volumes and including several of his own poems. He wrote many letters to authors asking permission to include their poems. He occasionally responded to other authors' queries to decline their works or to express sorrow that they had sent them to him too late to be used. The whole work, which at first he was delighted to be putting together, ultimately cost him much time, annoyance, grief, and money.

POEMS ON SLAVERY (1842). Eight poems, seven of which were written during Longfellow's voyage from Bristol, England, back home (1842). "The Warning" was composed later. Well aware of their tepid contents, Longfellow described his *Poems on Slavery* in a letter (23 May 1843) to Isaac Appleton Jewett (1808-53), his wife Fanny's cousin (whom Longfellow had first met in Switzerland in 1836), that they are "so mild that even a Slaveholder might read them without losing his appetite for breakfast." The little book sold well and generated much commentary, both favorable and otherwise. John Greenleaf Whittier,* popular poet and fiery Abolitionist, liked the booklet so much that he asked Longfellow to become a candidate for Congress on the Liberty Party ticket. Longfellow declined. Margaret Fuller* reviewed the booklet adversely in the *Dial*, calling it "the thinnest of all Mr. Longfellow's thin books." Nathaniel Hawthorne* wrote Longfellow a letter (24 Dec 1842) expressing surprise, since "You have never poetized a practical subject hitherto." *Poems on Slavery* were omitted from Longfellow's *Poems* (1845), because, as Carey & Hart,* his publishers, explained, including them would ruin sales in the South and the West. Apropos of all this, it is of interest that Longfellow wrote Charles Sumner* (20 Apr 1864) the following: "Until the black man is put upon the same footing as the white, in the recognition of his rights, we shall not succeed, and what is worse, we shall not deserve success."

Bibliography: Harris, Arvin; Janet. "Longfellow's *Poems on Slavery.*" *Colby Library Quarterly* 14 (Jun 1978): 84-92; Hilen, ed.; S. Longfellow; O'Neill, Joseph. "Longfellow: Preacher and Poet." *Thought* 31 (winter 1956-57): 567-600; Wagenknecht, 1986.

The poems are as follows:

"To William E. Channing." The poet praises William E. Channing* for his "well done" book *Slavery* (1845), compares his words to those of Martin Luther, and urges him to continue fighting against "The feudal curse, whose whips and yokes / Insult humanity." Longfellow feels that Channing was doubtless as inspired to write as "John in Patmos" was. Slavery threatens an apocalyptic "dire eclipse."

"The Slave's Dream." The slave, worn out and resting in the rice field, dreams of his home by the Niger River, where he was a king; dreams of his queen and children; dreams of a furious ride well armed on his stallion; and dreams of following flamingoes to the ocean, of the roar and scream of lions and hyenas, of some kind of triumph of liberty. The master's whip doesn't rouse the slave now, for his soul has just been unfettered by death. This poem has eight clever six-line stanzas, rhyming abcbdb, with internal rhymes in some of their third lines. Its meaning, however, is unclear. Does the slave dream of galloping to free himself, of returning to free his family, or simply of enjoying a bellicose horseback ride?

"The Good Part, That Shall Not Be Taken Away." A woman, formerly rich, now teaches in a girls' school, puts off "village churls / By her angelic looks," and tells her pupils about the coming of freedom for slaves. Inspired by "her beloved Lord," she sold her possessions and freed her enslaved servants and field hands. They have sailed "beyond the Southern Sea" and clothe her in "their prayers," and she happily works for "her daily bread." This poem was deemed so controversial that the New England Anti-Slavery Tract Association omitted it from its reprint of Longfellow's *Poems on Slavery* (1843).

"The Slave in the Dismal Swamp." An old, lame, infirm, scarred, ill-clad slave crouches in a mossy, vine-tangled swamp. He hears his pursuers' horses and bloodhounds. Above him, squirrels scamper freely and birds sing "songs of Liberty!" He alone is stricken by "the curse of Cain." This poem closely parallels "The Lake in the Dismal Swamp" (1803) by Thomas Moore (1779–1852).

Bibliography: Morrison, Robert Haywood. "An Apparent Influence of Thomas Moore on Longfellow." *Philological Quarterly* 35 (Apr 1956): 198–200.

"The Slave Singing at Midnight." A clear-voiced "Negro . . . enslaved" sings "the psalm of David," about "Israel's victory," about free Zion, about "triumph." His impressive tones are both glad and sad. When imprisoned, Paul and Silas sang about "the Lord arisen," and an earthquake freed them; but "what earthquake's arm of might" will shatter this slave's dungeon?

"The Witnesses." In ocean depths "the black Slave-ship swims." Its dead cargo of manacled slaves, "necks . . . galled" and flesh gone, "glare from the abyss" and "cry, from unknown graves, / 'We are the Witnesses!'"

"The Quadroon Girl." A slaver, whose boat is anchored in the lagoon, is dickering with a planter, whose "soil is barren." "A Quadroon maiden" stands before them. She is timid, puzzled, scantily dressed. Her slight smile is meek, saintly. As for the planter,

> His heart within him was at strife
>   With such accursed gains:
> For he knew whose passion gave her life,
>   Whose blood ran in her veins.

Even so, he takes "the glittering gold," and the slaver leads her away "To be his slave and paramour / In a strange and distant land!"

Bibliography: Arbery, Glenn Cannon. "Victims of Likeness: Quadroons and Octoroons in Southern Fiction." *Southern Review* 25 (Jan 1989): 52–71.

"The Warning." Remember Samson, the lion-killing Israelite who was blinded, "Shorn of his strength," made "to grind / In prison," and mocked by the Philistines. He shook down the temple and died with "thousands . . . in the fall." Slaves in our land are "Shorn . . . and bound" and may likewise one day "shake the pillars of this Commonweal" into rubble. "The Warning" was originally part of Longfellow's "The Past and the Present," the poem he delivered at Harvard's Phi Beta Kappa Society meeting (1833).

Bibliography: Thompson.

"THE POET AND HIS SONGS" (1880). Poem, in *AM,* Jun 1880; as "L'Envoi," in *Thule.* Where do things come from? Birds from spring, rain from clouds, fruits from vines and branches, sails and foam from waters. So with the poet's song—out of "the misty realm, that belongs / To the vast Unknown." The lines and their fame are "His, and not his." When voices pursue him, he must obey the Angel's command to write.

"POETIC APHORISMS" (1846). Twelve poems, translated from the German poet Baron Friedrich von Logau (1604–55), in *Bruges.* "Money": Money bothers those who have it or lack it. "The Best Medicines": The joyful, temperate, and restful rebuke the doctor. "Sin": Men, Christ, and God respond to sin differently. "Poverty and Blindness": The blind see no one, and the poor no one sees. "Law of Life": The poet says he lives and dies "heartily" to God, "faithfully" to his "Prince," and "honestly" to neighbors. "Creeds": Where is Christianity in various distinct creeds? "The Restless Heart": Grinding away are millstones and hearts. "Christian Love": Fiery love, once "quenched, . . . bites . . . like . . . smoke." "Art and Tact": Intelligence and good manners aren't always found together. "Retribution": God is patient and grinds slowly but exactly. "Truth": "Truth silences the liar" the way fire stops the croaking of frogs. "Rhymes": Words sound best in a familiar setting. These aphorisms were reprinted, titled "Epigrams," in the Supplement of *Poets and Poetry of Europe,* ed. by Longfellow.

Bibliography: Arvin.

"POETRY OF THE DARK AGES" (1832). Poem, unrecovered, written at Bowdoin and perhaps related to his Phi Beta Kappa poem, delivered at Bowdoin (Sep 1832). It is also referred to as "The Dark Ages."

Bibliography: Thompson.

"THE POETS" (1877). Sonnet, in *Golden Songs of Great Poets,* published privately by Sarah H. Leggett (1877); *Kéramos.* Dead poets and living poets, alike, answer if not neglected. Though even when crowned with thorns, are you not happy to fulfill "your errand"? Poetic talent is a divine gift. Therefore, "Not in the shouts and plaudits of the throng, / But in ourselves [poets themselves], are triumph and defeat."

Bibliography: Wagenknecht, 1986.

***POETS AND POETRY OF EUROPE* (1845).** Anthology assembled by Longfellow, containing translations of almost 400 poems originally in Anglo-Saxon, Danish, Dutch, French, German, Icelandic, Italian, Portuguese, Spanish, and Swedish. Forty of the translations, from Anglo-Saxon, Danish, French, German, Italian, Portuguese, Spanish, and Swedish were by Longfellow. The following five translations by Longfellow were first published in *Poets and Poetry of Europe:* "Blessed Are the Dead," "Death of Archbishop Turpin," "Rondel: Hence, Away," "Silent Love," and "Song: If Thou Art Sleeping, Maiden." For various introductions, Longfellow compressed several of his essays published earlier (*NAR,* 1830s). He and Cornelius Conway Felton* prepared the numerous biographical notices. Longfellow wrote several letters to Carey & Hart,* the Philadelphia publishing firm that issued this book, to complain about terms of payment. He also disputed with his publishers about illustrations. The historian William Hickling Prescott* in a letter to Longfellow (25 Jun 1845) describes his gift copy as "a delightful bouquet of wild-flowers, picked off from old tumble-down ruins and out-of-the-way nooks and by-paths where the foot of the common traveler seldom treads." The big book proved popular, and an English edition followed (1855). It was with great pleasure that Longfellow prepared a second American edition (1871), with a large Supplement, which contained nine more of his translations, from French, German, Italian, and Spanish originals. Among Longfellow's friends, translations from the following appeared: William Cullen Bryant* (6 in the first edition, 3 in the second); Felton (6 in the first); George Washington Greene* (1 in the first); William Dean Howells* (21 in the second); James Russell Lowell* (1 in the second); Thomas William Parsons (1819–92; 1 in the first); William Wetmore Story* (1 in the first); and Bayard Taylor* (1 in the second). By letter (8 Nov 1870), Longfellow thanked Porter & Coates, the publishers of the second edition, for their check in the amount of $555.

Bibliography: Hilen, ed.; S. Longfellow.

"THE POET'S CALENDAR" (1882). Poems, in *Harbor.* "January": Janus looks ahead and back and counts the years. "February": This is the time of cleansing waters. "March": "Martius," formerly first, was displaced, now makes war, "shake[s] the cities," and floods and drowns things. "April": Spring comes with flowers, birdsongs, sunshine, showers, and the advent of love. "May": "Maia" brings seabirds, bees, and tree blossoms; sailors sail away; and she "waft[s] o'er all the land" fragrances from "the Hesperides." "June": Fair June brings roses, marriages, and long evenings. "July": This month brings desert winds, drought, thirst, and fevers, and "The sky is changed to brass." "August": This virginal month is calmer, collects sheaves, and harvests. "September": Autumn brings the equinox, scatters the clouds, the harvest moon; birds head south. "October": This is the time of gold and red leaves, maturing fruit; summer is but a gentle memory. "November": Arrowy winds chase the dying leaves, which form a shroud. "December": Holly crowns this month; pinecones are fragrant; Christmas, with a proclamation of peace, follows.

"IL PONTE VECCHIO DE FIRENZE" (1875). Poem, in *Pandora, Birds* (1875). Longfellow wrote this sonnet in Italian and in English. *See* "The Old Bridge at Florence."

"THE POOR STUDENT. . . . A DRAMATIC SKETCH" (1824). Blank-verse play, signed "H.W.L.," in *American Monthly Magazine,* Apr 1824.

Part First: The moon is shining into the cottage room of Seymour, a poor, too-conscientious student. He regards himself as an overburdened genius, feels he has a crown of thorns, and predicts he will soon succumb to "the burthen of our gross mortality." Seeing his midnight lamp, Gertrude enters and urges him to rest. He gazes at the moon, offers Gertrude his hot hand as proof he is too feverish to sleep, and says his guttering lamp symbolizes his waning life. Gertrude says he is too gloomy and ought to be more considerate of "thy poor mother." He bids Gertrude goodnight with the hope that she will have pleasant dreams.

Part Second: Seymour wanders in pleasant woods, is cheered slightly, ponders his "link in the great chain of being," says "visionary fancy" soars above "reason's pinion," and exits. Gertrude and a peasant girl enter. The girl warns Gertrude that Seymour has been looking dangerous and might hurt her. Gertrude replies that she and Seymour have been friends since childhood and he'd never harm her. She adds, "And yet say on!" When the girl reports that Seymour has headed for the waterfall by "the left-hand path," Gertrude follows, lamenting that his "rich pride of dawning manhood" may dissolve. Seeing Gertrude, Seymour explains that he dreamed of life fighting death and also that the moon was Gertrude, whose cold brow he touched but to whom he tried unavailingly to speak. Gertrude counters that "love shall bring forgetfulness of this" and better days will follow. Seymour, however, predicts his early death and hopes she'll remember him.

Part Third: Gertrude stands beside Seymour's grave near the waterfall. She says that although the setting sun will rise and shine on his grave again, he will never awaken from his "dreamless sleep"; and further, that although the seasons will change, he is now "where youth can never dawn again" and nothing can change. Exiting, she follows a voice and "spectred form." Two peasants enter. The second peasant wonders if "troubled spirits always walk" and fears Gertrude "will die of grief." A stranger enters, says that he is a friend of Seymour's and has "tidings that will be of joy to him," and asks where

he lives. The second peasant points to Seymour's grave. The stranger says that his hand would have saved Seymour, who he heard "had an aged mother with him, and / A maid of somewhat greener years." The first peasant replies that the mother has unfaltering hope but that Gertrude is heartbroken. They see Gertrude's corpse plunge over the waterfall. The stranger will go comfort Seymour's mother.

"The Poor Student" is part of the once-popular literary tradition of presenting impoverished New England students studying themselves to death. In the same vein, the novel *Fanshaw, A Tale* by Nathaniel Hawthorne* followed Longfellow's lugubrious drama by four years but is only a little better. *See also* "To the Novice of the Convent of the Visitation."

Bibliography: Hilen, ed.; S. Longfellow.

PORTRAITS AND PHOTOGRAPHS OF LONGFELLOW. Longfellow quickly became popular and ultimately was America's most beloved poet. Images of him were soon sought. The following artists made portraits of him: Thomas Badger (1792-1868), oil, attributed, c.1829; Maria Christina Röhl (1801-75), pencil, 1835; Wilhelm Hendrik Franquinet (1785-1854), crayon, 1839, crayon, 1840; Cephas Giovanni Thompson (1809-88), oil, 1840; Joseph Alexander Ames (1816-72), oil, c.1840; Charles Octavius Coles (1814-?), oil, unfinished, 1842; Seth Wells Cheney (1810-56), charcoal, 1843; Eastman Johnson (1824-1906), crayon, 1846; Samuel Laurence (1812-84), crayon, 1854; Ernest Wadsworth Longfellow,* oil, undated; Thomas Buchanan Read (1822-72), oil?, c.1845; Thomas Hicks (1823-90), oil?, 1855; and Wyatt Eaton (1849-96), pencil, 1878. Longfellow's portrait, along with those of 129 other men, is in "Webster's Replying to Hayne" by George Peter Alexander Healy (1813-94), oil, 1862. The engraving of Longfellow (1866) by William Edgar Marshall (1837-1906), based on Marshall's own portrait of Longfellow, proved to be so popular that, according to a letter Longfellow wrote George Washington Greene* (14 Mar 1882), 10 days before Longfellow died, he autographed a thousand copies of the engraving for persons besieging him with letters. An early daguerreotype of Longfellow was made by Southworth and Hawes, Boston, c.1848. Among numerous photographs of Longfellow, the best are those by George K. Warren (1834-84), 1863; Julia Margaret Cameron (1815-79), 1868; Napoleon Sarony (1821-96), 1868; Elliott & Fry, London, c.1868; Frederick Gutekunst (1831-1917), 1876; Joseph Harrison Lampson (c.1841-1902), Portland. Longfellow also posed for many group photographs, usually with members of his family. In addition, he was the subject of busts and statues, notably by Edward Augustus Bracket (1818-1908), bust, 1855; Samuel James Kitson (1848-1906), bust, 1879; Bela Lyon Pratt (l1867-1917), unfinished clay model; and Franklin Simmons (1838-1913), statue, 1887.

Bibliography: Cameron, Kenneth Walter. *Longfellow among His Contemporaries.* . . . Hartford: Transcendental Books, 1978; *Emerson Society Quarterly,* no. 58, part 1 (1970): [23-30]; Hilen, ed.; Mann, Charles W. "The Poet's Pose." *History of Photography: An International Quarterly* 3 (Apr 1979): 125-27.

"POSSIBILITIES" (1882). Sonnet, as an "L'Envoi," beginning "Where are the poets . . . ?," in *Harbor.* Are they on "Olympian heights," with sure bow and arrow, with "argosies of song" voyaging to new lands? Perhaps an untaught lad, a "graduate of the field or street," will navigate "the high seas of thought" and steer unafraid toward lands still uncharted.

POTTER, BARRETT (1776–1865). Longfellow's father-in-law. Potter was a county judge of probate in Portland and the widowed father of three daughters, Elizabeth Ann Potter (1810-?), Mary Storer Potter (1812-35; she became Longfellow's first wife [1831]), and Margaret Louise Potter (1817-?), later the wife of Peter Thacher (1810-94).

POTTER, MARY STORER (1812–35). Longfellow's first wife. *See* Longfellow, Mary.

"PRAISE OF LITTLE WOMEN." Poem, translated from the Spanish poet Juan Ruiz de Hita (1283?-1351?), in Scudder. Small are precious stones, pepper, grains of gold, fragrant balsam, fine roses, and the best songbirds. So with tiny women. So with the lesser of two evils.

"PRAY FOR ME" (1877). Poem, translated from the French poet Charles-Hubert Millevoye (1782-1816), in *PP,* Scudder. The dying persona tenderly beseeches the cottagers to pray for him when they hear the prayer bells ring out. He is happy to be free of pain now. He was honest toward his one loyal friend. When she asks people to pray for her, take pity on her also.

"PRELUDE: AS TREASURES THAT MEN SEEK" (1882). Poem. Editors have placed this poem as an introduction to posthumous editions of *In the Harbor* and also to selections of translations by Longfellow. The poet says that treasures buried in ocean sands slip away from sailors' hands if they so much as speak. Isn't it therefore better to "let the treasures rest / Hid from the eyes of men"? So it also seems with foreign "songs." He as translator has simply "marked the place" where, "following this slight trace, / Others may find the gold."

"PRELUDE: PLEASANT IT WAS . . ." **(1839).** Poem, in *Voices.* The poet found it pleasant to lie under "some patriarchal tree, with the cloudy sky above, sunlight filtering through a canopy of leaves, and shadows on the ground. He enjoyed "Dreams that the soul of youth engage / Ere Fancy has been quelled." Later, when Pentacost would herald the spring, he used to leave "the city's throng" to seek the woods and hear the trees whisper. They asked him to become a child again. Nature seemed to be praying with him there. He resists the temptation to poetize his childish visions, realizes he is mature now, sees that "the heavens [are] all black with sin," and is told to "Look, then, into thine heart, and write!" His "theme" hereafter will be the "solemn Voices of the Night." The "Look, then" admonition is almost verbatim from "'Fool,' said my Muse to me, 'look in thy heart, and write!'" in Sir Philip Sidney's *Astrophel and Stella.* In each of the 11 stanzas in this "Prelude," Longfellow meets the difficult challenge of an *abaaab* rhyme scheme.

Bibliography: Wagenknecht, 1986.

PRESCOTT, WILLIAM HICKLING (1796–1859). Historian. Prescott was born in Salem, Massachusetts, the son of William Prescott, an attorney and a judge, and Catherine Green Hickling Prescott. Young Prescott moved with his family to Boston (1808) and soon enrolled at Harvard (1811). During some dining-hall skylarking, he was hit in the left eye by a crust of bread (1812) and suffered permanent blindness in that eye, followed by rheumatic inflammation and partial, to near, blindness in the right eye. He earned his Harvard B.A. (1813) and M.A. (1817). With family wealth behind him, Prescott followed a brief period in which he studied Italian literature by turning permanently (1814), inspired by lectures by George Ticknor,* to the field of Spanish history, concentrating on the reigns of Ferdinand and Isabella. Prescott traveled to the Azores, where his maternal grandfather was the American consul, then to the Continent (1815–17). In London he purchased a device called a noctograph, which enabled the visually challenged to write with a stylus on carbon paper ruled along brass wires. He married Susan Amory (1820); they had four children. Susan Prescott spent her life assisting her husband in his work, as did other family members and secretary-readers. Susan Prescott's grandfather was a British naval captain who (17 Jun 1775) participated in bombarding Bunker Hill, which was defended by Prescott's grandfather, Colonel William Prescott. Later, the two adversaries' crossed swords were placed over the Prescotts' fireplace and still later inspired William Makepeace Thackeray* to write *The Virginians.* Prescott's publishing successes were astounding: *The History of the Reign of Ferdinand and Isabella, the Catholic* (1837), *History of the Conquest of Mexico* (1843, perhaps his finest work), *Biographical and Critical Miscellanies* (1845), *History of the Conquest of Peru* (1847), *His-*

tory of the Reign of Philip the Second (vols. 1 and 2, 1855; vol. 3, 1858, incomplete), and *The Life of Charles the Fifth after His Abdication* (1857). During visits abroad (1850, 1856), Prescott was esteemed as a superb narrative historian. He suffered an apoplectic stroke (1858) and soon died. By 1860, his books had sold upwards of 90,000 copies. He has been widely acclaimed as a careful historian, using sources well, remaining impartial in his judgments, and artistic in his writings, which are more notable for structural, picturesque, and dramatic narrative effects than for much analytical profundity. A main effect of his histories has been to make American political thinkers aware of the dangers of jingoistic isolationism. Prescott remains the most widely translated American historian.

Not long after Longfellow began teaching at Harvard (Dec 1836), he met Prescott, whose father Longfellow's father knew well. In his journal (23 Mar 1838), Longfellow mentions encountering Jared Sparks* and Prescott, the latter "brimful of his book [on Ferdinand and Isabella]; glorious in his fame." Longfellow adds, "He is a striking example of what perseverance and concentration on one's powers will accomplish." Longfellow wrote his father again (30 Apr 1838), this time to report that Prescott was recently thrown off his horse, fell onto the pavement "all bent up like a Hindoo god," but was not seriously hurt. A few days later he encountered Prescott walking in the street and returned home to dine with the Prescotts. The historian soon was friendly enough with the poet to write him (30 Dec 1841) and offer, most courteously, his judgments as to the following: successful use of hexameters, "most doubtful"; Longfellow is too good a poet to spend much time translating; "the original tone of thought" in "The Children of the Lord," which Longfellow translated, lacks much "poetical character"; and "The Skeleton in Armor" and "The Wreck of the Hesperus" illustrate "the true coloring of the antique" and rival "The Rime of the Ancient Mariner" by Samuel Taylor Coleridge. According to his journal (20 Feb 1850), Longfellow was a dinner guest at Prescott's home, along with George Stillman

Hillard,* Charles Callahan Perkins,* Charles Sumner,* and a few other men. Prescott must have thrilled Longfellow when he sent the poet (28 Nov 1855) a copy of a letter from fellow historian George Bancroft* to Prescott praising *The Song of Hiawatha* for his skillful handling of Indian relations to animals and for his "delicious" depiction of Minnehaha. In his journal (23 Aug 1854), Longfellow expresses annoyance that in the absence of an international copyright Prescott earned too little abroad for his book on King Philip, parts of which he found "extremely interesting" (17 Jan 1856). In his journal (3 May 1856), Longfellow notes his presence, together with Louis Agassiz* and Cornelius Conway Felton,* among others, at a farewell dinner for Prescott before his voyage to Europe. When Prescott died, Longfellow commented in his journal (29 Jan 1859): "So departs out of our circle one of the most kindly and genial men; a man without any enemy; beloved by all and mourned by all." Sumner wrote Longfellow from France (4 Mar 1859) that Prescott's death occasioned much "grief and praise" there. In his journal (25 Jul 1859), Longfellow noted his intention to write a poem to be titled "The Ghost's Walk" about a locale where Prescott liked to walk; the work, if written, remains unpublished. Prescott's impact on Longfellow was far less professional than social. He regularly comments on the historian's amiable mien and youthful appearance. Prescott knew Spanish history far better than Longfellow, whose knowledge of Spanish literary figures, however, surpassed Prescott's. Fanny Longfellow,* Longfellow's wife, knew and revered Prescott and his works, both before her marriage and afterwards, and commented in writing on both more than Longfellow did.

Bibliography: Donald, Darnell, G. *William Hickling Prescott.* Boston: Twayne Publishers, 1975; S. Longfellow; *Mrs. Longfellow;* Williams, Stanley T. *The Spanish Background of American Literature.* New Haven: Yale University Press, 1955.

"PRESIDENT GARFIELD" (1881). Sonnet, in New York *Independent,* 6 Oct 1881; *Harbor.* Just as Dante's poet hears these words in Paradise—"e venni dal martirio a questa pace"—so the slain president, after "the discipline of pain," senses "infinite rest and infinite release," and can relieve "our suspense" by crying, "I came from martyrdom unto this peace!" For the reference to Dante, *see* the *Paradiso,* XV, l. 148, the poet being Cacciaguida, Dante's ancestor-soldier. On learning of James A. Garfield's death, Longfellow wrote George Washington Green* (20 Sep 1881) that the line from Dante kept running in his head. Longfellow had dinner with Garfield (Dec 1873) at the Cambridge home of their mutual friend William Dean Howells.* The editor of the *Independent* paid Longfellow $200 for the poem.

Bibliography: Arvin; Hilen, ed.; Leech, Margaret and Harry J. Brown. *The Garfield Orbit.* New York: Harper & Row, 1978; S. Longfellow.

PRESIDENTS LONGFELLOW MET. Longfellow was introduced to President Martin Van Buren in Washington, D.C. (Feb 1839) by Commodore Alexander Scammell Wadsworth,* the brother of Longfellow's mother. He probably met or at least saw John Tyler when he visited Boston (Jun 1843). Longfellow dined with John Quincy Adams at the home of John Gorham Palfrey* (Jun 1847). Longfellow and his wife attended a reception in the White House (17 May 1850), probably through the good offices of Angel Calderón de la Barca, the Spanish minister in Washington, D.C.; at that time, they met President Zachary Taylor, whom Longfellow describes in his journal as a "cordial old man" (17 May 1850). According to a letter Longfellow sent to Charles Sumner* (19 May 1850), the president, upon seeing Longfellow, "sprang forward, and said, 'This must be Mr. Longfellow.'" Taylor died less than two months later. According to a journal entry (15 Oct 1871), Longfellow drove Sumner to Boston to have dinner with President Ulysses S. Grant and several of his secretaries. Longfellow adds this: "The President is a quiet, unostentatious man, with a soft, pleasant voice." Longfellow had dinner with James A. Garfield (Dec 1873) at the Cambridge home of their mutual friend William Dean Howells.* Longfellow wrote to George Washington Greene* (20 Sep 1881) that ever since he learned of Garfield's assassination,

Dante's line has been running in my mind:—
   "E venni dal martirio a questa pace (I came from martyrdom to this peace)."
And what a martyrdom!

(*See* "President Garfield," Longfellow's sonnet.)

Bibliography: Arvin; Leech, Margaret and Harry J. Brown. *The Garfield Orbit.* New York: Harper & Row, 1978; S. Longfellow.

"PROMETHEUS, OR THE POET'S FORE-THOUGHT" (1855). Poem, in *PM,* Feb 1855; *Courtship, Birds* (1858). The myths and songs about Prometheus all portray him thus:

First the deed of noble daring,
   Born of heavenward aspiration,
Then the fire with mortals sharing,
Then the vulture,—the despairing
   Cry of pain on crags Caucasian.

The stories are all symbolic "Of the Poet, Prophet, Seer." Thus inspired, such people lead nations, write—like Dante, Milton, Cervantes—but are afflicted. They palpitate "With the rapture of creating" and are undeterred by "the vulture sailing" overhead. Bards of lesser talent celebrate and follow such daring pioneers. The singsong trochaic tetrameter of "Prometheus" is at odds with its profound burden. Longfellow's more realistic companion piece is his "Epimetheus, or the Poet's Afterthought."

Bibliography: Arvin.

"A PSALM OF DEATH: THE REAPER AND THE FLOWERS." *See* "The Reaper and the Flowers."

"A PSALM OF LIFE" (1838). Poem, in *KM,* Oct 1838; *Voices.* The subtitle is "What the Heart of the Young Man Said to the Psalmist." "A Psalm of Life," the most popular poem ever written in English, begins thus:

Tell me not, in mournful numbers,
   Life is but an empty dream!

For the soul is dead that slumbers,
   And things are not what they seem.

The soul refuses to believe that we become nothing but dust again. Our destiny is neither "enjoyment" nor "sorrow" but to be challenged to live actively, progressively. Time is short if we intend to be creative, artistic, triumphant. Neither trust the future nor lament the past. Be active now. Do as "great men" do, and upon "departing, leave behind . . . / Footprints on the sands of time." They may inspire a "shipwrecked sailor" coming upon them. Get going, confidently "Learn to labor and to wait." According to his journal (11 Aug 1850), Longfellow was delighted once when a certain minister quoted from "A Psalm of Life" during his sermon, but Longfellow's pleasure was lessened when a member of the congregation said that no one knew the source of the quotation. Longfellow's imagery in the poem is unfortunate. He says that we should fight well in our bivouacs, unlike cattle. Also, a lost sailor surely must be nimble to follow another's footprints before they are washed out. Nevertheless, "A Psalm of Life" was once immensely popular, was widely translated (once into Sanskrit), and is still anthologized even though now downgraded by contemporary critics as fragmentary pastiche. It had the virtue, also, of helping Longfellow persuade himself, after the death of Mary (1835), his first wife, to have "a heart for any fate."

Bibliography: Cargo, Robert T. "Baudelaire, Longfellow, and 'A Psalm of Life.'" *Revue de Littérature Comparée* 54 (1980): 196–201; Havey, Kenneth. "'A Psalm of Life' Reconsidered: The Dialogue of Western Literature and Monologue of Young America." *American Transcendental Quarterly,* n.s., 1 (Mar 1987): 3–19; Littlefield, Jr., Daniel F. "Longfellow's 'A Psalm of Life': A Relation of Method to Popularity." *Markham Review* 7 (spring 1978): 49–51; S. Longfellow; Wagenknecht, 1986; Williams.

"PSALM, THE FIFTH: MIDNIGHT MASS FOR THE DYING YEAR." *See* "Midnight Mass for the Dying Year."

Q

"THE QUADROON GIRL." *See Poems on Slavery.*

"A QUIET LIFE" (1882). Poem, translated from an anonymous French poet, in *Harbor.* Let others connive and advance. As for the poet, he will meditate quietly and age serenely. Unlike many, when he dies he will, though obscure, know himself.

QUINCY, JOSIAH (1772–1864). Politician, educator, and author. He was born into an influential and wealthy family in Braintree, Massachusetts. After attending Phillips Andover Academy, he was educated at Harvard (B.A., 1790; M.A., 1793), studied law, and passed the bar but seldom practiced. He married Eliza Susan Morton (1797); they had seven children, many of whom, and their offspring, were talented and influential people. His wife died in 1850. Quincy served in the State Senate (1804–05, 1820–21) and in between as a Federalist in the U.S. Congress (1805–13). He was an effective mayor of Boston (1823–27). He served for a long while as president of Harvard (1829–45), during which time he was progressive but was often at odds with some administrators and faculty because of his Unitarianism, and with the student body because of his refusal to permit horseplay. High jinks of this sort resulted, much earlier, in the expulsion of Richard Henry Dana Sr.* Quincy was responsible for recruiting several distinguished professors to Harvard, including Jared Sparks*

and Longfellow. The student body commissioned the sculptor Thomas Crawford* to prepare a bust of Quincy at the time of his retirement (1845). Quincy wrote *The History of Harvard University* (1840; it was intended to thwart orthodox Congregationalists in his midst), a biography of John Quincy Adams (1858), and much else.

Longfellow's association with Quincy began when in Portland he received Quincy's letter from Cambridge (1 Dec 1834) inviting him to replace George Ticknor,* who was resigning, as Smith Professor of Modern Languages. Terms included $1,500 per annum, provided Longfellow first spend 12 to 18 months in Europe again, at his own expense, to improve his knowledge of German. Following a flurry of letters clarifying details, Longfellow accepted. Once he started teaching, he occasionally dickered with Quincy about money, appointments of language instructors under his supervision, and a leave of absence for himself owing to sickness (1842). After retiring from Harvard, Quincy wrote Longfellow a prolix letter (21 Feb 1848) about the unique beauties of "the English hexameter lines" and in the process mentioned that reading *Evangeline* gave him "pleasure." Longfellow's journal records at least one occasion when he visited Quincy at his home; he found the old fellow "eighty, but hale and hearty" (6 Mar 1852).

Bibliography: Hilen, ed.; Johnson, Carl L. *Professor Longfellow of Harvard.* Eugene: University of Oregon Press, 1944; S. Longfellow; Morison.

R

RACHEL (1820–58). (Real name: Elizabeth Felix.) French actress. Born to poor Jewish peddlers in Mumpf, Switzerland, she and her older sister Sarah Felix sang in cafés, moved to Paris (1830), and became street singers. They were given free singing lessons and studied in the Conservatoire. Rachel's stage debut was mediocre (1837); but as Camille in Pierre Corneille's *Horace,* as Roxane in Jean Racine's *Bajazet* (both in 1838), and especially starring in Racine's *Phédre* (1843), she was spectacular. Gabriel Legouvé (1807-1903) and Augustin Scribe (1791-1861) wrote *Adrienne Lecouvreur* (1849) as a contemporary vehicle for her. She was successful on the London stage (1841, 1842) in tragic dramas by Corneille and Racine. Rachel's tour in the United States (1855), however, was regarded as a professional failure. She died of tuberculosis near Nice, France.

While in Paris, Longfellow attended a performance by Rachel, and in a letter (8 Jun 1842) about the event to Catherine Eliot Norton, the mother of Charles Eliot Norton,* said this: "I saw with perfect delight Mlle Rachel the actress, in Racine's Mithridate, and discovered, for the first time in my life, that one of Racine's plays could be made interesting." Nor was Longfellow disappointed when he attended at least four performances in Boston by Rachel (Oct 1855), relishing her in *Phédre* and *Adrienne Lecouvreur,* and also in *Angelo,* which was an 1833 failure by Victor Hugo. In his journal (24 Aug 1855) he labeled Rachel "A great actress; the best I ever saw." Incidentally, Longfellow treasured a letter from Hugo (22 April 1867), whom he admired, to whom he had sent a book, and who wrote Longfellow, in part, this: "Vous êtes un des hommes qui honorent la grand Amérique."(You are one of the men who are honoring America the grand.)

Bibliography: Brownstein, Rachel M. *Tragic Muse: Rachel of the Comédie Française.* New York: Alfred A. Knopf, 1993; Hilen, ed.; S. Longfellow.

"RAIN IN SUMMER" (1845). Poem, in *GM,* Aug 1845; *Bruges.* After a hot day, streets and lanes welcome the rain, as it clatters and pours into "a muddy tide." The sick man sees it with relief. Boys sail their "mimic fleets" in "the wet streets." In the country the rain is welcomed, by dry plains, "patient oxen," and farmers. But "The Poet" understands the rain uniquely. He sees "Aquarius old / Walking the fenceless fields of air," pouring "showery rain." The poet foretells the future, since "his thought . . . never stops." He can follow raindrops into graves and rainbows. "Thus the Seer" recognizes natural cycles: "From birth to death, from death to birth, / From earth to heaven, from heaven to earth," until revealed is the wheel of "The Universe . . . Turning forevermore / In the rapid and rushing river of Time." Notable in this eleven-stanza poem, of between 4 and 13 lines each, is their varied rhyme schemes—from a simple *aaabbb* to ones of complexity, for example, aaabccbdbdeffe. It has been suggested that aspects of Longfellow's verse form here anticipates what Gerard Manley Hopkins (1844–89) developed and called "Running Rhythm."

Bibliography: Arvin.

"THE RAINY DAY" (1842). Poem, in *Ballads;* Scudder. The poet compares the cold, dark, dreary, rainy, windy day, with its wall-clinging vines and falling leaves, to his cold, dark, dreary life, with its clinging thoughts and falling hopes. He must "cease repining," however, since the sun is behind the clouds and, inevitably, "Into each life some rain must fall, / Some days must be dark and dreary." This three-stanza poem is divided mathematically into description, analogy, and interpretation, a formula Longfellow often employs.

Bibliography: Wagenknecht, 1986.

"THE REAPER AND THE FLOWERS" (1839). Poem, as "A Psalm of Death: The Reaper and the Flowers," in *KM,* Jan 1839; *Voices.* Death is a sharp-sickled "Reaper" who cuts down not only "bearded grain" but also fragrant, "drooping" flowers. He binds the latter "in his sheaves" for Christ, who needs these "Dear tokens of the earth . . . / Where he was once a child." He will transplant them "in fields of light," and saints will wear their blossoms on "their garments white." The Reaper, who took flowers one day from a weeping, anguished mother, was neither cruel nor wrathful in doing so, but was in reality an angel. Longfellow originally subtitled this poem "The Psalm of Death." The first image comes from a line in a German hymn—"*Es is ein Schnitterr under er heisst Tod.*" Longfellow recorded in his journal (6, 7 Dec 1838) that "The Reaper and the Flowers" came to him "in a gush," having "seemed to crystallize at once" in his mind, and that he wrote it "with peace in my heart and not without tears in my eyes." Eliza Henderson Bordman Otis (1796–1873), a Boston social leader, wrote Longfellow (4 July 1841) to report that the little daughter of a friend recited "The Reaper and the Flowers" to her mother one night and asked whether she might combine it with her prayer.

Bibliography: Hilen, ed.; S. Longfellow; Thompson; Wagenknecht, 1986.

"RECOLLECTIONS OF THE METROPOLIS" (1837). Review of *The Great Metropolis* by James Grant (1807–79), in *NAR,* Apr 1837. Longfellow admired Grant's solid and practical depiction of London.

Bibliography: Thompson.

"REMARKS OF MR. LONGFELLOW" (1860). Eulogy, in *Proceedings of the Massachusetts Historical Society* (1860). At a meeting of the Massachusetts Historical Society* (1859), Longfellow praises the personality and writings of Washington Irving* and discusses Irving's personal influence on him.

"REMINISCENCE OF GENIUS" (1825). Essay, in Portland *Advertiser,* 27 May 1825. This essay, containing brief comments relating to Thomas Chatterton (1752–70), appeared in a column titled "Pedestrian" and conducted by William Browne, Longfellow's boyhood friend and occasional collaborator.

Bibliography: Thompson.

"REMORSE" (1870). Poem, translated from the German poet Count August von Platen Hallermund (1796–1835), in *AM,* Sep 1870; *Three.* The poet becomes startled "in the night, in the night," wanders into the street, through a medieval gate, and to a rushing brook. He leans over a bridge, watches the forward-gliding waves, gazes at the "melodious" stars and the "serene" moon, senses a waste of someone's "days in delight," and urges "thou light" to quiet "The remorse in thy heart that is beating." The use of the word "light" is puzzling. The poet walks "so light"; the waves move "so light"; stars sparkle "so light"; then "thou light" is asked to become silent. The phrase "in the night" is sounded 10 times.

Bibliography: Arvin.

"RENOUVEAU: GENTLE SPRING . . ." *See* "Spring."

"RENOUVEAU: NOW TIME . . ." *See* "The Return of Spring."

"RESIGNATION" (1850). Poem, in *S/F.* Every flock has a dead lamb; every fireside, an empty chair. We should assume such losses to be "celestial benedictions" in "dark disguise," and funeral candles to be "heaven's distant lamps." Death is only a "transition." The child we love is not dead but is merely gone to Christ's school, free now of all temptation, led by angels, and growing to maidenly maturity "in her Father's mansion." We will recognize and embrace her in heaven. While our hearts may moan like a restless ocean meanwhile, we will be patient. We should not conceal grief, but sanctify it. This elegiac poem was occasioned by the death of Longfellow's first daughter, Fanny Longfellow* (11 Sep 1848 [9/11!]). Sturdy in it is the expression of Longfellow's faith in immortality.

Bibliography: Arvin; Wagenknecht, 1986; Williams.

"THE RETURN OF SPRING" (1839). Poem, translated from the French poet Charles d'Orléans (1391–1465), in *Voices.* "Now Time throws off his cloak again / Of ermined frost, and wind, and rain." He puts on "the embroidery / of glittering sun and clear blue sky." Birds and animals sound again. Rivers, fountains, and brooks don "dainty livery / . . . of silver jewelry" and look merry again. The initial couplet is repeated twice. When Longfellow republished this poem in his edition of *Poets and Poetry of Europe,* he titled it "Renouveau."

"REVENGE OF RAIN-IN-THE-FACE" (1878). Poem, in *Kéramos, Birds* (1878). Near the waters of the Yellowstone and the Big Horn, Sioux chiefs are in a bellicose mood. Rain-in-the-Face calls for revenge against "the White Chief with yellow hair." Lying in ambush are Sitting Bull and three thousand warriors, resembling "bison among the reeds." Into the trap ride the yellow-haired leader and his three hundred soldiers. Death quickly engulfs them, "like the breath / And smoke of a furnace fire." That night Rain-in-the-Face rides off with his trophy, the heart of the yellow-haired leader. Which side was right? Which was wrong? Let's "say that our broken faith / Wrought all this ruin and scathe." The yellow-haired officer is obviously George Armstrong Custer (1839–76). Longfellow makes a point of dating the action when he concludes the poem "In the year of a Hundred Years."

Bibliography: Dippie, Brian W. "Bards of the Little Big Horn." *Western American Literature* 1 (fall 1966): 425–36; Eastman, Charles Alexander. "Rain-in-the-Face: The Story of a Sioux Warrior." *Outlook* 84 (27 Oct 1906): 507–12; Wagenknecht, 1986.

"R.H.D." *See* "The Burial of the Poet."

"THE RHYME OF SIR CHRISTOPHER." *See* "The Landlord's Tale" in *Tales of a Wayside Inn,* Part Third.

"ROBERT BURNS" (1880). Poem, *Harper's New Monthly Magazine,* Aug 1880; *Thule.* In his imagination, the poet sees a plowman in a field in Ayr. Regardless of the weather, the fellow sings as he works. More than simply grain, he harvests birdlike songs; weeds turn to flowers, and gorse becomes brighter when "Touched by his hand." He sings about love, which illuminates his dark cottage, despite—to be sure—also causing treachery, waywardness, and remorse. The brush hung above the tavern entrance drops bitterness on his tongue. His voice was "harsh," inevitably, but never "with hate." His songs are about "Manhood, Freedom, Brotherhood." Perhaps it is better that he died young, because he thus avoided an old age of poverty and illness. He remains immortally youthful as "he haunts his native land," which is filled with grateful farmers and echoing brooks. In fact, he is in the poet's room this moment and is saluted thus:

> Welcome beneath this roof of mine!
> Welcome! this vacant chair is thine,
>   Dear guest and ghost!

Bibliography: Wagenknecht, 1986.

"ROMAN DU PARAPLUIE PERDU" (1982). Poem. A messenger asks various people where the umbrella is that Samuel Ward* borrowed from Longfellow and either lost or mislaid. Longfellow sent the poem, composed of four five-line doggerel stanzas, as a letter to Ward (31 Dec 1873).

Bibliography: Hilen, ed.

"RONDEL" (1845, BY CHARLES D'ORLÉANS). *See* "Rondel: Hence, Away . . ."

"RONDEL" (1831, BY JEAN FROISSART). *See* "Rondel: Love, Love . . ."

"RONDEL: HENCE, AWAY . . ." (1845). Poem, translated from the French poet Charles d'Orléans (1391–1465), in Longfellow's edition of *Poems and Poetry of Europe;* Scudder. The poet tells "Carking care and melancholy" to get out. He intends for reason to "have the mastery."

"RONDEL: LOVE, LOVE . . ." (1831). Poem, translated from the French author Jean Froissart (1338–1410?), in *NAR,* Apr 1831; Scudder. Addressing his beloved, the poet is uncertain whether to "be mute, or vows with prayers combine." This, because he sees nothing "fixed," "sure," or "permanent" in her; so he asks, "Love, love, what wilt thou with this heart of mine?"

"THE ROPEWALK" (1858). Poem, in *Courtship, Birds* (1858). Inspired by his recollection of the mill in Portland, Maine, in which workers wove ropes, Longfellow spins, spider-like, "Cobwebs brighter and more fine" and while doing so imagines different uses for the ropes the workers produce. Two girls in a swing laugh at the shadow they make on the grass beneath. A circus girl, "in spangled dress," is "posed high in air." A farm woman draws water from her well. An old bell ringer in a tower tugs on his rope. In the yard of a prison is a gallows with a noose. A boy flies his kite with a strand. Horses are pursued with lassoes. Hunters make snares. Fishermen have their lines. Sailors drag their anchors, "feeling for the land." Made sleepy by the mill wheel's "dreamy sound," the poet "All these things . . . behold[s]." It has been suggested that whereas the picture of the "faded loveliness" of the "weary" female aerialist is inappropriate, Longfellow's desire that "Breath of Christian charity [should] . . . / Blow, and sweep it [the gallows] from the earth!" is right on.

Bibliography: Wagenknecht, 1986.

"A ROSARY OF SONNETS" (1877). Five sonnets, in *AM,* Mar 1877. I. "Nature." II. "In the Churchyard in Tarrytown." III. "Eliot's Oak." IV. "The Descent of the Muses." V. "Venice" (also in *Youth's Companion* [22 Mar 1877]).

S

"THE SAGA OF KING OLAF." *See* "The Musician's Tale," in *Tales of a Wayside Inn,* Part First.

"SAGGI DE' NOVELLIERI ITALIANI D'OGNI SECOLO" (1832). Reader that Longfellow prepared for his Bowdoin students.

"ST. JOHN'S, CAMBRIDGE" (1878). Sonnet, in *Kéramos.* The poet stands beneath a tree. Its branches provide shade for the west window of the Chapel of St. John. Its leaves whisper a prayer for the mason who laid the chapel stones. This causes the poet to recall the coming of the Son of God during "the world's darkest hour." The poet sees him, as he waits to hear not only the apostles' words about "love and light" but also what the leaves say about the abiding peace of God.

SALES, FRANCIS (1771–1854). Professor. Sales, born near Perpignan, France, migrated to the United States when he was twenty. He was teaching French and Spanish at Harvard when Longfellow became Smith Professor of Modern Languages there (1836) and hence was Sales's academic supervisor. Sales published language textbooks and an edition of *Don Quijote de la Mancha* (1836). Years later Longfellow learned that Sales was old and ill. So he initiated a drive (May 1851) to obtain a purse for him and, with a letter in gracious Spanish closing "de / Algunos amigos y discípulos" (12 de Junio de 1851), sent him $200 in gold, so that he could spend the summer resting at the seashore. A journal entry (15 Feb 1854) reveals that Longfellow visited Sales when the old professor was dying: "He clasped both my hands and said in a feeble voice, 'Kiss me,' and then, Don't forget me'; and I took my leave of him forever." All of this is an instance, among scores, of Longfellow's friendly, loyal, and generous nature.

Bibliography: Hilen, ed.

"SALUTATORY ORATION IN LATIN—ANGLI POETAE" (1824). Oration. Longfellow delivered this speech at part of the "Exercises at Exhibition, October 29, 1824," at Bowdoin College. "De Patribus Conscriptis Romanorum (of Roman senators)," by Nathaniel Hawthorne,* came later in the ceremony.

Bibliography: Hilen, ed.

"SANDALPHON" (1858). Poem, in *AM,* Apr 1858; *Courtship, Birds* (1858). Have you ever read about Sandalphon, the angel of glory and of prayer? He stood near the "Celestial City," beside "the ladder of light" that only Jacob could see, and then only while he was slumbering. Sandalphon stands now, with dead angels all about, and listens serenely "To sounds that ascend from below." He hears the prayers of heartbroken, weary people. As he gathers their prayers, they turn into flowers, and their fragrance wafts into the streets of the city. This account is only a rabbinical legend, of course; but its beauty is haunting. So, as the poet looks through his window at night, he sees Sandalphon amid the "throbbing and panting . . . stars." This legend, grasped at by those who are hungry, thirsty, feverish, and pained, resembles "forbidden" fruit and "The golden pomegranates of Eden." Each of the nine stanzas comprising "Sandalphon" rhymes *aabccb,* with each rhyme being hauntingly feminine. In advertisements, the poem was sometimes titled "Sandalphon, the Angel of Prayer."

Bibliography: Arvin; Wagenknecht, 1986.

"SAND OF THE DESERT IN AN HOUR-GLASS" (1850). Poem, in *S/F.* In his hourglass the poet sees sand from an Arabian desert. It spies for time and encourages thought. This sand could tell about Ishmaelites' camels, Moses's burned feet, the wheels of pharaohs, Mary holding the infant Nazarene in her arms, anchorites from near the Dead Sea, caravans from Bassora, pilgrims heading to Mecca. All these may have trod this sand, now captured here. As the poet gazes through the glass, he sees desert and "unimpeded sky" beyond. The tiny "golden thread" of sand expands into a frightening column. It runs with its shadow across a plain that thought cannot pursue. The vision ends. Thirty minutes have run by.

Bibliography: Arvin; Wagenknecht, 1986.

"SAN MIGUEL, THE CONVENT (SAN MIGUEL DE LA TUMBA)." Poem, translated from the Spanish poet Gonzalo de Berceo (1180?–after 1246), in Scudder. Within the walls of the wild convent of San Miguel de la Tumba, surrounded by the groaning sea, "pious, fasting monks" have built an altar to the Virgin Mother and her Child. Beside their figures, "kings and wise men of the East" have knelt. Beneath the Holy Mother's face is a fan. It was for keeping flies away and is made of glistening peacock feathers. One night, because of "the people's sins," a bolt of lightning smashed the convent's four walls and burned up robes, missals, and sacred books. The monks barely escaped with their lives. But the fire never touched the Virgin Mother, her Child, or the feathery fan. Nor did smoke even reach them, any more "Than the bishop hight Don Tello has been

hurt by hand of mine." Longfellow included his translation of this poem in his edition of *Poets and Poetry of Europe.*

"SANTA FILOMENA" (1857). Poem, anonymously, in *AM,* Nov 1857 (*AM'*s first issue); *Courtship, Birds* (1858). Noble deeds and nobly expressed thoughts lift us above "meaner cares." The poet thinks about all this while he reads about starved and frozen dead soldiers, and about the wounded lying in "cheerless corridors" of "dreary hospitals." Suddenly he sees "A lady with a lamp," whose shadow "speechless sufferer[s] . . . kiss." Her passing by seems to open heaven's door. England's history will record Saint Filomena's goodness and nobility. This is Longfellow's tribute to Florence Nightingale (1820–1910), "Philomela" being Latin for nightingale.

Bibliography: Wagenknecht, 1986; Williams.

"SANTA TERESA'S BOOK-MARK" (1871). Poem, translated from the Spanish of Saint Teresa (1515–82), in the Supplement to Longfellow's edition of *Poets and Poetry of Europe; Three.* The bookmark should not be disturbed or frightened. Everything but God changes. Patience "Attaineth to all things." Those who possess God lack nothing.

THE SATURDAY CLUB. A Boston literary club. Horatio Woodman (1821–79), a lawyer, publishing agent, and friend of many men in Boston's and Harvard's intellectual community, suggested (1855) having a small group of friends meet one Saturday a month at Parker's Hotel, for fine food, drink, and talk. At the outset, two clubs developed— one to socialize, the other to plan a literary magazine. The original 11 members included Longfellow's friends Louis Agassiz,* Richard Henry Dana Jr.,* and James Russell Lowell* (as of 1856). In 1857, the men called their club the Saturday Club, established their magazine, which they called the *Atlantic Monthly,* and invited Cornelius Conway Felton,* Oliver Wendell Holmes,* and Longfellow to become members. More members were added later, including the following close friends of Longfellow: William Hickling

Prescott* (1858), John Greenleaf Whittier* (1858), Thomas Gold Appleton* (1859), Nathaniel Hawthorne* (1859), Charles Eliot Norton* (1860), Samuel Gridley Howe* (1861), Charles Sumner* (1862), and James T. Fields* (1864). By 1870 the early phase of the Saturday Club was at an end. William Dean Howells* was elected (1874).

Bibliography: Emerson, Edward Waldo. *The Early Years of the Saturday Club, 1855-1870.* Boston and New York: Houghton Mifflin, 1918.

"SCANDERBEG." *See* "The Spanish Jew's Second Tale," in *Tales of a Wayside Inn,* Part Third.

SCHERB, EMMANUEL VITALIS (?–?). Swiss poet, lecturer, and critic. Scherb migrated to the United States (mid-1840s). Longfellow, according to his journal (8 May 1848), welcomed a visit from Scherb, identifies him only as "a poet from Basle," says he supposedly "has a tragedy on the *Bauernkrieg* [peasants' war] in his inkstand," and adds that the two "had much talk about the German poets." Scherb came to tea and recited "some of the Psalms, in Hebrew," which Longfellow goes on to describe as a "strange, mysterious language, building up its poems with square blocks of sound" (8 Nov 1849). Longfellow attended Scherb's lecture titled "Dante and the Worship of the Virgin" but objects to his "overstepping the bonds of reasonable, temperate warmth, into the tropics of a rather wild growth of enthusiasm" (1 Dec 1849). One evening, Scherb enjoyed conversation about Alfred, Lord Tennyson* with Charles Sumner* at the Longfellows' home, then "read some of his [Scherb's] poems with great enthusiasm of delight" (22 Dec 1850). Over tea at Longfellow's, Scherb reported that an assistant of Samuel Gridley Howe* "read . . . Evangeline on her fingers to Laura Bridgman" (23 Jan 1852). Laura Dewey Bridgman (1829-89) was a pupil, deaf, dumb, and blind, of Longfellow's friend Howe. Scherb taught modern literature courses (early 1850s) at Franklin College (now University of Georgia, Athens). Probably in part owing to Longfellow's recommendation, Scherb was appointed to give eight lectures at the Lowell Institute, Boston, on modern religious and philosophical poems (Mar–Apr 1856). Longfellow's journal sheds further light on Scherb. He suggested that Longfellow "write a poem on the Puritans and the Quakers," which Longfellow agreed was "A good subject for a tragedy" (16 Mar 1856). The indirect result was "Giles Corey and the Salem Farms" (1868). (*See The New England Tragedies,* part of *Christus: A Mystery.*) The Longfellows had Scherb, James T. Fields,* Frederick Swartwout Cozzens (1818-69), who had just published *The Sparrowgrass Papers; or, Living in the Country* (1856), and a few others as dinner guests (12 May 1856). When Scherb wrote Longfellow (1 Sep 1857) that he was ill in Portland, Longfellow wrote his brother Alexander (5 Sep) asking him to visit Scherb and provide him all the money he needed for treatment; Longfellow sent Alexander (1 Oct) $130 to cover any such gifts. Longfellow admired Scherb's essay "Dante's Beatrice as a Type of Womanhood" (*Christian Examiner,* Jan 1858). Scherb spoke in English (16 Nov 1859) at a festival at Boston's Music Hall to commemorate the hundredth birthday of Johann Christoph Friedrich von Schiller (1759-1805). Longfellow's wife hardly shared her husband's tolerance of Scherb, about whom little is now known. In her journal, she notes that "George Sumner dines with us every Wednesday, and Scherb (who is a bore and self-invited) every Monday" (15 May 1860). The Longfellows' friendship with Scherb cooled (1862), perhaps because he owed them money.

Bibliography: Hilen, ed.; S. Longfellow; *Mrs. Longfellow.*

"THE SCHOOLMASTER" (1831–33). Series of six sketches, each titled "The Schoolmaster," in *NEM* some of which Longfellow used in *Outre-Mer,* as follows: 1 Jul 1831— one paragraph; 1 Sep 1831—revised and becoming the chapter titled "The Norman Diligence"; Apr 1832—subtitled "The Village of Auteuil," slightly revised and becoming the chapter titled "The Village of Auteuil"; Jul 1832—subtitled "Recollections of the Metropolis," about Paris, not used; Oct 1832— story translated from Germain François Poullain de Saint-Foix (1698–1776), not used; Feb 1833—subtitled "The Walk Continued" used as part of the chapter titled "Père La Chaise."

Bibliography: Thompson.

SCUDDER, HORATIO (1838–1902). (Full name: Horatio Elisha Scudder.) Editor and author. Scudder was born in Boston, Massachusetts, the son of a successful merchant, and Sarah Lathrop Coit Scudder. He attended local Latin schools and Williams College (graduating 1858). Suffering from chronic, intermittent deafness, he tutored in Brooklyn, read in Manhattan, wrote a few articles, and anonymously published *Seven Little People and Their Friends* (1862), his first juvenile book—and a big success. When his father died (1863), Scudder returned to Boston to become the family leader. The year 1864 was pivotal. In it he published a biography of his brother, David Coit Scudder, a Congregational missionary who had drowned in India two years earlier. Scudder also published *Dream Children,* another novel for young readers, and an essay on William Blake for the *North American Review.* And he became literary adviser for the Boston publishing firm Hurd & Houghton, for which he founded and edited the *Riverside Magazine for Young People* (1867), until it was absorbed by *Scribner's Magazine* (1870). While Hurd & Houghton was evolving into Houghton, Osgood & Co. (1878) and then Houghton, Mifflin & Co. (1880), Scudder worked for the firm in editorial, advisory, and managerial assignments (to 1890). Meanwhile, he married Grace Owen (1873), had two children with her, wrote eight more juvenile books featuring "the Bodley family" (1875–85), and edited successful anthologies of six American poets (1879), eight American prose writers (1880), and a potpourri for children (1881). When William Dean Howells* resigned (1881) as editor of *Atlantic Monthly,* which Houghton, Mifflin published, Scudder wanted the job; but the popular Thomas Bailey Aldrich (1836–1907) was chosen instead. Biding his time, Scudder wrote biographies of Noah Webster (1882), Bayard Taylor* (2 vols., 1884, coauthored with Tay-

lor's widow), and George Washington (1889), juvenile histories of the United States (1884, 1890), and *Men and Letters: Essays in Characterization and Criticism* (1887), and edited the works of Longfellow (1886) and of William Makepeace Thackeray* (1889). Scudder became editor of the *Atlantic Monthly* (1890), for which he accepted works by a stream of up-and-coming American authors and for which he also wrote an astounding 185 reviews and articles. At the same time, he continued to edit trade books of works by authors too numerous to list but including John Greenleaf Whittier* (1895), James Russell Lowell* (1897), and Nathaniel Hawthorne* (1901). His last book was a biography of Lowell (1901).

Longfellow evidently had only indirect connections, at most, with Scudder. But Scudder did much to popularize and make widely available Longfellow's works, edited many of them, and also made astute editorial and annotative comments on them.

Bibliography: Ballou, Ellen B. *The Building of the House: Houghton Mifflin's Formative Years.* Boston: Houghton Mifflin, 1970; Howe, M. A. DeWolfe. *The Atlantic Monthly and Its Makers.* Boston: Atlantic Monthly Press, 1919; Wagenknecht, 1955; Wagenknecht, 1986.

"THE SEA-DIVER" (1825). Poem (as "The Sea Diver"), in *USLG,* 15 Aug 1825; Scudder. The dark-winged, mist-cleaving bird says that he has listened to "the sea-shell breathe" over "living myriads," which are surrounded by coral, pearls, and sea grapes, and are far down in "the splendid deep." He once flew on "storm-drench'd wing" over "a helmless bark," which sank "without a signal-gun." Its sailors' hearts stopped beating, although the ocean's heart did not. Peace to them under "the bright and silver sea." They descended without "vain pride and pageantry." Longfellow wrote James T. Fields* (12 Apr 1852) asking him to omit this poem from the 1852 London edition of *The Poetical Works of Henry Wadsworth Longfellow.*

"THE SEA HATH ITS PEARLS" (1845). Poem, translated from the German poet

Heinrich Heine (1797–1856), in *Bruges*. The sea has pearls. The heavens have stars. The poet's heart has love. The sea and the heavens are great, but the poet's heart is greater, and his love "flashes and beams" more beautifully than pearls or stars. Young girl, enter my heart, which, together with the sea and the heavens, is "melting away with love!"

THE SEASIDE AND THE FIRESIDE (1850). Collection of poems: *By the Seaside:* "The Building of the Ship," "The Evening Star," "The Secret of the Sea," "Twilight," "Sir Humphrey Gilbert," "The Lighthouse," "The Fire of Driftwood." *By the Fireside:* "Resignation," "Sand of the Desert in an Hour-Glass," "Birds of Passage," "The Open Window," "King Witlaw's Drinking-Horn," "Gaspar Becerra," "Pegasus in Pound," "Tegnér's Death," "Sonnet on Mrs. Kemble's Readings from Shakespeare," "The Singers," "Suspiria," "Hymn for My Brother's Ordination," "The Blind Girl of Castèl Cuillè," "A Christmas Carol from the Noel Bourguignon de Gui Barozia (I hear along our street . . .)."

"SEAWEED" (1845). Poem, in *GM,* Jan 1845; *S/F.* Equinoctial storms stir the Atlantic, which, surging and laden with seaweed, lashes the shores. Oceanic currents bring it from Bermuda, the Azores, the Bahamas, San Salvador, the Orkneys, and the Hebrides, and from shipwrecks. Whatever the waves bear rests eventually in coves and "reaches / Of sandy beaches." Similarly, stormy emotions lash the poet's soul, and from caves and rocks come "fragment[s] of . . . song[s]." They also come from faraway islands which "Heaven has planted / With the golden fruit of Truth," and from surfs near "the tropic clime of Youth." Willpower and effort "Wrestle with the tides of Faith," and wrecked hopes float desolately. Like "Currents of the main" are "Currents of the restless heart." In time, though, the heart's burdens are recorded in books, and then "no more depart." Longfellow's description of the turbulent ocean, burdened with seaweed, is more satisfying than his attempt to equate poetry with seaweed.

Bibliography: von Abele, Rudolph. "A Note on Longfellow's Poetics." *American Literature* 24

(Mar 1952): 77–82; Arms; Arvin; Wagenknecht, 1986.

"A SECOND PSALM OF LIFE: THE LIGHT OF STARS." *See* "The Light of Stars."

"THE SECRET OF THE SEA" (1850). Poem, in *S/F.* When the poet looks at the sea, legends and dreams return to him. He thinks about old ships and sailors' songs, especially the Spanish ballad about Count Arnaldos. The count had a hawk on his hand when he saw "a stately galley / Steering onward to the land." An old helmsman was chanting a wild song so beautifully that a seabird lit on the mast to listen. Arnaldos begged the helmsman to teach him that wonderful song. The helmsman replied that "Only those who brave . . . [the] dangers [of the secretive sea] / Comprehend its mystery!" The poet also now sees "that stately galley" and "Hear[s] those mournful melodies," and his soul now longs to fathom the ocean's pulsing heart.

Bibliography: Arvin; Wagenknecht, 1986.

"SERENADE." *See* "Stars of the Summer Night."

"THE SERMON OF ST. FRANCIS" (1875). Poem, *Pandora, Birds* (1875). St. Francis heard the song of an upsoaring lark. To him the lark symbolized the upward-moving seraphim, seeking light, warmth, and "the heart's desire." Birds from near and far came to Assisi's gate in search of crumbs from Francis. He replied that the birds would be fed that day not with bread alone, but from God through him with the "manna of celestial words." Francis said that the birds should sing their Creator's praise. He gave them their crimson and brown plumage, wings to seek out "purer air," and no cause to worry. The birds flew up and sang, all right; but the saint wonders if they understood his "homily." At any rate, he "knew that . . . one ear" did.

SEVEN SONNETS AND A CANZONE, FROM THE ITALIAN OF MICHAEL ANGELO (1878). *See Kéramos and Other Poems.*

"A SHADOW" (1875). Sonnet, in *Pandora, Birds* (1875). At first the poet wonders what fate would befall his children if he should die. "Their lives, I said, / Would be a volume," of which he could have read only the beginning, and its later chapters would contain both "beauty" and "dread." But then he feels comforted by the knowledge that generations come and go in this old world, that the world "belongs to those who come the last," and that "They will find hope and strength as we have done."

"SHAKESPEARE" (1875). Sonnet, *Pandora, Birds* (1875). The poet has a vision of streets crowded with people, of battle trumpets, of sailors landing safely, of bells, of children and flowers. All this when he opens "The volume of the Poet paramount." All the muses loved him, gave him a golden lyre and "sacred laurel," and "Placed him as Musagetes on their throne." Musagetes is an epithet of Apollo as leader of the nine muses. A New York bookworm named Rebekah Owen (1858-1939) wrote Longfellow (18 Nov 1879) objecting to his assigning "Voices of children" to Shakespeare's presentation of life and offered "Voices of lovers" instead. Longfellow replied to her (18 Nov 1879), agreed that her emendation was "a decided improvement," but never made the change—either because he never intended to do so or because he died before he could thus revise and then republish his sonnet.

Bibliography: More; Weber, Carl J., "Rebekah Corrects a Sonnet of Longfellow's." *New England Quarterly* 14 (Mar 1941): 141-44.

"SICILIAN CANZONET" (1832). Poem, translated from an anonymous Italian poem, in *NAR,* Oct 1832; Scudder. The poet begs Nici to say whether she will respond to his love with "love or hate."

"THE SIEGE OF KAZAN" (1870). Poem, translated from the prose version of the Polish poet Aleksander Chodzko (1804?-91), in *AM,* Sep 1870; *Three.* The persona looks at "the moors before Kazan," smells blood in "their stagnant waters," but determines to swim through its shallows "with horse and man." When he looks back, he sees that his followers had all "sunk in the black morass!" He knows that his "maidens fair" are imprisoned. They cannot be heard, because on this "black day" his horses and men are "buried deep in the dark abyss!"

"THE SIFTING OF PETER" (1880). Poem, in *Harper's New Monthly Magazine,* Mar 1880; *Thule.* In the gospel of Luke is the account of how Peter thrice denied Christ. Ages later, Satan tempts everyone to deny "The Man of Sorrows, crucified and bleeding." When we observe his suffering, we will feel that weakness is a disgrace, conceit will turn meek, and wounded souls will heal. Their scars will remain and "make / Confession." Be aware that

> Lost innocence returns no more;
> We are not what we were before
> Transgression.

However, "noble souls" emerge out of "disaster and defeat," stand upright with new strength, and feel "the divine / Within them." Longfellow was paid $200 for this poem.

Bibliography: Hilen, ed.

"SILENT LOVE" (1845). Poem, translated from an anonymous German work, in *Poets and Poetry of Europe,* ed. Longfellow. If you want love, then love quietly. If you don't let "Silence . . . reign," love will pain your heart.

"THE SINGERS" (1850). Poem, in *S/F.* God sent singers to sing about "sadness and . . . mirth" to touch people's hearts and return them to heaven. A youth sings about dreams. A bearded fellow sings stirring songs in the marketplace. A gray old fellow sings in church to the accompaniment of the organ. When listeners wonder who sings the best, "the Master" replies that the "great chords" of the three, singing "To charm, to strengthen, and to teach," combine into "perfect harmony." To a query from an Englishwoman identified as H. M. Bird, Longfellow replied by letter (9 Dec 1880) that this poem was not about any three different poets but about "classes [of poetry] only,—the Lyric, the Epic, and the Devotional or Didactic."

Bibliography: Arms; Hilen, ed.

"SIR HUMPHREY GILBERT" (1848).
Poem, in *GM,* Jun 1848; *S/F.* Sir Humphrey
Gilbert, this "corsair of Death," sails his icy
fleet southward. It is glistening, misty, and
dripping with rain. Then east from Campo-
bello. After three days, no land wind. Sir
Humphrey sits on deck, with a book, and
says, "Heaven is as near / . . . by water as by
land!" Suddenly at night, Death's fleet of
ships rises and surrounds him, its masts rak-
ing the clouds under moon and evening star.
They grapple with Sir Humphrey's vessel,
embrace it, and all drift southward "through
day and dark," until they vanish and sink,
together, "like a dream, in the Gulf-Stream."
Sir Humphrey Gilbert (c.1539–83), English
navigator, soldier, and half-brother of Sir
Walter Raleigh, established the first British
colony in North America, at St. John's, New-
foundland (1583). While he was trying to
return to England aboard the ten-ton frigate
Squirrel and accompanied by the *Golden
Hind,* a forty-ton frigate, a tempest off the
Azores threatened both ships. Humphrey refused to transfer to the *Hind,* shouted to her
captain, "We are as near to heaven by sea as
by land," and soon sank.

"THE SKELETON IN ARMO[U]R" (1841).
Poem, in *KM,* Jan 1841; *Ballads.* The poet
asks a guest, who approaches "in rude armor dressed" and with "fleshless palms"
reaching out, "Why dost thou haunt me?"
The dull-voiced creature replies that he has
sought out the poet and threatens him with
a curse unless "in thy verse / Thou dost the
tale rehearse." The woeful story follows. He
was a Viking. As a child he trained gerfal-
cons, skated, hunted bears, and followed
larks. When of age, he joined "a corsair's
crew" and became a murderous pirate and
a hearty wassailer. Then, one day, he and a
"blue-eyed maid" fell in love, until,

> Under its loosened vest
> Fluttered her little breast,
> Like birds within their nest
> By the hawk frightened.

When he asked her father, the aged Norseman Hildebrand, for her hand in marriage,
he was refused, since "She was a Prince's
child, / I but a Viking wild." Oh, the father's
friends should have guarded that little dove's

nest! Escaping by sea, the pair were followed by Hildebrand and 20 of his men,
pledged to kill the Viking. He rammed and
sank the enemy vessel, sped like a "fierce
cormorant" ever westward for three weeks,
voyaged through a hurricane, and finally
made landfall. He built his lady a "lofty
tower" for her bower, and they lived there
for years and years. Her tears dried. Her fears
vanished. She became a mother. But she
died, and he buried her under "that tower."
His heart grew "Still as a stagnant fen." Shun-
ning all companionship, he donned his armor, entered "the vast forest here," and fell
on his spear. His soul burst through his
battle-scarred body, ascended "to its native
stars," and now drinks "from the flowing
bowl" and shouts *Skoal!* to the Northland!"

Longfellow recorded in his journal (24
May 1839) that he told Cornelius Conway
Felton* about his "plan of a heroic poem on
the Discovery of America by the Northmen,
in which the Round Tower at Newport and
the Skeleton in Armor have a part to play."
Bones had been recently discovered, were
called "the Fall River [Massachusetts] skeleton," were thought to be those of a Norseman, and had a brass breastplate; Longfellow saw the skeleton (1848). For his poem,
Longfellow borrowed the rollicking meter
of "The Battle of Agincourt" (c. 1605) by Michael Drayton. He ignored the advice not
only of Felton but also that of Charles Sumner* not to publish "The Skeleton in Armor,"
since it had no moral message. Samuel
Ward,* however, was excited by the poem,
and arranged for it to be accepted, for $25,
and published. In its first form, Longfellow
included marginal notes (dropped later), in
obvious imitation of similar notes alongside
"The Rime of the Ancient Mariner" by Samuel Taylor Coleridge. Longfellow's poem remains one of his most effective early works.

Bibliography: Arvin; Hatfield, Robert Griffith.
"The 'Old Mill' at Newport: A New Study of an
Old Puzzle." *Scribner's Monthly Magazine* 17
(Mar 1879): 532–641; Hilen; Thornstenberg, Ed-
ward. "'The Skeleton in Armor' and the *Frithiof
Saga.*" *Modern Language Notes* 25 (Jun 1910):
189–92; S. Longfellow; Wagenknecht, 1986.

"THE SLAVE IN THE DISMAL SWAMP."
See Poems on Slavery.

"THE SLAVE'S DREAM." *See Poems on Slavery.*

"THE SLAVE SINGING AT MIDNIGHT." *See Poems on Slavery.*

"A SLEDGE-RIDE ON THE ICE" (1837). Poem, translated from the Swedish poet Esaias Tegnér,* in *NAR,* Jul 1837; Scudder. Even though a stranger warns him about thin ice. King Ring, accompanied by his reluctant queen, takes his horse-drawn sledge onto the "mirror-clear" ice. Meanwhile, the stranger, shod with steel shoes, passes them easily and even "carves many runes" on the ice, while "Fair Ingeborg o'er her own name doth glide." *See Drift-Wood.*

"SLEEP" (1875). Sonnet, in *Pandora, Birds* (1875). The poet asks the winds of sleep to lull him and "Seal up the wakeful eyes of thought." He is "weary, and . . . overwrought / With too much toil." He feels "distraught" and anguished. He asks sleep to caress his face and induce "uninterrupted breath." The Greeks were correct when they called sleep "the lesser mystery at the feast / Whereof the greater mystery is death!"

Bibliography: Reed, Kenneth T. "Longfellow's 'Sleep' and Frost's 'After Apple-Picking.'" *American Notes and Queries* 10 (May 1972): 134–35.

"SNOW-FLAKES" (1847). *See* "Fragments."

"SNOW-FLAKES" (1863). Poem, in *Tales of a Wayside Inn,* 1863; *Birds* (1863). Snow falls from the air and from clouds on forsaken fields and bare woods. Our fancies and our worried hearts grieve, also, like the sky. This poem, long hoarded, likewise expresses "the secret of despair." "Snow-Flakes," one of Longfellow's most successful poems, follows a typical pattern. It is in three stanzas. The first sketches the natural scene. The second provides the explicit analogy. The third offers the didactic statement.

Bibliography: Arms; Arvin; Wagenknecht, 1955.

"SO FROM THE BOSOM OF DARKNESS OUR DAYS COME ROARING AND GLEAMING." *See* "Fragments."

"SOFT THROUGH THE SILENT AIR DESCEND THE FEATHERY SNOW-FLAKES." *See* "Fragments."

"A SOLDIER'S SONG" (1832). Translated from a Neapolitan song, *NAR,* Oct 1832; Scudder. Who's knocking at my door? Your lover; let me in. I can't; mother's not home; I'll listen at the window. But "My cloak is old, and the wind blows cold, / So open the door to me."

"SOME DAY, SOME DAY." *See* "From the [Spanish] Cancioneros."

"SOMETHING LEFT UNDONE" (1863). Poem, in *Tales of a Wayside Inn,* 1863; *Birds* (1863). Even though we work zealously, we leave some things unfinished. Such assignments wait for us, like beggars. Finally, some chores seem as heavy as the sky that dwarfs in "Northern legends" are said to hold "On their shoulders."

"SONG: AH, LOVE! . . ." (1843). Poem, translated from the Spanish poet Gabriel López Maldonado (?–1615?), in *The Spanish Student* and reprinted in Longfellow's edition of *Poems and Poetry of Europe.* Love is "false, treacherous." It betrays those faithful to it. We should see through its deceits, because it is "Thorns below, and flowers above!"

"SONG: AND WHITHER GOEST THOU, GENTLE SIGH . . . ?" (1835). Sonnet, translated from an unidentified French source, in *Outre-Mer;* Scudder. The poet asks the "gentle sigh" if it is proceeding to some martyred lover. If so, pray "Pierce deep,—but oh! forbear to kill."

"SONG: HARK! HARK!" (1831). Poem, translated from "The Paradise of Love," an anonymous French poem, in *NAR,* Apr 1831; Scudder. The pretty lark sings away but pays little attention to the poet's pain. He would be happy if his love would smile and yield. He languishes but remains faithful. It would be acceptable if his love would even frown at him again. The lark chirps away, heedless of "my pain!"

"SONG: IF THOU ART SLEEPING, MAIDEN" (1835).

Poem, translated from the Portuguese poet Gil Vicente (1470?–1536), in *The Spanish Student* and reprinted in Longfellow's edition of *Poets and Poetry of Europe.* The poet at dawn asks his "maiden" to wake up, open the door, and not bother with slippers. The two have to "pass through the dewy grass, / And waters wide and fleet."

"SONG: LET THEM KNOW, MY NOBLE BARONS" (1871).

Poem, translated from a poem in Provençal by Richard I, the Lion-Hearted (1157–99), while he was imprisoned; in the Supplement to *Poets and Poetry of Europe,* ed. Longfellow. The captive hero tells his "noble barons" to remind everyone that he would buy the freedom of the lowliest "yeoman." He tells his friendly troubadours to relay this message to the enemy: It is not brave to blow out a dim candle; fighting a chained enemy brings "more shame than glory."

Bibliography: Hilen, ed.

"SONG: MURMURING WIND THAT EVERYWHERE" (1982).

Poem, translated from a Spanish poem. The sad persona asks the wind to make restful music, through the leaves, for his fair lady, who is sleeping. Longfellow sent this poem in a letter (25 Apr 1877) addressed to Clara Kathleen Barnett (*see* Doria, Clara).

Bibliography: Hilen, ed.

THE SONG OF HIAWATHA (1855).

Epical, lyrical poem. It contains an "Introduction" and 22 numbered and titled cantos.

"Introduction": If asked about sources of these stories, legends, and traditions, the poet would say that they arose from the prairies, North-Land lakes, Ojibway and Dacotahs, mountains, moors, and swamps where the Shuh-shuh-gah, the heron, lives; and that he heard them repeated by Nawadaha, the sweet-singing musician. He derived them from beavers' lodges, tracks of the bison, and many nests and songs of birds. Nawadaha lived in the green, silent Tawasentha valley, near Indian villages, well watered, forested, and beautiful through the changing seasons. He sang of Hiawatha, of his birth, prayers, fastings, and labors to "advance his people." You lovers of Nature, listen to this song of "wild traditions." It tells of the blind gropings of those with "human heart[s]" in "savage bosoms," as they longed, yearned, and strove for the uncomprehended good. This song resembles half-legible inscriptions in country churchyards, "Written with little skill of song-craft" but telling much "Of the Here and the Hereafter."

I. "The Peace-Pipe": Gitchie Manito, "the Master of Life," wants all tribes to assemble, traces rivers through meadows, makes a peace pipe out of red stone broken from a quarry, fills it with willow bark, breathes fiery life into a forest for a light, and smokes his calumet. An enormous cloud ascends as a signal summoning tribes from Tawasentha, Wyoming, Tuscaloosa, the Rocky Mountains, and Northern bodies of water. From prairies and rivers come Delawares, Mohawks, Choctaws, Comanches, Shoshonies, Blackfeet, Pawnees, Omahas, Mandans, Dacotahs, Hurons, and Ojibways—all armed, defiant, full of old hatreds and thirsting for revenge. Wise Gitchie Manito warns, chides, and urges his "poor children," to whom he has given fish, bear, bison, roe, reindeer, brant, beaver, and wild birds, to stop quarreling with , seeking out, and killing each other, and instead to live in peace. Sending a prophet to them, he says this:

> If you listen to his counsels,
> You will multiply and prosper;
> If his warnings pass unheeded,
> You will fade away and perish!

Following his orders, they wash off their war paint, bury their weapons, make peace pipes from the quarry and smoke them together, bedeck themselves with feathers, and return to their homes. Gitchie Manito, the mighty creator, smiles on "his helpless children!"

This episode is based on Longfellow's reading of *Letters and Notes* by George Catlin. (For bibliographical details concerning Catlin and other sources Longfellow consulted in writing *Hiawatha,* see below.)

II. "The Four Winds": The warriors praise Mudjekeewis for stealing the sacred wampum belt from the bear Mishe-Mokwa as he slept, "Like a rock with mosses on it," in the North-Wind region. It seems that Mudjekeewis smote the bear between the eyes with his club, woke him up, taunted him for whimpering like a woman, boasted of the recent unification of the formerly rival tribes, and killed the bear with another blow. The people rename Mudjekeewis "the West-Wind," Kabeyun, the father of all heavenly winds. He keeps the West-Wind for himself, and the other winds for his children. Thus, Wabun gets the East-Wind, Shawondasee the South, and ferocious Kabibonoppa the vicious North-Wind. Wabun is beautiful, brings lovely dawn, has his face painted crimson, and calls both deer and hunter. Now lonely, Wabun sees a solitary maiden in a meadow, is attracted to her blue eyes—lakes gazing in return at him—descends from heaven and wooes her with sighing music and sweet fragrances, enfolds her in his rosy robe, and rises and transforms her into the Star of Morning. Wild Kabibonoppa paints the trees with autumnal colors, sends hissing snow through them, and drives the birds away. Among reedy vegetation he finds Shingebis, the brave diver, trailing his catch of fish through deserted moorlands. He rebukes Shingebis for staying around and shakes down his smoky lodge. But Shingebis merely laughs, turns the log in his fire, cooks and eats some fish, and calls Kabibonoppa nothing but his "fellow-mortal." Kabibonoppa rushes in, cannot stand the heat and merriment, and stamps off. Shingebis follows and wrestles naked with him in the chilly fens until, bewildered and defeated, he retreats north to the land of the White Rabbit. Shawondasee is listless "In the drowsy, dreamy sunshine, / In the never-ending Summer." He sends various birds and fruits to the North-Land and even provides its "rugged hills" with Indian Summer. Shawondasee, though lazy, has a unique sorrow. He once saw a tall prairie maiden with yellow hair standing in sunshine and greenery, was too careless to do more than gaze—until one day he saw her covered with snow, then gone, and therefore passionately accused his brother Kabibonoppa of frosting her and stealing her. But not so. It was not a woman he saw but the prairie dandelion,

which he "puffed away forever" by sighing toward it. Thus were the Four Winds divided and stationed "At the corners of the heavens," with stalwart Mudjekeewis keeping the West-Wind as his own.

This canto contains material Longfellow found in several works by Henry Rowe Schoolcraft and in *A Narrative of the Captivity and Adventures of John Tanner* (1830).

III. "Hiawatha's Childhood": One evening Nokomis, married but childless, fell from the moon onto a meadow, gave birth to a beautiful daughter, named her Wenonah, and when she grew slender and tall, and displayed moonlit and starlit beauty, warned her to beware of the West-Wind, Mudjekeewis. While he was walking over the prairies he came upon Wenonah and wooed her successfully with sweet words and gentle caresses. In "love and sorrow" she bore the wondrous Hiawatha and died. Sad Nokomis wept for her abandoned, dead daughter; though old, she reared Hiawatha in her wigwam, called him her "little owlet," and taught him about the stars, Ishkoodah the fiery comet, and flaring plume-like lights in the northern sky. The boy listened in rapture to nature's varied sounds, especially when a pine tree whispered "Minne-wawa." He watched the fireflies, saw the moon and rainbows, and learned the language and secrets of birds and animals. Iagoo, the well-traveled, boastful storyteller, made Hiawatha a bow of ash and arrows of oak, well tipped and feathered, and with a deerskin cord. Hiawatha, sent out to kill a red deer, spared birds and little animals along the way, and spied a deer. As he shot, it "Leaped as if to meet the arrow." Hiawatha proudly returned with it and hosted a village banquet. His guests "Called him Strong-Heart, Soan-ge-taha."

Hiawatha, introduced here, is based on the semidivine Native American culture hero, known by the Algonquins as Manabozho and, according to Schoolcraft, by the Iroquois as Tarenyawagon or Hi-a-wat-ha. Hiawatha's birth is described in Schoolcraft's *Algic Researches*. Hiawatha's parents have mythic qualities paralleling those of Väinämöinen, the hero of *Kalevala*.

IV. "Hiawatha and Mudjekeewis": Now behold Hiawatha in glorious manhood. He is

> Skilled in all the craft of hunters,
> Learned in all the lore of old men,
> In all youthful sports and pastimes,
> In all manly arts and labors.

Hiawatha can shoot an arrow and run on ahead of it, can fire 10 arrows into the sky before the first falls to the ground, has deerskin mittens which help him crush rocks, and has deerskin moccasins enabling him to step a mile at a time. When made aware of his father Mudjekeewis's treachery toward his mother Wenonah, Hiawatha's "heart was hot within him, / Like a living coal his heart was." Well-armed, he goes to the North-Wind's sunset portals, outrunning deer and antelope and bison in the process, crossing prairies, and climbing into the Rocky Mountains. He finds Mudjekeewis, with his streaming, "cloudy tresses," and is welcomed, for the father, "lonely" and "frosty," sees the son, who is "lovely" and "fiery." Though irate, Hiawatha silently listens to his father's boasts and learns that only Wawbeek, a nearby black rock, can hurt him. Hiawatha replies that only Apukwa, the bulrush, can hurt him. Mudjekeewis tells Hiawatha about his three brothers, who control, respectively, the east, south, and north winds, and then recalls Hiawatha's mother's beauty. Outraged, the son requires the father to confess, which, now abashed, he does. Hiawatha crushes the black rock with his mittens and hurls the fragments at Mudjekeewis, who merely blows them back, uproots the bulrush, and flourishes it. The two fight. Mudjekeewis retreats for three days, finally to where the sun sinks much the way "a flamingo / Drops into her nest at nightfall." The immortal father says he cannot be killed and persuades his valorous son to return home, clean the earth, clear the waters, and kill all inimical creatures and forces; when the son dies, the father will share his kingdom with him, where the son can rule "the Northwest-Wind, Keewaydin, / . . . the home-wind, the Keewaydin." Hiawatha heads for home, no longer feverish and vengeful, but stops on the way in the Dacotahs, near the Falls of Minnehaha, to buy arrowheads of sharpened sand-

stone, chalcedony, flint, and jasper, from a fabulous arrowmaker. Mostly, however, Hiawatha stays there a while to gaze at the arrowmaker's dark-eyed daughter, Minnehaha, who has swift feet and flowing tresses, smiles and frowns moodily, laughs musically, and glances at him through tree branches. "Who shall say what thoughts and visions / Fill the fiery brains of young men?" Home again, Hiawatha tells his grandmother all about his father but "Not a word of Laughing Water."

V. "Hiawatha's Fasting": Hiawatha prays, not for skill in hunting, fishing, or doing battle, but rather "for profit of the people, / For advantage of the nations." He builds a forest wigwam and begins a seven-day fast. On the first day he wanders in the woods, which are filled with birds and animals, and wonders: "Master of Life! . . . / Must our lives depend on these things?" On the second day he wanders in a meadow of rice and berries and repeats his question. He asks it again on the third day, beside a lake and while observing many fish. On the fourth day he is visited by a youth "Dressed in garments green and yellow," with "soft and golden" hair. He calls himself Mondamin, smiles at Hiawatha, praises his selfless prayer, says "the Master of Life" has sent him here, and tells Hiawatha that he is to gain what he prayed for "by struggle and by labor." The two must wrestle. In doing so, Hiawatha, though feeble at first, gains strength "in his brain and bosom," despite Shuh-shuh-gah, the heron, as it "scream[s] of pain and famine." The next evening, after sunset, and the next evening as well, the two wrestle again, and again the heron screams. Mondamin says that on the seventh day Hiawatha will win the conflict and must strip off Mondamin's green and yellow garments and his plumage, bury him with "Soft and loose and light" earth above him, and keep Kahgahgee, the would-be molesting raven, and also worms and insects, away from his grave. Hiawatha sleeps peacefully; next morning declines food brought by Nokomis, his grandmother, and at sunset defeats and kills Mondamin, though dizzy himself from fasting. He buries his adversary precisely as directed, returns home briefly, and then keeps the grave inviolate as promised. Soon green feathers shoot from the covering soil, and in the summer "Stood the maize in all its beauty." Recognizing the "shining robes" and the "long, soft, yellow tresses" of Mondamin, Hiawatha rightly names him "the friend of man." He calls both Nokomis and boastful Iagoo to him, tells them of his triumph, and explains "this new gift to the nations, / Which should be their food forever." When the crop matures, its "soft and juicy kernels," "This new gift of the Great Spirit," provides "the first Feast of Mondamin."

The ritual of fasting and the legend of Mondamin are in several works by Schoolcraft. Väinämöinen in *Kalevala* introducing his people to barley-corn is echoed, here, in Hiawatha's gift of maize to his people.

VI. "Hiawatha's Friends": Hiawatha's two best friends are Chibiabos, a musician, and Kwasind, an unusually strong man. The three speak to each other in total confidence, "Pondering much and much contriving / How the tribes of men might prosper." When Chibiabos, who "Brave as man is, soft as woman," sings and plays on his homemade flute, animals and waters are quiet, and bluebirds, robins, and whippoorwills ask him to teach them better singing. He softens the hearts of men when he sings of peace, freedom, beauty, love, longing, death and especially life without death

> In the Islands of the Blessed,
> In the kingdom of Ponemah,
> In the land of the Hereafter.

When he was a boy, muscular Kwasind's mother asked him to squeeze her half-frozen fish nets, but in doing so he broke them. His father complained that the boy also broke bows and arrows but still wanted to go hunting with him. When they came upon a log-blocked passage, Kwasind surprised his father by tossing pines and cedars as though they were arrows and lances. When his youthful friends asked Kwasind to toss quoits with them, he instead tossed a gigantic rock into the river. Once, to catch the King of Beavers, he swam underwater to grab and kill it.

In Schoolcraft's *History of the Indian Tribes,* Chibiabos is said to be Manabozho's brother, but his musicianship derives from that of Väinämöinen in *Kalevala.* There are many super-strong men in epic poetry worldwide, but Kwasind's qualities and actions closely parallel some of tough-man Kullervo in *Kalevala.* Kullervo, however, lacks anything like Kwasind's crown, his patch of vulnerability, which makes him akin to Achilles, with vulnerable heel, and Siegfried, with vulnerable back.

VII. "Hiawatha's Sailing": Hiawatha decides to make a canoe. He persuades the reluctant birch to be stripped for a start, a cedar to release boughs for a frame, a larch to give roots for sewing the birch, and a fir for balsam and resin for waterproofing. He gets Kagh, the hedgehog, to shoot out some quills so that Hiawatha can put together a girdle with stars for his beloved. Hiawatha needs no paddles, because his thoughts propel the finished canoe. Kwasind wades ahead of him to clear sunken branches, logs, dead trees, sandbars, and tangled bottom ooze. Thus is "Made a pathway for the people," from mountain springs to Taquamenaw bay.

There are many magic boats in myth and legend. Schoolcraft summarizes the Iroquois legend of Hiawatha's boat. Hiawatha and Väinämöinen build their respective boats in parallel ways, and both steer them by voice command.

VIII. "Hiawatha's Fishing": "Forth upon the Gitche Gumee, / On the shining Big-Sea-Water," Hiawatha goes fishing for the vicious sturgeon, Mishe-Nahma, in his birch canoe, with a cute little squirrel on its bow. Hiawatha sees perch and crawfish, and deep down Nahma, with purple, fanning fins and sand-sweeping tail. His armor-like bones have spikes, and he sports yellow, red, and azure warpaint and brown and sable spots. Seeing Hiawatha afloat above him and hearing his challenge, Nahma orders a pike to grab Hiawatha's bait and break his cedar fishing line. Hiawatha pulls up the pike but releases him. The same thing happens when Nahma sends a sunfish as decoy. Hiawatha shouts defiance; so Nahma wrathfully leaps into the air and swallows Hiawatha, canoe, peppy squirrel, and all. Inside Nahma's dark belly, Hiawatha pounds its throbbing heart and, with the squirrel's help, turns his canoe crosswise for safety. In gratitude, Hiawatha names the squirrel Adjidaumo, meaning "Tail-in-air." Weakened, Nahma beaches itself amid grating pebbles ashore and dies. Friendly seagulls see Hiawatha through the fish's ribs, and peck and claw its flesh until Hiawatha and Adjidaumo are freed. Hiawatha praises the seagulls, lets them feed all they wish on dead Nahma, and tells Nokomis, who happens to be nearby, to boil what is left of the fish flesh for oil to use when winter comes.

Longfellow closely followed Schoolcraft here. In addition, both Hiawatha and Väinämöinen are swallowed alive (the former by a fish, the latter by a giant), torture their enemies, and escape. Longfellow later learned that his description of the sturgeon was inaccurate and wrote Ferdinand Freiligrath,* his translator and friend (29 Jan 1857), about his error.

IX. "Hiawatha and the Pearl-Feather": Nokomis points westward, where the fiery sun is setting. The moon follows the sun's "bloody footprints." Nokomis tells Hiawatha to follow the moon, find Megissogwon, known as the "Pearl-Feather," "the Magician, / Manito of Wealth and Wampum," and destroy him. He is guarded by fiery snakes emerging from dangerous "black pitchwater." Megissogwon killed Nokomis's father and now spews forth fever, pestilence, poison, fog, disease, and death. Hiawatha arms himself with his bow, arrows, club, mittens, and some oil from Nahma, and sails away in Cheemaun, his happily leaping birch canoe. Overhead screams Keneu, the mighty, forward-hurtling war-eagle. When the flaming serpents offer trouble, Hiawatha shoots them dead with his jasper-headed arrows. Smearing Nahma's oil on the bow and sides of eager Cheemaun, Hiawatha glides through the pitch-water, undeterred when mosquitoes, fireflies, and bullfrogs try to lead him astray. The moon reveals Megissogwon's wigwam in the land ahead. Stepping ashore on dry moccasins, Hiawatha fires a warning arrow into the wigwam. Megissogwon steps out, tall, broad, terrifying, armored in wampum, and brandishing multicolored weaponry. He recognizes Hiawatha,

boasts of killing Nokomis's father, and offers to kill Hiawatha. "Nothing daunted, fearing nothing," Hiawatha shouts defiance, and a uniquely ferocious day-long battle follows. Hiawatha's arrows cannot penetrate Megissogwon's wampum. At sunset Hiawatha is tattered, exhausted, and wounded, and with only three arrows left. The woodpecker, called Mama, tells him to fire arrows into Megissogwon's one vulnerable spot, at the root of his tuft of long black hair. As Megissogwon stoops for a rock to hurl at him, Hiawatha sends his three arrows at their target; Megissogwon, answering the voice of death, called Pauguk, dies. In gratitude to Mama, Hiawatha stains his head feathers crimson. Hiawatha strips off Megissogwon's wampum as a trophy, and also takes from his wigwam his other wampum, and also his skins, furs, belts, pouches, beaded quivers, and silver-headed arrows. Welcomed back home by Nokomis, Chibiabos, and Kwasind, Hiawatha is accorded a hero's plaudits, for he has slain Megissogwon and thus cleansed the land of fever, fog, and disease.

Longfellow was partly inspired to write this canto by minor passages in Catlin and Schoolcraft and much in *Kalevala,* notably about Tuonela, its Stygian River and area of death, and its evil woe-spreading occupants.

X. "Hiawatha's Wooing": Hiawatha recites these lines to himself:

> As unto the bow the cord is,
> So unto the man is woman;
> Though she bends him, she obeys him,
> Though she draws him, yet she follows;
> Useless each without the other!

He thinks a great deal about Minnehaha, the Dacotah maiden. Nokomis advises him to choose someone as nearby as a hearth fire, not someone as distant as moon- and starlight. No, says Hiawatha. Nokomis suggests a wife who would be useful, willing, and eager to run errands. He replies that a Dacotah maiden would run errands just fine. When Nokomis says that Dacotahs are traditional enemies of their Ojibway tribe, Hiawatha counters that his projected marriage will unite Dacotahs and Ojibways. Off he goes, over moors and meadows and through silent forests, until he hears the falls of Minnehaha.

He shoots a deer as a gift for Minnehaha's old arrow-maker father. These days, the fellow has been contrasting his glorious past and the effeminate present, whereas his mat-weaving daughter's thoughts are on that stalwart hunter from another tribe. In he walks, throws down the deer, is welcomed, shares water and food, talks of Ojibway-Dacotah peace, and simply says, "Give me as my wife this maiden." The sad father agrees, if the daughter is willing. She answers simply, "I will follow you, my husband." They leave the lonely father, pass the laughing waters of the falls, find their path as Hiawatha clears the way, and sleep on hemlock boughs during their journey. Squirrels and rabbits watch "with curious eyes the lovers." The bluebird tells Hiawatha he is happy to have a loving wife; the robin tells Minnehaha she is happy to have a noble husband. The sun, shining down benignantly, tells the couple that "Love is sunshine, hate is shadow, / Life is checkered shade and sunshine," and advises Hiawatha to "Rule by love." The moon tells them that "Day is restless, night is quiet, / Man imperious, woman feeble," and advises Minnehaha to "Rule by patience." They find Nokomis's lodge at last. Hiawatha's people feel that he has "Brought the moonlight, starlight, firelight, / Brought the sunshine," to them.

Longfellow's sources here include Mrs. Mary Eastman and Schoolcraft, but especially *Kalevala,* in which the mother of a lover named Lemminkäinen warns her bride-seeking son in ways Nokomis employs in cautioning Hiawatha.

XI. "Hiawatha's Wedding-Feast": Nokomis invites many village guests. They come richly attired and enjoy a sumptuous feast of sturgeon, pike, pemican, deer, bison, buffalo marrow, maize cakes, and wild rice. Nokomis, Hiawatha, and Minnehaha serve their guests before they partake of anything. Nokomis fills pipes with tobacco, willow bark, and fragrant herbs and leaves. Pau-Puk-Keewis, handsome, gorgeously dressed, but of such a girlish manner that the warrior-guests call him an idle gambling coward, plays games and then dances, first solemnly, and finally beside the water in a sand-whirling frenzy. Chibiabos sings "of love and

. . . longing"; likens the fair Minnehaha to a dewy flower, a wild bird, a soft-eyed fawn; and says that her sadness darkens the land, her smile, sunny and rippling, causes the earth to rejoice. Iagoo, the "old and ugly" storyteller, is jealous of Chibiabos's charm and therefore boasts of his own prowess in archery, swimming, traveling, sightseeing, and hunting. The guests tolerate him, though, because when Hiawatha was an infant he made the child his cradle and later taught him how to fashion bows and arrows. When asked to tell them "a tale of wonder," Iagoo offers the account of how the magician Osseo "From the Evening Star descended."

Longfellow used material from Eastman and Catlin here but mainly feast details from *Kalevala,* concerning food and serving etiquette, singing, and storytelling. Pau-Puk-Keewis, with his love of gambling, derives from Schoolcraft's *Algic Researches* and *Oneóta;* his good looks and jovial recklessness echo aspects of Lemminkäinen, who is Väinämöinen in *Kalevala.*

XII. "The Son of the Evening Star": The sun sets in the level water like a bleeding swan, whose plumage makes the air splendid. Above it is the trembling Star of Evening, like "a bead of wampum / On the robes of the Great Spirit." Seeing all this inspires Iagoo to recite the following story.

Near the beginning of everything, Osseo, the Evening Star's son, marries the lovely but "wilful" Oweenee, who spurned other suitors. She has nine sisters, all of whom wed handsome, haughty young warriors. Osseo is ugly, poor, and old, coughs a lot, but has a beautiful spirit, is passionate, and speaks splendidly. When Oweenee's disappointed suitors deride her, she simply says, "I am happy with Osseo!" At a family feast in a lodge, Osseo prays to the Star of Evening and asks for pity. The nine other couples hear him, and the forest rings with their mocking laughter. Osseo sees an uprooted, hollow tree, leaps into one end of it, and comes out the other end—young, tall, handsome, and strong. But the lovely and faithful Oweenee turns weak, ugly, and old. More laughter follows. Osseo, now young, tenderly escorts his old wife back to the feast. While others make merry, he ponders his fate, but only until he hears his father's voice out of "the starry distance" inviting him to rise to the heavens. Once there, he will taste divine food from gleaming silver kettles; there, the women, toiling no more, will all be glistening birds. The banquet lodge rises above the dark treetops "into the dewy starlight" and becomes a birdcage with silver rods instead of roof poles. Osseo sees the nine couples—now jays, magpies, thrushes, and blackbirds—twittering and strutting in their fine feathers. Seeing Oweenee still wrinkled and aged, Osseo cries out. Lo, both she and he are young and attractive together. The lodge cage flutters back down and comes to rest like a leaf on water. Osseo's father explains that he converted those 18 cocky ones into imprisoned birds for mocking Osseo when he was old and for not recognizing his "heart of passion" and his "youth immortal," as Oweenee did. Osseo's father also warns him to beware of Wabeno, the evil magician whose enchanted arrows converted Osseo into an old man. Years pass, and Oweenee and Osseo have a son, "With the beauty of his mother, / With the courage of his father." The boy grows. Osseo trains him to use bows and arrows. One day Osseo releases the caged birds—his aunts and uncles—as target practice for the boy. When he shoots one, the victim falls, a beautiful maiden, now, with an arrow in her bosom. Her blood stains "the sacred Star of Evening," thus breaks the magic spell, and causes "the fearless bowman" to land onto a grassy island in the big waters of the Gitche Gumee. Down also come kind Osseo and dutiful Oweenee, and the 18 birds as well, which are changed into human pygmies, called Puk-Wudjies. The lodge remains, near which fishermen occasionally hear and sometimes see the happy little creatures singing and dancing in the starry night.

Thus ends the story told by Iagoo, who warns those who engage in the sport of ridiculing "great men" they do not understand that they may also suffer "the fate of jesters." The wedding guests applaud but also wonder if they are "the aunts and uncles." Chibiabos sings a final song, about a maiden with an Algonquin lover who promised to go with her to her native land but then left her. Her sad refrain is "O my sweetheart, my Algonquin!" Such was Hiawatha's wedding party. When the guests leave, "Hiawatha [is] happy / With the night and Minnehaha."

In Schoolcraft, Longfellow found details concerning the red swan and Osseo's story.

XIII. "Blessing the Cornfields": The nations are at peace. Hunters and fishermen go out freely, while the women make maple sugar, gather rice, and dress animal skins. In the spring the women "Buried in the earth Mondamin," and in the fall they strip the ears of maize "as Hiawatha taught them." One night, he tells Minnehaha, his happy wife, what to do. When all are asleep, she must disrobe, walk "Covered by your tresses only," and quietly stamp a "magic circle" around the cornfields to keep away all insects and crawling creatures, especially "the mighty caterpillar." Darkness wraps "his sacred mantle" around Minnehaha so that no one can later boast of seeing her beautiful body. Kahgahgee, the monstrous raven, laughs at her efforts. At dawn he leads his army of ravens, crows, blackbirds, and jays down into the fields, eager to exhume and devour Mondamin; but Hiawatha, saying, "I will teach you all a lesson / That shall not be soon forgotten," catches the whole flock in well-laid snares. Except for Kahgahgee, he slaughters them all and makes scarecrows out of them. He ties Kahgahgee to his ridge pole "As a hostage for his people." Kahgahgee flaps about, sulks, and caws for help; but when summer passes, Shawondasee, the ardent south wind, breathes upon the land, wafts warm kisses, and helps the maize mature. Old Nokomis announces harvest time. Minnehaha recruits the youthful boys and girls, and they all husk and harvest their crop while warriors and elderly men sit under the pines, smoking and watching. Finding a red ear signals to a maiden that she will soon wed. Anyone finding a misshapen ear bends down and limps like a cripple. Laughter rings throughout the fields. Kahgahgee continues to scream angrily. His thwarted cohorts croak their frustration from the trees. The old men emit a simple "Ugh!"

Details of handling corn come directly from Schoolcraft's *Oneóta.*

XIV. "Picture-Writing": Hiawatha is sad that memories of "great traditions" are lost when death takes warriors, hunters, wise men, and craftsmen, and especially prophets who have "dreams and visions." So he gathers a pouch of colors and paints "shapes and figures" on birch bark. The egg symbolizes "Gitche Manito the Mighty, / He, the Master of Life"; the serpent stands for evil; white and dark, for life and death; a bow, for the sky, with white for day and stars for night; and wavy lines for rain and clouds. Hiawatha directs his people to paint their totems and grave poles with individual household symbols. Prophets, magicians, and medicine men decorate bark and deerskins meaningfully, to record their songs about war, hunting, medicine, and magic. Love songs are well treated, with pictures showing men and women standing, holding hands, maidens on islands casting passion spells, and other maidens sleeping near their respective lovers. The final figure "Was a heart within a circle," meaning "Naked lies your heart before me, / To your naked heart I whisper!" Thus does wise Hiawatha teach his people.

Details come from Schoolcraft and Tanner.

XV. "Hiawatha's Lamentation": Hiawatha warns his beloved friend, the singer Chibiabos, that evil, jealous spirits intend to "molest them and destroy them." But Chibiabos is "young and heedless," hence fears nothing, and goes off hunting alone in winter. The evil spirits catch him on Gitche Gumee's "treacherous ice," break it beneath him, and drown him in its sandy depths. Hiawatha laments so loudly that the bison pause, wolves howl, and thunder echoes. Hiawatha blackens his face and, while the purple-coned firs fan in sympathy, eulogizes his friend thus:

> He has moved a little nearer
> To the Master of all music,
> To the Master of all singing!
> O my brother, Chibiabos!

When spring comes, bluebirds, robins, and whippoorwills sing dirges. Medicine men, magicians, and prophets visit the downcast Hiawatha, build him a holy lodge, and persuade him to enter "slowly and in silence." They have him quaff a magic potion of spearmint, yarrow, roots, and herbs; sound drums and rattles before him; chant, with a responding chorus, to heal and strengthen him; and shake their pouches and dance. Hiawatha rises as from a dream, afflicted no longer. They call up Chibiabos's spirit, give him a burning brand, and tell him to lead the dead "On their solitary journey / To the kingdom of Ponemah," the place "of the Hereafter." Like smoke, Chibiabos drifts silently through villages and forests, over silvery waters, to the ghost- and shadow-haunted blessed isles. Along the way, the dead, who are burdened with gifts of weapons and food from well-meaning mourners, say that better it would be to proceed naked on this journey. Hiawatha, well again, teaches his people varieties of medicine.

Much here comes from Schoolcraft. More important, in *Kalevala* Väinämöinen's beloved Aino drowns, as Chibiabos does.

XVI. "Pau-Puk-Keewis": The mischief-maker Pau-Puk-Keewis, who danced at Hiawatha's wedding, plans some new adventures. He leaves his lodge near Gitche Gumee and finds Iagoo busy telling some young men the story of how Ojeeg, the Fisher Weasel, made a hole in the sky to "let out the summer-weather." Otters, beavers, lynxes, and badgers all tried to leap up and pierce the sky, but only Ojeeg succeeded. Pau-Puk-Keewis says he is tired of Iagoo's yarns and Hiawatha's wise remarks, and challenges everyone present to a game of bowl and counters. He explains that he has nine flat pieces of bone variously identified—serpent, "wedge-men," club, fish, duckling—painted white on one side, vermilion on the other; and he also has four pieces of brass—one side burnished, one black. These objects have various values when cast and totaled. Iagoo takes the bait and boasts of his gambling experience; then he and his friends play all day and night. They bet their clothes, weapons, wampum, belts, feathers, pipes, and pouches. They lose everything, whereupon Pau-Puk-Keewis wagers his winnings against getting Face-in-a-Mist, who is Iagoo's "stripling" nephew, and whom Pau-Puk-Keewis fancies as a companion, attendant, and pipe-bearer.

Iagoo rolls only a five. Pau-Puk-Keewis rolls five tens, wins, and orders Face-in-a-Mist to tote his loot, and off they go to Hiawatha's lodge. Finding Hiawatha, Minnehaha, and old Nokomis gone, Pau-Puk-Keewis taunts them by strangling the captive raven, hanging it to the ridge pole, and scattering all the household things. He goes to a handy headland perch and while "Waiting full of mirth and mischief / The return of Hiawatha" kills Hiawatha's considerable flock of "mountain chickens." A seagull witness sends Hiawatha a message.

Pau-Puk-Keewis comes from Schoolcraft's *Algic Researches.*

XVII. "The Hunting of Pau-Puk-Keewis": When Hiawatha gets home, he is furious and leads some hunters after Pau-Puk-Keewis. From the headlands they see and hear his derisive gestures and shouts. He runs to a pond where some beavers, ruled by Ahmeek, their king, have built a dam. He persuades them to convert him into a beaver, 10 times their size, and to let him live with and be their leader. Hiawatha and his band trample the dam, and all the beavers escape through a little doorway, except Pau-Puk-Keewis, "puffed with pride and feeding," and therefore too big. Hiawatha clubs him to death, just the way "maize is pounded"; but his ghost rises, reassumes his human shape, and flies away like the wind, pursued by Hiawatha, like the rain. In a lake, Pau-Puk-Keewis finds a brant and talks the black-beaked fellow into changing him into his like but 10 times larger. Hiawatha shouts at the brant flock from the shore, and off they fly. Pau-Puk-Keewis's fellow-fliers warn him to proceed steadily and not look down. The flock lands, feeds, and sleeps among some "reeds and rushes." Next morning onward they fly, borne along with the South-Wind. When they are miles above a village, Pau-Puk-Keewis spots Hiawatha and Iagoo, forgets his warning, foolishly draws in his neck, and looks down. The wind catches his "fan of feathers," as wide as a doorway, and down he plunges, crashes, and breaks his wings. Up pops his ghost again, assumes his same old handsome shape, and rushes off. When Hiawatha tries to grab him, Pau-Puk-Keewis dances up a dusty whirlwind that disorients

Hiawatha. Pau-Puk-Keewis hides in a hollow tree, wriggles out as a serpent, and escapes just as Hiawatha is smashing the tree into kindling. Pau-Puk-Keewis, human again, escapes into the rocks past Gitche Gumee and into the cave of the Old Man of the Mountains. Hiawatha bangs ineffectually at its sandstone opening, gets nowhere, and prays to the tempest, the lightning, and the thunder. They all combine to blast the Old Man's cavern into bits and kill Pau-Puk-Keewis, permanently. Hiawatha picks up his corpse, upbraids him for his manifold naughtiness, generously changes him into a war-eagle, and launches him aloft. In wintertime, when storytellers see whirling snow and hear tumultuous winds, they say Pau-Puk-Keewis is out dancing again.

XVIII. "The Death of Kwasind": Kwasind is famous far and wide. This makes the weak pygmy Puk-Wudjies envious, and therefore with the fairies they plot his death. They learn that nothing but "his crown" contains his unique strength but that it also is his one vulnerable spot, and further that only pine tree cones make up a weapon that can kill him. They pile a heap of cones together and lie in wait. Kwasind drifts by in his canoe and gets drowsy. Nepahwin, the sleep spirit, hovers above him like a dragonfly and orders his legions to club him into unconsciousness. He reels upright, floats blindly, and becomes the Puk-Wudjies's easy victim. They shower him with pinecones, and he dies. The people remember him, and when winter storms roar outside they say the Strong Man is gathering firewood.

Kwasind's story comes from Schoolcraft's *Algic Researches.*

XIX. "The Ghosts": It seems that "disasters come not singly" but like vultures, one following another down to their "sick and wounded" prey. Winter breathes snow across the land. Hunters don snowshoes. Women grind maize. Youngsters frolic outside. One evening while Minnehaha and Nokomis are awaiting Hiawatha's return in their wigwam, two strange women, "pale and haggard," enter, tremble, and crouch in a corner. Something mutters from above into the wigwam. Is it Koko-Koho, the owl in "the dismal forest"? Something says the women are ghosts from the Hereafter. Hiawatha enters with a red deer for food, wonders about the strangers, but welcomes them and courteously watches them devour the "choisest portions" of venison with neither requests nor thanks. Then they flit back into a corner. Time passes, and the ghosts sit by day and gather firewood each night, "in storm or starlight." Hiawatha offers no reproof, Nokomis no impatience, and Minnehaha no resentment. They regard guests as having rights. One midnight Hiawatha, ever sleepless, hears the strangers sighing and weeping, slips from under his bison hides, and asks what troubles his guests. They say they "are ghosts of the departed" and have come from Chibiabos's realm to explain something. Since the dead have "no place among the living," they ask that no heavy furs, wampum, pots, and kettles be placed as gifts on graves. All that the dead need are food and firelight to help them on their four-day journey to the shadow land. They praise Hiawatha for enduring their outrageous actions in his home and ask him to "Fail not in the greater trial, / Faint not in the harder struggle." His doorway curtain lifts, and the ghosts are gone.

Parts of this canto reflect Longfellow's reading in Catlin and Schoolcraft.

XX. "The Famine": During a dreadful winter of deep snow, the hunter can find no game, falls, and dies "from cold and hunger." Above the hungry air, "the hungry stars in heaven / Like the eyes of wolves glared." Two more guests visit Hiawatha's wigwam and look at Minnehaha. They introduce themselves as "Famine, Bukadawin," and "Fever, Ahkosewin." Minnehaha lies down, "trembling, freezing, burning." Hiawatha rushes into the forest, "maddened," with the sweat freezing on his face. When he prays to "Gitche Manito, the Mighty," for food, "there came no answer." Hiawatha recalls his pleasant past. In delirium, Minnehaha hears the Falls calling, sees her father beckon, and feels the "icy fingers" of Pauguk, the fatal stalker. Hearing Minnehaha's cry, Hiawatha hastens home, "Empty-handed, heavy-hearted," sees Nokomis rocking hopelessly, and sees "his lovely Minnehaha / Lying dead and cold before him." He

sits in mourning for seven days, then dresses his wife in rich raiment, buries her, and covers the grave with snow. He prepares a fire to light her four-day journey to the Blessed Isles. He cries,

> Farewell, O my Laughing Water!
> All my heart is buried with you,
> All my thoughts go onward with you!

He promises to follow her soon "To the Land of the Hereafter!"

XXI. "The White-Man's Foot": An old man is sitting in his wintry lodge when a rosy-cheeked youth enters. His smile fills the place with sunshine. The old man expresses pleasure in seeing the lad, calls him "my son," and offers to exchange stories of adventure and prowess with him. The old man fills his red-stone pipe and says his breath frosts the land. Smiling, the youth says that when he breathes on the land, flowers bloom and rivers flow. The old man says that when he shakes his "hoary tresses," snow descends, leaves fade and fall, and birds and animals disappear. The laughing youth says his shaken "ringlets" cause warm showers, which urge plants to rise, birds to return, trees to put on foliage, and the woods to "ring with music." Night departs; and soon Gheezis, the sun, rises like a painted warrior. The old man is quietly warmed by the pleasant air, hears the birds sing and the streams murmur, and smells new grasses. The young stranger, Segwun, recognizes the old man, who is "Peboan, the Winter." Peboan weeps, melts, and is transformed to "the Spring." Swans, geese, loons, grouse, and Shuh-shuh-gah, the heron, fly back "in long lines waving, bending / Like a bow-string snapped asunder." Bluebirds, robins, and pigeons pipe, sing, and coo. Hiawatha, in mute sorrow, hears them calling him. Iagoo returns and tells a disbelieving audience that he went to broad, salty waters on which he saw a tall, winged canoe. It saluted him with lightning and thunder, and white-faced, hairy-chinned men disembarked. Hiawatha confirms Iagoo's story, having had a vision of a "great canoe with pinions" and white faced people "From the regions of the morning, / From the shining land of Wabun." He says that "Gitche Manito, the Mighty," has sent them here and that they should be greeted with "the heart's right hand of welcome." He adds that wherever "they tread, beneath them / Springs the White-Man's foot in blossom." These white people, talking many tongues, will toil, cut down the woods, build smoky towns, and do battle on "lakes and rivers." Also, he saw "our nation scattered," fighting each other, and swept "westward" like "withered leaves of autumn."

Accounts of the momentous arrival of white men appear in Catlin, Heckewelder, Schoolcraft, and of course elsewhere. In his journal (13 Sep 1849), Longfellow noted that Louis Agassiz* told him that when roads or railway lines are built in the United States, European weeds appear and that Native Americans call a certain weed of this sort "the white man's foot." In an unpublished work, called "Book of Suggestions," Longfellow noted (1849) that "The White Man's Foot" would be a good title for a poem.

XXII. "Hiawatha's Departure": Behold Hiawatha near Gitche Gumee, smiling in the broad sunlight. What does he see "floating, flying" on the water? Not birds, but a black-robed, pale-faced prophet, with "guides and . . . companions," and "the cross upon his bosom." Welcoming these visitors, Hiawatha says that because of them the earth and sun shine uniquely, the lake is uniquely calm, tobacco has become uniquely flavorful, and the cornfields are uniquely beautiful. Black-Robe replies:

> Peace be with you and your people,
> Peace of prayer, and peace of pardon,
> Peace of Christ, and joy of Mary!

Hiawatha and old Nokomis generously offer them bowls of food and the well-filled peace pipe. Black-Robe preaches to his hosts about the Virgin Mary and the Savior, and how the Savior was scourged and crucified by "the tribe accursed," but "Walked again with his disciples, / And ascended into heaven." The chiefs promise to give thought to these "words of wisdom," return to their wigwams, and relay to others what was told them. The visitors, lulled by the summer heat, slumber long. When cool evening comes, Hiawatha quietly tells Nokomis that

he is going to the Sunset's portals, where Keewaydin, the Northwest-Wind, rules. Nokomis is to feed and shelter their guests and keep them from harm. To his warriors and youths, Hiawatha explains that he will be away a long time and that they must listen to the guests, "For the Master of Life has sent them / From the land of light and morning!" Hiawatha boards his faithful birch canoe and orders it to dart forward. The people watch until he disappears "in the purple distance." They say, "Farewell forever!," and hear their words repeated by the lonely forests, the rippling waves, and the screaming heron, Shuh-shuh-gah. And so their beloved Hiawatha journeyed

> To the Islands of the Blessed,
> To the Kingdom of Ponemah,
> To the Land of the Hereafter!

Longfellow didn't use accounts by American missionaries of their bringing Christianity to Native Americans; instead, Väinämöinen's acceptance of Christianity and his disappearance in *Kalevala* provides Longfellow's model for Hiawatha's nearly identical behavior. Longfellow was well aware that this ending, disturbingly sudden, glosses over the thematic conflict of legendary and historical events.

Although Longfellow expressed interest in Native Americans as early as 1837, it was not until 17 years later that he began writing *The Song of Hiawatha.* While in Germany (Jun 1852), Longfellow took pleasure in reading several German translations of Finnish poetry with Ferdinand Freiligrath.* Longfellow had access (1854) to the German translation (1852) by Franz Anton Schiefner (1817–79) of *Kalevala,* the great Finnish epic. Journal entries record Longfellow's progress toward *Hiawatha.* He was reading *Kalevala* with joy (5 Jun 1854), hit on his plan to weave together traditions of "American Indians" and to use the trochaic tetrameter of *Kalevala* (22 Jun), might use the title "Manabozho" for what he then called his "Indian Edda" (25 Jun), began writing it (26 Jun), then decided to name it "Hiawatha" (28 Jun). He relished writing *Hiawatha* and finished doing so (21 Mar 1855). He and Freiligrath, who published his translation into German of *Hiawatha* (1857), were avid correspondents about the poem and much else.

Of Longfellow's many sources concerned with Native American culture and traditions, the following are the most important: George Catlin, *Letters and Notes on the Manners, Customs, and Condition of the North American Indians* (1841); Mrs. Mary Eastman, *Dahcotah, or, Life and Legends of the Sioux* (1849); J. G. E. Heckewelder, *Account of the History, Manners, and Customs of the Indian Nations, Who Once Inhabited Pennsylvania and the Neighbouring States* (1819); *Kalevala;* and Henry Rowe Schoolcraft, *Algic Researches: Comprising Inquiries Respecting the Mental Characteristics of the North American Indians* (1839), *Oneóta, or Characteristics of the Red Race of America* (1845), *Personal Memoirs of a Residence of 30 Years with the Indian Tribes* (1851), and early parts of what became *Historical and Statistical Information Respecting the History, Condition, and Prospects of the Indian Tribes of the United States* (6 vols., 1851–57). Shortly after Longfellow's *Hiawatha* was published, Schoolcraft edited *The Myth of Hiawatha and Other Oral Legends* (1856). Longfellow also read widely in pertinent if less significant geographical, missionary, and literary works concerning Native Americans in the region of Lake Superior.

The Song of Hiawatha was an enormous success, with 30,000 copies sold in the first six months. It was quickly translated into several languages, first into Swedish (1856), most notably by Freilingrath into German (1857), then French and Polish (1860), Italian (1867), Russian (1878), Hungarian (1885), and, most curiously in an abridged unpublished version, Latin. The sing-song trochaic tetrameter Longfellow chose for *Hiawatha* derived, with notable variations, from that of *Kalevala,* and has inspired more parodies than that of any other poem in history. The spoofs soon began coming, but they bothered Longfellow rather little. When Karl Knortz (1841–1918), a German emigrant who was teaching in Oshkosh, Wisconsin, wrote Longfellow, listed paro-

dies of *Hiawatha,* and asked him to name any others he knew about, Longfellow replied (30 Sep 1877) and named two more. *Hiawatha* has also inspired songs and plays. The name "Hiawatha" has been given to babies, schools, and streets. From Scotland, Charles Sumner* wrote Longfellow (22 Oct 1858) that a famous cattleman there had named a prize bull and cow Hiawatha and Minnehaha (respectively). When *Hiawatha* first appeared, charges of plagiarism from *Kalevala* were raised in various quarters, about which, at this date, the less said the better. It is now obvious that Longfellow used, but didn't abuse, many sources and analogues. Instead, he created an American masterpiece, at once popular and controversial, more revered once than it is now, but still capable of being read with great pleasure, especially for its depiction of the American woods, rivers, and lakes in successive seasons, and for giving the world an American culture-hero of considerable charm and magnanimity.

Bibliography: Arvin; Carr, Helen. *Inventing the American Primitive: Politics, Gender, and the Representation of Native American Literary Traditions, 1789–1936.* New York: New York University Press, 1996; Carr, Helen. "The Myth of Hiawatha." *Literature and History* 12 (spring 1986): 58–78; Ferguson, Robert A. "Longfellow's Literary Fears: Civic Authority and the Role of the Artist in *Hiawatha* and *Miles Standish.*" *American Literature* 50 (May 1978): 187–215; Higginson; Hilen; Hilen, ed.; Hirsh; Jackson, Virginia. "Longfellow's Tradition; or, Picture-Writing a Nation." *Modern Language Quarterly* 59 (Dec 1998): 471–96; Keiser, Albert. *The Indian in American Literature.* New York: Oxford University Press, 1933; Legler, Henry E. "Longfellow's *Hiawatha:* Bibliographical Notes Concerning Its Origins, Its Translations, and Its Contemporary Parodies." *Literary Collector* 9 (Jan 1904): 1–19; S. Longfellow; Millward, Celia and Cecelia Tichi. "Whatever Happened to Hiawatha?" *Genre* 6 (Sep 1973): 313–32; More; Moyne; Moyne, Ernest J. "Parodies of Longfellow's *Song of Hiawatha.*" *Delaware Notes* 30 (1957): 93–109; Rees, John O. "[T. S.] Eliot's 'Cousin Nancy' and *The Song of Hiawatha.*" *Etudes Anglaises* 34 (Oct-Dec 1981): 454–57; Schramm, Wilbur L. "*Hiawatha* and Its Predecessors." *Philological Quarterly* 11 (Oct 1932): 321–43; Thompson, Stith. "The Indian Legend of Hiawatha." *PMLA* 37 (Mar 1922): 128–

40; Tichi, Cecilia. "Longfellow's Motives for the Structure of 'Hiawatha.'" *American Literature* 42 (Jan 1971): 548–53; Vogel, Virgil J. "Placenames in Longfellow's 'Song of Hiawatha.'" *Names* 39 (Sep 1991): 261–68; Wagenknecht, 1986; Williams.

"A SONG OF SAVOY" (1825). Poem, signed "H.W.L.," in *USLG,* 15 Mar 1825; Scudder. When twilight darkens the mountains, "voices hail the evening-bell." Wind stirs the trees. Cymbals accompany dancers at a "scene of love." The persona's lover broke his "frail" promise and left her. She feels that "'T were better ne'er to love at all, / Than love and then forget!" But she departs when he waves her away from him and "comes for his mountain maid."

Bibliography: Little.

"SONG OF THE BELL" (1839). Poem, translated from an anonymous German source, in *Hyperion; Voices.* Bells ring "merrily" at weddings and when evening comes. Bells ring "solemnly" on Sunday mornings and at funerals. Bells, though of "metal dull," feel all of our emotions. God gave bells the power to raise our sinking hearts when "Trembling in the storm!"

"SONG OF THE BIRDS" (1827). Poem, in *AS,* 1827; Scudder. One night, perched on a tree over a brook, a bird sings sadly and yet merrily, like "those that love hath crazed." The song evokes in the poet thoughts of someone faraway, someone dead, an unrequited lover. In the "sad and dark" morning, the "delicate rich voice" of a thrush chants sweetly through the rain and the mists. Similarly, a loving woman's voice, flowing like a gentle fountain, is rendered all the "more delicious" if melancholy casts a shadow over "bright flowers round our way."

Bibliography: Little; Thompson.

"SONG OF THE RHINE" (1834). Poem, in *KM,* 1834; Scudder. Rivulets join the "strong and deep" Rhine as it moves proudly toward the sea. But its progress is thwarted by the "sidewards" movement of "rebellious" "waters"; and the Rhine sinks in the sand near "Leyden's wall."

"SONG OF THE SILENT LAND" (1839). Poem, translated from the German of the Swiss poet Johann Gaudenz Salis (1762–1834), in *Hyperion; Voices.* Who leads us "Into the Silent Land" by "a gentle hand"? When we see clouds and beached wrecks, and visions of beauty, when we battle but have hopes, and when we are heartbroken, the one with "gentle hand" and holding an "inverted torch" leads us "To the land of the great Departed." The syntax of this translation is tortured.

"SONGO RIVER" (1875). Poem, in *Pandora, Birds* (1875). This stream, uniquely devious, "Links together lake and lake." It is more winding than a lost knight's path, than the route of a nut- or nest-seeking truant. Underbrush is mirrored, "inverted," in it. Swallows fly above it; loons, in it. Although hidden, "thy tranquil waters teach / Wisdom deep as human speech," with neither "haste [n]or noise." It invites heat-escaping city dwellers to take their ease, stop imitating "brawl[ing] rivulets, and instead "in quiet self-control / Link together soul and soul." The Songo Locks are northwest of Portland, Maine. Longfellow and his brother, Samuel Longfellow,* fretted in an exchange of letters (late Sep 1875) about the moralizing final lines.

Bibliography: Hilen, ed.

"SONG: SHE IS A MAID OF ARTLESS GRACE" (1832). Poem, translated from an unidentified Spanish source, as "La Doncella," in *Token,* 1831; Scudder. The poet asks an "ancient mariner," a "gallant cavalier," and a "swain" if sail or star, weapon or battleground, flock or valley "Be half so fair" as this artlessly graceful maiden. Longfellow includes his translation, untitled, in *Outre-Mer,* in the chapter titled "A Tailor's Drawer," where he calls the "little ditty . . . as delicate as a dew-drop."

"SONG: STAY, STAY AT HOME, MY HEART, AND REST" (1878). Poem, in *AM,* Feb 1878; *Kéramos, Birds* (1878). The poet adjures his heart to rest at home. Wanderers are troubled, full of doubts, defeated. Birds are safest in their nests. When they fly away, hawks hover above them.

"SONG: WHERE, FROM THE EYE OF DAY" (1826). Poem, in *USLG*, 1 Apr 1826; Scudder. A mist over the woods reveals the path the dark and quiet river takes. Similarly, thoughts emerge from hidden emotions, "unseen at first, / From our cold hearts . . . stealing." Just as quickly, Love, from "darkness flowing," breaks through concealing clouds to express hidden thoughts.

Bibliography: Hilen, ed.; Thompson.

"SONNET ON MRS. KEMBLE'S READINGS FROM SHAKESPEARE" (1850). Sonnet, in *S/F.* Longfellow praises the actress for "giving tongue unto the silent dead." Her readings make "our hearts glow." Shakespeare is "the great poet who foreruns the ages, / Anticipating all that shall be said!" The reader is happy in her text, while the poet, "by no critic vext," is happily "rejoic[ing]. . . / To be interpreted by such a voice!" Longfellow often attended dramatic performances by Frances Kemble.* After she read from *The Merchant of Venice* (26 Feb 1849), she was the Longfellows' supper guest at Craigie House,* together with George Stillman Hillard* and Charles Sumner.*

"THE SOUL'S COMPLAINT AGAINST THE BODY" (1838). Poem, translated from the Anglo-Saxon, in *NAR,* Jul 1838; Scudder. "Each one of mortals" should ponder "his soul's journey" before death separates it from his body. Long ago God put the soul's "woe or . . . weal" into "its earth-vessel." The soul will seek the body after death and complain to its dust that it worked and thought too little about the soul earlier.

"THE SOUND OF THE SEA" (1875). Sonnet, in *Pandora, Birds* (1875). The poet hears the sea awaken, rise, and rush forward. From "the unknown" comes its "sound mysteriously multiplied," just as

> . . . comes to us at times, from the unknown
> And inaccessible solitudes of being,
> The rushing of these sea-tides of the soul.

We call such "inspirations" ours, but in truth they represent "divine foreshadowing and foreseeing / Of things beyond our reason or control."

"SPANISH DEVOTIONAL AND MORAL POETRY" (1832). Article, in *NAR,* Apr 1832. This essay served as a preface to Longfellow's translation of *Coplas de Manrique. See also* "The Devotional Poetry of Spain," in *Outre-Mer.*

"SPANISH LANGUAGE AND LITERATURE" (1833). Article, in *NAR,* Apr 1833.

***THE SPANISH STUDENT* (1842).** Play, in three acts.

Act I. In his chambers in Madrid, the Count of Lara tells his friend Don Carlos that he attended a dull play this evening. It was livened by the gypsy Preciosa's delightful dancing. When Lara labels the girl a half-naked sinner whose voluptuous dancing excites young men, Don Carlos defends her purity. Don Carlos leaves. Lara suspects Victorian, the Spanish student from Alcalá, of being her lover and intends to supplant Victorian tomorrow and many days thereafter. Francisco, Lara's servant, brings Lara's jewels back from Preciosa, who has thus refused his advances. When Francisco says he saw Victorian buy a gold and ruby ring, Lara orders him to buy one just like it.

Chispa, Victorian's servant, drafts four musicians to serenade beside Preciosa's garden wall.

Their "Serenade" begins by telling the "Stars of the summer night" to stop shining because "My lady sleeps!" Victorian climbs to Preciosa's chamber. They kiss chastely. She saw him tonight when she was dancing. He is jealous of the audience for looking at her. He sees her in the books he studies and also at chapel. She tells him that the Pope has ordered the Archbishop of Toledo and a cardinal to come and judge her Spanish dancing, which has been regarded in Rome as lewd. As soon as Preciosa saw Victorian in Córdova, she regarded Bartolomé Román, her gypsy boyfriend, as dreadful. Yet she feels inferior to Victorian's intellect. He replies that brain power is finite, even in ambitious men, whereas the affections, especially women's, especially hers, are inexhaustible. When the watchman cries "Ave Maria Purissima" at midnight, Victorian gives Preciosa the gold and ruby ring and leaves for Alcalá; but he will return. She gives him her handkerchief.

On the road to Alcalá, Chispa calls the supper of rabbit and wine, offered by Baltasar the innkeeper, in reality kitten and vinegar. He orders water for his horse and Victorian's and explains that Victorian travels to Madrid often because he is in love.

Sleepy Hypolito, Victorian's fellow student at Alcalá, awaits Victorian. When he enters, he reveals that he is in love with Preciosa, whom both saw dance with Bartolomé at Córdova. Hypolito laughs gently at Victorian's high praise of Preciosa, his "precious jewel . . . found / Among the filth and rubbish of the world." When Hypolito recalls that Victorian wooed Victorian's cousin Violante, he blurts out that she may marry elsewhere or enter a convent. At three in the morning, Hypolito leaves. Victorian muses on fame, willpower, genius, and then—best of all—love. Some knights await their beloved in vain. But Victorian has faith in Preciosa, his "bright ideal." He sleeps.

Act II. In her room, Preciosa welcomes a poor but decent girl named Angelica, warns her against Lara, the girl's immoral landlord, and gives her a purse of gold. Enter Beltran Cruzado, Preciosa's father—the so-called count of the gypsies. He cannot believe that she gave gold to the girl, warns her to provide for him instead, and also demands that she marry Bartolomé Román. Preciosa says she can't stand the fellow.

The Archbishop, in his palace, is talking with a Cardinal about bullfights and lewd dancing. The Pope has suppressed the former, as barbarous and disgraceful in a Catholic country, but the people still relish energetic dancing. The Cardinal has asked Preciosa to come and dance a sample before the two of them. Preciosa enters and surprises the Cardinal with her modesty and discretion. Queried, she recalls certain "Gardens and palace walls" in her infancy and names Cruzado as her father. The Archbishop says that the walls were of the Alhambra and remembers Cruzado as "A sun-burnt Ishmael." Surprisingly, Preciosa dances so gracefully that the holy men lose their gravity, rise, toss their caps, and applaud.

At the Prado, Don Carlos meets Hypolito, gives the poor student some gold, and asks about Victorian. In love, is the answer. Don Carlos wonders, "Well, well! who is this doll?" Not cousin Violante but Preciosa, is the revelation. Don Carlos counters that Lara says Preciosa is not pure. When Victorian enters and Don Carlos and Hypolito kid him about Lara's conquest of Preciosa, he warns both to desist.

While Preciosa is reading, lamenting Victorian's absence, and listening to her caged bird sing, Lara sneaks in. She asks him to leave her poor and friendless self alone. He tells her that he is influential enough to save her from gossip about a lover climbing into her balcony. She pulls her gypsy dagger. Victorian slips in unseen. He misunderstands Preciosa's urging Lara to accept her respectful love, and her hope that Lara will turn his passion to holiness. Victorian reveals himself; threatens Lara, who leaves; rebukes Preciosa for encouraging Lara; and storms out.

Francisco tells Lara that he has persuaded a bunch of men to disrupt Preciosa's dance tonight.

On the street, Victorian tells Hypolito that Preciosa probably wanted gold from Lara, not love. Hypolito replies that Lara has that gold and ruby ring. Lara enters with Francisco. Victorian and Lara quarrel and have a duel. Defeated, Lara says Preciosa was false to both men, shows his ring, and says Preciosa gave it to him. Victorian, grateful for the truth, leaves. Lara smells amorous victory.

In Madrid, Cruzado greets Bartolomé, here from the mountain village of Guadarrama, after two years, still lusting for Preciosa, and now planning to kill her lover, Lara.

Preciosa, about to dance but hissed on stage, faints.

Lara and his male dinner guests, back from the theater where Preciosa was embarrassed, toast her name. Lara anticipates seducing her.

As serenading musicians pass by Preciosa's wall, Lara enters her gate with Francisco's help. Bartolomé climbs over, and Cruzado follows.

Preciosa, feverish and watched over by Dolores, her servant, calls for Victorian deliriously. In the garden below, Lara is attacked and mortally wounded by Bartolomé.

Act III. On the road to a village, Hypolito sings about false love to Victorian, who wishes he were a soldier, rather than a scholar, and could die in battle. Village church bells ringing "Ave Maria" beckon them.

The ruler of Guadarrama delivers an order from the King of Spain banishing all gypsies on pain of enslavement. The Padre Cura is lecturing on the origin of gypsies as Hypolito and Victorian enter. By flattering the padre effusively, Hypolito obtains lodgings for himself and his love-lorn companion.

Once inside, Hypolito continues his flattery. The padre introduces Martina, his lovely niece. Hypolito takes her hand to tell her fortune. Victorian enters. A muleteer brought him a letter: Preciosa is exonerated, but, hissed off the stage, is now wandering with gypsies. The padre says the local gypsies include Cruzado and Preciosa. Victorian will find her, apologize, and declare his fond love.

Chispa, now working for Don Carlos and seeking Preciosa, gets fresh horses on his way to the gypsies near Guadarrama.

At the gypsy camp, Cruzado gives some men singing at their forge orders to sneak into town at night. They all leave. Entering, Preciosa expresses inchoate hopes. Bartolomé enters, having long hidden after killing Lara, and comes to spirit Preciosa to safety. She says a price is on his head, says she never loved him, says only Cruzado promised her to him, says he should find a compatible wife. He leaves, in anger. She prays. Victorian enters, with Hypolito behind and cautioning him. Disguising his voice, Victorian calls her. Recognizing him, she disguises her voice, pretends she is a fortuneteller, accuses him of wronging a loving maid. He says the girl was no maid. She says marry that maid. He tries to buy her ring as a gypsy memento. No, never; keeping it proves her honesty. Ah, they embrace. He asks and receives her forgiveness. Hypolito

admires their tenderness. Chispa enters with news from court: Preciosa was stolen when little by a hag; her real father, a nobleman, is back in Spain, rich; Don Carlos has the official proofs. All take in this fabulous news.

In a mountain pass, a muleteer sings, a shepherd leads a monk to San Ildefonso, and a smuggler rides along singing. Victorian, Preciosa, and the others, some armed, ride and walk on toward Segovia, where Preciosa's father awaits them. Bartolomé rushes in, fires his carbine at Preciosa, but misses. A returning shot kills him.

Longfellow confided this in his journal (28 Mar 1840): "Yes, I will write a comedy,— 'The Spanish Student!'" He enjoyed working on it but was often interrupted by teaching and other duties. He was stimulated to resume work on it, especially on his heroine Preciosa, modeled on Fanny Elssler (1810–84), an Austrian ballet dancer, when she went on a money-making tour of the United States. Samuel Ward* sent Longfellow a letter (8 July 1840) alerting him to Elssler's contrasting beauty and ugliness, and her good and evil nature. Once in Boston, she both dazzled and saddened Longfellow. He wrote his father (4 Oct 1840): "Her Spanish dances are exquisite; and remind me strongly of days gone by." But he added this: "She has five hundred dollars a night;—consequently makes with her heels in one week just what I make with my head in one year." After many delays, he offered his play (Feb 1842), tentatively titled "The Student of Alcala," to George Rex Graham,* founder of *Graham's Magazine,* which was edited at that time by Edgar Allan Poe.* Graham proposed paying $150 for it. Longfellow wanted more, delayed, left the play in the hands of George Stillman Hillard* and departed for Europe (Apr 1842). Rufus Wilmot Griswold,* who briefly succeeded Poe as Graham's editor, offered to pay the $150 (Jun 1842) and publish it in October. As it worked out, the play was published, one act at a time (Sep, Oct, Nov 1842). Reappearing in book form (May 1843), it caused some distress in parents of young readers because of its alleged candor in treating sexual matters and, perhaps therefore, sold 38,000 copies (by 1857). In a preface to the book, Longfellow notes that in "La Gitanilla," by Miguel de Cervantes, a Spanish student loves a gypsy girl by the name of Preciosa. Longfellow also mentions *The Spanish Gypsy* by Thomas Middleton (1570?-1627), among a few other sources and analogues. Longfellow's play is a curious mixture of competent blank verse, fine lyric lines, several exquisite figures of speech, Elizabethan slapstick leg-pulling, and dialogue wreckers such as "Fie," "Hist," "Heighho," "where wast thou?," and "wot of." One stage direction has Preciosa sleeping "in an undress." Poe in an unsigned essay ("The American Drama," *American Review* 2 [Aug 1845]) enjoyed skewering *The Spanish Student* for being an antiquated, unoriginal work with neither plot nor characters. Notwithstanding, a German translation of it by Carl Vilhelm Böttiger (1807-78) was published (Dessau, 1854) and staged at Dessau's Ducal Court Theater (28 Jan 1855), at the height of Longfellow's popularity abroad. Many of the scenes in Longfellow's play could have coalesced into a ringing Giuseppe Verdi grand opera. In some of his bantering letters to Longfellow, Ward addressed Longfellow as Victorian and signed himself as Hypolito, which name Longfellow therefore used to address Ward for a while.

Bibliography: Arms; Arvin; Crosby, Robert Ray. "Longfellow as a Dramatist." Ph.D. diss., Indiana University, 1958; Hilen, ed.; Tanselle, G. T. "Longfellow's 'Serenade' (*The Spanish Student*)." *Explicator* 23 (Feb 1965): 48; Thompson; Thompson, Lawrance R. "Longfellow Sells *The Spanish Student.*" *American Literature* 6 (May 1934): 141-50; Wagenknecht, 1986.

SPARKS, JARED (1789–1866). Man of letters, educator, and clergyman. Sparks was the illegitimate son of Eleanor Orcutt, who nine months after his birth in Willington, Connecticut, married Joseph Sparks, a local farmer who was not the boy's father. He was sent, aged six, to his mother's married but childless sister, whose husband was a drifter. After living in Camden, New York, with his aunt and uncle, Sparks returned to his mother (1805), attended school, was obviously bright, taught school in Tolland, Connecticut, and also was a carpenter (1807-09). Willington ministers helped finance

Sparks's attendance at Phillips Exeter Academy in New Hampshire (1809-11). He then not only attended classes at Harvard but also taught and tutored elsewhere, until he graduated from Harvard (1815). He studied theology intermittently there, finally achieving a master's degree in the subject (1819). He tutored in mathematics and science (1817-19), and edited the *North American Review* (1817-18). Sparks was an unhappy Unitarian minister in Boston, Baltimore, and Washington, D.C. (1818-23), returned to Boston, purchased the *North American Review* partly with borrowed money, and edited it skillfully (1823-30). Meanwhile, he published an essay on colonizing Africa with African Americans (1824), received permission to examine George Washington's papers at Mount Vernon, assembled papers of the explorer John Ledyard (1751-89) as part of a biography (1828), did research in England and France (1828-29), and issued profitable annual scientific almanacs (from 1829). Astonishingly prolific work as editor, author, and publisher then followed: *The Diplomatic Correspondence of the American Revolution . . .* (12 vols., 1829-30), *Life of Gouverneur Morris* (3 vols., 1832), *The Life and Writings of George Washington* (12 vols., 1834-37), *The Works of Benjamin Franklin; with Notes and a Life of the Author* (10 vols., 1833-40), and *The Library of American Biography* (25 vols., 1833-49). Most of these works earned him enormous royalties. Sparks was a popular lecturer (from 1838) and taught minimally at Harvard (1838-53) as the first professor of history in the United States. As president of Harvard (1849-53), he combined reactionary administrative decisions with valuable reorganization of the archives. Outside criticism began to diminish his reputation. The *New York Evening Post* published articles (1851) to the effect that Sparks had "improved" Washington's hasty and colloquial wording and also altered other documents; meanwhile, a British historian exposed similar tampering. Sparks rationalized, in print, on the grounds of editorial judgment—this, in keeping with the editorial practice common among Romantic historians. A congressional committee (1888) presented detailed evidence of

Sparks's altering documents concerning the American Revolution. Sparks married Frances Anne Allen (1832); they had a daughter. To death he lost both wife (1835) and daughter (1846). In 1839 he married Mary Crowninshield Silsbee (1809–?); they had five children, one not surviving infancy. Undeterred by criticism of his editorial alterations, he published *Correspondence of the American Revolution, Being Letters from Eminent Men to George Washington . . .* (4 vols., 1853) having corrected "errors" in the text he thought were the result of haste in those writing to General Washington. Worse, however, was his longstanding unprofessional practice of cutting off signatures here and there, destroying naughty passages from diaries, and sending other samples to his friends. After a research trip and family vacation in Europe (1857–58), Sparks quietly died back in Cambridge, Massachusetts. Controversial Sparks may be, but without his efforts in America and abroad, countless items in his assembly of historical documents, many items shedding light on the American Revolution, would undoubtedly be unrecovered.

Longfellow's friendship with Sparks started tentatively and was never close. Sparks, when editor of the *North American Review,* rejected an essay by Longfellow (Feb 1825), on the grounds that his thoughts were immature and his style too elegant. To a query from Sparks, Longfellow replied by letter from Portland (30 Jul 1825) that evidently nothing was known in America about the English poet Thomas Chatterton (1752–70) and that something ought to be published about "so wonderful a genius," and sent an essay by him on Chatterton—which Sparks rejected. In a letter to Sparks (8 Feb 1831), Longfellow mentioned their having met and asked for help in securing publication of his translation of a French grammar. Sparks was unable to assist, but Longfellow got it published anyway. Knowing of Sparks's work on Franklin, Longfellow sent him (22 Mar 1833) the copy of a letter by Franklin (which Sparks didn't use). When Longfellow moved to Harvard (Dec 1836) to start teaching there, Sparks was in Cambridge doing research on Franklin and Wash-

ington, and the two men often met. Abbott Lawrence (1792–1855), a prosperous textile manufacturer, politician, and Harvard benefactor, invited Longfellow, Sparks, and others (including ex-President John Quincy Adams and Edward Everett*) to what young Longfellow described in his journal (13 Oct 1838) as "A grand dinner, with exquisite wines." Longfellow records strolling with Sparks and his (second) wife and receiving a book from them which he didn't like (3 May 1840). He attended Sparks's inauguration as Harvard's president and recorded his impression that the requisite "address [was] very substantial, but retrograde" (20 Jun 1849). During Sparks's presidency, Longfellow frequently conferred with him over administrative matters. Guests at a dinner (1 Jun 1859) honoring America's phenomenal chess champion Paul Morphy (1838–84) were Sparks, Louis Agassiz,* and Longfellow.

Bibliography: Green; S. Longfellow; Morison.

"THE SPIRIT OF POETRY" (1828). Poem, in *AS,* 1828; *Voices.* In the woods "a quiet spirit" dwells, inspired by winds, trees, flowers, the morning star, and the departing evening. This spirit moves along valleys, brooks, under storms. It lifts one's thought above the silent, majestic woods into "the pure bright air." Talented bards have always found "an eloquent voice" in woods, sun, flowers, leaves, rivers, sky and clouds, winds, slanting sunlight, groves, mountains, "shattered cliff[s]," valleys, lakes, fountains, and trees. The poet likens this spirit to "a bright image of the light and beauty / That dwell in nature," to divine forms we "worship in our dreams," and to colors on birds' wings and sunlit clouds. This spirit's eye is like lights in April; her hair, like summer tree "tresses"; her cheeks, autumnal blushes; her breath, spring air; her voice, that of a musical summer bird. The blank verse of this juvenile poem is more notable than its mix of imagery.

Bibliography: Hilen, ed.; Little; Thompson.

"SPRING" (1939). Poem, translated from the French poet Charles d'Orléans (1391–1465), in *Voices.* Winter, with "his gloomy train," made us sad, with its cold, ice, rains, sleet, snow, storms, and winds. Spring, "in sunshine clad," tears away "surly" winter's shroud-like "mantle of cloud" and merrily steps closer. When Longfellow republished this poem in his edition of *Poets and Poetry of Europe,* he retitled it "Renouveau."

"THE STARS." Poem, translated from the German poet Martin Opitz (1597-1639), in Scudder. Night brings rest to others but sorrow to the poet. The moon and stars gladden much, but the poet still grieves. He can't find his beloved Kunigund's "lovely eyes" in the stars. When they shine on him, he needs "Neither moon nor stars."

"STARS OF THE SUMMER NIGHT" (1843). Poem. The stars and the moon should hide their light, and the wind should cease. The poet's lady is sleeping. This poem, titled "Serenade," is in *The Spanish Student.*

"THE STATUE OVER THE CATHEDRAL DOOR" (1843). Poem, translated from the German poet Julius Mosen (1803-67), in *GM,* Apr 1843; *Bruges.* Above the door of the cathedral the poet sees statues of saints and kings, but only one figure "soothed my soul with love." It is of a man standing calmly, in a wild storm, and in his mantle are birds, flowers, and weeds. If the poet were exalted like him, he would shelter "these birds of air" and his songs would carry blossoms and leaves to heaven's door. This poem is syntactically confused.

STEPHENSON, COLONEL SAMUEL (1776–1858). The husband of Abigail Longfellow Stephenson, Longfellow's aunt. Longfellow enjoyed the Stephenson family's hospitality. In a letter (29 May 1858) to his sister Anne Longfellow Pierce,* he says that the colonel's death was like "part of my youth taken away suddenly."

Bibliography: Hilen, ed.

STEPHENSON, MRS. SAMUEL (1779–?). Longfellow's aunt, born Abigail Longfellow. She married her cousin, Colonel Samuel Stephenson* (1776-1858). They had a daughter, Elizabeth Ware Stephenson (1802-?).

STORER, DR. EBENEZER (1803–82). Longfellow's second cousin. His mother, Catherine Stephenson (1774-1850), was the daughter of Tabitha Longfellow Stephenson (1752-1817), who was Longfellow's father's sister. Ebenezer Storer, while studying medicine in Paris, engaged a room for Longfellow with a pleasant Parisian family (Jun 1826-Feb 1827). Storer began to practice medicine in New York City (by 1834) and was in New York as late as 1876.

Bibliography: Hilen, ed.

STORY, JOSEPH (1779–1845). Juridical scholar and U.S. Supreme Court justice. Story was born in Marblehead, Massachusetts, graduated from Harvard (B.A., 1798), prepared for and passed the bar (1801), and began an extensive practice in Salem. His first marriage was to Mary Lynde Oliver (1804), who died six months later. Story married Sarah Waldo Wetmore (1808); they had two surviving children: Mary Oliver Story (1817-1849) and William Wetmore Story.* Joseph Story was elected to the Massachusetts legislature (1805, 1810-11) and also served in the U.S. Congress (1808-09). He served on the U.S. Supreme Court (1811-45). In accordance with the practice then, he was allowed to live in Salem (1811-29) and thereafter in Cambridge. He was a bank president, was a Harvard administrator, and taught in its law school (1829-45). He edited legal texts, wrote reviews, and published commentaries on the law so distinguished that the Lord Chief Justice of England called his work the best since that of Sir William Blackstone. Story's best books are *Commentary on the Constitution of the United States* (1833) and *Commentary on the Conflict of Laws* (1834).

Longfellow's father was Story's classmate at Harvard. Story used his influence to get Joshua Quincy,* president of Harvard, to appoint Longfellow to replace George Ticknor* as Smith Professor of Modern Languages there. Longfellow socialized with Story in a limited way. William Wetmore Story, a student of Longfellow's at Harvard, from which he graduated (1838; law degree, 1840), worked in the law office of Charles Sumner* for a while, married Emelyn Eldredge (?–1894) in 1843, inherited family wealth, and became an expatriate sculptor and author. Longfellow wrote a letter to Joseph Story (4 July 1844) to recommend, without success, Joseph L. Bosworth,* Anglo-Saxon scholar, for an L.L.D. degree from Harvard. When Longfellow and his wife were in Washington, D.C., he wrote his father (9 Feb 1839) that they called on Judge Story, who welcomed them and even "sent for all the judges of the Supreme Court to come down and see us."

Bibliography: Hilen, ed.; S. Longfellow; Newmyer, R. Kent. *Supreme Court Justice Joseph Story: Statesman of the Old Republic.* Chapel Hill: University of North Carolina Press, 1985; Thompson.

STORY, WILLIAM WETMORE (1819–95).
Sculptor and man of letters. He was born in Salem, Massachusetts, the son of Joseph Story.* Young Story attended Harvard (B.A., 1838; L.L.B., 1840), and then practiced law and wrote a few legal treatises, unenthusiastically. He preferred literature and sculpture. He married Emelyn Eldredge (1843); they had three children. In 1847 he published *Poems* and visited Rome briefly, commissioned to create a statue in his father's honor, returned to Boston to edit his father's *Life and Letters* (2 vols., 1851), and went back permanently to Rome (1856). A thorough going expatriate, he devoted his considerable energy but only moderate talents to sculpture, literature, and music. A complete list of his friends, among travelers, fellow expatriates in the various arts, and hangers-on, would be too extensive to present here, but would include Robert Browning and Elizabeth Barrett Browning, Nathaniel Hawthorne,* Harriet Hosmer,* Walter Savage Landor, James Russell Lowell,* John Lothrop Motley, and Charles Eliot Norton.* Hawthorne describes what evolved into Story's statue *Cleopatra* (1852) in *The Marble Faun* (1860). Story dedicated his *Poems* (1856) to Lowell, who in turn dedicated his *Fireside Travels* (1864) to Story. Much of Story's verse is vapid, but his *Roba di Roma* (1862) contains charming descriptions. When Story revisited the United States briefly, he was acclaimed in Boston and New York as a great artist (1877).

Longfellow knew Story only slightly. Longfellow's various journal notes indicate the following. He saw Story and Lowell on their way to Boston, "looking so young and full of strength and hope!" (25 Nov 1850). He enjoyed "a pleasant chat on Italy and art" with both Storys, at Lowell's home (26 Nov 1850). Calling on the Storys when they were vacationing in a cottage at Nahant, Massachusetts, he found them "shiver[ing] and think[ing] of Sorrento" (14 Jul 1851). On one occasion, he enjoyed tea and the sunset, as did Ralph Waldo Emerson,* with the Storys in their cottage (31 Aug 1851). At the inauguration of the statue of *Beethoven* by Thomas Crawford,* Story presented "an introductory poem . . . [which was] very good and very well delivered" (1 Mar 1856). When Longfellow saw Story's bust of Browning, he called it "good; but not so good as that of Mrs. Browning by the same artist" (1 Jun 1867). Walking past Story's statue of Edward Everett* in Boston's public garden, he regarded it as "good" (22 Nov 1867). Finally, "A hazy autumn day. W.W. Story, the sculptor, called" (31 Oct 1877).

Bibliography: James, Henry. *William Wetmore Story and His Friends, from Letters, Diaries, and Recollections.* 2 vols. Boston: Houghton, Mifflin & Co., 1903; S. Longfellow.

STOWE, HARRIET BEECHER (1811–96).
American author. She was born Harriet Elizabeth Beecher in Litchfield, Connecticut. Lyman Beecher, her father, was a conservative Calvinist minister opposed to Unitarianism. After her mother died (1815), leaving eight living children, her father remarried and produced three more children. Harriet attended the Hartford Female Academy, founded and run by her sister Catharine Beecher, and then taught there herself. When Beecher was appointed president of the Lane Theological Seminary in Cincinnati (1832), the family moved there, Catharine established the Western Female Institute there (1833), and Harriet taught there (1833–36). Harriet had begun publishing stories in the *Western Monthly* and also items in the Cincinnati daily *Journal,* run by her brother Henry Ward Beecher. In 1836 Harriet married Calvin Ellis Stowe (1802–

86). A fellow student at Bowdoin College with Longfellow, he had graduated (1824), studied at the Andover Theological Seminary, and taught at Dartmouth College, before teaching biblical literature at Lane Theological Seminary (from 1831). He married Eliza Taylor (1832); she died two years later. Harriet Beecher Stowe collected some of her New England tales as *The Mayflower; or, Sketches of Scenes and Characters among the Descendants of the Puritans* (1843). Her husband, with whom she was to have seven children, returned to Bowdoin to teach (1850). She had observed the treatment of slaves in Kentucky, was distressed by the Fugitive Slave Act and the Compromise of 1850, and was sympathetic to the abolitionist movement. She published *Uncle Tom's Cabin; or, The Man That Was a Thing* in serial form in the *National Era* (5 Jun 1851–1 Apr 1852) and then in book form (1852). She wrote the novel in a house in Brunswick in which Longfellow and his brother Stephen boarded (1822–23). Mrs. Stowe negotiated poor terms, and even though she soon received $10,000 and more later, her publisher fared much better; the book sold 3,000,000 copies (by 1860), then millions more. An unauthorized 1852 dramatization of the novel had racist overtones, for which Mrs. Stowe was irrationally blamed. Questions about the authenticity of *Uncle Tom's Cabin* led her to publish *A Key to Uncle Tom's Cabin; Presenting the Original Facts and Documents upon Which the Story Is Founded* (1853) and a sadly hasty follow-up slave novel, *Dred: A Tale of the Great Dismal Swamp* (1856). By this time, her husband was teaching at the Andover Theological Seminary (from 1852), and Mrs. Stowe, internationally known and admired, had taken to traveling and writing about foreign subjects. She visited England and toured Europe (1853), published *Sunny Memories of Foreign Lands* (2 vols., 1854), and revisited England (1856). She published *The Minister's Wooing* (1859), a fine New England historical novel cast shortly after the American Revolution and exploring Calvinism; resided briefly in Italy (1859); and as a consequence wrote *Agnes of Sorrento* (1862), a melodramatic medieval romance

unsympathetic to Catholicism. *The Pearl of Orr's Island* (1862) is a beautiful local-color idyll about fisherfolk and mariners off the Maine coast. By this time, the Civil War had commenced. President Abraham Lincoln welcomed Mrs. Stowe to the White House and allegedly called her "the little lady who made this big war." After her husband's retirement, the couple moved to Hartford (1864). She continued publishing: *Home and Home Papers* (1865) suggests that a wife can be more than just a homemaker; *Men of Our Times* (1868) is a potboiler of biographies, including ones of her brother Henry and her friend Charles Sumner;* *Oldtown Folks* (1869) contains superb local-color sketches, soon followed by *Sam Lawson's Oldtown Fireside Stories* (1872); and *Lady Byron Vindicated* (1870) is a sensational work based on Lord Byron's wife's extensive revelations to Mrs. Stowe about Byron's illicit relations (the word "incest" doesn't appear) with his half-sister (unnamed). Mrs. Stowe's family had its own scandal when brother Henry got sued (1874) by a parishioner for committing adultery with said parishioner's wife. The jury couldn't reach a verdict, but gossip was nationwide nonetheless. Mrs. Stowe wrote more, lived off and on in Florida (1867–83), survived multiple family tragedies, was widowed (1886), and suffered senility and mental derangement. Her friend Annie Adams Fields,* the widow of James T. Fields,* edited *Life and Letters of Harriet Beecher Stowe* (1898).

Longfellow had known Calvin Ellis Stowe from their Bowdoin college days together. Longfellow's relationship with Harriet Beecher Stowe began when he started reading *Uncle Tom's Cabin,* which he defined in his journal (9 May 1852) as "a pathetic and droll book on Slavery; a book of power." Later journal entries: "Every evening we read ourselves into despair in that tragic book, Uncle Tom's Cabin. It is too melancholy, and makes one's blood boil too hotly" (22 May 1852); "How she [Mrs. Stowe] is shaking the world with her Uncle Tom's Cabin! At one step she has reached the top of the stair-case up which the rest of us climb on our knees year after year. Never was there such a literary coup-de-main as this. A million copies of a book within the first year of its publication" (24 May 1852). Longfellow wrote Mrs. Stowe (29 Jan 1853) praising the commercial success of her novel, "to say nothing of the higher triumph of its moral effect." Fanny Longfellow,* the poet's wife, perceptively wrote her sister-in-law Mary Longfellow Greenleaf* (Apr 1853) that Mrs. Stowe's *Key to Uncle Tom's Cabin,* being factual, is "more painful than the softened fiction of *Uncle Tom,* and I think the South will be sorry to have provoked such a reply by denying her statements." The Longfellows invited the Stowes to dinner, and the Longfellows first met Harriet then (24 May 1853). As for Mrs. Stowe's *Sunny Memories of Foreign Lands,* Longfellow noted in his journal (29 Aug 1854) that "we like them very much. They are very frank and fresh, with touches of her genius in them and deep poetic feeling." Evidently Mrs. Stowe rewrote in monologue form a section of *Uncle Tom's Cabin,* which Longfellow, according to his journal (6 Dec 1855), heard performed by a mulatto, whom he calls "this Cleopatra," before what he critically labels "a great, unimpassioned, immovable Boston audience." Mrs. Stowe moved in fine New England circles. For example, according to his journal (9 Jul 1859), when Longfellow dined at a big Boston hotel, he looked around and saw Oliver Wendell Holmes,* James Russell Lowell,* John Greenleaf Whittier,* the daughter of William Hickling Prescott,* and Mrs. Stowe and her husband ("with his patriarchal gray beard"). Longfellow comments in his journal (25 Jul 1859) that "Mrs. Stowe's Minister's Wooing continues very charmingly."

Bibliography: Green; Hedrick, Joan D. *Harriet Beecher Stowe: A Life.* New York: Oxford University Press, 1994; Hilen, ed.; S. Longfellow; *Mrs. Longfellow;* Strout, Cushing. "*Uncle Tom's Cabin* and the Portent of Millenium." *Yale Review* 57 (spring 1968): 375–85; Tryon; Williams.

"A SUMMER DAY BY THE SEA" (1875). Sonnet, in *Pandora; Scudder.* At sunset a small "gray and gold" cloud falls like a prophet's mantle. Lighthouses, "The streetlamps of the ocean," are gleaming. Darkness is overhead. Another day has gone "into the land of dreams." This delightful day has been "full of gladness and . . . pain," for some, a delight's tombstone for others, the mark of something new for still others.

SUMNER, CHARLES (1811–74). Politician and reformer, Sumner was born in Boston, Massachusetts, graduated from Harvard College (1830), graduated from Harvard's law school (1833), practiced law with George Stillman Hillard* and others (1834–37), but began to develop an interest in being an author. He wrote reviews, revised law textbooks, and enjoyed literary friendships with Ralph Waldo Emerson,* Samuel Gridley Howe,* John Greenleaf Whittier,* and especially Longfellow. Sumner both relished and intellectually profited from a prolonged European sojourn (Dec 1837–May 1840). He traveled, studied European politics and legal structures, cultivated friendships with various American expatriates, and mastered French, German, and Italian. He befriended the sculptor Thomas Crawford* by commissioning a statue and by asking Longfellow to puff Crawford's talents. Back in Boston, Sumner practiced law and annotated 13 volumes (1844–45) of the 20-volume *Reports of Cases Argued and Determined in the High Court of Chancery* . . . by Francis Vesey (1765?–1845). Sumner took up the cudgels for prison and education reform, for pacifism, and for abolition of slavery, often in a tactless, quarrelsome way. He helped found the New Soil Party (1848), was elected by Democratic-Free Soilers to the U.S. Senate (1851), and became a long-serving, forceful, but too-scornful orator there (to 1874). He argued against the Compromise of 1850, unsuccessfully sought the repeal of the Fugitive Slave Act that accompanied it, failed to prevent the Kansas-Nebraska Act (1854), and then delivered his famous "Crime Against Kansas" speech (19, 20 May 1856), in which he denounced proslavery compromisers. His calling slavery "the harlot" of Senator Andrew P. Butler caused Butler's young cousin, a South Carolina congressional representative named Preston Smith Brooks (1819–57), to sneak up behind Sumner and beat him over the head with a cane until he was bloody and unconscious. Brooks's name is now in history books only because of his cowardly act.

Sumner and Cornelius Conway Felton* had argued when Felton defended the Fugitive Slave Act and stopped speaking, despite Longfellow's efforts at mediation; but after Sumner was attacked, Felton renewed their friendship. Sumner was so severely injured that, despite medical treatment abroad, he could not resume his senatorial seat—kept active though vacant—until late 1859. On the eve of the Civil War, Sumner wanted to be minister to England, and he—and Longfellow—were disappointed when President Abraham Lincoln instead sent Charles Francis Adams (1807–86). Sumner's conduct during and after the Civil War indicates his high-principled inflexibility. Having opposed appeasing proslavery politicians, he generally supported Lincoln, influenced the issuance of the Emancipation Proclamation (1863) and the use of African American troops in the Union Army, denounced British aid to the Confederacy (1863), espoused harsh Reconstruction policies fomented by the Radical Republicans (from 1865), favored the impeachment of President Andrew Johnson (1868), and frequently (from 1869) incurred the displeasure of Ulysses S. Grant, about whom he fulminated in speeches and in print. Sumner was married (1866) to an attractive young widow named Alice Mason Hooper (1838–1913), but differences soon led to an icy separation (1867) and eventual divorce (1873).

Soon after arriving in Cambridge (Dec 1836) to teach at Harvard, Longfellow made the acquaintance of Sumner, who was then lecturing in the law school. The two, plus Hillard, Felton, and Henry Russell Cleveland began socializing and soon formed "The Club of Five." When Cleveland died, Samuel Gridley Howe* replaced him. When Sumner was in Europe the first time, Longfellow wrote to ask George Washington Greene* (6 Aug 1838) to welcome him in Rome and described him "as a very lovely character, . . . full of talent; with a most keen enjoyment of life; simple, energetic, hearty, good; with a great deal of poetry and no nonsense. You will take infinite delight in his society [he

added], and in walking old Rome with him." Welcoming Sumner back in Boston, Longfellow noted in his journal (7, 8 May 1840) that he appeared "more manly, more European," and "vastly improved by foreign travel; more ease, more *aplomb,* and no affectation." Sumner soon became Longfellow's closest friend by far. He traveled with Longfellow and Longfellow's bride Fanny Longfellow* during part of their wedding journey (summer 1843); at Springfield, Massachusetts, the three visited the arsenal, and while Sumner told the attendant that federal money spent there would be better spent on a library, Longfellow mentally sketched what became the poem "The Arsenal at Springfield." Longfellow often dined with notables in Sumner's company; wined and dined him personally; discussed politics, economics, literature, education, philanthropy, prison reform, slavery, and much else with him; attended many of his numerous lectures; and when the two were apart wrote dozens of letters to and received as many from him. When Sumner failed to be elected senator (Jan 1851), Longfellow regarded him as too good to be a senator; but when he was elected (Apr 1851), Longfellow rejoiced. With affectionate attention, he followed Sumner's political speeches in Washington, D.C.; defined his "Crime Against Kansas" Speech in a letter to him (28 May 1856) as "the greatest voice, on the greatest subject, that has been uttered since we became a nation"; and welcomed letters from Sumner during his slow convalescence after having been savagely clubbed. Sumner distressed Longfellow by writing graphically about having his nervous system treated by Parisian physicians who applied white-hot irons along his spine (Jun 1858). During Sumner's times abroad, Longfellow wrote him to express his sympathy, to be newsy about their mutual friends, and to entertain him with witty remarks often accompanied by quotations from foreign literatures.

Upon Sumner's return to Boston, Longfellow happily recorded in his journal (21 Nov 1859) that his friend regarded himself as a "'a well man'" again and described his visit to Alfred, Lord Tennyson* on the Isle of Wight. Longfellow applauded Sumner's renewed vigor back on the Senate floor. He read Sumner's speech denouncing slavery in Kansas and wrote him about it thus (14 Jun 1860): "Its great simplicity gives it awful effect. In rhetoric you have surpassed it before; in forcible array and arrangement of arguments, never!" Longfellow shared Sumner's despondency in the dark days of the Civil War. After peace came, Longfellow asked Sumner to push for an international copyright law. "If I were a senator," began one pitch (18 Dec 1866); Sumner tried, but to no avail. Longfellow wrote Sumner (8 Dec 1867) that the absence of an international copyright law cost him the loss of £40,000. He sympathized when Sumner's marriage ended, responded to Sumner's lugubrious letters, and agreed when he griped about President Grant, "Grantism," and malfeasance. Longfellow followed the ongoing publication of Sumner's fiery speeches, comparing the first three volumes in a letter to Sumner (25 Jan 1870) to "the rounds of a ladder; let me rather say steps hewn in the rock, one after the other, as you toiled upward." Reminiscing over the three volumes, Longfellow wrote Sumner again (22 Mar 1871), saying that they are "a noble monument of a noble life!" An indication of bookish Longfellow's profound love for Sumner is beautifully indicated in this statement in a letter he sent Sumner (25 Feb 1872): "When I have a noble thought in my reading, I instinctively think of you." Longfellow, however, couldn't agree when Sumner declared his support of Horace Greeley, the Liberal Republican Party candidate opposing Grant in the presidential election (1872).

Longfellow was devastated by Sumner's death. He soon wrote the sonnet "Three Friends of Mine," memorializing Sumner, along with Felton and Louis Agassiz.* Sumner's will, of which Longfellow was named as executor, included bequests to Longfellow's daughters. Longfellow declined requests to write Sumner's biography and at various times suggested any of the following to do it: James Freeman Clarke (1810–88), reformer and transcendentalist; George William Curtis*; Richard Henry Dana Jr.;* John Lothrop Motley, the historian; Edward Lillie

Pierce;* or John Greenleaf Whittier. James T. Fields* preferred James Parton (1822–91), English-born man of letters working in New York. Pierce, who was processing Sumner's papers anyway, was finally selected. When the last of the ongoing *Memoir and Papers of Charles Sumner* (15 vols., 1870–83) were being readied for publication, Longfellow proofread parts and, according to a letter he wrote to George Washington Greene (26 Sept 1881), helped index the finished volumes. The journals and letters of Longfellow's wife Fanny are full of genial comments about Sumner, whom she evidently liked very much. For example, in a letter to a neighbor and friend named Emmeline Austin Wadsworth (16 Apr 1852), she writes this: "We so miss Sumner's Sunday visits, with their free, fresh variety of topics and nice literary talks which he loves best."

Bibliography: Blue, Frederick J. "The Poet and the Reformer: Longfellow, Sumner, and the Bonds of Male Friendship." *Journal of the Early Republic* 15 (summer 1995): 273–97; Donald, David. *Charles Sumner and the Coming of the Civil War.* New York: Alfred A. Knopf, 1960; Donald, David. *Charles Sumner and the Rights of Man.* New York: Alfred A. Knopf, 1970; Green; Hilen, ed.; S. Longfellow; *Mrs. Longfellow;* Wagenknecht, 1955.

"SUNDOWN" (1882). Poem, in *Harbor.* At sunset, the treetops and the church spire are red, but "All is in shadow below." The summer day has been both "beautiful, [and] awful." It has brought life, love, happiness, gaiety, and good, but also death, hatred, desolation, sadness, and evil. Nothing can alter the added milestone, the finished page on "the book of life."

"SUNRISE ON THE HILLS" (1825). Poem, in *USLG,* 1 Jul 1825; *Voices.* The poet is standing on a hill when the sun marches up. Winds kiss the valleys. Light-bathed clouds gather below. Pinnacles thrust through mist like lances. Parts of the river gleam, while other parts are dark. Faraway waters "dash / . . . and flash." A bittern spins away. Bells, horns, and smoky shots ring out. Those who are sad should visit "the woods and hills," where "No tears / Dim the sweet look that Nature wears."

Bibliography: Little.

"SUNSET AFTER RAIN." *See* "The Past and the Present."

"SUSPIRIA" (1850). Poem, in *S/F.* The poet tells Death to go ahead and grab what it can, because its image is on our clay; tells the Grave to accept our bodies, which are our souls' discarded clothes; and tells Eternity that we know our lives merely bend its tree branches, merely scatter our "blossoms in the dust!"

***SYLLABUS DE LA GRAMMAIRE ITALIENNE* (1832).** Text Longfellow prepared for his Bowdoin students.

T

TALES OF A WAYSIDE INN **(1863, 1872, 1873).** Collection of narrative poems, in three parts.

Part First (1863).

"Prelude: The Wayside Inn." In Sudbury is an ancient hostelry, marked by the sign of the Red Horse. One autumn evening the place is filled with many guests "of different lands and speech." They are before a pleasant fire, which casts a bronze light over everything. They applaud the violinist. His music almost makes the spinet echo. The Landlord—"A Justice of the Peace he was, / Known . . . as 'The Squire'"—points to his grandfather's proudly displayed sword, which was active "Down there at Concord in the fight," and mentions the name Howe as that of some of his forebears. A Student is there, "With many a social virtue graced, / And yet a friend of solitude." He loves to read books, especially when they concern "the twilight that surrounds / The borderland of old romance." A youthful, well-moustached Sicilian remembers Boccaccio, other Italian writers, and music full "Of vineyards and the singing sea / Of his beloved Sicily." A mysterious-looking Spanish Jew sells "silks and fabrics rare / And attar of rose from the Levant," and is steeped in stories, parables, fables, and religious books. A Theologian, believing that "the deed, and not the creed, / Would help us in our utmost need," would like to establish "the Universal Church." A Poet is present and has "thoughts so sudden, that they seem / The revelations of a dream"; he envies no one

and accepts "but does not clutch" personal praise. The Musician, blond and blue-eyed, stands by the fire, with "every feature of his face / Revealing his Norwegian race." His words are "not speech, but song," and his thoughts are about "elves and sprites." His beautiful instrument is signed "Antonius Stradivarius." When his music ends, the guests "clamor for the Landlord's tale." The bashful fellow agrees.

"The Landlord's Tale: Paul Revere's Ride." The Squire begins his story thus: "Listen, my children, and you shall hear / Of the midnight ride of Paul Revere." Revere tells a friend to signal the route of the British foe, by lantern, from the North Church tower: One, if by land, and two, if by sea. Revere will watch from the other shore, ready to rouse "every Middlesex village and farm." The friend watches, climbs the tower, and lights one "lamp in the belfry," then a second. Revere sees, and soon his steed strikes sparks on the pebbles. "The fate of a nation was riding that night." Twelve o'clock: Medford. One: into Lexington. Two: at the Concord bridge. Well, "You know the rest." The enemy "fired and fled," while the armed farmers followed, "only pausing to fire and load." When our people are ever in peril, they "will waken and listen to hear," "borne on the night-wind of the Past," that "midnight message of Paul Revere."

This poem first appeared in the *Atlantic Monthly* (Jan 1861) and has proved to be incredibly popular. In it, however, Longfellow, purposely and systemically played fast and loose with historical facts, in order to recast Paul Revere as a solitary hero. In reality, Revere didn't get lantern signals from the Old North Church but helped send them; didn't row himself alone across the Charles River but was rowed over by others; and didn't reach Concord but failed in his effort, while another messenger got there; moreover, other midnight riders were involved. Longfellow's poem, a burnished chestnut, has been severely criticized by historians and has been the subject of countless parodies.

Bibliography: Fischer, David Hackett. *Paul Revere's Ride.* New York: Oxford University Press, 1994.

"Interlude" The Landlord displays the sword from that first battle. The Poet handles it; explains that it is a grand weapon even though it is unnamed, as, for example, "Joyeuse" and "Excaliber" are; and calls it more precious than the Landlord's coat-of-arms. The Student assuages the Landlord's annoyance by saying that "The arms, the loves, the courtesies, / The deeds of high emprise, I sing!" He remarks that the Landlord spoke of armed conflict, whereas his tale, from the *Decameron,* will be "of love . . . / Blending the human and divine."

Bibliography: Wagenknecht, 1986.

"The Student's Tale: The Ballad of Ser Federigo." Ser Federigo rests from his garden work and gazes at Florence by the Arno. Its buildings are nothing to him but a tomb over his wasted fortune and lost love, the fair Monna Giovanna, who married his rival. Only his faithful falcon returns his devotion now. One summer day "a lovely child" walks past a trellis, admires Federigo's falcon, and asks if he may hold it and also watch it fly. When asked, the boy, in a voice Federigo recalls, says his mother is Monna Giovanna, and they live "In the great house behind the poplars tall." The three—man, boy, and bird—become firm friends. It seems that Monna Giovanna, "widowed in her prime," is vacationing in her hillside villa. Her sadness is relieved when she sees her son, the image of her dead husband, maturing with charm, not least when he is watching the swoop of the neighbor's falcon. One sad day

the boy falls ill, grows worse, and asks if he may have Federigo's falcon to keep. Though reluctant to ask her "luckless lover" for the unique falcon, "the sole pursuivant of this poor knight," she promises to do so. On a glorious September morning, accompanied by a pretty young lady, Monna Giovanna calls upon Federigo. To him, his garden turns Edenic; the Arno, "the Euphrates watering Paradise!" She timidly asks to share breakfast with him. Knowing he has only wine, bread, and some juicy fruits, Federigo kills his falcon, stuffs it with spices, and serves it with the rest. Monna Giovanna casts pride aside and says if he gives her the falcon for her son, the lad "perchance may live." Federigo, having "tears of love and pity in his eyes," tells her what he did. She grieves because of what he sacrificed for her morning meal and yet feels proud of what he did for her. She leaves. Three days later Federigo hears the little boy's funeral bells. But three months later, Christmas bells ring out, and Federigo sits with Monna Giovanna, "his beloved bride," in the beautiful villa. At the back of his throne-like chair is carved a wooden falcon, and the inscription to the effect that good things come to those who wait.

The source of this story is one of Fiammetta's tales from the *Decameron* by Giovanni Boccaccio. Alfred, Lord Tennyson* liked Boccaccio's falcon story enough to convert it into a one-act play titled *The Falcon* (1879). Longfellow planned to have the Student recite "Galgano: A Tale of Giovanni Fiorentino" (*which see*) but substituted "The Ballad of Ser Federigo" instead.

Bibliography: Allaback, Steven. "Longfellow's 'Galgano.'" *American Literature* 46 (May 1974): 210–19; Arms; Arvin; Hilen, ed.; Wagenknecht, 1986.

"Interlude." Some guests praise the Student's story, but many are critical of it, including the Theologian, who opines that "These old Italian tales" are "trifling, dull, or lewd." To this gripe the Student replies that Shakespeare himself was not above making use of plots from the same Italian "reservoirs and tanks" for "His Moor of Venice [*Othello*], and the Jew [*The Merchant of Venice*], / And Romeo and Juliet," in addition to some of his comedies. When a guest says, "An Angel is flying overhead," the Spanish Jew voices his hope that it is not the Angel of Death. He is reminded of a haunting story from the Talmud.

"The Spanish Jew's Tale: The Legend of Rabbi Ben Levi." Rabbi Ben Levi reads in a law book that no one can look upon a certain "face" and live. He prays that he may see God's face and not die. A shadow falls on his page. The Angel of Death is there, with naked sword. The rabbi asks one favor first. All right. The rabbi wishes to see his place in Paradise. Very well. The rabbi asks Death to give him his sword for safety along the way. Agreed. Arriving at "the Celestial Town," the rabbi waves the death sword through it, making its inhabitants aware of the unknown something "men call death." He won't leave. All the angels are aghast, until God says the rabbi may indeed see His face and not die. Death asks for his sword. No. God tells the rabbi to surrender it. So he does but then persuades Death to keep all humans from seeing the sword and instead to "take . . . away the souls of men, / Thyself unseen, and with an unseen sword." Thereafter Death "walks on earth unseen."

Bibliography: Appel, J. J. "Henry Wadsworth Longfellow's Presentation of the Spanish Jew." *Publication of the American-Jewish Historical Society* 45 (Sep 1955): 20-34; Arvin; Wagenknecht, 1986.

"Interlude." A spell falls on the Spanish Jew's listeners, for "The spiritual world seemed near." They fear to look about. Is the Angel's sword near? The Sicilian says the Spanish Jew's story reminded him of "The legend of an Angel" that his old teacher, an Abate, told him about when he was little.

"The Sicilian's Tale: King Robert of Sicily." King Robert of Sicily is the brother of Pope "Urbane" and of Valmond, "Emperor of Allemaine." When during vespers Robert hears the monks chant "*Deposuit potentes / De sede, et exaltavit humiles,*" he asks for a translation. A clerk replies, "He has put down the mighty from their seat, / And has exalted them of low degree." Robert proudly says that nobody can get him off his throne. He falls asleep, then awakens in darkness and solitude. His shouts bring the

sexton, who opens the door and sees a half-clad fellow rush into the night and disappear like a ghost. Robert wanders around until he comes to a well-lighted banquet hall. On a dais sits an angel, robed like King Robert and accepted as such by all. He mildly identifies Robert as the king's jester and orders him bells, a cape, and an ape for his counselor. He is laughed at and mocked, sleeps on straw, and eats leftovers, but remains haughty and defiant for almost three years. Pope Urbane summons Valmond and the angel King Robert to Rome for Holy Thursday. The jester Robert tags along, riding "a piebald steed," dressed in a "cloak of fox-tails flapping in the wind," with his ape "perched behind." At Saint Peter's Square he claims to be king but is denounced as mad by Urbane. Sunshine brightens Easter morning and shines on Robert, kneeling humbly before the angel. Valmond returns to the Danube. The angel, through "land . . . made resplendent with his train," returns to Palermo. Enthroned again and while hearing the angelus, the angel calls Robert to him. When they are alone, he asks, "Art thou the King?" Robert admits his scarlet sins and offers to walk penitently until "my guilty soul be shriven!" The angel smiles, listens to the chant about the mighty being put down and the lowly exalted, and says that he isn't the king but an angel and that Robert is king. Robert finds himself alone, robed in ermine. His returning courtiers find him kneeling in quiet prayer.

Jacques Pantaléon (c.1200–64) became Pope Urban (1261–64). Robert, Duke of Anjou (1275–1343), born after Pope Urban's death and still later King of Sicily (1309–43), was not historically connected to Pope Urban; King Robert was a learned patron of literary men, including Petrarch. Longfellow's main source for "King Robert of Sicily," which he cast in excellent heroic couplets, was one of the tales, titled "Of the Emperor Jovinian," in *Gesta Romanorum*. In a letter (1 Nov 1875) to Katherine Maria Sedgwick Washburn (1831–84), the novelist-niece of Catharine Maria Sedgwick (1789–1867), Massachusetts romantic novelist, Longfellow identifies his source and adds that the popular story also appeared in publications by George Ellis (1753-1815), Leigh Hunt (1784-1859), and Thomas Warton (1728-90). Dom Pedro II (1825-91), emperor of Brazil (1831-89), translated "King Robert of Sicily" into Portuguese in 1864 (as "O Conde Siciliano"). Longfellow wrote Dom Pedro (25 Nov 1864) to acknowledge receipt of an autographed copy of the translation and to sign himself "Your Majesty's Obt. Sert.," etc. Years later, Longfellow wrote George Washington Greene* (11 Jun 1876) that Dom Pedro, Ralph Waldo Emerson,* and Oliver Wendell Holmes* were his guests for dinner.

Bibliography: Edgren, Hjalmar. "Antecedents of Longfellow's 'King Robert of Sicily.'" *Poet Lore* 14 (Jan-Mar 1903): 127-31; Hilen, ed.; Runciman, Steven. *The Sicilian Vespers: A History of the Mediterranean World in the Later Thirteenth Century.* Cambridge: Cambridge University Press, 1958); Swan, Charles, trans. and ed. "Tale LIX: Of Too Much Pride. . . ." In *Gesta Romanorum: or, Entertaining Moral Stories. . . .* 1876. New York: Dover Publications, 1959; Wagenknecht, 1986; Williams.

"Interlude." The Musician explains that the source of his tale is *Heimskringla,* a wonderful volume "Of Legends in the old Norse tongue, / Of the dead kings of Norroway." As he recites his tale, he punctuates it with musical interludes on his violin. These "Fragments of Norwegian tunes" resemble woodbines climbing a crumbling wall "and keep[ing] the loosened stones in place."

"The Musician's Tale: The Saga of King Olaf." I. "The Challenge of Thor": Thor announces that he is the god of war, reigns in his northern fastness, and has for accoutrements hammer, gauntlet, girdle, scary red beard, and noisy-wheeled chariot. He says that "Force rules the world still" and that "Meekness is weakness," and challenges the divine Galilean to a fight.

II. "King Olaf's Return": Aboard his ship, young King Olaf hears this challenge while he is heading northward to avenge the murder of his father (Trygve Olafsson). He remembers his mother Astrid's escape, Queen Gunhild's annoyance, sea fights and his captivity, and being greeted and recognized in Estonia by Astrid's brother Sigurd. Olaf was

Queen Allogia's page and then her warrior. Olaf voyaged far. He was a mighty rower, a two-sword fighter, a two-javelin hurler. Now he returns to beautiful Norway and shouts his acceptance of Thor's challenge.

III. "Thora of Rimol": Olaf is seeking Jarl Hakon, who begs the fair Thora to conceal him. Through love of him, she tells him, along with Karker, his disloyal thrall, to hide in a cave under the pig sty. Olaf arrives. Thora weeps. That night Karker stabs Hakon to death. Olaf hangs two heads—Hakon's and Karker's—on a gibbet, to the accompaniment of singing priests and a shouting mob. Thora swoons.

IV. "Queen Sigrid the Haughty": The proud queen sits disconsolate in her kingdom near "Norroway." Olaf has asked for her hand, to make peace. Court women sit nearby, weaving, while a maiden sings the rune of Brynhilda's love and Gudrun's anger. Olaf sent Sigrid a ring, for a wedding present. But goldsmiths test it and call it copper, not gold. So when Olaf walks in, kisses her hand, and swears true love, she asks him to swear as Odin once did. No, says Olaf, and says his wife must be a Christian. She voices her preference for her old faith, whereupon Olaf calls her "A faded old woman, a heathenish jade!," slaps her with his heavy gauntlet, and stamps down the stairs. Sigrid vows revenge.

V. "The Skerry of Shrieks": At home in Angvalds-ness, Olaf invites his warriors to have a drinking party at Easter. The waters on the Skerry roar an accompaniment. Olaf likes the song the Skerry makes; orders "his Scald, / Halfred the Bald," to learn and sing this ocean dirge; but when Halfred offers to sing it at once, Olaf yawns and sleeps until dawn. Meanwhile, his yard guards mistake the approach of inimical blue warlocks under Eyvind Kallda for mist and fog. They surround the place. Olaf stirs and wonders who "these strange people" are. Once identified, they are captured by Olaf's men-at-arms. That evening "the sorcerers were christened!" by being drowned in "the bursting surge." Now, Olaf tells Halfred, is the time to sing his "ocean-rhyme." But Halfred turns pale and complains that "The Skerry of Shrieks" are too loud for him to be heard.

VI. "The Wraith of Odin": During a loud, ale-filled feast, Olaf's door swings wide, and in comes a one-eyed, gray-bearded stranger. Olaf warms him with a hearty draft and gets him to sit down and recite some "Tales of the sea, and Sagas old." Sigurd the Bishop thinks it's bedtime. They put out the lights and send the pages away. The old stranger continues, with tales of heroes and heroic deeds, faraway places, and dangerous seas in between. Suddenly "The Havemal of Odin" rolls musically from his lips, and he asks whether "the great Scalds teach / That silence better is than speech." Olaf counters by saying he has never been "so enthralled / Either by Saga-man or Scald" as by his strange guest. Finally everyone goes to sleep. In the morning, they discover that the guest has departed through the barred door and left no footprint anywhere. Crossing himself, Olaf explains that "our Faith" is triumphant and that the stranger was the "wraith" of dead Odin. The refrain "Dead rides Sir Morten of Fogelsang" ends each of the thirteen stanzas of this poem.

VII. "Iron-Beard": When Olaf blows his bugle defiantly in Drontheim, farmers arm themselves to confront him there. Iron-Beard, "the churliest of the churls," quits his plowing, swears by Thor's Hammer, leaves his flaxen-haired daughter Gudrun, joins the farmers, and bravely tells Olaf to emulate previous kings by making ritualistic sacrifices to Odin and Thor. Olaf replies that this is to become a Christian land and the only sacrifices he plans to make are of rebellious noblemen. Fighting between the peasants and his soldiers breaks out behind him as he enters the Temple. Inside, Olaf shatters wooden statues of Odin and Thor with his gold-inlaid war-axe. Outside, Iron-Beard lies dead. Olaf offers the wailing farmers baptism or slaughter. They beg to be baptized. Thus Drontheim became "Christian . . . in name and fame." For "a blood-atonement," Olaf marries Gudrun.

VIII. "Gudrun": On their bridal night, Gudrun stands in the moonlit chamber. She looks fixedly on the cairn in which her father lies. She clutches a cold, sharp object. Odin awakens from his couch and asks what she is holding. The bodkin from her hair, she answers, adding that it fell and woke her up. Odin replies that "treachery lurking lies / Underneath the fairest hair!" and warns her. After a predawn blast from his bugle, "forever sundered ride / Bridegroom and bride!"

IX. "Thangbrand the Priest": Olaf's priest, short and burly, is learned and able but so contentious that Olaf sends him to Iceland to convert the pagans there. He doesn't like their bookish pretensions and grumbles with a leer over his beer in the alehouse. "Scalds and Saga-men" overhear him, praise their island as the best place "the sun / Doth shine upon!," and write satires ridiculing him. When they caricature him with a charcoal drawing, Thangbrand goes wild and kills two men. Fearful of execution, he escapes to Norway and meekly informs Olaf that he holds "little hope" for Icelanders.

X. "Raud the Strong": Olaf feels that his policy of converting the heathen has succeeded, but he dreams about Thor's continued defiance. Sigurd the Bishop pitches in to the effect that Raud the Strong, a bold Viking in the Salten Fiord up north, rules the Godoe Isles with wind-controlling sorcery. Olaf says he will go chat with Raud, and "Preach the Gospel with my sword, / Or be brought back in my shroud!"

XI. "Bishop Sigurd at Salten Fiord": Into the mouth of Salten Fiord plunge Olaf's ships, loaded with loyal men. When demon winds spin them about, Sigurd the Bishop stands on the bow of one vessel, surrounded by choristers, tapers, and incense. Holy water helps, and the fleet reaches land. The invaders find Raud's home. "Up the stairway, softly creeping, / To the loft where Raud was sleeping," they proceed. They grab the drunken fellow, and Olaf asks him to "Choose between the good and evil," and "Be baptized, or . . . die!" Raud defies God, the Devil, and "thy Gospel." Olaf feeds him an adder, which fatally poisons the blasphemer. After that they baptize every "Swarthy Lap and fair Norwegian" along the Salten Fiord's salmon streams, then pulverize the regional Thor and Odin temples. Olaf commandeers Raud's "carved and gilded / Dragon-ship" and in it leads his crew back to Drontheim.

XII. "King Olaf's Christmas": Olaf and his Berserkers celebrate the Yule-tide with "nut-brown ale" and songs. Over his drinking horn Olaf makes the sign of the cross, but his men make the sign of Thor's Hammer over theirs. Olaf orders Halfred the Scald to "Sing me a song divine / With a sword in every line." Olaf flourishes his own sword and praises it as superior to "Quern-biter of Hakon the Good," which cut through a millstone and also Thoralf the Strong. Halfred sings lustily. The men praise both Olaf and his sword. Olaf demands that the song make mention of Christ's cross, with these words: "Thor's hammer or Christ's cross: / Choose!" Halfred kisses the cruciform hilt of Olaf's sword. The men shout the name of Christ. The noonday sun rises over the mists, "Like the lifting of the Host" almost hidden by "incense-clouds." Seeing the shadow of Olaf's sword hilt cast a cross on the wall, the men offer "Was-hael! / To the Lord!"

XIII. "The Building of the Long Serpent": Olaf orders Thorberg Skafting, master shipbuilder, to build him a serpent ship twice as long as Raud's beached Dragon. The fame-seeking builder supervises busy carpenters, flax spinners, blacksmiths, and tar boilers. But warlocks send "an ill wind" from Thorberg Skafting's farm home. He briefly leaves his work. And when he returns, he finds his ship sabotaged with deep gashes everywhere. Outraged, Olaf starts blaspheming, until Thorberg Skafting tells him to calm down, takes the blame, repairs everything perfectly, and soon presents the finished vessel: over seventy ells long, gilt, gorgeous, with a steel-crested figure-head. The Long Serpent is launched. Thorberg Skafting is praised for the next hundred years.

XIV. "The Crew of the Long Serpent": Behold the ship in Drontheim bay. Olaf's crew includes Ulf the Red, forecastle man; mailed Kolbiorn, near him; Thrand Rame of Thelemark, tattooed and with a hand like Thor's hammer; tender-eyed, blond Einar Tamberskelver, at the mainmast; and Biorn and Bork, in command of 30 "horny-handed" oarsmen each. Olaf commands these men and others, all of whom are devoted to him and love the freedom he inspires. When ashore at Drontheim, they roar through the streets, stamp in the taverns, and toss down ale astonishingly. They outdo the crews of "Old King Gorm" and "Blue-Tooth Harald."

XV. "A Little Bird in the Air": A bird sings to this effect: Thyri, Svend the Dane's beautiful, fair-haired sister, married King Burislaf the Vend, but grew so unhappy in "his town by the stormy sea" that "after a week and a day, / She has fled away and away." Rumor has it that Thyri went to Olaf's court and that Olaf has married the beauty. Doing so will mean war with Svend and Burislaf. Each of the five stanzas of this poem ends with this refrain: "Hoist up your sails of silk, / And flee away from each other."

XVI. "Queen Thyri and the Angelica Stalks": The sun is shining, the birds are singing, and the meadows are green. But Thyri, Olaf's queen, is lonely and tearful. Olaf enters her chamber, smiling and bringing her fragrant angelicas. She throws them on the floor and upbraids him, saying that King Harald Gormson gave her mother, the queen, far better presents "When he ravaged Norway" and gathered "treasure / For her royal needs." She scorns him for not seizing her "domains . . . / From King Burislaf" and adds that he probably feared her brother, the fork-bearded King Svend of Denmark, would defeat Olaf and "Scatter" his "vassels / As the wind the chaff." Insulted and challenged, Olaf gathers his forces, steers his Long Serpent to Thyri's domain, and takes it from Burislaf. Returning, Olaf jests that women "draw us" better than oxen can and "confess[es]" that his queen deserves jewels, not angelica stalks.

XVII. "King Svend of the Forked Beard": After Gunhild, his queen, died, King Svend "Plighted . . . his faith / To Sigrid the Haughty." Her face still has an "angry scar" from Olaf's heavy slap. She orders Svend to get revenge. Spring comes, and he leaves his farm work and recruits the Swedish king, Eric the Norseman, and Earl Sigvald to join him. They all anchor "under [the Isle of] Svend" to plot, and Sigvald proceeds "On a foul errand bent."

Longfellow wrote a canto entitled "The Revel of Earl Sigvald," in which Sigvald and his fellow Vikings drink "in honor to Christ and Saint Michael," and which the poet probably would have placed immediately following "King Svend of the Forked Beard." But he suppressed it, since it would have weakened his characterization of Olaf by having his political enemies be Christians.

Bibliography: Hilen.

XVIII. "King Olaf and Earl Sigvald": Waiting ashore, Olaf points toward the north. Sigvald is at sea. Historians record that on that day "Seventy vessels / Sailed out of the bay." Billows scatter them, until Olaf and Sigvald "Sailed side by side." Sigvald treacherously offers to pilot Olaf into the deep channels. Enemy ships, and Sigrid's revenge, await him.

XIX. "King Olaf's War-Horns": Olaf sees the danger, orders his sails struck, the war-horns sounded, and a ship to be lashed to each side of his Long Serpent. The three vessels drift toward the Danish fleet. Olaf identifies the Danish King Svend, the Swedish king's Earl Eric, and Eric the Norseman as his three main enemies, but regards only Eric as formidable. Eric cuts loose Olaf's companion vessels and pledges "A death drink salt as the sea" to Olaf.

XX. "Einar Tamberskelver": Einar Tamberskelver aims arrow after arrow at Eric, who, his mail grazed, orders a Laplander to shoot at Einar. He does and breaks Einar's bow. Olaf gives his bow to Einar, who finds it too thin and instead of using it climbs aboard Eric's ship.

XXI. "King Olaf's Death-Drink": The gory battle rages all day. Boarders use grappling irons. Shouts grow weaker. All of Norway's sailors are wounded, lying dead, or drowned. Olaf and Kolbiorn, his brave marshal, stand side by side with identical shields. Eric, aboard the Long Serpent, cuts down its mast, and the sails fall like forest snow. Olaf and Kolbiorn raise their shining shields together and leap like meteors into the sea. Eric grabs Kolbiorn's shield and calls it Olaf's. Olaf's floats off, resembling a jewel in the "Sea-current's eddying ring." Although legend says that Olaf stripped his mail away and swam underwater, he is never seen again.

XXII. "The Nun of Nidaros": While praying at midnight in the Drontheim convent, Abbess Astrid hears a strange voice, which proves to be that of Saint John. He says that although conflict is recognized—for example, "Cross against corselet, / Love against hatred"—patience will overcome. God is approaching, and the spirit and truth and love are stronger than swords and arrows in this ephemeral world. The saint's final message is this:

> The dawn is not distant,
> Nor is the night starless;
> Love is eternal!
> God is still God, and
> His faith shall not fail us;
> Christ is eternal!

Very much as is the case with "The Knight's Tale" in Geoffrey Chaucer's *Canterbury Tales,* "The Saga of King Olaf" is disproportionately lengthy to be part of a collection of tales. Longfellow's main source for "King Olaf" was the translation by Samuel Laing of *Heimskringla; or, Chronicles of the Kings of Norway* (3 vols., 1844), which Longfellow turned to (Feb 1849). Written by the Icelandic statesman-historian Snorri Sturluson (1178-1241), *Heimskringla* is a poetic chronicle of Norse mythology and early history. Longfellow had, however, already read parts of the Swedish version of it a decade earlier and was fascinated by the conflict between Jarl Hakon, the pagan, and King Olaf, the fierce Christian. Often interrupted by other matters, Longfellow composed the 22 cantos of his saga piecemeal (1849, 1860, 1862). All but its first and last cantos are based on *Heimskringla.* The poetic virtuosity Longfellow displays throughout is brilliant; no canto has the same stanzaic form. King Olaf in real life was Olaf I, known as Olaf Tryggvesson (969-1000; king 995-1000). The popularity of Longfellow's treatment of him led the poet to plan, abortively, a lyric poem on Olaf II (Olaf Haraldsson, 995-1030), Olaf I's nonrelated successor. Dudley Buck (1839-1909), the Boston composer, set "The Nun of Nidaros" to music. Longfellow learned of this, wrote John Sullivan Dwight (1813-93), the Boston music critic (20 Jul 1879) to ask him unavailingly to use his influence in getting it performed, and wrote Buck (21 Sep 1879) to express gratitude for sending him a copy of the composition.

Bibliography: Arvin; Hilen, ed.; S. Longfellow; Wagenknecht, 1986.

"Interlude." The Theologian comments on how glad he is that "war and waste of clashing creeds / Now end in words, and not in deeds." He prefers the Lord's Prayer, plain faith in Christ, not "councils and decrees," but simple "human charity." All of which reminds him of a tragic tale from "the chronicles of Spain."

"The Theologian's Tale: Torquemada." When Ferdinand and Isabella ruled Spain, Torquemada (Tomás de Torquemada [1420?–98])—he of the "subtle brain"—was the Grand Inquisitor. Outside Valladolid, a widowed Hidalgo, "proud and taciturn," improved each day by attending church, praying, and honoring each religious holiday. His only fun was hunting boars and watching "When Jews were burned, or banished from the land." He often heard the demonic cry, "Kill! kill! and let the Lord find out his own!" The Hidalgo had two lovely daughters, just released from a convent school and back in his castle "in the dawn of womanhood." A presentiment came upon him of impending doom and death. So he spied on his daughters, questioned his servants, and believed their gossip that the girls met a gypsy in the woods and also a mendicant monk. He deliberately listened when his daughters were "talking in the dead of night / In their own chamber, and without a light." He branded their talk "Heresy!" and reported them to a priest, who queried the pair in their father's presence. They answered briefly, "Nor when accused evaded or denied." The Hidalgo said, "The Holy Office, then, must intervene!" Behold, coming to Valladolid, "the Grand Inquisitor of Spain, / With all the fifty horsemen in his train." He heard the Hidalgo's report and compared him to Abraham when told "To sacrifice his only son." The Hidalgo accused his daughters, who were condemned to death by fire. The Hidalgo requested permission to gather the wood, did so, and then asked to be allowed "to light the funeral fire!" Agreeing, Torquemada said that churchmen "through all ages" would "magnify thy deed." The scaffold was made ready in the market place. Church bells rang. Monks chanted. Crowds gathered. The Hidalgo burst forward, lit the fagots, and then ran off. Why did the skies not weep rain? Why did no abyss open to hide this crime? That very night, the Hidalgo's castle was wrapped in flames. He was seen at a window praying until all was consumed. More than 300 years have passed. His name has been lost, "and no trace / Remains on earth of his afflicted race." But the name of Torquemada "Looms in the distant landscape of the Past, / Like a burnt tower upon a blackened heath." The source of this gruesome tale is *Historia de los Protestantes Españolas; see* Adolfo De Castro, *Geschichte der spanischen protestanten und ihrer verfolgung durch Philipp II* (1866).

Bibliography: Wagenknecht, 1986.

"Interlude." The listeners are all quiet. The Spanish Jew remembers past persecutions, his eyes expressing "wrath and tears of shame." The Student breaks the silence by saying that tragic tales seem out of place for this pleasant group and adds that a merry Italian story, of the sort disdained, would be more fun. But the Poet interrupts and says he has a tale with "meaning in it, if not mirth."

"The Poet's Tale: The Birds of Killingworth." In spring, God, called by Caedmon "the Blithe-heart King," writes songs for many a bird—merle, mavis, robin, crow, raven, and even "birds of passage" up from "tropic isle[s]." One spring a century ago the farmers of Killingworth got tired of crows feeding on their gardens and pastures and "set a price" on them. The proud Squire, the mean Parson, the Preceptor (love-struck by Almira, his favorite upper-class girl), and the cocksure Deacon all assembled in the town hall to address the worried farmers. The Squire recommended killing the birds. The Preceptor rose. He eloquently argued against depriving crows of a little food, praised the "sweet music" of various birds, wondered what woods and orchards would be like without them, preferred them to "the incessant stir / Of insects," was glad that crows aided harvests by crushing beetles, and felt that seeing birds treated nicely would teach children "reverence / For life." However, the farmers ignored all this "fine-spun sentiment" and voted to put a bounty on crow heads. Even as the "fair Almira" read her Preceptor's speech in the papers and praised him for it, the fusillade caused a veritable "Saint Bartholomew of Birds," a Herod-like slaughter of the innocents. Hot summer followed. So did a horde of insects that devoured fields and gardens. Worms dropped from trees on ladies' bonnets. The farmers repealed their edict, but too late: Autumn leaves fell blushing in shame. In the spring, however, the farmers brought birds from all around in cages, released them to the "woods and fields . . . they loved best." Whether their songs were "canticles" or "satires," their music accompanied the wedding ceremony of Almira and her teacher. Alone among the narratives in *Tales of a Wayside Inn,* "The Birds of Killingworth" did not come from a literary source. Rather, it seems to have been based on a tradition in Killingworth, Connecticut, and certainly reflects Longfellow's lifelong reverence for all forms of life. Ralph Waldo Emerson* included the poem in *Parnassus,* which he assembled and edited (1874).

Bibliography: Arvin.

"Finale." It is late now at the inn. The Landlord snores, stirs, and insists he heard everything. All say their goodnights. A servant rakes the fire and puts out the parlor light. The village clock strikes one.

Part Second.

"Prelude." It rains the next morning on the Sudbury Inn. The Poet hears the mail coach stop, then go on. The Squire is reading the paper when one after another his guests report for breakfast. The Sicilian draws the Jew's portrait and labels it "'Edrehi, / At the Red Horse in Sudbury.'" The Theologian busily feeds some caged robins. The Student and the Musician discuss the sources of various stories. The Poet studies the cloudy sunrise. When the Sicilian sees an old, neglected horse, he is inspired to tell his story.

"The Sicilian's Tale: The Bell of Atri." King John of Italy once hung a bell in the public square at Atri, in Abruzzo, and said that if anyone felt wronged he should ring the bell and John would order the Syndic to hear the case. Time passed, and the bell rope frayed; so someone mended it with a leafy vine. See,

now, the proud Knight of Atri, whose faithful horse served him well, on hunts, and at camps and court, but who is now so stingy that he has turned the old beast out to graze wherever it can. It nibbles on the bell-vine tendrils and thus rouses the Syndic from his siesta. The cocky old Knight is soon admonished to right matters. Shamed by the crowd's laughter, he agrees "to provide / Shelter in stall, and food and field beside." King John is delighted when he hears what happened. The source of this story is *Canto Novelle Antiche* by Carlo Gualteruzzi (?– c.1577). This poem was published, as "The Alarm-Bell of Atri," in *AM,* Jul 1870, for which Longfellow received $150.

Bibliography: Hilen, ed.

"Interlude." The Poet praises all those who defend abused beasts. The Sicilian asks Edrehi to speak. In response, the Jew only smiles querulously but then tells his story.

"The Spanish Jew's Tale: Kambalu." Alau, a brave captain, brings his caravan laden with treasure from Kandahar to the palace of his brother, the Tartar Khan, in Kambalu. Alau explains that the Khan's enemies are all dead. Only the Kalif of Baldacca resisted the Khan. So Alau lured "the gray old" miser into attacking outside his gate, ambushed his forces, chased him back into a tower where he had his gold, silver, and jewels, locked him in his own dungeon, and let him die there, "clutching his treasure." This was "the story, strange and true," that Alau told. Longfellow's source for "Kambalu" is *Il Milione . . .* by Marco Polo (c.1254–1324). This poem, titled "The Kalif of Baldacca," was first published in *AM,* Jun 1864.

Bibliography: Wagenknecht, 1986.

"Interlude." The Student expresses surprise at the Jew's story, says he expected something from another source, adds that the story was pleasant enough, but offers "a merrier tale to clear / The dark and heavy atmosphere."

"The Student's Tale: The Cobbler of Hagenau." In the quaint old town of Hagenau in the "Alsatian hills," a contentious cobbler, well read in secular works, worries his God-fearing little wife because he is "inclined /

Somewhat to let the next world drift." One afternoon, while the cobbler is mending some shoes and singing a song about how we enter "the world / . . . naked and bare" and go at death "nobody knows where," a religious procession passes by. John Tetzel, the monk, rides by in a coach, accompanied by musicians and horsemen. The cobbler tells his wife not to buy any indulgence from "that reverend bird." That night at the church, filled with light and burning incense, Tetzel spreads out his indulgences, for sale "Like ballads at a country fair," exhorts his congregation, mostly women, to buy forgiveness of sins and thus "ransom" their dead from Purgatory. Gold and silver coins fall into his strongbox "Like pebbles dropped into a well." The cobbler's wife pays a gold florin into the box and takes her "Letter of Indulgence" home. Tetzel leaves. Seasons come and go. The meek wife dies, secure in her heart that she merits Paradise. But the village priest reports her to the village magistrate that no funeral mass has been heard for her soul's salvation. The magistrate hauls the cobbler before him on a charge of heresy. The cobbler produces his wife's indulgence, which she carefully preserved, along with her wedding dress and other mementoes "of past hours." The magistrate and then the priest read the indulgence, which removes all sins from the woman and guarantees her admission to heaven. The cobbler reminds the officials that he has read about "Reynard the Fox." In medieval beast-epic cycles in popular Dutch, French, and German literature, Reynard stories satirized the Catholic Church, especially monks and nuns. The main source for this tale was *Histoire de la réformation du seizième siècle* by Jean Henri Merle d'Aubigné (1794–1872).

Bibliography: Wagenknecht, 1986.

"Interlude." When the Poet wonders how the tale ended, the Student explains that Reynard fought the Wolf, won, and became the Keeper of the Seals. The Sicilian says the moral of the fox story is that cunning succeeds. He adds that his own tale had a better moral, while the Jew aimed merely to amuse. The Musician apologizes for the

length of his saga, plays some tender melodies on his violin, and tells the following story—again punctuated by varied strains from his instrument.

"The Musician's Tale: The Ballad of Carmilhan." Sailors aboard the *Valdemar* in the Baltic Sea are spinning tales. One concerns Klaboterman, "a spright / Invisible to mortal sight," who helps busy sailors but torments the idle. The skipper answers with a yarn about the spectral ship the *Carmilhan,* near which in mid-Atlantic are three rocks perilous to careless ships. The *Valdemar* captain swears that if he ever found the *Carmilhan,* he would run her down. Such talk scares the Bible-clutching cabin boy. Off sails the *Valdemar,* past "Skager-rack," beyond Finistere, on under black skies, into a hurricane, and through the *Carmilhan,* undamaged. The Klaboterman moves from her bowsprit to board the *Carmilhan.* Down she goes with all her crew—save the cabin boy, soon "picked up at sea" "To tell the tale." This lively poem relates both to German folktales of Phantom Ships and to "The Rime of the Ancient Mariner" by Samuel Taylor Coleridge. The care with which Longfellow handled details in his poetry is revealed by the fact that he wrote a letter (3 Apr 1872) to his German friend Francis Lieber* to ask whether the Baltic Sea had an appreciable tide. Told no, he revised an original line in this poem from "The tide was at its flood" to "Serene o'er field and flood."

Bibliography: Arvin; Hilen, ed.; Wagenknecht, 1986.

"Interlude." The applause that followed causes the Poet to complain about too many "Old World" narratives and proposes to offer a New England one, with "A sweetness as of home-made bread." The Student gripes that too often what is old is wrongly decried, that people too often demand what is "new in prose and verse," usually "half baked" at that. The Poet's unhappiness is only momentary.

"The Poet's Tale: Lady Wentworth." It is a century and more ago. Behold the Earl of Halifax in old Portsmouth. He gazes on Mistress Stavers in amorous desperation. Her husband is on his way to Boston. But suddenly he sees a charming, barefooted "thin slip of a girl, like a new moon, / Sure to be rounded into beauty soon." She is carrying a pail of dripping water along the street. Mistress Stavers calls her Martha Hilton and rebukes her for appearing half dressed thus. Laughing, the girl says she will ride in her very own chariot one day. Halifax smiles at her "benignly." Now see Governor Wentworth, with a pageant of carriages and outriders, approach his official mansion. Mistress Stavers curtsies "low and fast." For seven "slow years" the lonely governor resides in his beautifully appointed colonial residence, during which time Martha, "not wholly unobserved," was a hardworking "maid of all work" there. "By day, by night, the silver crescent grew, / Though hidden by clouds, her light still shining through." Time grinds on. For his sixtieth birthday one day in May, Governor Wentworth gives a lavish banquet. Guests include many of the elite, not least Reverend Arthur Brown, the rector. After they toast the king, festivities conclude "as none other I e'er knew." The governor introduces Martha; "how queen-like she appears; / The pale thin crescent of the days gone by / Is Dian now in all her majesty!" Explaining that this is not only his birthday but also his wedding day, the governor commands the rector to perform their ceremony, whereupon Martha becomes "Lady Wentworth of the Hall!" Longfellow found the story of Lady Wentworth in *Rambles about Portsmouth . . .* (1859–69) by Charles Warren Brewster (1802–68). The poem, for which Longfellow received $150, was first published in *AM,* Jan 1872.

Bibliography: Hilen, ed.; Wagenknecht, 1986.

"Interlude." The audience was delighted, including the Theologian, who, however, says many legends recorded by monks have "sweetness as of home-made bread." To make up for his grim story about Torquemada, he will present the loveliest one he knows. The Student says it will probably have some baleful fire in it, but "go forward."

"The Theologian's Tale: The Legend Beautiful." While praying devoutly in his chamber, a monk sees a vision of "our Lord, with light Elysian / Like a vesture wrapped about

him." The monk would rather stay but instead, when the convent bell rings, goes to feed the poor clamoring at the door. The beggars are ragged, "bestial" in appearance, and terrified at the possibility of being neglected. But will the Vision be there when the monk gets back to his room? The monk prays for these neglected, homeless persons, then hears these words:

> Whatsoever thing thou doest
> To the least of mine and lowest,
> That thou doest unto me!

Returning to his cell, the monk now understands the meaning of the Vision's words: "Hadst thou stayed, I must have fled!" Longfellow's source for this tale is "The Legend Beautiful" by Jeremy Taylor (1613–67). This poem was first published in *AM,* Dec 1871.

Bibliography: Wagenknecht, 1986.

"Interlude." When audience response is varied, the Theologian says it is true that different friends will advise one differently. The Sicilian says that they have just heard six stories and a seventh will complete "A cluster like the Pleiades." He can't find the Landlord to tell a tale; so he asks the Student for a second one since he "tell[s] them better than the rest." Flattered like "a child / When he is called a little man," the Student "unclosed / His smiling lips, and thus began."

"The Student's Second Tale: The Baron of Castine." One spring the Baron Castine left his castle in the Gave Valley of the Pyrenees. Time passes. Cardinal Mazarin (1602–61) has died. It is winter now, and the Baron's old father misses his "wild boy." Then a letter comes from "beautiful . . . Acadie." The lad has married Chief Madocawando's daughter. The old man is aghast; blessing his son with "His latest breath," he dies. Spring comes, and so, at last, does the Baron, with his bride. The Curate thought she would be "a painted savage" with "a robe of panther's hide." But no, she is "beautiful beyond belief," with gold-bronze skin as though it were "lighted by a fire within." When the Curate learns the Baron got married Indian-fashion by buying the lady with a pair of weapons, all is put right; they are married in the local church, with bells, a choir, and much rejoicing. There is a Castine, Maine. The plot for "The Baron of St. Castine" Longfellow found in *The History of the State of Maine . . .* (1832) by William D. Williamson (1779–1846). James T. Fields* paid Longfellow $150 for "The Baron of Castine," which first appeared in *AM,* Mar 1872.

Bibliography: Arvin; Hilen, ed.; Miller, Roscoe B. "Baron of Castine, American Pioneer." *Americana* 28 (Jan 1934): 92–97; Wagenknecht, 1986.

"Finale." Finished, the Student requests and receives applause. But the clapping is mainly because the sun has just "Burst from its canopy of cloud." Wind rattles the inn windows. The rain disappears "down the valley." Seeing "a shattered rainbow," everyone happily rushes outside.

Part Third.

"Prelude." Evening comes. A golden sunset is followed by darkness, then moonlight. The fireplace glows, and the chimney sings like an actor. The Sicilian asks the Jew what he was muttering at supper; "the Manichaean's prayer," he answers. He adds that all life is one, that we die "into life," that bread has life. The Poet says that birds and flowers have souls, but that creaking hinges, roaring chimneys, and rattling windows don't. Asked whether he was dreaming along those lines, the Jew says perhaps and offers this "vision of my waking dream."

"The Spanish Jew's Tale: Azrael." King Solomon is walking near his palace with Runjeet-Sing, a strange rajah from Hindostan, when they see Azrael, the Angel of Death. The rajah, afraid, wants to return home. Solomon lifts his blazing ring to the skies, whereupon a wind bears the rajah away. Azrael, smiling, tells Solomon that he was on his way to Hindostan to look for the rajah there.

Bibliography: Arvin; Wagenknecht, 1986.

"Interlude." The Sicilian asks the Jew to put his Talmud to rest and plays a Neapolitan air on the spinet. The Poet offers to tell about "my Azrael," a mortal angel, namely Charlemagne, when he charged "across the Lombard plain" to attack Pavia.

"The Poet's Tale: Charlemagne." When Desiderio, the King of the Lombards, sees a huge army approaching from the north, he asks Olger the Dane, his long-time hostage, whether Charlemagne is leading such a host. No, says Olger, and says the same when the Paladins of France likewise draw near. Soon some bishops, abbots, and priests appear, with several counts, at which Desiderio suggests they go hide. Olger replies that when the harvests shake and the Po and Ticono rivers lash at the walls, then it will be Charlemagne. Suddenly out of "a black and threatening cloud" bursts Charlemagne, "Man of Iron!," clothed in iron, bearing iron arms, riding a horse possessed of the strength of iron, and leading iron-hearted men. Olger exclaims that this is Charlemagne and "falls as one dead at Desiderio's feet." Longfellow's source here is *Storia Degli Italiani* (6 vols., 1854) by Cesare Cantù (1804–95), who quotes therein from *De Factis Caroli Magni.* In a journal entry (12 May 1872), Longfellow says that his friend Charles Callahan Perkins* first acquainted him with the story. "Charlemagne" is the only poem in *Tales of a Wayside Inn* written in blank verse, a form Longfellow never felt comfortable using.

Bibliography: Wagenknecht, 1986.

"Interlude." The Student praises the story because it came "from the ancient myth / Of some one with an iron flail," or perhaps from the legend of Hyphaestus, who "Heated himself red-hot with fire" and embraced his attackers. No, answers the Poet, it came from "the hunger and the thirst / In all men for the marvellous." Such "ideal[s]" are "truer than historic fact." Thus, Charlemagne embodied what people feared. But no, he adds; the "iron flail" allusion is to "Talus in the Faerie Queene." The Theologian offers as a possible source the description of Artaxerxes in "the Anabasis." Anyway, says the Student, he has a rosier yarn about Charlemagne, from the Latin of "the good Monk of Lauresheim."

"The Student's Tale: Emma and Eginhard." Alcuin teaches Charlemagne's sons and other students many subjects. One brilliant pupil is Eginhard, a Frankish youth. He becomes so adept in astronomy, grammar, logic, mathematics, and music that Charlemagne makes him his valued scribe. Eginhard was unschooled in "the one art supreme, whose law is fate." Here comes Princess Emma, fresh from the convent to the palace. Eginhard observes her, with knights, at banquets, and soon in the garden, where they discuss roses and meet secretly "in the twilight park." "O mystery of love!" One night he makes his way to her room. They pledge their love. But by dawn a snow has blanketed the courtyard. Charlemagne, "sleepless with the cares / And troubles that attend on state affairs," happens to spy Emma first carrying Eginhard on her shoulders to his quarters and then returning by stepping on her outgoing footprints. In the morning, Charlemagne tells Eginhard to await until the councilmen pronounce sentence for his offense. Although some want exile, others death, Charlemagne suggests mercy, not justice, and says that "Over those fatal footprints I will throw / My ermine mantle like another snow." His terrified, blushing daughter enters but is soon happy; for Charlemagne places her hand in that of his loyal, affectionate, and zealous scribe and calls him his son. Thus the poem ends with what may be called a happy shotgun wedding. Emma and her lover were the subject of "La Neige," an earlier poem by Alfred de Vigny (1797–1863).

Bibliography: Arvin; Johnson, Carl L. "Three Notes on Longfellow." *Harvard Studies and Notes in Philology and Literature* 14 (1932): 249–71; Wagenknecht, 1986; Williams.

"Interlude." Some doubt the yarn's veracity, but all liked it. The Musician hears two of his violin strings break. The Landlord, long out of sight doing chores, enters with firewood and says it comes from apple trees "the first Howe of Sudbury" planted. The Theologian says he will "tell a tale worldwide apart / From that the Student had just told." All the same, it too will reveal that all hearts beat alike. While the clock is slowly striking eight, the Theologian has time to quote Horace on necessity and fate. Then he "sing[s] his Idyl of the Past."

"The Theologian's Tale: Elizabeth." Elizabeth Haddon, a Quaker, lives in a home by the Delaware River, built but never lived in by her father. She looks out and comments on the "spotless . . . snow" falling outside.

But her maid, Hannah, complains that the roads will soon be blocked and wonders how Joseph, Elizabeth's servant, will get back home. Elizabeth reprovingly says that "the Lord will provide." Hannah prepares dinner. When Elizabeth comments that Joseph has gone to the village with food and clothes for the poor, Hannah expresses concern that Elizabeth is overly generous, to which the pious woman says what she has is the Lord's, not hers. Somehow Hannah is moved to recall John Estaugh, who spoke inspiringly at a large Quaker meeting one May in London.

Joseph returns by horse-drawn sleigh and brings in a stranger. Elizabeth, as though drawn by "an unseen power," names and welcomes John Estaugh. He explains that he felt conducted here by the Lord. John saw Joseph's sleigh, climbed up, and here he is, "led by the light of the Spirit." Joseph stamps in, and the three share supper. Around the mellow fireplace, Elizabeth explains that she obeyed "the voice imperative" and "cast in her lot with her people / Here in the desert land." Elizabeth, hearing Hannah upstairs preparing the bedrooms, jokes about the girl's awkward feet; this makes Joseph laugh to himself, but he says nothing. In the morning, Joseph is busy plowing out the snowdrifts; John says farewell and promises to return in May; and in the attic, Hannah, "the homely," looks down at Joseph and laughs.

Spring comes. The robin chirps about "his Babes in the Wood," while Elizabeth sings only inwardly. One morning a procession of worshippers is heading toward "the Quarterly Meeting." They stop at Elizabeth's and freely partake of her wine, bread, and honey, and then continue. Halting John briefly, Elizabeth whispers frankly to him that the Lord has laid her under the obligation of telling him she loves him. He praises her frank speech and her "soul's immaculate whiteness" but adds that neither inward light nor voice is yet leading him toward her. He is going away and will wait for the Lord's "guidance." She is content, knowing that he will cross the sea and assured that the Lord will decree what is to be.

Elizabeth remains quiet and uncomplaining and dutifully works more for others than for herself. Homely Hannah keeps healthy with the vigorous housework. When she disparages Joseph's obvious virtues, Elizabeth reproves her. In the Old World, John carries a priceless secret in his heart. Why did he doubt and delay so long? Finally, "the light shone at last," and he returns to accept "the gift that was offered, / Better than houses and lands, the gift of a woman's affection." They are married. So too with Joseph. When he rushes "his bashful wooing," Hannah first says, "Nay," and adds, "But thee may make believe, and see what will come of it, Joseph."

"Elizabeth" is based on "The Youthful Emigrant," a story by Lydia Maria Child (1802–80), which in turn was based on *A Call to the Unfaithful Professors of Truth* by John Estaugh (1676–1742).

Bibliography: Arvin; Wagenknecht, 1986.

"Interlude." When the Student calls "Elizabeth" "a winsome tale" though untrue, the Theologian denies the accusation and says he read it in an old newspaper. The Jew says it doesn't matter, since "The cloak of truth is lined with lies." The Sicilian stops the argument by promising "a tale / That's merrier than the nightingale" and at the same time a "falsehood."

"The Sicilian's Tale: The Monk of Casal-Maggiore." Two monks are walking back to their convent at Casal-Maggiore, carrying their heavy "beggar's sacks." Brother Anthony is thin and quiet. Brother Timothy is strong, coarse, and illiterate. They come upon an ass. Its owner, Gilbert, is gathering fagots in the forest. Timothy ties himself to the ass's tree with its halter, orders Anthony to load their sacks on the ass, take it to the convent, and say Timothy stayed back resting and the farmer loaned them his ass. When Gilbert returns, Timothy persuades him to believe that Timothy, as a punishment for gluttony, was demonized into an ass but, fully penitent now, is human again. Apologizing for ignorant mistreatment, Gilbert takes Timothy home to Cicely, his wife, their children, and his father, a veteran of the French and Milanese war. Timothy is welcomed as saintly and dines on their last chickens and some nice wine. By morning,

however, he has "cast such [lewd] glances at Dame Cicely" that Gilbert becomes enraged. He orders Timothy to return to Casal-Maggiore and, moreover, "Since monkish flesh and asinine are one," to fast and scourge himself so as not to become an ass again. A pretty morning dawns over the Apennines. Timothy tells his prior that their ass was a gift to the convent. Not wanting to feed it, the prior decides to sell it at a neighboring fair. "It happened now by chance, as some might say, / Others perhaps would call it destiny," that Gilbert is there. He sees his ass, thinks it ate too much again and reverted to ass status, and—encouraged by scoffing witnesses—buys it, and takes it home, where his children "hung about his neck,—/ Not Gilbert's, but the ass's." Gilbert feeds it well; it grows selfish, even vicious, breaks its halter, and raids the family cabbage patch. Gilbert beats it and overworks it again, "Until at last the great consoler, Death," ends its "sufferings." Gilbert's father hopes "Heaven [will] pardon Brother Timothy, / And keep us from the sin of gluttony."

Longfellow found the original of this coarse fabliau piece in a group of Italian stories by Michele Colombo (1747–1838). The poem is cast in brilliantly sustained ottava rima.

Bibliography: Arvin; Wagenknecht, 1986.

"Interlude." The Jew calls the Sicilian "Luigi" and says werewolves are well known "But the were-ass is something new." Still, if beasts can take human form, humans can be punished by being converted to beasts. The Jew adds that since his first story was "not acceptable to all," he will try another. He hopes the Landlord will stay seated this time.

"The Spanish Jew's Second Tale: Scanderbeg," in *AM,* May 1873. After King Ladislaus, a Hun, defeats the Turkish army of King Amurath on the day of Pentecost, Scanderbeg, also known as Iskander and George Castriot, gathers his ruined forces and plans to revolt. When a scribe from Amurath arrives, Scanderbeg explains that the defeat was God's will, lays hold of the scribe—that "man of books and brains"—and orders him to write an official command to the Pasha of

Croia, the city where Scanderbeg was born, to surrender the place—known as Ak-Hissar. In fear, the scribe does so, seals the order with his official ring, but expresses fear that Amurath will be furious and offers to escape. Scanderbeg promptly kills him with his bejeweled "scimetar" and merrily leads 300 followers past Argentar and the Drin river to moated Croia. Albanians and Turkomen eat and drink with Scanderbeg, and he presents the order to the Pasha, who says "Allah is just and great," and gives over both city and surrounding lands. Scanderbeg's flag, displaying a double-headed black eagle, replaces the crescent flag, because "men's souls are tired of the Turks, / And their wicked ways and works." The people hail their new leader. News spreads. As recorded by Ben Joshua Ben Meir, other cities, "far and near," were also easily grasped.

Skanderbeg (c.1404–68), the revered Albanian chief and national hero, was also known by various authorities as Iskander, Iskander Beg, Iskander Bey, and George Castriota, and was from Kroja. Ladislaus III (or VI) (1424–44) crusaded against the Turks (1443).

Bibliography: Arvin; Hilen, ed.; Wagenknecht, 1986.

"Interlude." The Poet says he loved the story about "swarthy" Scanderbeg. The Theologian liked it too except for the hero's "treason with the Scribe." The Student praises its "hoofbeat" rhymes and would like to hear more about Ben Meir. The Musician talks again about Viking heroism. The Sicilian calls the story a cobweb fabrication. The uneasy Landlord wonders if he can avoid having to tell another tale. The Student relieves the Landlord by asking the Musician to stop worrying about his popped violin strings and come up with another yarn—perhaps about a shipwreck. The Musician reluctantly agrees but says that it will be "a song almost divine," one his nurse lulled him with when he was little.

"The Musician's Tale: The Mother's Ghost." Svend Dyring woos and wins a fair maid. His refrain is "*I myself was young!*" After they have six children in seven years, the mother dies. He finds a second wife, but she is bitter and proud and treats her stepchildren cruelly. She gives "neither ale nor bread" to them and forces them to sleep on straw in the dark. Their dead mother hears their crying and obtains God's permission to visit them, but only until the cock crows. As she whisks through town, the watchdogs howl. She appears before her children, scaring them at first but then treating them tenderly. She tells the oldest daughter to summon her father. Speaking "in anger and shame," she reminds him that she never kept her children hungry, cold, and in darkness. "If I come again unto your hall, / As cruel a fate shall you befall!" Now, when the watchdogs wail and bay, they think the dead are returning and provide the children with "bread and ale."

Longfellow translated "The Mother's Ghost" from a Danish ballad he found in *Danmarks Gamle Folkeviser* (5 vols., 1853–83), collected by Svend Hersleb Grundtvig (1824–83).

Bibliography: Arvin; Wagenknecht, 1986.

"Interlude." The Theologian praises such touching old ballads, plain and simple. The Student agrees in part but also feels that poets "are birds / Of passage," not "fowls in barnyards born / To cackle," and therefore must range "where their instinct leads." The Theologian, though agreeing in part, says "what is native still is best" and therefore says let's listen to the Landlord.

"The Landlord's Tale: The Rhyme of Sir Christopher." Sir Christopher Gardiner, a Knight of the Holy Sepulchre, comes to Boston as though "his august presence lent / A glory to the colony." He cuts quite a figure on the street in "Winthrop's time," with his rapier, doublet, hose, boots, ostrich-plumed hat, perfumed gloves, and fancy curls, and sporting "superior manners now obsolete!" As though weary of the ways of the world, he establishes what he calls "his country-seat" (really a log cabin) out of town. While pretending he wants to join the Puritan church, he roysters with Morton of Merry Mount, that "Lord of misrule and riot and sin," and in addition harbors a pretty blonde lady in his cabin. He calls her his cousin, although she is actually a woman "he had wed / In the Italian manner, as men said."

Worse, it's also said he's "a Papist in disguise." When word reaches Governor Winthrop (John Winthrop [1588-1649]) from England that Sir Christopher "carelessly left behind" two additional wives, some advisers suggest deportation while others argue for execution. Winthrop orders Sir Christopher seized, but the marshal and his bailiffs can find only the lady. They carry her through the streets weeping, and Winthrop scolds her and sends her off to England—to Sir Christopher's other wives—in search of him. But, no; he's off in the woods shooting pigeons with a certain "noble savage." Hearing of a bounty on his feathery-hatted companion, the Indian would bring in his scalp until he learns the fellow is wanted alive. Brought in, now melancholy, dishevelled, and dusty, Sir Christopher still manages "an unblushing face" before the authorities. Winthrop courteously listens as the fellow suggests "colonial laws were too severe / When applied to a gallant cavalier," but immediately thereafter orders him to depart from Salem and return "To Merry England over the sea, / As being unmeet to inhabit here." This Knight of the Holy Sepulchre is remembered as "The first who furnished this barren land / With apples of Sodom and ropes of sand."

In 1627, Thomas Morton (c.1590-1667) ridiculed his Puritan neighbors by setting up a maypole in his yard on the site of Quincy, which he renamed Ma-re-Mount. He was arrested by Captain Miles Standish (1628), was sent to England, returned to America (1629), was tried and convicted by Winthrop (1630), and was exiled to England (1631). He wrote his descriptive and satirical *New English Canaan* (Amsterdam, 1637), returned to Plymouth (1634), went to Rhode Island and Maine, and was arrested and jailed (1644-45). Nathaniel Hawthorne* treats Morton in "The May-Pole of Merry Mount" (1836) and in "Main Street" (1849) but does not mention Sir Christopher Gardiner in either work. In "The Rhyme of Sir Christopher," Longfellow handles the clash between Puritan and Cavalier in a more sprightly manner than Hawthorne does, especially in his beautifully ambivalent "The May-Pole of Merry Mount."

Bibliography: Arvin; Wagenknecht, 1986.

"Finale." Such were the tales—well, ill; new, old—"In idle moments idly told." The friendly guests watch the fire, hesitant to leave but finally saying their drowsy goodnights. Only the clock stirs in the parlor. In the morning, the guests leave by coach. They exchange farewells with "the portly Landlord," unaware that they will forever scatter. Two are now abroad. Three are dead. Some may see themselves in this book like reflected faces in a brook looking up at them as in a dream.

The Wayside Inn, built (1686) by the Howe family from England, was a famous way station in Sudbury, Massachusetts, 20 miles from Cambridge, an easy destination for travelers heading west from Boston. After Lyman Howe, a fifth-generation descendant of the family, died unmarried (1861), the place was not used as an inn again until Edward R. Lemon, its owner, reopened it (1897). When Longfellow visited the place with James T. Fields* (1862), he described it in his journal (31 Oct 1862) as "A rambling, tumble-down building, two hundred years old; and till now in the family of the Howes," and added that it had been converted into the Red Horse Tavern. He evidently wanted to see the place, because a few days earlier, according to his journal (11 Oct), he planned to "Write a little upon the Wayside Inn,—a beginning only." Continuing with his accustomed speed, he wrote Fields (11 Nov) that "The Sudbury Tales go on famously. I have now five complete, with a great part of the 'Prelude.'" Before the first part was published, he wrote Fields (25 Aug 1863) that he wanted the title changed to *Tales of a Wayside Inn.* It was published (Nov 1863), with a print run of 15,000 copies. For rights to produce their London edition of the first part of *Tales of a Wayside Inn* (1864), George Routledge (1812-88) & Sons, publishers, paid Longfellow £2,000.

Longfellow based his tale-tellers on real persons. Thus, the Landlord was Lyman Howe; the Spanish Jew, Isaac Edrehi (?-1884; scholar and Boston peddler in the 1850s); the Sicilian, Luigi Monti;* the Musician, Ole Bornemann Bull;* the Poet, Thomas William Parsons (1819-92; dentist, poet, translator of Dante's *Inferno,* and friend of James Russell Lowell* and Charles Eliot Norton*); the Student, Henry Ware Wales (1818-56; Harvard man and traveler-scholar, who died young and willed a sizable library to Harvard); and the Theologian, Daniel Treadwell (1791-1872; Harvard physics professor).

The second and third parts of *Tales of a Wayside Inn* sold well enough but were less popular than the first part. Longfellow's nicely interlinked 22 tales have been mentioned in the same breath with Giovanni Boccaccio's *Decameron* and Geoffrey Chaucer's *Canterbury Tales.* They are less ambitious, dramatic, or successful than the works by Boccaccio and Chaucer have proved to be; nor are they, fortunately, so long as the interminable *Arabian Nights,* to which they have sometimes been compared. Longfellow's work, however, remains the best combination of narrative poems ever written by an American. His eclectic reading is evident in any consideration of the sources he consulted for the originals of many of his tales. Moreover, spectacular is the virtuoso prosodic variety he displays—blank verse, ballad stanzas, dactylic hexameters, heroic couplets and simpler iambic pentameter, octosyllabic lines, ottava rima, and permutations thereof. Henry Ford, the American auto-making billionaire, bought the Wayside Inn and 90 acres surrounding it from Lemon's widow for $65,000 (1923). He restored it, refurnished it to something closely resembling its original appearance, purchased additional property near it, established schools and built a gristmill, a sawmill, a smithy, and a modern dairy, all as part of a local community. Ford said that in all he contributed $1,616,956.11 to the Wayside Inn project and that from 1923 to 1945 the hostelry business, including the farms and schools, lost $2,848,177.

Bibliography: Arvin; Axon, W. E. A. "On the Sources of Longfellow's *Tales of a Wayside Inn." Royal Society Literary Transactions* 30 (1911): 159-72; Higginson; Hilen, ed.; Hirsh; S. Longfellow; Nevins, Allan and Frank Ernest Hill. *Ford: Expansion and Challenge: 1915-1933.* New York: Charles Scribner's Sons, 1957; Schaick, Jr., John Van. *The Characters in "Tales of the Wayside Inn."* Boston: Universalist Publishing House, 1939; Wagenknecht, 1986; Williams.

TAYLOR, BAYARD (1825–78). Travel-book writer, fiction writer, poet, diplomat, and lecturer. He was born in Kennett Square, Pennsylvania, moved with his family to nearby West Chester (1837-40), studied French, Latin, and Spanish, worked for a printer, and published juvenile items (1840, 1841). Encouraged by Rufus Wilmot Griswold,* Taylor published *Ximena . . .* (1844), a collection of poetry. A trip abroad (1844-46), sponsored in part by Horace Greeley of the New York *Tribune* (1844-46), resulted in newspaper dispatches by Taylor and also his popular *Views Afoot . . .* (1846) and in addition solid fluency in German and Italian. Home again, Taylor bought and sold a newspaper in Phoenixville, Pennsylvania, entered New York City's respectable and also bohemian literary circles, and made friends everywhere. Greeley sent Taylor to cover the California Gold Rush; Taylor's *Eldorado . . .* (2 vols., 1850) followed. Taylor wrote the lyrics for the greeting song which Jenny Lind,* the fabulous singer, used to inaugurate her initial U.S. appearance (1850). Taylor's marriage to Mary S. Agnew (1850) ended when she died of tuberculosis two months later. Distraught, Taylor traveled (1851-53) and wrote furiously, on Africa (1854), Mediterranean and Middle Eastern regions (1854), and the Far East (1855). He also edited a hack work titled *Cyclopedia of Modern Travel . . .* (1856) and wrote much else, including his popular *Poems of the Orient* (1854). He lectured successfully (1854) and went abroad again (1855-57), the results being books on Scandinavia (1857) and Greece and Russia (1859), other items, and marriage in Germany to Marie Hansen (1857; they had one child). Taylor was secretary of legation and then chargé d'affaires in St. Petersburg, Russia, early in the Civil War (1862-63), was miffed when he was not named minister, resigned, and returned home (1863) to write three novels of value mainly for their local-color touches (1863, 1864, 1865). He published his superb translation of Johann Wolfgang von Goethe's *Faust* (2 vols., 1870, 1871)—perhaps Taylor's finest literary accomplishment. He lectured on German literature at Cornell (1870-77), was appointed minister to Germany (1878), but died in Berlin soon after arriving there. Taylor's widow and Horatio Scudder* coedited *Life and Letters of Bayard Taylor* (2 vols., 1884); she also wrote *On Two Continents: Memories of Half a Century* (1905). Taylor's many important friends included Ralph Waldo Emerson,* James T. Fields,* William Dean Howells,* James Russell Lowell,* John Greenleaf Whittier,* and Longfellow.

When Longfellow was introduced by Fields to Taylor, he noted in his journal (14 Sep 1846) that "the young poet . . . has a book in press called Views Afoot" and added that "He seems modest and ingenuous." Longfellow often welcomed and dined the far-ranging Taylor and commented on him in his journal: "A very modest youth, rising fast in the literary world . . . [and] has real merit and quick, impressionable feelings" (11 Oct 1848); "He is looking fresh, vigorous, and young" (1 Dec 1854); "grown stouter, and looking as large as [Charles] Sumner[*]" (18 Nov 1858). When George William Curtis* asked Longfellow to write President Abraham Lincoln to promote Taylor to the rank of minister to Russia, Longfellow replied (3 Oct 1862) that "it would be useless for me to write." Longfellow attended Fields's dinner to honor Taylor on the publication of the first volume of his translation of Goethe's *Faust* (14 Dec 1870). Betweentimes, Taylor sent Longfellow a copy of *Views Afoot,* for which Longfellow thanked him by a letter (25 Dec 1846) in which he graciously praises the venturesome traveler-author for showing in it "strength of will,—the central fire of all great deeds and words,—that must lead you far in whatever you undertake." Longfellow goes on to hope that Taylor will translate enough poems by Ferdinand Freiligrath* to make up a fair-sized book (which Taylor, though translating a few such poems, never did). Longfellow thanks Taylor for a copy of his *A Journey to Central Africa . . .* (1854), which he says he and his wife "are reading with great interest and pleasure" (4 Oct 1854). Taylor read Longfellow's *Song of Hiawatha* and sent him a letter of extravagant praise from New York between lecture stints (23 Nov 1855); Taylor likes Longfellow's handling of sources, mingling of the "grotesque" and "simple" in Native American "legends," using the "poetical" but eschewing the "repulsive" therein, employing "apt and descriptive" imagery, etc. Irrationally, Taylor says Longfellow's "repetitions" of his chosen "measure" only "relieve it from monotony." Taylor is obliged to add a few carping "strictures," concerning Indian names, occasional lack of the "passionate," and so on. To make amends, he exalted Longfellow's *Christus* to the heavens, in a grandiose letter from Kennett Square (27 Nov 1871). Beginning "I know not who else before you has so wonderfully wedded Poetry and the Religious Sentiment," Taylor adds that John Milton "only half succeeded," while Friedrich Gottlieb Klopstock (1724–1808, author of *Messias* [The Messiah] in hexameters) "entirely failed." Taylor adds that the Finale in *Christus* demonstrates "the power which perfect rhythm adds to language." Longfellow was meanwhile writing Taylor dutifully, but uncritically, to praise his now-forgotten works, especially *The Picture of St. John* (1866), his first long narrative poem; *The Masque of the Gods* (1872), a verse drama, which Longfellow calls in a letter to Taylor (19 Apr 1872) "lofty," "solemn," "impressive," but "a puzzle" for "the common and careless reader"; and *Prince Deukalion, a Lyrical Drama* (1878), his last published item. Longfellow respected Taylor's translation of *Faust* so much that he obtained Taylor's permission (1870) to publish an excerpt from it in the Supplement to his edition of *Poets and Poetry of Europe.* When Taylor died, Longfellow wrote a short elegy titled "Bayard Taylor," comprising 16 mild couplets in trochaic tetrameter.

Bibliography: Hansen-Taylor, Marie. *On Two Continents: Memories of Half a Century.* New York: Doubleday, Page, 1905; Tryon; Wermuth, Paul C. *Bayard Taylor.* New York: Twayne, 1973.

TEGNÉR'S DRAPA" (1850). Poem, in *S/F.* The poet sees the funeral pyre of "Balder the beautiful" on a ship "With horse and harness" and floating into the sunset. It sinks, and "Balder returned no more!" Preferring "a new land of song," which rises from the sea and fosters "the new Song of Love!," the poet adjures the new age, inspired by "the meek Christ," to "Preserve the freedom only" of former days and "Not the deeds of blood!" It has been noted that Longfellow first treats in "Tegnér's Drapa" the message that love is superior to force, and, further, that its dozen six-line, irregular, unrhymed stanzas, may be called Longfellow's first effort at free verse.

Bibliography: Arvin; Hilen.

TEGNÉR, ESAIAS (1782–1846). Swedish poet, bishop, and educator. He was born in Kyrkerud, Sweden. Although his father, a pastor, died when Tegnér was nine, the boy's brilliance was recognized early, and he was fortunately well educated. He graduated from the University of Lund (1802), was professor of Greek there (1812-24), became a member of the Swedish Academy, and served as bishop of Växjö (1824-46). Tegnér's poetry at first reflected the romantic tradition; but, soon disliking its emotional ingredients, he criticized the mystical elements in works published in the magazine *Phosphoros* (1810-13) and became more classically oriented. His major works are the following: *Sweden* (1811), a popular epic poem concerning the events of the Russo-Swedish War (1808-09); *Children of the Lord's Supper* (1820); *Axel* (1822), a lyric, epic poem glorifying a Swedish soldier's love for a Russian girl; "Ode to Melancholy" (c.1826); and *Frithiofs Saga* (1825), based on an Old Icelandic saga celebrating the heroic Viking heritage, with lyric, dramatic, and epic elements. Tegnér's final years were marked by increasing interest in prefeudal Scandinavia and ultraroyalism, and by moroseness and mental instability (from 1840).

Longfellow may have known about Tegnér earlier, but, in any event, shortly after he arrived in Stockholm (Jun 1835) he bought a copy of *Frithiofs Saga*. He soon grew discontent with translations of it. He published an article on Tegnér's *Frithiofs Saga* (*NAR,* Jul 1837), included translations of fragments of the *Saga* in it, and sent a copy to Tegnér. The Swedish poet, recovering from temporary insanity, replied in a letter in Swedish (10 Jul 1841) in which he complimented Longfellow for his unique skill as translator, expressed the hope that "Herr Professor" would translate the saga in full, sent a copy

of his "edition of Frithiof," and promised to send additional, newly published volumes in the hope that "Herr Professorn" would find additional poems also worthy of being translated into English—"of all languages the one which is best adapted to translation from Swedish." Longfellow published his translation of Tegnér's *Children of the Lord's Supper* (1841) and translated, but never published, six epigrammatic poems by Tegnér, in hexameters and concerning the differing qualities of different languages (1844). When he heard that Tegnér had died, Longfellow composed "Tegnér's Death," later retitled "Tegnér's Drapa," "drapa" meaning eulogy, although Longfellow said the word meant death song or dirge.

Bibliography: Arvin; Hilen; Leighly, John. "Inaccuracies in Longfellow's Translation of Tegnér's 'Nattsvardsbaren' ["Children of the Lord's Supper"]." *Scandinavian Studies* 21 (Nov 1949): 171-80; Massengale, James. "Tegnér's, Esaias." In *Dictionary of Scandinavian Literature,* ed. Virpi Zuck, 600-602. Westport: Greenwood, 1990; S. Longfellow; Thorstenberg, Edward. "*The Skeleton in Armor* and *The Frithiof Saga*." *Modern Language Notes* 25 (Jun 1910): 189-92; Warme, Lars G., ed. *A History of Swedish Literature.* Lincoln: University of Nebraska Press, 1996.

"TEGNÉR'S FRITHIOFS SAGA" (1837). Essay, in *NAR,* Jul 1837. An analysis of *Frithiofs Saga* by Esaias Tegnér.* Part was reprinted as "Life in Sweden," in *The Boston Book* (1840) and revised and reprinted at Longfellow's Preface to "The Children of the Lord's Supper."

Bibliography: Thompson.

"TELL ME, TELL ME, THOU PRETTY BEE" (1832). Poem, translated from the Italian physician-poet Giovanni Meli (1740-1815), untitled, in *NAR,* Oct 1832; in Scudder. The poet asks the bee why, though tired, it seeks honey even on arduous predawn flights. It can more easily "sip" "Endless sweetness" from the bright lips of a certain "beloved maid."

TENNYSON, ALFRED, LORD (1809–92). English poet laureate. He was born in Somersby, Lincolnshire, where his father was rector. Writing precociously, he began studying at Trinity College, Cambridge (1827), where he met and was profoundly influenced by Arthur Henry Hallam, through whose influence he wrote after the fashion of John Keats. After he and his two brothers published the incorrectly titled *Poems by Two Brothers* (1827), Tennyson alone issued *Poems, Chiefly Lyrical* (1830), *Poems* (1832), and the highly successful *Poems* (2 vols., 1842). Meanwhile, Tennyson's father died (1831) and Hallam died (1833); Tennyson became engaged to Emily Sellwood (1838) but married her only 12 years later and only after anonymously publishing his sequence of melancholy elegies for Hallam titled *In Memoriam A.H.H.* (1850). Tennyson was named poet laureate (1850), lived comfortably on the Isle of Wight (from 1853) with his wife and their two sons, and became Lord Tennyson (1884). Among his numerous splendid poems both long and short, the following, many of which Longfellow must have taken unexpressed delight in, may be mentioned: "The Kraken" (1830), about monster-infested ocean depths; "The Hesperides" (1832), about the nymphs and their golden apples in Greek mythology; "The Lotos-Eaters" (1832), a warning against indolence; "St. Simeon Stylites" (1842), concerning severe asceticism; "Ulysses" (1842), about unending adventuresomeness (Dante half-admired Ulysses but put him in his *Inferno* for evil counseling); "Morte d'Arthur" (1842); "Tears, Idle Tears" (1847), which may relate to Longfellow's "The Tide Rises, the Tide Falls"; "Lucretius" (1868), in which the conflict expressed between epicureanism and antimaterialism may have troubled the moral but comfort-loving Longfellow; "Crossing the Bar" (1889), about oncoming death, hence relating to Longfellow's "Morituri Salutamus" and poems in his *Ultima Thule* and *In the Harbor.* Fanny Longfellow* wrote a neighbor and friend Emmeline Austin Wadsworth an undated letter (spring 1850) that "Henry is feasting on it [*In Memoriam*] with eyes full of tears." Many quatrains in *In Memoriam* must later have made him think of his two deceased wives.

Longfellow treasured his copy of the rare 1832 edition of Tennyson's *Poems.* James T. Fields* introduced Tennyson to a wide American readership by publishing his two-volume *Poems* (1842) and paid him well for doing so. Fields later published several other works by Tennyson. As for evidence of Longfellow's relationship to Tennyson, the following actions may be summarized. In his journal (7 Feb 1848), Longfellow records his excitement after Fields gave him a copy of Tennyson's "The Princess" (1847); Longfellow relished "the gentle satire" and the "flowing blank verse" in it, but was inexplicably "disappointed . . . [because of] a discordant note somewhere." Longfellow was pleased when the English poet Henry Taylor (1800–1886) wrote him from London (31 Dec 1851) that he admired Longfellow's *The Golden Legend* and lent a copy to Tennyson. Both Tennyson and Longfellow wrote about the death of the Duke of Wellington. "The Warden of the Cinque Ports" by Longfellow is regarded as a better elegy than Tennyson's "On the Death of the Duke of Wellington" (1852). According to his journal (5 Aug 1855), Longfellow liked the beauty evident in Tennyson's *Maud: A Monodrama* (1853), although "there is in parts a spirit of ferocity which I do not like" (probably the excesses of its unbalanced wild-lover male narrator). Fanny Longfellow wrote her brother-in-law Samuel Longfellow* (5 Nov 1855) to suggest that *The Song of Hiawatha* might be abused by the critics much as Tennyson's "poor *Maud* seems to be." The ending of *Hiawatha* echoes Tennyson's "Morte d'Arthur." Charles Sumner* must have delighted Longfellow when he wrote him from Scotland (22 Oct 1857) that Tennyson just told a friend that he and his wife "wish much that you could come with your wife and children"—obviously to visit them. According to his journal (19, 20 Jul 1859), as soon as Longfellow got his hands on "Tennyson's new poem, Four Idyls of the King ['Enid,' 'Vivien,' 'Elaine,' 'Guinevere,' 1859]" he "devour[ed] the first," compared it to "Chaucer's 'Griselda,'" soon read the rest, and opined that "The First and third could have come only from a great poet. The second and fourth do not seem to me so good." In a letter to Fields (12 Aug 1859), Longfellow described Tennyson's *Idylls of the King* as "a brilliant success. Rich tapestries, wrought as only Tennyson could have done them, and worthy to hang beside The Faerie Queene [by Edmund Spenser]." Some days after Fanny burned to death in 1861, Longfellow penned these undated lines from "To J.S." (Tennyson's 1832 elegy commemorating his friend James Spedding): "Sleep sweetly, tender heart, in peace! / Sleep, holy spirit, blessed soul!" Longfellow wrote Sumner (1 Jan 1867)—proudly, no doubt—that he had just received a letter from Tennyson saying that Englishmen and Americans should all be brothers and that he trusts "some of us" will be. To Longfellow's promise (21 May 1867) to provide a copy of his translation of *The Divine Comedy,* Tennyson replied (12 Jun 1867) with thanks but appended his belief that "to transfer the Commedia successfully into English is beyond the power of the greatest poet living."

When Longfellow was last in England— together with two sisters, one brother, three daughters, one son and his wife, and one brother-in-law—the entire assemblage visited Tennyson and his wife on the Isle of Wight for two days (16–17 Jul 1868) before heading for Dover and the Continent. Longfellow wrote to Annie Adams Fields* (19 Jul 1868) that their time with Tennyson was "not at his house, but mostly with him. He was very cordial, and very amiable; and gave up his whole time to us." In a letter to Fields (24 Dec 1869), Longfellow humorously calls Tennyson "King Alfred." Tennyson gave Longfellow permission to include some of his poems in Longfellow's edition of *Poems of Places* (1876–79). After Longfellow wrote Tennyson (21 Dec 1876) to praise his *Harold: A Drama,* saying of its fifth act "I know not where to look for anything better," Tennyson gratefully replied (14 Jan 1877) and expressed the hope that the two might "come together again before we pass away forever." Longfellow's sonnet "Wapentake: To Alfred Tennyson" is a late, sincere tribute, a copy of which he enclosed in a letter to Tennyson (27 Nov 1877).

Bibliography: Arvin; Eidson, John Olin. *Tennyson in America: His Reputation and Influence from 1827 to 1858.* Athens: The University of Georgia Press, 1943; Hilen, ed.; Lang, Cecil Y. and Edgar F. Shannon, eds. *The Letters of Alfred Lord Tennyson.* 3 vols. Cambridge: The Belknap Press of Harvard University Press, 1981–90; S. Longfellow; *Mrs. Longfellow;* Tryon; Williams.

THACHER, MARGARET LOUISA POTTER (1817–?). (Nicknames: Madge, Marge.) Longfellow's sister-in-law. She was the younger sister of Mary Storer Potter (*see* Longfellow, Mary). Margaret helped Longfellow in his courtship of Mary. Early in their association, he sent Margaret letters in the form of ditties (one from Göttingen [Mar 1829], another from Bowdoin [Mar 1834]). After Mary's death, the two remained friendly. She was married (1841) to Peter Thacher (1810–94). A graduate from Bowdoin (1831), he practiced law in Machias, Maine. In a letter to his father (2 Apr [May] 1841), Longfellow refers to Margaret's husband as "St. Peter." In a letter to his sister Anne Longfellow Pierce* (9 May 1841), Longfellow mentions "Don Pedro . . . [,] radiant as he should be." Over the years, Longfellow and Margaret remained in touch. He helped Mary Potter Thacher (1844–1941), her niece, publish *Seashore and Prairie* (1877), through his friendship with publisher James Ripley Osgood,* and also admired her later books.

Bibliography: Hilen, ed.

THACKERAY, WILLIAM MAKEPEACE (1811–63). English novelist. He was born in Calcutta, India, where his father was in the civil service; his mother was nineteen at his birth, was soon widowed (1816), and remarried (1818). Thackeray was educated in England (from 1817) at the Charterhouse and Cambridge, from which he left without a degree (1830). He traveled, read briefly for the law (1831), inherited a goodly sum (1832), soon lost it, and studied drawing in Paris (c.1834). He married Isabella Shawe (1836); they had three daughters, two surviving. Thackeray's wife, whom he always treated tenderly, became mentally unbalanced (1840) and died decades later (1892). Thackeray did a great deal of hack writing but then produced a string of brilliant novels: *Barry Lyndon* (1844); *Vanity Fair* (1847–48); *Pendennis* (1848–50); *Esmond, the History of Henry Esmond, Esq.* (1852);

The Newcomes (1853-55); *The Virginians* (1857-59); *The Adventures of Philip* (1861-62); and *Denis Duval* (unfinished, 1864). Thackeray was on the staff of *Punch,* the London weekly comic periodical, and was the first editor of the influential *Cornhill Magazine* (1860-62). Before Thackeray was well known, he published for low pay in American periodicals edited by Nathaniel Parker Willis.* When he was famous in the United States, having been published by James T. Fields,* Thackeray lectured there (1852-53, 1855-56). When Thackeray first lectured in Boston, Fields was his de facto impresario.

Before meeting Thackeray, Longfellow read *Vanity Fair,* which he defines in his journal as "clever, cutting, amusing, disagreeable" (7 Aug 1848). Longfellow called on Thackeray in his Boston hotel, noting in his journal that the novelist had come over from England "in the same steamer with the Lowells" (13 Nov 1852—*see* Lowell, James Russell). According to journal entries, Longfellow attended two of Thackeray's lectures and read a few of his novels. Thackeray's lecture on Jonathan Swift was "very clever, playing round the theme with a lambent flame, that scorched a little, sometimes" (21 Dec 1852); the one on William Congreve and Joseph Addison was "light, graphic . . . [and] pleasant to hear from that soft, deep, sonorous voice of his" (24 Dec 1852). Longfellow attended Lowell's wit-studded supper (5 Jan 1853) in Thackeray's honor; other guests included Arthur Hugh Clough,* Richard Henry Dana Jr.,* Cornelius Conway Felton,* and Fields. Longfellow did not go to Thackeray's final lecture of the series (7 Jan 1853) but spent parts of a week reading *Esmond,* which he avers "shows a freedom of touch . . . beyond his other books" (18 Jan 1853). In due time came *The Newcomes,* "how pleasant" (14 Oct 1854) and an episode of *The Virginians,* "full of life" (17 Dec 1857). In between, Thackeray, back lecturing in Boston again, was escorted by Thomas Gold Appleton* to Longfellow's house; Appleton's horses ran away with his carriage, and Longfellow ordered a carriage and drove Thackeray to the lecture hall, where he expounded "on the times of the first George"

(7 Dec 1855). Next evening, the Longfellows had Thackeray, Ole Bornemann Bull,* and Fields to dinner. From London, Thackeray wrote Longfellow (16 Nov 1859) to plead for a contribution to the *Cornhill,* which he was starting to edit. Longfellow declined (19 Dec 1859) on the grounds that the *Atlantic Monthly* had exclusive rights to all items he would be writing for periodical publication.

Bibliography: Elwin, Malcolm. *Thackeray: A Personality.* London: Jonathan Cape, 1932; Hilen, ed.; S. Longfellow; Monsarrat, Ann. *An Uneasy Victorian: Thackeray the Man, 1811-1863.* New York: Dodd, Mead, 1980; Tryon.

"THANKSGIVING" (1824). Poem, in *USLG,* 15 Nov 1824; Scudder. In olden times, when "Jubal's tongue" began to sing, listeners responded with hymns, whether it was "Soft Spring or hoary Autumn." Nature responded in "adoration," because "The Deity was there." For accompaniment were the sounds of the wind, birds, rivulets, and "listless wave[s]" among rank weeds. Air and light "Became religion" to everyone, "for all was love." Stars, moon, day, night, the "beautiful forms of nature," ocean with tides and storms—all combined in eloquent adoration. Now, "have *our* hearts grown cold?" Do we see any "heavenly light" or sing any hymns? Let youth remain pure so that "in the nightfall of his years" he will praise God "in peace." This seventy-line juvenile poem, which was the first Longfellow published in the *Gazette,* is in competent blank verse.

Bibliography: Thompson.

"THERE'S NOT A CLOUD IN YON BLUE SKY" (1824). Poem, signed "H.," in Portland *Advertiser,* 14 Jan 1824. Winter broke summer's lute and autumn's reed and now urges the New Year forward. The poet sees cloudless sky, "sentry stars," and "crescent moon," and all the while thinks that our spirits might well leave "the gross earth" with "The sorrows of its days," be purified, and "Fly off to worlds of bliss."

Bibliography: Little.

"THERE WAS A LITTLE GIRL . . ." (c.1865–70). Poem, immensely popular and attributed, without solid proof, to Longfellow, about a little girl who had a little curl on her forehead and who was sometimes horrid.

Bibliography: Kramer, Sidney, "'There Was a Little Girl': Its First Printing, Its Author, Its Variants." *Papers of the Bibliographic Society of America* 40 (1946): 287–310.

"THESE ARE THE BUNNS" (1982). Poem. This six-line ditty tells the recipient to eat the buns that accompany this poem, when "she dips / Her sweet rosy lips / In . . . Cocoa." Longfellow sent the package (around Christmas 1881) to Lilian Kirk McDowell (1871–1922), his godchild. (*See* Bonner, Sherwood.)

Bibliography: Hilen, ed.

"A THIRD PSALM OF LIFE." *See* "Footsteps of Angels."

"THIS BOOK, BOUND IN VERMILION" (1982). Poem. This four-line ditty, cutely rhyming "vermilion," "cover," "dearest Lilian," "faithful lover [i.e., Longfellow]," Longfellow sent (20 Apr 1881) to accompany a book he mailed as a gift to Lilian Kirk Mac-Dowell (1871–1922), his godchild. (*See* Bonner, Sherwood.)

Bibliography: Hilen, ed.

THOREAU, HENRY DAVID (1817–62). Transcendental author. Thoreau was born in Concord, Massachusetts, graduated from Harvard (1837), taught in Concord (1839–41), lived in the home of Ralph Waldo Emerson* (1841–43, 1847–48), lived part of the interval in a hut beside Walden Pond (1845–47), and then resided in his father's home (1849–62). During his lifetime, Thoreau published *A Week on the Concord and Merrimack Rivers* (1849); *Walden, or Life in the Woods* (1854); and scattered periodical items. Much in *The Writings of Henry David Thoreau* (20 vols., 1906), including his unique journals, combine with *Walden* to make Thoreau a figure of international significance.

For obvious reasons, the minds of Longfellow and Thoreau could seldom meet. However, when Nathaniel Hawthorne* answered Longfellow's invitation to dinner (20 Nov 1848) by a letter (21 Nov 1848) suggesting that he bring Thoreau along, Longfellow agreed. Two evenings later, Longfellow entertained Hawthorne, Thoreau, the uneasy Transcendental writer William Ellery Channing,* and Longfellow's brother Samuel. In his journal (29 Jun 1849), Longfellow writes, "In the evening F.[Fanny, his wife] read me . . . Thoreau's account of his one night in Concord jail . . . [,] extremely good." Out of Thoreau's night in jail (24? or 25? Jul 1846), the result of his refusal to pay his poll tax, came his world-famous essay "Resistance to Civil Government" (1849) retitled "Civil Disobedience."

Bibliography: Hilen, ed.; S. Longfellow.

THORP, ANNE ALLEGRA LONGFELLOW (1855–1934). *See* Longfellow, Anne Allegra.

THREE BOOKS OF SONG (1872). Collection of poems. *Book First: Tales of the Wayside Inn* [Book First]: "Prelude," "The Sicilian's Tale, The Bell of Atri," "Interlude," "The Spanish Jew's Tale," "Kambalu," "Interlude," "The Student's Tale," "The Cobbler of Hagenau," "Interlude," "The Musician's Tale," "The Ballad of Carmilhan," "Interlude," "The Poet's Tale," "Lady Wentworth," "Interlude," "The Theologian's Tale," "The Legend Beautiful," "Interlude," "The Student's Second Tale," "The Ballad of St. Castine," "Finale." *Book Second: Judas Maccabaeus. Book Third: A Handful of Translations:* "The Fugitive," "The Siege of Kazan," "The Boy and the Brook," "To the Stork," "Consolation," "To Cardinal Richelieu," "The Angel and the Child," "To Italy," "Wanderer's Night-Songs," "Remorse," "Santa Teresa's Book-Mark."

"THREE FIFTHS OF TWELVE" (1982). Poem. Longfellow sent James T. Fields* an eleven-line poem about attending a performance of *Faust,* the opera by Charles François Gounod (1818–93). The clever ditty rhymes "20," "went he," and "spent he."

Bibliography: Hilen, ed.

"THREE FRIENDS OF MINE" (1875). Five sonnets, in *Pandora, Birds* (1875). I. When the poet remembers his three friends, now gone, he mostly remembers, with a smile, a shining, archetypical something, ample and majestic, about them. II. He says that one of his friends, apostrophized as "Philhellene," should have been born in ancient Greece, where he would have seen Poseidon and Jason, and would have been friendly with Homer and Plato. III. The poet stands by the seashore, welcomed there by rocks, seaweed, willows, and Atlantic winds. Why should his friend "come no more?" IV. His friend has the same name as the river (Charles). He cannot say goodnight to him now. His friend has taken a lamp and gone to rest, and "I stay a little longer, as one stays / To cover up the embers that still burn." V. Doors are open. Lilacs blaze. The meadows of Brighton are hazy. The river seems to await the friends, as does the poet. They cannot remember the path to his place, and "Something is gone from nature since they died, / And summer is not summer, nor can be." In a letter to George Washington Greene* (10 Nov 1874), Longfellow says that the three friends about whom he wrote, as a "small tribute to their memory," were Louis Agassiz,* Cornelius Conway Felton,* and Charles Sumner.*

Bibliography: S. Longfellow.

"THE THREE KINGS" (1878). Poem, in *PP, Kéramos, Birds* (1878). Baltasar, Gaspar, and Melchior, richly caparisoned, ride westward and follow the unique, prophetic star. They carry golden caskets. Wishing to worship the King of the Jews, they ask about the child. But the people know only about King Herod. When the three kings get to Jerusalem, Herod tells them to find out about this new king in Bethlehem. Arriving there, they find Mary of Nazareth in a stable, watching, with both joy and terror, her baby's even breathing. The three kings offer gold, frankincense, and myrrh, then leave—but not to return by way of malicious Herod. This singularly dull redaction has little to recommend it.

"THE THREE SILENCES." *See* "The Three Silences of Molinos."

"THE THREE SILENCES OF MOLINOS: TO JOHN GREENLEAF WHITTIER[*] (1877). Sonnet, as "The Three Silences," in Boston *Literary World,* 1 Dec 1877; *Kéramos.* The Spanish monk wrote about the three silences—of speech, desire, and thought. The three silences join to form "the perfect Silence" and enable the monk to hear "Mysterious sounds from realms beyond our reach." Longfellow says that the "Hermit of Amesbury" is similarly endowed and therefore speaks "only when thy soul is stirred!" Whittier was Longfellow's close and respected friend. Miguel de Molinos (c.1640-97) was a Spanish priest, mystic, and apostle of Quietism. He was investigated during the Spanish Inquisition, publicly professed his errors (1687), was sentenced to prison for life, and died in prison. Longfellow read his poem at a party (17 Dec 1877) celebrating Whittier's seventieth birthday. However, the occasion is now remembered only because that was the time when Mark Twain delivered his uproarious but inappropriate speech about three derelict miners in the Far West pretending to be Ralph Waldo Emerson,* Oliver Wendell Holmes,* and Longfellow. (For details, *see* Whittier, John Greenleaf.)

TICKNOR, GEORGE (1791–1871). Ticknor, educator and author, was born in Boston. His parents were both teachers until his father became a successful merchant and banker. Tutored at home, Ticknor, an only child, studied Latin and Greek, then French and Spanish, before entering Dartmouth College as a junior (1805). After graduating (1807), he was tutored further in Latin and Greek and read for the law in the office of William Sullivan, a Federalist and son of James Sullivan (1744-1808), the governor of Massachusetts (1807-08). Ticknor was admitted to the bar (1813) but practiced for only a year. With family connections, Ticknor traveled to New Haven, New York, Philadelphia, Washington, D.C., and Virginia (winter 1814-15); met President James Madison; and visited ex-President Thomas Jefferson at Monticello, with whom he later became especially close. Ticknor sailed for England with Edward Everett* and other talented young men (1815). Jefferson had given Ticknor letters of recommendation to significant European friends. After meeting many writers in England and Germany, including Lord Byron, Chateaubriand, Johann Wolfgang von Goethe, Sir Walter Scott, Madame de Staël, and William Wordsworth, Ticknor became a zealous student at the University of Göttingen (1815–16). Offered a professorship at Harvard (1816) in belles lettres, French, and Spanish, Ticknor left Göttingen. Everett remained and received the first Ph.D. awarded an American there (1817). Ticknor studied languages in France, Spain, and Portugal, then returned home (1817) to commence a career as teacher and administrator, bibliophile, and author of erudite articles for the *North American Review* and elsewhere. His students at Harvard included James Russell Lowell,* Charles Eliot Norton,* the future historian John Lothrop Motley, and Henry David Thoreau.* Ticknor was successfully innovative but often at odds with Harvard's conservative administration, not least when Jared Sparks* was president. When Ticknor resigned his professorship (1835), Longfellow replaced him. Ticknor had married Anna Eliot (1821), the daughter of Samuel Eliot, a prosperous Boston merchant-banker whose death that year provided her with an $84,394.50 inheritance. Ticknor's wife's sister, Catherine Eliot, was the wife of Andrews Norton and the mother of Charles Eliot Norton.* Ticknor and his wife had four children (two dying in infancy). He returned to Europe (1835–1838) with his wife and their two daughters, and traveled, made and renewed many friendships, impressed scholars and other observers by his knowledge and pro-American manners, studied Spanish culture, and purchased rare Spanish books. Back home, he reviewed his pertinent lectures, consulted and added volumes to his personal library of 14,000 books, and wrote his enormous, exhaustively annotated *History of Spanish Literature* (3 vols., 1849; 2nd ed., 1854; expanded editions, 1863, 1872). His thesis concerns the morality, honor, and religious extremism of Spaniards, but also their love of coarseness and violence, and implies his espousal of American civil liberty

and moral restraint. Ticknor was active in establishing, funding, and developing the Boston Library (1852–60), in part by returning to Europe (1856–57) to gather more books and also by donating 2,400 of his own. Ticknor began to have grave doubts as to America's healthy future, admired the efforts at compromise by Daniel Webster,* feared that politics during the Civil War would destroy the Constitution, and believed that the emancipation of southern slaves would have adverse political and social effects on blacks as well as on whites. He published a biography of his friend the historian William Hickling Prescott* (1864). Ticknor advanced from member of the board of trustees of the Boston Public Library to president of the board (1865), willed his Spanish collection to it, and sadly died months before the library moved to larger quarters. George Stillman Hillard,* Ticknor's and Longfellow's close friend, edited *Life, Letters, and Journals of George Ticknor* (1876).

When Longfellow was preparing to go to Europe the first time (1826) to study languages there, he dined with Ticknor and obtained not only letters of introduction from him to Washington Irving,* Robert Southey, and a professor in Germany, but also advice to study literature for a year at Göttingen. Longfellow pleased Ticknor by sending him a copy of the first number of *Outre-Mer* and his translations of certain Spanish poems. His doing so elicited a complimentary letter from Ticknor (6 Dec 1833), to which Longfellow replied too ingratiatingly from Bowdoin (15 Dec 1833). His later letters to Ticknor are more eye-to-eye, though always excessively courteous. Ticknor knew Longfellow's accomplishments sufficiently to recommend him for a teaching position at New York University. Longfellow briefly toyed with the idea (1834). Instead, however, upon his own resignation from his Harvard chair (1835), Ticknor recommended Longfellow as his replacement. Josiah Quincy,* Harvard's president at the time, included in his written invitation to Longfellow (1 Dec 1834) the information that Ticknor would continue in the chair while Longfellow polished his linguistic abilities some more in Europe and then returned. Once in the class-room at Harvard, Longfellow followed Ticknor's practice of using lecture notes in class instead of reading fully written-out lec-tures. From a distance, Ticknor watched Longfellow's teaching habits, commending him graciously, for example, for editing small French and Spanish readers for his stu-dents. The two men continued their friend-ship; however, it was evidently never inti-mate. Longfellow privately regarded Ticknor as affable but dogmatic. Longfellow com-mented on Ticknor's biography of Prescott in his journal (2 Jan 1864) tersely: "Very in-teresting." Responding to Longfellow's gift of the first volume of his translation of *La Divina Commedia* by Dante, Ticknor sent a letter (1 June 1867) to "My Dear Sir," fol-lowed by astonishing praise and closing with a curiously phrased hint that between the lines of the translation will be "thoughts and recollections . . . always legible."

Bibliography: Green; Hilen, ed.; S. Longfellow; Morison; Tyack, David B. *George Ticknor and the Boston Brahmins.* Cambridge: Harvard Univer-sity Press, 1967.

"THE TIDE RISES, THE TIDE FALLS" (1880). Poem, in *Thule.* As the tide forever rises and falls, twilight and darkness come, the curlew and the dark sea call, waves erase footprints in the sand, and steeds neigh. Days return, but the traveler never does. This lovely lyric, often anthologized, is one of Longfellow's most impressive short poems.

"THE TIDES" (1875). Sonnet, in *Pandora, Birds* (1875). At the shore line, the poet sees seaweed, shells, and rocks exposed by the ebb of the tide, which he thinks will rise no more. Then he hears the vast ocean breathe and watches it roar over "the defenceless land" again. Similarly, he once believed that thoughts, emotions, and desires had "ebbed from me forever." But, no, they sweep in again and buoy him up on waves as "strong / As youth, and beautiful as youth."

"TO A BROOK." *See* "A Brook."

"TO A CHILD" (1846). Poem, in *Bruges.* The poet observes a child on his mother's knee. He looks at pictures painted on some

tiles. He shakes his rattle like a commander, little aware that it was made of coral some thousands of years old, and of silver from "darksome mines," and was shipped from far away. The little boy wanders through an open door, no longer imprisoned in his nurs-ery. He patters through a hallway, chattering merrily. "The Father of his Country" once "dwelt" here. His footsteps echoed along these stairs. He sat, troubled "in heart and head." Just beyond could be seen "fires of the besieging camp." But the little boy doesn't care. He only wants to get out "into the open air." He looks at the apples, flow-ers, bees, and garden. The wheels of his car-riage efface little anthills. After returning for a nap, he drifts into sleep like his toy boat down a creek. He is at the threshold of "the future's undiscovered land." Hopes and fears lie ahead. The poet cannot cast the little fel-low's horoscope. Perhaps he will weep and sweat. If so, he should realize that rest fol-lows labor. If he has a life of ease, he should be sympathetic to those less fortunate and wisely learn to "discern / True beauty in util-ity." The poet thinks he has said enough and will simply fear less than he will hope. Crai-gie House,* in which Longfellow lived and also wrote this poem, was General George Washington's headquarters when he was commanding troops in and around Boston. According to Longfellow's brother Samuel Longfellow,* the child the poet had in mind was Charles Appleton Longfellow,* his first son.

Bibliography: Longfellow, [Rev.] Samuel. "Long-fellow with His Children." *Wide Awake* 24 (Feb 1887): 161–65; More.

"TO A MOUNTAIN BROOK" (1831). Poem, signed "L.," in *NEM,* Aug 1831; Scud-der. Spring lays Winter's shaggy head on her breast and warms it the way "the fair Roman girl" comforted her aged father.

Bibliography: Thompson.

"TO AN OLD DANISH SONG BOOK" (1846). Poem, in *Bruges.* The poet remem-bers when he first encountered this book "beneath the skies of Denmark." He wel-comes it to his autumnal fireside. It has been smudged by thumbprints and stained with drinks. In it are ballads, "songs of love and friendship," Viking "staves," and "ditties" once sung in King Hamlet's court. Soldiers, sailors, students, and laborers, who sang them long ago, have deserted it now. But not so the poet. These songs rest in his heart, the way birds live in "old-fashioned chimneys," bothering no one and "recalling by their voices / Youth and travel." This charming poem, unrhymed and oddly metered, resembles free verse.

"TO CARDINAL RICHELIEU" (1871). Poem, translated from the French poet François de Malherbe (1555–1628), in the Supplement to Longfellow's edition of *Poets and Poetry of Europe; Three.* Do realize, "mighty Prince of Church and State," that one can choose a road but fate controls him; our days and seasons combine sadness and pleasure; we cannot avoid all perils; and wisdom teaches only that "Fortune and Adversity" alternate.

"TO IANTHE" (1824). Poem, in Portland *Advertiser,* 28 Aug 1824; Scudder. The persona thinks sadly about her at twilight. A "slighted lover," he will never love again. Memories may cheer him, but love when it "decays" is forever "departed." His heart resembles a frozen flower, "unchanged" in appearance but never to bloom again. Do think about "those that love thee!" We, but not our hearts, must separate for years.

Bibliography: Little; Thompson.

"TO ITALY" (1871). Sonnet, translated from the Italian poet Vincenzo da Filicaia (1642–1707), in the Supplement to Longfellow's edition of *Poets and Poetry of Europe; Three.* Italy is destined to combine beauty and wretchedness. It would be better if it were stronger and less attractive, so as to be feared more and coveted less. If so, the poet would not see Italy invaded and fighting and, whether "Victor or vanquished, slave forevermore."

"TO MORROW: LORD, WHAT AM I . . . ?" (1833). Irregular sonnet, translated from the Spanish poet Lope de Vega (1562–1635), in *Coplas; Voices.* The poet apolo-gizes to his "Lord," who unceasingly sought him, often on bleeding feet. The poet's good angel kept telling him to notice that "he persists to knock and wait for thee!" Always, the poet said he would accept his Lord to-morrow.

"TO-MORROW: 'TIS LATE AT NIGHT" (1866). Sonnet, in *Flower.* It is late. The poet's "little lambs" are asleep. The clocks "Challenge" each hour like tower guards. Faraway cocks crow. A door seems to open for tomorrow's sweet breath. It warns the poet to "Remember Barmecide, / And tremble to be happy with the rest." The poet's answer is that he doesn't know what's best but trusts God, who has already decreed the future. Barmecide was a wealthy Persian in "The Barber's Sixth Brother," in the *Arabian Nights,* who invited a beggar to a feast of imaginary food.

"TO MY BROOKLET" (1877). Poem, translated from the French poet Jean François Ducis (1733–1816), in *PP, Kéramos.* The poet wishes to be like the shy, solitude-loving brooklet. His thoughts would be peaceful, like its peaceful flowers, waves, and nightingale. The poet's verse might then resemble its "waters, murmuring as they roll," and might replicate the shuddering of leaves near it and lapwings crying near it.

"TORQUEMADA." *See* "The Theologian's Tale," in *Tales of a Wayside Inn,* Part First.

"TO THE AVON" (1882). Poem, in *Harbor.* The poet adjures the "sweet river" to keep on flowing and not to wait for the person (obviously William Shakespeare) "who cannot hear thy call." The poet can visualize him—in Stratford's streets, thoughtful beside the river, wandering into "the wide world," and filling it "with his melodious song." He is now following a more vast river by "another shore."

"TO THE DRIVING CLOUD" (1845). Poem, in *Poems,* 1845; *Bruges.* The poet addresses Driving Cloud, the dark and gloomy Omaha chief. Wrapped in a red blanket, you once walked beside rivers, stalking "those birds unknown, that have left us only their footprints." Now you stride through crowded streets. Will your race soon be known only by its footprints? Stifled without sweet mountain air, you glare at city folks— "in vain." Deprived Europeans claim your hunting grounds for their living space. Return to the forests "west of the Wabash," breathe freely again, tame more horses, hunt the stag beside the Elkhorn. But what sounds come from "those mountainous deserts"? Human or animal? You are endangered, not by Fox, Crow, the behemoth, but by "these Saxons and Celts." Their withering breath, like an east wind, scatters "evermore to the west the scanty smokes of thy wigwams!" This dire poem is in effective hexameters.

Bibliography: Arvin.

"TO THE FOREST OF GASTINE" (1877). Poem, translated from the French poet Pierre de Ronsard (1524–85), in *PP,* Scudder. The poet loves to recline comfortably in Gastine's forest shadows. Here "The Muses answer" him unfailingly. Cares depart when he reads here. He hopes that "Satyrs and . . . Sylvans" remain and that no "sacrilegious flame" will ever spoil the place.

"TO THE NOVICE OF THE CONVENT OF THE VISITATION" (1824). Poem, signed "H.W.L.," in *American Monthly Magazine,* Apr 1824. The persona bids his "last farewell" to the sister in the convent. She should remember "Love's broken urn," be aware that "A broken heart [is] the sacrifice," and realize that time has merely "effac'd" her beauty but has sounded his death knell. Be devout. Hope is winging toward Heaven. This is the first poem Longfellow signed "H.W.L." James McHenry (1785–1845), Irish-born Philadelphia physician and businessman, also edited the *American Monthly Magazine* and published this poem and then Longfellow's verse drama "The Poor Student. . . . A Dramatic Sketch" and his essay "Youth and Old Age." McHenry encouraged Longfellow to submit some more work, but the magazine folded with the December 1824 issue.

Bibliography: Hilen, ed.; Little; S. Longfellow.

"TO THE RIVER CHARLES" (1842). Poem, in *Ladies' Companion,* Jan 1842; *Ballads.* Longfellow has worked and rested for four years near this river. It taught him much. So he gives it a song. Its celestial hue has lightened his hours. But he loves it best because it reminds him "Of three dear friends, all true and tried," once living near it.

"TO THE RIVER RHONE" (1877). Sonnet, in *PP, Kéramos.* The "Royal River," coming as it does from the purple Alps, wrapped in snowy, unspotted ermine, charges "like a steel-clad horseman" and accepts the demanded tribute of "vassal torrents." Towns, bridges, and vineyards attend its "progress to the sea!"

"TO THE RIVER YVETTE" (1877). Poem, in *PP, Kéramos, Birds* (1878). This "lovely river" resembles a bride, "dimpled, bashful, fair." It avoids solicitous but overly haughty Maincourt, Dampierre, and Chevreuse, and rushes on "as one in haste to meet / Her sole desire, her heart's delight."

"TO THE ROSE OF ROSES" (1982). Poem. Longfellow wishes "the Rose of Roses" joy and a long healthy life. Longfellow sent this six-line ditty as a holiday greeting (Christmas 1876) to Rose Emily Fay (1852–1929), a family friend. Her sister Harriet Melusina ("Zena") Fay Peirce was the wife of the distinguished American philosopher Charles Santiago Sanders Peirce (1839–1914). Rose later married Theodore Thomas (1835–1905), the symphony conductor.

Bibliography: Hilen, ed.

"TO THE STORK" (1870). Poem, translated from the English prose version by Ghevont M. (Rev. Leo M.) Alishan(ian) (1820–1901) of an Armenian song, in *AM,* Sep 1870; *Three.* Stork, you are welcome, as evidence of the return of spring. When you flew away, "withering winds did blow, / And dried up all the flowers." Skies grew dreary. Snows covered everything.

"TO VITTORIA COLONNA: LADY, HOW CAN IT CHANCE . . . ?" (1878). Sonnet, translated from the Italian of Michael Angelo, in *Kéramos.* Curiously, a statue out-lives the sculptor. The artist can create images "in color or in stone" of the lady and of himself, before both die. Thus Art outlasts Nature.

"TO VITTORIA COLONNA: WHEN THE PRIME MOVER OF MY MANY SIGHS" (1878). Sonnet, translated from Michael Angelo's Italian, in *Kéramos.* When death took the poet's "prime mover," nature became ashamed and the poet grew hopeless. "Earth holds in its embrace / Thy lovely limbs." Lethe cannot destroy "thy virtuous renown." In Heaven you have "a refuge and a crown."

"TO WILLIAM E. CHANNING." *See* Channing, William Ellery, and *Poems on Slavery.*

TRAVELS BY LONGFELLOW. In addition to enjoying visits to several U.S. cities along the Atlantic seaboard and inland and up into Canada, Longfellow was an inveterate traveler abroad—and in an age when such voyages were arduous, protracted, and sometimes dangerous. Longfellow went to France (Apr 1826), where he studied and traveled widely. He went on to Madrid (Mar 1827) and toured throughout Spain. He proceeded to Italy (Dec), settling in Florence but also visiting other major cities. He went to Austria, Czechoslovakia, and Germany, before returning home in August (1829). Longfellow sailed to England (Apr 1835), then proceeded to Germany, Denmark, Sweden, and the Netherlands, where his first wife, Mary Longfellow,* died. Longfellow went on with friends to Germany, Switzerland, and Austria. He returned home (fall 1836). He traveled in France, the Netherlands, Belgium, and Germany, settling in Marienberg and returning via England (Apr–Nov 1842). From June 1868 through August 1869 he went to England, France, Belgium, Germany, Switzerland, Italy, and Austria. After that tour, Longfellow remained close to his Cambridge home and never ventured farther than to Philadelphia, to take in the Centennial Exposition (1876).

Bibliography: Hilen, ed.; S. Longfellow; Wagenknecht. 1955.

"TRAVELS BY THE FIRESIDE" (1975). Poem, in *Pandora, Birds* (1875). Three days of rain have driven the poet in on himself. He reads old books about places he saw in his youth: the Alps, Spain, Elsinore, convents, castles near the Rhine, parks, spires, old trees, poppy fields, the sea. He never grows tired when he travels "with another's feet." Others toil to travel, while reading enables him to "turn the world round" in his hand. Their eyes "see . . . / Better" than his.

TROLLOPE, ANTHONY (1815–82). English novelist, born in London. His father was a failed barrister and then a failed farmer, who died in 1835; his mother, Frances Trollope (1780–1863), was a prolific novelist and travel writer. Her sensational *Domestic Manners of the Americans* (1831) aroused ire in American readers because much of its shrewd criticism, though on target, was offensively sarcastic. Anthony Trollope worked intermittently in the postal service (1834–67) and published a prodigious amount of fiction (from 1847). In 36 years he produced 63 titles in 129 volumes, in the following divisions: Barsetshire chronicles, novels of social manners, satirical fiction, Irish- and Australian-based novels, historical and romantic novels, and miscellaneous pieces. Both before and after retiring from the postal service, Trollope traveled extensively—often on official assignments—and visited the United States twice (1861–62, 1875). During the earlier of his trips to America, Trollope met Louis Agassiz,* Richard Henry Dana Jr.,* Ralph Waldo Emerson,* Nathaniel Hawthorne,* Oliver Wendell Holmes,* James Russell Lowell,* William Hickling Prescott,* and Longfellow, among others.

In his journal, Longfellow mentions Trollope briefly. Lowell gave a lecture which Trollope attended, after which Lowell took Trollope, along with Charles Eliot Norton,* to Longfellow's home for a visit (29 Nov 1861). After Trollope returned from traveling in the American West, Longfellow encountered him at the office of James T. Fields* (3 Mar 1862). From London Trollope sent Longfellow a copy of his *North America* (1862), which, though critical of the United States, didn't offend Longfellow.

When Trollope revisited the United States years later, Longfellow casually wrote, "In the afternoon Anthony Trollope, the novelist, calls" (16 Oct 1875). The two men amiably corresponded later. Trollope's novels, often realistically coming to grips with clerical, social, and political problems in England, didn't appeal to Longfellow. Trollope weirdly begins his essay titled "Henry Wadsworth Longfellow," in *North American Review* (Apr 1881), thus: "I not unnaturally feel disinclined to speak in public of the character and genius of Longfellow, as he is happily still among us"; but he proceeds thereafter to carp at pathos in Longfellow, to analyze *Evangeline, The Song of Hiawatha,* and *The Courtship of Miles Standish* with considerable averse comment, and to close by only briefly praising "The Skeleton in Armor." Years earlier, Longfellow's wife Fanny noted in her journals that she found Trollope's mother's *Domestic Manners of the Americans* excessive but her novel *The Widow Barnaby* (1838) "Admirable" (20 Jun 1833, 24 Jul 1840).

Bibliography: Hall, N. John. *Trollope: A Biography.* Oxford: Clarendon Press, 1991; S. Longfellow; *Mrs. Longfellow.*

TUCKER-MACCHETTA, BLANCHE ROOSEVELT (1853–98).

Opera singer and novelist. As the leading light of the Blanche Roosevelt English Opera Company, she sang the title role in the production of the short-lived musical based on *The Masque of Pandora* presented in Boston (10 Jan 1881). In subsequent letters to her, Longfellow addresses her as "Dear Pandora." When she was in Paris with her Italian-born husband August Macchetta (late 1881), and when she was in New York (early 1882), Longfellow wrote her. Her book *The Home Life of Henry W. Longfellow: Reminiscences of Many Visits at Cambridge and Nahant, During the Years 1880, 1881, and 1882* (1882) appeared shortly after the poet's death.

Bibliography: Hilen, ed.

"TWILIGHT" (1848).

Poem, in *The Opal: A Pure Gift for the Holy Days,* 1848; *S/F.* At a cloudy twilight, while the wind is whipping up the sea, a child peers through a fisherman's cottage window and a woman's shadow waves about. What is the wind telling the child? Why does the loud ocean make the woman's face turn pale?

"THE TWO ANGELS" (1858).

Poem, in *Courtship, Birds* (1858). "Two angels, one of Life, and one of Death," approach two separate houses in the village. Though alike in appearance, one angel is "crowned with amaranth," the other "with asphodels." The poet grows fearful, when the one with asphodels knocks at his door. He will accept whatever God ordains, without lamenting or rejoicing. The angel smiles radiantly, says he brings life, and speeds away. The other, with amaranth, goes to the house of the poet's friend. The word "death" is whispered there. From the house of gloom two angels leave. Who, believing that God orders both angels, would bar the door from such messengers? Longfellow wrote this solemn poem on the occasion, five days apart, of the birth of his daughter, Edith Longfellow* (22 Oct 1853) and the death of Maria White Lowell (27 Oct 1853), the first wife of his friend James Russell Lowell.*

Bibliography: Arvin.

"THE TWO HARVESTS" (1833).

Sonnet, translated from the Italian poet Francisco de Medrano (1570–1607?), in *Coplas;* Scudder. Only yesterday the poet saw the plant grow, spread leaves, and mature, only to be cut down by "the reaper's sickle." We are the same, though harvested after a longer while; moreover, some "fall before . . . ripened."

"THE TWO LOCKS OF HAIR" (1832).

Poem, translated from the German poet Gustav Pfizer (1807–90), in *Token,* 1842; *Ballads.* The persona defines himself as "Arab-like," young and wandering around the world, "light-hearted and content." But he often dreams of a wife's brown hair, and of a child's blond hair, and of their cold graves. When he beholds "that lock of gold" and "the dark lock," he wishes he were dead. After his first wife and child died, Samuel Ward* sent Longfellow a copy of Pfizer's

"Junggesell" and asked him to translate it. Longfellow did so, wrote him (24 Jun 1841), and sent him a copy.

Bibliography: Hilen, ed.; S. Longfellow.

"THE TWO RIVERS" (1878). Sonnet, in *Kéramos.* The clock's hour hand moves slowly. The ship sails slowly. But "both arrive." The watchman strikes the midnight hour. It is "The watershed of Time." From it flows yesterday, "to the land of darkness and of dreams"; from it also flows tomorrow, "to the land of promise and of light."

U

ULTIMA THULE (1880). Collection of poems: "Dedication to G[eorge]. W[ashington]. G[reene].[*]" *Poems:* "Bayard Taylor[*]," "The Chamber over the Gate," "From My Arm-Chair," "Jugurtha," "The Iron Pen," "Robert Burns," "Helen of Tyre," "Elegiac," "Old St. David's at Radnor." *Folk-Songs:* "The Sifting of Peter," "Maiden and Weathercock," "The Windmill," "The Tide Rises, the Tide Falls." *Sonnets:* "My Cathedral," "The Burial of the Poet, R[ichard]. H[enry]. D[ana Sr.*].," "Night." *L'Envoi:* "The Poet and His Songs."

V

"VALENTINE" (1825). Poem, in Portland *Gazette,* 1 Oct 1825. The persona feels that he deserves the lady's love; but his heart is "cleft," "Life's cheerful banquet" is off-limits for him, and after a while his tomb will read "Here rests a Troubadour." But it's all right, since his death will be a blessing for her. This unsigned poem was published together with the poem "On a Lock of Hair" in an essay titled "Valentine Writing."

Bibliography: Little.

"THE VENETIAN GONDOLIER" (1825). Poem, in *USLG,* 15 Jan 1825; Scudder. The gondolier readies "his tuneful viol" at midnight, plies his oar, and sends his "light bark" forward. Nearby, nuns pray for those hurt by "life's rude storms" and never know the "calm repose" of this Venetian canal. Church bells sound "Love's midnight hour," and the gondola hastens "To seek Genevra's balcony."

Bibliography: Little.

"VENICE" (1877). Sonnet, in *Youth's Companion,* 22 Mar 1877; *PP, Kéramos.* Venice is a white swan nesting in lagoon reeds, a water lily cradled by the ocean and sending up spire-like blossoming filaments, a "phantom city" with rivers for streets and shadows for pavements. The poet "wait[s] to see thee vanish" like fleets in a mirage and towers made of clouds.

"VENICE, AN ITALIAN SONG" (1820). Poem. This is Longfellow's earliest recorded poem. It is dated Portland Academy (17 Mar 1820).

Bibliography: Little.

"VICTOR AND VANQUISHED" (1882). Sonnet, in *Harbor.* The poet is tired of running away from Death. With his back to the wall, without weapons, and wounded, he "stand[s] unmoved"—this he tells Death. Resigned but unyielding, he says that "This is no tournament where cowards tilt; / The vanquished here is victor of the field."

"VICTOR GALBRAITH" (1855). Poem, in *PM,* Jul 1855; *Courtship, Birds* (1858). Bugles sound the call for the execution by firing squad of Victor Galbraith, a shamed bugler, in front of a wall at Monterey. Galbraith marches firmly, with head erect, and tells the riflemen to shoot accurately. The first volley only wounds him in the chest and the head. He gets up, has a drink of water, and tells the men to put him out of his pain. They do so, with a second round of firing. Afterwards, although Galbraith answers no more roll calls, a phantom bugle sounds, and the sentinels say, "That is the wraith / Of Victor Galbraith!" According to his journal, Longfellow wrote this poem on 1 April 1855. Much earlier, he had been sent a newspaper account describing the execution—perhaps one that happened during the 1846–48 Mexican War.

Bibliography: S. Longfellow.

VICTORIA, QUEEN (1819–1901). Alexandrina Victoria, queen of Great Britain (1837–1901). Soon after Longfellow and his family arrived in London (26 Jun 1868), Queen Victoria invited him to a private audience at Windsor Castle. She received him without unusual ceremony and managed to compliment him. To say something in reply, he expressed surprise that he was so well known in England. To this the queen asseverated, "Oh, I assure you, Mr. Longfellow, that all my servants read you." Relaying this anecdote to Oscar Wilde (1882), Longfellow said, "Sometimes, I will wake up in the night and wonder if it was a deliberate slight." Wilde concluded that it was "the rebuke of Majesty to the vanity of a poet." It is of incidental interest that Longfellow wrote Helen Mar Bean* (5 Feb 1882) and Mary Appleton Mackintosh* (7 Feb 1882) that when Wilde visited him, he impressed the aging poet as "very agreeable." Longfellow was not, however, even allegedly slighted elsewhere in England during his busy June of 1868. He had been awarded the honorary degree of Doctor of Laws at Cambridge University (16 Jun 1868); while in London breakfasted with William Gladstone (1809–98), Queen Victoria's prime minister (1868–74 and for three periods later); and also called by request on Edward (1841–1910), Prince of Wales, Queen Victoria's eldest son and later King Edward VII (1901–10). Through the hospitality of Charles Eliot Norton,* Longfellow had met the Prince of Wales earlier at a dinner and ball held in his honor in Boston (18 Oct 1860).

Bibliography: Ellman, Richard. *Oscar Wilde.* New York: Alfred A. Knopf, 1988; Hibbert, Christopher. *Queen Victoria: A Personal History.* New York: Basic Books, 2000; Hilen, ed.; S. Longfellow.

"VIDA DE SAN MILLAN." Poem, translated from the Spanish poet Gonzalo de Berceo (1180–after 1246), in Scudder. A small army of Christians is about to be attacked by hordes of fierce Moors. Looking to the skies in uncertainty, the Christians see two angelic figures on white horses. One holds a crosier and wears "a pontiff's mitre"; the other has a crucifix. They gallop down among the Moors. The Christians are encouraged. The angels smite the foe, cause terror in their ranks, and even make their arrows fall back and wound themselves. The one with the papal crown is "the glorified Apostle, the brother of Saint John"; the other, "the holy San Millan of Cogolla's neighborhood." Longfellow included his translation of this poem in *Outre-Mer.*

Bibliography: Dutton, Brian. *La "Vida de San Millan de la Cogolla" de Berceo.* London: Tamesis Books Limited, 1967.

"THE VILLAGE BLACKSMITH" (1840). Poem, in *KM,* Nov 1840; *Ballads.* The smithy of the brawny village smith stands beneath "a spreading chestnut-tree." The blacksmith works hard and proudly, has no debts, and when he "swing[s] his heavy sledge" it makes sounds like the sexton tolling the evening hour. After school, children delight in looking at the blacksmith's forge, hearing his bellows, and chasing after his "burning sparks." He glories in hearing his daughter's voice in the church choir. It reminds him of his dead wife, and he wipes a tear. Each evening, he knows that a day's work is completed well. This "worthy friend" teaches an important lesson. We must work "at the flaming forge of life" and shape every "deed and thought" on "its sounding anvil." Although this poem commemorates Longfellow's paternal great-great-grandfather (*see* Longfellow, Stephen [1685–1764]), the smithy described was the one on Brattle Street between Craigie House* and Harvard Square in Cambridge. For Longfellow's seventy-fifth birthday, the children of Cambridge gave him a chair made out of wood from the chestnut tree above the smithy (*see* "From My Arm-Chair"). "The Village Blacksmith," commonplace though some have called it, has retained its vigor over the years and is frequently anthologized. Longfellow was paid $15 for it.

Bibliography: Arms, George. "'Moby-Dick' and 'The Village Blacksmith.'" *Notes & Queries* 192 (3 May 1947): 187–88; Arvin; Masheck, Joseph. "Professor Longfellow and the Blacksmith." *Annals of Scholarship* 10 (summer-fall 1993): 345–561; Thompson; Wagenknecht, 1986; Williams.

"VIRE" (1877). Poem, translated from the French poet Gustave le Vavasseur (1819–96), in *PP,* Scudder. For "a poet of Normany the Low / It is good to rhyming go" along the valleys of Vire and Bures. In the humble but delightful town of Vire, you would find Olivier (a fuller), Le Houx (a lawyer), and Thomas Sonnet (a physician). Olivier mainly "fulled his tub." Olivier advocated "dry and sweet" wines. Sonnet prescribed avoidance of bad wine. They represent, respectively, "Peace, and Tavern, and Poesy." Vire, with its many taverns, "is the fresh cradle of the Song, / And mother of the Vaudeville."

"VIRGIL'S FIRST ECLOGUE" (1878). Poem, translated from the Latin poet Virgil, in *Kéramos.* Meliboeus and Tityrus express distress and confusion following distribution of their lands. Meliboeus worries that "gentle susurrus to fall asleep shall persuade" Tityrus and is irate that "an impious soldier [shall] possess these lands newly cultivated." Longfellow converted Virgil's lines into awkward, unsyntactical hexameters. In a letter to George Washington Greene* (24 Feb 1878), Longfellow said he was afraid that if he included this translation in his volume titled *Kéramos and Other Poems* (1878), readers might regard it as "rather a school-boy performance."

"VITTORIA COLONNA" (1878). Poem, in *PP, Kéramos, Birds* (1878). The poet praises Vittoria Colonna (1490–1547), who after her husband, (Marchese di) Pescara, died, returned to Inarimé (i.e., Ischia), where "she / . . . [had] lived and loved so long ago." Death "only closer pressed / The wedding-ring upon her hand," and she dreadfully missed the "one to come / Who nevermore would come again." Sea breaths and air "caresses" made her more despairing until she found "voice in one impassioned song / Of inconsolable lament." Vittoria Colonna's ode on her husband's death is so moving that she was called "Divine." (*See also Michael Angelo: A Fragment.*)

VOICES OF THE NIGHT **(1839).** Collection of poems: "Prelude," "Hymn to the Night," "A Psalm of Life," "The Reaper and the Flowers," "The Light of Stars," "Footsteps of Angels," "Flowers," "The Beleaguered City," "Midnight Mass for the Dying Year."

"VOICES OF THE NIGHT: A THIRD PSALM OF LIFE." *See* "Footsteps of Angels."

"VOX POPULI" (1871). Poem, in *AM,* May 1871; *Aftermath, Birds* (1873). The magician Mazárvan when he is west of Cathay hears about Badoura exclusively, but in Khaledan people talk only about Prince Camaralzaman. Explanation? "Every province hath its own" poet.

W

WADSWORTH, ALEXANDER (1806–?). The son of Charles Lee Wadsworth,* the brother of Longfellow's mother Zilpah Wadsworth Longfellow,* and hence Longfellow's cousin.

WADSWORTH, ALEXANDER SCAMMELL, JR. (1828–62). The son of Commodore Alexander Scammell Wadsworth* and hence Longfellow's cousin. He attended Harvard, was rusticated for academic infractions, but graduated (1848). Longfellow seems to have lost interest in him thereafter.

Bibliography: Hilen, ed.

WADSWORTH, CHARLES (1800–1880). The son of Charles Lee Wadsworth* and hence Longfellow's cousin.

WADSWORTH, CHARLES LEE (1776–1848). The brother of Longfellow's mother, Zilpah Wadsworth Longfellow,* and hence Longfellow's uncle.

WADSWORTH, CHRISTOPHER. Longfellow's great-great-great-great-great-grandfather, who migrated from England and settled before 1632 in Duxbury, Massachusetts.

Bibliography: Higginson.

WADSWORTH, COMMODORE ALEXANDER SCAMMELL (1790–1851). The brother of Longfellow's mother, Zilpah Wadsworth Longfellow,* and hence Longfellow's uncle. He married Louisa Denison (1786–?) in 1824; they had three children: Alexander Scammell Wadsworth Jr.* (1828–62), Louisa ("Luly") Denison Wadsworth (1833–?), and Anne Denison Wadsworth (1841–?). Alexander Wadsworth entered the U.S. Navy (1804), served on the frigate *Constitution* and other men-of-war (by 1823), and did duty in the Washington Navy Yard (1823–25). He achieved the rank of commodore. Longfellow and his wife Fanny visited Wadsworth in Washington (Feb 1839) and had a pleasant time. Wadsworth introduced Longfellow to President Martin Van Buren. Longfellow wrote his mother (27 Feb 1839) that "Aunt *Louisa* is a very lovely woman." As for Luly Wadsworth and Anne Wadsworth—Luly was married (1853) to Charles G. Baylor (c.1826–?). Baylor, a Texan, was appointed American consul in Manchester, England (1858–60). According to Longfellow's sister, Anne Longfellow Pierce,* Baylor wanted his sister-in-law, Anne Wadsworth, to avoid living with Anne Pierce and instead move to Manchester with Luly and him, so as to control his sister-in-law's inherited income. However, Anne Wadsworth remained with Anne Pierce and was soon married (1860) to John Doane Wells (1834–1911). Just as the Civil War was erupting, Baylor, according to Anne Pierce, was somewhere in the South and his poor wife, Luly, was living outside Baltimore with their three little daughters. Luly had been separated from Baylor for several years (by 1874); beginning then, Longfellow helped support her, ultimately sending her $1,885 by the time of his death.

Bibliography: Hilen, ed.

WADSWORTH, HENRY (1785–1804). Longfellow's uncle. He was a naval lieutenant and was killed when a fire ship exploded before the walls of Tripoli, during the Tripolitan War (1801–05). The future poet was named after this young man.

Bibliography: Higginson.

WADSWORTH, LOUISA DENISON (1833–?). The daughter of Commodore Alexander Scammell Wadsworth* and hence Longfellow's cousin. After visiting the Wadsworth family in Washington, D.C., Longfellow wrote his mother (27 Feb 1839) that "Little *Luly* is more lovely than ever."

Bibliography: Hilen, ed.

WADSWORTH, LUCIA (1783–1864). The sister of Longfellow's mother, Zilpah Wadsworth Longfellow,* and hence Longfellow's aunt. Never marrying, she was invited to become a member of the Longfellows' household. Aunt Lucia was a beloved figure in the family while Longfellow and his siblings were born and were maturing in their various ways. She also helped care for Henry Wadsworth Longfellow II* for a while after the boy's father, Stephen Longfellow (1805–50),* died.

Bibliography: Hilen, ed.

WADSWORTH, PELEG (1715–99). Longfellow's maternal great-grandfather.

WADSWORTH, PELEG (1748–1829). Longfellow's maternal grandfather. He was the son of the elder Peleg Wadsworth,* was born in Duxbury, Massachusetts, graduated from Harvard (1769), and taught school at Plymouth. He married Elizabeth Bartlett (1753–1825),* who was the daughter of Nathaniel Bartlett (1723–?) and lived in Plymouth. During the American Revolution, the younger Peleg Wadsworth became a captain of a minuteman company and rose to the rank of major general. He was captured on the eastern frontier, was imprisoned, but es-

caped. After the war ended, he bought 7,500 acres of wild land from the state, lived in Hiram, Maine, and represented his district in Congress. Through Wadsworth and Bartlett ancestors, Longfellow traced his descent to four pilgrims on the *Mayflower,* including John Alden and Elder Brewster.

Bibliography: Higginson.

WADSWORTH, ZILPAH (1778–1851). Longfellow's mother. *See* Longfellow, Zilpah Wadsworth.

THE WAIF: A COLLECTION OF POEMS **(1845).** An anthology of 50 fugitive poems, selected and edited by Longfellow. He regarded their calm and gentle contents with special affection. He introduces the book with "The Day Is Done," called here "Proem by Henry W. Longfellow."

"WALT[H]ER VON DER VOGELWEIDE" (1846). Poem, in *Bruges.* When he died, Walther von der Vogelweide (c.1170–c.1230), the German poet and minnesinger, gave money to the monks of Würzburg and asked them to feed his beloved birds, which flocked around his tomb. For a time, these "poets of the air," nicely fed, gathered on trees, pavement, tombstone, Walther's sculptured face, windows, and lintels. Later, however, "the portly abbot" figured that the bequest should be used to buy "loaves . . . / For our fasting brotherhood." The birds flocked vainly. Time passed. "And tradition only tells us" the location of the poet's body. However, birds still "repeat the legend" all "around the vast cathedral" by their "sweet echoes."

"WANDERER'S NIGHT SONGS" (1870). Poem, translated from the German poet Johann Wolfgang von Goethe, in *AM,* Sep 1870; *Three.* The poet hopes that something may come from the heavens and refresh the wretched and himself. All is quiet. The birds are asleep. Soon you will also rest. Longfellow included an early version of his poem in a letter to Samuel Ward* (17 Sep 1841).

Bibliography: Hilen, ed.

"WAPENTAKE: TO [LORD] ALFRED TEN-NYSON[*]" (1877). Sonnet, in *AM,* Dec 1877; *Kéramos.* Longfellow wishes to "touch thy lance with mine," not in combat but in "homage to the mastery, which is thine, / In English song." The poet calls Tennyson's "verse divine," never emulating "howling dervishes of song." He is the "sweet historian of the heart," ever faithful "to the poet's art." Longfellow, who always revered Tennyson's poetry, spent two delightful days with him at his home on the Isle of Wight (Jul 1868). The word "wapentake," deriving from the Old English "waepentaec," means "take weapon," that is, brandish a weapon as a show of approval when a chief enters upon his office.

WARD, SAMUEL (1814–84). Adventurer, politician, and lobbyist. Samuel Ward was the son of Samuel Ward Sr. (1786–1839) and Julia Rush Cutler Ward. The father was a partner in the well-known banking firm of Prime, Ward, and King. Young Ward was the brother of Julia Ward Howe* (the wife of Samuel Gridley Howe*), Louisa Ward Crawford (the wife of Thomas Crawford*), and Anne Eliza Ward (the wife of Adolph Mailliard, grandson of Napoleon Bonaparte's son Joseph Bonaparte [1768–1844], ex-king of Naples and Spain). Samuel Ward was born in New York City, attended Round Hill School in Northampton, Massachusetts, where he was instructed in Greek by Cornelius Conway Felton* and proved to be skillful in languages and mathematics, and later graduated from Columbia University (1831). His father indulged him in a four-year stay in Europe (mostly France and Germany), where he gormandized, womanized, collected books, was an informal diplomatic secretary, made numerous friends—including Longfellow, by chance—and wrote a dissertation in Latin on mathematical equations (Ph.D., University of Tübingen). Ward returned home and worked in his father's bank (1836). He married Emily Astor (1838), the granddaughter of John Jacob Astor.* The couple had one daughter; then his wife died (1841). Ward married Medora Grymes (1843); her gossiped-about past caused a rupture with the Astor family, who took custody of his daughter. Medora and Samuel

Ward proceeded to have two sons. Ward split off from his father's banking house to start his own firm, failed, went bankrupt, and separated from his wife and children (1847–48). He went into politics and business in San Francisco (1849–51), failed because of the 1851 fire there, engaged in trading with Native Americans (1851–52), and returned to San Francisco (1852–54). He tried but failed to rescue a French friend condemned to be executed in Mexico City for filibustering (1854), resumed relations with his wife (1854–56), and pursued diplomatic and commercial work in Europe (1854–58). Fluent in Spanish, among other languages, Ward junketed on secret cases between Paraguay and Washington, D.C. (1858–60). During the Civil War, he accomplished covert work for William Henry Seward, President Abraham Lincoln's secretary of state, may also have acted as a liaison between military-supply manufacturers and the U.S. government, and published his *Lyrical Recreations* (1865).

From this time on, Ward was dubbed "King of the Lobby," whose vaunted successes are documented only partially, because in his will he ordered papers destroyed that would have shed much light. It is said that he worked for Hugh McCullough, President Andrew Johnson's secretary of the treasury; may have helped Johnson gain acquittal after he was impeached; and aided railroad financiers, steamship subsidy-seekers, other businessmen, and foreign agents seeking advantageous congressional tariff and land-grant votes. The 1870s found Ward in New York much of the time, well financed partly through the generosity of friends; but a ruinous investment (1882) caused him to feel the need to escape process-servers by going to Rome, to live with his sister Louisa. She was Crawford's widow and was married (since 1861) to Luther Terry, an American expatriate painter. With her at the time was her son, Francis Marion Crawford (1854–1909), the popular novelist, whose first book, *Mr. Isaacs: A Tale of Modern India* (1882), Ward had persuaded and encouraged him to write. Gravely ill, Ward tried to convalesce in Pegli, west of Genoa, but soon died there.

During his second trip to Europe, Longfellow was visiting the wife and family of William Cullen Bryant* in Heidelberg (Mar 1836) when he chanced to meet Ward. Their personality differences attracted each to the other, and they became fast friends. Since they seldom met, given Ward's propensity to travel and socialize with the politically and commercially influential, it is mainly through their 350-letter correspondence (1836–82) that their often interlocking lives are known. Ward was easily the wildest friend Longfellow ever had, and Longfellow's letters to him are among his most exuberant. Shortly after meeting Ward, Longfellow wrote George Washington Greene* (25 Mar 1836), into whose Rhode Island family Ward's grandfather had married; Longfellow said that Ward had "a *temperament* of at least sixty-horsepower." Among the blizzard of letters Longfellow wrote Ward, often about their family members, friends, work (done and proposed), infrequent get-togethers, gifts, dinners, travels, money, and publications (theirs and others'), several are of special note. Longfellow appears to have started their correspondence by writing Ward a chatty letter (3 Apr 1836) about his reading, the weather, beautiful scenery, and peppy Ward's need to get married. Ward sent Longfellow an original, erotic poem; Longfellow replied (22 Jun 1836) to say, before turning to other topics, that "these matters belong to the great volume of unwritten sensations which ought to remain unwritten." Home again, Longfellow wrote Ward again (2 Apr 1837) to gripe— "Why the devil have you not written to me?"—and then to ask the status of Greene's translation of *Histoire de la Civilisation en Europe* (1828) by François Pierre Guillaume (1787–1874), which Ward said he would try to get published in New York. It remained unpublished. Ward was often Longfellow's literary agent (from c.1838), selling his poems to New York periodical editors. When Ward complained that an essay of his own had been adversely reviewed, Longfellow replied, uncandidly (21 Apr 1839): "I have one excellent remedy on all such occasions, which I commend to you likewise. I never read what is written against me." Longfellow was Ward's guest in New York when he de-livered two lectures on Dante and one on Jean Paul Richter (the last, Jan 1840). During that time, Longfellow met Ward's three sisters, Julia, Anne, and Louisa. Feeling hopeless because of Fanny Appleton's protracted aloofness, he cast a romantic eye on Anne. Ward took Anne with him for a visit to Boston (May 1840), during which time Longfellow saw her again, thought a lot about her, but regarded himself as too old for her. While *The Spanish Student* by Longfellow was still in manuscript, Ward read it and in letters to Longfellow called himself Hypolito and Longfellow Victorian, after two characters in the play. Ward placed Longfellow's "The Skeleton in Armor" *(KM,* Jan 1841) for $25. In a letter to Ward (7 May 1843), Longfellow alluded to Medora Grymes, whom Ward was to marry in September, as Preciosa, the heroine of *The Spanish Student.*

For years thereafter, Ward's personal and commercial life took him away from Longfellow and his circle. They did meet when Ward's sister Julia invited both to dinner (14 Dec 1848), shortly before Ward left for California. With his second marriage in temporary ruins along with another personal fortune (1857), he evidently applied for money to Longfellow, who in September sent what he could. Ever peripatetic, Ward wrote Longfellow from Switzerland (25 Aug 1870) reminding him—without explicable figurative sense—that "you are more or less a child of mine,—at least I have been the family physician of some of your bairns; notably 'The Skeleton in Armor,' 'The Children of the Lord's Supper,' 'The Two Locks of Hair,' and 'Hyperion.'" Home again, Ward visited Longfellow, who noted in his journal (14 Apr 1871) that "He looks like a prime minister or a European diplomat." Ward helped Longfellow a final time by negotiating for the New York *Ledger* to pay Longfellow $3,000 to publish "The Hanging of the Crane" (1874); Ward helped himself too, by being paid $1,000 for brokering the sale. Coming into some cash (1880), Ward sent two checks to Longfellow and asked him to forward the money, one sum anonymously, to Greene. Soon after Longfellow's death, Ward published a mellow essay titled "Days with Longfellow" *(NAR,* May 1882).

Bibliography: Elliott, Maud Howe. *Uncle Sam Ward and His Circle.* New York: Macmillan Company, 1938; Hilen, ed.; Tharp; Thompson.

"THE WARDEN OF THE CINQUE PORTS" (1853).

Poem, unsigned, in *PM,* Jan 1853; *Courtship, Birds* (1858). The "autumn sun" dawns red over the English Channel, streams through windows, and glances on flags and ships' sails. Cannons roar. French warships steam toward British Channel cities, and their guns salute the shore, saying "all was well." Faraway forts fire, but nothing can "summon from his sleep the Warden / And Lord of the Cinque Ports." No sun, drum, or "morning gun" can rouse him. Nor will anyone see "the gaunt figure of the old Field Marshal" again. "In sombre harness mailed," Death has climbed the wall and taken him. When Death entered the sleeper's room, "the gloom" became "darker . . . and deeper." Death's thrust at "the Warden hoar" caused "all England [to] tremble / And groan from shore to shore." And yet outside, "Nothing in Nature's aspect intimated / That a great man was dead." Longfellow, normally anti-militaristic, quickly wrote this forceful tribute (14 Oct 1852) to Arthur Wellesley, the Duke of Wellington, who had died only a month earlier (13 Sep 1852). For this poem, Longfellow was paid $50 by the editors of *Putnam's Magazine.*

Bibliography: Arvin; Hilen, ed.; S. Longfellow; Wagenknecht, 1986; Williams.

"THE WARNING." *See Poems on Slavery.*

"THE WAVE" (1839).

Poem, translated from the German poet Christoph August Tiedge (1752-1841), in *Hyperion, Voices.* Where is the wave going in haste like that of a thief? The answer? "I am the Wave of Life," eager to escape "the narrow stream . . . / To the Sea's immensity," and "wash from me" Time's slime. When Longfellow republished this poem in his edition of *Poets and Poetry of Europe,* he titled it "The Wave of Life."

"THE WAVE OF LIFE" (1839). *See* "The Wave."

"THE WAYSIDE INN." *See* "Prelude," in *Tales of a Wayside Inn,* Part First.

"WEARINESS" (1863).

Poem, in *AM,* Nov 1863; *Tales of a Wayside Inn,* 1863. The poet grows weary thinking how far little feet have yet to walk, how busy little hands have yet to be, how little hearts must contend with "strong desires" later, and how close little souls still are to "their source divine." The poet's feet are near death's "wayside inn"; his hands have written much; his once-glowing heart now "covers and conceals its fires" with ashes; and his soul is like a setting sun, "Refracted through the mist of years" and made "lurid."

Bibliography: Wagenknecht, 1986.

WEBSTER, DANIEL (1782–1852).

Lawyer and statesman. He was born in Salisbury, New Hampshire. During minimal early schooling, he read voraciously and developed a photographic memory. He attended Phillips Exeter Academy and then graduated from Dartmouth College (1801). He read for the law in Salisbury and Boston, was admitted to the bar in Boston (1805), but practiced in New Hampshire (1805-13). During the War of 1812, which he opposed moderately, he skillfully defended American shipping interests. He represented New Hampshire as a Federalist in the U.S. House of Representatives (1813-17), practiced law in Boston (1817-23), and became an able constitutional lawyer and a spellbinding orator. He represented Massachusetts in the U.S. House of Representatives (1823-27) and in the U.S. Senate (1827-41, 1845-50). During part of this time, he ran unsuccessfully for president (1835) against Martin Van Buren. Webster allied himself with Henry Clay as a Whig Party leader, fought against the annexation of Texas (1845) and the ill-starred Wilmot Proviso (1846), opposed the pro-slavery policies of John C. Calhoun, and argued against the Mexico War (1846-48). Webster served as secretary of state under presidents William Henry Harrison (1841) and John Tyler (1841-43), resigning because of opposition to Tyler's advocacy of states' rights. Webster opposed the Clayton Compromise (1848), which, if not defeated, would have opened Oregon, California, and New Mexican territories to slavery. He continued to seek the presidency and was disappointed when the Whigs nominated the successful Zachary Taylor instead (1848). Eager to save the Union even if it meant appeasing Southern slave owners, Webster supported the Compromise of 1850 in his disastrous speech on 7 Mar 1850. This cost him the friendship and admiration of countless New Englanders, including Ralph Waldo Emerson,* John Greenleaf Whittier,* and Longfellow. However, Oliver Wendell Holmes,* along with several hundred other New England intellectuals, including clergymen and Harvard faculty members, signed a letter commending Webster's action; some of them even called him "the godlike Daniel." When President Taylor died, Webster served as President Millard Fillmore's secretary of state (1850–52). Webster was again frustrated when the Whigs ignored his presidential ambitions and nominated the unsuccessful Winfield Scott (1852). Webster correctly predicted the Whig Party's demise and died himself soon thereafter. Webster married Grace Fletcher (1808). They had five children, two dying in childhood and a third predeceasing him. His wife died (1828). He married Caroline Le Roy (1829), a young New York heiress who survived him by 30 years. Webster speculated irresponsibly in western lands, was involved in shady commercial actions, and suffered from alcoholism. His collected writings were published (6 vols., 1851), as were his private correspondence (2 vols., 1857), his letters (1902), and his *Writings and Speeches . . .* (18 vols., 1903).

Longfellow, 25 years younger than Webster, never knew him well. Longfellow briefly vacationed in Washington, D.C. (Feb 1839), and Commodore Alexander Scammell Wadsworth,* his uncle, showed him around. He was introduced to President Van Buren, heard several speeches in the Senate, saw the Supreme Court judges, and spoke personally with Webster. Longfellow, never actively concerned with politics, did write this in his journal about early Northern steps toward compromise with the Southern states: "what a great and fatal mistake was

that first compromise of the Constitution by which slavery was tolerated; and what a fatal one will be this second one [the Clayton Compromise], if passed, which God forbid!" (31 Jul 1848). As for Webster's seventh of March speech, Longfellow snidely asked in his journal "what has there been in Webster's life to lead us to think that he would take any high moral ground on this Slavery question?" (9 Mar 1850). However, a couple of months later Longfellow and his wife visited Washington, D.C., where they were the Websters' breakfast guests. Longfellow cutely rationalized in a letter to Charles Sumner,* who loathed Webster: "You see I put social matters before political, because I like them better" (19 May 1850). Breakfasting soon again with Webster, Longfellow described him in his journal as "ponderous and silent" (21 May). When Longfellow called on Webster back in Boston, he commented in his journal on "his face of infinite woes. He always reminds me of Dante [Longfellow continues], though he has written no *Divina Commedia*" (5 Nov 1850). Longfellow clearly disliked Webster's part in the ruin of the Whig Party and, worse, his support of the infamous Fugitive Slave Act (1850), which required arrests of Southern slaves seeking freedom in the North. Revulsed by enforcement of the law in Massachusetts, Longfellow notes in his journal, "Troops under arms in Boston . . . This is the last point of degradation. Alas for the people who cannot feel an insult! While the 'great Webster' comes North to see that the work is done!" (5 Apr 1851). After Webster's death, Longfellow remained unforgiving; when Anthony Burns, a fugitive slave, was arrested in Boston by federal authorities, Longfellow laments in his journal: "Ah, Webster, Webster, you have much to answer for!" (27 May 1854). Richard Henry Dana Jr.,* Longfellow's friend and later the father-in-law of his daughter Edith Longfellow Dana,* vigorously but unsuccessfully defended Burns in court (May–Jun 1854) and was slugged and nearly blinded by a pro-Southern street thug for doing so.

Bibliography: Fuess, Claude Moore. *Daniel Webster.* 2 vols. Boston: Little, Brown, & Company, 1930; Hilen, ed.; S. Longfellow; Remini,

Robert V. *Daniel Webster: The Man and His Times*. New York: W. W. Norton & Company, 1997.

"THE WHITE CZAR" (1878). Poem, in *PP, Kéramos, Birds* (1878). If you see some wreath-like mist on the ramparts, it is the White Czar. He has heard his dead soldiers, tramping and beating their drums. He has heard voices of the dead crying for him to awaken. Responding, he leads armies through deserts to the mountains and points "o'er the land / Of Roumili." He boasts of former shipbuilding, promises to sail past Gibraltar and free the Bosphorus, and swears to help the crushed Christians throw off the "iron rule" of Istanbul's sultan. Longfellow makes a refrain of "Batyushka! Gosudar!," which is Russian for "father dear" and "sovereign." The czar celebrated here was Peter the Great (1672-1725).

"WHITHER?" (1839). Poem, translated from the German poet Wilhelm Müller (1794-1827), in *Hyperion, Voices*. The poet hears the brook and "must hasten downward" to find it. Its "soft murmur," which has stolen away his senses, is the voice of water nymphs. Let them sing "roundelays." After all, brooks do turn mill wheels.

WHITTIER, JOHN GREENLEAF (1807–92). Man of letters, born on a farm outside Haverhill, Massachusetts. With only a country-school education, he read privately, John Bunyan and Robert Burns being his favorite authors. Whittier also sharpened his considerable native intelligence by meditating on the firm Quaker faith of his family. He published his first poem in the *Newburyport Free Press* (1826), edited in Newburyport, Massachusetts, by William Lloyd Garrison, who became the future fiery abolitionist and was one of Whittier's closest friends. Whittier studied at the Haverhill Academy (1827), taught school, and held editorial positions in and around Boston, Hartford, Connecticut, and elsewhere (1828–44). During this span of years, Whittier was a delegate to the National Anti-Slavery Convention held in Philadelphia (1833), served in the Massachusetts legislature (1835), and found time and energy to write steadily. His

publications during these years included the following: *Legends of New-England in Prose and Verse* (1831); *Mogg Megone* (1836), concerning the Indians in colonial times; *Justice and Expediency* (1833), advocating the abolition of slavery; *Poems Written during the Progress of the Abolition Question in the United States* (1837); and *Poems* (1838). After his *Voices of Freedom* appeared (1846), Whittier became a contributing editor of the *National Era* (1847–60). Next, he published *Leaves from Margaret Smith's Journal in the Province of Massachusetts Bay, 1678-9* (1849), a beautiful, half-fictional rendering of a British girl's visit to colonial New England; *Songs of Labor and Other Poems* (1850), containing "Ichabod," his awesome denunciation of Daniel Webster* for supporting the Compromise of 1850; *The Chapel of the Hermits and Other Poems* (1853); *The Panorama and Other Poems* (1853), featuring the classic "Barefoot Boy" and "Maud Muller"; "The Gift of Tritemius," a poem advocating Christian charity and appearing in the first issue of the *Atlantic Monthly* (Nov 1857; he helped establish the periodical); *Home Ballads and Poems* (1860), with the popular "Skipper Ireson's Ride" and "Telling the Bees"; and book-length reprints of his *National Era* articles. During the Civil War, Whittier wrote pro-Union verse. His *In War Time and Others Poems* (1864) includes "Barbara Frietchie," a patriotic but historically ridiculous effort. *National Lyrics* (1865) contains his "Laus Deo!," which celebrates the passage of the constitutional amendment ending slavery. Whittier was so popular that his beloved "Snow-Bound" (1866) quickly earned him $10,000, while his *Tent on the Beach* (1867), partly a narrative cycle of recycled poems, sold so well—a thousand copies a day for a time—that he wrote James T. Fields,* his publisher, and Longfellow's, thus (28 Feb 1867): "This will never do. The swindle is awful. . . . I am . . . ashamed to look an honest man in the face." In his last years, Whittier grew mellow and wrote lovingly about colonial life and his own youthful days on the farm. He wrote too much, and often too sentimentally and didactically; but his best verse is strong and

enduring, and he remained unbelievably beloved. On his eightieth birthday, almost 600
visitors called on him and he received two
thousand letters.

Whittier knew and wrote poems about
and letters to many friends whom Longfellow also knew, including Fredrika Bremer,*
William Cullen Bryant,* William Ellery Channing,* Fields, Oliver Wendell Holmes,* James
Russell Lowell,* Charles Sumner,* Bayard
Taylor,* and Webster. Whittier wrote Longfellow (4 Sep 1844) to praise his *Poems on
Slavery* (1842) for their help in advancing
the cause of the Liberty Party and to ask
whether he would agree to run for the U.S.
Congress on its ticket. Longfellow replied at
once (c.6 Sep 1844) to express gratitude
that the poems were regarded as having
"some salutary influence," to assure Whittier
that he hated slavery, but to reject the idea
of his ever "entering the political arena,"
which he defined as "too violent, too vindic-
tive, for my taste." The two men became casual friends. Whittier wrote an enthusiastic
review of *Evangeline* in his *National Era*
(25 Nov 1847), saying that it was America's
answer to British critics who carp that Americans couldn't produce literature. Longfellow wrote Whittier in gratitude (17 Dec
1847): "You alone of all my brother bards,
have hailed it with any warmth of welcome,—at least so far as I have heard." Longfellow must not have been pleased, however, when Whittier opined that the story of
Evangeline could have been told in poetic
prose, of the sort Longfellow used in his *Hyperion,* as effectively as in poetry. Whittier
added, however, that if he had written up
the story of Evangeline he would have
spoiled any artistry by showing too much
indignation at the treatment of the Acadians.
Whittier's poem "Marguerite" (1871) does
treat the expulsion of the Acadians in violent
language.

Longfellow and Whittier occasionally saw
one another. Longfellow's journal is therefore dotted with Whittier's name. When
they once chanced to meet at Fields's office,
Longfellow felt (4 Dec 1857) that Whittier
"grows milder and mellower, as does his poetry." Longfellow noted Whittier's presence
at a Saturday Club* meeting (9 Jul 1859). In

a self-deprecating letter to Fields (12 Dec
1870), Whittier said he was not worthy to
untie Longfellow's "poetical shoestrings."
Whittier's seventieth birthday was celebrated (17 Dec 1877) at a big party held in
Boston's Hotel Brunswick; Longfellow read
"The Three Silences of Molinos: To John
Greenleaf Whittier," the poem he wrote for
the occasion. The whole event was made
more historic, however, when Mark Twain
read his marvelously funny but allegedly unacceptable skit featuring three derelict Far
Western miners professing to be Ralph
Waldo Emerson,* Oliver Wendell Holmes,
and Longfellow. Twain called Emerson "a little seedy bit of a chap" and Holmes "fat as a
balloon." As for Longfellow, he "was built
like a prizefighter. His head was cropped
and bristly-like as if he had a wig made of
hair brushes. His nose lay straight down his
face, like a finger, with the end joint tilted
up." The audience seemed appalled, and
Twain soon turned so chagrined that he felt
obliged to mail apologies to his three targets
of humor. Longfellow, however, far from being offended, replied (8 Jan 1878) that nobody "was much hurt," that he surely was
not, that the dinner was "very pleasant," and
that "I think Whittier enjoyed it very much."
In a letter to Elizabeth Stuart Phelps* (21 Aug
1878), Longfellow commends Whittier for
his "In School Days" (1870), in which he
suggests that there is more to education than
reading school texts. Whittier's poem "The
Poet and the Children: Longfellow" (1882)
is a loving picture. Whittier sent Longfellow
a letter (27 Feb 1882) to celebrate his
friend's birthday (destined to be his last); in
it he wrote "I cannot let the occasion pass
without expressing my gratitude for the
happy hours I have spent over thy writings,
and the pride which I share with all Americans in view of thy success as an author and
thy character as a man." When Longfellow
died, Whittier wrote his niece (3 Mar 1882)
that his death was "a national loss. He has
been an influence for good; all the Christian
virtues his verse and his life exemplified."

Bibliography: Kaplan, Justin. *Mr. Clemens and
Mark Twain.* New York: Simon and Schuster,
1966; S. Longfellow; Fatout, Paul, ed. *Mark
Twain Speaking.* Iowa City: University of Iowa

Press, 1976; Smith, Henry Nash. "That Hideous Mistake of Poor Clemens." *Harvard Library Bulletin* 9 (spring 1955): 145–80; Tryon; Wagenknecht, 1955; Wagenknecht, Edward. *John Greenleaf Whittier: A Portrait in Paradox*. New York: Oxford University Press, 1967; *The Complete Writings of John Greenleaf Whittier*. 7 vols. Boston and New York: Houghton Mifflin Company, 1888–89.

"WILL EVER THE DEAR DAYS COME BACK AGAIN?" (1882). Sonnet, translated from an unidentified French poem, in *Harbor*. Though the poet knows not whether those sweet June days will return, he is aware of "a presence," like a phantom fragrance, in his room. Those old days were lovely, when at the heart came a knocking,

> . . . and we heard
> In the sweet tumult of delight and fear
> A voice that whispered, "Open, I cannot wait!"

WILLIS, NATHANIEL PARKER (1806–67). Author, journalist, and editor. Willis was born in Portland, Maine, moved with his family to Boston (1812), attended Andover Academy (1821–22), entered Yale (1823), and graduated and published a book of poems titled *Sketches* (both 1827). For many years, "Natty" Willis combined editorial work, an assignment as a foreign correspondent ($10 per weekly letter), pleasant travel, and non-journalistic writing. He edited the *Legendary* (1828) and the *Token* (1829), founded and edited the *American Monthly Magazine* (1829–31), occasionally edited the *New York Mirror* (1831–42), coedited the *Corsair* (1839–40), helped edit the *Dollar Magazine* (1840), helped establish the *New Mirror* (1843), helped establish the *Weekly Mirror* and the *Evening Mirror* (1844), and helped start the *National Press* (1846, later titled the *Home Journal*). He sent articles to the *New York Mirror* from France, Italy, the Near East, Malta, and England (1831–34, 1839–40); wrote for the *Court Magazine* and other English periodicals (from 1831); wrote for *Brother Jonathan* (1840) and the *Opal* (1848); and coedited *The Prose and Poetry of Europe and America* (1848). Willis's closest associate

during these years was George Pope Morris (1802–64), editor and poet.

Between 1836 and 1859 Willis published 16 books of prose (about travel, manners, social pleasures, and one novel, *Paul Fane* [1857]); between 1837 and 1868, three books of poetry. He also wrote *Bianca Visconti, or the Heart Overtasked* (1837) and *Tortesa: or, the Usurer Matched* (1839), two successful melodramas in blank verse. Edgar Allan Poe* called *Tortesa* the best drama by an American. Willis engaged William Makepeace Thackeray* to write for the *Corsair* (1845). Willis published Poe's "The Raven" (1845, *Evening Mirror*). After Poe's death, Willis wrote a fine defense of him (1849, *Home Journal*). While in England, Willis married Mary Stace, British General William Stace's daughter (1835); she died in childbirth (1845). Willis married Cornelia Grinnell (1846), almost 20 years his junior, and the two became Manhattan society leaders. Willis printed such careless criticism of the marital life of the popular but irascible American actor Edwin Forrest (1806–72) that Forrest beat him up on the street. Willis sued for assault and battery and won $1; Forrest sued for libel and won $500. Willis's sister Sara Payson Willis (1811–72), after being widowed, remarried wretchedly, and, when divorced, asked Willis to hire her as a writer. He spurned her; so she got revenge after becoming the popular Fanny Fern by casting him as Hyacinth Ellet, a popular editor and the heroine's selfish brother in *Ruth Hall: A Domestic Tale of the Present Time* (1855), her popular autobiographical roman à clef. Willis bought an estate at Cornwall-on-the-Hudson (1853), entertained lavishly there with his wife, and welcomed such literary visitors as James T. Fields,* Washington Irving,* and Bayard Taylor.* James Russell Lowell* in *A Fable for Critics* tersely calls Willis "The topmost bright bubble on the wave of the Town." Willis's stylistic weaknesses included digressions, frivolity, triviality, gossip, and padding; he was, however, a clever travel writer.

Longfellow had professional associations with Willis. In letters to George Washington Greene,* Longfellow shared information about Willis. In one letter he gripes that

"Willis is writing a Tragedy . . . *'to order,'* for Miss [Josephine] Clifton [1813–47], who gives him one thousand dollars. I can hardly tell you how *very* sorry I am for this. I do not like to see Poetry sold like a slave." More tersely, he adds that "Willis is in good spirits, and fat" (21 May 1837). In actuality, Willis when young was a handsome dandy. Longfellow reported to Greene again: "Willis has bought a farm on the Susquehanna, and writes plays for Miss Clifton, and letters for the New York Mirror, and the text to Views of American Scenery. We do not correspond, though he is very pleasant when we meet" (22 Oct 1838). A touch of envy comes next: Willis "says he has made ten thousand dollars the last year by his writings. I wish I had made ten hundred" (28 May 1840). Longfellow calls Willis's *A l'Abri* (later titled *The Tent Pitch'd* [1839]) "a collection of letters written from his country-seat on the Susquehanna" and praises them as "very racy and beautiful" (23 Jul 1839). Willis wrote Longfellow a chatty letter, half respectful and half impudent, in which he slowly gets around to praising Longfellow's *Voices of the Night* (1839)—"I see perfectly the line you are striking out for a renown, and it will succeed"—and wondering if his mentioning the book in a column "would make your topsails belly" (15 Sep 1840). Fields occasionally lured Longfellow into Willis's presence, because Willis and Fields were mutually helpful editors. Pallbearers at Willis's funeral in Boston included Oliver Wendell Holmes,* Lowell, and Longfellow.

Bibliography: Auser, Cortland P. *Nathaniel P. Willis.* New York: Twayne 1969; S. Longfellow; Thompson; Tryon.

"THE WINDMILL" (1880). Poem, in *Youth's Companion,* 27 May 1880; *Thule.* See me. I am a giant. I have "granite jaws," which turn maize, rye, and wheat into flour. When I gaze at farms, I realize that the harvests are for me. With my foot on a rock beneath me, I turn my face so that my sails can meet the changing, roaring wind. The hands of my master, the miller, feed me; in turn, I make him "lord of lands." When Sunday comes, I rest my arms across my chest, hear church bells, and am at peace. Longfel-low sent George Washington Greene* a copy of "The Windmill" and says in the letter (18 Apr 1880), "I think this is the first poem ever written on the subject." (Is it?) Hezekiah Butterworth (1839–1905), editor of *Youth's Companion,* paid Longfellow $100 for this poem and "The Maiden and Weathercock" together.

Bibliography: Hilen, ed.

"THE WIND OVER THE CHIMNEY" (1865). Poem, in *AM,* Jan 1865; *Flower.* The poet "cower[s]" over the embers of his dying fire. A black log sings about June. The wind over the chimney trumpets fiercely, like Iskander. The flames whisper "Aspire!," but the wind replies that such thoughts die quickly. In response, the flames illuminate the "majestic pages" the poet has been reading and proclaim their authors "prophets, bards, and seers." The wind insists that writers' efforts are mere "flying sparks" and that the hands of their creators soon turn to dust and their laurels quickly wither. The poet, determined to try anyway, answers that "No endeavor is in vain" and that "the rapture of pursuing / Is the prize the vanquished gain."

"THE WINE OF JURANÇON" (1877). Poem, translated from the French poet Charles Coran (1814–83), in *PP, Harbor.* The poet, who enjoyed some sweet wine in Jurançon 20 years ago, returns to the region and finds the same "host" singing the same song. Why, when they sample the same sweet wine again, is it sour? "It was you, O gayety of my youth, / That failed in the autumnal flask!" Jurançon is a commune in the Basses Pyrénées, famous for its white wine.

"WINTER" (1821). Sonnet, signed "H." in Portland *Gazette,* 22 Jan 1821. After autumn comes winter, with "fleecy snow," "piercing storms," and frozen streams. Nature surrenders "meek[ly]" and is "bound with icy chain." Wanderers at such a time wish to return to "fertile spot[s]" and friends. This sonnet, neatly rhyming *abbaabbacddccd,* is a remarkable work by Longfellow, aged thirteen.

Bibliography: Little; Thompson.

"A WINTER'S NIGHT" (1825). Poem, in Portland *Advertiser,* 19 Jan 1825. Night welcomes "the new-born year" with icy breeze, bright stars, mist on a hill, white clouds. "Nature [is] . . . mute to those / That hear not in the wintry sky" what is no less than "The still voice of humanity!"

Bibliography: Little.

"THE WITNESSES." *See Poems on Slavery.*

"THE WONDROUS TALE OF A LITTLE MAN IN GOSLING GREEN" (1834). Tale, as by Charles F. Brown, in *The New Yorker,* 1 Nov 1834. It is a satirical depiction of the backcountry manners and the general indolence of villagers in and around Bungonuck, near Merry-meeting Bay. The village has a main street, lazy and gossipy inhabitants, tired visitors, a multi windowed meeting-house, and a tower with a dial lacking hands and a weathercock shaped by a bootjack. Beyond Bungonuck are pines full of barking squirrels and twittering birds. The hero, John Schwartkins, in gosling-green attire, was based on a Dutchman who arrived in Brunswick (for Bungonuck read Brunswick) years ago. Longfellow was awarded $50 for his prize tale.

Bibliography: Hatfield, J. T. "An Unknown Prose Tale by Longfellow." *American Literature* 3 (May 1931): 136–48; Thompson.

"WOODS IN WINTER" (1825). Poem, in *USLG,* 15 Feb 1825; *Voices.* The poet trudges over the wintry hill, sees icicles where summer vines hung, sees the half-frozen river, and hears skaters. Birds aren't singing, but the winds make "hoarse accord" and are cheering.

Bibliography: Hilen, ed.; Little.

"WOODSTOCK PARK" (1878). Sonnet, in *Kéramos.* In this "little rustic hermitage," Alfred the Great set aside politics and translated "The Consolations of the Roman state." Here, also, Geoffrey Chaucer, when old, penned his "unrivalled Tales." All imitators of them fail. These men were both kings—"one in the realm of Truth, / One in the ream of Fiction and of Song." Who can

possibly "Their glory . . . inherit and prolong?" Here Longfellow, late in his life, is alluding obliquely to his inability to rival *The Canterbury Tales* with his own *Tales of a Wayside Inn.*

Bibliography: Arvin.

"A WRAITH IN THE MIST" (1876). Poem, in *PP, Kéramos, Birds* (1878). The persona sees a person big of body and with a pained face walking proudly here on the island of Inchkenneth. He is not Sir Allen McLean, its laird. He is the author of "the Rambler, / The Idler," who hails from Bolt Court and once said that if he lived on Inchkenneth he would "wall himself round with a fort." The reference is to Dr. Samuel Johnson, who when visiting Scotland with his biographer James Boswell said as much about Inchkenneth. In a letter to James T. Fields* (23 Nov 1876), Longfellow complained that to beef up the parts of *Poems of Places* he occasionally had to write some pieces himself and says "a specimen of this patchwork" is "A Wraith in the Mist."

Bibliography: Hilen, ed.

"THE WRECK OF THE HESPERUS" (1840). Poem, in the *New World,* 11 Jan 1840; *Ballads.* The skipper has taken his lovely little daughter aboard his *Hesperus.* He indifferently notes when the wind veers from west to south, and he laughs when an experienced sailor says that he ought to seek "yonder port" because a hurricane is brewing. When a gale blows in from the northeast, the skipper tells his trembling daughter not to worry. He wraps her in his coat and ties her to the mast. He has easy answers when she asks about the bells and the guns she hears. He steers "for the open sea"; but he cannot answer when she asks about a certain "gleaming light," because by now he is frozen to death. What she sees is a lantern, tied to the helm. She prays to Christ, recalling that he once "stilled the wave, / On the Lake of Galilee." All night long the ship sweeps "Tow'rds the reef of Norman's Woe." A mighty wave wipes "the crew / Like icicles from her deck." Vicious rocks gore the vessel "Like the horns of an angry bull." Icy shrouds and masts vanish. The vessel sinks like broken glass. At dawn a shocked fisherman sees the child tied "to a drifting mast." On her breast and in her eyes is frozen sea water. Her hair waves in the billows like seaweed. May "Christ save us" from the fate of the *Hesperus*.

Longfellow noted in his journal (14 Dec 1839) that several ships, including "the schooner Hesperus," wrecked on a reef named Norman's Woe, near Gloucester, and that 20 bodies had washed ashore. He adds, "I must write a ballad upon this." In truth, the vessel wrecked elsewhere. According to a subsequent journal entry (30 Dec 1839), he began writing this famous poem—its title is now a cliché—at midnight the night before, went to bed, got up again at 3:00 A.M., and added more lines that had been running in his head. He concludes, "I am pleased with the ballad. It hardly cost me an effort. It did not come into my mind by lines but by stanzas." Longfellow cast it in conventional ballad form, which he rarely used. Such stanzas have four lines, with iambic tetrameter altering with iambic trimeter, and rhyming *abcb*. Park Benjamin,* editor of the *New World,* paid Longfellow what he had asked—$25—(7 Jan 1840) for the poem and published it four days later. Longfellow took many liberties with historical events in this work. A violent storm hit the Massachusetts coast during the night of 15–16 December 1839. The schooner *Favorite,* from Wiscasset, Maine, was wrecked and 17 bodies were washed ashore at Gloucester. One victim was Mrs. Sally Hilton, found tied to a windlass bitt. *Hesperus,* another schooner, from Gardiner, Maine, broke from her anchorage in Boston harbor during the storm but was not involved in the tragedy. Longfellow could have read about both vessels in the Boston *Morning Post* (17 Dec 1839). In a rare burst of cockiness, perhaps only jocose, Longfellow wrote his father (20 Dec 1840) that "The Wreck of the Hesperus" "is a National Ballad." For many years, readers wrote Longfellow asking him to provide details about the wreck, especially about Norman's Woe; he answered with uncommon patience.

Bibliography: Arvin; Beston, Henry. "The Real Wreck of the Hesperus." *Bookman* 61 (May 1925): 304-6; Hilen, ed.; Hollahan, Eugene. "Intertextual Bondings between 'The Wreck of the Hesperus' and [Gerard Manley Hopkins's] *The Wreck of the Deutschland.*" *Texas Studies in Language and Literature* 33 (spring 1991): 40-63; Hugenin, Charles A. "The Truth About the Schooner Hesperus." *New York Folklore Quarterly* 16 (1960): 48-53; S. Longfellow; Wagenknecht, 1986; Williams.

Y

"YOUTH AND AGE" (1878). Sonnet, translated from the poet Michael Angelo, in *Kéramos.* If "Amor" would like to have him "burn and weep," he must again have "blind passion," a certain "angelic face," quickness of foot, and above all "fire and moisture in the heart and brain." Perhaps Amor lives alone, nourished by "the sweet-bitter tears of human hearts." If so, Amor cannot "wake desire" in him, because "Souls that have almost reached the other shore" ought to "be as tinder to a holier fire."

"YOUTH AND OLD AGE" (1824). Essay, signed "L.," in *American Monthly Magazine,* May 1824. As we age, "we look with a kind of melancholy joy at the decay of things around us." Mutability "excites within us mournful but pleasant feelings for the past, and prophetic ones for the future." Suggesting that he is much older than he is, Longfellow mourns for friends who have "crossed the threshold of the grave in youth, and in manhood, at home and abroad"; while other friends are still young, some "like myself [are] slowly descending the declivity of years." He hopes to die "and to rest in the peaceful bosom of that spot which was the scene of my sports in childhood." *See also* "To the Novice of the Convent of the Visitation."

Bibliography: Hilen, ed.; S. Longfellow.

"THE YOUTH OF MARY STUART" (1835). Essay, signed "L.," in *Token,* 1835.

Longfellow describes the Loire Valley, where Mary Stuart was born, then discusses her parents, education, and happy life at court. She returned to Scotland, where Chastelard, a male attendant, grew too amorous and was executed. Soon after her marriage in Paris (1558) to Francis II, dauphin of France, he died. Her return to Scotland began with a bad omen, when a bark sank in front of her vessel out of Calais. This essay was reprinted in different form in *Harper's New Monthly Magazine,* Feb 1905, mistitled "A Hitherto Unpublished Essay."

"YOUTHFUL YEARS" (1825). Poem, in Portland *Advertiser,* 30 Dec 1825. After "years of pain and tears," the poet would like to play his harp; but time has spoiled its chords. Earlier joys have faded, just the way twilight turns to night over a "storm-troubled ocean." He has wasted his feelings, and his pride is broken. He thought that joys would "wither never," that "hopes . . . / Would live and bloom forever," that winds would never "wake time's silent lake," that those he loved would never die. But now he knows that "Sorrow is for the sons of men, / And weeping for earth's daughters." In a headnote, Longfellow reports this poem was written by a young man who recently died of dysentery; then Longfellow cryptically signed the poem "Y.S.W.K.W."

Bibliography: Little; S. Longfellow; Thompson.

General Bibliography

Allaback, Steven. "Mrs. Clemm and Henry Wadsworth Longfellow." *Harvard Library Bulletin* 18 (Jan 1970): 32–42.

Allen, Gay Wilson. *American Prosody.* New York: American Book Company, 1935.

Austin, George Lowell. *Henry Wadsworth Longfellow: His Life, His Works, His Friendships.* Boston: Lee and Shepard, 1883.

Bellavance, Thomas Eugene. *The Periodical Prose of Henry Wadsworth Longfellow.* Ph.D. diss., Michigan State University, 1969.

Blanck, Jacob. "Longfellow, Henry Wadsworth." In *Bibliography of American Literature,* 9 vols. New Haven and London: Yale University Press, 1955–91, V: 468–640.

Brooks, Van Wyck. *New England: Indian Summer, 1865–1915.* New York: E. P. Dutton, 1940.

———. *The Flowering of New England.* 1936. Rev. ed. Cleveland and New York: The World Publishing Company, 1946.

Cameron, Kenneth Walter, ed. *Longfellow among His Contemporaries: A Harvest of Estimates, Insights, and Anecdotes from the Victorian Literary World and an Index.* Hartford: Transcendental Books, 1978.

Carpenter, George Rice. *Henry Wadsworth Longfellow.* Boston: Small, Maynard, 1901.

Chamberlain, Jacob Chester. *A Bibliography of the First Editions in Book Form of the Writings of Henry Wadsworth Longfellow.* New York: Burt Franklin, 1908.

Clarke, Helen Archibald. *Longfellow's Country.* New York: Baker and Taylor, 1909.

Flibbert, Joseph. "Poetry in the Mainstream." In *America and the Sea: A Literary History,* ed. Haskell S. Springer, 109–26. Athens: University of Georgia Press, 1995.

Gale, Robert L. *A Cultural Encyclopedia of the 1850s in America.* Westport: Greenwood Press, 1993.

Gebbia, Alessandro. *La citta' teatrale.* Rome: Offician Edizioni, 1986.

Gioia, Dana. "Longfellow and the Aftermath of Modernism." In *The Columbia History of American Poetry,* eds. Jay Parini and Brett C. Millier, 64–96. New York: Columbia University Press, 1993.

Gorman, Herbert S. *A Victorian American: Henry Wadsworth Longfellow.* New York: George H. Doran, 1926.

Green, Martin. *The Problem of Boston: Some Readings in Cultural History.* New York: W.W. Norton & Company, 1966.

Greenslet, Ferris, ed. *The Sonnets of Henry Wadsworth Longfellow.* Boston: Houghton Mifflin, 1907.

Griffith, John. "Longfellow and [Johann Gottfried von] Herder and the Sense of History." *Texas Studies in Literature and Language* 13 (summer 1971): 249–65.

Haralson, Eric L. "Mars in Petticoats: Longfellow and Sentimental Masculinity." *Nineteenth-Century Literature* 51 (Dec 1996): 327–55.

Hatfield, James Taft. *New Light on Longfellow: With Special Reference to His Relations to Germany.* Boston: Houghton Mifflin, 1933.

"Henry Wadsworth Longfellow. Seventy-Fifth Birthday. Proceedings of the Maine Historical Society, February 27, 1882." Portland: Hoyt, Fogg and Donham, 1882.

Higginson, Thomas Wentworth. *Henry Wadsworth Longfellow.* Boston and New York: Houghton Mifflin, 1902.

Hubbell, Jay B. *Who Are Our Major Writers?: A Study of the Changing Literary Canon.* Durham: Duke University Press, 1972.

Johnson, Carl L. *Professor Longfellow of Harvard.* Eugene: University of Oregon Press, 1944.

——. "Longfellow's Studies in France." *Emerson Society Quarterly,* no. 58, part 1 (1970): 40-48.

Johnson, Harvey Leroy. *Longfellow and Portuguese Language and Literature.* Eugene: University of Oregon Press, 1965.

Kennedy, W. Sloane. *Henry W. Longfellow: Biography, Anecdote, Letters, Criticism.* Cambridge: Moses King Publisher, 1882.

Kramer, Michael P. "'A Fine Ambiguity': Longfellow, Language, and Literary History." In *Imagining Language in America,* ed. Michael P. Kramer, 64-89. Princeton: Princeton University Press, 1992.

Ljungquist, Kent P. "The 'Little War' and Longfellow's Dilemma: New Documents in the Plagiarism Controversy of 1845." *Resources for American Literary Study* 23, no. 1 (1997): 28-59.

"Longfellow." [Boston] *Literary World* (26 February 1881): 74-88.

Matthiessen, F. O. *American Renaissance: Art and Expression in the Age of Emerson and Whitman.* New York: Oxford University Press, 1941.

M'Ilwraith, J. N. *A Book about Longfellow.* London, Edinburgh, and New York: Thomas Nelson and Sons, 1900.

Monteiro, George. Introduction to *The Poetical Works of Longfellow,* [xvii]-xxvii. Boston: Houghton Mifflin, 1975.

More, Paul Elmer. "The Centenary of Longfellow." In *Shelburne Essays,* 5th ser., 132-57. Boston and New York: Houghton Mifflin, 1908.

Morin, Paul. *Les sources de l'oeuvre de Henry Wadsworth Longfellow.* Paris: Émile Larose, 1913.

Mott, Frank Luther. *A History of American Magazines, 1741-1930.* 5 vols. Cambridge: Harvard University Press, 1939-68.

Papers Presented at the Longfellow Commemorative Conference, April 1-3, 1982. Washington, D.C.: U.S. Government Printing Office, 1982.

Pearl, Matthew. *The Dante Club.* New York: Random House, 2003.

Pearson, Norman Holmes. "Both Longfellows." *University of Kansas City Review* 16 (summer 1950): 245-53.

Reynolds, Davis S. *Walt Whitman's America: A Cultural Biography.* New York: Alfred A. Knopf, 1995.

Riewald, J. G. "The Translational Reception of American Literature in Europe, 1800-1900: A Review of Research." *English Studies* 60 (Oct 1979): 572-74.

Robbins, J. Albert, ed. *American Literary Manuscripts,* 2d ed. Athens: University of Georgia Press, 1977.

Robertson, Eric S. *Life of Henry Wadsworth Longfellow.* London: Walter Scott, 1887.

Sears, Donald A. "Folk Poetry in Longfellow's Boyhood." *New England Quarterly* 45 (Mar 1972): 96-105.

Shepard, Odell, ed. *Henry Wadsworth Longfellow: Representative Selections, with Introduction, Bibliography, and Notes.* New York: American Book Company, 1934.

Stauffer, Donald Barlow. *A Short History of American Poetry.* New York: E. P. Dutton, 1974.

Thompson, Lawrance. *Young Longfellow (1807-1843).* New York: Macmillan, 1938.

Tosi, Ina. *Longfellow e l'Italia.* Bologna: N. Zanichelli, 1906.

Underwood, Francis H. *Henry Wadsworth Longfellow: A Biographical Sketch.* 1882; New York: Haskell House, 1973.

Vanderbilt, Kermit. *American Literature and the Academy: The Roots, Growth, and Maturity of a Profession.* Philadelphia: University of Pennsylvania Press, 1986.

Wagenknecht, Edward. *Longfellow: A Full-Length Portrait.* New York: Longmans, Green & Co., 1955.

Ward, Robert Stafford. "The Influence of [Giovanni Battista] Vico on Longfellow." *Emerson Society Quarterly,* no. 58, part 1 (1970): 57–62.
———. "Longfellow's Roots in Yankee Soil." *New England Quarterly* 41 (Jun 1968): 180–92.
Westbrook, Percy. *The New England Town in Fact and Fiction.* Madison: Fairleigh-Dickinson University Press, 1982.
Whitman, Iris Lilian. *Longfellow and Spain.* New York: Instituto de las Españen los Estados Unidos, 1927.

Index

Note: Poems with long titles or subtitles are usually given in a shortened form. Unless otherwise noted, all works in quotation marks or italicized are by Longfellow or translated by him. Alternate or discarded titles are usually not indexed. Extensive personal names are often shortened to first and last only. Peripheral and incidental references, including nonsubstantive ones of persons or titles that did not evidently influence Longfellow, are not included. Guests and hosts of Longfellow and recipients of letters from him are usually not indexed. Page references to main or significant entries are in **boldfaced** type.

About the Author

ROBERT L. GALE is Professor Emeritus of English at the University of Pittsburgh. His previous books include *A Rose MacDonald Companion* (2003), *A Dashiell Hammett Companion* (2000), and *A Mickey Spillane Companion* (2003), all available from Greenwood Press.